MW01618610

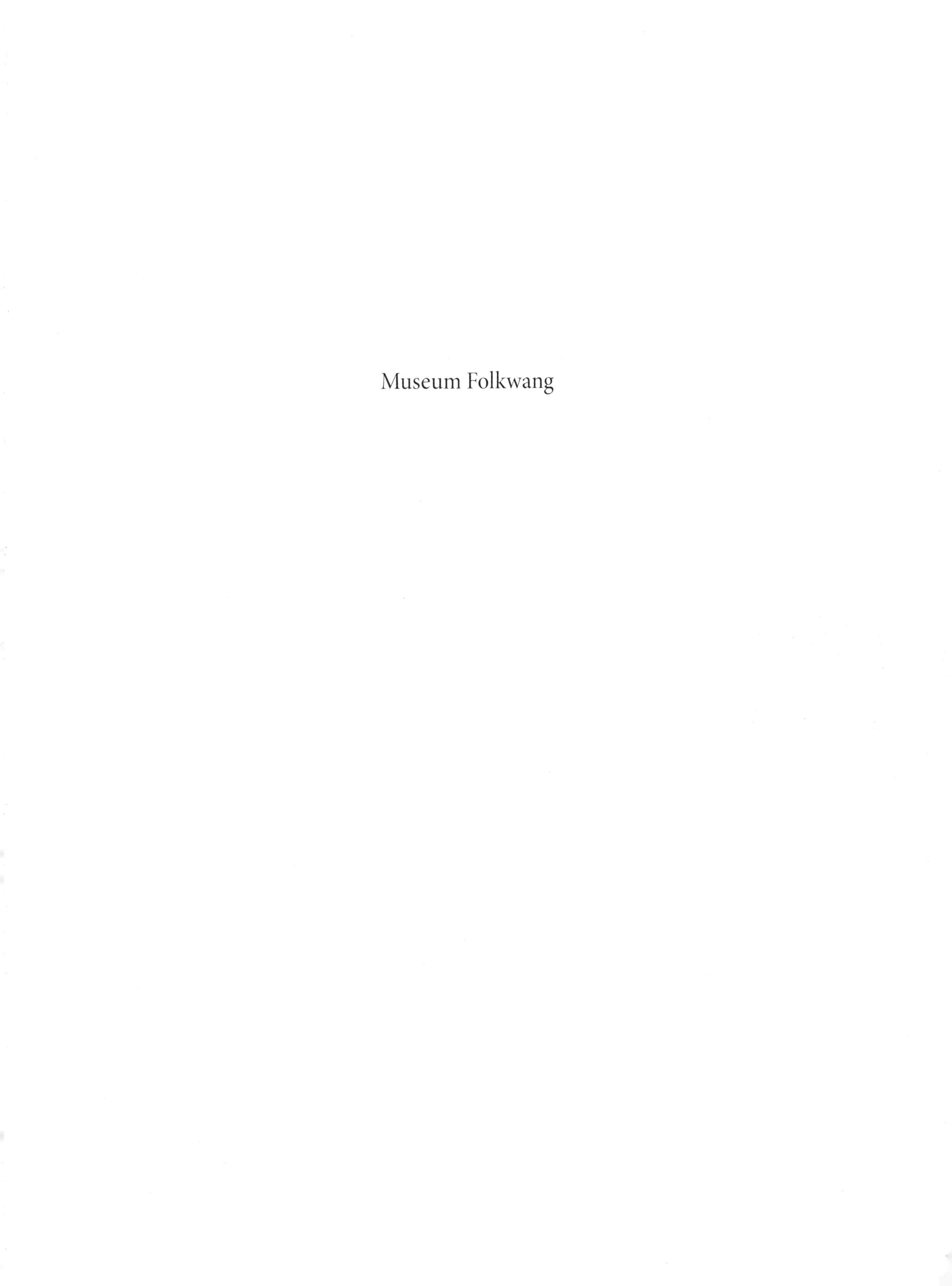

Museum Folkwang

Monet, Gauguin, Van Gogh ...
Japanese Inspirations
Museum Folkwang

Edition Folkwang / Steidl

Table of contents

CATALOGUE

APPENDIX

Greeting

Museum Folkwang in Essen has dedicated this marvellous special exhibition to *Japonisme*, one of the most exciting chapters in art history at the end of the nineteenth century. In a time when business and culture have become increasingly global, the exhibition *Monet, Gauguin, Van Gogh ... Japanese Inspirations* shows the cultural influences of a "different world" that had an enlivening and inspiring effect on the perception and creativity of European artists in their time and still offers a great deal to us today.

The exhibition features key works by the most important European artists of the age in dialogue with the Japanese art that inspired them. The integration of objects from Japanese art and everyday life into the artists' own works, the adoption of pictorial subjects used by artists such as Kitagawa Utamaro or Utagawa Hiroshige, or the adaptation of the visual language of Japanese woodblock prints characterise the reception of Japanese art during the late nineteenth century, particularly in France. This special exhibition reveals the creative influence of Japan linked to a changing attitude towards life and the pictorial traditions of the French impressionists and post-impressionists, which are the primary focus of the show.

The partnership between Museum Folkwang and E.ON stretches back to 1985, when the first conversations were held in preparing the exhibition *Edvard Munch*. With the opening of this exhibition on the Norwegian painter, marking the tenth jubilee year of the delivery of natural gas from the Scandinavian country, Ruhrgas was the partner and sponsor. From 1987 until today, Museum Folkwang and E.ON have collaborated on twelve special exhibitions. Alongside shows focusing on the oeuvres of Vincent Van Gogh, Claude Monet, Pablo Picasso and Paul Gauguin, the exhibitions from 1990 to 1996 have also included shows of the works of William Turner, Paul Cézanne and Caspar David Friedrich. Fittingly to mark the opening of the new museum building, E.ON, as the main sponsor of the European Capital of Culture 2010, also supported the project *"The Most Beautiful Museum in the World" – Museum Folkwang until 1933* and, later that same year, the exhibition *Images of a Capital – The Impressionists in Paris*.

The history of this productive collaboration is marked by a mutual understanding and respect – indeed, friendship – and an awareness that both partners can draw their own benefits from this alliance, a win-win relationship in every way. This means that Museum Folkwang, for example, can not only rely on funding to put on renowned exhibitions but can also use the resources and relationships at E.ON's disposal. As a prominent player in the Rhine-Ruhr region with its roots in Ruhrgas, E.ON in turn profits from the international distinction of Museum Folkwang and the attraction of a culturally powerful urban centre known around the world and which excels not only in terms of commitment, social responsibility and fair competition but also in art, education and scholarship.

The exhibition *Monet, Gauguin, Van Gogh ... Japanese Inspirations* at Museum Folkwang presents world-famous artworks in the special context of tradition and modernism in Japan and France. As in Japan, we in the Ruhr region have a long tradition of the integration of business and culture, periods of structural transformation and their influence on art and society.

We would like to express our thanks to Hartwig Fischer, the former director of Museum Folkwang under whom this project was initiated, and to the current director of the museum Tobia Bezzola and his team, in particular Sandra Gianfreda, for their highly committed and thorough work, as well as to generous lenders from all over the world for their readiness to provide the artworks shown in this project. We dedicate this show to the residents of the Ruhr region, as they and the region deserve to call themselves a home for both quality and art.

Ingo Luge *Chairman of the Board, E.ON Deutschland*

Acknowledgements

Museum Folkwang, Essen, and Kunsthaus Zürich would like to thank the following lenders who have generously supported the exhibition:

Musée Toulouse-Lautrec, Albi, Danièle Devynck • Van Gogh Museum, Amsterdam, Axel Rüger, Leo Jansen, Fleur Roos Rosa de Carvalho • Pinacoteca Giuseppe De Nittis, Barletta, Santa Scommegna, Giusy Caroppo • Kunstmuseum Basel, Bernhard Mendes Bürgi, Nina Zimmer • Staatliche Museen zu Berlin, Museum für Asiatische Kunst, Klaas Ruitenbeek, Alexander Hofmann • The Barber Institute of Fine Arts, University of Birmingham, Nicola Kalinsky, Robert Wenley • Kunsthalle Bremen, Der Kunstverein in Bremen, Christoph Grunenberg, Anne Buschhoff • Ackland Art Museum, The University of North Carolina at Chapel Hill, Emily Kass, Peter Nisbet • Ordrupgaard, Charlottenlund, Anne-Birgitte Fonsmark • Ville de Cherbourg-Octeville, musée Thomas Henry, Louise Le Gall • The Art Institute of Chicago, Douglas Druick, Gloria Groom • Cincinnati Art Museum, Aaron Betsky, Esther Bell • Designmuseum Danmark, Copenhagen, Anne-Louise Sommer, Ulla Houkjær • Ny Carlsberg Glyptotek, Copenhagen, Flemming Friborg, Line Clausen Pedersen • Kupferstich-Kabinett, Staatliche Kunstsammlungen Dresden, Hartwig Fischer, Bernhard Maaz, Petra Kuhlmann-Hodick • Lehmbruck Museum, Duisburg, Söke Dinkla, Marion Bornscheuer • Museum DKM, Duisburg, Dirk Krämer, Klaus Maas • Private Collection, courtesy Galerie Beck & Eggeling, Düsseldorf • Hetjens-Museum, Deutsches Keramikmuseum, Düsseldorf, Sally Schöne, Daniela Antonin • Stiftung Museum Kunstpalast, Düsseldorf, Beat Wismer, Gunda Luyken, Dedo v. Kerssenbrock-Krosigk • The George Economou Collection, Athens • Scottish National Gallery, Edinburgh, Michael Clarke, Frances Fowle • Museum Angewandte Kunst, Frankfurt am Main, Matthias Wagner K, Stephan Graf von der Schulenburg • Städel Museum, Frankfurt am Main, Max Hollein, Felix Krämer • Baur Foundation, Geneva, Jean-Pierre Zehnder, Monique Crick, Helen Loveday • Bibliothèque de Genève, Alexandre Vantautgaerden, Brigitte Grass • Collection Musée Ariana, Ville de Genève, Isabelle Naef Galuba, Anne-Claire Schumacher • Musée d'art et d'histoire, Genève, Jean-Yves Marin, Laurence Madeline • Fondation Claude Monet, Giverny, Académie des Beaux-Arts, Hugues R. Gall, Claudette Lindsey • Musée de Grenoble, Guy Tosatto, Hélène Vincent • Hamburger Kunsthalle, Hubertus Gaßner • Museum für Kunst und Gewerbe Hamburg, Sabine Schulze, Nora von Achenbach, Claudia Banz, Jürgen Döring, Thomas Gilbhard • Sammlung P. + R. Herzog, Basel • The Museum of Fine Arts, Houston, Gary Tinterow • Museum für Angewandte Kunst Köln (MAKK), Petra Hesse, Patricia Brattig • Museum Ludwig, Köln, Katia Baudin, Miriam Halwani • Wallraf-Richartz-Museum & Fondation Corboud, Köln, Marcus Dekiert, Barbara Schäfer • E.W.K. Bern • Sammlung Viktor und Marianne Langen • Fondation Jean et Suzanne Planque, Lausanne, Florian Rodari • Tate, London, Nicholas Serota, Caroline Collier • Collection Adrien Maeght, Saint Paul • Collection Jules Maeght, San Francisco • Kunsthalle Mannheim, Ulrike Lorenz, Thomas Köllhofer • The State Pushkin Museum of Fine Arts, Moscow, Marina Loshak, Tatiana Potapova • Bayerische Staatsgemäldesammlungen – Neue Pinakothek, München, Klaus Schrenk, Joachim Kaak • Yale University Art Gallery, New Haven, Jock Reynold, Laurence Kanter • The Metropolitan Museum of Art, New York, Thomas P. Campbell, Susan Alyson Stein • The Museum of Modern Art, New York, Glenn Lowry, Ann Temkin, Leah Dickerman • Stadtmuseum Oldenburg, Grafiksammlung, Andreas von Seggern • Galleri K, Oslo, Ben Frija • The National Museum of Art, Architecture and Design, Oslo, Audun Eckhoff, Nils Ohlsen, Frode Ernst Haverkamp • Les Arts Décoratifs, musée des Arts décoratifs, Paris, Olivier Gabet, Audrey Gay-Mazuel, Jean-Luc Olivié, Évelyne Possemé • Bibliothèque nationale de France, Paris, Bruno Racine, Sylvie Aubenas, Valérie Sueur-Hermel • Institut national d' histoire de l'art, Bibliothèque, collections Jacques Doucet, Paris, Antoinette Le Normand-Romain • Musée Carnavalet – Histoire de Paris, Paris, Valérie Guillaume, Jean-Marie Bruson • Musée Clemenceau, Paris, Valérie Joxe, Lise Lentignac • Musée National des Arts Asiatiques Guimet, Paris, Sophie Makariou, Hélène Bayou, Cristina Cramerotti • Musée d'Orsay, Paris, Guy Cogeval, Caroline Mathieu, Leïla Jarbouai • Musée Rodin, Paris, Catherine Chevillot, François Blanchetière, Sophie Biass-Fabiani, Geneviève Aitken, Bénédicte Garnier • Petit Palais, Musée des Beaux-Arts de la Ville de Paris, Christophe Leribault, Dominique Morel • Museen der Stadt Regensburg, Historisches Museum, Peter Germann-Bauer • Arp Museum Bahnhof Rolandseck / Sammlung Rau für UNICEF, Remagen,

Oliver Kornhoff, Susanne Blöcker • Fondation Beyeler, Riehen/Basel, Sam Keller • Museum Boijmans Van Beuningen, Rotterdam, Sjarel Ex, Patty Wageman • Musée Départemental Maurice Denis, Saint-Germain-en-Laye, Frédéric Bigo, Christine Martinez • Saint Louis Art Museum, Brent R. Benjamin • Staatsgalerie Stuttgart, Christiane Lange, Christofer Conrad, Hans-Martin Kaulbach • Collection D. Travert, France • Collection Triton Foundation, Marlies Cordia-Roeloffs • National Gallery of Art, Washington, Earl A. Powell III, Mary Morton • Sterling and Francine Clark Institute, Williamstown, Massachusetts, Michael Conforti, Richard Rand • Collection of Diane B. Wilsey • Hahnloser/Jaeggli Stiftung, Winterthur • Coninx-Stiftung, Zürich, Silvia Orthwein-Erhard, Tania Camenzind • Private Collection, courtesy Thomas Ammann Fine Art AG, Zürich • Stiftung Sammlung E. G. Bührle, Zürich, † Hortense Anda-Bührle, Lukas Gloor

We also thank those who prefer to remain anonymous.

We extend our sincere gratitude to all those who contributed to the preparation of this exhibition with their help and dedication:

Paola Aeschlimann-Rebstein; Hélène E. Alexander and Jacob Moss, The Fan Museum, London; Doris Ammann, Galerie Thomas Ammann Fine Art AG, Zurich; Kristina Barekyan, The State Pushkin Museum of Fine Arts, Moscow; Michael Beck and Ute Eggeling, Galerie Beck & Eggeling, Düsseldorf; Carrie Becker, Japanisches Generalkonsulat, Düsseldorf; Edwin Becker, Van Gogh Museum, Amsterdam; Anisabelle Berès-Montanari and Marie-Christine Bonola, Galerie Berès, Paris; Therese Bhattacharya-Stettler; Frédéric Bigo; Katharina Büttiker; Mathias Chivot, Archives Vuillard, Paris; Landa Crommelynck; Hannah Darvin, Sotheby's, London; Jill De Vonyar; Leah Dickerman, The Museum of Modern Art, New York; Irene Dimitrakopoulou, Athens; Ann Dumas; Christian Dunkel, Staatsbibliothek zu Berlin – Preußischer Kulturbesitz; Katharina Epprecht, Museum Rietberg, Zurich; Christiane Ernek, Staatliche Kunstsammlungen Dresden, Schloss Pillnitz; Ute Eskildsen; Walter Feilchenfeldt; Manuela Fellner-Feldhaus, Historisches Archiv Krupp, Essen; Sabine Flaschberger, Museum für Gestaltung, Zurich; Matthi Forrer; Peter and Brigitte Fortmann, Duisburg; Tatyana Franck; Ingrid Gilgenmann, Lempertz, Cologne; Laura Gutman; Giulio Haas and Christina Fischer, Embassy of Switzerland, Tehran; Widar Halén, The National Museum of Art, Architecture and Design, Oslo; Florence Half-Wrobel; Corina Hein, Christie's, Düsseldorf; Josef Huber, Bibliothek Museum Rietberg, Zurich; Conor Jordan, Christie's, New York; Richard Kendall; Thomas Ketelsen, Wallraf-Richartz-Museum & Fondation Corboud, Cologne; Albert Kostenevich, Hermitage Museum, Saint Petersburg; Ulf Küster und Anna Szech, Fondation Beyeler, Riehen/Basel; Geneviève Lacambre; Paul Lang and Anabelle Kienle Poňka, National Gallery of Canada, Ottawa; Monika Leonhardt; Hendrick Lühl; Isabelle Maeght; Eva Mahler and Andrea Staub, Thomas Ammann Fine Art AG, Zurich; Marc Maison, Paris; Markus Müller, Kunstmuseum Pablo Picasso Münster; David Nash, Mitchell-Innes & Nash, New York; Monique Nonne; Geneviève Noufflard; Payam Parishanzadeh; Margareta Pavaloi, Völkerkundemuseum der J. & E. von Portheim-Stiftung, Heidelberg; Christine Pinault, Picasso Administration, Paris; Tanja Pirsig-Marshall; Ulrich Pohlmann, Münchner Stadtmuseum; Katia Poletti, Fondation Félix Vallotton, Lausanne; Marc Olivier Ranson Bitker; Françoise Reynaud, Musée Carnavalet, Paris; Esther Ruelfs, Museum für Kunst und Gewerbe Hamburg; Christian Rümelin, Cabinet d'arts graphiques du Musée d'art et d'histoire, Geneva; Sabine Runde, Museum Angewandte Kunst, Frankfurt am Main; Aurélie Samuel, Musée Guimet, Paris; Polly Sartori, Sotheby's, New York; Dorit Schäfer und Alexander Eiling, Staatliche Kunsthalle Karlsruhe; René Scharf, Berlin; Thomas Schrader, Kunsthalle Bremen; Jutta Schütte, Städel Museum, Frankfurt; Heinrich Schulze Altcappenberg, Staatliche Museen zu Berlin – Preußischer Kulturbesitz, Kupferstichkabinett; Véronique Serrano, Le musée Bonnard, Le Cannet; Howard Shaw, Hammer Galleries, New York; Kim Sitzler and Markus Leitner, Embassy of Switzerland, Cairo; Katy Spurrell, Arthemisia Group, Rome; Fabienne Stahl; Christine E. Stauffer, Galerie Kornfeld, Berne; Benjamin Steinitz and David Langeois, Galerie Steinitz, Paris; Andreas Stolzenburg, Hamburger Kunsthalle; Anne Terrasse and Jérôme Faucheux; Simon Theobald, London; Hans Bjarne Thomsen, Universität Zürich, Kunsthistorisches Institut; Florence Valdès-Forain; Sara Vignale, Galerie Maeght, Paris; Ruprecht Vondran; Gabriel P. and Yvonne Weisberg; Uta Werlich, Linden-Museum, Stuttgart; Adalbert Wruck; Yoshii Kazuhito, Yoshii Gallery, New York

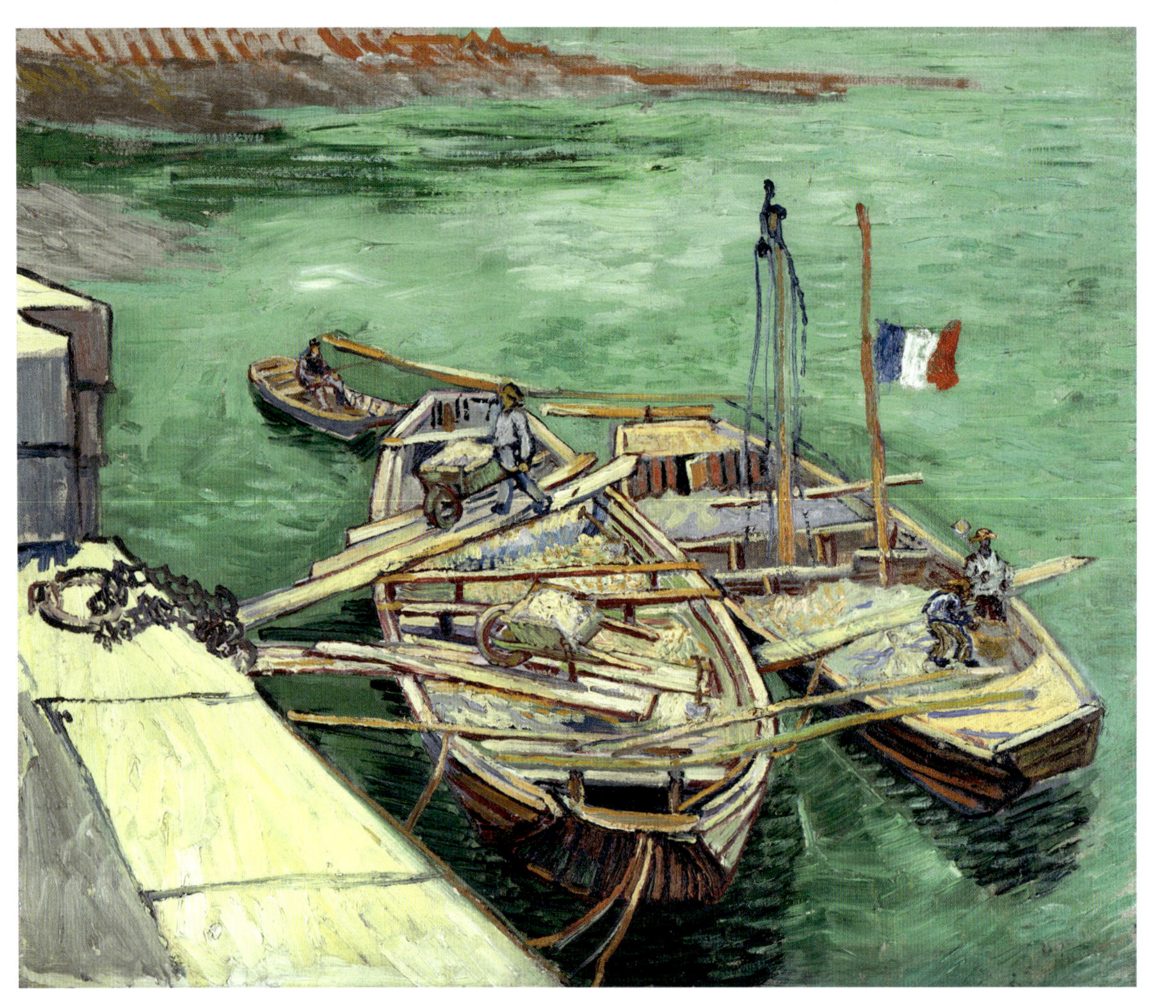

39 Vincent Van Gogh, *Quay with Men Unloading Sand Barges*, 1888

Foreword

With *Monet, Gauguin, Van Gogh ... Japanese Inspirations*, Museum Folkwang is devoting a major exhibition to one of the most fascinating chapters of French art in the second half of the nineteenth century. The show focuses on the period between 1860 and 1910, the development and heyday of the craze for Japanese art in France. For the first time since the groundbreaking show held at the Galeries nationales du Grand Palais in Paris in 1988, therefore, the phenomenon known as *Japonisme* is once again the subject of a multifaceted exhibition.

Why, then, an exhibition on *Japonisme* at the Folkwang? The dialogue between European and non-European cultures has been fundamental for Museum Folkwang since its inception. Karl Ernst Osthaus himself, founder of Museum Folkwang, began collecting Japanese art early on. Thus, our museum possesses a substantial collection of Japanese artefacts such as scrolls, ceramic vessels, lacquerware, masks, sculptures, baskets and much more. Some of these objects were already presented and evaluated in the exhibition entitled *"The Most Beautiful Museum in the World" – Museum Folkwang until 1933*, which was held after the inauguration of the new wing in 2010. Other artefacts, such as the hanging scrolls, baskets and tsubas previously in the Osthaus Collection and transferred to Essen in 1922, have now been classified in terms of their period and style and restored for the show. Thanks to his infallible intuition, Christoph Dorsz was able to research both the history and provenance of this extensive inventory in preparation for the exhibition.

Together with the museum's own paintings by Monet, Gauguin, Van Gogh and Courbet as well as photographs from the studio of Felice Beato and posters by Toulouse-Lautrec from the German Poster Museum, it was the hitherto-unexplored collections that prompted us to dedicate a special exhibition to the phenomenon of *Japonisme*, thus making it accessible to a wider public and a new generation. Tied into the project is the intention that the dialogue between global cultures be the subject of regular discussion at the Folkwang. Last but not least, the exhibition is a wonderful opportunity to display an inspiring collection of diverse artistic genres alongside one another – be it painting, graphic art, photography, sculpture and the decorative arts.

This large-scale project could not have been realised without the collaboration of a great number of committed people. Our very special thanks go to all contributors – both museums and private collectors – who generously agreed to lend their artworks to us for the duration of the exhibition; we truly appreciate their valuable support.

The concept, exhibition set-up and catalogue lay in the hands of Sandra Gianfreda who was also responsible for the entire project management. We are grateful to her and her two assistants, Ulrike Hofer and Claire Guitton, who not only carried out intensive research but also helped with the organisation. We also thank Wilko Beckmann for his technical database assistance with our Japanese inventory, Fabian Knierim for his research in the field of photography as well as the two academic interns, Jennifer Buchholz and Juliana Gocke, all of whom worked temporarily on the project. Mario-Andreas von Lüttichau always proved to be an approachable and cooperative colleague, and we would like to thank him warmly.

Thanks also go to the following experts in Far Eastern art for their assessment of our collections: Nora von Achenbach, Alexander Hofmann, Gregory Irvine, Else and Heinz Kress, Akiko Mabuchi, Antje Papist-Matsuo, Petra Rösch and Melanie Trede. We thank all authors for their essays and text contributions that illuminate new aspects of *Japonisme* and bring to light important new findings: Geneviève Aitken, Sabine Bradel, Ricard Bru, Christoph Dorsz, Sandra Gianfreda, Claire Guitton, Ulrike Hofer, Gregory Irvine, Peter Kropmanns, Mario-Andreas von Lüttichau, Mae Michiko, Antje Papist-Matsuo, Ursula Perucchi-Petri and Belinda Thomson. For essays translated into German, we thank Stefan Barmann, Daniela Böhmler and Stephan Glietsch; for translations into English, we thank Ariane Kossack, who was also in charge of copy-editing the English catalogue, as well as Helen Atkins, Brian Currid, Ishbel Flett, Carolyn Kelly, Benjamin Letzler and Judith Rosenthal. We are very grateful to Gerhard Steidl and his team for the design and production of the catalogue and, in particular, to Daniela Böhmler for her extremely thorough copy-editing and Sarah Winter and Julia Melzner for the layout. We thank Hans Hansen and Jens Nober for the photography of the Japanese artefacts.

The exhibition advertising was entrusted to the advertising agency Espey, and our thanks for this go to Karsten Espey, Anke Espey and their team.

Finally, we are very grateful to all the staff of Museum Folkwang. Anka Grosser was responsible for communications and marketing, an assignment she took over from Doerthe Ramin. They were assisted by Anna Littmann for press work, Asja Kaspers for the website maintenance as well as Ineke Klosterkemper and her successor Pia Terstappen for all further work regarding press, communications and marketing. Peter Daners and his team put together a multifaceted education and information programme. As always, the colleagues in charge of visitor services, under the direction of Stefanie Dixon, responded to all our visitors' wishes and requirements and also coordinated our extensive team of freelance colleagues. The registrars Susanne Brüning and Alexandra Seese expertly coordinated the transport and insurance of the precious loans, the in-house care of which lay in the responsible hands of our restorers Silke Zeich, Frederike Breder and Christiane Schneider. Severine Modes always accurately followed up the invoices. All administrative and technical staff of the museum have reliably contributed to the success of this exhibition; on behalf of all of them, we express our thanks to Holger Peters, head of administration.

We sincerely thank the architect Dieter Thiel for presenting the works in an exhibition architecture that he especially designed for this show. We are deeply indebted to GVE Grundstücksverwaltung Stadt Essen GmbH – in particular, Andreas Hillebrand and Kay Zetzsche and his facility management team for their continued reliable handling of all technical concerns and everyday security.

Again, the board of the Folkwang-Museumsverein e. V. supported us in holding the exhibition; our special thanks go to its head Achim Middelschulte, its treasurer Ulrich Blank and its legal adviser Jürgen Simon, as well as his successor Ulrich Irriger.

And once again, a special exhibition of this size and format would not have been realisable without the long-standing partnership of E.ON. Our thanks, therefore, go to the chairman Ingo Luge and his predecessor Klaus Schäfer, as well as Christian Wülfing and his team – notably, Rita Hofmann-Credner, Michael Oberbacks, Ursula Ratzko, Lisa Rosche and Gabriele Herlyn for their continued trustful cooperation.

Finally, we are very pleased that Christoph Becker, the director of Kunsthaus Zürich, already showed great interest in our project at an early date so that this exhibition will subsequently also be shown at Kunsthaus Zürich. To him and his team, in particular Oliver Wick, we extend our sincere thanks.

Tobia Bezzola *Director Museum Folkwang*

Introduction

"*Japonisme*! Attraction of the era, disorderly rage that has invaded everything, taken control of everything, confused everything in our art, our fashions, our styles, even our sanity"[1] – these are the words the art patron and ceramics enthusiast Adrien Dubouché used in *L'Art* magazine, on the occasion of the Paris World Fair of 1878, to describe the ubiquitous phenomenon of the Japan craze of his day in France. Six years later, the writer Edmond de Goncourt testified to the significance of this movement in his diary: "And when I said that *Japonisme* is in the process of revolutionising the optics of the Western nations, I affirmed that *Japonisme* brought the Occident a new *colouration*, a new *system of decoration*, briefly, if you will, a *poetic fantasy* in the creation of an art object that never existed in the most consummate objects of the Middle Ages and the Renaissance"[2] (19 April 1884).

Japonisme designates neither a uniform style nor a truly self-contained epoch. On the contrary, the term stands for a veritable passion for Japanese art and culture that began to manifest itself in France and Great Britain after the Americans forced Japan to open up to the rest of the world in 1854. From the beginning, *Japonisme* – as a collecting passion as well as a literary and artistic manner of dealing with Japan – exhibited widely different facets. It could almost be said that there are as many *Japonismes* as there are people who abandoned themselves to the charm of the "newly discovered" land. *Japonisme*, so to speak, is an attitude.

The term was verifiably first used by the art critic and *Japonica* collector Philippe Burty for the title of a series of articles appearing in the magazine *La Renaissance littéraire et artistique* from May 1872 to February 1873.[3] In these issues, Burty elucidates various aspects of Japanese customs and traditions. It was not until 1875, however, that he provided a definition of the term in the English magazine *The Academy*: "The study of the art and genius of Japan, what is called here *le Japonisme*."[4] It was the art critics Jules Claretie and Ernest Chesneau who, in 1873, first used the term "Japonisme" as we understand it today: in the sense of a creative manner of dealing with Japanese art on the part of French artists. Claretie made use of the neologism in his book *Peintres et sculpteurs contemporains* and Chesneau in his article "Le japonisme dans les arts" appearing in the illustrated weekly *Musée universel*; in the latter article, the author claimed to have invented it.[5] The Goncourt brothers, for their part, had created the term "japonaiserie" in 1867 (letter of 1 August from Jules de Goncourt to Burty) after the example of the seventeenth- and eighteenth-century chinoiseries.[6] With this coinage, however, they were referring primarily to the Japanese objects themselves. Both terms existed in the nineteenth century side by side, as is also true of the words used to describe Japan enthusiasts: "japoniste" and "japonisant". It was only after the second half of the twentieth century that these designations – "japonisme"/"japonaiserie" and "japoniste"/"japonisant" came to be defined differently, although the distinctions thus introduced are historically completely unfounded. In any case, this is how the phenomenon that began to take hold in the 1860s got the name by which it is known today. In this publication, we have given preference to the French term "Japonisme" over the English "Japonism", since the focus here is primarily on the reception of Japanese art in France, and the term was originally French.

Several persons claimed to have "discovered" Japanese art. On the one hand, as early as 1868 (on 29 October), the Goncourt brothers wrote in their *Journal*: "It was we who first had a taste for things Chinese and Japanese. Who perceived, preached and propagated that taste, which has meanwhile reached even the bourgeoisie, better than we? Who was passionate about the first Japanese albums and had the courage to purchase them?"[7] The Goncourt brothers reportedly bought a Japanese album as early as 1852;[8] in 1861, they visited the collection of Philipp Franz von Siebold – who had travelled Japan and was well informed about it – in Leiden.[9] Léonce Bénédite, on the other hand, in his essay about the artist Félix Bracquemond published in 1905, declared that the latter had kindled the enthusiasm for Japan, as Bracquemond supposedly discovered one of Katsushika Hokusai's *Manga* volumes in the workshop as his printer Auguste Delâtre, and lost no time in showing it to his artist friends.[10] Claude Monet, for his part – in a conversation that took place in 1924 – told Marc Elder that he had purchased his first Japanese woodblock prints in Le Havre, where the French *Compagnie des Indes Orientales* was based, in 1856, at the age of sixteen.[11]

Since Japanese woodblock prints made their way to France around 1860 by various channels, the question of their "true discoverer" must go unanswered. We can assume, in fact, that several persons were responsible for inflaming the passion for Japan at around the same time. Painters such as François Millet and Théodore Rousseau were likewise fascinated with the Japanese art of woodblock prints at a very early stage, and began collecting it in 1863.[12] And even if individual artists showed appreciation for the Japanese woodblock prints of *ukiyo-e* ("pictures of the floating world") before 1860, it was not until the following decades that those works came to have a wide impact.

One of the most important catalysts for this development among artists was undoubtedly the *Recueil de dessins pour l'art et l'industrie* published by Adalbert de Beaumont and Eugène V. Collinot. A collection of motifs of various origins, this work was intended primarily for the decorative arts and, ultimately encompassing 247 plates, appeared in several instalments from 1859 to 1873. The first Japanese motifs turned up in the 1861 instalment; a few of them can be identified as direct adaptations from Hokusai's first two *Manga* volumes. Beaumont and Collinot had most likely found their sources in the Japanese books and albums brought back from Japan by the French diplomats Baron Gros and Baron de Chassiron upon their return to France.[13] The collection was printed in the workshop of Auguste Delâtre, where Félix Bracquemond and James McNeill Whistler regularly dropped by as visitors, but also to print. It is thus conceivable that both of them first saw Japanese albums on Delâtre's premises.

European artists had already acquainted themselves previously with non-European art. The above-mentioned chinoiserie of the past two centuries – manifest primarily in the adoption of motifs and forms of Far Eastern character in the decorative arts and architecture – but also so-called orientalism, which likewise moved the subject into the foreground, had been fundamental sources of inspiration for European artists. With *Japonisme*, however, the artists went beyond the level of the motif and formal imitation by internalising Japanese stylistic devices to such an extent that, from within this inspiration, they created something new and developed pictorial and formal languages of their own.

The reasons for the different course taken by *Japonisme*, as compared to that of chinoiserie and orientalism, are a complex matter that has been investigated in depth by Elisa Evett and Diane N. Towle in their dissertations of 1982 and 2013, respectively.[14] Despite Japan's self-imposed isolation of 215 years, cultural exchange and a reciprocity of stylistic attributes took place between Japan and the West over centuries (with particular intensity after 1860). This and the fact that Japan was never colonised by a European nation are factors of fundamental importance to the issue under discussion. Thus, *Japonisme* is a model case of a phenomenon today referred to as "transculturality".[15]

Through the relations with the Netherlands – the only Western nation permitted to carry out trade with Japan during the period of isolation – art and East Asian objects, primarily porcelain, were already circulating in Europe before Japan's opening. The sheer quantity of commercial goods and art objects that became available after 1854 – and particularly after the Meiji government declaration of 1868 that led Japan to develop from a feudal agrarian state to an internationally competitive industrial nation within a few short decades – sparked a veritable euphoria for Japanese products in Europe, and especially in Paris. In his article "Le Japon à Paris" from 1878, Chesneau observed in retrospect: "The enthusiasm conquered every studio at the speed of a flame on a fuse. We were never tired of admiring the unexpected compositions, that science of form, the richness of tone, the originality of the painterly effect and, at the same time, the simplicity of the means of attaining those effects."[16] The members of what was initially a small group of artists in the France of the time, among them Félix Bracquemond, Edgar Degas and Édouard Manet, were looking for new ways of liberating art from its academic constraints. It is conceivable that the pictorial aesthetic of Japan, and particularly of the colour woodblock print, appealed to those artists above all because they saw in it an "authentic", "original" art unspoiled by Western civilisation.[17] They strove for a return to a supposedly "pure" art that was to facilitate the renewal of art in France. The productive contemplation of a different culture's pictorial language, however, presupposes an inner willingness to open up to all things "foreign". Many artists of the period around 1860 evidently possessed that willingness.

The discovery of Japanese art presumably not only provided a fundamental inspiration to those of France's artists aspiring towards renewal, but also validated their endeavours. The world of Japanese imagery and form thus played an important role in the development of modernism in Europe in two respects: on the one hand, it served as an inexhaustible inspirational source of subjects and stylistic devices previously unfamiliar to European eyes and, on the other hand, it provided confirmation of artistic approaches already being pursued by artists in France. In his above-mentioned article of 1878, Chesneau accordingly wrote: "Every one of them adopted those qualities of Japanese art that proved to possess the closest affinity with his own gifts. [...] And they all found in it less an inspiration than a confirmation of their own ways of seeing, feeling, understanding and interpreting nature. What we have here is thus more a reinforcement of individual originality than cowardly submission to Japanese art."[18] This quotation helps us to understand the significance that Japanese art held for the development of contemporary art – but also the degree to which many critics endeavoured to play down that significance. Like Chesneau, other art critics[19] were also afraid that French art would deteriorate into a mere imitation of a foreign culture, a fear that would prove entirely unjustified. For it was precisely within the context of their study of this unfamiliar culture that French artists launched a creative process leading not only to an inspired adoption of motifs, but – far more consequentially – to an internalisation of stylistic devices with which these artists formulated new pictorial and formal languages, each in their own way.

The Japanese artists, conversely – especially Katsushika Hokusai and Utagawa Hiroshige – had studied the compositional devices of Western art, such as perspective, and put them into practice in their own woodblock prints.[20] They themselves had thus already opened up to the pictorial language of a culture that was foreign to them, creating the foundation for the inspirational reception of their art in the West. For it is possible that the reason for the strong impact borne by Japanese art on the Western artists lies in the fact that the latter encountered something familiar in it. The "Japanised" work of an artist like Van Gogh, in turn, set off a new wave of reception in early twentieth-century Japan.[21] This open, constantly evolving "transcultural" process resulted in the productive intercultural dialogue that makes the phenomenon of *Japonisme* so fascinating and vibrant to this day.

Only very few European artists were actually in Japan, however, or explored the meanings of the artworks they admired in any depth. They were laypersons who often could not distinguish between Chinese and Japanese artefacts. Their chief concern was not with understanding Japanese art and culture correctly, but with the respective visual stimuli. In fact, there were presumably a lot of things that they misunderstood. Van Gogh, for example, set out for the south of France in the belief that he would find there the bright light and clear colours that he imagined were typical of Japan[22] – a misunderstanding, to be sure, but a very productive one for the development of his art and that of European modernism.

Naturally, Japan was only one of the many sources of inspiration that contributed to this development of such far-reaching significance. Artists also found orientation elsewhere – for example, in Greek art, the old masters, folk art or the relatively new medium of photography, to name just a few. These various impulses went hand in hand with industrial, urban and social developments. By concentrating in our exhibition *Monet, Gauguin, Van Gogh ... Japanese Inspirations* on the reception of Japanese art in France from its beginnings to its heyday (1860–1910), we are thus directing our attention solely to *one* aspect – albeit a very important one – in the development of European modernism in art.

In *Monet, Gauguin, Van Gogh ... Japanese Inspirations*, we are focusing primarily on three different kinds of artistic preoccupation concerning the inspiration from Japan that have hitherto never been presented as such in an exhibition or discussed in a publication: the depiction of Japanese objects and motifs in the works of Western artists, the transfer of Japanese-inspired pictorial themes and forms to the artists' own surroundings, and the internalisation of Japanese stylistic devices and techniques. Such a differentiation will aid us in making this fascinating – and simultaneously complex – phenomenon accessible to a broad public. We have been validated in our approach by Klaus Berger's groundbreaking study on *Japonisme in Western Painting from Whistler to Matisse*, originally appearing in German in 1980. At the end of his chapter on impressionism, which primarily revolves around Monet, Berger distinguishes between three "stages" of *Japonisme*: "If we regard the 'quotations' of kimonos and Japanese articles by Stevens, Bracquemond, Tissot, by the early Whistler and by Monet himself as the first stage, then the adaptation of Japanese motifs marks the next lengthy segment of the process; in the last stage, a purely stylistic interpretation and transposition completely dissolves and transcends the Japanese raw material."[23] Geneviève Lacambre, one of the most important *Japonisme* scholars of our day, arrives at a similar differentiation in her article "Les milieux japonisants à Paris" of 1980, although she adds a fourth aspect: the imitation of Japan's sophisticated techniques.[24] For our presentation of the works in this exhibition, we have taken as our orientation these three approaches to Japanese art, which were practised by artists concurrently until well into the early twentieth century.

The representation of art, objects and flowers imported from Japan in the artists' paintings – or, in the case of Van Gogh, the translation of Japanese colour woodblock prints into the painting medium – is one expression of the enthusiasm for Japan in the period under discussion. The unusual subjects and compositional elements they encountered in the Japanese woodblock prints moreover showed them an alternative to the aesthetic that had prevailed in European art until that time. The exploration of the highly sophisticated imagery of the Japanese woodblock prints inspired artists to try out new pictorial forms for the representation of their own surroundings, and to develop correspondences for the particular richness and aesthetic rigour of the Japanese examples. They therefore adapted Japanese pictorial themes for their own works (women at their toilette, waves, or rocks in the sea). Inspired by the serial depiction of a motif (Mount Fuji, bridges, waterfalls, etc.) in the work of Hokusai or Hiroshige, artists such as Courbet, Monet, Cézanne and Rivière likewise began repeating the same subject over and over again and – in the case of Courbet and Monet – exhibited the resulting works as series. They also adopted the stylistic devices of the Japanese woodblock prints, internalised them and employed them entirely in their own ways. Among the most important compositional devices to have undergone reinterpretation in the West in this manner are the planar juxtaposition of the foreground and background, the steep view from above or below, the negation of classical perspective, the radical cutting off of the main motif with the edge of the picture, the division of the pictorial plane by diagonal elements, the simplification of forms through large, compact colour areas and strongly emphasised contours or the employment of empty zones, the asymmetrical arrangement of the pictorial elements, the decorative arrangement of the pictorial space, and extremely vertical or horizontal formats. Many artists, such as Vincent Van Gogh, also admired the vibrant and extremely nuanced colours of the woodblock prints and adopted them in their own works. In a letter to his brother of 31 July 1888, Van Gogh described a scene he had observed in the harbour of Arles which inspired him to paint *Quay with Men Unloading Sand Barges* (p. 10): "I saw a magnificent and very strange effect this evening. A very large boat laden with coal on the Rhône, moored at the quay. Seen from above it was all glistening and wet from a shower; the water was a white yellow and clouded pearl-grey, the sky lilac and an orange strip in the west, the town violet. On the boat, small workmen, blue and dirty white, were coming and going, carrying the cargo ashore. It was pure Hokusai."[25]

A conspicuous aspect of the idiosyncratic reception of this new, unfamiliar art is the fact that the pictorial aesthetic of the Japanese colour woodblock prints was initially applied in paintings, and only adopted or imitated in printmaking by the succeeding generation of artists. Then it was particularly Toulouse-Lautrec, Rivière, Cassatt and Vallotton who helped the printing techniques to new prestige within the context of their practice of looking to Japanese examples for orientation.

Finally, in 1893, Monet designed his property in Giverny with a pond and bridge inspired by Japanese colour woodblock prints. The vegetation he planted was also Far Eastern in character. Irises, Japanese woodland poppies, azaleas and, above all, chrysanthemums grew in his garden. It was there that he executed the water-lily paintings, which rank among the masterpieces of early twentieth-century art, influencing entire generations of artists. These paintings would have been inconceivable without the in-depth exploration of Japanese art.

Concurrently with the fine arts, the decorative arts also underwent a development stimulated by ceramics, lacquerware, fans and partition walls imported from Japan. Not only artists such as Gallé, Rousseau, Carriès or Jeanneney drew inspiration from these objects for their motifs and forms, but also Degas, Bonnard, Denis, Vallotton and Rodin, to merely name a few.

Naturally, the respective pictorial themes and stylistic devices can also be encountered in the European art of earlier centuries. Consider, for instance, Albrecht Dürer's *Women's Bath* of 1496 (Kunsthalle Bremen), Jean-Auguste-Dominique Ingres's *Valpinçon Bather* of 1808 (Musée du Louvre, Paris), examples of trees serving to divide the composition diagonally in paintings by Jean-Antoine Constantin (1756–1844) or of figures cut off by the picture's edge in the works of El Greco (1541–1614) or Federico Barocci (1526/1536–1612). Yet in view of the fact that – owing to the woodblock prints and albums that were circulating in France in the second half of the nineteenth century – the Japanese pictorial aesthetic was omnipresent there, the Japanese can be considered true impulse-givers and eye-openers. The art critic Théodore Duret aptly summed up this state of affairs in his text *Les peintres impressionnistes* of 1878, writing: "It took the arrival of the Japanese prints among us for someone to dare to sit down on the bank of a river, to juxtapose on one canvas a boldly red roof, a high white wall, a green poplar, a yellow road and some blue water. Before the example of the Japanese, it was impossible."[26] In the decorative arts, the practice of employing materials previously somewhat neglected, such as stoneware, played a major role as a stimulus in the work of artists such as Jean Carriès or Paul Jeanneney.

Nearly all of the artists who permitted themselves to be inspired by the imagery and formal language of the Far East collected Japanese art themselves, especially *ukiyo-e* colour woodblock prints. Today regarded as masterpieces and traded for large sums, back then these prints were available for very little money. The source material of these artists' collections varies greatly. Whereas the holdings of Whistler, Monet, Van Gogh, Rivière, Rodin, Denis, Vuillard and Bonnard have remained almost intact, others were scattered to the four winds after the artist's respective deaths, as in the case of Degas, Tissot, Stevens, Bernard or Gauguin.

For our exhibition, we have included only Japanese masters whom the artists of the nineteenth century are known to have been acquainted with, either from exhibitions or publications or because they collected them themselves. In ideal cases, a work on view here exhibits the exact pictorial subject verifiably included in one of the artists' collections or is even a print once belonging to such a collection. At any rate, in our choice of pictorial themes, we have endeavoured to approximate the situation the artists in France will presumably have encountered themselves, so as to permit dialogue with the paintings, prints and objects by French artists likewise on display. One aspect that has only become a focus of interest in European art history in recent years[27] is "erotic" *Japonisme*, which we have taken into account here by juxtaposing *shunga* ("pictures of spring") with Picasso.

In addition to the above-described aims of our show, however, the visitor can also gain an overview of the development of the Japanese colour woodblock print from the early masters such as Harunobu to Utamaro and the well-known greats of the nineteenth century, Hokusai and Hiroshige, and finally the most important exponents of the late nineteenth century, Kunisada and Kuniyoshi – all of whose works together constitute an exhibition within the exhibition, so to speak.

Not least importantly, this project presented us with an opportunity to study the history and origins of the Japanese objects in Museum Folkwang's holdings. Karl Ernst Osthaus, who founded the museum in Hagen in 1902, had begun acquiring Japanese artefacts in 1898. In the years that followed, he significantly expanded the Japanese Collection. To our great delight, more than twenty objects have now proven to stem from the collections of the early *Japonistes* – for instance, a Noh robe from the Charles Gillot's Collection, two tsubas from that of Philippe Burty, and hanging scrolls, statuettes, bowls, lacquerware items and tsubas from the holdings of Paul Brenot and Edmond Taigny. Except for the Noh robe, Osthaus purchased these objects through the agency of Siegfried Bing. A lacquered desk from Bing's own collection also made its way into Osthaus's possession. All of these objects bear direct witness to *Japonisme* in nineteenth-century France.

Yet the rage for things Japanese took hold not only in France, but also elsewhere in Europe such as in Great Britain, Germany, Austria, Spain, Poland, the Czech Republic and the Scandinavian countries, and even in the United States. It also had an impact on other art forms – such as photography, architecture, textile art, theatre and film – none of which we can take into account within the framework of our show.

In many countries, the preoccupation with Japan lasted until well into the twentieth century. These extremely suspenseful developments go beyond the scope of our present project; they have, however, given rise to exhibitions of their own – many quite comprehensive – over the past ten years. Our show accordingly concludes with a brief look at the twentieth century, again from the French perspective, as mirrored in works by Bonnard, Matisse and Picasso.

As is so often the case at the end of a project, we realise that, despite the abundance of publications on the subject in question, and despite the new deliberations undertaken for this catalogue, many questions remain unanswered. The historiography of *Japonisme* is accordingly far from complete; further aspects have yet to be investigated in depth. One of these aspects is the recently postulated theory (Susan J. Napier and Mae Michiko) that the mass enthusiasm for Japanese colour woodblock prints in the nineteenth century exhibits similarities to the manga and anime boom of the late twentieth century.[28] The impact borne by this reception of Japanese pop culture on Western visual arts – today or in the future – is an exciting new topic for coming exhibitions and publications.

Sandra Gianfreda *Exhibition curator*

Essays

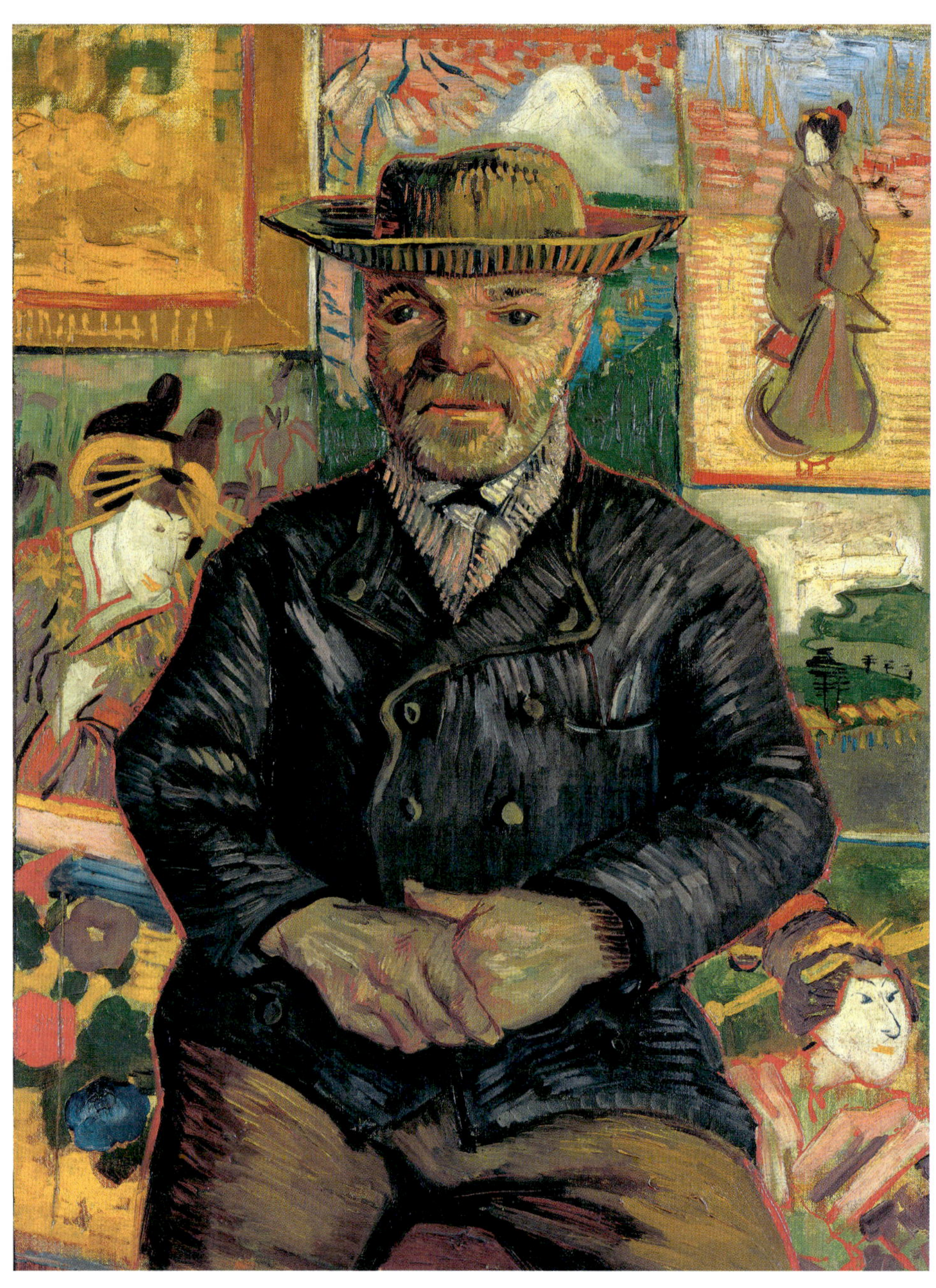

38 Vincent Van Gogh, *Portrait of Père Tanguy*, 1887

Japonisme as a transcultural process – Odano Naotake, Katsushika Hokusai and Vincent Van Gogh

Mae Michiko

To regard *Japonisme* from a transcultural perspective means to ask how and why it succeeded in leading European art to a "revolution in seeing".[1] What made this breakthrough to modern art possible?

In the mid-nineteenth century, many artists began to sense that – owing to the constraints of academic classicism, historicism, naturalism and what could be referred to as "illusionism" – art in Europe had reached an impasse. These artists sought a new beginning beyond an artistic tradition characterised by such compositional principles as central perspective. In this crisis, Japanese colour woodblock prints known as *ukiyo-e* presented Western artists with a way of seeing free of the restrictions posed by the hierarchical ranking of pictorial subjects and genres as adhered to by the European art tradition. Artists realised that this liberation from the conventions of the European tradition represented an opportunity for creating a new art.

Japonisme took Japanese culture beyond its own boundaries and made it a significant part of Western culture. At the same time, by absorbing Japanese culture and transforming it into something all its own, Western culture opened itself to another tradition and overcame its self-referentiality. The influences, effects, encounters, exchanges and inspirations that transpired between these two cultures were thus *transcultural* rather than *intercultural* processes and phenomena. Only in these terms can the phenomenon of *Japonisme* be understood productively. If we regard *Japonisme* as a transcultural phenomenon – and even go so far as to regard it as a model of transculturality – its productive potential for cultural change and the emergence of modern culture in the twentieth and twenty-first centuries becomes clear.

How can we describe the transcultural dynamic of *Japonisme*? Did the "discovery" of the Japanese colour woodblock prints in the mid-nineteenth century trigger the development that led to modern art? Or, conversely, did the crisis in Western painting "make the aid" of East Asian art "imperative"?[2] Did the crisis generate a kind of "inner motivation" and "inner disposition" in the artists for new ways of seeing and depicting things, leading them in turn to the "discovery" of the *ukiyo-e*? Or was it Japanese art that brought forth the disposition, motivation and necessity that led Western artists to the development of modern art?

These questions bring us directly to an understanding of *Japonisme* that permits us to regard it as a transcultural process. *Japonisme* created new visual perspectives, presented new means of composition and expression, and it was an inspiration for the Western artists' own creative processes. The recognition, adoption and implementation of the Japanese way of seeing can be understood as having brought about an "integration of the Japanese vision into Western modernism".[3] What was decisive here was the fact that this "integration" led to what Klaus Berger calls a "completely new and original visual form".[4] He writes: "The new artistic discoveries gave rise to the visual form appropriate to modern conditions."[5] The artists were amazed to discover "that the Japanese had already achieved much of what they were striving

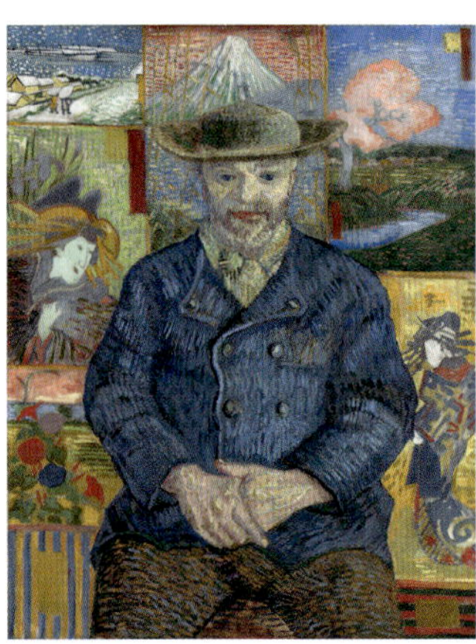

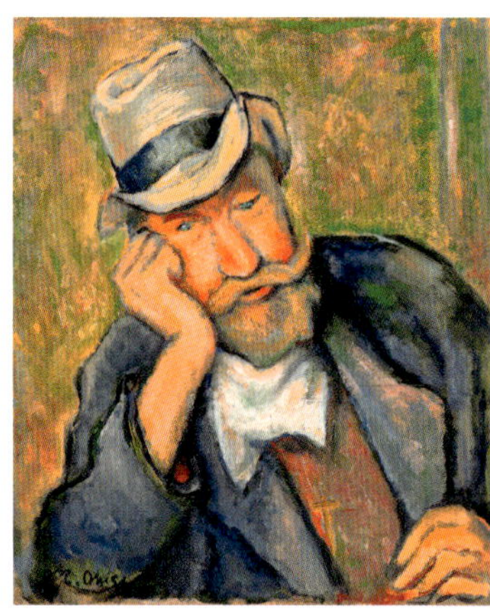

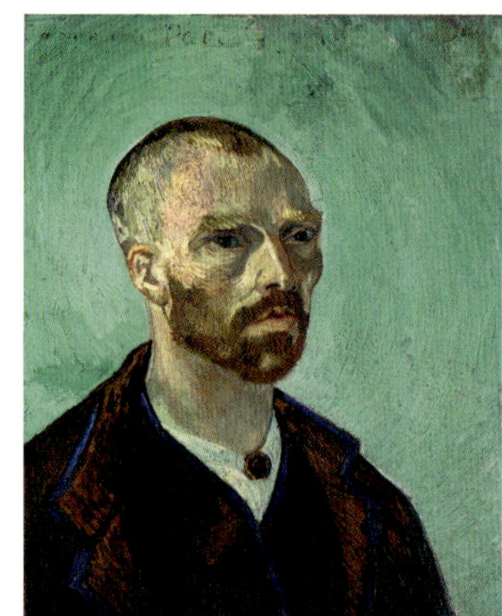

1 Vincent Van Gogh, *Portrait of Père Tanguy*, 1887, Musée Rodin, Paris
2 Ōishi Terukazu, *Self-Portrait on my Mind*, 1972, Ōtani Memorial Art Museum, Nishinomiya City
3 Vincent Van Gogh, *Self-Portrait Dedicated to Paul Gauguin*, 1888, Harvard Art Museums/ Fogg Museum, Bequest from the Collection of Maurice Wertheim

for, that the Japanese […] had got ahead of the European art movement",[6] as the Viennese art historian Franz Wickhoff observed in the late nineteenth century. In other words, European artists recognised in Japanese art the modernism they themselves were aiming for. This "insight"[7] was the inspiration, motivation and creative stimulus for the development of modernism in their own art.

Van Gogh's Japan and Japan's Van Gogh

Vincent Van Gogh can perhaps be considered the best-known and most popular *Japoniste*. He projected his vision and utopia of the south (Provence) onto Japan, and he projected Japan onto the south. "[Y]ou know", he wrote to his brother Theo, "I feel I'm in Japan".[8] For Van Gogh, to become acquainted with the south meant "to understand the Japanese better",[9] because in the south he aimed to seek and put into practice the way toward a new art that the Japanese showed him.

Understanding the Japanese was not, however, his only concern. More than any other artist, Van Gogh sought "to adopt [their] spirit".[10] "If we study Japanese art, then we see an undoubtedly wise and philosophical and intelligent man who spends his time – on what? […] he studies a single blade of grass. But this blade of grass leads him to draw all the plants – then the seasons, the broad features of landscapes, finally animals, and then the human figure. He spends his life like that, and life is too short to do everything."[11] This passage from a letter by Van Gogh referring to a text by Siegfried Bing[12] recalls Katsushika Hokusai's description of his life as an artist: "From the time I was six years old, I had the inclination to sketch objects, and at the age of fifty I frequently presented my pictures in public. But among the pictures I completed before I was seventy, hardly any were remarkable. It was not until I was seventy-three that I recognised the skeletons of animals and the origins of plants. When I am eighty I will develop my art further, at ninety I will get to the bottom of things, and at a hundred I will achieve a spiritual art. And when I'm a hundred and ten, every dot and every line in my work will be alive."[13]

Entirely in the spirit of Hokusai's statement, Van Gogh writes: "I envy the Japanese the extreme clarity that everything in their work has. It's never dull, and never appears to be done too hastily. Their work is as simple as breathing, and they do a figure with a few confident strokes with the same ease as if it was as simple as buttoning your waistcoat. Ah, I must manage to do a figure with a few strokes."[14] Van Gogh, in other words, wanted to become like a Japanese artist himself. And even if the "search for himself" and the "finding of himself" in ("his") Japanese artists was partly based on a misunderstanding – according to Kōdera Tsukasa, he seems to have projected "his own ideal onto the Japanese painters"[15] – that projection and his enthusiasm about all things Japanese made him open for what was different and new in Japanese art.

What the Japanese showed him appeared to Van Gogh like a "new religion".[16] Yet the admiration for Van Gogh cultivated by many Japanese artists and intellectuals could likewise be called a "new religion".

Van Gogh's biography and his works move people all over the world, but the Japanese sense a very special affinity with him – possibly because they recognise the "Japanese" in him. The art critic Théodore Duret, who wrote a biography of Van Gogh in 1916, mentioned in the second edition of 1924 that Van Gogh was celebrated in faraway Japan as though he had been born there.[17] Van Gogh himself dreamed of becoming like a Japanese painter.[18] And if he were to live a long life, he once mused, he would like to be like "père Tanguy", the art dealer who was for him the intermediary "on the way to an imaginary Japan"[19] (fig. 1). Conversely, for many Japanese artists and men of letters, Van Gogh was not only a model to be emulated, but a kind of spiritual father. As early as 1912, the magazine *Shirakaba* caused a great wave of enthusiasm and admiration for Van Gogh. *Shirakaba* was published by young individualist poets, men of letters and artists, in order to spearhead their new artistic and literary movement that was influenced by European culture, seeking to create a new art in Japan whose chief focus was the assertion of themselves as individual subjects. The magazine introduced Western artists such as Auguste Rodin, Paul Cézanne and Paul Gauguin in Japan and, in 1912, published a special issue on Van Gogh. Although at the time it was not possible to see his works in the original, even copies had a tremendous impact. The famous literary critic Kobayashi Hideo, who later wrote *Van Gogh's Letters* (1952), described his first experience of Van Gogh as such a shock that, at the sight of the Dutch artist's last painting, *Wheatfield with Crows*, he sank to his knees; it was as if he "had been stared at and paralysed by a great eye".[20] The artist Ōishi Terukazu painted a self-portrait in the manner of Van Gogh and called it *Self-Portrait on my Mind* (fig. 2) – just as, conversely, Van Gogh portrayed himself as though he were a Japanese monk (*bonze*) (fig. 3). Japanese artists were deeply impressed by both Van Gogh's art and life. They even considered his "madness", which tended to alienate people in the West, a logical and necessary element in the realisation of his artistic passion.[21]

If transcultural understanding involves asking what Western artists such as Van Gogh *wanted* to see in Japanese art and what they projected onto the other culture, then we must also ask what they *were capable* of seeing in it. Was it possible for them to "discover" the *ukiyo-e* woodblock prints precisely because the works of Hokusai, Hiroshige and others already contained Western elements? Was Claude Monet, for instance, aware that the Hokusai and Hiroshige prints in his collection already manifested the "absorption" of Western concepts?[22] And did the assimilation of Western concepts and forms make these works more accessible to him? According to Gary Hickey, what Monet saw in the *ukiyo-e* paintings he owned was in part a reinterpretation of his own artistic tradition.[23] The following section offers an overview of the factors leading to this reinterpretation of Western art by Hokusai and Hiroshige and the transcultural context from which they emerged.

The openness for the West in the isolated Japan of the Edo period (1603–1868)

In the period between 1639 and 1854, Japan was almost completely cut off from the outside world. Afraid that Christianity might spread in Japan, the Tokugawa had introduced this policy of isolation in the early seventeenth century. Via the artificial island of Dejima in Nagasaki (south-western Japan), however, restricted trade with Chinese and Dutch merchants enabled limited contact to the outside world. It was through this small window that information about Western science and technology made its way to the isolated mainland, where it was controlled and monopolised by the Tokugawa government. The strict ban on the import of Western publications was relaxed in 1720 in connection with the reform measures of the Kyōhō period (1716–1736); Western science, technology and culture thus became somewhat more accessible by way of Nagasaki. As a result, Japanese culture – and art –underwent a transformation in the second half of the eighteenth century.

By what routes did artists like Hokusai and Hiroshige obtain the knowledge of Western painting that they were able to integrate into their own art? Here, the Akita Ranga school based in Akita (north-western Japan) – and thus, far from the centre, Edo – played an important role. *Ranga* means "Dutch painting"; it was called "Dutch" because at the time everything Western came to Japan by way of Holland. Odano

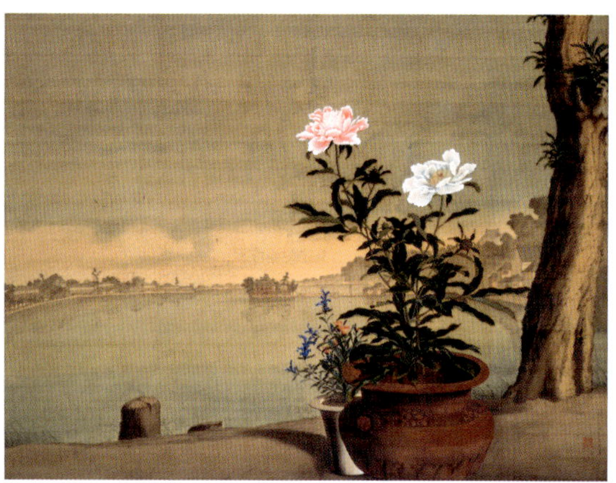

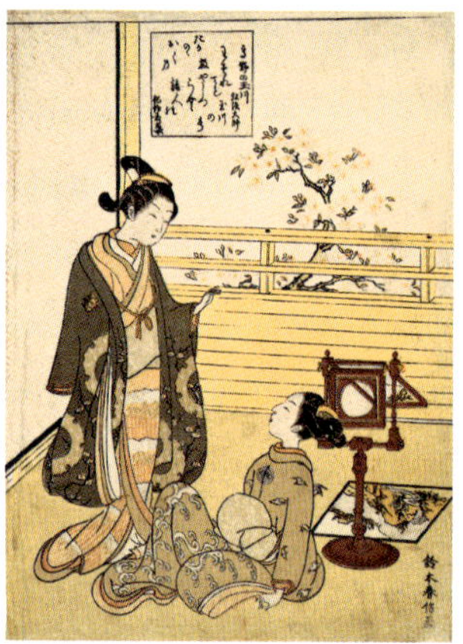

Naotake (1749–1780) was the central figure in the small circle of *ranga* painters. In his early phase, Odano painted in the traditional manner of the Kanō school before becoming acquainted with Western painting through Hiraga Gennai (1728–1779). Hiraga, a "Renaissance man" in Japan, possessed an exceptionally wide range of talents and was active as a geologist, doctor, painter, writer, inventor and entrepreneur. He had been to Nagasaki, where he had acquired knowledge of Western science. In Akita, where he went from Edo at the invitation of the feudal lord and painter Satake Yoshiatsu (pseudonym: Shozan; 1748–1785), he made the acquaintance of Odano and recognised the young artist's exceptional artistic abilities. Odano soon followed Hiraga to Edo and, in 1774, he began painting in the Western style under his mentor's guidance.

In his most representative work, *Shinobazu-no-ike-zu* (*A View of Shinobazu Pond*, circa 1778/1780), Odano harmoniously combines Japanese tradition with Western techniques such as central perspective, chiaroscuro and realistic detail (fig. 4). This picture is considered the first successful integration of the Japanese tradition and the Western painting technique in Japan. Odano succeeded in adopting Western stylistic elements, combining them with the Japanese tradition, and thus developing a new and independent style. This style is characterised by a boldly depicted, large motif in the foreground, set against a background consisting of a faraway landscape shown according to the laws of perspective; this juxtaposition of near and far creates a special sense of pictorial depth.

Odano's painting technique did not come about solely through the teachings of Hiraga Gennai, but had its origins in East–West connections of a more complex nature. In a number of Odano's realistically painted works, for example, the influence of the painter Sō Shiseki (1715–1786) is evident. Sō had gone from Edo to Nagasaki to learn the realistic painting technique of the Chinese Shin-Nanbin (Chinese: Shen-Nanpin) school from the Chinese painter Sō Shigan (1682–1760). The Nanbin school had already assimilated the Western painting style by this time. An important intermediary in this development had been the Italian painter Giuseppe Castiglione (1688–1766), who had gone to China in 1715 as a Jesuit missionary and worked at the Qing court (later as a mandarin) until he died there. In China, Castiglione became completely assimilated into the Chinese culture and way of life. He painted in a new style that made use of Western techniques but was strongly adapted to the Chinese style. For Japanese painters such as Odano, the Nanbin school that emerged in this context prepared the ground for their reception of Western painting techniques. What the Japanese so appreciated about Western art and science – the art historian Kōno Motoaki writes of an almost "religious profession of faith"[24] – thus did not come directly from the West, but in part by way of China as well.

Japanese artists particularly admired Western painting for its realistic representation and use of central perspective. The famous Western-style painter Shiba Kōkan (1747–1818), who wrote a theoretical treatise entitled *Seiyōgadan* (Discussion of Western Painting), observed that, whereas Eastern art was frivolous and purposeless, Western art represented the truth of the objects. Only Western painting, he concluded,

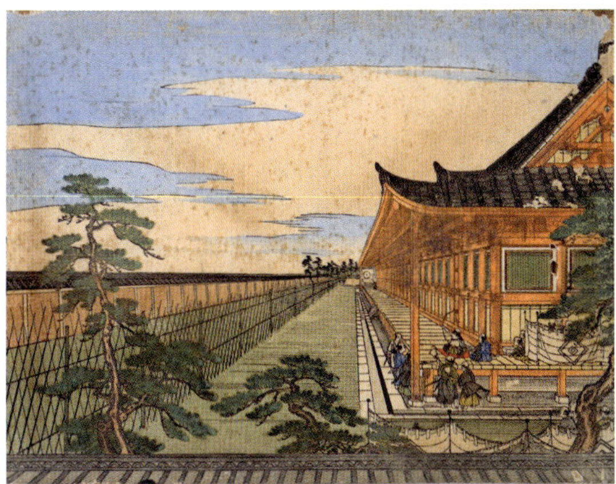

4 Odano Naotake, *A View of Shinobazu Pond*, circa 1778/1780, Akita Museum of Modern Art
5 Suzuki Harunobu, *The Tamagawa River in Kōya (Two Girls with a Zograscope)*, from the series *Six Tama Rivers*, circa 1767, The Metropolitan Museum of Modern Art, Harris Brisbane Dick Fund
6 Maruyama Ōkyo, *Archery Contest at the Sanjūsangendō*, 1760s–1795, Kobe City Museum

was a truly practical art, as was the "technique of science".[25] And indeed, in the European Renaissance, art was considered an applied science. It was from this context that, according to Hans Belting, artistic perspective had emerged, "probably Western culture's most important pictorial idea".[26] In Belting's view, the art of perspective was based on the Arab theory of seeing, from which Western pictorial theory evolved in the Renaissance.[27] He regards perspective as "the signum of what distinguishes Western paintings from others".[28]

The Japanese, too, considered perspective "the most important attribute of the Western style".[29] At the end of the sixteenth century, the Jesuits had undertaken teaching the cultural technique of perspective as part of their effort to evangelise China and Japan. In the period from around 1590 to 1615, the Jesuit Giovanni Nicolò established a painting school "for instructing Japanese artists in perspective".[30] But it was not until the second quarter of the eighteenth century that "perspective [became] a recognised mode of representation"[31] in Japan. For the broader public, the concept of perspective was shaped by the so-called *uki-e* pictures, in which central perspective was indicated by lines (linear perspective). *Uki-e* means pictures that "protrude"; such images were used primarily to depict interiors, such as those of theatres. The illusion of three-dimensional perspective was intensified by so-called zograscope images (*vues d'optique*), which, together with zograscope devices, made their way from Europe to China in the mid-eighteenth century, where they were modified and then introduced in Japan. An *ukiyo-e* work by Suzuki Harunobu entitled *Kōya no Tamagawa* (*The Tamagawa River in Kōya,* circa 1767) depicts an apparatus equipped with a convex lens and designed for viewing pictures (prints) with a three-dimensional effect (fig. 5). Pictures of this kind were referred to as *megane-e* (literally: "eyeglass pictures") (fig. 6). Japan's first theoretical treatises on Western painting were written by Odano's pupil, Satake Shozan. In his writings, he praised Western painting's naturalistic mode of representation and criticised Eastern painting as "impractical" and "symbolistic", pointing out that the concern of the latter was not the realistic depiction of the objects themselves, but the expression of their "spirit". He considered a scientific empirical basis so important that he wrote: "Anyone who wants to become a painter must first study astronomy and geography". For him, the way to painting began with the precise observation and objective representation of reality. Satake explained the importance of the central-perspective projection, describing perspective – which he considered the core of the Western painting technique – as the "degree of distance and proximity" (*enkin no dosū*).[32] In Japan, perspective – literally "looking through", in the sense of looking through space – was understood as the division of space into near and far.

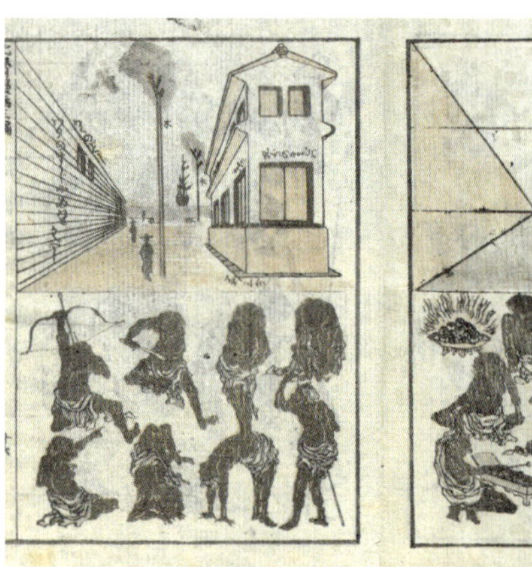
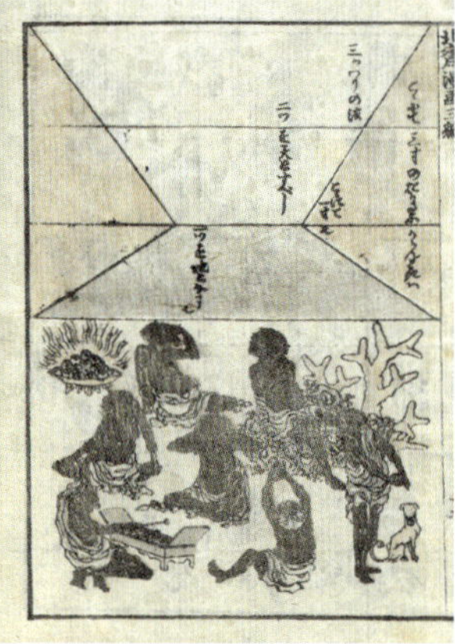
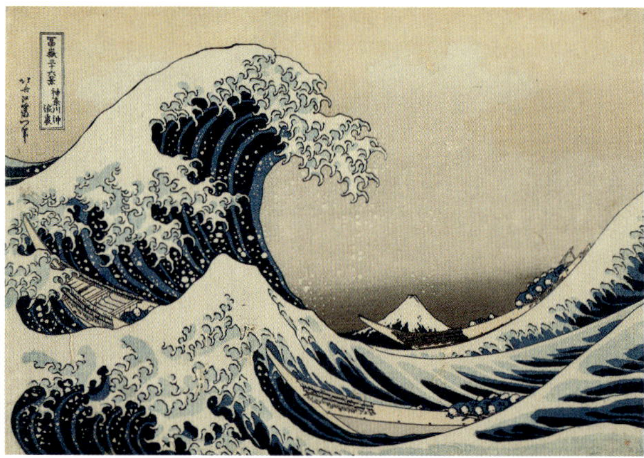

Hokusai as a "pioneer" of modern art

The ingenious artist Katsushika Hokusai mastered Western techniques such as perspective and chiaroscuro so well that he could draw upon them freely in developing his individual style. Hickey writes that "Hokusai has creatively appropriated Western methods to achieve his own ends", ascertaining that "[…] the creative potential offered by Western techniques was to be fully exploited by *ukiyo-e*-artists such as Hokusai and Hiroshige, particularly in their use of perspective".[33] In his famous *Manga*, Hokusai revealed his interpretation of perspective in sketches. Rather than visualising perspective as a construction organised according to spatial depth and a vanishing point, he divided the picture surface horizontally into three parts ("method of division into three parts") and vertically into two parts (fig. 7).

Hokusai went beyond the perspective-oriented mode of pictorial composition cultivated by Odano and Shiba Kōkan by directing attention to what is taking place in the foreground. In one of his most well-known scenes of Mount Fuji, the waves in the foreground are shown creatively, decoratively and disproportionally large, in excess of any realistic representation; the contrast between the foreground (waves) and the background (Mount Fuji) is thus heightened to an extreme (fig. 8). According to Inaga Shigemi, Hokusai transformed perspective (or, more precisely, the Japanese distance-proximity technique's rendition of it) into a method of "deliberately exaggerated, special presentation of space" that served as the underlying compositional principle for his *36 Views of Mount Fuji*.[34] Breaking with the European tradition's continually receding spatial depth, Hokusai developed a means of creating the effect of spatial depth through a particular arrangement of surfaces or surface elements and by varying the shading of two-dimensionally applied colours.

For Western artists, this must have seemed like the revelation of an artistic truth, since in their own tradition the perspectival picture presents the illusion of three dimensions on a two-dimensional surface. Perspectival space "is generated only by looking and for the purpose of looking",[35] as Belting shows; in the picture itself, it "exists only on a surface that is not space and does not possess space".[36] Could it be that, with the aid of Hokusai's and Hiroshige's pictures, Western artists became aware of precisely this problem? Did these pictures provide them a means of achieving a new two-dimensional pictorial space and the two-dimensional deployment of colour that represented an important step on the way to abstraction in twentieth-century art?

The creative transformation of Western artistic concepts, forms and techniques by Hokusai and Hiroshige not only made their art more easily accessible to Westerners in general, but was the very means by which artists such as Van Gogh, Monet and others succeeded in liberating themselves from their own artistic tradition. Monet owned many prints by the two Japanese artists. With the help of what he saw in those pictures, he was able to overcome traditional Western perspective by applying Hiroshige's perspective – a displaced perspective, concealed and deconstructed by a curve – in his own paintings (fig. 9 and fig. 10).[37]

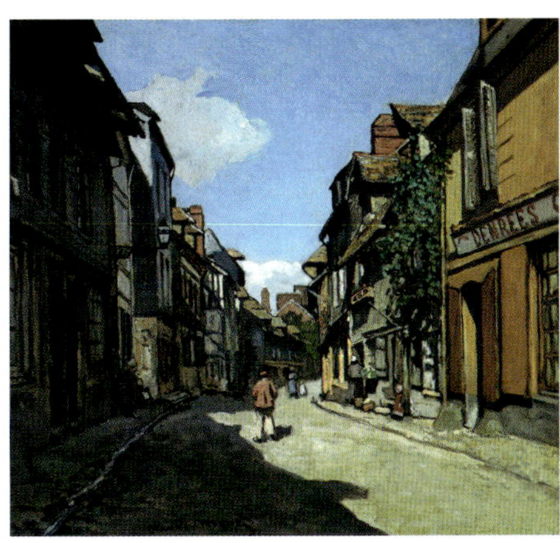

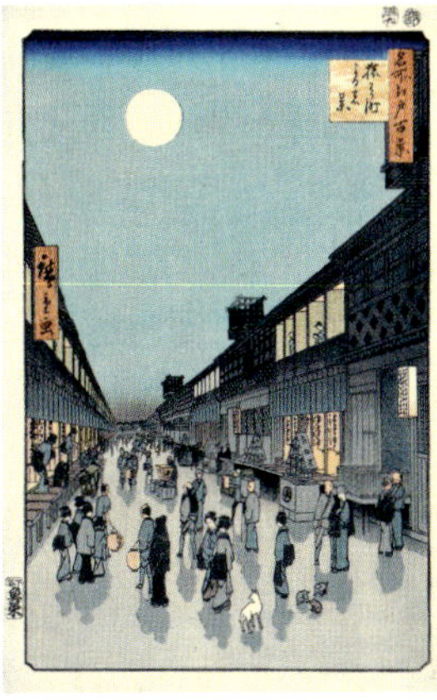

7 Katsushika Hokusai, *Studies on the Central Perspective*, in: *Hokusai Manga*, vol. 3 (15 v / 16 r), 1815, Ostasienabteilung, Staatsbibliothek zu Berlin – Preußischer Kulturbesitz
8 Katsushika Hokusai, *Under the Wave off Kanagawa* from the series *36 Views of Mount Fuji*, 1830–1831, Museum für Kunst und Gewerbe Hamburg
9 Claude Monet, *Rue de la Bavolle, Honfleur*, circa 1864, Museum of Fine Arts, Boston, Bequest of John T. Spaulding
10 Utagawa Hiroshige, *Night View of Saruwaka-machi* from the series *One Hundred Famous Views of Edo*, 1856, Museum für Kunst und Gewerbe Hamburg

Cultural elements such as central perspective and chiaroscuro, as well as Japanese and East Asian pictorial elements transcend cultural boundaries and spread freely through other cultures, entering into new relationships and bringing forth new meanings in the process. Thus, perhaps it is not so important whether Western artists understood Japanese art and culture "correctly" in the strictly scientific sense; what is far more important is what they "wanted to see and were capable of seeing"[38] and how they responded to the other culture by creating new relationships and meanings in their art.

Indeed, the transcultural interpenetration of Western and Japanese art represented a decisive step in the development of modern art on its path to abstraction.

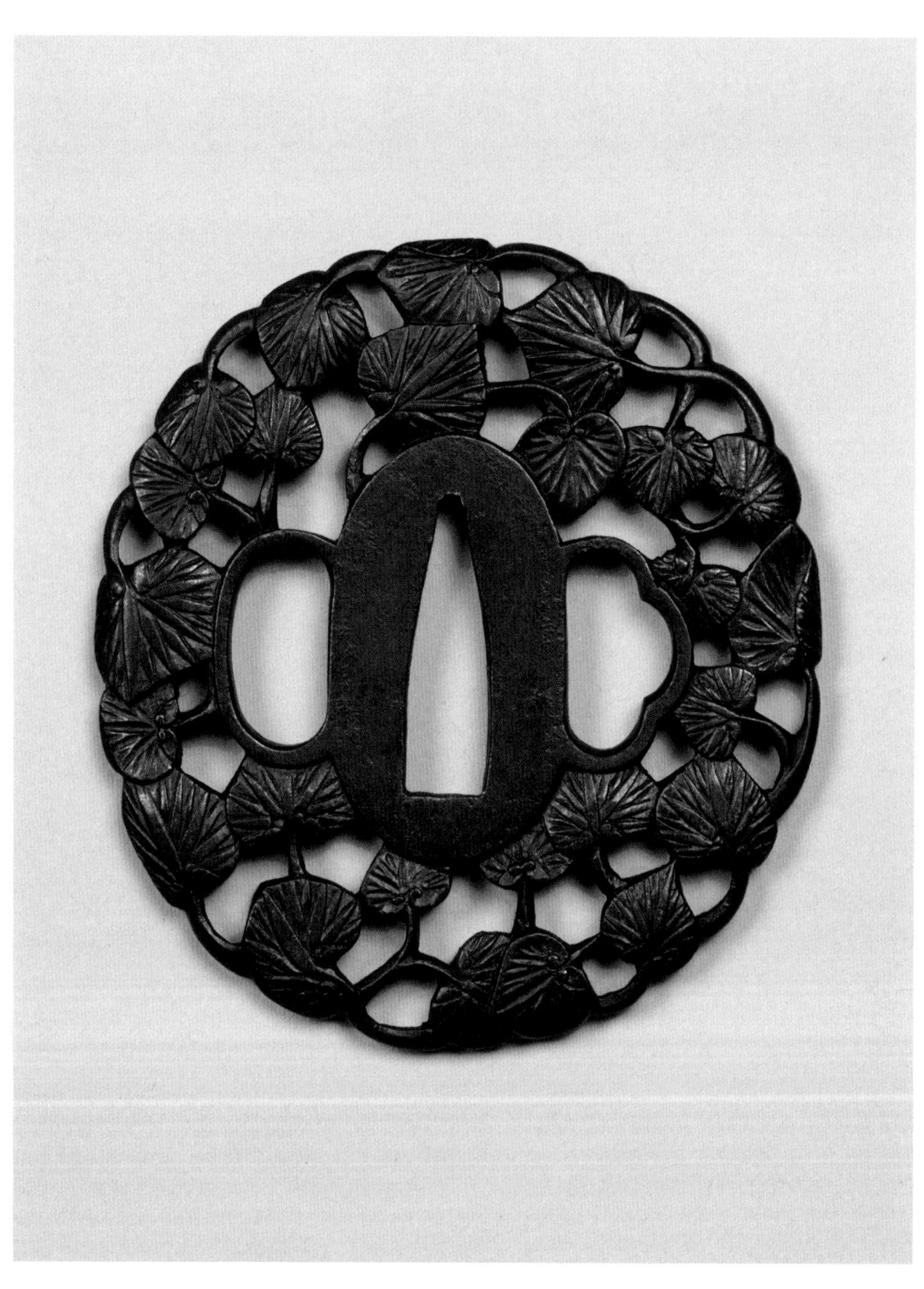

349 Japan, *Tsuba*, circa 1650–1700,
formerly in the Philippe Burty Collection

The presentation, perception and collection of Japanese art in nineteenth-century France

Gregory Irvine

In 1853, the American Commodore Perry arrived in Edo Bay with a powerful squadron of ships in an attempt to open up trade with Japan. In 1854, he returned with an even more powerful fleet, and a Treaty of Peace and Amity (the so-called Kanagawa Agreement) was eventually signed that opened up two ports to the Americans and allowed for an official consul. By the end of 1855, the British, Russian and Dutch governments had set up similar arrangements, thereby precipitating the end of Japan's long period of self-enforced seclusion from the outside world. Prior to this period, the West had seen little of the arts of Japan – save for export porcelain and lacquer, the trade in which had been controlled since the seventeenth century by the Dutch. Now, however, the potential for a greater export of Japanese goods to the West was beginning to open up.

Between 1858 and 1859, there followed the establishment of (generally regarded unequal) further agreements and trading partnerships between Japan and other Western powers. The Treaty of Amity and Commerce between France and Japan was signed in Edo on 9 October 1858, by Jean-Baptiste Louis Gros, the commander of the French expedition in China, assisted by Charles de Chassiron and Alfred de Moges, thereby opening up diplomatic relations between France and Japan. In 1859, Gustave Duchesne de Bellecourt became the first official French representative in Japan, and a French consulate opened later that same year in Edo.[1]

Japan at the world fairs in Europe

In 1862, the British diplomat, Sir Rutherford Alcock, "her Majesty's Envoy Extraordinary and Minister Plenipotentiary to the Court of the Taikoon of Japan",[2] had organised the display of over six hundred Japanese objects at the London International Exhibition of Industry and Art, mostly with material from his own collection which he had acquired while serving in Japan (fig. 1). Alcock probably had little idea of the quality and date of manufacture of these objects, many of which – as we can see in illustrations of the displays – were rather mundane and unrepresentative of Japanese contemporary arts. Moreover, they were displayed in a highly Western nineteenth-century fashion, and some of the objects (porcelain, bronzes, prints and material which might be considered "ethnographic") were in fact already aiming at a Western market or were already showing distinct Western influence.[3] The success of these displays catering to an undiscriminating British public, who were confronted with these art forms for the first time, was significant; but it was not so with the visiting Japanese ambassadors who thought the selection and display of objects demeaned Japan, commenting that "it was such a ramshackle assortment of artefacts that it looked just like an old antique shop and I could not bear to look".[4]

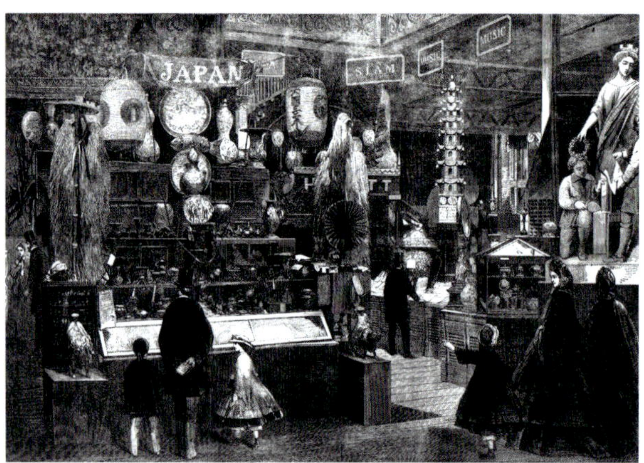

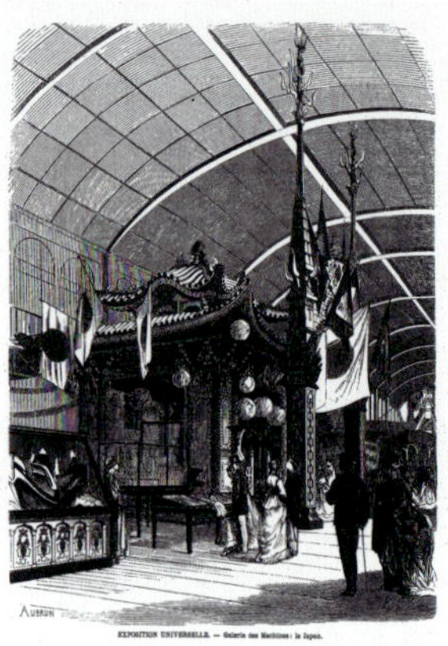

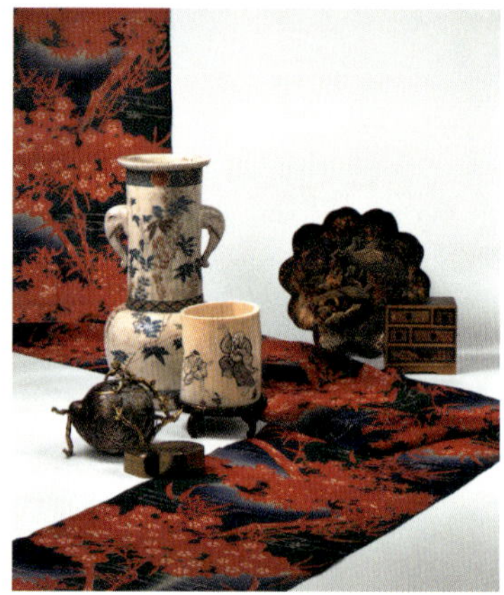

The *Illustrated London News* devoted two pages to its glowing description of the objects on display: "Of the skill and workmanship displayed in the ornamental lacquering we can speak with the greatest praise; it is at once rich, tasteful and solid in appearance, while the articles themselves are in reality remarkably light and handy [...] Attention may next be directed to the numerous lacquered and enamelled objects in ivory, tortoiseshell, mother-of-pearl &c such as boxes, pedestals, saucers, buttons and so on [...]".[5]

Japan was still in political turmoil, and dissatisfaction with the ruling Tokugawa shogunate as well as pressure to restore the emperor to full power resulted in civil war. In 1868, power passed from the ruling samurai classes to the young Prince Mutsuhito (later named Emperor Meiji), thereby ending almost seven hundred years of samurai control of the country. In 1876, laws were passed which saw the final abolition of the samurai as a class; Japanese artisans had now lost their centuries-old traditional patrons and had to find new markets for their skills. Collectors in the West quickly developed an almost insatiable appetite for Japan's artistic products, and as Japan struggled to throw off its feudal past and develop as a modern (Western) industrialised and economic power, so the trade in artworks expanded.

Serendipitously, this was also the time when great official fairs of art and industry were being held all over the world. At these occasions, Japan could now display its skills in the arts, crafts and other manufacturing forms. Thanks to the political and commercial insight of the Meiji government, these world fairs functioned as an important stage on which to promote Japanese art and culture.

The artistic and commercial successes which Japanese works of art gained at world fairs highlighted the importance of the decorative arts for the national economy. It has been estimated that, between 1870 and the early 1890s, the export of these handcrafted objects accounted for around one tenth of total national exports. However, the West often had preconceived ideas of what constituted Japanese art, and this "taste" was obligingly catered for by enterprising Japanese dealers. There was little true understanding of what was coming onto the market at the time, and many fakes and poor-quality works found their way into both private and museum collections. Often even what were known to be contemporary objects were perceived as "ancient" by Western collectors – or indeed passed off as such by unscrupulous dealers.

Despite the civil wars preceding the restoration of the Emperor Meiji, Japan had sent objects with representatives of the ruling Tokugawa shogunate as well as works from the feudal domains of Satsuma and Saga to the Paris World Fair of 1867 (fig. 2). The displays of the Tokugawa government included lacquerware, ceramics, swords, armour, textiles, paper products and cloisonné enamels. There were also more than five thousand (mostly contemporary and possibly especially commissioned) *ukiyo-e* woodblock prints and several hundred fans, both folding and fixed round forms. The independent domains of Satsuma and Saga sent many thousands of ceramic pieces. As with the London World Fair of 1862, among these displays of traditional artworks were a considerable number of objects that already showed Western influence or were already being aimed directly at a Western market (fig. 3).

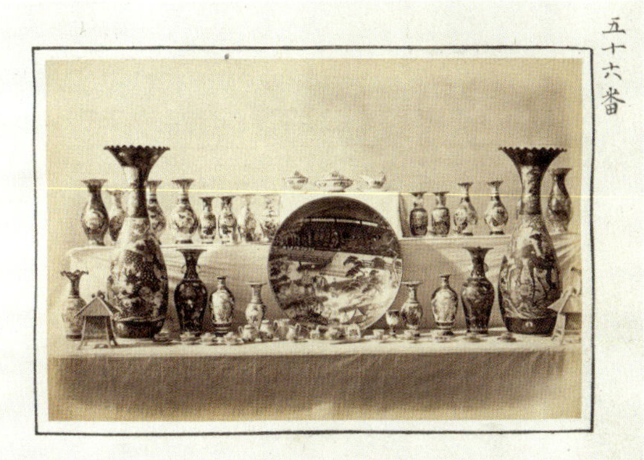

1 Japanese Court at the London World Fair of 1862, in: *The Illustrated London News*, 20.9.1862, p. 320, Victoria and Albert Museum, London
2 "Galerie des Machines: le Japon" at the Paris World Fair of 1867, in: *L'Illustration*, 21.9.1867, p. 188, Bibliothèque nationale de France
3 Japanese artefacts acquired by the Victoria and Albert Museum at the Paris World Fair of 1867, Victoria and Albert Museum, London
4 Display of Japanese ceramics at the Vienna World Fair of 1873, Tokyo National Museum

These displays were a phenomenal success, and over nine million people attended the fair: the craze in Europe for all things Japanese had now begun. An interesting feature of the displays at the Paris World Fair of 1867 was that, as well as the Western-influenced works being shown by the Japanese, Western manufacturers were already exhibiting works that showed clear Japanese influence. For instance, a superb dinner service designed by Félix Bracquemond for Eugène Rousseau was decorated with fish, animals, insects and other scenes from nature; these images had been taken directly from Japanese woodblock *ukiyo-e* prints and from the series of woodblock printed books, *Hokusai Manga* (pp. 252, 253). It was Bracquemond who, perhaps apocryphally, had found a copy of *Hokusai Manga* around 1856 being used as packing material in a consignment of Japanese ceramics that had been shipped back from Japan by French residents.[6] In his *Notes sur le Japon, la Chine et l'Inde* of 1861 – a book that took shape during his diplomatic mission to Japan between 1858 and 1860 – Baron Charles de Chassiron had reproduced pages from *Hokusai Manga*, a book with which he was obviously familiar and which was now brought to prominent light for the European public.[7] However, this was not the first time *Hokusai Manga* had been sighted in Europe, as copies had already been displayed at the Siebold Museum in Leiden some nineteen years before Braquemond's alleged "discovery".[8]

Given the obvious success and reception of this exhibition, from this date onwards the Japanese government sought to promote their interests through participation in world fairs, primarily through the display of virtuosic and often large-scale objects clearly aimed at a Western market. These objects were frequently decorated with just enough Japanese imagery to cater for the "exoticism" required by this burgeoning market, but often the subject matter would have been lost on the Western audience, although totally familiar to the Japanese themselves. Japan's next major contribution to international exhibitions in Europe, where they built upon their earlier success in the promotion of Japanese art manufactures, came at the Vienna World Fair of 1873. This was the first official participation in a world fair by the new Meiji government.

The Japanese displays were again diverse and included lacquerware, ceramics and silk, as well as dolls and models of houses; the latter are held today in the National Museum of Ethnology, Vienna (Weltmuseum Wien). The displays, which included traditional ceramics and contemporary bronzes, were presented in a manner that appealed to Western taste, and many of the works were also of a size, shape and design aimed specifically at this audience (fig. 4).[9] There was an eager market for such "exotic" pieces throughout Europe, and objects were of course also available for sale to an enthusiastic public directly from Japanese sources. In 1874, the Meiji government had set up the commercial enterprise Kiryū Kōshō Kaisha (the First Manufacturing and Trading Company); this company commissioned prominent artists and gave them both the time and the resources to develop designs in their particular crafts, notably lacquerware, ceramics, porcelain, metalwork and cloisonné enamel.[10]

The successes of the Japanese participation in the Paris World Fair of 1867 and the Vienna World Fair of 1873 had made the Japanese government all too aware of the potential for huge sales of artworks at

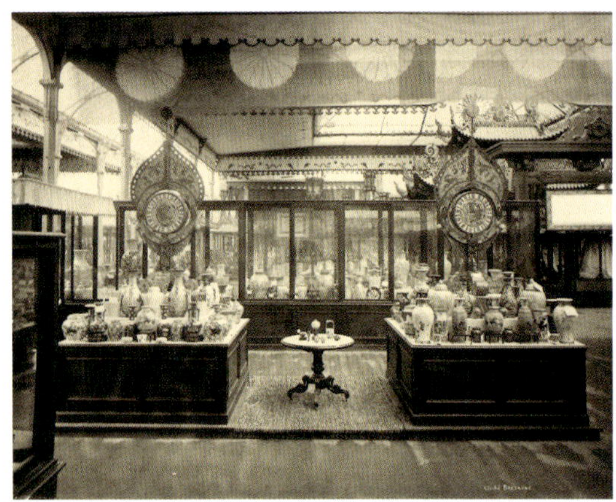

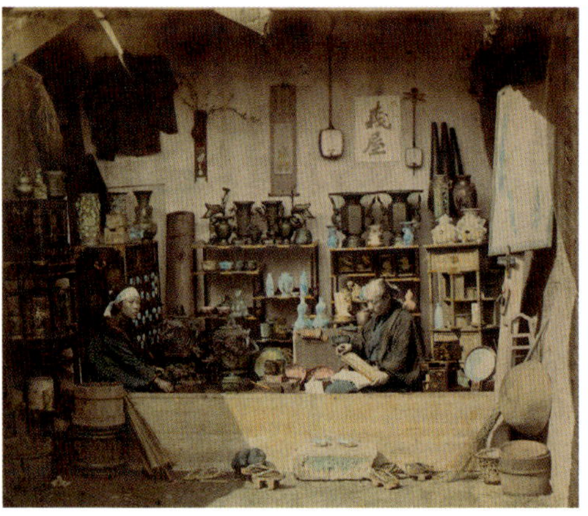

such occasions, and both traditional and contemporary works of art and craft were offered up for exhibition and retail. World fairs were occasions when Japan's Meiji government could display its country's skills in the arts, crafts and other manufacturing industries to the world, thereby showing how quickly Japan had become a "modern" power. The official Meiji government's outline for applicants to exhibit at the Paris World Fair of 1867 stated that "this exhibition should increase the honours received at the Vienna and Philadelphia exhibitions, attempt to leave a deep impression on viewers with objects suitable for the demand of various countries, and prices should be kept low to increase export".[11] Japanese artistic objects had a high reputation with the Western audience and were also seen as potential inspiration for Western manufacturers. They were highly praised for their elegant design, meticulous craftsmanship and attention to detail. Following the Vienna World Fair of 1873, interest had been further raised by the arts of Meiji Japan, but it was with the Paris World Fair of 1878 that a full-blown craze began. Japanese artworks were now imported in great quantities and sold through specialist dealers and shops: Paris was to become the centre for the development of the craze for Japan that now began to take Europe by storm.

As a result of Japan's participation in the Paris World Fair of 1878, the craze for Japan and the fashion for *Japonisme* in Europe were now at their peak. The fair had focused on artistic achievements (rather than including industrial products and design as in previous world fairs), and Japanese artworks were now displayed in two separate areas: the Palais de l'Industrie on the Champs-Élysées exhibited newly created works, while older, more traditional works were shown at the Palais des Beaux-Arts at the Trocadéro. The latter venue included a "Japanese House" (depicted in the *Illustrated London News* on 15 June 1878) together with displays assembled by Parisian collectors such as Émile Guimet, Henri Cernuschi and Philippe Burty, as well as Japanese objects from Siegfried Bing, a collector and influential dealer (fig. 5).

The Paris World Fair of 1878 attracted more than sixteen million visitors, who could all have potentially seen the arts of Meiji Japan on display. Following the event, museums, private collectors and indeed the general public were by now actively acquiring Japanese art from whatever source they could find, and enormous sums were often paid. The range and styles of so many new objects available to Western markets, and produced by the numerous schools of Japanese craftsmen who had by now begun to adapt their traditional craft techniques to new forms for the Western market, appealed to Western collectors who were additionally obsessed with the taxonomy of objects; the new schools of Japanese craftsmen provided a fresh and exciting source for classification (p. 260). Japanese artworks from the Meiji era frequently used new materials and techniques (and used familiar methods in entirely novel ways), employing approaches in design and subject matter that were different from what the West had been accustomed to from Japan. Westerners had an ideal image of the arts of Japan and fantasised about "pure" Japanese art, yet often what was in fact collected was a fusion of art, craft and ethnography (fig. 6).

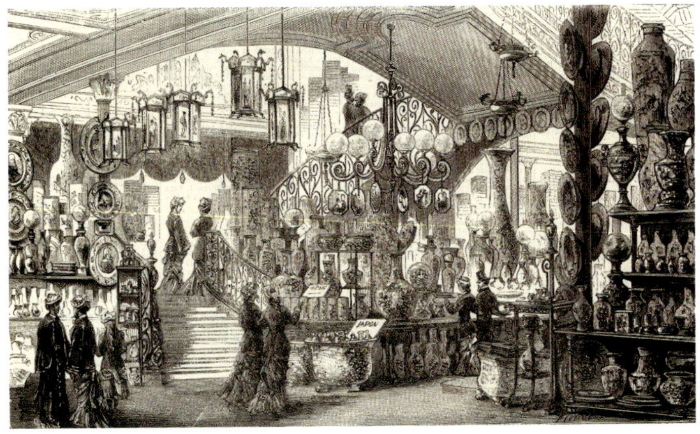

5 Japanese installation at the Paris World Fair of 1878, Victoria and Albert Museum, London
6 Felice Beato, *Merchant's Shop, Yokohama*, circa 1868, Victoria and Albert Museum, London
7 Gallery for Japanese porcelain in the new space of Le Bon Marché in Paris, in: *L'Illustration*, 9.10.1880, p. 245, Victoria and Albert Museum, London

The commercial availability of Japanese art

Japanese artworks had been available in Paris from sources such as Decelle's À l'Empire chinois at 55, rue Vivienne, which had opened in 1856 and was one of the first places in Paris to sell Japanese wares. After 1878, however, Japanese art was imported in vast quantities and sold through specialist dealers and shops in London such as Liberty's and Yamanaka (with shops in several countries), and in France through established commercial enterprises in Paris such as À la Porte chinoise and Le Bon Marché (fig. 7). Curiously, although Paris was the centre of European interest and trade in Japanese artworks, Yamanaka did not have a shop there, only an agent from the rather late date of 1905 onwards. Other important commercial enterprises in Paris included the auction houses of Hôtel Drouot (which had several premises), the shop of Madame Desoye in rue de Rivoli, Au Céleste Empire in rue Saint Marc and the premises of Philippe Sichel in rue Pigalle. All these establishments were not merely sources for Japanese art but served as meeting places where respectable connoisseurs could gather to discuss their recent purchases and share and develop their taste in Japanese art – although Madame Desoye's shop was once referred to as a "rendez-vous des couples adultères".[12] The contemporary craze for and availability of Japanese art was a heaven-sent opportunity for collectors to pursue their passion. Ever since the "reopening" of Japan, the market for Japanese objects there had responded with Japanese dealers more than willing to part Western collectors from their money.

One of the main suppliers of Japanese art in Europe was the German collector and dealer Siegfried Bing (1838–1905).[13] In the 1860s, Bing's family ran, amongst other concerns, a porcelain-manufacturing business in Paris. Following several disruptions, business expanded, and by the early 1870s, Bing was collecting oriental artworks. At this time, the European vogue for artworks coming out of Japan was beginning to peak, especially in France where artists and craftsmen were already producing wares in Japanese style or decorated with Japanese motifs. We know for certain that Bing had begun dealing in oriental art by 1875, as the archive at the Victoria and Albert Museum (known at that time as the South Kensington Museum) has papers dating from October of that year regarding transactions from Bing's premises in Paris at 19, rue Chauchat (fig. 8).

The Victoria and Albert Museum – henceforth referred to as the V&A – presents a well-documented example of the types of Japanese art readily available to the Parisian collector from Bing. It also shows how Bing's "empire" was expanding, disclosing details of both his business acumen and strategy at the height of the demand for Japanese art in Europe. The V&A was sent two consignments of objects "on loan and approval with a view to their ultimate purchase by the Museum" (fig. 9).[14] Bing had not at this time visited Japan (this first took place in 1880), thus would have assembled his collection from other dealers (of which there were several in Paris), perhaps from the Vienna World Fair of 1873 or from an as-yet-unidentified source. However, it should be noted that his brother-in-law, Michael Martin Baer, was

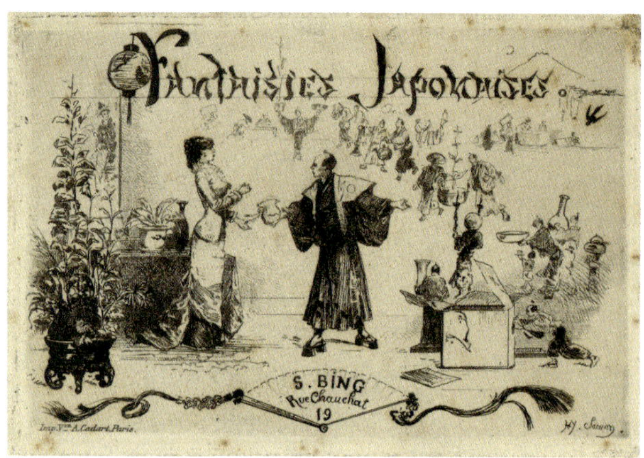

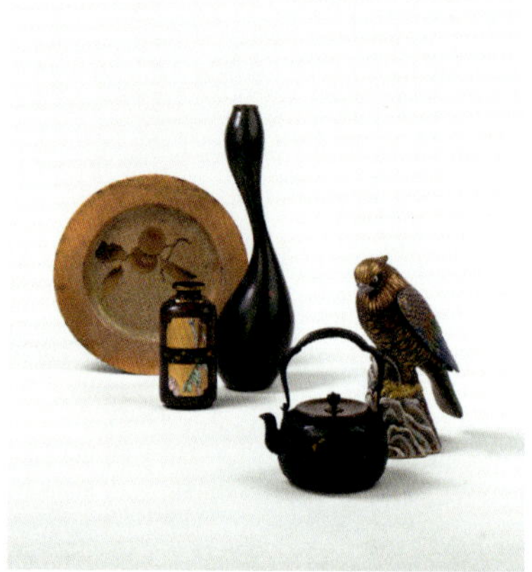
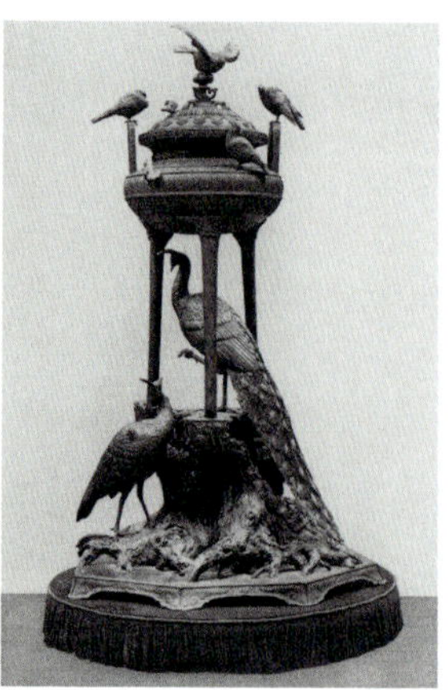

acting consul for the German Legation in Tokyo from 1870 to 1874 and again from 1877 to 1881.[15] Baer was extremely rich and, a collector himself, was able to access excellent private Japanese collections and was known to have acquired objects for Bing and other European import and export companies.[16]

Bing is best remembered for the seminal part he played in the development of art nouveau, the shop he opened in 1895 giving its name to the style. He was a great champion of Japanese art and was also the first European dealer to gain direct access to collections in Japan, perhaps through the diplomatic connections of his brother-in-law. His Oriental Art Boutique, which opened in Paris in 1875, was an important meeting place for French Japanophiles. From 1888 to 1891, he published the influential journal *Le Japon artistique* which made an important contribution to the growing appreciation and understanding of Japanese art. A major supplier of Japanese objects to private clients in Europe and America, Bing also sold objects to many European museums including the Musée des Arts décoratifs in Paris, the Victoria and Albert Museum in London and Museum Folkwang in Hagen. The V&A, for example, acquired a considerable number of Japanese objects from Bing in the 1870s and 1880s, including ceramics, textiles and lacquerware, although the majority were bronzes; Museum Folkwang acquired lacquerware, ceramics, tsubas, hanging scrolls and sculptures from 1900 onwards.

In a letter from Paris dated 27 January 1876, Bing wrote to the Museum Director Sir Philip Cunliffe-Owen: "I am offering you a collection of thirty exceedingly beautiful old masks sculpted from wood which actors wore dancing the religious Noh dance before the Taikoon. There are thirty various types of masks, all executed by the hands of a master. The price of the collection is 1,800 francs for your museum (marked price: 2,200 francs)."[17] It is interesting to note that 1876 was the year that the Haitōrei Edict was issued, which finally abolished the samurai as a class. Noh performance had been the preserve of the samurai class and suddenly the performers were out of work and many sold off their family heirlooms simply in order to live. On 17 February 1876, a Mr Fortnum, acting in the capacity of Art Referee (a system whereby the Museum employed independent authorities on a freelance basis to search out and recommend artworks for acquisition), wrote from Paris to the Director: "I have, as requested by you given some time to an inspection of M. Bing's numerous collections of Chinese and Japanese objects, amongst which are many that I consider desirable for purchase by the South Kensington Museum [...] I would also recommend a selection of 12 or more carved wood masks (750 francs for 12)."[18]

The whereabouts of the other eighteen masks offered by Bing has not yet been established but several European museums are potential owners. Together with the masks, the V&A acquired bronzes and porcelain – altogether some fifty-seven objects were purchased from Bing for the hardly inconsiderable sum of £850. This was but one of several occasions when Bing found the South Kensington Museum to be a reliable source of income at a time when he seemed the foremost authority (and indeed he promoted himself as such) on the subject and to control the European trade and understanding of Japanese art. In the opinion of the Art Referee, Mr Fortnum, the objects offered by Bing in 1875 "ought, in my opinion,

8 Henry Somm, *Fantaisies Japonaises* (design for Bing's business card), 1879, Van Gogh Museum, Amsterdam
9 Sample artefacts from Bing's Collection, Victoria and Albert Museum, London
10 Suzuki Chōkichi, Incense burner (*kōro*) on display at the Paris World Fair of 1878, in: Jean-Baptiste Giraud, *Les Arts du Métal, Recueil Descriptif et Raisonné*, 1881, Bibliothèque nationale de France

to be purchased from M. Bing at any reasonable cost, as they would be of great value to our English manufacturers as examples of the extraordinary perfection to which this art is carried out by Japanese workmen."[19] This observation neatly sums up the prevailing attitude of the West towards Japanese art objects.

The Kiryū Kōshō Kaisha had a large display in the Japanese pavilion of the Paris World Fair of 1878, and it was here that a superb bronze incense burner by Suzuki Chōkichi, one of the greatest bronze casters of Meiji-period Japan, was displayed (fig. 10). The English guide to the fair stated that "the Japanese have a man always at hand to answer questions and to inscribe the name of the purchaser". This was Hayashi Tadamasa, who had been directly involved with Suzuki on the production of this magnificent bronze. Hayashi's employment by the Kiryū Kōshō Kaisha lasted only some 180 days before he left to work for Mitsui Bussan and eventually set up his own gallery in 1884. From 1886, he was based in rue de la Victoire, from where he established himself as one of the greatest authorities on Japanese art at the time. He particularly focused on Japanese prints, of which it has been estimated that he sold in excess of 160,000.[20] His wealthy and distinguished clientele included Claude Monet, Auguste Renoir, Louis Gonse, Edmond de Goncourt and Henri Vever.[21]

Suzuki Chōkichi's incense burner attracted much attention, being illustrated in a number of journals. One British reviewer praised the "richest and rarest treasures" to be found in the Japanese section and commented on this "chef-d'œuvre [...] a magnificent censer in bronze, with two peacocks, natural size [...]".[22] Soon after the exhibition closed, the Kiryū Kōshō Kaisha sold the incense burner to Bing who – on 1 February 1883 – wrote to Sir Philip Cunliffe-Owen: "I sent you yesterday the photographs of a large bronze which you saw at the Paris Exposition of 1878. In time I acquired this object and I entertain a boundless admiration for it. In fact I consider this bronze, in conjunction with Mitford's eagle now in your possession, to be the finest piece of bronze which an artist's hand has ever produced. In consequences of changes which I am obliged to make, I am now prepared to dispose of it. I have thought of you, and my regret would be diminished if this marvellous piece of work could find a place in your museum where it would provoke a considerable sensation [...]".[23]

Sir Philip Cunliffe-Owen, Director of the V&A since 1874, had been Secretary of the Royal Commission for the Paris World Fair of 1878. The many important Japanese acquisitions made under his directorship certainly reflect the general vogue for Japan that existed at the time, but also points to his personal enthusiasm for Japanese art and design.[24] The V&A paid the astounding sum of £1,568.7s.2d for the incense burner, special permission from the Treasury being required. It is difficult to calculate the equivalent sum today, but certainly this would be in excess of £1.5 million and would indeed have helped Bing with "the changes I am obliged to make".

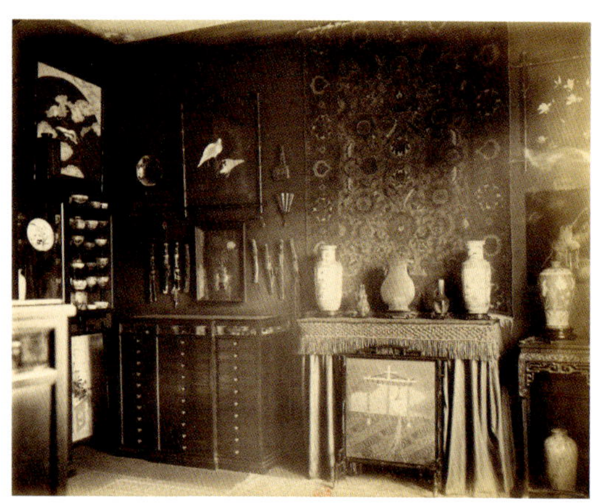

11 Interior with Far Eastern objects at Edmond de Goncourt's house in Auteuil, 1886, photograph by Ferdinand Lochand, Bibliothèque nationale de France

Collectors of Japanese art

But what of private collectors of Japanese art in Paris in the second half of the nineteenth century? As the centre for trade in Japanese art, Paris was not short of sources to acquire the art; in addition to the pre-eminent establishments of Bing and Hayashi, there was the shop of Madame Desoye in rue de Rivoli, the gallery of Philippe Sichel and the Hôtel Drouot salesrooms – all frequented on a regular basis by avid rich and influential collectors and by curators from the newly established museums like those of Émile Guimet (1889) and Henri Cernuschi (1898).[25] Collectors such as the jeweller and writer Henri Vever – who assembled a large collection of Japanese sword hand guards (tsubas), netsukes and over 8,000 *ukiyo-e* prints – and the Goncourt brothers, who were among the most enthusiastic collectors and promoters of Japanese arts and crafts, were also regular patrons of the Japanese art scene in Paris (fig. 11).

In his diary entry of 20 December 1882, Edmond de Goncourt mentions that he had spent some 30,000 francs that year on Japanese art.[26] Another leading figure in the Parisian world of Japanese art was Louis Gonse (1841–1926). Gonse was editor in chief of the influential magazine *Gazette des Beaux-Arts*, and in 1883 he helped organise the Retrospective Exhibition of Japanese Art at Galerie Georges Petit in Paris. This exhibition was a large-scale display of many of the private French collections of Japanese art such as those of Edmond Taigny, Théodore Duret or Charles Haviland. Among the many visitors to the Paris World Fair of 1867 was Philippe Burty (1830–1890), the collector and art critic who had an immense enthusiasm for the arts of Japan. It was Burty who was later to coin the term "Japonisme", which he defined in an English journal as "the study of the art and genius of Japan".[27] Fascinated by Japanese art, he lectured and published prolifically.[28]

From around the middle of the nineteenth century, Paris had become the European epicentre for the understanding, appreciation and collection of the arts of Japan. As the venue for four major world fairs (1867, 1878, 1889 and 1900) and the location of the most influential dealers of the time, its influence spread across the globe. Contemporary collectors all knew each other and often vied – not always amicably – to be the best in their fields. It will take a more focused and lengthier publication to deal with the intricacies and machinations of the art world at the time. But the entire period certainly harboured a passion for the subject and, although absorbed by the "craze" that afflicted so much of Europe, it was addressed in a serious and academic way. Not always "correct" by today's understanding, the collectors successfully laid the groundwork for future generations of those who study and admire the arts of Japan.

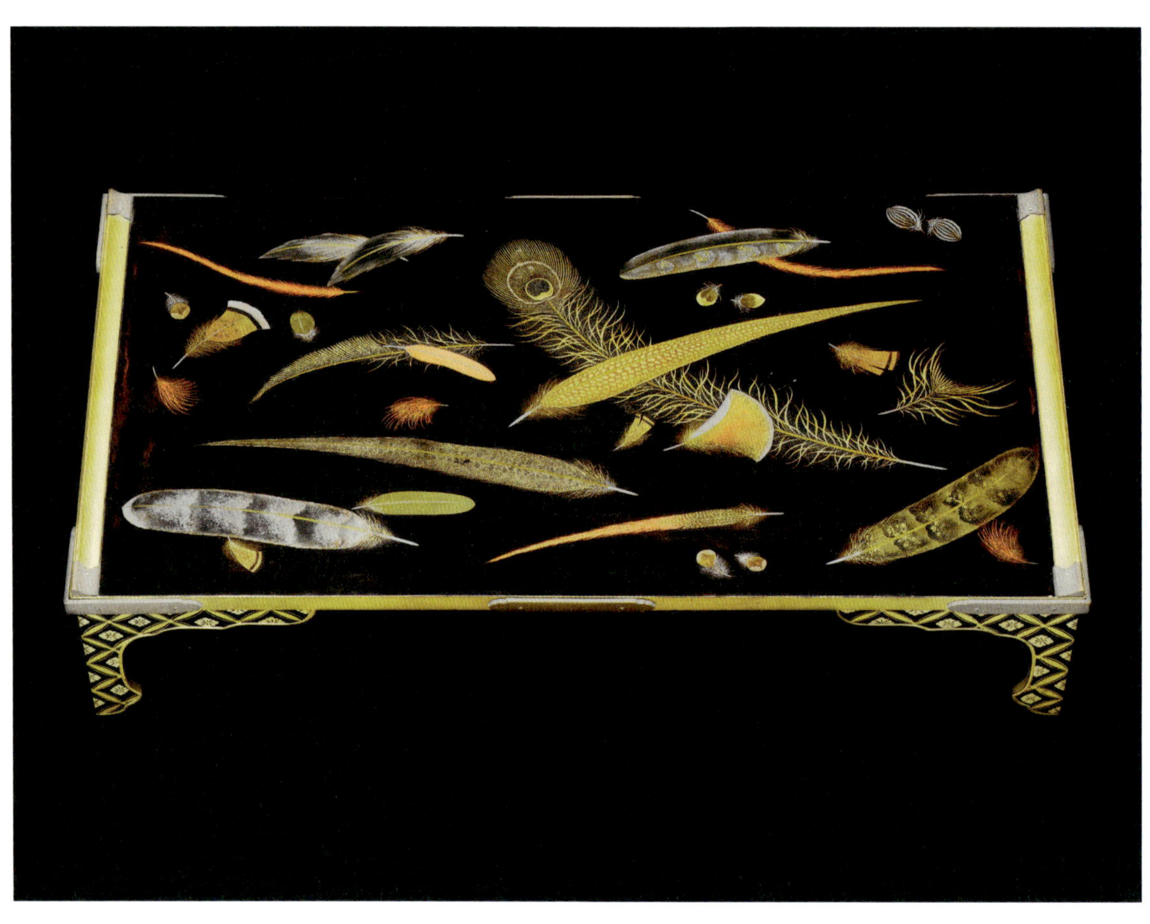

309 Japan, *Low Writing Table (bundai)*, Meiji period, late 19th c., formerly in the Siegfried Bing Collection

The museum as a school of vision – Karl Ernst Osthaus and Museum Folkwang's Japanese Collection

Christoph Dorsz

The opening of Museum Folkwang on 9 July 1902 took place during a time of increasing aesthetic interest for Japanese art in Germany. The latter had an important place in the Folkwang Collection, which included art from all cultures and periods. The museum's founder Karl Ernst Osthaus saw Japanese art as an important inspiration for design and form in the present age. The viewing of Japanese art – focusing on colour, form, material, structure and craftsmanship – promoted the early reception of modernist art at Museum Folkwang, largely no longer narrative. A revolution of vision, the comparative "new vision" of modernism, ensured an epochal paradigm shift: early on, Osthaus moved aspects of technique and craftsmanship to the background, and he was one of the first art historians in Germany to focus on the aesthetic qualities of Japanese art.

Initial steps – Karl Ernst Osthaus in the world of European *Japonisme*

In August 1898, the young millionaire heir Osthaus, who had developed a plan to found a museum for natural history and the arts and crafts, visited the nestor of Germany's enthusiastic reception of all things Japanese, Justus Brinckmann (fig. 1). With the director of the Museum für Kunst und Gewerbe Hamburg, he discussed the scope and profile of a collection of applied arts in great detail. His stay led to the first acquisitions of Japanese art for the emerging Folkwang collections. From among the duplicates in the Hamburg Collection, Osthaus chose five ikebana baskets, ten sword hand guards, two sword accessories and a gold lacquer case, to which Brinckmann added a "few more complimentary baskets".[1] For Osthaus, who in early September 1899 spent two weeks of practical instruction in the museum, the well-networked Brinckmann served as both a mentor and an advisor, providing him with duplicates, giving him instruction, establishing contacts, contributing his expertise for important purchases and, above all, training the eye of the young collector.

During a joint trip to Berlin in the summer of 1899, Brinckmann invited the Folkwang founder to the art dealer Hermann Paechter, who had been director of the company R. Wagner, specialising in Japanese artefacts, since the 1880s. With purchases that can no longer be reconstructed in detail, Osthaus here established the foundation of his Japanese Collection.[2] Paechter, who also had modern French artists like Édouard Manet and Paul Signac on offer, was the most important dealer of Japanese art in Germany until his death in 1902.[3] An indication of the breadth of this network of connections were the five netsukes acquired in 1901 from the former Collection of Marcus B. Huish, a friend of James McNeill Whistler.[4] From 1899 to 1903, the company R. Wagner was the exclusive purveyor of Japanese objects to Museum Folkwang. At least two hundred objects such as kakemonos, woodblock prints, small sculptures, netsukes, bronzes,

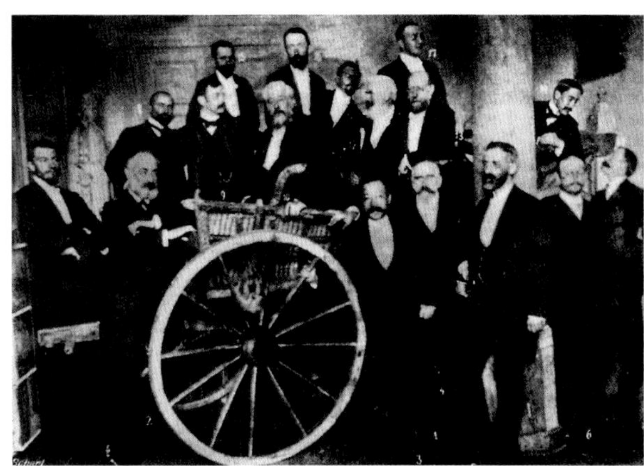
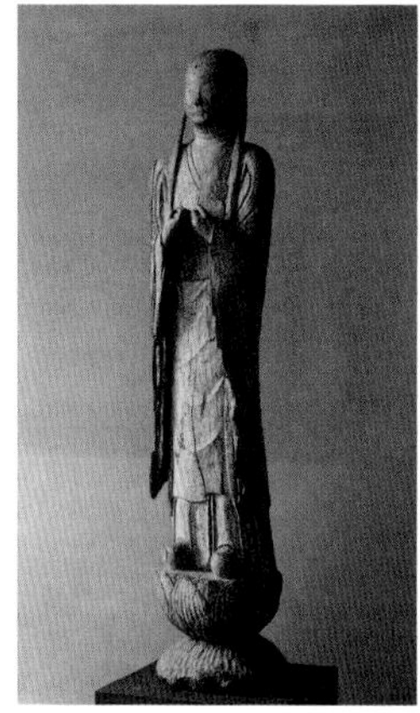
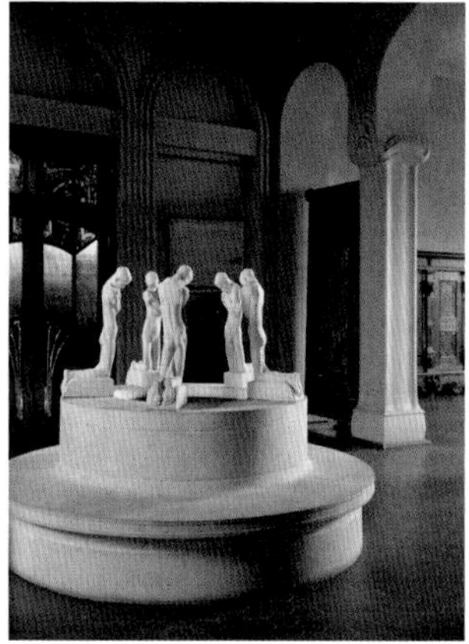

tsubas, lacquer pieces, ceramics, ikebana baskets and fabrics found their way to Hagen via Berlin. Paechter repeatedly offered objects from Siegfried Bing's Collection, which the important Japan dealer and collector "did not want to place on the Parisian market, for reasons of prestige".[5] In this way, Osthaus acquired precious lacquer pieces from the Bing Collection, including a desk (*bundai*) from the early Meiji period with a lacquer surface, completely covered in ornamentation (p. 38).

The friendship of the young collector with the Belgian art nouveau artist Henry Van de Velde, who was also friends with Paechter, was in many ways a turning point for the Folkwang aspirations. Osthaus himself emphasised that "in terms of an energetic change of direction in his collecting activity, [he] owed a great deal to the superior experience of its architect".[6] Ever since his stay in Paris in 1884 at the latest, Van de Velde had become a profound connoisseur of Japanese art. During his visit to Van de Velde's home in early May 1900, Osthaus was able to convince himself of the programmatic integration of Japanese art in the modern milieu of the artist's interiors as "a joint exhibition of all arts from East and West".[7] The three mentors Brinckmann, Paechter and Van de Velde revealed for Osthaus the meaning of Paris as the capital of the art world at the time and the centre of the cult around Japan. Directly after his first meeting with Van de Velde, Osthaus travelled to the French capital, where he made the acquaintance of Bing, from whom he was able to make fifty acquisitions of Japanese art, some of them very crucial to the collection. Later, he was even given access to Bing's private quarters, in which "the cabinets full of gold lacquer cases glowed when you opened their doors".[8] In April of 1903, Osthaus acquired a dozen mostly Japanese paintings and an equal number of ceramics from the Collection of Edmond Taigny (1828–1906).[9] Taigny, an influential art historian and collector of Asian art and impressionist painting, was one of the leading figures in *Japonisme*. Six weeks later, Osthaus acquired several lacquer pieces, Chinese bronzes and other items from the Collection of Paul Brenot (1838–1902), the former treasurer of the Société des Amis du Louvre, at an auction.[10] From the important Collection of Charles Gillot (1853–1903), a graphic artist and friend of Bing's, Osthaus acquired three ancient Japanese theatre masks in 1904 and a silk dancing gown from the Noh theatre (p. 235) interwoven with gold.[11] In the eyes of Osthaus, the objects up for auction were the equivalent of a "sensation". Much more decidedly than before, he now recognised the quality of Japanese art from before the Edo period.[12] Thus, he definitively departed from the nineteenth-century view that saw the perfect craftsmanship of Japanese art as exemplary for inspiring design and form in the present. At the same time, he turned away from the nineteenth-century French passion for collecting, which was fixated on smaller heirlooms or bibelots and often on special areas, now focusing on select individual pieces from all genres which he acquired for their formal, aesthetic qualities.

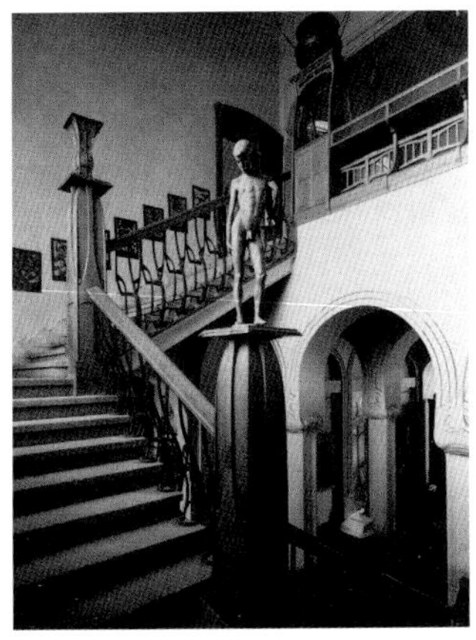

1 Karl Ernst Osthaus (far left) with friends and students of Justus Brinckmann at the celebration of the 25th jubilee of the founding of the Museum für Kunst und Gewerbe Hamburg, 30.9.1902
2 Japan, *Monk*, called *Shōtoku Taishi*, 19th c., Museum Folkwang, Essen
3 Entrance foyer, Museum Folkwang, Hagen, before 1917
4 View of the stairway, Museum Folkwang, Hagen, 1910

The re-evaluation of Japanese art after 1905

The year 1905 – which is today seen as marking the end of a *Japonisme* dominated by the Parisian culture of taste, and which was also the year of Bing's death – marked a decisive turn in the history of the Hagen Japanese Collection.[13] For a collector of such varied interests as Osthaus, the overheated European market with "prices rising at an increasingly fantastic rate"[14] had been exhausted – even if he did not cease from visiting the relevant galleries and art dealers or the renowned collectors and museum officials on his visits to the world's major cities, in order to exchange thoughts with them or to make select acquisitions. The discoverer of ever-newer, usually non-European artistic landscapes increased the desire for greater expression in the arts, which was no longer offered exclusively by the Japanese art dealt in Europe. In subsequent years, Osthaus favoured the art of China, but continued to maintain an interest in Japanese sculpture, which he found possessed expressive qualities of "the greatest intimacy".[15] From now on, in Osthaus's view, "the true recognition of the lofty things that we suspected could only be gained in Japan".[16] This search for "true" Japanese art explains why German museums were more and more eager to acquire things overseas. In January 1910, Osthaus secured twenty-nine theatre masks, several lacquer pieces and almost a dozen ceramics from Paul Vautier, who worked in Tokyo for the Hamburg trading house Illies & Co. and was able to build up an exquisite collection of Japanese art.[17] Of special importance here was his relationship to Karl With, who already began working as a volunteer in Hagen during his student years and who managed Museum Folkwang during Osthaus's stays in a sanatorium, which began in 1919, and finally after the death of the museum's founder on 27 March 1921, when he took over the directorship. On the invitation of Oskar Vonwiller, his classmate and collector of painting and Japanese objects, he travelled to Japan in 1913 for almost a year of research.[18] Once there, he acquired "three cases containing Japanese artistic creations" for Museum Folkwang.[19] Among the purchases were two miniature masks, three scrolls, fans and "lacquered boxes" (*tebako*). Karl With identified the main acquisition, a wooden statue, as a depiction of the *Shōtoku Taishi* (fig. 2).[20] This attribution, no longer maintained today, was of great importance for the young researcher; he saw in the figure a representation of Prince Umayado, a pioneer of Buddhism and one of the founders of Buddhist art in Japan.[21] The museum's final acquisition for the Japanese collection can be attributed to Karl With as well.[22] On 28 February 1921, he also had the final word during the lifetime of the museum founder when he spoke in the museum's lecture hall on Asian sculpture.

Staging practices

Like no other museum of its time, the presentation of art objects at Museum Folkwang followed artistic principles (fig. 3). After the visitors entered the museum's foyer, they were greeted by a scroll by Kanō

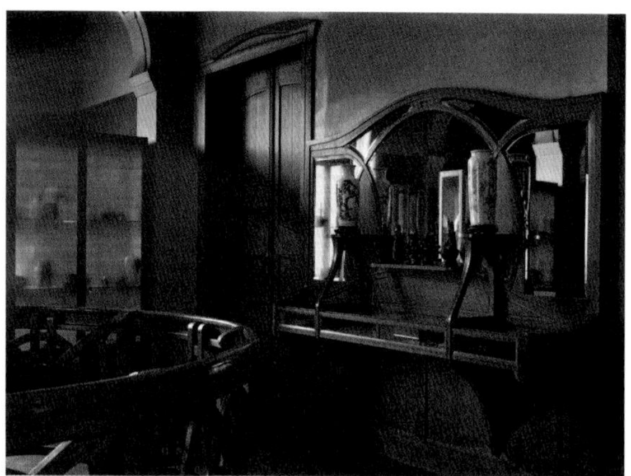
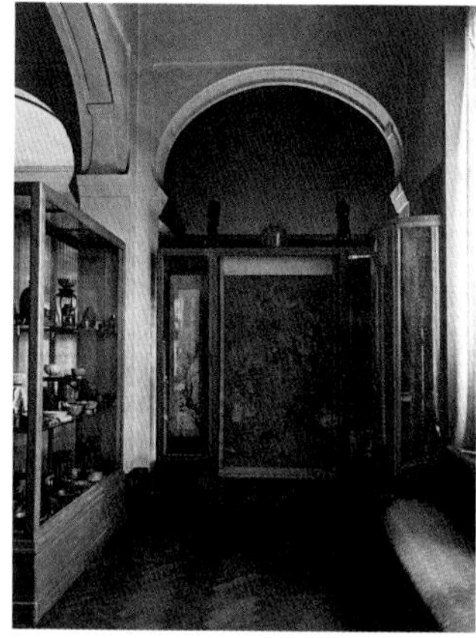
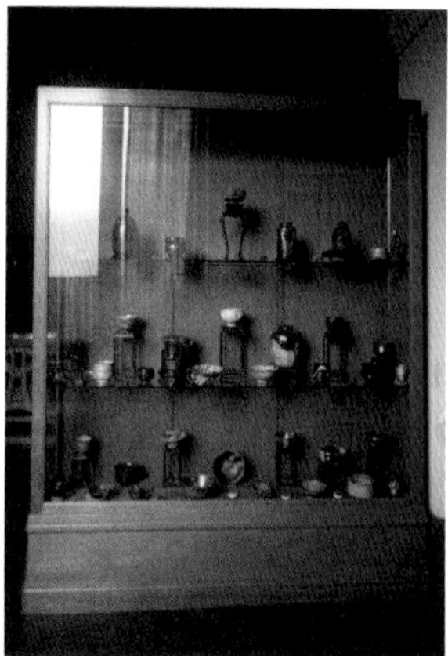

Yōsen-in Korenobu with a depiction of a cut bamboo and four herons (p. 231) visualising the play of figure and background. The exaggeratedly thin figures of George Minne's *Boy Kneeling at the Spring*, Paul Gauguin's *Barbaric Tales* (1902) and Henri Matisse's *Still Life with Daffodils* (1907) – later replaced by Ferdinand Hodler's painting *Lake Geneva Seen from Chexbres* (1904), purchased in 1917 – responded to the design principle of flatness. Upon entering the upper floor, the visitor passed by Aristide Maillol's filigreed *Young Cyclist* from 1909, borrowing the formal vocabulary of Greek antiquity, inherently at rest, whose pose responded in an almost kindred sense to the turn of the approaching visitor and the moving outlines of the pedestal (fig. 4).[23] A richly patterned *gu*, a Chinese cloisonné vase, anticipated the abstract linear aspect of the paper stencils that led in the East Asian cabinet to the upper vestibule, where cases in yellow, untreated oak housed the exhibits (fig. 5).[24] The colour triad of the upper roof light in yellow, green and violet stained Tiffany glass corresponded to the general decorative principle, where the wall surfaces and ceilings of the exhibition spaces served as a unifying foil for the exhibits. The colour scheme found its continuation in the display cases: Japanese gold lacquer pieces were placed on "purple Chinese silk", while other artefacts were placed against a "green background".[25] A side room was added to the vestibule (fig. 6). With lower ceiling heights, a cushioned bank invited the visitor to spend time in contemplation in this *Cabinet de l'Extrême-Orient*. The design of the room corresponded to the "simulation of a modern culture of living", as had emerged in impressionism, already presented in 1893 by the *Exposition des Estampes d'Outamaro et de Hiroshighé* at Galerie Durand-Ruel in Paris.[26]

The presentation of the objects was subject to a decorative, virtually pictorial arrangement (fig. 7). It was committed to "the law of proportion and order" and assembled the "variety of forms to a unity".[27] In so doing, Osthaus did not refuse a hieratically centred exhibition. He always began from the middle, from where the objects were organised from bottom to top in a paratactic alternation, arranged front and back. On a third level, allowing for a particularly close-up examination, small-format objects were placed at eye level. The rhythmic play of "placing, laying and hanging various objects",[28] seeking harmony, subverted the standard monotonously linear practice of staging an exhibition and interwove the objects with the modern milieu of the surrounding room.

The (former) Japanese Collection at Museum Folkwang

Based on aesthetic aspects, Osthaus integrated a comprehensive cross section of Japanese art consisting of almost five hundred objects into the collections of his museum; around two hundred of these remain in Museum Folkwang's Collection today.[29] His attention was focused on Japanese painting early on. The flat, linear composition on a hanging scroll after Isoda Koryūsai from the Taigny Collection seems like a predecessor of the strikingly flat images of Maurice Denis, Paul Gauguin (pp. 211, 224), Edvard Munch and Henri

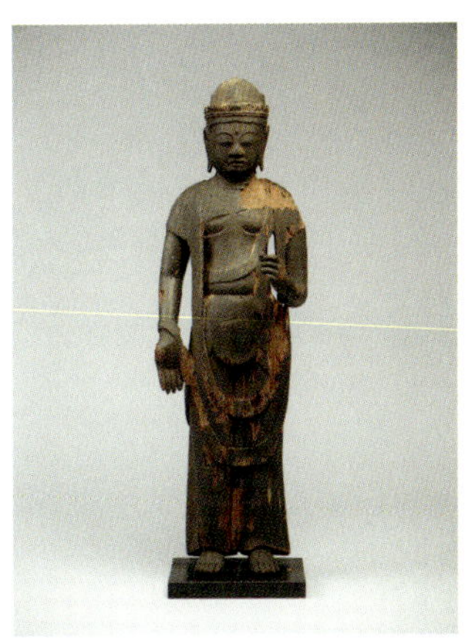

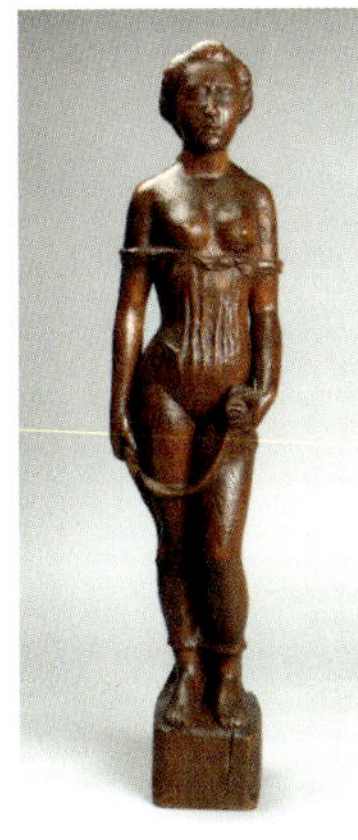

5 East Asian Collection in the upper vestibule, Museum Folkwang, Hagen, 1917
6 Window wall in the side room, East Asian Collection, Museum Folkwang, Hagen, 1917
7 Exhibition cabinet in the side room, East Asian Collection, Museum Folkwang, Hagen, 1917
8 Japan, *Shō Kannon*, circa 900, Museum Folkwang, Essen
9 Aristide Maillol, *Young Woman Standing*, 1902, Museum Folkwang, Essen

Rousseau – works which, with their cut-off views, overlaps and leaps in proportion, where the figures act on the foremost layer of a visual space that lacks all depth, testify in different ways to the influence of Japanese art.[30] In this context, the most modern European painting and most ancient Japanese painting seem like two sides of a coin. The light sensitivity of the scrolls, the limited space in the museum and, above all, the enormous increases in price might explain why this part of the collection, which cannot have contained more than twenty works, was not later expanded.

It consisted of less than fifty woodblock prints, which are no longer in the collection, based on a lot comprising a twenty-sheet portfolio that Osthaus assembled as a block together with seventeen paper stencils (*katagami*) from Paechter.[31] He acquired a second extensive collection in 1904 from the renowned Leipzig bookseller Karl W. Hiersemann, whose offerings came "largely from the collections of Hayashi, Bing, Bowes, Goncourt and others".[32] These woodblock prints were all characteristic *ukiyo-e* master sheets from the late Edo period. Examples from the beginnings of multicolour printing (*nishiki-e*) can be found in three prints by Suzuki Hanurobu. The collection contained at least four sheets by Torii Kiyonaga, one from the Taigny Collection.[33] The beautifully lined works of Kitagawa Utamaro were present in large numbers, too. We also know that the collection comprised a sheet from the twelve-part series *Twelve Views of Beautiful Girls, Compared With Famous Regions* (*Meisho fūkei bijin jūni-sō*) (cf. p. 187) and the *ōban Young Woman Painting her Lips Red, Holding a Mirror in Her Left Hand*,[34] purchased in 1904. The titles of the other named prints, *Woman and Child* or *Lovemaking* and perhaps *Female Koto Player*, are not clear enough to identify them properly. Osthaus owned at least three sheets by Hosoda Eishi – one from the collection of Hayashi Tadamasa, the most important Japanese art dealer in Europe, alongside Bing.[35] Utagawa Toyokuni (Toyokuni I) und Utagawa Hiroshige were included as prominent representatives of the Utagawa school.[36] Osthaus was able to acquire a sheet from the Taigny Collection by the founder of the Katsakuwa school, Hishida Shunsō,[37] and possessed at least five prints by Katsushika Hokusai. Of these, at least one can be identified with certainty – the illustration of a poem by Ono no Takamura from the sequence *One Hundred Poems Explained by a Wet Nurse* (*Hyakunin isshu uba ga etoki*) from 1835/1836.[38] Unlike art museums at the time, Osthaus did not place the collection of woodblock prints at the centre of interest. However, a changing series of prints, due to conservational reasons, was kept on permanent display.

Among the small number of sculptures, the figure of the *Jizō Bosatsu* should be emphasised, which Osthaus purchased in 1910 together with a large set of Javanese shadow puppets from the Amsterdam art dealer Douwe Komter.[39] The figure, which only remains in fragments, with its very fine colourful execution with gilding (*kirigane*) is an eighteenth-century replica of a statue from the Kamakura period. The wooden figure of a *Shō Kannon* from the Heian period around 900 – resting in a pose of concentration with its closed, strikingly flat forms (fig. 8) – seems like a psychological relation of the sculpture *Young Woman Standing* (1902), also acquired in 1904, by Aristide Maillol (fig. 9).[40] Both works reflect Osthaus's enthusiastic response to the execution of human emotion in the medium of art, as in the sculptures of

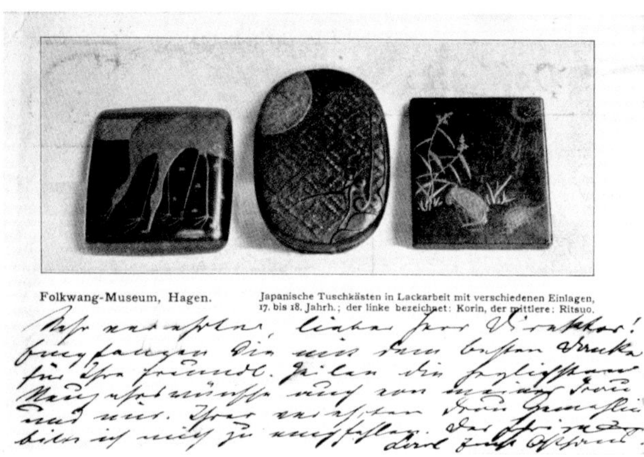

10 Postcard from Karl Ernst Osthaus to Justus Brinckmann, 9.1.1905, Museum für Kunst und Gewerbe Hamburg

August Rodin, which are accompanied by a series of small sculptures. The two expressive ceramic statuettes of a beggar and the depiction of *Daruma* (p. 232) stem from the Taigny Collection.[41] No less impressive is the wooden figurine of the poet Hitomaro, partially gilded (p. 233), from the Brenot Collection.[42] The more than thirty theatre masks from the Gillot and Vautier collections correspond to the collector's interest in the visualisation of typical physiognomies and human expressive gestures, as shown in the portrait of the Japanese dancer Sada Yacco by Kees van Dongen.[43]

The collection of ceramics stands out as a collection of select individual pieces that came primarily from three sources: Paechter, Bing and Vautier. Almost without exception, these are tea ceremony ceramics. The acquisitions show Osthaus as a sophisticated collector who only rarely chose overly decorated works. Rather, the individual *chawan* are striking for their highly individual shapes and the blurring colours of the glazing (pp. 246, 265, 268). The special appreciation for the asymmetric Raku ceramics with their rough surface and their diverse visual charms correspond to a fashion of the period (p. 268).[44] Porcelain pieces, unlike the first Paris collections of the nineteenth century, are scarcely present.[45]

Lacquerware is represented by inros, stacked writing boxes that predominantly date from the Edo period. The finely decorated lacquers are almost all executed using a wealth of decorative material that evokes the "inner rhythm of the surface".[46] One multicoloured case already acquired in 1900 via R. Wagner, originally intended for sheets of poetry (*shikishi bako*), was exhibited as "one of the most outstanding pieces on view in Europe" (p. 245).[47] Today attributed to the workshop of Ritsuō, Osthaus claimed that the work stemmed directly from this master, just like the writing box with a cover imitating basketry, in moving relief with the depiction of two stylised monkeys, which he acquired from Bing in May 1903 (fig. 10 and p. 243).[48] At the same time, he acquired a writing set with the depiction of two egrets in lead and gold lacquer by Ogata Kōrin (fig. 10).[49] The dozen or so inros, most of them black lacquer works, can be divided into two groups: one with perspectival landscape motifs in glowing colours, the other with abstract, linear and highly delicate flat motifs (pp. 238, 239).

Highly popular not only in Germany, the sword hand guards (tsubas) combined with the other sword decorations to make up a relatively small collection. No more than around thirty specimens, of which only eighteen remain in the collection today, represented this particular branch of Japanese craftsmanship. This focused selection includes objects of an impressive provenance: most importantly, the seven extant tsubas, which all stem from the Paris collections of Philippe Burty (p. 28) and E. L. Montefiori, which come from the Brenot Collection (p. 260).[50]

Osthaus knew how to choose select treasures for his collection in agreement with Ernst Große, who thought it best to focus on collections that were intended to serve "artistic pleasure", "for here it is only worth choosing works that are able to generate the greatest and most lasting impact possible".[51]

A comparative vision – the museum as a school of vision

As Osthaus began to acquire Japanese artworks, Franz Wickhoff speculated on the future of museums of applied art. The Viennese art historian promoted a fundamentally new evaluation of Japanese art, granting it a status equal to the Greek.[52] Wickhoff pleaded for a turn away from biographically based art history to a general history of forms that takes account of artistic expressions from all periods and cultures. The popularity of a largely authorless Japanese art advanced these considerations that were taken up by Heinrich Wölfflin in his *Kunstgeschichtliche Grundbegriffe* (1915), in which he projected his concept of an "art history without names" as an "interior history of forms".[53] Osthaus sought to implement this demand in his own museum: "The arrangement – which brings things that are very disparate in terms of temporal origin, but cohere inherently, in an often surprising relation to one another – does its part to make a stroll through the Folkwang a revelation of modern artistic life."[54] This principle of "combining the psychologically related", the "recognition of the commonality of intellectual and formal problems",[55] found its convincing realisation in the Gauguin room beyond the music salon, where Osthaus "showed the holy silence of Japanese cemetery figures before deep blue walls amidst dreamy images of the South Sea".[56]

The interest of the first years in a general renewal of form gave way in 1912 to a speculative and emphatic way of regarding art. A presentation that relies on viewing and empathy, with a consistent refusal to label the objects, focused on aesthetic qualities. The lines separating the old and the new, the historical and the modern, and the European and the non-European became, if not entirely obsolete, at least less binding. The integration of Japanese art was of key significance in creating a museum of a new kind, understood as a living organism, and which interpreted the past from the perspective of the present, whilst allowing creations of the artistic cultures of the past to sharpen the modern sense of taste. The modern museum as a tool of vision is thus the legacy of Karl Ernst Osthaus, and it remains alive today.

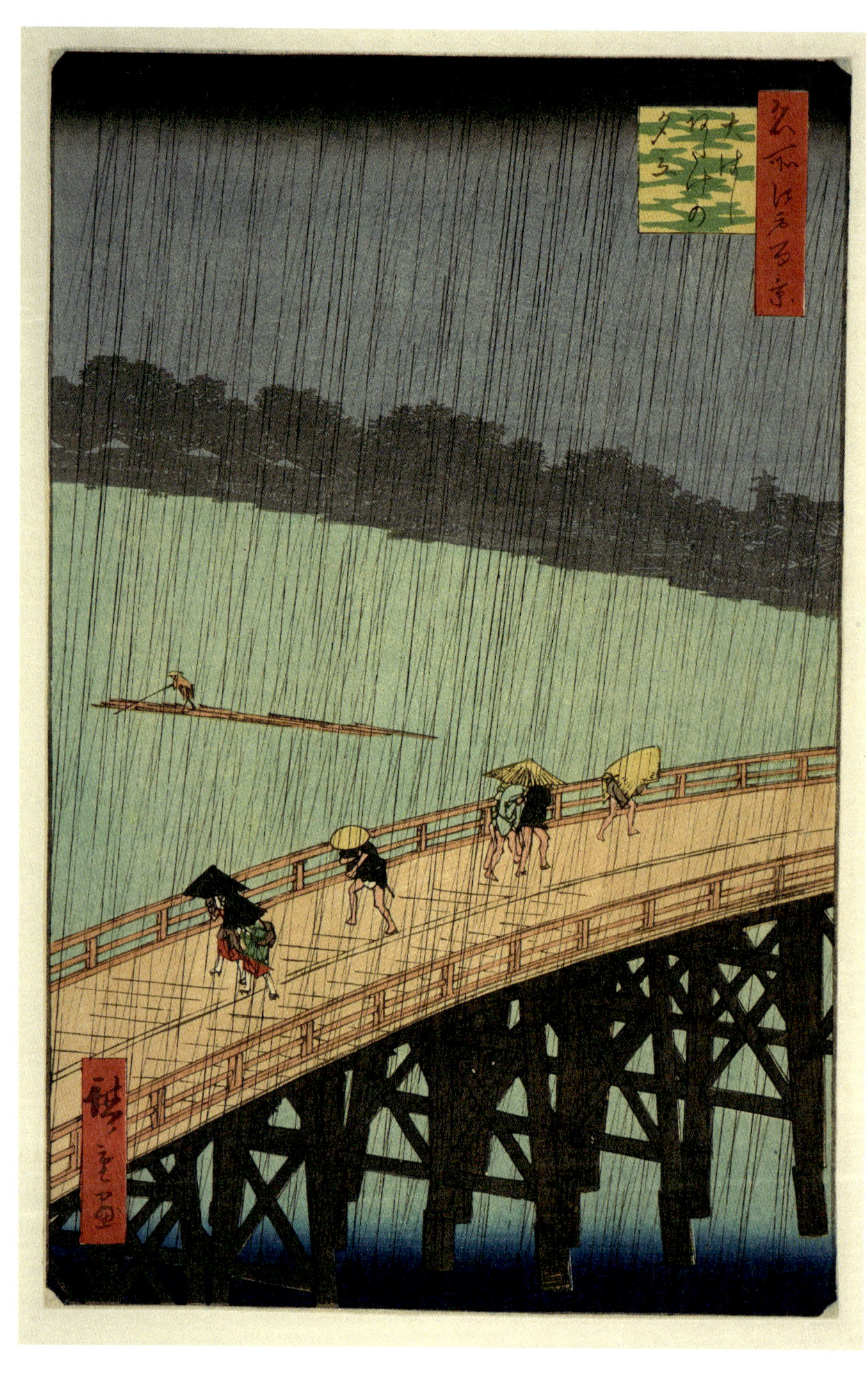

203g Utagawa Hiroshige, *Rain Shower above the Great Bridge at Atake*, 1857, formerly in the Henri Rivière Collection

Claude Monet, Vincent Van Gogh, Henri Rivière and Auguste Rodin as collectors of Japanese woodblock prints

Geneviève Aitken

In the second half of the nineteenth century, artists were overcome by the passion for Japan that had captivated all of Europe after 1858, when the archipelago emerged from its isolation and opened itself to the world as a result of the signing of trading agreements with the West.[1] In this respect, the world fairs held in Paris in 1867 and 1878 represented two key moments in the emergence of a phantasmagorical Japan. In 1867, Nippon's government commissioned pupils of Utagawa Hiroshige and Utagawa Toyokuni – among them, Utagawa Hiroshige III and Utagawa Kunisada II – to create around one hundred woodblock prints, in order to stir up the interest of the European public;[2] the first collections were already assembled by 1878, especially by industrialists, writers and painters such as James McNeill Whistler, Édouard Manet, Edgar Degas, Giuseppe De Nittis, Claude Monet and Camille Pissarro. At the end of the nineteenth century, artists as diverse as Vincent Van Gogh, Paul Gauguin, Henri de Toulouse-Lautrec and the Nabi as well as Henri Rivière and Auguste Rodin collected Japanese colour woodblock prints. In the following essay, we shall focus on the four collections of Monet, Van Gogh, Rivière and Rodin. Why, one might ask, have we restricted ourselves to the – inevitably reduced – selection of precisely these four artists?

First, they belong to different generations. Monet, like Rodin, was born in November 1840, Van Gogh in 1853 and Rivière in 1864. They worked with different media – Monet and Van Gogh painted, Rodin sculpted and Rivière, known for his illustrations, created woodcuts and lithographs. Thus, these artists represent the wide spectrum of artistic techniques predominant in the late nineteenth century. Furthermore, they are also connected by their appreciation for or even friendship with each other. Rodin owned three works by Van Gogh, thus demonstrating his interest in the latter's painting;[3] Rivière mentions the name Rodin frequently in *Les détours du chemin*[4] and visited the sculptor in the Parisian marble depot or at his house in Meudon; Van Gogh speaks repeatedly in his letters to Theo of Monet,[5] who in turn congratulated Vincent via Theo on his paintings, which were exhibited at the Salon des Indépendants in 1890.[6] Finally, Monet and Rodin were also very close, considering themselves connected by "the same love of art". During an extensive correspondence, each of the artists expressed his admiration for the other; they exchanged works[7] and even exhibited together in 1889 with Georges Petit.[8]

By means of a comparative analysis, this study of Monet's, Van Gogh's, Rivière's and Rodin's collections of Japanese woodblock prints should help to expand our knowledge of *Japonisme*. These artist-collectors also benefited from the emergence of a market for Japanese art in France following the opening up of Japan to foreign trade. While they shared an interest in the woodblock prints of Kitagawa Utamaro, Katsushika Hokusai and Utagawa Hiroshige, their collecting and artistic approaches to the works differed. In order to understand these four ensembles in light of the history of the Japanese woodblock print and of *Japonisme*, we shall therefore begin with a qualitative and quantitative study of the collections, which already reveal how these artists

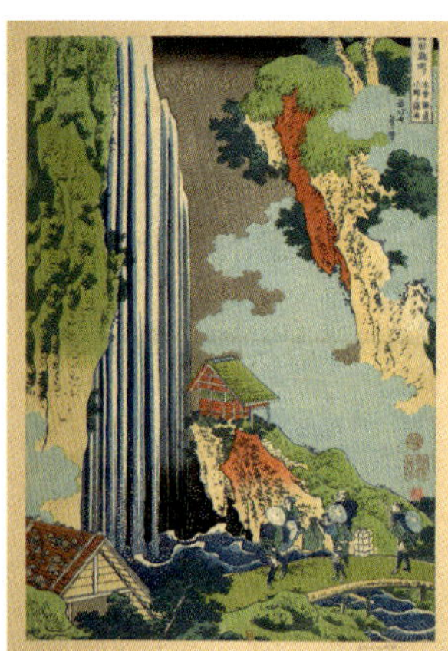

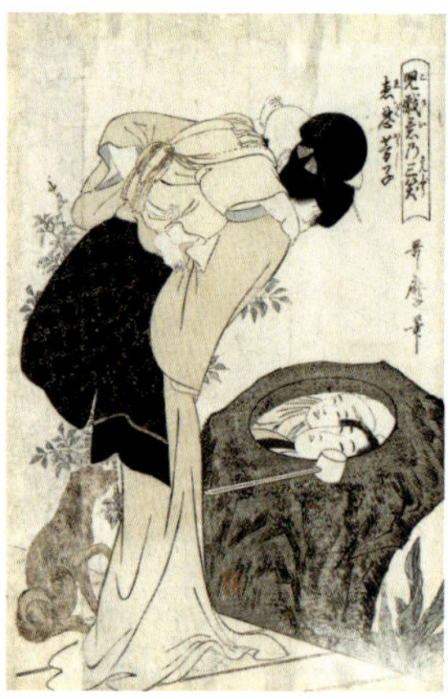

1 Katsushika Hokusai, *The Waterfall at Ono on the Kisokaidō Road*, from the series *A Tour of Waterfalls in Various Provinces*, circa 1833, Bibliothèque nationale de France (formerly Rivière Collection)

2 Kitagawa Utamaro, *Eon Hoshi (The Priest Huiyuan)*, from the series *Three Laughers at Children's Playful Spirits*, circa 1802, Fondation Claude Monet, Giverny, Académie des Beaux-Arts (formerly Monet Collection)

differed in their respective dedication to collecting. Then we shall extend our examination to the economic, social and cultural context of the late nineteenth century that was fixated on a phantasmagorical Japan, thus coming to the sources and motivations for such acquisitions. Finally, we will concentrate on the status of the colour woodblock print in the everyday lives of the artists before, ultimately, exploring their effect on the artistic practice in the works of Rivière; separate essays in this catalogue deal with Monet and Van Gogh.

Origin and analysis of the collections

We begin with a brief history of the origins of the four collections under examination, which are kept albeit not completely, but still quite extensively in museums, libraries or foundations. Since 1916, the Musée Rodin in Paris has preserved the sculptor's Japanese Collection, donated by the artist personally. In 1958, the Musée Guimet in Paris acquired an album of Japanese colour woodblock prints entitled *Souvenir of Van Gogh*, which contains the works that accompanied the artist until his death in Auvers-sur-Oise.[9] In 1962, the descendants of Vincent and Theo Van Gogh assigned the rest of the collection to the Vincent Van Gogh Foundation, which was then placed in the Van Gogh Museum in Amsterdam. Michel Monet also bequeathed the woodblock prints that belonged to his father to the Académie des Beaux-Arts of the Institut de France in 1966, and they are now held by the Fondation Monet in Giverny. Rivière's partial collection, in turn, found its way into the prints and photographs department of the Bibliothèque nationale de France[10] in 2006, thanks to a donation. Because these collections have been inventoried or published in the form of books[11] and exhibition catalogues,[12] they are now accessible for study.

In terms of quantity, Rivière's Collection is by far the most significant. The exceptional aesthete compiled 749 (766) woodblock prints,[13] 49 illustrated books and two paper stencils (*katagami*). The works collected by Rodin, who had less specialist knowledge, comprised only 280 (288) woodblock prints[14] and 15 stencils. The sculptor and draughtsman was primarily interested in the graphic dimension, the linear and curved forms of Japanese art, and he procured 112 ink drawings that came from unstitched booklets or which served as preliminary sketches for graphic works (*hanshita-e*). Monet's Collection and the bundle of woodblock prints gathered by Vincent and Theo Van Gogh[15] are similar in quantity: the former amounts to 231 units, namely, 156 individual – or detached – sheets as well as two pentaptychs, 66 triptychs and 7 diptychs; the latter contains 451 items, divided into 321 individual sheets, 17 triptychs as well as 32 complete and countless incomplete diptychs.

An examination of the content of these collections shall demonstrate the main focus of interest placed by each of the artists in *ukiyo-e* with regard to the development of the polychromous print (*nishiki-e*). In line with a generally accepted classification, this development can be divided into three historical periods (see chart, pp. 50–51).

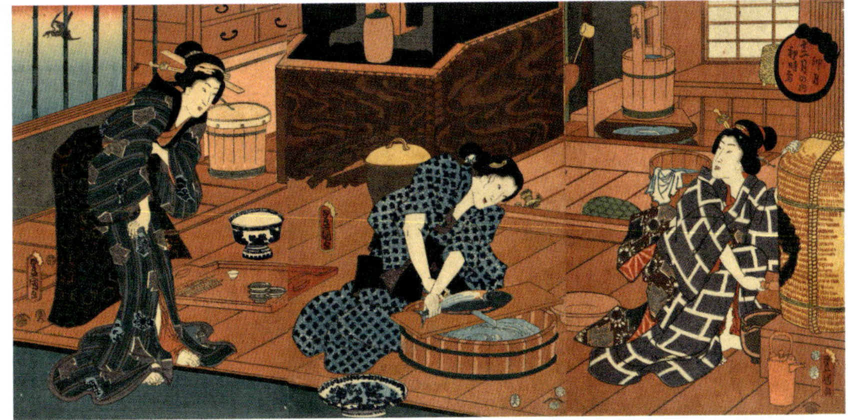

3 Utagawa Kunisada (Toyokuni III), *The Fourth Month: The First Call of the Cuckoo*, triptych from the series *The Twelve Months*, 1854, Van Gogh Museum, Amsterdam (Vincent van Gogh Foundation) (formerly Van Gogh Collection)

We notice that Rivière appreciated the prints from the period between 1760 and 1800, a period characterised by the origin of the polychrome print, but also those from the period between 1800 and 1870, the peak of polychromy in the works of Hokusai (fig. 1) and Hiroshige. Due to their both aesthetic and technical qualities, marked by the subtlety and perfection of the woodblock prints and by their blind blocking and simmer effects, he was also interested in the "beautiful" prints of Suzuki Harunobu or Kitagawa Utamaro, which were completed somewhat earlier. He was the only one to collect a small number of so-called "primitive" woodblock prints (1720–1760), which were characterised by the use of two to three colours; in contrast, he disregarded the woodblock prints of the final period (1870–1910), in which the use of chemical pigments generally prevailed, including among Utagawa Hiroshige III, Utagawa Sadahide or Utagawa Yoshiiku, of which most of Rodin's and Van Gogh's collections are comprised. In that respect, Monet could be regarded as the most eclectic of the four: he was interested in the woodblock prints of all three periods, and his collection is the most varied in terms of their proportions, with a preference for the artists of the period from 1760 until 1800 (fig. 2).

The technical features of the woodblock prints are inseparably connected with their subjects and their development, which must in turn be seen against the background of a political power that more or less strictly controlled the production of the prints.[16] Thus, the history of the Japanese colour woodblock print is accompanied by a thematic development that ranges from the soon-to-be censored presentations by actors and courtesans from the eighteenth century to the contemporary scenes of battle from the Sino-Japanese War (1894–1895), not forgetting the landscape image that unfolded throughout the entire nineteenth century in the course of the travel and pilgrim trend. Therefore, all of the very varied subjects of *ukiyo-e* – these "pictures of the floating world" – are represented, but in each of the collections they are significant to a greater or lesser degree.

With the painters Monet and Van Gogh, for example, the beauties, courtesans, bathing women or popular folk scenes come to the fore, as shown by the woodblock prints by Torii Kiyonaga, Kikugawa Eizan and Utagawa Kunisada (fig. 3). In Rodin's Japanese Collection, pictures of actors, engraved by Utagawa Toyokuni or Kunisada, are more prominent, as are battle scenes. And Rivière's Collection is mostly dominated by landscapes. Four extremely successful series are of particular note here: the *36 Views of Mount Fuji* by Hokusai and Hiroshige's *53 Stations of the Tōkaidō Road*, *Famous Places in the Sixty-Odd Provinces* and *One Hundred Famous Views of Edo*, which are also found in the collections of Monet, Van Gogh and Rodin. Also worth mention are other topics that pervade the entire complex of these collections: fish, bird and flower depictions (*kacho-e*) or bathing women or, as a variation, the female Awabi fishers, who dived without breathing aids in order to harvest conches known as "ear shells".

This initial overview of the Japanese woodblock print collections of Monet, Van Gogh, Rivière and Rodin demonstrates different degrees of depth in each of their collecting activities with regard to the abundance of their content and the quality of the prints. The somewhat dilettantish taste of Van Gogh and

Composition of collections according to period

Period 1: 1760–1800	Artists	Dates	Monet	%	van Gogh		Rivière	%	Rodin	%
	Harunobu	1725–1770	2	4%	0		14	13%	0	
	Koryusai	1735–1790	0	0	0		9	8%	0	
	Shunsho	1726–1793	0		0		6	5%	0	
	Shunjo	died 1787	0		0		1	1%	0	
	Shuncho	active circa 1783–1795	1	2%	0		7	6%	0	
	Shunzan	active circa 1780–1790	0		0		1	1%	0	
	Shunko	1743–1812	0		0		1	1%	0	
	Kiyonaga	1752–1815	3	5%	0		6	5%	1	33%
	Utamaro	1753–1806	37	67%	0		45	41%	2	67%
	Toyoharu	1735–1814	0		0		1	1%	0	
	Shunman	1757–1820	0		0		1	1%	0	
	Utamaro II	died circa 1831	1	2%	0		1	1%	0	
	Eishi	1756–1829	6	11%	0		11	10%	0	
	Enshi	active circa late 1780s	0		0		1	1%	0	
	Eisho	active circa 1780–1800	1	2%	0		3	3%	0	
	Eisui	active circa 1790–1823	0		0		1	1%	0	
	Eiri	active circa 1791	1	2%	0		1	1%	0	
	Sharaku	active circa 1794–1795	3	5%	0		0		0	
Sum of Period 1			55		0		110		3	
Percentage of Period 1 in the overall inventory of the collection			24%		0%		15%		1%	

Period 2 : 1800–1870	Artists	Dates	Monet	%	van Gogh	%	Rivière	%	Rodin	%
	Hokusai (and school)	1760–1849	22	18%	0		129	20%	4	2%
	Toyokuni	1769–1825	3	3%	6	1%	14	2%	7	4%
	Shuntei	1770–1820	0		0		0		1	0,60%
	Shinsai	circa 1764–1830	1	1%	0		1	0,10%	0	
	Hokuba	1771–1844	0		0		1	0,10%	0	
	Kunimasa	1773–1810	1	1%	1	0,30%	1	0,10%	0	
	Toyokuni II	1777–1835	1	3%	3	1%	0		2	1%
	Hokkei	1780–1850	1	1%	0		1	0,10%	0	
	Gakutei	1786–1868	0		0		2	0,31%	0	
	Kunisada (= Toyokuni III)	1786–1864	10	8%	159	51%	1	0,10%	78	44%
	Kiyomine	1787–1868	0		0		1	0,10%	0	
	Eizan	1787–1867	1	1%	6	2%	1	0,10%	1	0,60%
	Eisen	1791–1848	0		10	3%	15	2%	1	0,60%
	Juniyasu	1794–1834	0		3	1%	0		0	
	Hiroshige	1797–1858	51	42%	43	14%	457	72%	34	19%
	Kuniyoshi	1797–1861	12	10%	35	11%	0		44	25%
	Kuniteru	1808–1876	0		0		0		1	0,60%
	Kunihiro	active circa 1810	1	1%	0		0		0	
	Yoshikuni	active circa1813–1832	0		1	0,30%	0		0	
	Ashiyuki	active circa 1814–1833	0		1	0,30%	0		0	
	Sadakage	active circa 1818–1844	0		1	0,30%	0		0	
	Kunitomi	active circa 1818–1845	0		1	0,30%	0		0	
	Shunko	active circa1820 (or 1790)	0		0		1	0,10%		
	Hokuei	active circa 1824–1837	0		1	0,30%	0		0	
	Taigaku	active circa 1825–1840	0		0		0		1	0,60%
	Sencho	active circa 1830–1850	0		3	1,00%	0		0	
	Hokuju	active circa 1830	1	1%	0		1	0,10%	1	0,60%
	Shunsho	active circa 1830–1854	0		3	1%	0		0	
	Yoshitsuya	1822–1866	1	1%	0		0		1	0,60%
	Kagematsu	active circa 1840–1841	0		1	0,30%	0		0	
	Hirokage	active circa 1851–1866	0		2	1,00%	0		0	
	Hiroshige II	1829–1869	3	3%	11	4%	8	1%	2	1%
	Kunimori I or II	active circa 1818–1843 or circa 1848–1860	0		1	0,30%	0		0	
	Kunisada II (=Toyokuni IV)	1823–1880	10	8%	21	7%	0		0	
	Kuninao	1795–1854	0		0		0		1	
Sum of Period 2			119		313		634		179	
Percentage of Period 2 in the overall inventory of the collection			52%		70%		85%		64%	

Period 3: 1870–1910	Artists	Dates	Monet	%	van Gogh	%	Rivière	%	Rodin	%
	Sadahide	1807–1873	6	14%	1	1%	0		13	34%
	Yoshifuji	1828–1887	1	2%	2	3%	0		1	3%
	Toyohiro	1829–?	0		0		1	20%	0	
	Yoshimori	1830–1884	1	2%	1	1%	0		0	
	Yoshiiku	1833–1904	2	5%	4	5%	1	20%	0	
	Yoshiyuki	1835–1879	0		0		1	20%	0	
	Kunichika	1835–1900	2	5%	15	20%	0		2	5%
	Chikanobu	1838–1912	1	2%	1	1%	0		0	
	Yoshitsuru	active circa 1835–1855	0		1	1%	0		0	
	Yoshikazu	active circa1850 1860	1	2%	4	5%	0		1	3%
	Fusatane	active circa 1850–1860	1	3%	0		0		0	
	Yoshitomi	active circa 1850–1870	4	10%	17	23%	0		4	11%
	Yoshitora	active circa 1845–1880	5	12%	9	12%	1	20%	1	3%
	Naomasa	active circa 1850–1870	0		0		0		4	11%
	Shigetoshi and Shigekiyo	?	1	2%	0		0		0	
	Yoshitoshi	1839–1892	3	7%	4	5%	0		0	
	Hiroshige III	1843–1894	0		4	5%	1	20%	1	3%
	Toshihide	1863–1925	2	5%	0		0		0	
	Toshikata Mizuno	1866–1908	2	5%	0		0		2	5%
	Kuniteru II and III	1829–1874	2	5%	4	5%	0		2	5%
	Yoshimaru II	1844–1907	0		1	1%	0		0	
	Kuniaki	active circa 1850	1	2%	1	1%	0		1	3%
	Kunimaro	active circa 1850–1875	0		1	1%	0		0	
	Kuniharu	active circa 1852–1854	0		1	1%	0		0	
	Sadakoma	active circa 1854–1860	0		1	1%	0		0	
	Ikkei	active circa 1870	1	2%	0		0		0	
	Gekko	1859–1920	1	2%	0		0		0	
	Ginko	active circa 1874–1897	1	2%	0		0		2	5%
	Akika	undated	1	2%	0		0		0	
	Baido	undated	0		0		0		1	3%
	Gyokuei	undated	0		2	3%	0		0	
	Hosho	undated	0		0		0		1	3%
	Koju	undated	0		0		0		2	5%
	Minehide	undated	1	2%	0		0		0	
	Nobukazu	undated	1	2%	0		0		0	
	Toshimasa	undated	1	2%	0		0		0	
Sum of Period 3			**42**		**74**		**5**		**38**	
Percentage of Period 3 in the overall inventory of the collection			**19%**		**16%**		**0,20%**		**14%**	
	Unknown artists/Sheets from an album/Miscellaneous		14		64		–		59 (incl. drawings)	
Percentage in the overall inventory of the collection			**5%**		**14%**		**0%**		**21%**	

Works by the Japanese artists highlighted in colour are represented in at least two of the collections of Monet, Van Gogh, Rivière or Rodin.

Diagram of subject distribution according to artist

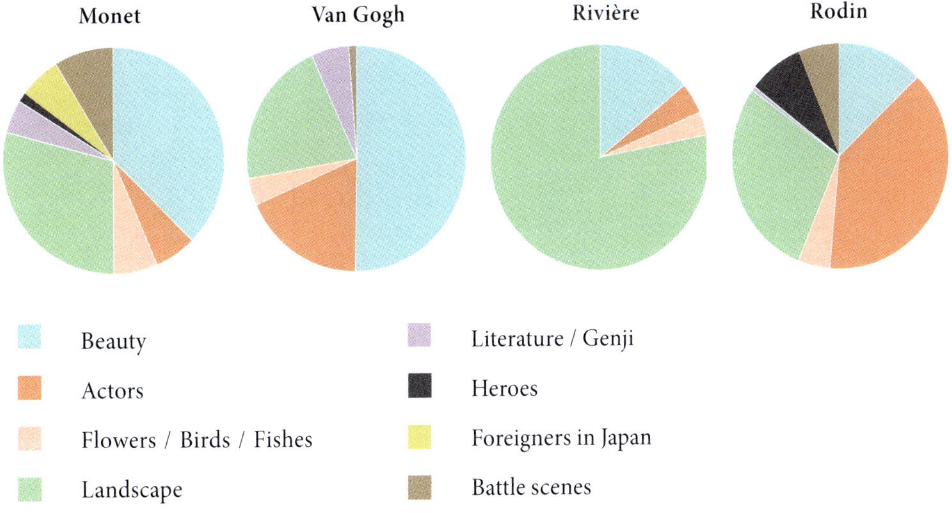

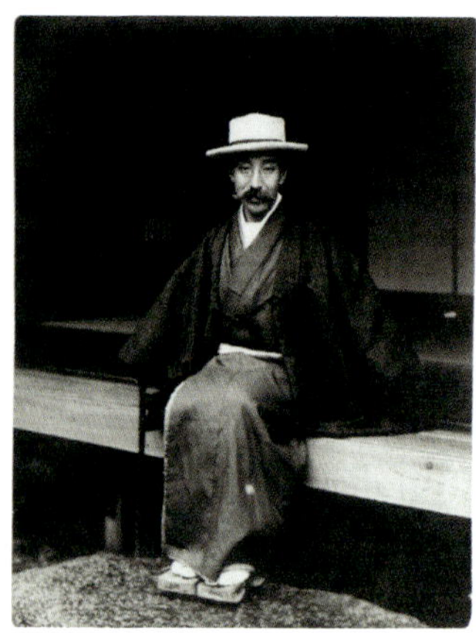

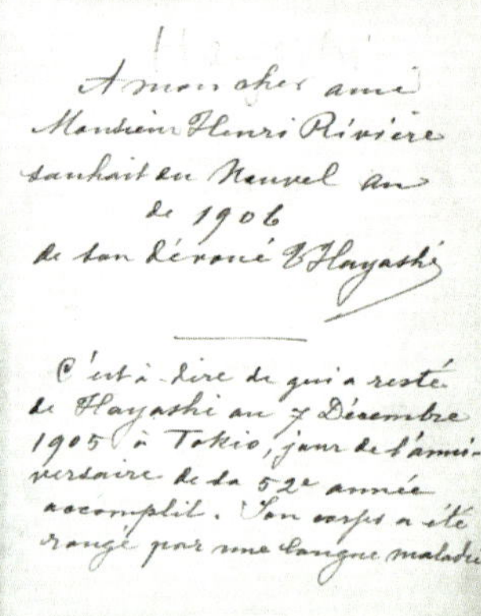

A mon cher ami
Monsieur Henri Rivière
souhait du Nouvel An
de 1906
de son dévoué T. Hayashi

C'est à dire ce qui a resté
de Hayashi au 7 Décembre
1905 à Tokio, jour de l'anni-
versaire de sa 52e année
accomplit. Son corps a été
rongé par une longue maladie

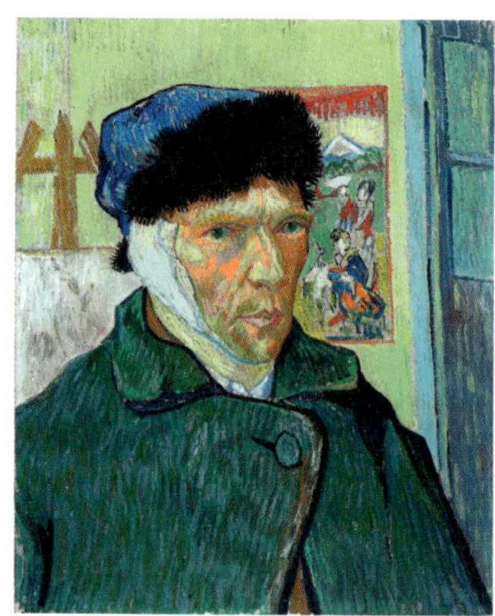

Rodin in Japanese woodblock prints remains difficult to define. Here, the appeal of a Japan that was equated with exoticism refers to criteria that require no engagement on the part of the artist for a better understanding of the art. Rivière and Monet, however, behaved like true collectors. While the former was interested in high-quality historical creations, the latter regarded the woodblock prints across their entire range; and for each, their fascination with the works was accompanied by an intellectual understanding. Thus, just like Raymond Koechlin, Charles Gillot or Henri Vever, they held their ground as veritably enlightened amateurs. All further considerations must be seen in light of the social and cultural context of *Japonisme* in order to understand how Monet, Van Gogh, Rivière and Rodin built up their collections.

On trading and bartering – complementary values

The market for Japanese woodblock prints – which were initially not distinguished from the Chinese counterparts, called "Chinoiserie" in France – developed in the mid-1860s and spread pursuant to the world fairs of 1867 and 1878 when expert traders began settling in Paris. While the new Japan network that had settled in Paris was quite widespread, the sources are too few as to allow a full understanding of how Monet, Van Gogh, Rivière and Rodin accumulated their collections in detail. However, Van Gogh's correspondence as well as the collection stamps and labels on the woodblock prints belonging to Monet and Rivière mention the names Siegfried Bing, Hayashi Tadamasa and Florine Langweil – dealers from whom these artists were able to acquire Japanese woodblock prints. Monet claimed to have discovered his first Japanese woodblock prints at the age of sixteen in Le Havre in a shop "in which the curiosities brought by the ocean liners were flogged".[17] He declared further that he had purchased a bundle of prints during his stay in Amsterdam in 1886. Rodin's acquisitions, by contrast, which began in 1900 and are documented by bills and statements kept in the museum, were made via other networks that came about later.

Edmond de Goncourt reported in his *Journal* that he often met "Monet [...] at Bing's, in the small attic with the Japanese prints".[18] In 1878, Bing opened a shop for Japanese art in 19, rue Chauchat in Paris, which is listed in the *Annuaire du Commerce* under the category "curiosités". As Goncourt attests, this place became a true social meeting place for artists and writers. Along with Monet, Rivière also visited Bing's store, and, here, during his stay in Paris from March 1886 to February 1888, Vincent Van Gogh also admired the Japanese albums and woodblock prints which he had already discovered for himself and had started to procure in the Netherlands no later than 1885;[19] he perused the monthly magazine *Le Japon artistique*, which Bing published from 1888, and soon invited his friends, the "painters of the *Petit Boulevard*", Louis Anquetin, Émile Bernard and Henri de Toulouse-Lautrec along, who were in turn fascinated by this art. Thus, an expert dealer such as Bing was able to sell his woodblock prints in Parisian cultural circles; in the process, he also instructed and advised the artists and writers in setting up their own collections. Henri

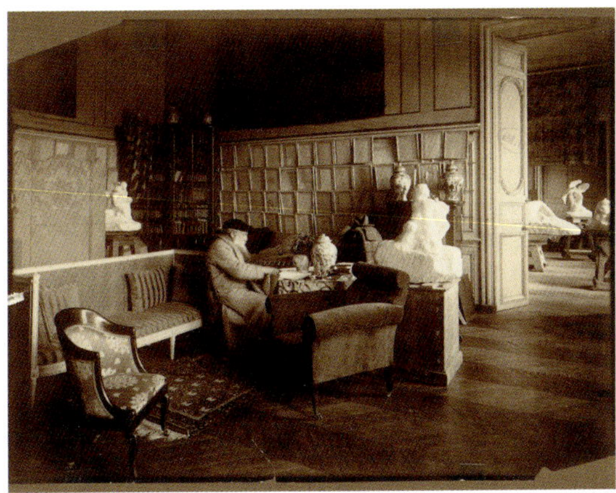

4 Hayashi Tadamasa, photograph sent as postcard to Henri Rivière for the new year 1906, Private Collection
5 Vincent Van Gogh, *Self-Portrait with Bandaged Ear,* 1889, The Samuel Courtauld Trust, The Courtauld Gallery, London
6 Cl. Lemery, Rodin in the Hôtel Biron, 22.4.1912, Musée Rodin, Paris

Rivière, for example, recalls: "We were allowed to browse through albums and woodblock prints over long afternoons, simply for the purpose of our initiation; it was clear that we were not buyers, but it was a way to train new disciples."[20] This shows how artists were not only instructed in their love for the Japanese woodblock print – beyond all economic considerations – but that they also had an important role as mediators, thus supporting the dealers. We can see the perspicacity of Bing who, in order to expand his market, not only expected the writers, industrialists and museum people to be enthusiastic about these prints, but also expected the painters to act as disseminators of this aesthetic. Van Gogh, for example, organised an exhibition of his woodblock prints and crepe prints in the Café du Tambourin around February/March 1887.[21]

Therefore, the passion of the artists for Japanese art went well beyond strictly artistic bounds, especially when Van Gogh harboured some commercial hopes in his letters that did not at all fit in with the prescribed image of an ostracised artist. Let us not forget that he worked for Goupil's offices in The Hague, London and finally Paris from 1869 to 1876, and he "speculated" tenaciously with his brother Theo, manager of the Parisian gallery of Boussod, Valadon & Cie – Goupil's successors – on the growing value of this art: "There's not much to be earned from it, and that's why nobody takes it up. Nevertheless, after a few years it will all become quite rare, will be sold more dearly."[22]

We can see once more from the spectrum that ranges from the speculating Van Gogh to the selfless love held by Rivière and Monet for Japanese woodblock prints, the serious qualitative differences – mentioned at the outset – between each of the collections. These came about due to trade and bartering – the latter a practice that Vincent Van Gogh contemplated, writing to Theo: "And that will procure you a Claude Monet and other paintings, because if you take the trouble to dig out the Japanese prints, you certainly have the right to do exchanges with them, with the painters, for paintings."[23] Monet and Rivière cooperated in this manner with the Japanese Hayashi: Monet exchanged paintings with him "for" woodblock prints,[24] and in 1904, Rivière put the seal on an agreement with his Japanese friend (fig. 4). The graphic artist designed the decor for his house, and in return Hayashi opened up his entire fundus to him. By these means, Rivière was free to help himself to one of the most extensive sets of Japanese woodblock prints present in Paris at the time, which is also reflected in the quality of his own collection. That is why Hayashi's little red stamp can often be found on the illustrated books from Rivière's estate, whereby the latter frequently placed his own monogram beside it – a sign of veneration and common belongingness. Equally, among the approximately fifteen very rare woodblock prints that belonged to Monet, we find one from the inventories of the expert and dealer Wakai Kenzaburō, who had worked with Hayashi until 1886; and some triptychs by Hosoda Eishi as well as some of the most beautiful Utamaros and Hokusais from Monet's Collection also came from Hayashi. He had come to the French capital as an interpreter in 1878, on the occasion of the Paris World Fair, and Japan enthusiasts often enlisted him to find very rare items, inform them on the customs and traditions of the Japanese, explain the meaning of the *ukiyo-e* pictures and "translate" them for non-Japanese

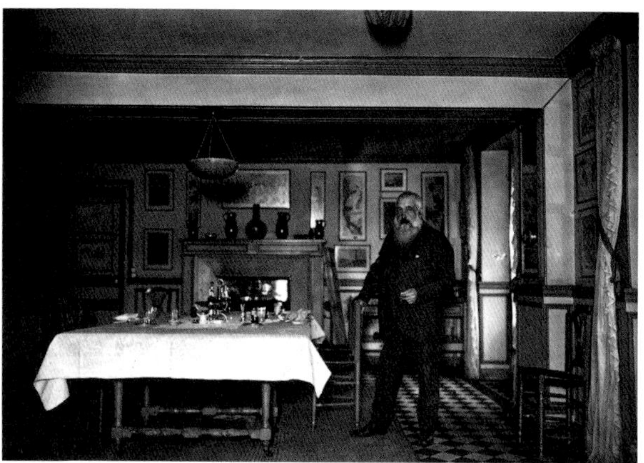

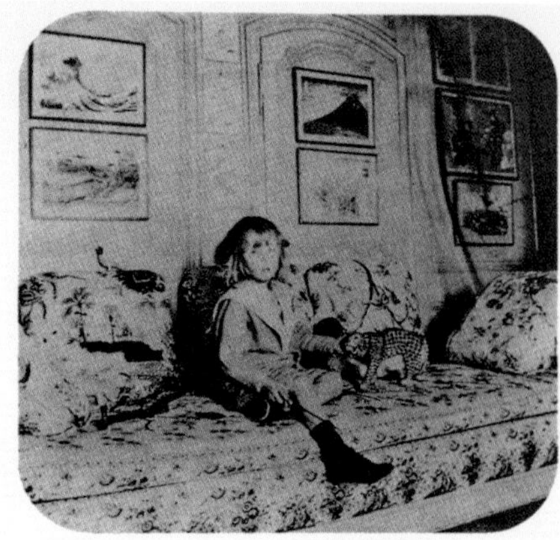

mentalities. The books on *L'Art japonais* by Louis Gonse (1883) or on *Outamaro* (1891) and *Hokousaï* (1896) by Edmond de Goncourt could never have existed without Hayashi's erudition and devotion, and the same could be said of the collections of Monet and Rivière. In other words, the dealings with him (and since 1880, in the case of Rivière, with Langweil, another key personality of *Japonisme* in Paris) explain the richness of their collections and their intimate knowledge of Japanese woodblock prints.

As far as the aforementioned great difference between Rodin's Collection and those of Rivière and Monet is concerned, it can be explained by the thoroughgoing change in context that took place between the end of the nineteenth and the beginning of the twentieth centuries. Bing died in 1905, Hayashi had already returned to Japan, where he died in 1906, and *Japonisme* had gone out of fashion in France when Rodin decided – after 1900 – to buy Japanese objects and woodblock prints. At the time of the purchase of his first two albums, on the occasion of the Paris World Fair of 1900, the market had changed fundamentally. The beautiful woodblock prints by Utamaro and Hokusai had become rarer and existed only in private collections and museums. Rodin therefore built up his collection using other channels. Attracted by the reputation of the sculptor, some young Japanese scholars wanted to pay homage to him in 1911 by dedicating an issue of their journal *Shirakaba* to him. On this occasion, they made him a gift of thirty woodblock prints, which had been procured properly by the editorial team,[25] and which were representative of the best Japanese artists – from Harunobu to Utamaro and Kunisada. Other Japanese Rodin admirers, such as the painter Mori Oghihara, who turned to sculpture after meeting him, or European collectors like Max Linde, also offered Rodin such prints as a sign of their appreciation.

But how can this late interest in Japanese prints be explained? It is possible that the sculptor and draughtsman turned his attention to erotic graphic works for artistic reasons in 1908 when he, probably parallel to the development of his own erotic drawings, purchased three scroll paintings; but his personal concern for cultural heritage is also a reason. With a view to his future museum, Rodin acquired (until 1911) woodblock prints by Hiroshige for the modest price of 10 or 20 francs, while greatly enlarging his collection of Greek and Roman antiques. And although the Japanese woodblock prints owned by Rodin are not exhibited in his museums today, but instead almost exclusively show sculptures, it might well be that the sculptor, like his friend Monet, also wanted to link his name with Japan. In such a case, his acquisition of Japanese art would have contributed to the establishment of his posthumous fame as an artist.

The relationship between collectors and collections

We now want to turn our attention to other aspects – namely, the possibly very different aesthetic pleasure given by the Japanese woodblock prints to Monet, Van Gogh, Rivière and Rodin. The manner in which these artists kept their prints and integrated them into their personal surroundings always reveals much

7 Claude Monet's house in Giverny, dining room, Philippe Piguet Collection, Paris
8 Claude Monet's house in Giverny, Salon Bleu, Jim Butler at his grandparents' house, Claire Joyes Collection

about their respective personalities, their *Weltanschauung* and their idea of art. For that reason, we shall examine the collections within the space of the *maison d'un artiste*, a subject honoured by decadent writers at the beginning of the 1880s,[26] before addressing the impact of the woodblock prints on the creative practice of these four artists.

"My studio's quite tolerable, mainly because I've pinned a set of Japanese prints on the walls that I find very diverting,"[27] wrote Vincent Van Gogh as early as 1885 to his brother Theo. In some of his paintings, such as the two painted versions of *Portrait of Père Tanguy* (pp. 20, 22) or *Self-Portrait with Bandaged Ear* (fig. 5), Japanese woodblock prints even found their way into his artistic work as backgrounds in his private or creative space. Rodin also introduced some works from his collection into his personal living space and his studio, which then merged with his own works and antiques in his house in Meudon or in the Hôtel Biron. We know from Hofbauer's report[28] that the *Carps (katagami)* hung on a wall in Rodin's apartment. The state of preservation (yellowed paper and faded colours) of some of the prints given by the *Shirakaba* group also indicates that they were probably exposed to light. Thus, the artist lived in the midst of his works and collections. However, it is true that Rodin tended to exhibit art objects, "Chinoiseries" and "Japonaiseries" in his dwelling rather than woodblock prints (fig. 6). It was a different matter with Monet, who decorated the walls of the salon and the dining room of his house in Giverny with an ensemble that was highly representative both of his collection and for the history of the Japanese woodblock print. Among others, Gustave Geffroy also reported of an "abundance of the most beautiful and rare Japanese woodblock prints, placed simply behind glass".[29] This ensemble of the *ukiyo-e* style, gathered together in the dining room, included Utamaro's female images, Kunisada's Kabuki actors, Kōrin's animal representations and Hiroshige's landscapes, as well as Yoshitomi's scenes of foreigners and a couple of battle scenes by Yoshitoshi.

A photograph also shows Monet standing proudly in the middle of his dining room (fig. 7), where he dined together with Gustave Geffroy, Georges Clemenceau, Octave Mirbeau or with the Japanese Matsukata Kōjirō and his niece, Princess Kuroki. Thus, the colour woodblock prints that Monet acquired in Hayashi's small individual cabinets now developed into a convivial space, similar to Bing's "store". This also means that the collection became an environment that imprinted itself on the viewing habits of the artist in his everyday life.

However, such an observation should not be generalised, since, whereas the woodblock prints were found in Van Gogh's creative space and in the living environments of Monet and Rodin, in Rivière's Parisian apartment they were completely protected from the light and not as accessible to view. As a collector concerned with the sensitivity of his sheets, he protected his woodblock prints in bound slipcases, which occasionally bore the name of the corresponding series. Rivière conserved, but one might say that he did so "as an artist and craftsman". He commissioned his friend Georges Auriol to make suitable cardboard portfolios, which were decorated with stylised blossoms in the style of the decorative motifs found on the *katagami*. At the same time, he was a lender to large exhibitions of Japanese woodblock prints, especially those

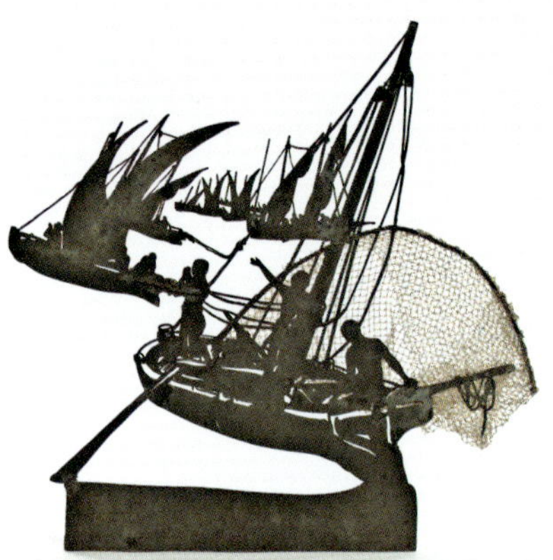

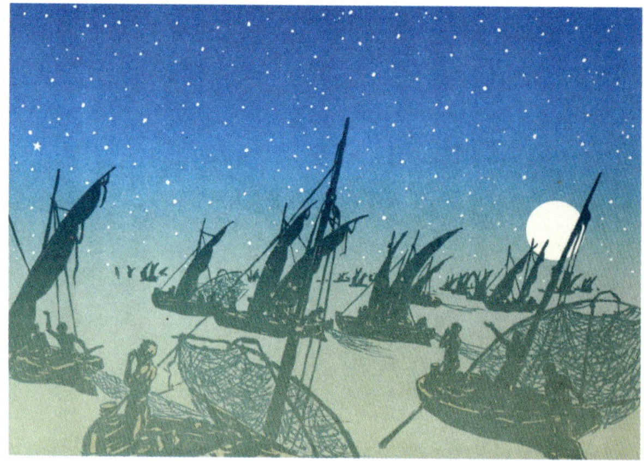

organised by the Musée des Arts décoratifs between 1909 and 1914.[30] While others behaved like amateurs, Rivière acted almost like a professional conservator.

Yet the Japanese element did not disappear from Rivière's decorative projects. Quite the contrary, it was the central focus of the furnishing of his house in Brittany: the graphic artist borrowed iris motifs from Hokusai and Hiroshige and used them to paint a frieze that lined the ceilings in some rooms, invoking a "Japanese" world and giving the house its name – "Landiris".[31] Thus, an artist's house was named after a Japanese motif, and what first seemed like a fashion or decoration eventually led to an everyday matter of course. In this respect, Monet – with his pond covered in reflections and water lilies, including a Japanese bridge – was a prime example of this immersion into the Japanese world. Beyond the realm of purely aesthetic pleasure, the artist was particularly interested in Japanese flora, for example, when he wrote to Maurice Joyant: "I thank you for thinking of me with regard to the Hokusai flowers [...] admittedly, you don't mention corn poppies, but that is what is important, as I already have irises, chrysanthemums, peonies and morning glory."[32] So Hayashi not only provided him with woodblock prints, but also with the bulbs of Japanese plants, which he planted in Giverny.[33] From the print to the garden, from the interior to the exterior, from the two-dimensionality of art to the three-dimensionality of nature – the flourishing of Japanese culture was no longer merely visual, but rather spread across the entire complex of the body, the living space and the image.

We might therefore ask what impact such a heartfelt and everyday relationship with Japan, at times reaching even beyond the pictures, had on the world view of these artists. Many of them believed to have found Japan in some European landscapes. In Norway, Monet took the Kolsås mountain for Mount Fuji,[34] Rodin opined of the meanders of the Loire that "the Loire forms Japanese ornaments",[35] and Van Gogh ultimately felt like he was in Japan, even though he was only staying in southern France. As a convinced idealist and utopian, he created his own "floating world" in his Yellow House in Arles. Incidentally, the colour of the yellow sun of the south was reflected in the colour of the walls in Monet's dining room, as Julie Manet reports: "The salon is panelled in violet wood, many Japanese woodblock prints hang there, as in the dining room, which is painted completely yellow"[36] (fig. 7 and fig. 8). Here, we can see the exceptional discrepancy between the image of Japan as dreamed by the artists in France and the Japanese reality. The Land of the Rising Sun had transformed into a dazzling apparition.

At the end of this essay, we wish to address the influence of this "Japanese dream" on Rivière's artistic practice. When Rivière erected – with the help of the illustrator and Japan enthusiast Henry Somm – his shadow theatre for the cabaret Le Chat Noir in 1887, he may well have been thinking of the colour woodblock prints in which the Japanese envelop the entire background – both landscape and figures – in all-encompassing fog, in order to suggest depth. The silhouettes made by Rivière from a zinc plate (fig. 9) and Hiroshige's woodblock print *Mishima* display the same shadow effect in the style of *ombres chinoises* or Chinese shadows (p. 148).

9 Henri Rivière, *Fishermen*, cut and painted zinc plate, 8th scene of *La Marche à l'étoile*, mystery play in ten scenes, poem and music by Georges Fragerolle; premiere on 6.1.1890 in Le Chat Noir cabaret theatre by Rodolphe Salis, Les Arts Décoratifs, Paris

10 Henri Rivière, *Fishermen*, plate 29 of the illustrated score of *La Marche à l'étoile*, 1890, Bibliothèque des Arts décoratifs, Paris

In fact, the relationship with the Japanese art of the woodblock print was reflected in Rivière's work in a very different way. The graphic artist and collector neither "dreamed of" Japan – like Monet – nor was he stimulated to create a "new art" – like Van Gogh – but instead he himself reproduced the Japanese print technique and made it his own. In a very long production process, he combined the four crafts (drawing, engraving, printing and publishing) that were involved in the processing of a woodblock print in Japan. In this manner, he created numerous views of Brittany, and his *36 Views of the Eiffel Tower* (p. 193), based on Hokusai's *36 Views of Mount Fuji* (p. 192), also emerged according to the same principle and with the help of a technique adapted to lithography. By these means, the artist also achieved a colour gradation in his illustrated score *La Marche à l'étoile*, which corresponded with the Japanese *bokashi* (fig. 10). We can therefore say that Rivière did not set up his "dreamed" Japan like Monet and Van Gogh, but instead painted French cityscapes and landscapes with a "Japanese eye". Incidentally, he was the only one of this group of four artists to sign his own works personally in the "Japanese manner" with a monogram – an artistic avowal and a sign of the internalisation of Japanese art in his own practice, just as with Toulouse-Lautrec and the Nabi.

Therefore, the collections of these four artists provide a complete panorama of the 150-year history of the Japanese woodblock print. The Westerners' enthusiasm for Japanese art – from the simple illustrated sheets to the search for refined techniques – was what created the prerequisite for a flourishing *Japonisme*. Whereas the *ukiyo-e* generally represented for publishers a commercial and promotional product that was popular among the Japanese in the Edo period, the status of these woodblock prints changed upon crossing the oceans, and they became veritable works of art. Yet the Japanese woodblock prints were more than mere collectables; they entered everyday life and even, in some cases, the creative atmosphere of the artist, in whose works they appeared, so that they became the subject of dreams and inspiration for Monet and Van Gogh, and especially for Henri Rivière, who rediscovered his artistic practice based on the objects of his passion.

I wish to express my absolute gratitude to Valérie Sueur, curator in the prints and photography department of the Bibliothèque nationale de France, for her warm reception and the trust she placed in me by allowing me access to Henri Rivière's collection of Japanese woodblock prints; a warm thank you is also due to Christian Lahanier for his valuable advice and to Olivier Schuwer for his efficient and discreet cooperation.

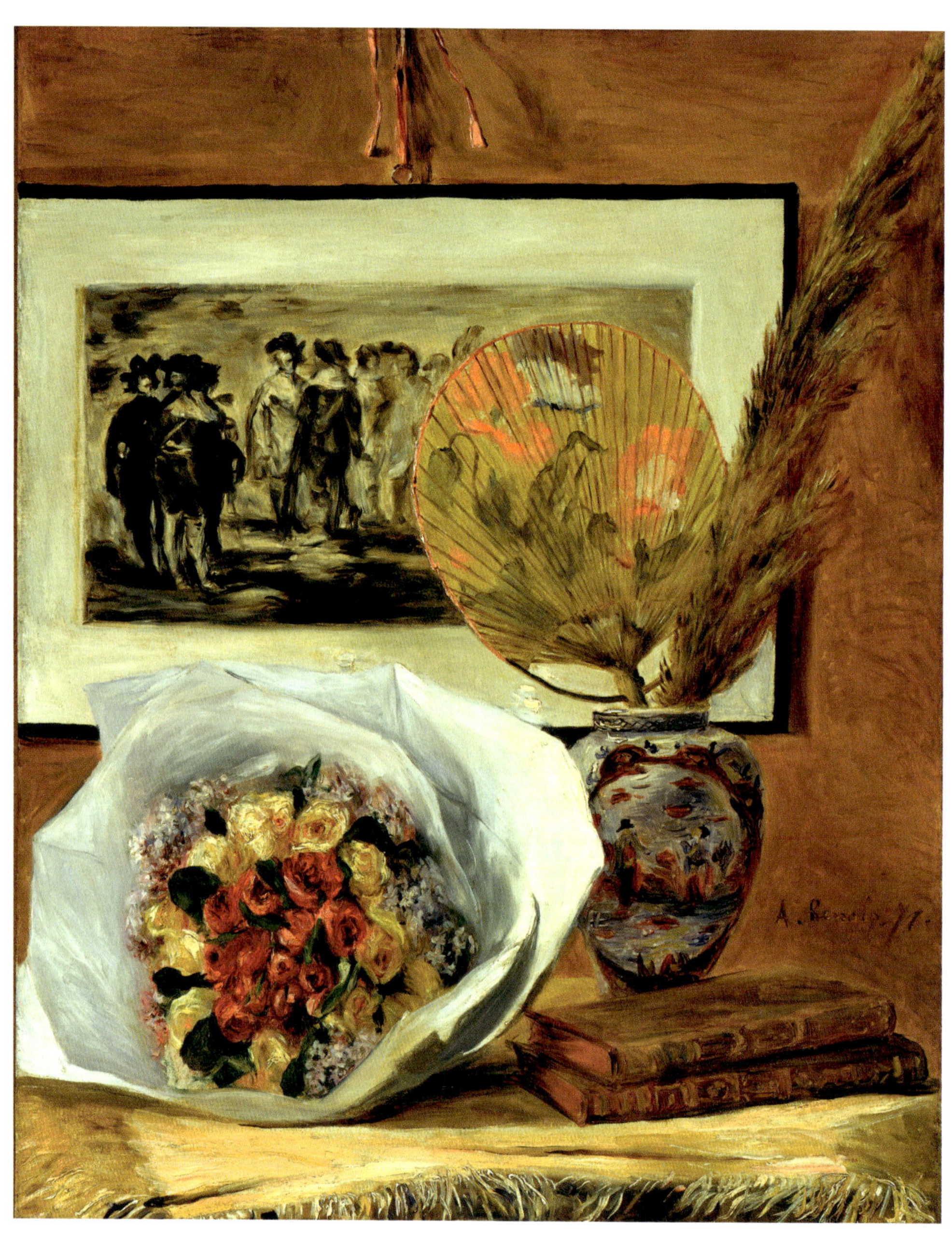

62 Pierre Auguste Renoir, *Still Life with Bouquet*, 1871

The early *Japonistes*

Sandra Gianfreda

Surrounded by Japanese art – a sign of *modernité*

Once the first European countries had concluded trade agreements with Japan (Great Britain and France in 1858), the import of art and objects from this Far Eastern country got underway on a large scale in major cities such as London and Paris. The presence of those artefacts – but even more so, the readiness of what began as a small circle of devotees to examine them more closely – triggered an interest of unprecedented dimensions in the culture of a far-distant land. The enthusiasm for the unknown world of imagery of Japan and its unaccustomed articles will presumably have taken hold of artists and scholars at around the same time. Primarily men of letters such as Zacharie Astruc, Charles Baudelaire, the Goncourt brothers and Émile Zola, and artists such as Félix Bracquemond, Edgar Degas, Giuseppe De Nittis, Henri Fantin-Latour, Édouard Manet, Alfred Stevens, James Tissot and James McNeill Whistler were among the first *Japonistes*.[1] They all began acquiring *Japonica* and furnishing their homes or studios with them in the 1860s. Their common interest soon brought them together in friendships and associations – and it was in this context, for example, that the *Société Japonaise du Jing-lar* was founded in 1867.[2]

After the Paris World Fair of 1867, at which Japan presented itself to a broad public in France for the first time, anybody who was anybody among the bourgeoisie began following the trend. To be "modern" in the late 1860s meant to buy interior decoration items and trinkets in such shops as À la Porte chinoise, À l'Empire chinois or La Jonque chinoise, the latter run by Madame Desoye. Therefore, it is hardly surprising that objects from the Far East also made their way into Western imagery.

Among the earliest paintings of Far Eastern character is Whistler's *Princess from the Land of Porcelain* (fig. 1), a work he began in London in the winter of 1863. It is possible that the artist first came into contact with Japanese woodblock print books through Auguste Delâtre, whom Whistler commissioned to print his etching series *The French Set* in 1858.[3] No information has come down to us about what type of *Asiatica* Whistler may have acquired before moving from Paris to London in 1859, and to what extent he collected them. What we know for certain is that his first home in London was decorated with objects of Chinese and Japanese art. In a photograph of his drawing room from around 1865, we can identify a low, five-part partition screen with a classical Far Eastern bird and flower motif, three *uchiwa* fans and four hanging scrolls (kakemonos) with peacock motifs on the wall, as well as a lacquered cabinet holding various objects (fig. 2).[4] What inspired him to paint Christine Spartali – one of the most beautiful women in the London of his day – in a kimono before the backdrop of his drawing room is unclear. However, the title with the addendum "from the land of porcelain" (i.e. China) suggests that the painting was not necessarily intended as a portrait.[5] In a letter to Fantin-Latour of February/March 1865, Whistler referred to the work as "La japonaise" ("The Japanese Lady").[6] Exhibited at the Paris Salon in the spring of 1865, the painting thus oscillated between portrait and fiction.[7] In the period that followed, paintings in which Japanese objects were illustrated became a trend in Paris.

In the same period, Tissot likewise painted a large-scale "Japonaise", *Japanese Lady in the Bath* (fig. 3), which he dated 1864. In view of the fact that Whistler had been in contact with Tissot since 1856, the choice

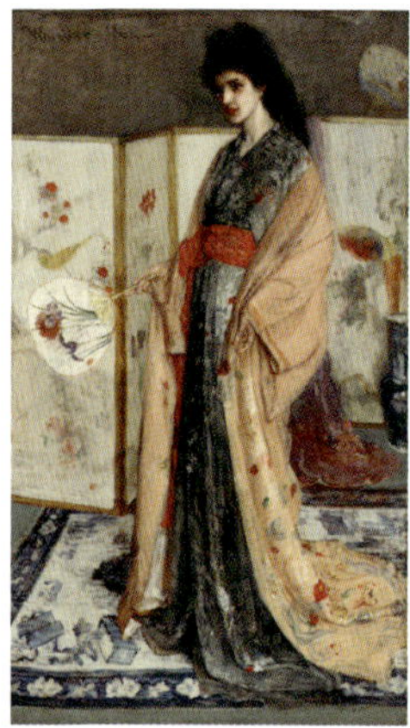
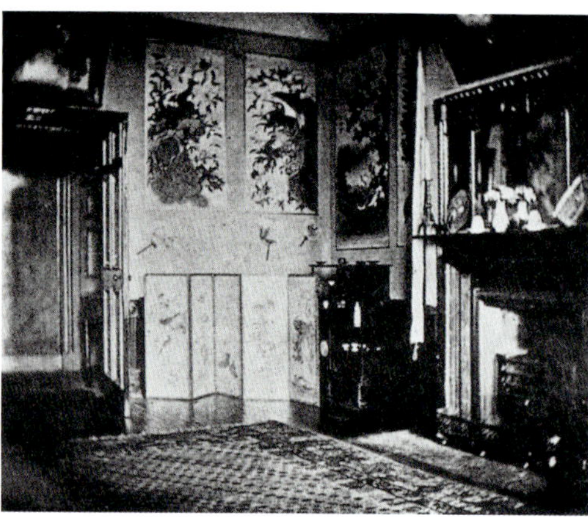
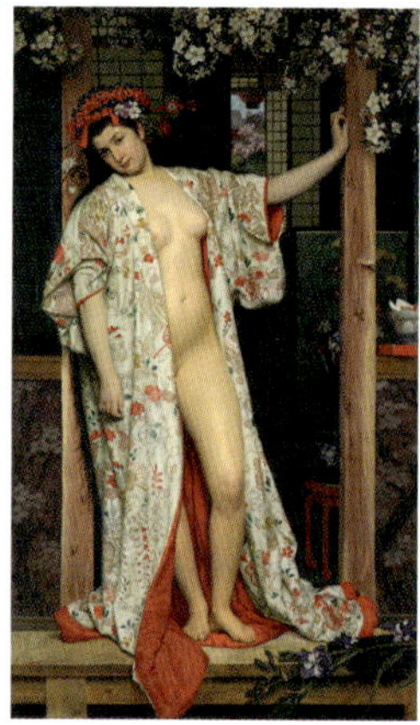
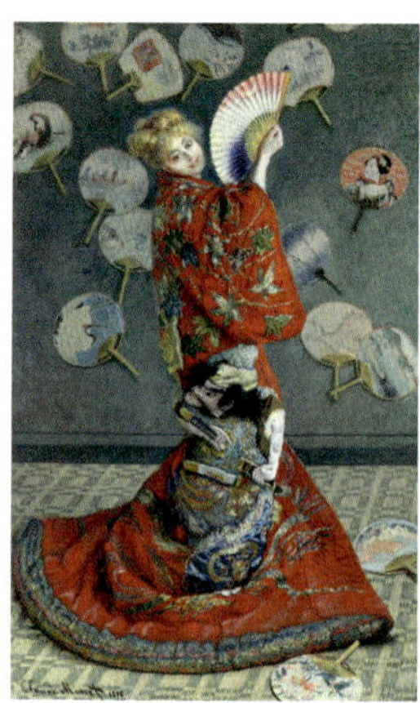

of subject was presumably not entirely coincidental. The work is quite likely to be one of three paintings with Japanese motifs that Madame Desoye raved about in late 1864 and referred to as being in competition with Whistler.[8] As in the latter's work, a European woman in a Far Eastern costume served Tissot as a model; here, however, she has been placed in an imaginary bathhouse. Climbing roses blooming in full splendour decorate the veranda and accentuate the erotic voluptuousness of the young lady who looks at the viewer with a lascivious gaze. She wears her kimono open to show off her charms. Tissot presumably bought the kimono in Madame Desoye's shop; indeed, Dante Gabriel Rossetti complained that the Frenchman had bought out all of the beautiful costumes in that establishment.[9] In both paintings, Whistler and Tissot seem to have been imagining a scene taking place in Japan or at least in the Far East. Whistler suggested this primarily in his addendum to the title, "from the land of porcelain", and Tissot with the window looking out on a landscape with a pagoda and blossoming cherry trees. On the one hand, both works mirror the images the artists had of Japan in the 1860s and, on the other hand, they also thus cater to the image Western Europe *wanted* to have of Japan.

Despite their efforts to reproduce the Far Eastern elements precisely, both Whistler's *Princess* and Tissot's *Japonaise* have an element of disguise about them, which, however, will presumably not have bothered their contemporaries.[10] It was in the same spirit that Monet painted his famous *La Japonaise (Camille Monet in Japanese Costume)* (fig. 4) about ten years later. Here, the artist's wife Camille is modelling in a splendid kimono and, with the open fan, in a typical Japanese pose. Rigid Japanese fans decorate the wall and lie scattered on the floor, embedding the figure in an interior furnished with Japanese objects. The blonde wig, for its part, forms a drastic contrast to this setting, virtually turning the scene staged by the painting into a mockery. Is the work to be understood as a humorous commentary on the all-encompassing Japan fad of the time or as a serious endeavour by Monet to confess himself in public as a *Japoniste*?[11] In any case, it is the only depiction of its kind in Monet's oeuvre, and he later dissociated himself from it, calling it "une saleté" – a "piece of filth".[12]

Tissot's *Japonaise* likewise represents an exception in his work:[13] the following paintings with "Japanese content" all depict contemporary ladies contemplating Japanese objects with fascination. One of these works is *Young Women Looking at Japanese Articles* of 1869 (p. 107). In it, two young ladies are looking at a Japanese model ship. The room is furnished almost entirely with items of Japanese origins. Behind the two protagonists is a shrine with dolls *(ningyo)* in it. In view of the hat, muff and gloves she is wearing, the lady towards the front appears to have just entered the room, evidently to pay a visit. The other, presumably the lady of the house, is dressed in a white gown and laying her arm across her visitor's back in a friendly manner. She proudly indicates her ownership of the objects by propping her right hand on the little table bearing the model ship. It is uncertain whether this interior really existed. It may have been a room in Tissot's house in Avenue de l'Impératrice, to which he had moved in 1868 and which he had elaborately decorated with Japanese articles.[14]

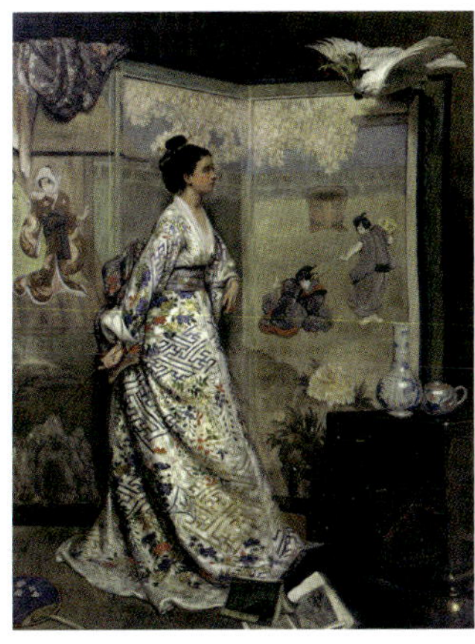
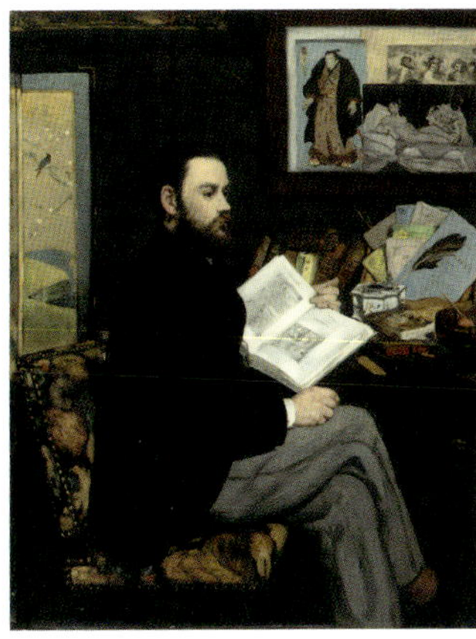

1 James McNeill Whistler, *The Princess from the Land of Porcelain*, 1863–1865, Freer Gallery of Art, Smithsonian Institution, Washington DC, Gift of Charles Lang Freer
2 Anonymous, *The Drawing Room in Whistler's House in London, Chelsea, 7 Lindsey Row*, circa 1863/1865
3 James Tissot, *Japanese Lady in the Bath*, 1864, Musée des Beaux-Arts de Dijon
4 Claude Monet, *La Japonaise (Camille Monet in Japanese Costume)*, 1876, Museum of Fine Arts, Boston, 1951 Purchase Fund
5 Gustave Léonard de Jonghe, *The Japanese Fan*, circa 1865, The Cummer Museum of Art and Gardens, Jacksonville (FL), Gift of the Francis & Miranda Childress Foundation
6 Édouard Manet, *Portrait of Émile Zola*, 1868, Musée d'Orsay, Paris

Around 1864, Tissot had stopped depicting medieval subjects to devote himself to the representation of women in modern dress. Thus, it is hardly surprising that he painted Japanese objects in conjunction with contemporary fashion as an expression of *modernité*. From the mid-1860s, *Japonisme* and *modernité* were virtually synonymous.[15] As late as 1886, in *Impressions sur la peinture* published in that year, the Belgian painter Stevens referred to Japanese art as a "strong element of modernity",[16] by which he presumably also meant what the Western viewer thought of as stylistic "modernity".

In addition to Whistler and Tissot, but also Stevens (pp. 110, 115) and De Nittis (p. 111), there must have been quite a number of other artists who devoted themselves to the depiction of Japanese objects in contemporary genre scenes – artists who have meanwhile fallen into oblivion, such as Auguste Toulmouche (1829–1890) or Gustave Léonard de Jonghe (1829–1893; fig. 5). Be that as it may, in as early as 1868, Jules Champfleury – himself an impassioned *Japoniste* – complained about the excessive presence of *Japonica* in contemporary painting: "Even professed painters of the elegant life meanwhile bore us with their Japanese cabinets, Japanese flowers, and Japanese lacquer and bronze works which appear on their canvases as protagonists and play a more important role than the persons depicted."[17]

That same year, Manet exhibited his *Portrait of Émile Zola* (fig. 6) at the Salon. The likeness, thought to have been painted by Manet as a token of appreciation for Zola's defence of his art, shows the art critic surrounded by various objects arranged in the artist's studio for this purpose. In a frame at the upper right are three prints representing three different currents in art advocated by both Zola and Manet: a reproduction of Diego Velázquez's *Triumph of Bacchus* standing for the Spanish art of the seventeenth century, a woodblock print of a Sumo wrestler by Utagawa Kuniaki II representing the Japanese art of woodblock printing, and a reproduction of Manet's own *Olympia* as a hallmark for contemporary French painting.[18] We can no longer determine today whether the two peacock feathers stuck in behind the frame (as a symbol of Asia) and the Japanese screen in the style of the Rimpa school at the left of the painting belonged to Manet or Zola. Both collected *Japonica*, as we can deduce from various written and pictorial sources (p. 121).[19] In Zola's portrait, the concern is accordingly not with the depiction of an interior "à la mode japonaise" in the manner of Tissot or Stevens, but with the declaration of Japanese art as an example and inspiration for contemporary French painting. The formative importance of Japanese art for the artists of the period's avant-garde, and especially for Manet, is also manifest in the still life by Auguste Renoir that is to be understood as a homage to Manet (p. 58).[20]

Japanese woodblock prints as a source of inspiration

Manet was among those artists who studied Japanese woodblock prints intensively and drew impulses from it for their own work. Their chief aim was not the direct imitation of motifs or compositions, but the

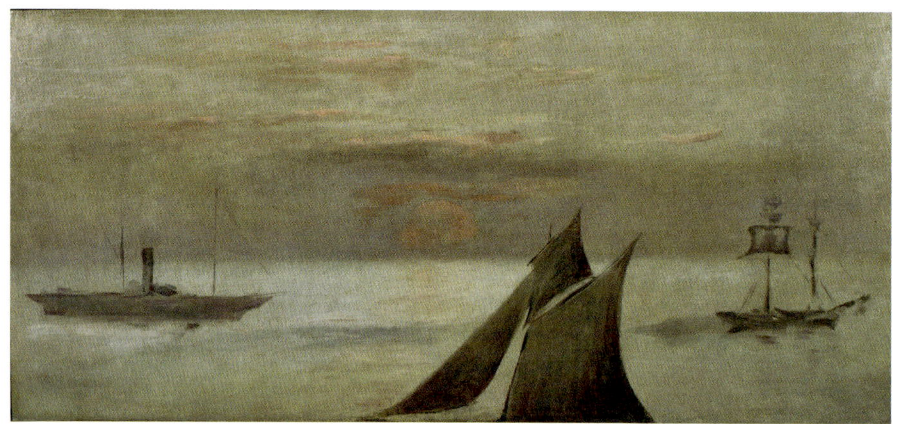

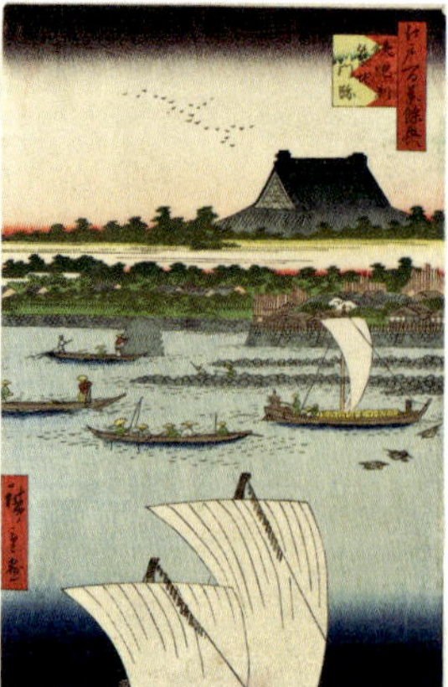

free adoption and further development of individual Japanese stylistic devices that, in turn, bore a relation to other sources of inspiration (for example, the art of the Middle Ages or the old masters, but also the relatively new technique of photography). Triggered by the imagery of Japan, which had hitherto received little notice, this creative process led to the internalisation of Japanese stylistic devices and provided one of the cornerstones for the development of modern European art.

Manet's in-depth preoccupation with Japanese woodblock print artists is reflected in his adoption of their compositional practices, such as the placement of the horizon at the upper edge of the picture, the isolation of figures and the radical cutting off of motifs. Manet experimented with these methods above all in paintings executed after sketches made during his stays on the northern French coast in 1868 and 1873. The painting *Boats at Sea, Sunset* (fig. 7), for which a sketch produced in Boulogne-sur-Mer in 1868 has survived,[21] uses delicate shades of colour to depict three different vessel types at sea. What is unusual for the tradition of European marine painting is the fact that the sailing boat in the foreground is abruptly cut through the middle, which is not the case in the sketch. The sails loom up into the scene as if from the middle of nowhere, shifting the viewer's vantage point upward. What led Manet to change his vertical-format sketch – depicting the ships in their entirety – in this fashion? Both the bold lopping-off of the main motif and the elevation of the viewer's standpoint, but also the wide horizontal format, are stylistic devices of Japanese art found in strongly pronounced form in the work of Utagawa Hiroshige (fig. 8; pp. 172–173). The brushstroke and the monochrome tonality are moreover reminiscent of Far Eastern ink painting. No information has come down to us as to whether Manet had a personal collection of Japanese woodblock prints, but it is highly probable that he did. We can assume that, as an artist who moved in *Japoniste* circles, Manet could never have escaped the sight of Japanese woodblock prints. Still, his preoccupation with specific Japanese pictorial sources is apparent in his early printmaking oeuvre as well as in his late sketches of the years 1875 to 1878.[22]

Unlike Manet, Degas is known for certain to have collected Japanese woodblock prints and books by such artists as Kikugawa Eizan, Hosoda Eishō, Utagawa Hiroshige, Katushika Hokusai and Kitagawa Utamaro.[23] We have no information about when he began collecting. In 1878, however, Chesneau ranked him among the early collectors of Japanese art.[24] When his collection was auctioned off in 1918, it contained more than a hundred Japanese artworks and albums. The latter included Nishikawa Sukenobu's *Studies of One Hundred Women* (*Hyakunin Joro shina sadame*) in two volumes of 1723, in which women are depicted performing everyday activities – a subject also encountered in Degas's oeuvre.[25] It is virtually impossible to determine whether Degas's predilection for the depiction of women at their toilette (pp. 157, 158, 159, 161) – which began to appear in his work in the mid-1870s – can be attributed to his study of Japanese woodblock prints such as those of Eizan (p. 144), Hokusai, Sukenobu or Utamaro (p. 142), or whether, conversely, he found confirmation in them for this penchant. In any case, before Degas, the motif of women washing themselves and combing their hair did not belong to the repertoire of European artists, at least not to this degree.

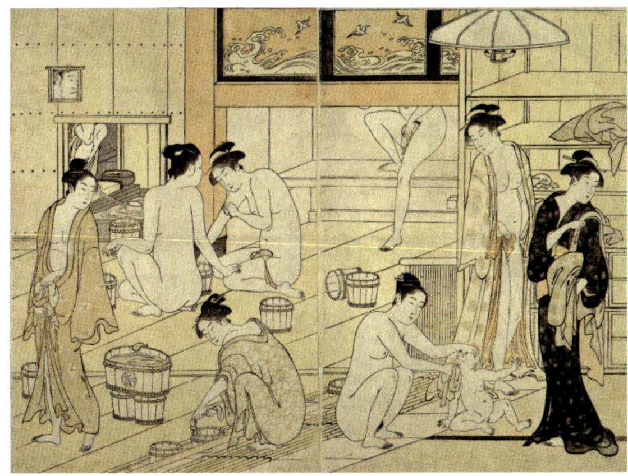

7 Édouard Manet, *Boats at Sea, Sunset*, 1869/1873, Musée Malraux, Le Havre (dépôt du Musée d'Orsay, Paris)
8 Utagawa Hiroshige, *Teppōzu and Tsukiji Hongan-ji Temple*, from the series *One Hundred Famous Views of Edo*, 1858, Museum of Fine Arts, Boston, William Sturgis Bigelow Collection
9 Torii Kiyonaga, *Interior of a Bathhouse*, circa 1787, Museum of Fine Arts, Boston, William Sturgis Bigelow Collection, by exchange (formerly Degas Collection)

Comparison with Utamaro's *Hour of the Snake* (p. 156), however, strongly suggests that – at any rate for the motif of the maidservant offering her mistress a hot beverage upon the latter's emergence from the bath – Degas received a decisive impulse from Japanese art. Tellingly, Hayashi Tadamasa – one of the chief protagonists in trade with *Japonica* in late nineteenth-century Paris – gave Degas Torii Kiyonaga's diptych *Interior of a Bathhouse* (fig. 9) in exchange for works by the Frenchman, because it reminded his of Degas's bathing scenes.[26] The significance the diptych held for Degas is evident in the fact that he hung it along with figural drawings by Ingres and landscapes by Corot – two other artists he strongly emulated – in his bedroom.[27]

Not only the subject matter, but also the stylistic devices of Japanese art were an important source of inspiration for Degas. Like Manet, he was evidently so fascinated by the manner in which Hiroshige, for example, cut off his motifs at the edge of the picture or juxtaposed close-up and distant views (pp. 214, 220, 221) or Hokusai's use of pictorial elements to divide his compositions vertically (p. 146) that he made frequent use of them himself. He thus heightened the sense of the momentary – or indeed, the unintentional or incidental – in his works. In the literature on Degas, the unusual mode of framing the scene in a number of his works is often seen in relation to snapshot photography.[28] It is quite true that Degas exhibited a great interest in photography – but only many years later.[29] The invention of stereoscopy made it technically possible to produce snapshot-like images as early as around 1850, but it took conventional photography until the 1880s to reach that stage. What is more, the early examples of "photographie instantanée" appear not to have intended the radical cutting-off of figures or objects; on the contrary, the latter was a side effect of the shorter exposure time that made it possible to capture moving subjects on film.[30] Woodblock prints by artists like Hiroshige, by contrast, are compositions in which a living creature or an object are cut off at the edge of the picture quite deliberately.

Orchestra Musicians of 1872 (p. 205) is one of the first paintings in which Degas placed the main motif, the musicians, so far in the foreground that they are boldly cut off on both sides. He originally executed the work in a wide format; two years later, he cut it on all sides and extended it by one third at the top so as to include the ballerinas.[31] In comparison to his other paintings of the same subject matter,[32] *Orchestra Musicians* represents his most radical compositional solution. For the iconography, we can cite Daumier's lithograph *The Orchestra during the Performance of a Tragedy* of 1852 by way of comparison;[33] without knowledge of Japanese woodblock prints, however, it is hard to imagine Degas cutting into the scene to such a radical degree. Even twenty years later, Degas made use of pictorial elements placed in the immediate foreground and partially cut off – for example, in *Dancers Mounting a Staircase* (p. 206) or the small-scale painting *Ballet Dancer* (p. 204), in which two scrolls of bow instruments loom up into the scene right before the viewer's eyes.

However, in his ballet scenes – for example, *Before the Ballet* of 1890/1892 (p. 207) – there is yet another element that may well have been inspired by the artist's study of Hokusai's *Manga*, in particular. In volumes 3, 4 and 6 (fig. 10), Hokusai depicts figures in various poses and sequences of movement. In one instance, there are two men wrestling, in another a man performing the so-called "sparrow dance", in a third fighters with kendo sticks. Here, Hokusai was working his way through various body movements that could serve as models for other works.[34] As shown by the exhibition *Degas and the Ballet – Picturing Movement* presented in London in 2011, Degas was primarily interested in ballet because of the dancers' movements. The girls with their tutus and nearly identical appearances struck the same poses again and again, unceasingly, allowing Degas to resume his study of the moving body as often as he liked. Many paintings accordingly seem to show the various sequences of a certain movement all performed by the same girl.[35] Degas encountered a similar preoccupation with the depiction of movement in the Japanese *Manga*, but he also took an interest in the chronophotography developed by Eadweard Muybridge and Étienne-Jules Marey in the late 1870s.[36] With the aid of a special exposure technique, these photographs virtually "dissect" movement – for example, that of a walking man or a galloping horse – to make it comprehensible for the human eye. After the publication of Muybridge's *Animal Locomotion* in 1887 (fig. 11), Degas made a number of drawings after photographs by the Englishman. In addition to Hokusai's *Manga* figures, the latest developments in photography thus presumably also served him as a visual impulse for his later frieze-like ballet scenes.

Degas and Whistler are considered the two great individualists of the second half of the nineteenth century. Perhaps that is the reason for their lifelong friendship. Whereas in the 1860s Whistler had expressed his enthusiasm for the Far East primarily by depicting Asian objects and models in kimonos, in around 1870 he directed his attention to East Asian pictorial aesthetics. Now he began painting views of the Thames (which he could see directly from his house in Lindsey Row) in the twilight, just as William Turner – one of the artists he most emulated – had done before him. Not only Turner's atmospheric landscapes, however, but also Asian works played a decisive role in the development of Whistler's *Nocturnes*, as he called his paintings from the early 1870s onwards at the suggestion of his patron at that time, Frederick Richards Leyland. To begin with, mention should be made here of two works from Hiroshige's *One Hundred Famous Views of Edo* of 1856–1858, specifically the *Kyōbashi Bridge* and *Fireworks at Ryōgoku*. As is well known, these two prints served Whistler as inspirations for the paintings *Nocturne: Blue and Gold – Old Battersea Bridge* of around 1872/1875, and *Nocturne in Black and Gold, the Falling Rocket* of 1875 (fig. 12). Whistler translated Hiroshige's nocturnal scenes into views of his own surroundings – in one case, the bridge across the Thames; in the other case, the Cremorne pleasure grounds – and interpreted them in his own way.[37] The greatest difference between his works and those of Hiroshige – who paid great attention to detail not least of all because of the woodblock print medium – consists in the fact that Whistler shrouded his scenes in a diffuse mist of colour. The adherence to a single colour scheme and the fading away of pictorial elements in the distance are both characteristics of Far Eastern ink painting. They are particularly evident in one of Whistler's earliest night-time landscapes, *Nocturne: Blue and Silver – Cremorne Lights* of 1872 (p. 202). In order to achieve the harmonious blending of colours, Whistler developed a painting technique with whose aid he could apply the oil paints in an especially thin consistency. In some instances, he was even compelled to lay the canvas down flat because the paint was so fluid. It is difficult to know which examples of Far Eastern ink painting he might have been inspired by, and Whistler scholarship has apparently taken little interest in the matter to date.[38] In his two paintings entitled *The Artist in His Studio* (1865, Dublin City Gallery The Hugh Lane; The Art Institute of Chicago), we see hanging scrolls which may have featured ink paintings. In any case, Whistler emphasised the inspiration of the Far East in *Nocturne: Blue and Silver – Cremorne Lights* by placing two stalks of bamboo in the left foreground and signing the work with a butterfly in a painted cartouche. The American's chief concern in his *Nocturnes* was to create chromatic harmonies with the aid of ever-recurring shades of colour, a practice for which he greatly admired the Japanese.[39] In his speech for the defence at the 1878 trial against the art critic and painter John Ruskin, which had come about not least of all as a result of his *Nocturnes*, Whistler defined these works "first" as "an arrangement of line, form and colour".[40]

Whistler's variations on the nocturnal Thames landscapes were rooted chiefly in his striving for a harmonious combination of the three fundamental elements of a picture – line, colour and form – with which he repeatedly experimented. At the same time, his *Nocturnes* anticipate a method other artists would later come to practise downright obsessively: the painting of the same subject in series. Naturally, artistic oeuvres had always comprised variations on and versions of the same motif. The reason for the repetition was usually that the customer so desired it or the motif sold well on the art market. What distinguishes artists like Whistler – but also Courbet and Monet – from their predecessors was that they exhibited the similar paintings as groups, thus underscoring their serial nature. In 1873, Whistler showed at least two of his Thames landscapes at Galerie Durand-Ruel in Paris.[41] As Charles Stuckey emphasised in his eye-opening essay on Monet's series in 2007, in state-organised art exhibitions such as the Salon this would not have been possible, owing to the limited exhibition space at each individual artist's disposal.[42] The only artist to have exhibited such a series before Whistler was Courbet. In his 1866 show held at Galerie Luquet in Paris, Courbet presented a number of the seascapes he had painted the previous year in Trouville. Whistler had spent two months in Trouville with him, and will accordingly have had knowledge not only of the works executed there, but also of this exhibition.

Considering he was a sea enthusiast who was painting on the coast, there is nothing particularly surprising about Courbet's repetition of the subject of the sea view. His preoccupation with the motif of the wave during his second stay on the coast in Étretat in 1869 and later, however, raises certain questions. Some forty versions of the wave motif have come down to us,[43] of which the Frankfurt example (p. 169) is one of the most striking. What moved Courbet – four years after the quiet "paysages de mer", as he called them – to turn his attention to a subject such as the wave and paint it unceasingly until 1872? In and of itself, the motif of the wave seen from close up was not new; artists such as Paul Huet and even Whistler had already painted it. Around 1856, the wave had also become a pictorial theme in photography.[44] What was new was the obsessive recording of it in different variations. It is highly probable that Courbet would have placed a large group of his waves on exhibit if the Franco-Prussian war had not broken out in 1870. In a large percentage of the relevant literature, Courbet's investigation of the sea is seen in the historico-cultural context around Jules Michelet's work *La Mer* (1861) and the interest in the ocean that was emerging at the time.[45] The authors of more recent publications, however, recognise a connection with the wave depictions in Japanese art, especially that of Hokusai (pp. 167, 175).[46] Courbet was in close contact with persons who verifiably pursued an interest in Japan and particularly in the Japanese art of woodblock printing, such as Whistler, Fantin-Latour, Degas and Monet, but also art critics and writers such as Théodore Duret or Champfleury.[47] In 1865, Courbet moreover sojourned in Trouville concurrently with Whistler and Monet, whom Zacharie Astruc referred to in an article from 1868 as a "loyal emulator of Hokusai" ("fidèle émule d'Hoksai [sic])".[48] Thus, Japanese art will certainly have been a topic of their conversations.

Hokusai's *One Hundred Views of Mount Fuji*, which includes a prominent depiction of a wave (p. 170), was undoubtedly known in France by 1861 at the latest, since that is when Baron Charles de Chassiron published two motifs from it in his *Notes sur le Japon, la Chine et l'Inde*.[49] However, it is not clear when his earlier series of *36 Views of Mount Fuji*, with *Under the Wave off Kanagawa* (p. 167), began circulating in France. If Monet did indeed look to Hokusai's woodblock print *Sazai Hall at the Temple of the Five Hundred Arhats* for orientation for the composition of his *Garden at Sainte-Adresse* (1867, The Metropolitan Museum of Art, New York), as is generally postulated, then artists will already have been familiar with it as early as 1867.[50] What is more, in view of the fact that sheets from Hiroshige's series *Famous Views in the Sixty-Odd Provinces* are to be found in Whistler's painting *Caprice in Purple and Gold: The Golden Screen* of 1864 (Freer Gallery of Art, Washington DC), it can be assumed that Hokusai's series were also already known in Europe at that early date. In addition to the wave motif, the serial depiction of the same subject in countless variations – as in the case of Hokusai's Mount Fuji series, but also in series of bridges, waterfalls and seas[51] – can thus be considered the strongest influence exerted by the Japanese art of woodblock printing on Courbet's oeuvre.

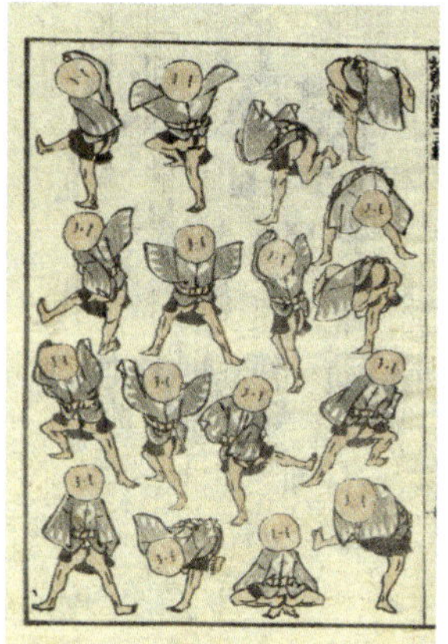

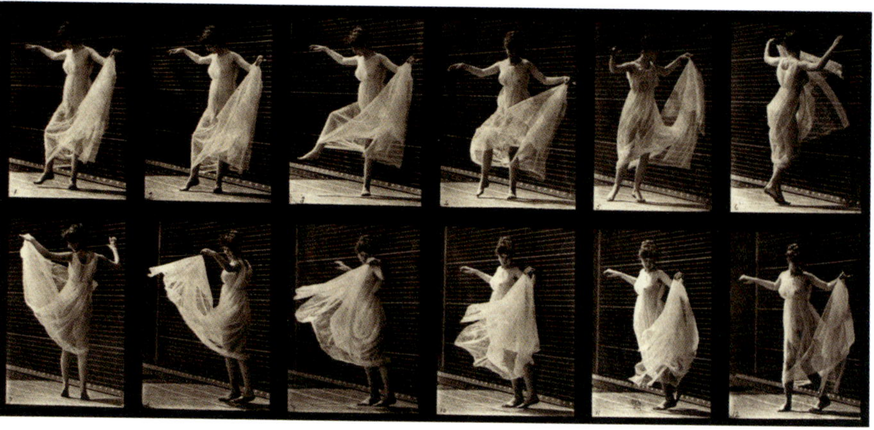

Hokusai's and Hiroshige's series made an even deeper impression on Monet. He is the artist who planned, executed and exhibited entire groups of works as series.[52] In May 1891, Monet showed fifteen of more than thirty paintings of *Haystacks*. The exhibition was *the* event of the spring season in Paris and a sweeping success for the gallery.[53] Monet had already begun painting individual motifs repeatedly a few years earlier – for example, the rock "pyramids" at Port-Coton (pp. 176, 177). Six versions of this subject are known; they differ only slightly from one another with regard to the framing, depiction and handling of the light. For the motif, Monet may have been inspired by comparable Hiroshige depictions (pp. 172–173, 174), which he also had in his collection. At any rate, the Japanese artist could well have directed his gaze to motifs that had always existed but had never before come to the attention of French artists. What we do not find in the works Monet executed on Belle-Île, however, is the depiction of the same object from various perspectives and in differing light and weather conditions in the manner he would systematically undertake five years later with the haystacks. The serial approach was a logical further development within his painting oeuvre. In October 1890, Monet wrote to his later biographer Gustave Geoffroy: "I am grinding away, bent on a series of different effects [(haystacks)], but at this time of year, the sun goes down so quickly that I cannot keep up with it […] I am becoming a very slow worker, which depresses me, but the further I go, the more I understand that it is imperative to work a great deal to achieve what I seek: 'instantaneity', above all […] the same light present everywhere and more than ever easy things that come in a single stroke disgust me."[54] Monet recorded the different atmospheres created by the light in countless brushstrokes, working directly from nature, and he was compelled to interrupt his work again and again when the light conditions changed. In order to be more productive, he ultimately developed a method of working simultaneously on several canvases. He had the paints for each mixed and ready for use, and when the mood of the light changed he simply switched to a different canvas. At the same time, Hokusai's oeuvre could well have provided Monet not only with confirmation but also inspiration.[55] Although we cannot determine when he acquired them, we know that Monet had altogether nine of Hokusai's *36 Views of Mount Fuji* (1830–1831) in his possession. He also owned a copy of the Japanese artist's three-volume work *One Hundred Views of Mount Fuji* of 1834–1835.[56] In the closing remarks to his series of *Modern Designs for Combs and Pipes (Imayō kushi kiseru hiinagata)* published in 1823, Hokusai had already announced a series on "Fuji in eight forms", which he never realised. His plan was to show "landscapes as they differ according to the movements of the heavens, in clear skies, under rain, wind, snow, and mist, through the four seasons".[57] Depiction according to seasons was a convention in Japanese art. Hokusai later rejected it, but his statement reveals his intention – already at that early date – to work with the motif of the holy mountain in serial form. In the series of Fuji he embarked on seven years later – which initially consisted of 36 sheets and was later expanded to 46 on account of its great success – he depicted Fuji from various perspectives, now alone as the main motif, now incorporated in a landscape animated with human beings, and in a range of different weather conditions. The analogy to Monet's approach of conceiving landscape elements – whether haystacks, poplars,

10 Katsushika Hokusai, *The Yakko-Odori (Servant) Dance*, in: *Manga*, vol. 3 (7v / 8r), 1815, Ostasienabteilung, Staatsbibliothek zu Berlin – Preußischer Kulturbesitz
11 Eadweard Muybridge, *Woman Dancing*, from *Animal Locomotion*, 1887, Victoria and Albert Museum, London
12 James McNeill Whistler, *Nocturne in Black and Gold, the Falling Rocket*, 1875, Detroit Institute of Arts, Gift of Dexter M. Ferry Jr.

cathedrals, bridges or the like, in which, unlike Hokusai, he consistently omitted the human figure – as series, and by varying the individual painting with regard to frame, light and weather, is remarkable. Whereas the fact that Hokusai cited the number of views in his titles (36 and 100) bears a connection to classical anthologies of Japanese poetry,[58] in the case of Monet the number bore no relevance. Monet's chief interest rather lay in the changing play of light and colour, which could be depicted best if the motif remained the same. Beginning in 1908, Monet would ultimately devote himself almost exclusively to various views of his garden in Giverny – the Japanese bridge, the flowers and the pond with the water lilies – in the form of series (pp. 302–315). The success Monet celebrated at Galerie Durand-Ruel will presumably have encouraged him to paint and exhibit other motifs as series – for example, the *Poplars* (1892), the *Cathedral of Rouen* and *Mount Kolsaas* (both 1895), the *Cliffs of Pourville* and *The Coastguard House at Varengeville* (both 1898), as well as the *Japanese Bridge* (1900) and the *Water Lilies* (1909).[59]

Cézanne likewise devoted himself unceasingly to the depiction of the same subject: he painted more than thirty views of Mont Sainte-Victoire. The summit of his native region first turned up in his paintings around 1870; after 1885, however, and from then on until the end of his life in 1906, there was something almost obsessive about his preoccupation with it. As in the case of Monet, the serial treatment of the same subject by the master of Aix-en-Provence can be explained solely in conjunction with the development of his oeuvre, as has been demonstrated often enough in the literature on Cézanne.[60] This explanation draws primarily on the fact that – as opposed to Monet – there is no evidence that Cézanne was particularly interested in Japanese art. On the contrary, it is said that Cézanne virtually despised Japanese colour woodblock prints because of the strong contour lines used in them.[61] Yet even if the woodblock prints by such artists as Hokusai did not appeal to him stylistically, he could very well have been interested in the fact that the serial treatment of a subject had already been conceived by the Japanese, and that his friend Monet had been following in their footsteps since 1886.[62] Be that as it may, not only did Cézanne – like Hokusai – paint his mountain from different perspectives, what is more, in many works compositional similarities can be discerned such as between *Chestnut Trees at Jas de Bouffan* (1885/1886; Minneapolis Museum of Art) and *Hodogaya on the Tōkaidō (Tōkaidō Hodogaya)* (p. 192).

Unlike the other artists discussed, Cézanne never exhibited his Mont Sainte-Victoire paintings as a series. That circumstance, however, does nothing to detract from the fact that Whistler's, Courbet's, Monet's and Cézanne's serial treatment of motifs – a method already practised by the Japanese much earlier[63] – is one of the greatest legacies they left to the art of the twentieth century.[64]

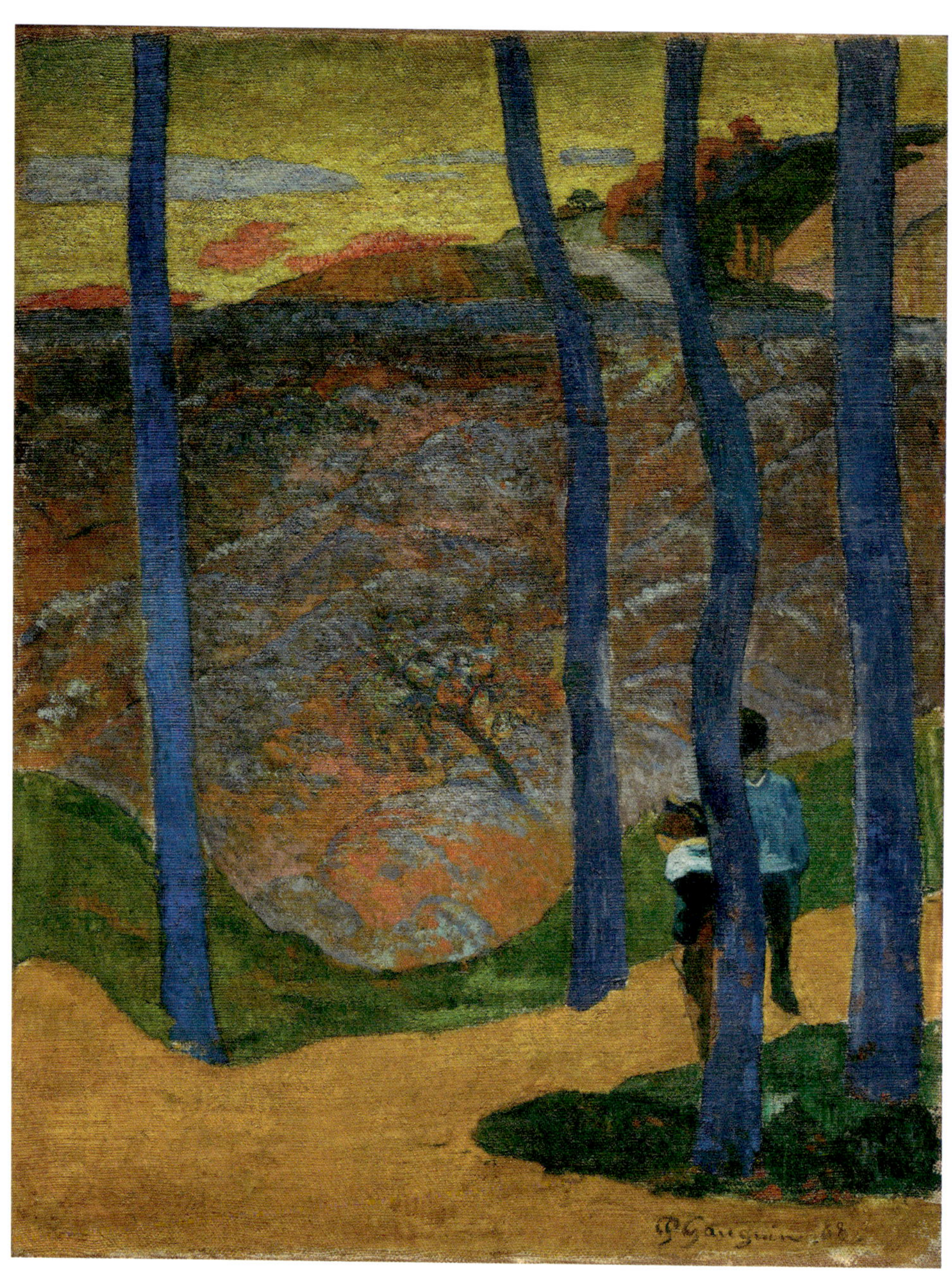

32 Paul Gauguin, *Blue Trees: "Your Turn Will Come, My Beauty!"*, 1888

Japonisme in the works of Van Gogh, Gauguin, Bernard and Anquetin

Belinda Thomson

In 1899, the French artist Félix Régamey, on an official visit to Tokyo's Fine Arts School, was pressed for information about the French impressionists. He had a striking reply for his Japanese hosts: "There is no question that Japanese print-making has opened up many people's eyes. You should not get so excited about our impressionism, you were the ones who invented it."[1] Régamey, an ardent Japanophile, was seeking to restore the Japanese artists' confidence in their own artistic traditions. On a previous extensive fact-finding trip to the Far East in 1876, he had already lamented the passing of "old Japan", convinced he was witnessing a "marvellous artistic, poetic, gentle world sinking under the dismal hotchpotch of Western civilisation."[2] Régamey was well placed to speak about Japanese influences on French art, as he, together with the industrialist and collector Émile Guimet, had played a major part in creating the receptive climate in France for all things Japanese. Whether Régamey had any knowledge of Van Gogh's work is doubtful, but Régamey's pioneering activism was well known to Vincent and formed the backdrop to his own veritable craze for Japan.

This essay looks at some of the ways in which Japanese art affected the generation of innovators who came after the impressionists – Van Gogh, Gauguin, Bernard and Anquetin. Each responded differently, in interesting and telling ways.[3] The Van Gogh brothers assembled an enormous collection of Japanese prints, and Vincent (1853–1890) referred to them regularly in his letters. But after 1888, the topic virtually disappears from his writing.[4] Upon moving from Arles to Saint-Rémy, the prints also carried less importance in his artistic practice.[5] For the younger artists Émile Bernard (1868–1941) and Louis Anquetin (1861–1932), documentary evidence is scant but suggests that their receptivity to Japanese influences was short-lived. Paul Gauguin (1848–1903) assimilated aspects of Japanese art over a longer period. His interest also peaked in 1888, yet a certain *Japonisme* was evident in his work as early as 1885 and, alongside other exotic and primitive influences, continued to play a part in his creative process for the remainder of his career.[6]

The case of Van Gogh

Van Gogh's relationship to Japanese art has critical importance because he was such a proselytiser, simultaneously seeing commercial opportunities in Japanese art and infusing his peers with a passion for things Japanese. In general, Van Gogh's zeal was something others found hard to equal, but, in July 1888, he could justifiably claim, echoing and prefiguring Régamey: "Japanese art, in decline in its own country, is taking new roots among French Impressionist artists. It's this practical side for artists that necessarily interests me – more than the *trade* in japonaiseries."[7]

It is usually assumed that Van Gogh's interest in Japanese art first took hold when he was living in the trading port of Antwerp over the winter of 1885/1886, where many dealers specialised in oriental wares. Certainly this was where he started to collect the prints in earnest, continuing in Paris in early 1886. But his

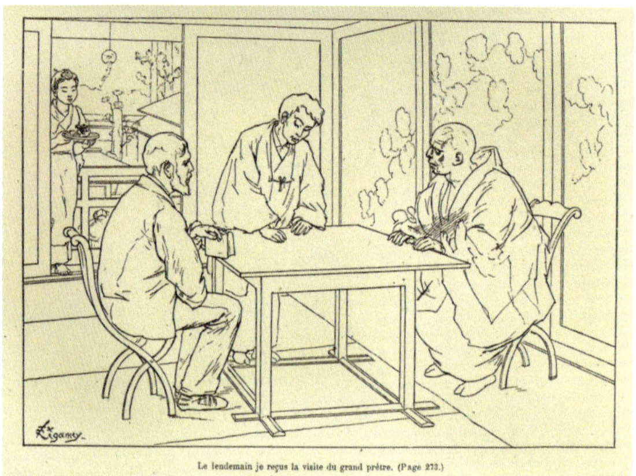

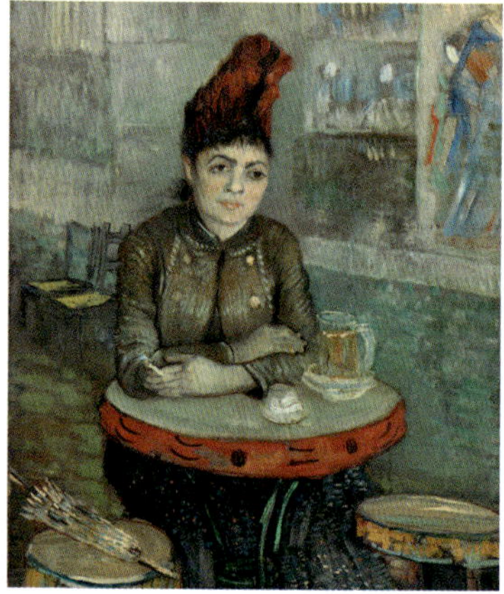

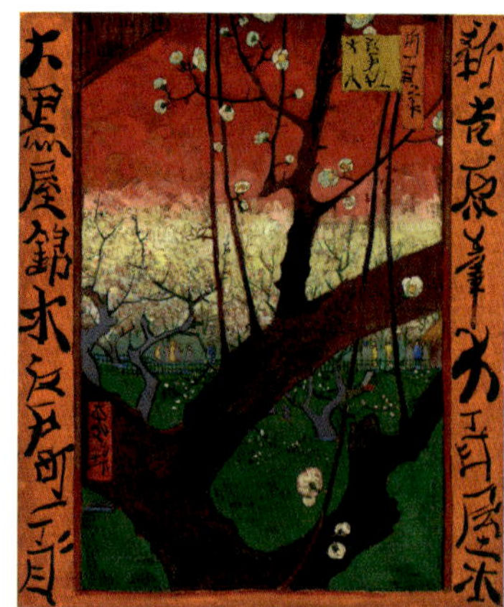

interest in Japan began earlier. Régamey is a name that crops up in Van Gogh's letters with surprising frequency, with eighteen direct or indirect references mostly dating from 1882 to 1885. There were three Régamey artist brothers, so it is not always clear which of them Van Gogh is referring to, but it was Félix, whose illustrations appeared in such journals as *The Illustrated London News* and *Le Monde illustré*, to whom Van Gogh was usually referring. "Félix Régamey travels a great deal and, as you know, is very strong in the Japanese", Van Gogh reminded his artist friend Anthon van Rappard in March 1883.[8] And in a letter to Theo of 7 July 1883, he commented, "Régamey is clever. This print is by Félix, who often does the Japanese things".[9] Vincent owned several Régamey wood engravings, including a series documenting aspects of contemporary Japanese life then in the throes of dramatic modernisation.

As well as producing documentary reportage, Régamey had so thoroughly absorbed Japanese woodblock print styles and techniques that he was able to reproduce their essential linear and compositional traits; Hokusai and Hiroshige were his favoured prototypes. The first of these pastiches appeared in *L'Art* in 1875.[10] He illustrated *Okoma*, the first Japanese "novel" to be translated into French by the prolific Japanese author Bakin, serialised in *Le Monde illustré* between 1879 and 1883, and in 1880 he collaborated with Guimet on the informative book *Promenades japonaises* (fig. 1). Thus, Van Gogh could find through Félix Régamey practical sources for an understanding of Japan – both its artistic techniques and its socio-religious practices. Indeed, Régamey perhaps provided a seamless transition for Van Gogh to absorb the world of Japanese art. For from 1885 on, Vincent's project of amassing a huge collection of Japanese *ukiyo-e* prints – which, by the mid-1880s, were available in Paris to him for as little as three sous, or fifteen centimes, a sheet – effectively took over from his collecting of contemporary magazine illustrations.[11] There was a difference, however. Whereas he readily identified with the individual magazine illustrators, he rarely mentioned a Japanese artist's name. His connoisseurship was limited, and he was aware of the gaps in his knowledge.[12] Nevertheless, the prints became a form of currency, as Van Gogh distributed them among friends or used them as bargaining chips in exchange for other artists' works.

In two important letters, both written to Theo from Arles on the same July Sunday in 1888, Van Gogh took stock, from a purely practical point of view, of the role "japonaiseries" had played in his career.[13] He recalled the exhibition of Japanese prints that he had organised in Paris, in Agostina Segatori's cafe *Le Tambourin*, an event recorded in the portrait of "La Segatori", where the prints can be made out on the wall behind the sitter (fig. 2). This was in the spring of 1887. For all that, he felt the venture had been a personal "disaster" (his relationship with La Segatori had broken down); it had, he maintained, a decisive impact on Bernard and Anquetin.[14] In the same letter, he advises Theo on how best to settle their debts with the dealer Siegfried Bing, Vincent having taken many prints on approval or possibly commission over the previous year, intending to sell them on. Clearly, he had been in the habit of foraging freely through Bing's stock. "There's an attic at Bing's, and in it there's a heap of 10 thousand Japanese prints, landscapes, figures, old Japanese prints too. One Sunday he'll let you choose for yourself, so take plenty of old sheets too."[15]

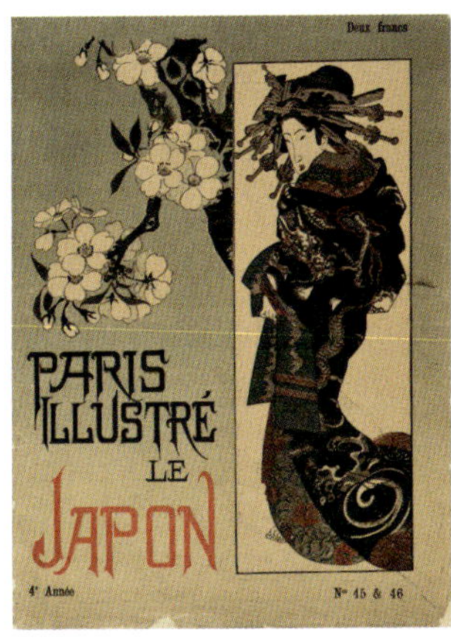

1 Félix Régamey, Guimet in dialogue with a "bonze" or high priest of the Buddhist temple, in: *Promenades japonaises,* 1880, p. 271
2 Vincent Van Gogh, *In the Café: Agostina Segatori in Le Tambourin,* 1887, Van Gogh Museum, Amsterdam (Vincent van Gogh Foundation)
3 Vincent Van Gogh, *Flowering Plum Tree (after Hiroshige),* 1887, Van Gogh Museum, Amsterdam (formerly Van Gogh Foundation)
4 Cover of *Paris illustré. Le Japon,* nos 45 and 46, May 1886, Van Gogh Museum, Amsterdam (Vincent van Gogh Foundation) (formerly Van Gogh Collection)

Vincent had an eye for quality and was now aware that the older prints, by such highly regarded artists as Hokusai, had greater value than the more contemporary examples in which their collection abounded, recognisable by their more garish colours. By the 1860s, Japanese artists were availing themselves of new, synthetic inks, enabling them to produce the vibrant reds one sees in certain kabuki prints. The Van Goghs, however, had no examples by the classic masters Hokusai and Utamaro.

Evidently, Van Gogh took certain Japanese prints to Arles and used them to decorate the Yellow House, but thought it likely that when Gauguin joined him, as he firmly hoped, they would want further prints sent down.[16] However, he seems not to have brought any of his self-consciously *Japoniste* paintings. Towards the end of his Paris stay in late 1887, he made three direct copies of Japanese prints, traced and squared up for transfer to canvases of a larger scale (fig. 3). In the two landscape subjects after Hiroshige, Van Gogh's interest was perhaps caught by the abrupt changes of scale, with the foreground tree or bridge dwarfing the minuscule human activity. Like Régamey, he remained true to the original compositions but, unlike him, he personalised them, transposing the medium to oil on canvas and adding painted decorative borders of Japanese characters. Those flanking the flowering plum tree, presumably borrowed from another Japanese print, refer to the address of a brothel.[17] The way colour was used by the Japanese woodblock print artists – applied in flat blocks and bright limpid tones – was a contrast to the confusing colour lessons in broken-toned, atmospheric brushwork and colour that Van Gogh found in impressionism and its derivatives. If anything, his copies heightened the colour and emphasised "la pâte", the materiality of the paint. His third *Japonaiserie* (p. 123) was copied at second hand from an Eisen print of a courtesan reproduced on a recent cover of *Paris illustré* (fig. 4), Van Gogh floating the vertical image over a decorative but incongruous pond setting of outsized bamboos, cranes and frogs on lily pads.[18] He copied the cranes and frogs from other Japanese sheets, such as one by Yoshimaru II which he owned (fig. 5).

The work that most obviously demonstrated Van Gogh's new faith in Japanese art was his *Portrait of Père Tanguy* (pp. 20, 22), of which he made two versions. Julien Tanguy, his colour merchant, was a valued friend who accepted canvases in lieu of payment, storing them in his untidy shop on rue Clauzel alongside canvases by older impressionists like Paul Cézanne and Armand Guillaumin and younger friends such as Bernard and Paul Signac. Van Gogh respected Tanguy's down-to-earth practicality and radical convictions (he was a former Communard), but the decision to pose him against a backdrop of Japanese prints – including clearly identifiable sheets by Hiroshige and Kunisada – says more about his preoccupations than those of the sitter. According to Bernard, sittings for this portrait began in his Asnières studio.[19] However, as Vincent later recalled, Japanese prints from their vast collection decorated the Van Gogh brothers' shared Paris apartment, pinned or pasted to the wall, edge to edge, which suggests that rue Lepic was the principal setting for the Tanguy portrait.[20]

Freed from his earlier preoccupation with atmosphere and tonal values, Van Gogh's first painted responses to Arles were hugely inspired by his ideas about Japan.[21] As he explained to his sister soon after arriving,

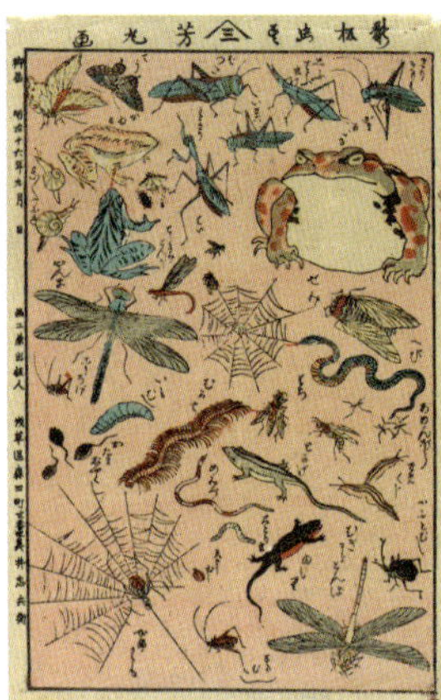

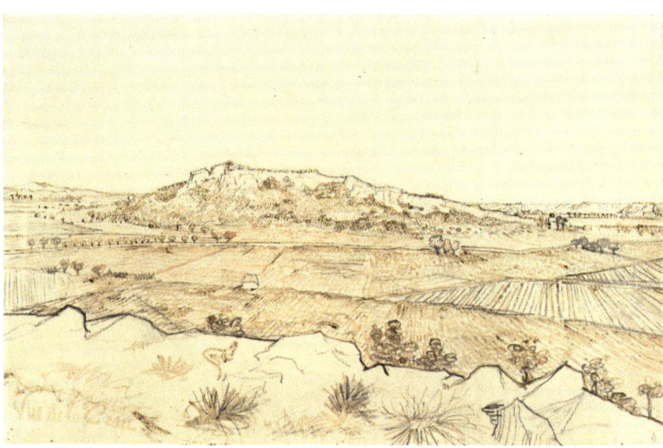

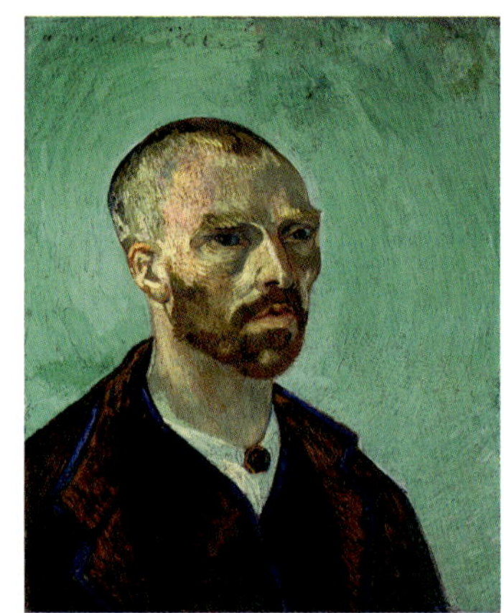

contemporary audiences were not interested in grey-toned Dutch-style paintings any more; they wanted colour because it was deemed "modern". He attributed this new trend to the impressionists, but rather than instancing the tints they used, he cited those of Japanese woodblock prints with which he now planned to fill his palette: "sky blue, pink, orange, vermilion, brilliant yellow, bright green, bright wine red, violet".[22] Seeing Provence through this borrowed Japanese lens, he was struck by the intensity and clarity of the light: just as in the prints, the colour of things in the far distance was as intense as objects in the foreground. Notably absent from his list, but prominent in Japanese art, are the two extremes – black and white – which he made a point of reinstating some months later.

Thus, Japanese art served Van Gogh at a number of levels, giving him confidence as he approached this new setting. It was an aesthetic complete in itself that suited the south. It was a way of "seizing the essential" in his drawing and of achieving a simplified, cheerful and harmonious palette.[23] It was a source of subject matter and style. All the motifs of his early Arles paintings – the orchards in blossom, rivers and canals with their bridges and barge traffic, the street scenes and panoramic landscapes – are familiar from Japanese woodblock prints. He consciously enlivened *Quay with Men Unloading Sand Barges* (p. 10), for example, by adopting a plunging viewpoint and peopling it with small "pure Hokusai" figures.[24] Indeed, such "figurines" give many of his own Provençal landscapes animation and scale.[25] In November 1888, he reprised the Milletesque subject of the sower in *Sower with Setting Sun* (p. 223), this time introducing the diagonal tree trunk, copied from Hiroshige's *Plum Estate, Kameido* (p. 221) print, to bisect the picture plane and radically alter the composition. Japanese art also affected his drawing, as he strove, with considerable success, to emulate its calligraphic fluency. Using a reed pen and brush with ink and working quickly, he made a number of smaller and more sizable drawings, some of which reproduced paintings that he deemed successful (fig. 6). Additionally, the passion for Japan served a social function. Van Gogh's ideal of a fraternal community of artists working in the Midi owed much to his reading about Japan – and, in particular, to the disciplined lives, leavened with occasional gaiety, of the Buddhist priests or bonzes which inspired the *Self-Portrait Dedicated to Paul Gauguin* (fig. 7) destined as a gift for Gauguin.[26] Using the pretext of Japanese artistic practice, he constantly urged his friends to exchange their works and thoughts with him, maintaining in this way and through correspondence, despite his almost total isolation, an extraordinary creative network. Van Gogh could not understand why the parallels he found between Provence and Japan were not motivating other artists to join him: "Look, we love Japanese painting, we've experienced its influence – all the Impressionists have that in common – and we wouldn't go to Japan, in other words, to what is the equivalent of Japan, the south? So I believe that the future of the new art still lies in the south after all."[27] But his contemporaries were managing to exploit the potential of Japanese art perfectly well without leaving the north. Perhaps this rueful realisation lay behind his somewhat fussy remark: "Apparently an article on Anquetin has appeared in the *Revue Indépendante* in which he seems to have been called the leader of a new movement in which Japonisme was even more marked, &c. I haven't read it, but after all – the leader of the Petit Boulevard is without any

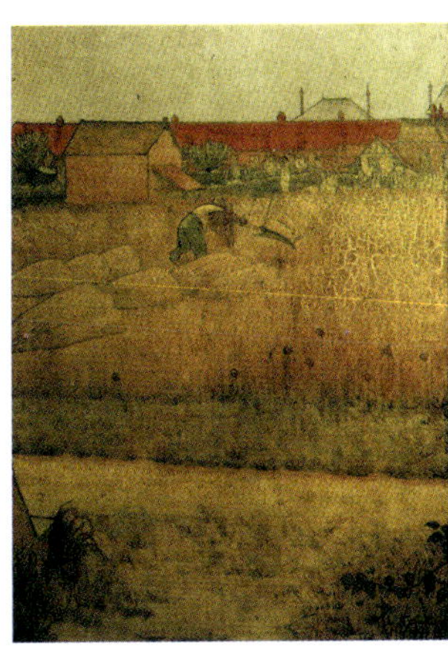

5 Utagawa Yoshimaru II, *New Prints of Worms and Insects*, Van Gogh Museum, Amsterdam (Vincent van Gogh Foundation) (formerly Van Gogh Collection)
6 Vincent Van Gogh, *The Plain of La Crau*, 1888, Museum Folkwang, Essen
7 Vincent Van Gogh, *Self-Portrait Dedicated to Paul Gauguin*, 1888, Harvard Art Museums/Fogg Museum, Bequest from the Collection of Maurice Wertheim
8 Louis Anquetin, *The Mower*, 1888, Private Collection

doubt Seurat, and young Bernard has perhaps gone further than Anquetin in the Japanese style."[28] The article in question, to which he had presumably been alerted by Bernard, signed by Édouard Dujardin, hailed the advent of a new artistic style, "Cloisonism", and attributed its exclusive paternity to Anquetin.[29]

Anquetin, Bernard and Cloisonism

Anquetin and Bernard had met Van Gogh at the Paris studio of Fernand Cormon in 1886. Anquetin, an extremely able, self-confident student and the atelier's "massier", commanded his respect, but he was on more fraternal terms with the younger, gifted but febrile Bernard. Like Van Gogh, they had briefly tried their hand at neo-impressionism with its radical simplification of form and systematic approach to impressionist colour broken down into its constituent complementary elements and painstakingly applied in dots. But their new manner of painting, Cloisonism, was diametrically opposed to impressionism. A combination of firm black outlines and solid blocks of bold colour, it tended towards a different kind of synthesis, much closer to Japanese prints. In November 1887, Anquetin had exhibited his first startlingly experimental Cloisonist works – including *Avenue de Clichy* (1887, Wadsworth Atheneum, Hartford, CT) and *The Mower* (fig. 8) – in a popular Montmartre eating-house exhibition organised by Van Gogh himself. Bernard, despite not wishing to exhibit with neo-impressionists, was persuaded to take part as well. Thus, it was under Vincent's aegis, in this off-piste location, that Cloisonism was revealed to fellow artists.[30] The public impact was only felt in 1888, however, when Anquetin showed the same works with the group Les XX in Brussels and then at the Salon des Indépendants. Anquetin was a savvy self-publicist who had undoubtedly primed Dujardin, an old school friend, to write his article. Cloisonism was described as a decorative art that had made a significant rupture with naturalism, its sources of inspiration identified as Japanese prints, popular prints (*images d'Épinal*) or the effects of looking at the world through coloured glass, this last insight being Anquetin's personal contribution: "It is obvious," Dujardin wrote, "that a different sensation will be produced by a different coloration [...] through a yellow pane of glass – as in *The Mower* – you'll get the sensation of full sun."[31]

Unsurprisingly, upon hearing Cloisonism hailed as the new artistic vogue, Van Gogh felt a proprietorial interest. He probably also felt wrong-footed, as Bernard did, by this public exposé of technical ideas he was still exploring in Arles in paintings like *Café Terrace at Night*, which owed its colour and dynamic perspectival composition both to Anquetin's *Avenue de Clichy* and to Hiroshige's *Night View of Saruwaka-machi* (p. 27).

The name "Cloisonist" proved to be short-lived. By the following year, when both Bernard and Anquetin took part in another alternative exhibition held by a group clustered around Paul Gauguin, the word "synthetist" had replaced it. At the Volpini show, *Japonisme* was again identified by critics as a crucial ingredient of the garishly coloured, heavily contoured works they saw on the walls.[32] The Volpini exhibition succeeded

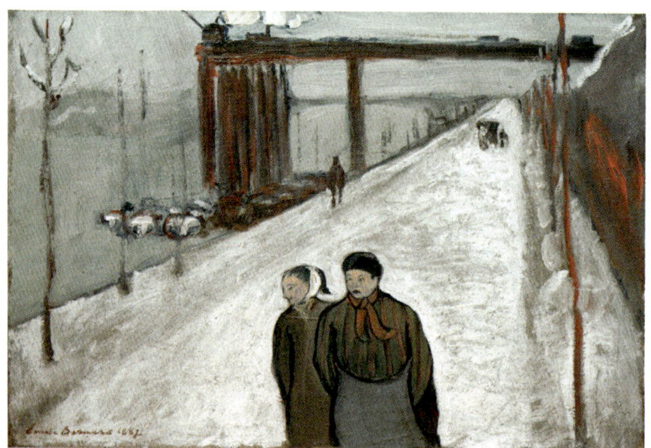

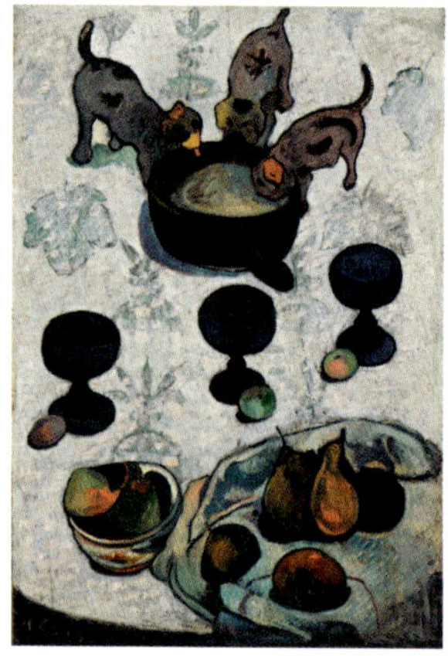

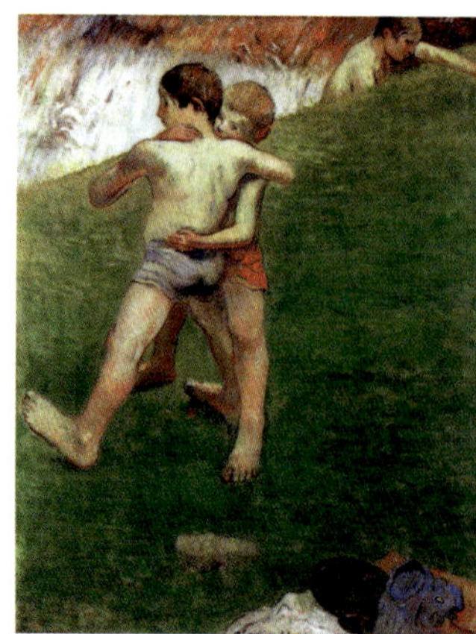

in alerting many young painters dissatisfied with naturalism and impressionism to the decorative possibilities of Japanese art.[33] Anquetin's *Japonisme* continued in a group of paintings of modern life depicting women with stylised sinuous silhouettes, but disappeared around 1891 when he entered a short-lived phase of Velazquez-inspired monochromaticism, followed in 1894 by an out-and-out, vocal return to the old masters – in particular, Rubens.

By late July 1888, challenged to defend his allegiances by Bernard, Van Gogh was starting to qualify his enthusiasm for Japanese art. He admitted it was an incomplete art when compared with the satisfyingly modelled wholeness of Dutch art.[34] Japanese art suited him insofar as it enhanced his appreciation of nature and his unswerving attachment to reality – the attention given to individual insects, heads of grass and thistles, for instance – but he was insensitive to the exotic per se and circumspect about the flattening, anti-naturalistic or abstracting aspects of the Japanese style: "the Japanese disregards reflection, placing his solid tints one beside the other – characteristic lines naively marking off movements or shapes."[35] The absence of shadows, crucial for giving forms solidity, was a feature of Japanese art that particularly bothered Bernard.[36] He exploited Japanese art selectively, borrowing its emphatic outlines and sharp diagonals in 1887 landscapes like *Afternoon at Saint Briac* (Aargauer Kunsthaus, Aarau) and *Ragpickers at Clichy* (fig. 9). But the "primitive" quality of Bernard's early Cloisonist works owes more to the lead interstices of stained glass and to Cézanne, and his admiration for Japanese art was ultimately eclipsed by his love of the Italian primitives. A decorative tendency and boldly silhouetted forms, seen in his *Bretonneries* zincographs (pp. 212, 213), still informed Breton works such as *The Wave* in 1892 (p. 215), but he had no use for the elegance of Japanese art. By 1893 – during his travels to Egypt – he could already look back dispassionately on the way *Japonisme* had served his generation's stylistic needs, as though it was all in the past. "Why did we love the Japanese so much?" he reflected. "Because they gave us back the syntheses we had lost in the course of 5 centuries of time-wasting concern with minutiae."[37]

Gauguin and Japanese art

Although Gauguin was aware of Japanese art earlier, it only really impinged on his way of working in 1888.[38] Always interested in the decorative arts, like other impressionists he took up the challenge of designing fans. The oblique asymmetrical compositions of certain fans, *Child with Mandolin* of 1885 (Private Collection), for instance, show a discreet *Japonisme*. By the time he painted *Little Cat Eating out of Bowl* (p. 216), however, Gauguin was introducing a wholly new, decorative playfulness to his composition, the disconnected elements arranged on a pale tabletop recalling Hokusai or Kuniyoshi.[39] Nevertheless, he retained the cast shadows beneath these circular objects and in the folds of the linen tablecloth. In *Still Life with Three Puppies* (fig. 10), this illusionism drops away as he allowed pattern and shape to dominate.

9 Émile Bernard, *Ragpickers at Clichy*, 1887, Musée départemental Maurice Denis, Saint-Germain-en-Laye (dépôt du Musée d'Orsay, legs de Pierre Farcy)
10 Paul Gauguin, *Still Life with Three Puppies*, 1888, Museum of Modern Art, New York, Mrs. Simon Guggenheim Fund
11 Paul Gauguin, *Boys Wrestling*, 1888, Private Collection

In July 1888, Japanese art suddenly provided Gauguin with the solution to certain technical problems. He had struggled to apply colour convincingly, most recently using small regular brushstrokes across the whole canvas rather than variegated strokes that might help the spectator establish distances. But *Boys Wrestling* (fig. 11), painted in flatter zones, at last liberated him from the influence of Degas and naturalism. He described the composition as "absolutely Japanese by a Peruvian savage," particularly the grass which he had treated with "pure Veronese green gradating to chrome yellow *with no visible brushwork*, as in the Japanese prints".[40] So what Gauguin at first took stylistically from Japanese art was this simplified *exécution*, laying down colours as blocks, using outlines to define forms, and dispensing with *trompe l'œil*. Now, combining Japanese art with broad effects seen in Puvis de Chavannes, Gauguin began to put his much-criticised tonal monotony to good use.[41] He dispensed with the impressionistic tendency to merge forms or suggest an ambient atmosphere. Instead, maintaining the firm contours of his drawings, he let his painted figures occupy their own separate zones on the picture surface, as one sees in paintings such as *Arlésiennes (Mistral)* from 1888 (p. 217) and *Beach at Le Pouldu* from 1889 (Private Collection). But unlike Anquetin and Bernard, Gauguin did not demarcate these zones with heavy black "cloisons". In contrast to Van Gogh, for Gauguin, Japanese art therefore offered a way to loosen his ties to naturalism, allowing him to explore the exotic and mysterious more fully. Several of his non-naturalistic colours – the startling reds, for instance, or arbitrary divisions of the pictorial space, as in the diagonal tree trunk in *Vision of the Sermon* from 1888 (National Gallery of Scotland, Edinburgh) and *Reclining Tahitian Women* (p. 225) – have Japanese precedents.[42]

Gauguin was presumably familiar with Hokusai and Hiroshige's landscape views, given the decorative screens of trees used in his Arles *Blue Trees* (p. 68), although to vitiate the composition's appeal, he gave it the menacing, enigmatic caption, "Vous y passerez, la belle" or "Your Turn Will Come, My Beauty!"[43] But he chiefly appears to have been interested in Japanese figurative prints depicting performers, actors and wrestlers. Unlike Van Gogh's wholesale approach, Gauguin seems to have collected sparingly and with an eye to his own interests. Several of his still lifes incorporate specific actor prints as part of their carefully assembled decor. He used them not as fashionable accessories but as minor players in the pictorial drama, much as he included his handcrafted pots to destabilise potentially pedestrian motifs and assert the "otherness" of his identity.[44] In *Still Life with Japanese Print* (p. 85), the warrior-like actor in the print seems to be in combat with the adjacent flowers.[45] A similarly literal intervention occurs in *Still Life with Onions* (p. 125), where Gauguin includes a print by Utagawa Toyokuni.[46] Here, the Japanese actor's arm – hidden by the still life in the foreground – seems to merge with the onion's tufted stalk.

Japanese art played its role in Gauguin's transportable imaginary museum. He is known to have had Japanese prints decorating the walls of his rented studio in Le Pouldu from 1889 to 1890.[47] His first biographer, Jean de Rotonchamp, also mentions seeing them in Paris, hung above Gauguin's own works in the home of his long-suffering host Schuffenecker. "The walls of the studio glowed with his light-toned gay studies, above which, two or three meters from the floor, ran a sort of frieze made up of juxtaposed prints by Hokusai

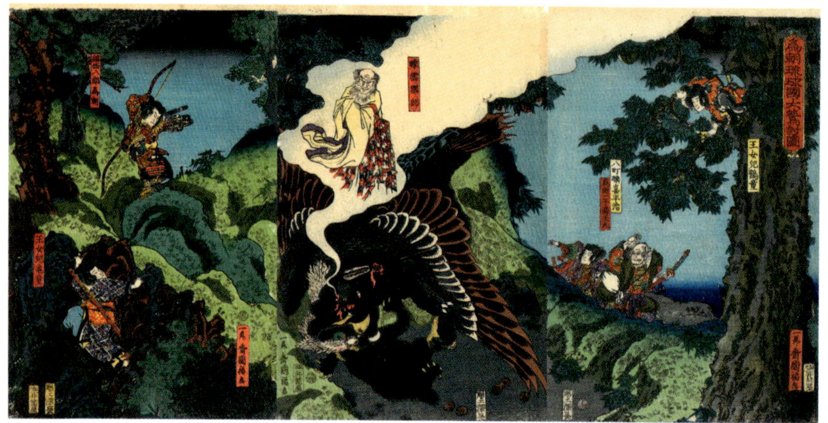

12 Utagawa Kunifuku, *A Battle between a Giant Eagle and a Bear*, circa 1860, Japan Print Gallery
13 Paul Gauguin, *Where Do We Come From? What Are We? Where Are We Going?*, 1897–1898, Museum of Fine Arts, Boston, Tompkins Collection – Arthur Gordon Tompkins Fund

and Utamaro. These prints, as well as some unusual original Japanese drawings, belonged to Gauguin and, here and there amongst them, he had pinned up a few photographs of well-known works by Manet and Puvis de Chavannes. He had obtained one print by Utamaro, worth 300 francs, from Joyant in exchange for canvases."[48] Unfortunately, the identity of this valuable Utamaro is unknown. However, two large triptych prints by Kunichika and Kunifuku were acquired by Victor Segalen in Tahiti at the posthumous auction sale of Gauguin's studio effects and brought back to France. Kunichika's clustered sumo wrestlers clearly amused Gauguin and were quoted in some of his satirical journals. But more telling is the Kunifuku, a dramatic and magical interpretation of a hunting scene in which an eagle carries off a small bear (fig. 12). Its tripartite composition, rich decorative colour scheme and imaginative merging of human and animal drama were surely pertinent to the gestation of Gauguin's testamentary masterpiece, *Where Do We Come From? What Are We? Where Are We Going?* (fig. 13).

On his walls and in albums, Gauguin enjoyed juxtaposing Hokusai's *Manga* prints with works by Daumier, Forain or Giotto; in his writings, he put Hokusai's draughtsmanship on a par with Raphael or Michelangelo.[49] Japanese artists' suave linearity and their free integration of image and text, the seen and the unseen as well as reality and dream remained important for Gauguin's later paintings and prints which freely combine oriental elegance with Polynesian barbarisms.

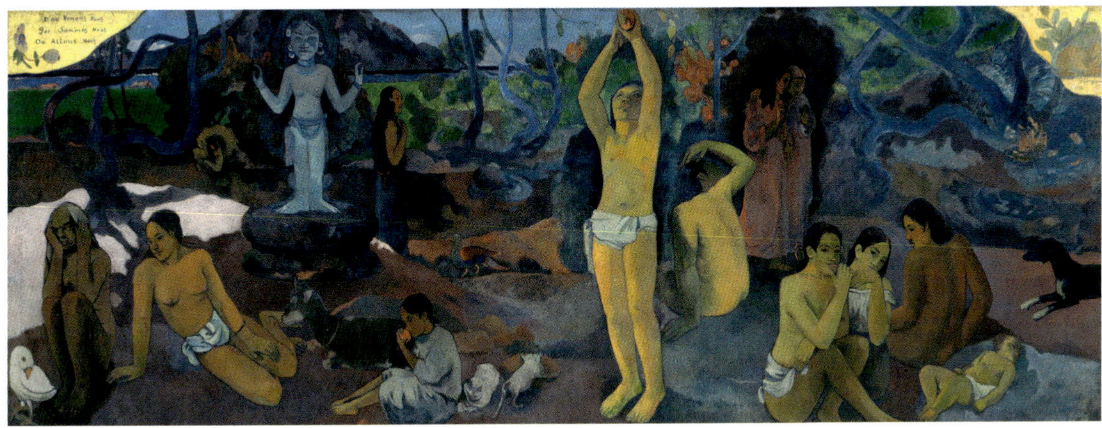

Conclusion

The impact of Japanese art on Van Gogh, Gauguin and their close associates in the late 1880s was intense and profound. It altered their use of line, colour application and composition. In Van Gogh's case, it so affected him that he contrived to see Provence with Japanese eyes. Japanese art offered them short- or longer-term solutions to perceived technical problems within naturalism and impressionism. Yet for this later generation, it was essentially regarded as another form of primitivism, despite their awareness of Japanese art's technical sophistication. In Bernard's view, Gauguin was still imitating Japanese prints in 1900, just as he continued to imitate Cambodian sculpture. While this was said dismissively, Bernard seeking to distance himself from his former comrade and assert his own profound engagement with the classic art of the European old masters, there was some truth in his observation.[50] As with Gauguin's fascination with the archaic traditions of Brittany or Polynesia, underlying this desire to assimilate the lessons of Japanese art lay the sense that it was a precious, centuries-old cultural tradition under threat.

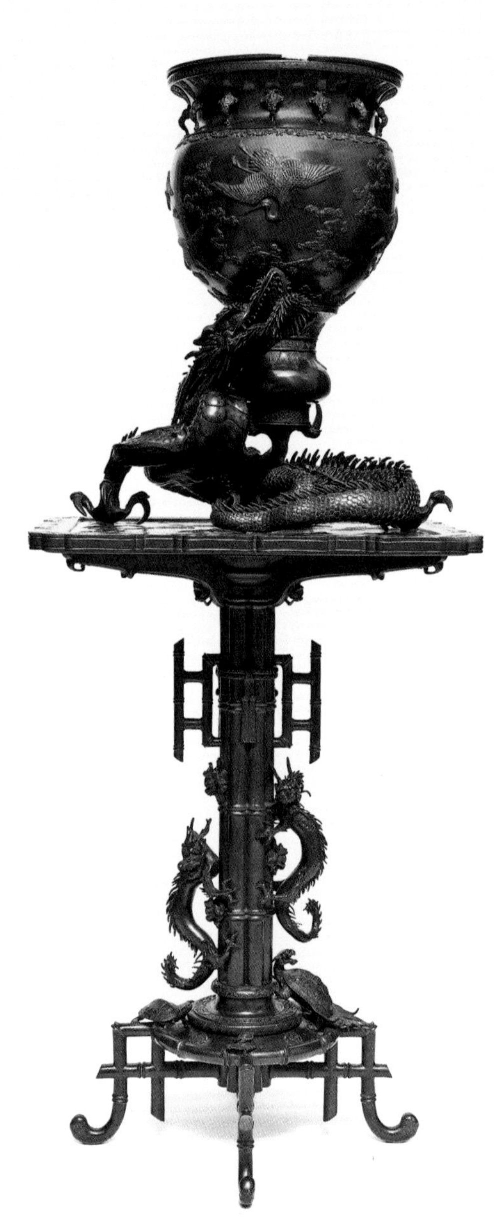

129 Édouard Lièvre, Maison Ferdinand Barbedienne, Japan, *Jardiniere*, 19th c.

"Discovering new horizons and liberties" – *Japonisme* and the decorative arts in France

Claire Guitton

After Japan had signed a succession of agreements with various different Western powers from 1854 (the agreement with France was sealed on 9 October 1858), objects from Japan started to arrive in ever-greater numbers on direct routes to the West. It was not long before people became enthusiastic about these "curiosities", which were a source of great fascination – not only because of their beauty, but also because of their otherness in comparison to Western tradition. Soon these objects received the highest of praise and were avidly collected and studied. Their discovery had a decisive influence on the decorative arts, as it soon became clear to artists – in the context of a lively and diverse kind of artistic creativity – that the precise observation and analysis of the iconography, style and technique of these so-called "bibelots" could only be conducive to the flourishing of the decorative arts.

The spread of Japanese models and their appropriation in the decorative arts

In 1905, Léonce Bénédite told the story that the painter and engraver Félix Bracquemond discovered "a small, strangely bound book with a red cover" at the printer Auguste Delâtre's shop in 1856, which was used "as padding to protect the porcelain tableware that had been sent by French settlers in Japan".[1] Even though this episode of the "discovery" of the *Manga* by Hokusai owes more to legend than to actual events,[2] Bracquemond is justifiably presented here as one of the very first protagonists of *Japonisme*. For example, many of the motifs that he designed for the *Service Rousseau*, which was shown for the first time at the Paris World Fair of 1867, were direct references to Hokusai's *Manga* as well as the woodblock prints of Hiroshige and other Japanese artists (pp. 252, 253). His bold use of white space, on which fish, insects, birds and flowers are arranged with a certain freedom, also testifies to an attentive study of Japanese woodblock prints.[3] The anecdote told by Bénédite must also be given credit for mentioning Auguste Delâtre's printing shop, whose role in the spread of the first Japanese motifs should not be underestimated. Starting in 1859, it was here, for instance, that Adalbert de Beaumont and Eugène V. Collinot published their *Recueil de dessins pour l'art et l'industrie* – an anthology that contained, from August 1861 onwards, some reproductions of Japanese motifs, which were taken from the first and second volumes of Hokusai's *Manga* in particular (fig. 1).[4] This *Recueil* was the first disseminating medium containing Japanese motifs that was aimed directly at artists and manufacturers.[5] Beaumont's and Collinot's *Recueil* was to be followed by numerous other works that contributed actively to the spread of Japanese models in the artistic milieu.[6] Some twenty years later, Siegfried Bing also tried to draw attention to Japanese art with his magazine *Le Japon artistique* by addressing artists directly.[7] His readership included Émile Gallé, Jean Carriès and René Lalique.

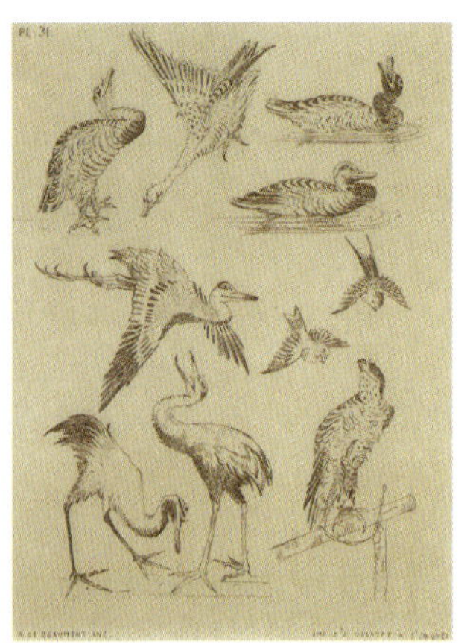

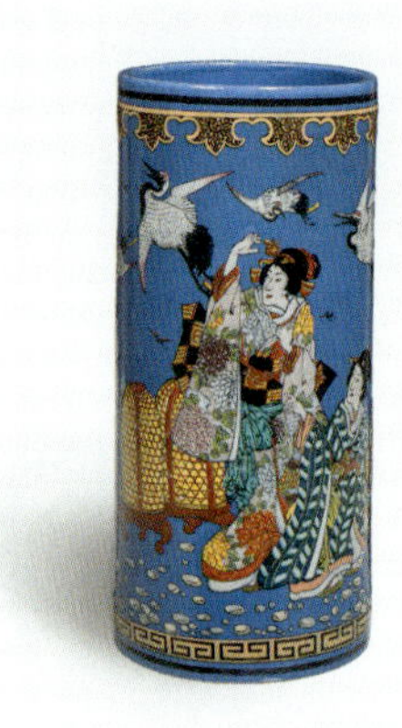

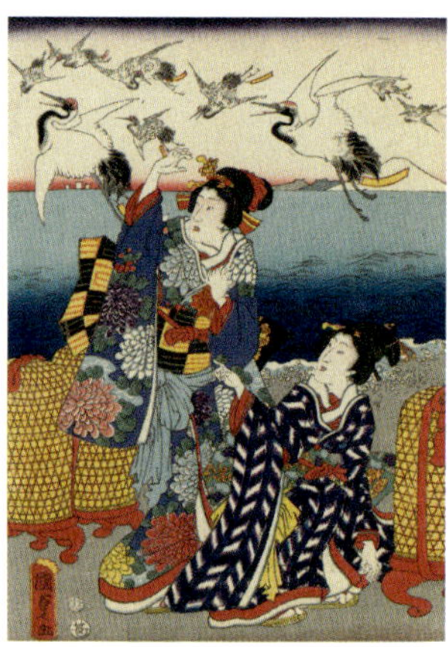

1 Adalbert de Beaumont and Eugène V. Collinot, *Recueil de dessins pour l'art et l'industrie*, Paris, 1861, plate 31 (left), Universitätsbibliothek Heidelberg
2 Genlis et Rudhard, *Vase*, 1865/1874, Les Arts Décoratifs, Musée des Arts decoratifs, Paris
3 Utagawa Kunisada II, *Pine, Bamboo and Plum for Eastern Genji: Parody of Yoritomo Releasing Cranes at Yuigahama*, 1864 (left part of a triptych), Museum of Fine Arts, Boston, William Sturgis Bigelow Collection

While Japanese models were being spread via pictorial anthologies, magazines and books, this art was simultaneously also being discovered by means of a direct examination of the works. Chinese and Japanese artefacts were becoming increasingly accessible from the 1860s onwards, especially in Paris. Curiosity shops, in which tea and other exotic goods could be purchased, now also began to sell objects from Japan – for example, the shop À l'Empire chinois owned by Monsieur Decelle or À la Porte chinoise, a shop run by Monsieur Bouillette. The shop La Jonque chinoise, owned by Monsieur Desoye and later his widow, was a meeting place for the first *Japonistes*. Some dealers, such as Siegfried Bing and Hayashi Tadamasa, also made a name for themselves as subtle connoisseurs.[8] Edmond de Goncourt's house in Auteuil is a testament to the great importance placed by *Japonistes* on having Japanese objects in their homes (p. 36).[9] Artists also became collectors, thus acquiring an almost inexhaustible source of inspiration. The collectors of Japanese woodblock prints included Félix Bracquemond, the entrepreneur and designer (*marchand-éditeur)* Eugène Rousseau, the ceramic artists Laurent Bouvier and Camille Moreau-Nélaton, the jeweller Alexis Falize and his son Lucien, as well as the glass artist and jeweller René Lalique. The collection of the caster Ferdinand Barbedienne contained around fifty Japanese pieces, including bronzes, porcelain, enamel pieces using cloisonné technique, lacquerware, albums and scrolls.[10] The collection of the draughtsman Édouard Lièvre contained bronzes and cloisonné enamel work, lacquerware, porcelain and ceramics from the Far East.[11] Paintings, woodblock prints and calligraphies, ceramics and lacquerware, as well as bamboo objects formed the collection of the glass artist, cabinetmaker and ceramicist Gallé.[12] The collection and study of these objects promoted those who directly cited certain Japanese motifs. For the decoration of a vase presented on the occasion of the Paris World Fair of 1878, Gallé was inspired by the carp motif in volume 13 of Hokusai's *Manga* (p. 256).[13] This kind of direct reference was no rarity, as shown by the vase by Julien Genlis and Charles Rudhard – the motif on one of the two sides is a reference to the left section of a triptych by Utagawa Kunisada II (fig. 2 and fig. 3).

The world fairs also played a key role in the discovery and dissemination of Japanese objects;[14] the same is true of various events that left a lasting impression, such as the establishment of the so-called "Musée Oriental" in 1869 by the Union centrale des Beaux-Arts appliqués à l'industrie (which was not open for long), the presentation of the collection of Henri Cernuschi in the Palais de l'Industrie in 1873, or the retrospective of Japanese art organised by Louis Gonse at Galerie Georges Petit in 1883. In an article on the Musée Oriental, published in the daily newspaper *Le Rappel* in 1869, Philippe Burty reports that ceramicists from Paris, artists from the factory of Sèvres and an important manufacturer from Limoges had come in order to study and sketch the works exhibited.[15] The presentation in 1873 of objects just brought back from a trip to Asia by Cernuschi also clearly demonstrates the artists' interest. This is especially true of Émile Reiber, head of drawing and design at Christofle from 1865 until 1878, who was fascinated by Cernuschi's collection. The co-director of the company, Henri Bouilhet, reported: "He [Reiber] spent over two weeks each morning sketching in the Palais de l'Industrie, and brought back the most wonderful drawings from

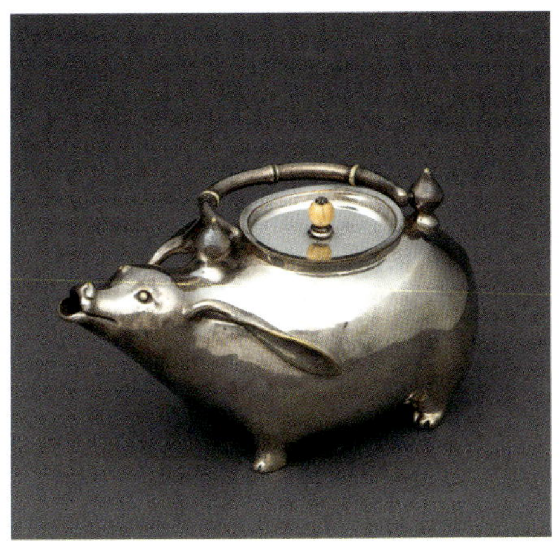

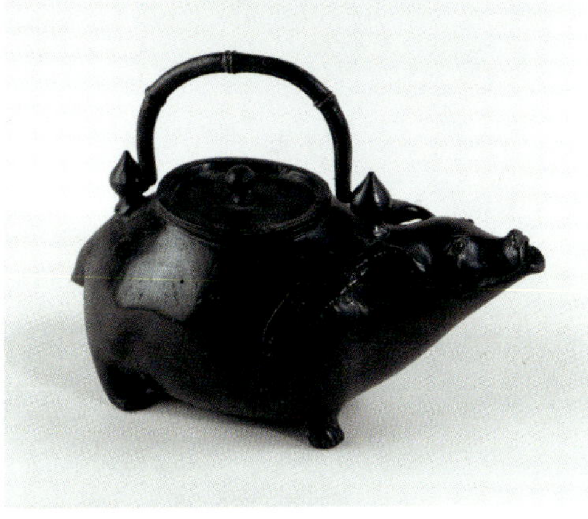

4 Émile Reiber (design), Christofle & Cie (execution), *Teapot*, circa 1882, Musée d'Orsay, Paris

5 Japan, *Kettle in the form of a Hare*, 18th/19th c., Musée Cernuschi, Paris

these sessions, which are sure to have served him well in his adaptions that he was to produce for Christofle."[16] Indeed, there were many of these adaptions.[17] Among the pieces completed by Reiber was an ensemble of objects that were inspired directly by certain items from the exhibition, such as a teapot made from metal and ivory in the form of a hare (fig. 4), whose shape was based on an eighteenth to nineteenth-century Japanese bronze kettle from the Cernuschi Collection (fig. 5).[18]

Some artists even went so far as to acquire authentic Japanese elements in order to then integrate them into their own designs. The *Jardiniere*, held in the Musée des Arts décoratifs in Paris, is a good example of this method (p. 78). The vase was made in Japan; its base can be dated back to the beginning of the nineteenth century. Its upper part, however, corresponds more with Japanese models from the second half of the nineteenth century intended for export. The dragon, in turn, resembles a censer that had been brought back by Cernuschi. Finally, this already motley ensemble was joined by a small round table designed by Lièvre and cast by Barbedienne. Its foot, a bamboo imitation, is decorated with dragons and turtles.[19] This object is characteristic of the freedom exercised by the artists in using certain Japanese elements for new designs, which were then mixed with thoroughly Western ideas and fantasies.

The eye of the critics

In view of an artistic production that was increasingly being influenced by the arts of Japan, critics and art historians set about describing the manifestations of *Japonisme* and analysing its development, with some warning openly against possible excesses. Jules Champfleury, for example, could not resist commenting ironically on this "fashion of *Japoniaiseries*" from 1868 onwards.[20] And on the occasion of a conference organised by the Union centrale des Beaux-Arts appliqués à l'industrie in 1869, Ernest Chesneau tried to convince his audience not "to imitate" the Japanese.[21] The warning against copying was to become a leitmotif in critical writings – albeit unsuccessfully. In his work *L'Art japonais*, Gonse strongly criticised "Japanese pastiche".[22] In *Le Japon artistique*, Bing, for his part, condemned "a blind aping".[23] Thus, the intellectuals turned against a – to use Gonse's words – "superficial Japan".[24] This criticism of a flat, empty *Japonisme* arose during a period of doubt in the decorative arts. Gonse, for instance, complained about the "impoverishment" of the inventive spirit in France.[25] Burty found fault with the fact that copies were being used to such an excessive extent that artists were no longer able "to pursue their own thoughts".[26] And Bing criticised the "restrictions" that were a result of the "rigorous rules [...] which we call our *style*".[27] In their study of Japanese art, these staunch *Japonistes* found a compelling element in their search for answers to those questions that confronted contemporary artists of the time. Yet the most important requirement was to first truly understand this Japanese art. Here, once again, it was the intellectuals who acted as advisers. While Chesneau spoke out against copying, he encouraged artists to simultaneously study the "conceptions" and "principles" of Japanese art.[28] And Gonse called on them to work out its "sound doctrines".[29] Thus, the precise study of Japanese art and the comprehension of its principles and methods seemed to be the way in which to draw helpful and favourable lessons from Japanese art for the renewal of the decorative arts.

By glorifying Japanese art, the intellectuals simultaneously also revealed the weaknesses in French production. Gonse could not avoid noting that the Japanese bronzes were "superior to an almost shattering extent for our craftsmen". The reasons he gave for this superiority are significant. According to the author, the Japanese did not have "any secrets or tricks that we would not have applied ourselves. What makes them so unique is their awareness whilst working, the respect and love for their work, but also the dexterity of their hands".[30] This criticism was directed straight at the system of the time, especially at the excesses of an industrial scale of production, whose dangers were now being recognised. By praising the preference of the Japanese artist for "well-made" work, alongside his veracity, commitment and skilful hands, Gonse also passed judgement on the rash, mechanical and anonymous industrial production with which "our steam-driven society" operated.[31] In contrast, Japan was the ideal nation for the further development of the decorative arts. In an article published by Ary Renan in *Le Japon artistique*, he pointed out that "the arts, both high and low [...] formed a perfect unity" there.[32] Thus, at a time when attempts were being made to revalue decorative artefacts, Japan seemed to be the model to follow. In addition, there was a feeling that the Japanese people as a whole were more receptive to art and beauty.[33] It appears as if the people of the time projected the ideals that they formulated for French art onto Japanese art. That also included the harmony between humans, art and nature, to which artists aspired so much at the end of the nineteenth century.

Back to nature

In the first issue of *Le Japon artistique*, Bing presented nature as the "sole lord and master" of the Japanese artist.[34] The fact that the observation of nature in Japanese art was given such fundamental significance soon aroused the interest of French artists, who saw the increasing necessity of a return to nature.[35]

They were fascinated by the exoticism of Japanese plants, whose splendour was now gradually being discovered in the West. At the time of his death, Gallé, for example, owned 422 original Japanese plant species.[36] In *L'Art japonais*, Gonse wrote a list of the trees and flowers that existed in Japan; in particular, these included wild plum trees, cherry trees, violet wisteria, orchids, chrysanthemums, camellias, peonies, water lilies, irises, poppies, morning glory, lilies, as well as ferns and mosses.[37] The artists were touched by the beauty and exoticism of these plant species, and it was not long before they adopted them as motifs in their work (pp. 117, 306, 312).

But they not only admired the beauty of Japanese flora; they were also riveted by the manner in which the Japanese observed nature so precisely. Japanese art therefore played a pioneering role; studying it prompted the artists to rethink their own way of observing nature. Or, as the jeweller Lucien Falize explained: "Japanese art shows us the way back to nature, to this endless world that surrounds us and which we do not notice. We had to look at the Japanese albums, observe their ceramics, lacquerware and bronzes, in order to remind ourselves that we also have a sky, fields, forests and waterways, just like them, which are inhabited by birds, flowers, all kinds of greenery, insects and fish in countless colours."[38] Studying Japanese art animated artists to observe nature just as it presented itself to them, in its entirety and without any prejudice. This uncompromising observation and authentic view emboldened the artists to question principles that had been anchored deeply in Western tradition. The Japanese model encouraged them to think anew about the hierarchy in the Western classification of the subject. For what astonished people more than anything else was the fact that there appeared to be nothing in Japanese art that was not worth illustrating, and therefore no distinction was made between "low" and "high" subjects. In an article dedicated to the *Manga* by Hokusai and published in *Le Japon artistique*, Ary Renan ascertained with delight that for Hokusai, "a flower [was] equal to a human".[39] Fascinated by Hokusai's *Manga* volumes, but also by the decoration of tsubas, netsukes and lacquerware, Western artists in turn discovered a delight for the world of the endlessly miniscule. Alexis Falize, for instance, followed the Japanese example and decorated his sumptuous enamel jewellery pieces with all kinds of small creatures – fish, tortoises, crabs, frogs, hens or grasshoppers (fig. 6).

By searching for their inspiration in nature, the artists hoped to overcome systems and conventions whose limits they now recognised. Lucien Falize admired how the Japanese were stimulated by all that nature offered. With the Japanese, according to the jeweller, "the form is not derived, as in our old world, from an architectural principle [...]; the Japanese form is more open; it is inspired by the blossom, the fruit, by things from nature, it is not corrected with the ruler or measured with a compass; it remains free, unusual, bold."[40] Falize draws attention here to the diversity, openness and freedom of the forms taken by the Japanese from nature. A deep-felt awareness of life flowed from the Japanese works, which presented a contrast to the prudish Western forms in the eyes of the people of the time. This feeling of organicity, so characteristic of Japanese art, can also be found in Gallé's work, for whom "nature itself is the starting point for everything".[41] A preliminary sketch held by the Musée de l'École de Nancy (fig. 7) very clearly shows how Gallé took his forms and motifs from nature. He was inspired for this design of a vase by the characteristic form of a columbine.[42] The curved elements that join the foot of the vase to its body are directly inspired by the spores at the end of the petals of this flower. The form of the object is derived directly from the painstaking observation of nature. Gallé drew his inspiration from the formal freedom provided to him by the columbine. This extreme sensibility to nature can also be seen in the manner in which the Japanese processed the material, especially clay.

Stoneware – the beauty of the material

"As far as ceramics from Japan are concerned, the International Exposition of 1878 opened our eyes to a circumstance that had completely escaped us beforehand," explained Burty in 1884 on the occasion of a conference on pottery and porcelain from Japan.[43] For it was at this world fair that the French public, which had hitherto only been accustomed to Japanese porcelain with multicoloured, gold-fringed decoration, was now acquainted with a previously unknown Japanese creation – namely, ceramics used in tea ceremonies. As Burty specified, the Japanese dealer Wakai Kenzaburō used this opportunity to erect a "narrow display case, without any special staging [...], containing pots, small vessels and small cups".[44] These unassuming objects, mostly stoneware, generated great astonishment and posed many questions. Incidentally, Burty admitted that "we could almost have thought they were coarse objects".[45] However, the enthusiasm for these ceramic pieces was not long in coming, and their discovery led to the fact that some, like Carriès, found their calling in this discipline. The art historian Arsène Alexandre wrote: "At the International Exposition of 1878, he [Carriès] was particularly impressed by the section on Japanese art, and especially by the art of pottery. He went there very often, full of enthusiasm and nervous curiosity, he spoke of it and thought a lot about it."[46] Both Japan devotees (such as Bing, Burty, Cernuschi, Goncourt, Gillot or Gonse) and artists (like Eugène Grasset, Henri Rivière, Jean Carriès, Paul Jeanneney or Georges Hoentschel) began to collect stoneware pots, bowls and receptacles. Many publications contributed to the spread of knowledge about these objects, which had barely – or indeed not at all – been known to the Parisian public until then. In his 1883 work *L'Art japonais*, Gonse provided his readers with a chapter on the subject of ceramics – the author was none other than Bing.[47] Bing, for his part, displayed Japanese stoneware frequently in his magazine *Le Japon artistique* (fig. 8) and entrusted Burty with the task of writing a two-part article on the subject of "Pottery in Japan".[48] In this article, the author referred, among other things, to the institutions in which some examples of this pottery could be admired – in particular, the Musée Guimet, the Union centrale des Arts décoratifs and the Musée Céramique in Sèvres. Burty could also have mentioned the Conservatoire national des Arts et Métiers, as this institution received a gift of Japanese objects from Bing in 1888, thus ensuring that Japan was also introduced as a model to this technical school.[49] In 1898, the Musée Cernuschi in turn opened its doors to the public. Of course, we should note that stoneware as a material had already risen to prominence in France in the 1840s – in other words, prior to the discovery of Japanese stoneware – thanks

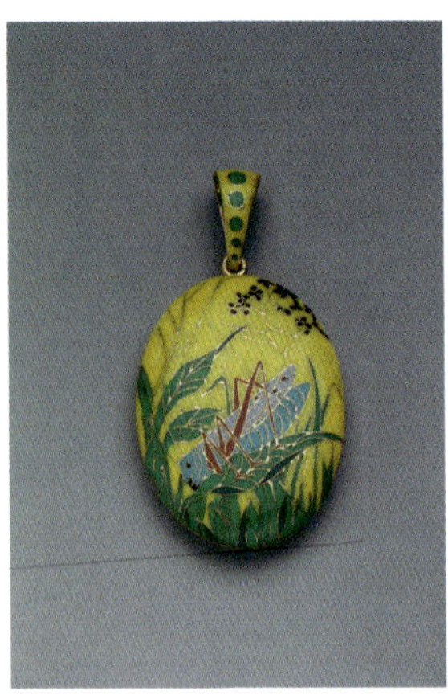

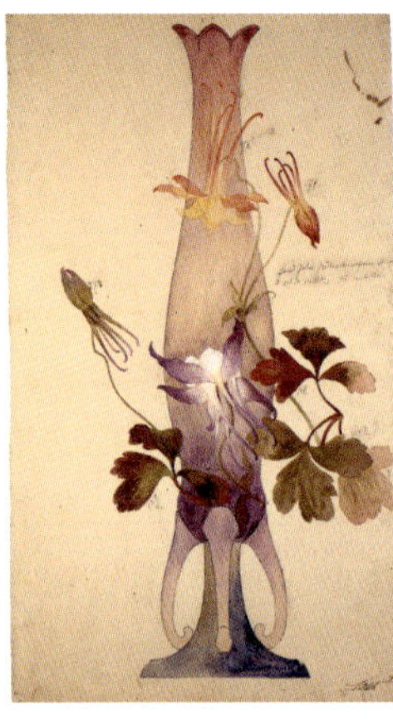

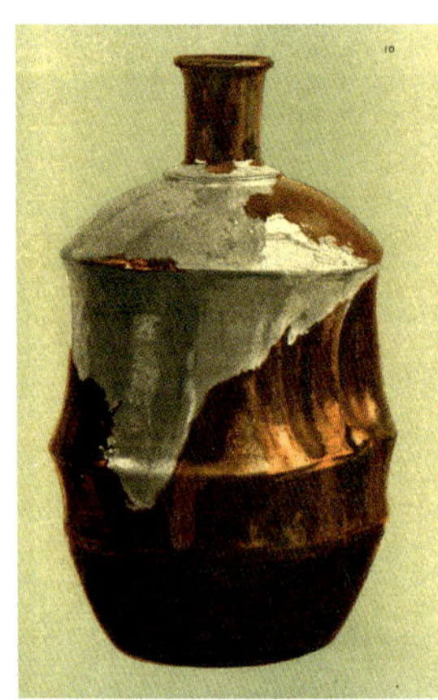

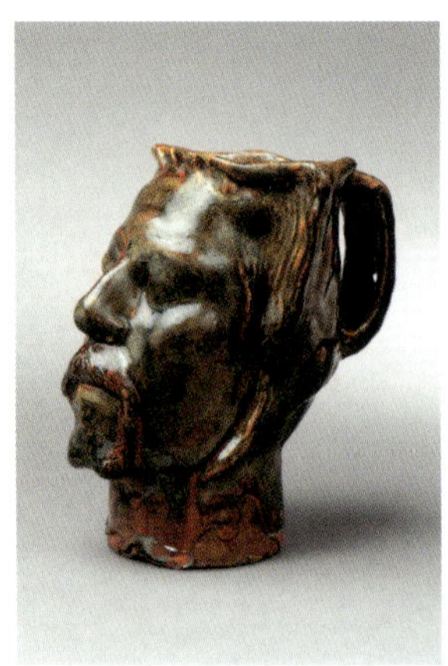

to the ceramicist Jules Ziegler. Nevertheless, although the national pottery tradition was to remain a reference for artists throughout the entire nineteenth century, the discovery in Paris in 1878 of ceramics used for the Japanese tea ceremony most certainly shaped the development of French artistic production.

Artists were particularly receptive to the simplicity of Japanese ceramics and their plain, fine shapes. Many ceramic artists were inspired by Japanese forms and particularly referred to the gourd form of the sake bottles (pp. 266, 267) or the shape of the *chaire*, the jars for Japanese tea powder (pp. 247, 269). Fine ivory lids, also based on the Japanese model, can be found in the artistic production of Paul Jeanneney (1861–1920) or Georges Hoentschel (1855–1915) (p. 264).[50] The technical aspect and the material effects of the Japanese production were also studied with great interest. For the execution of Rodin's *Monumental Head of Balzac* (p. 271) as stoneware, Jeanneney developed a glaze which represented that of Tanba or Bizen stoneware as much as possible, with its effect of yellow speckles on brown engobe resulting when burning pine ash dropped down inside the kiln.[51] The application of gold, used by the Japanese to restore their objects (p. 248, 262), also fascinated the ceramic artists who adopted this method for purely aesthetic purposes. The idea was no longer to patch up something, to fill a gap or to re-adhere a broken piece of ceramic, but rather to apply gold as an ornament in itself (p. 263).

For the artists, the study of Japanese pottery threw up the fundamental question of the essence of the ornament. Contemporaries were astonished at how abstract some Japanese ceramics were. This characteristic is particularly emphasised in the description of the bottle from Seto (mentioned above) in *Le Japon artistique* (fig. 8): "The only decoration on this bottle is the radiance of these glazes, which flow into each other with a casual charm."[52] Art critics and artists quickly understood the importance of the material to Japanese potters, prompting them as it did to develop its own decoration from itself. The ornament was not an "addition", but rather consisted in the transformation of the material itself. Motifs emerged from accidents, irregularities and distortions – surprises, offered up for view. Unplanned droplets, the random merging of glazes, bulges and dents became motifs that left the main role to chance, that "charming teacher whose cheerful moods have always challenged the Japanese artist".[53] But it was important not to be deceived: coincidence was not everything – in truth, it was an extremely controlled aesthetic of randomness. For this reason, Burty warned his audience: "We should protect ourselves against the misconception that these are simply accidents during production. It is quite often merely a flirt with negligence."[54]

Coarse, rough, crude, robust, uncivilised, folksy, naive, unfeigned, rustic, primitive – contemporaries were not short of adjectives to describe Japanese pottery. While some certainly used these terms in a negative sense, they were, however, suddenly transformed into praise by the pens of the advocates of Japanese art. In fact, it was precisely this unpolished appearance of the objects that fascinated people in the West, who regarded this coarseness as a sign of genuineness and authenticity. "I shall return to my former uncouth, wild, boorish life. I do not want to be a modern Frenchman at any cost, as that would mean being superficial," confided Carriès to his patron Aline Ménard-Dorian.[55] This aspiration towards the primitive and the desire

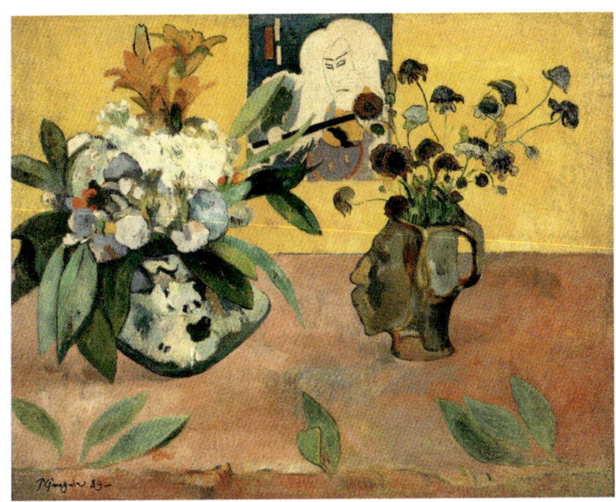

6 Alexis Falize (design and manufacture; Antoine Tard: enamel), *Locket*, 1868–1870, The Cleveland Museum of Art, Andrew R. and Martha Holden Jennings Fund
7 Atelier Gallé, *Study for a Vase with Columbine Decoration*, circa 1902, Musée de l'École de Nancy
8 *Bottle in Seto Ceramic*, plate ID in: *Le Japon artistique*, ed. Siegfried Bing, issue 8, Dec. 1888
9 Paul Gauguin, *Jug in the Form of a Head*, 1889, Designmuseum Danmark
10 Paul Gauguin, *Still Life with a Japanese Print*, 1889, Tehran Museum of Contemporary Art, Tehran

for direct contact with the material confronted an increasingly apparent industrial society, a conflict that was experienced as a separation between humans and nature. Gauguin – who explained to his friend Émile Schuffenecker that what he was trying to make was "very Japanese, by a wild man from Peru"[56] – also discovered in stoneware the material that allowed him to give free rein to his most primitive tendencies. The Japanese art of pottery thus joined the ranks of the various and most primitive sources which particularly included the French pottery tradition as well as medieval, Egyptian and Peruvian art. The violence of the transformation of the material, its distortions, its melting and its cracks – all of these are elements that contributed to the expressive power of the work. And it is a tragic, bleeding, barbaric kind of stoneware that can be seen in Gauguin's self-portrait *Jug in the Form of a Head* (fig. 9). Gauguin depicted this jug in a still life, in which a Japanese woodblock print of an actor can be seen on the wall (fig. 10).

"By enlightening us about its practices, Japan allows us to discover new horizons and liberties," Bing once confided.[57] This phrase refers to one of the most immaterial and significant manifestations of *Japonisme*: the new wind, this creative energy and liberating elan that meant so much to late-nineteenth-century artists.

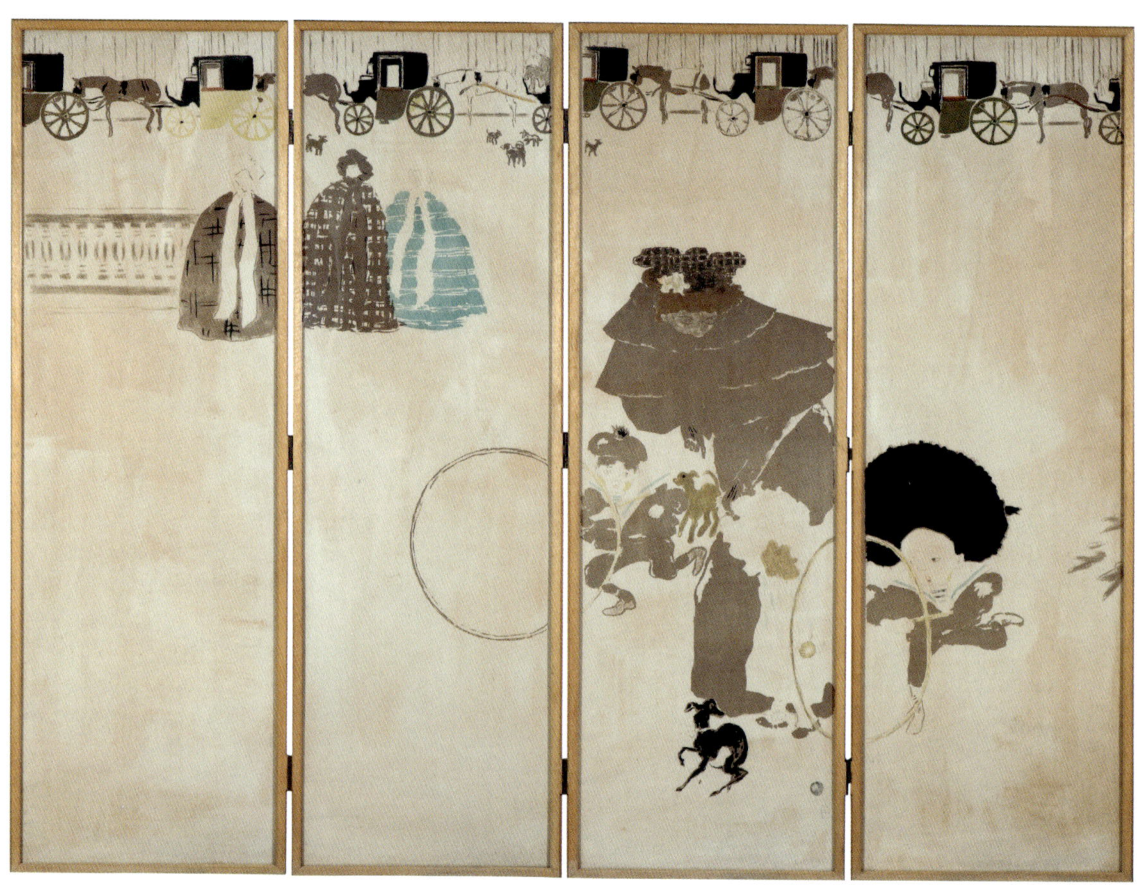

168a Pierre Bonnard, *Nannies' Promenade, Frieze of Carriages*, 1894/1897

The Nabi and East Asian art – Pierre Bonnard, Maurice Denis, Félix Vallotton and Édouard Vuillard

Ursula Perucchi-Petri

The Nabi played an important role in the reception of Japanese aesthetics and compositional forms. The early work of Pierre Bonnard, Maurice Denis, Félix Vallotton and Édouard Vuillard, in particular, was profoundly inspired by East Asian art. Because these artists simultaneously provided new impetus to twentieth-century art, an examination of their work gives us valuable insights into the phenomenon of *Japonisme*. The history of the Nabi is embedded within the wider, richly faceted era of Symbolism. Founded in 1888 at the Académie Julian in Paris, this group of artists took their name from the Hebrew word *nebiim*, meaning "prophet" or "enlightened one".[1] In response to the outmoded academic tradition of aesthetic mimesis and its illusionistic means of expression, the Nabi propagated a regeneration of art. Instead of the image being determined by literary subject matter and allegory, they sought expression through form. Maurice Denis, the theoretician of the group, summed this up in 1890 with the now-famous proposal: "Remember that a picture, before being a war horse, a female nude, or some anecdote, is essentially a flat surface covered with colours assembled in a certain order."[2] This maxim that can be interpreted in many ways posits, on the one hand, that the subject matter of the picture should be secondary to the actual means of expression. On the other hand, it extols the planarity of the picture, which spawned the need to develop new forms of portrayal to represent three-dimensional reality. Conscious of fin-de-siècle decadence, Denis and his friends seemed to consider that a renewal of art was possible only through "a return to the simplicity of its beginnings".[3]

Because Japanese woodblock prints were distinctive for their decorative planarity and their eschewal of the illusion of depth and plasticity so prevalent in European art, they tended to be regarded as an early and somewhat primitive form of art at the time. It was this misunderstanding that resulted in them being equated with the quest of the Nabi for simplicity, naivety and the archaic.[4]

The Japanese cultural traditions predating these woodblock prints first came to the attention of a wider public at the Paris World Fair of 1900, where Japan presented, for the first time in Europe, early Buddhist sculptures and ink paintings from the imperial collection and Buddhist temples. Japanese art introduced European artists to a hitherto-unknown aesthetic; at the time, in the later years of the nineteenth century, it proved a revelation, because this oriental formal syntax was interpreted as an approach that was more symbolic than representational and which dovetailed with the approach of the Symbolists.

Of all the major exhibitions introducing an interested public to this new art, the one that made the biggest impression on the Nabi was the *Exposition de la gravure japonaise* (p. 96) held at the École des Beaux-Arts in Paris in 1890 and organised by Siegfried Bing. It provided a comprehensive overview of the history of the art of Japanese woodblock prints by showing more than seven hundred individual woodblock prints and over four hundred illustrated books from private Parisian collections. At the same time, Bonnard and his friends began buying Japanese woodblock prints from department stores or art dealers in Paris.

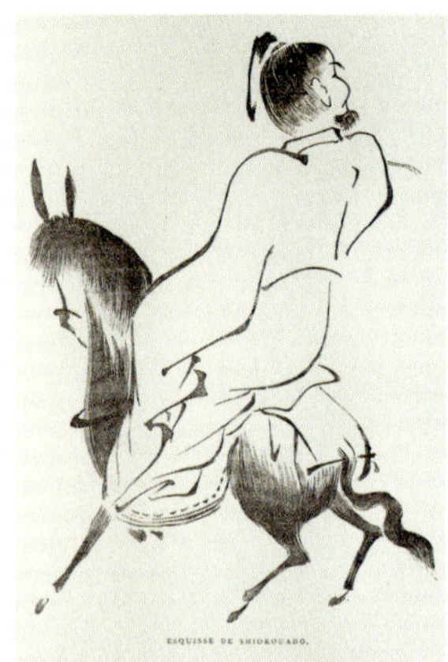

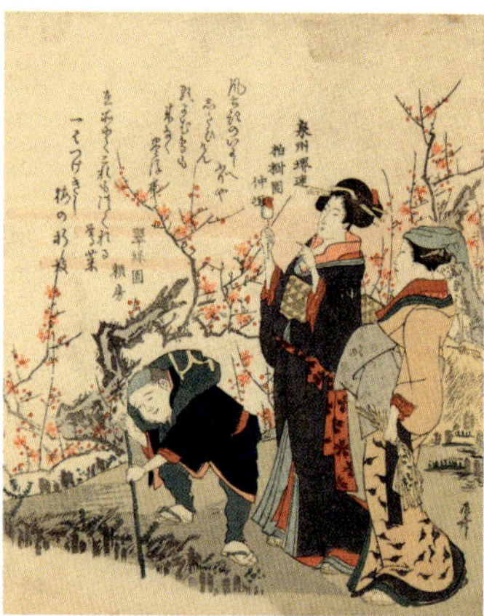

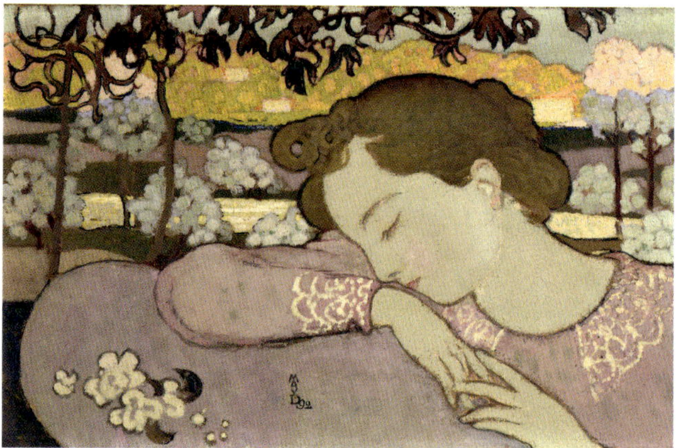

"For little money, I found crépons or wrinkled rice-papers in remarkable colours. I filled the walls of my room with this naive and lurid art," confessed Bonnard.[5] Photographs of the studios of Bonnard and Vuillard show Japanese woodblock prints on the walls (p. 330). As Bonnard would later put it, "Gauguin and Sérusier refer basically to the past. But what I had before me was something very vivid and extremely artistic".[6] In contrast to Denis, for example, this inspired Bonnard to embrace a more contemporary interpretation of his own time. It is interesting to note that both artists were stimulated by very different woodblock print artists: Bonnard was drawn towards the later, more realistically inclined artists such as Utagawa Kuniyoshi or Katsushika Hokusai, whereas Denis was attracted to the idealistic tendencies of Suzuki Harunobu and Kitagawa Utamaro.

Abandoning academic tradition in their quest for new forms of expression, the Nabi discovered in the Japanese woodblock prints an art form that affirmed their wish for a more original, less jaded, non-mimetic form of portrayal. Direct East Asian inspirations converged with the indirect influences of earlier *japonesque* artists such as Claude Monet, Edgar Degas, Paul Gauguin and Vincent Van Gogh, while at the same time merging with the new aesthetics of photography. The Nabi predilection for Japanese art also coincided with their appreciation of folk art, caricature and popular prints.[7]

The following text will address some of the fundamental influences of East Asian art on the new compositional structure of the Nabi. This involves, above all, an abandonment of traditional illusionistic three-dimensionality and central perspective as well as of the laws of proportion and movement entrenched since the Renaissance.

The arabesque as a new compositional form

The basic compositional element of East Asian art is "the line and the plane that relates to it", writes Dietrich Seckel in his *Einführung in die Kunst Ostasiens*.[8] East Asian artists distinguish mainly between two types of line: on the one hand, "the predominant line in the classic Buddhist painting, known as the wire-line, which is a smooth line of variable but constant width, with no expressive or shaded ebb and flow" and, on the other hand, the line that emerges in the later classical Buddhist painting, in the Sung and Kamakura periods, "which is a softer, gradually increasing but more strongly modulated and modulating, though less abstract or ornamental line".[9] In the dialectics of East Asian art, figure and object appear flat and incorporeal, while simultaneously possessing a certain volume and spatiality due to certain compositional devices. It is this aspect that must have impressed the Nabi, for, in spite of their radical insistence on the planarity of the image, their works are nevertheless projections of spatial foreshortening and three-dimensional volume within the plane. The arabesque became a key compositional element in this new formal syntax. The Nabi saw it as an alternative to illusionistic corporeal modelling with light and shadow.[10]

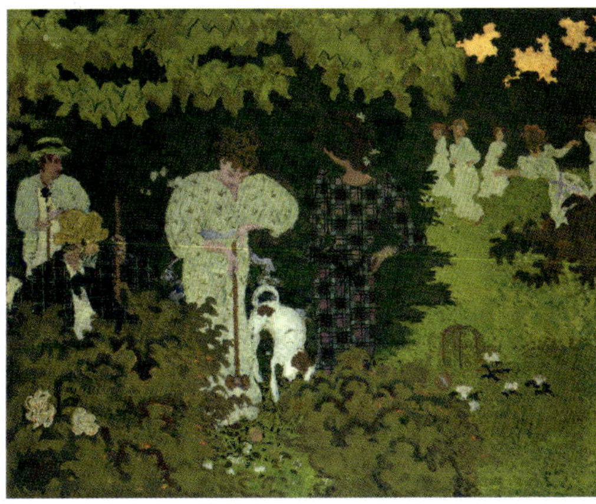

1 Shōkadō (Shōjō) (1584–1639), *Horse and Rider*, in: Louis Gonse, *L'Art japonais*, 1886, vol. 1, p. 211
2 Ryūryūkyo Shinsai, *surimono* with blind embossing, 1st quarter of 19th c., Private Collection (formerly Denis Collection)
3 Maurice Denis, *Sleeping Young Woman*, 1892, Musée Bonnat, Bayonne
4 Pierre Bonnard, *Twilight (The Game of Croquet)*, 1892, Musée d'Orsay, Paris

When Bonnard's poster *France-Champagne* (p. 197) first appeared on Paris billboards in 1891, it was immediately hailed as innovative. Henri de Toulouse-Lautrec was so excited that he went in search of the creator. Shortly afterwards, he created his own first modern poster, *Moulin Rouge*. On a bright yellow ground, Bonnard presents the half-figure of an exuberant young woman clutching an effervescently overflowing champagne glass. Without recourse to any illusionistic modelling, the artist succeeds in evoking the corporeality and movement of the figure by the use of increasing and diminishing contour lines alone. This language of lines can be traced directly to the influence of East Asian art. One example that Bonnard undoubtedly saw is the sketch by the seventeenth-century Japanese artist Shōkadō, also known as Shōjō, published by Louis Gonse in his famous book *L'Art japonais* from 1883 (fig. 1). He was also inspired by the subtly rendered curve and foam of Hokusai's famous *Under the Wave off Kanagawa*, echoes of which are cannily transposed to the frothing wave of champagne in his poster, making it highly eye-catching from a distance (p. 167).

A similar deployment of line can also be found in Bonnard's four panels of *Women in the Garden* (1890/1891), initially conceived as a screen but later separated (p. 279). In each one, in kakemono format, Bonnard presents a female figure in a garden setting.[11] The first panel features a young woman in a bright red dress with white polka dots, and a dog leaping by her side. The undulating, increasing and diminishing contour lines lend a certain corporeality, while the arabesque adds a dynamic slant to the figure, which seems to twist in a way that makes contour and contortion meld into a single form.

The "S" curve of the body is typical of female figures in Japanese woodblock prints. It is often emphasised by a bend of the waist and knees and by a distinctly forward-leaning upper body – a movement reminiscent of Japanese dance, which lends the figures a certain grace. Bonnard's female figure has affinities with the figures by Utamaro (p. 278). In comparison to the graceful, softly flowing lines of the Japanese original, Bonnard deploys a strongly ornamented contour to infuse the figure of the young woman with a sense of temperament and joyful excitement. At the same time, the arabesque is like a sign that suggests movement, going beyond the figure itself to incorporate the human, the dog, the branches and the flowers in equal measure, revealing a dynamism inherent in all living things.

The sweeping arabesques in Denis's religious and Symbolist paintings of 1891/1892 envelop not only the figures, but also the long trains of their robes. This is where the Japanese influence converges with other aspects that were also of importance to Denis – particularly the slender, "incorporeal" figures in the style of Fra Angelico.[12] In his *July* depiction of 1892 (p. 295) from the four-part cycle of the seasons *Panels for a Young Girl's Room*, graceful figures move delicately in an ornamentally evoked garden landscape. Here, Denis has used the arabesque as a very personal way of expressing his own religious ideal. The flat figures framed by a subtly regular and continuous contour line bear witness to his study of the elegant figures by Utamaro, Harunobu and Shinsai and their graceful bearing (fig. 2). Through these curved silhouettes and undulating hemlines, Denis portrays not only the dance-like movements of the women, but also their emotions in their rites of passage. The subtlety and sensibility of the line becomes an expression of the inner soul.

Other works from this period show how Denis gradually released the arabesque from the actual description of the subject matter, making it an element in its own right. In his *Sleeping Young Woman* of 1892 (fig. 3), the flow of the line illustrates her integration into the world of sleep and dream, while the pastel "unearthly" mauve and linden green of her dress and face further emphasise a state of reverie. The elegiac lengthening of the neck recalls the female figures of Suzuki Harunobu and Kikugawa Eizan (p. 141). His illustrations for André Gide's *Le Voyage d'Urien* in 1893 take this autonomy of line still one step further.[13]

The discovery of colour

The unreal atmosphere of *July* owes much to the nuanced palette of closely related greens and yellows that place the entire scene within the sphere of legend. Interestingly, in Bonnard's more realistic garden portrayal *Twilight (The Game of Croquet)* (fig. 4), also created in 1892, we find a similar palette of hues, ranging from dark green to a pale greenish-yellow. Through the use of multiple perspective, the light-filled image of the dancing girls in their white dresses, full of excitement and motion, evokes an imaginary and paradisiacal world far removed from the reality of the schematic and hieratic figures in the croquet game. A statement by Bonnard, cited by Antoine Terrasse, sums up how he was influenced by the unaccustomed colour of Japanese woodblock prints: "In my encounter with these simple, folkish images, I realised that the colour could express everything without requiring any recourse to relieve or modelling. I realised that it was possible to transpose light, form and character without 'valeurs', only through colour."[14] This statement clearly refers to the intensively luminous, almost lurid colours that had been introduced since the end of Japanese isolationist policies and with the introduction of the bright European aniline paints that had banished the subtle tones of earlier plant-based colours in Japanese woodblock prints.

A new concept of space

In his *Women with a Dog* from 1891 (p. 289), Bonnard devised spatial solutions that would become crucial to his later work. The main group in the foreground is portrayed at a steep angle from above and drawn so close to the viewer that the figures are cropped on all sides. This Japanese-inspired viewpoint allowed Bonnard to evoke a sense of spatial cohesion within the plane in spite of the exaggerated flatness of the chequered pattern,[15] in similar fashion to a theatre scene by Utagawa Kuniyoshi in the collection of Maurice Denis (p. 287). Surprisingly, the remaining family members in the background are seen from a different, slightly upward-slanting, angle. When the viewer's gaze leaps from one group to the other, a sense of space is created between the figures.

The direct influence of East Asian art in terms of no longer focusing on a single line of flight, as in the traditional Western system of central perspective, converges here with indirect impulses from Gauguin and Van Gogh. The Chinese and Japanese landscape paintings in the upright kakemono format – which are to be read compositionally more in a vertical direction than towards the depth of the background – do not possess a consistently uniform spatial structure. Instead, they have several focal points.[16] Chinese art theoreticians have developed the pattern of three viewpoints[17] uniting these angles in one and the same landscape painting. East Asian artists do not seek to represent a single aspect of the landscape viewed from one specific vantage point. Instead, they treat the image as a fragment of a greater whole that is to be viewed according to a holistic entity in which the viewer is also an integral part (fig. 5).[18] The Nabi, too, sought to capture the essence of things and to express the emotions they triggered instead of merely portraying their outward appearance. As Bonnard explained to his nephew Charles Terrasse, "the problem of drawing is portraying the dimensions and objects within a space on a flat surface [...] The eye of the painter lends the objects a human value and reproduces things the way the human eye perceives them. And that view is mobile. And that view is variable".[19] Bonnard would continue to pursue this multiple perspective throughout his career.

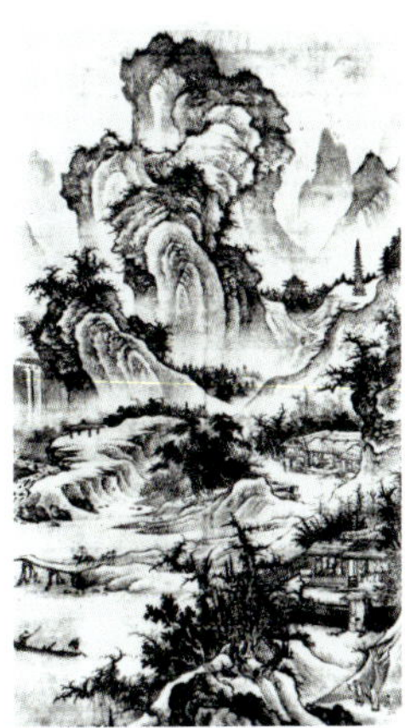

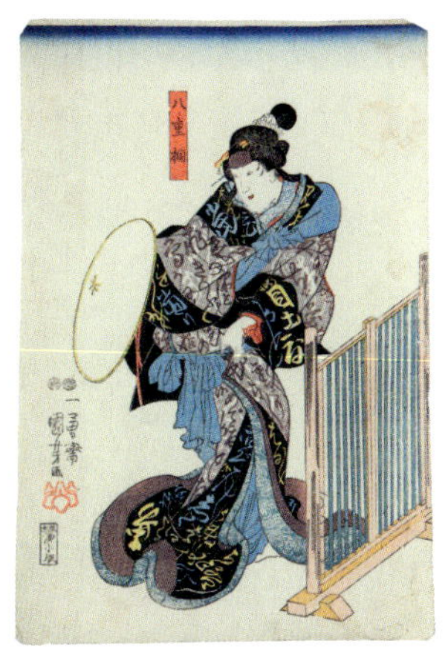

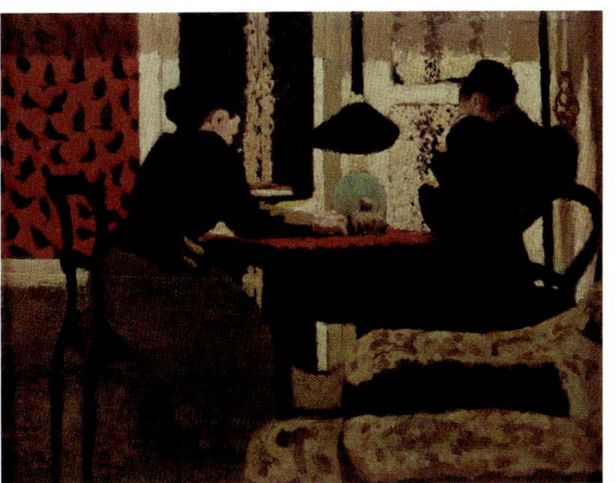

5 After Kuo Hsi (circa 1020–1075), *Literati living as Hermits in the Mountains*, probably Ming period, Taichung (Formosa), National Palace Museum Collection

6 Utagawa Kuniyoshi, *The Actor Ichimura Uzaemon XII in the Role of Princess Yaegaki*, 1848, Private Collection (formerly Denis Collection)

7 Édouard Vuillard, *Two Women under the Lamp*, 1892, Musée de l'Annonciade, Saint-Tropez

In 1893, Denis painted a portrait of the wife of his Nabi friend Paul Ranson in the tall and narrow format inspired by Japanese kakemonos: *Madame Ranson, in Green* (p. 277). While her upper body, in a chequered blouse, is seen from a slightly upward-looking angle, the view of her long black skirt slants sharply downwards and the angle of the patterned rug beneath her chair is so steep that it seems about to slip away. Few works by Denis are so strongly *japonesque*. In depicting the way Marie-France Ranson leans against the back of the starkly downward-sweeping chair, he has even adopted the slight twist between upper and lower body that is so often found in Japanese art. And he has signed the painting vertically, East Asian style. The unusual, reduced palette of green and black tones adds to the enigmatic atmosphere of the portrait. Around 1891, he had created a similarly proportioned work in horizontal format inspired by Japanese *emakimono* scrolls: *Self-Portrait beneath Trees* (p. 294).

The East Asian sense of space of the empty surface inspired Bonnard's composition for his four-panel folding screen from 1894/1897, *Nannies' Promenade, Frieze of Carriages* (p. 86). From 1893 onwards, Bonnard's female figures, especially those in his Parisian street scenes, are imbued with an unusually humorous, caricature-like sense of motion. The exaggerated poses, no longer adhering to the laws of *contrapposto*, are clearly inspired by later woodblock print masters such as Utagawa Kuniyoshi (fig. 6). In the screen from 1894/1897,[20] he characterises the movements of the elegant Parisian woman in similar fashion, with a bend of the knee and a twist of the hip, emphasising the countermovement of upper and lower body to create an impression of foreground and background, in spite of the flatness of the silhouette. The group of figures with dogs and children strolling across the Place de la Concorde develops freely on an empty plane, without any underpinning, so that their movement alone creates a tangible sense of space. The four panels of the screen are designed as a single uniform image to be read, in the East Asian manner, from right to left, whereby the aesthetic effect is altered depending on how the screen is positioned. The gaze is drawn from the foreground figures, seen from above, across the empty space towards the frontally viewed female figures by the balustrade and from there to the procession of carriages, portrayed almost in miniature. As the gaze shifts, the empty surface becomes a place the viewer wanders through. In this work, Bonnard puts one of the fundamental principles of East Asian art in the service of his new compositional approach. "East Asian formal structure is […] decisively determined by the dialectics of fullness and emptiness," writes Dietrich Seckel.[21] "Emptiness is manifested primarily as a surface […] but it usually has a sense of space, evoking mist, water or sky, for instance, but above all signifying the 'ground of all things'."[22]

Félix Vallotton often used "mobile" perspective in combination with a steep view from above, resulting in some surprising compositional solutions. His *Washerwomen at Étretat* from 1899 (Private Collection) presents a bird's-eye view of an expansive beach where the gaze sweeps across the group of washer women and the ornamental coastline towards the horizonless distance of the ocean. This highly unusual handling of space can also be found in many of the woodblock prints by Utagawa Hiroshige (p. 209). Such steeply angled viewpoints can be found, in especially striking forms, in Valloton's woodcuts like *The*

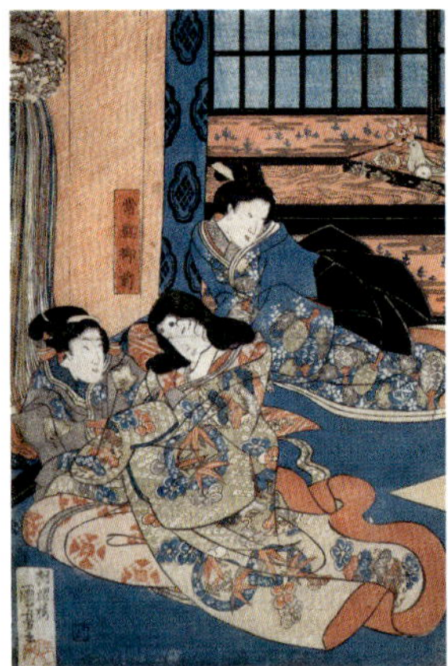
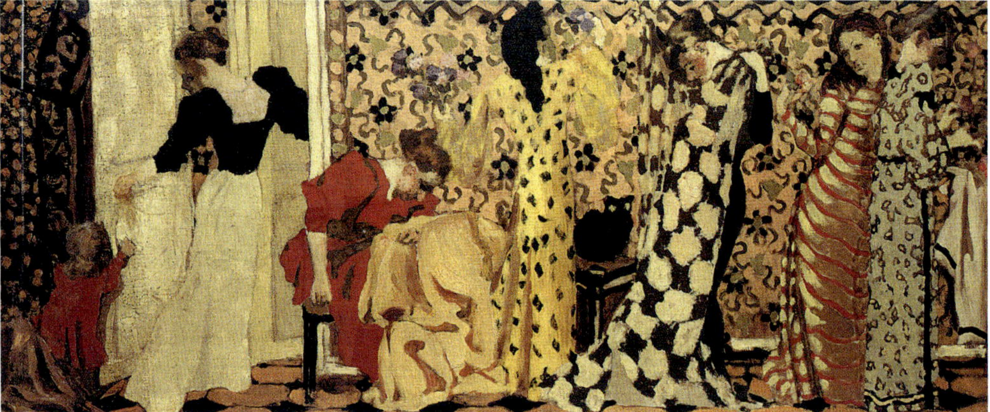

Demonstration of 1893, *The "Bon Marché" Department Store* of 1893 (p. 285) or *Laziness* of 1896 (p. 283). In the latter, Vallotton makes particular use of the multiple geometric patterns of Japanese *katagami* (paper stencils) (p. 282), spreading them out over the sofa beneath the seductive nude.

In other prints, he captures the crowds thronging the boulevards of Paris just as they are being buffeted by some outward force such as a sudden rain shower or a gust of wind. In *The Gust of Wind* of 1894 (p. 284), Vallotton stylises the dynamics of the wind by creating whorls of lines that seem to take on a life of their own. The figures – losing their balance – are caught up in the movement and sway in its rhythm. Japanese artists often created similar portrayals of the effects of a gust of wind – a theme that was especially beloved of Harunobu, Toyonobu, Kiyonaga, Hokusai and Hiroshige (p. 192). Like them, Vallotton often combines this effect with that of a rain shower, depicting the rain in heavy, parallel, diagonal strokes as can be seen in *The Shower*[23] from his series *Paris Intense* dating from 1894.

Ornamentalisation as a compositional device

Vuillard also deployed multiple perspectives. For instance, he integrated early interior scenes such as his *Two Women Under the Lamp* of 1892 (fig. 7) into a system of horizontals and verticals whilst using this linear system to create a deliberate spatial obfuscation. Similarly, Japanese artists such as Harunobu, Kiyonaga and Toyokuni also liked to place their figures against a background of house walls, sliding doors and screens, whereby the floor area, as in the work of Vuillard, appears to be on a level with the frontally viewed background wall (fig. 8). The enigmatic, shadowy deep-black figures of the artist's mother and sister, depicted in the style of *ombres chinoises,* conjure something of the unfathomable atmosphere of Symbolist theatre of the time. In Vuillard's *The Dressmaking Studio II* of 1892 (fig. 9) – an element in the six-part interior decor for Paul Desmarais – the busy seamstresses and vain clients, with their undulating contours and brightly coloured and patterned dresses, converge with the ornamental patterns of wallpaper, curtains and flooring in a way that seems to weave everything into a single overwhelming tapestry. Vuillard's ornamentalisation proves to be a new compositional device that binds the figures into their surroundings and, at the same time, presents a certain derealisation of the human individual. Late nineteenth-century Japanese woodblock print artists – most notably, Toyokuni, Kunisada, Kuniyoshi and Gakutei – taught European artists to recognise the ornamental in their surroundings and to transpose the visible into the ornamental (pp. 152–153, 290–291).

The fragmented image

One particularly distinguishing characteristic of many Nabi paintings is the way they are cropped. The portrayal continues beyond the edge of the picture, giving the impression that the picture itself is merely a

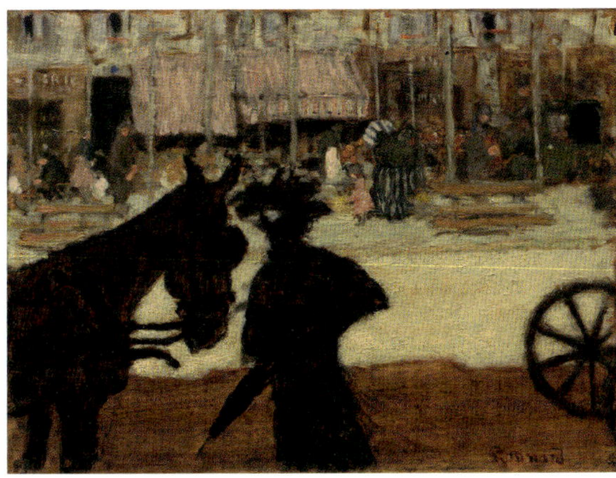

8 Utagawa Kuniyoshi, *Tokiwa Gozen, Courtesans of Minamoto no Yoshibune*, 19th c., Private Collection (formerly Bonnard Collection)
9 Édouard Vuillard, *The Dressmaking Studio II*, 1892, for the interior of Paul Desmarais, Private Collection
10 Pierre Bonnard, *The Cab Horse*, circa 1895, National Gallery of Art, Washington, Ailsa Mellon Bruce Collection

fragment of some larger context. In his endeavour to overcome the anonymity of the city, Bonnard occasionally picks out individual figures as they pass by fleetingly. In *The Passerby* from 1894 (p. 288), the head of the Parisian woman moving past, who wears a hat that seems to be created out of towering arabesques, is portrayed in close-up, taking in more than half of the entire picture plane. Portrayed at an angle slightly from above, this passer-by does not have eye contact with the viewer, thus avoiding any form of direct confrontation. Bonnard has clearly taken his inspiration from the so-called "large head portraits" or *hanshin-e* and *oku-bi-e* of Japanese actors (p. 124), but has interpreted them in a new way that embodies the urban lifestyle of the Parisian woman.

Whereas Degas and the impressionists used cropped images to convey a sense of some fleeting or chance impression, like a photographic snapshot capturing a moment in time, Bonnard's compositions are to be regarded more in the sense of an East Asian view "where the seemingly random and fragmentary aspects of life give a hint of the larger whole represented therein" (p. 214).[24] In his Parisian street scenes, the passers-by, horses, carriages and wheels cropped by the frame of the picture represent the irregular rhythms of city life that cannot be rendered in its entirety (fig. 10). According to Bonnard, "strict cropping of the view almost always gives a false impression. The second degree of composition consists of bringing in certain visual elements outside that rectangle".[25] In short, Bonnard was not interested in cutting anything out of the picture, but in evoking a wider world.

The inspiration that the four artists mentioned in this essay deduced from East Asian art is reflected in their fundamental decisions on certain key issues in painting. Each one of these artists developed their own formal syntax as a means of creating something new and distinctive. Their East Asian discoveries worked on each of them in very different ways right through to their later work – although in the case of Pierre Bonnard, this influence remains particularly evident.[26]

This essay is based in part on earlier publications by the author on this subject.

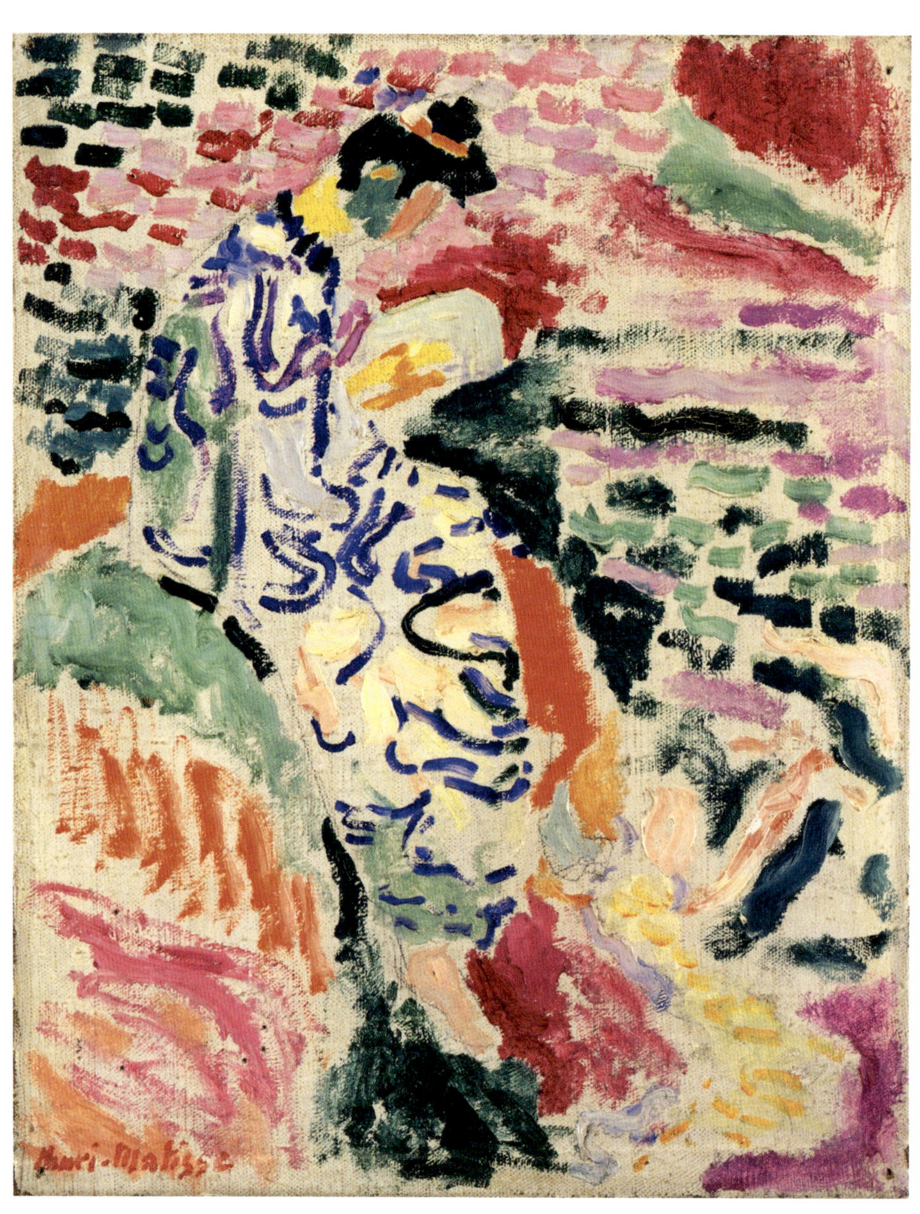

44 Henri Matisse, *La Japonaise: Woman beside the Water*, 1905

More confirmation than inspiration – *Japonisme* in French painting of the early twentieth century

Peter Kropmanns

in memoriam Antoine Terrasse (1928–2013)

The generation of French painters who were born in and shaped by the late nineteenth century, and who were destined to be active far into the twentieth century, included Pierre Bonnard, Henri Matisse, Albert Marquet, André Derain and Robert Delaunay. In their youth, they all had much easier access to Japanese colour woodblock prints than had been the case in the 1860s. By the end of the century, *Japonisme* had long since ceased to be reserved for a small circle of initiates.

The preceding essays in this catalogue have already provided a comprehensive presentation of the history of *Japonisme* and its different facets. Let us simply recall that Paris – the city where the new generation was educated and where it underwent its trial by fire – undoubtedly played a significant role in the transmission of Japanese art. Paris was the site of the World Fair of 1867 where Japan was represented for the first time, fourteen years after an American fleet forced the opening of the country and nine years after a trade agreement with France. Paris was also the city in which numerous articles and books on Japanese art were published, in particular on Utagawa Hiroshige and Katsushika Hokusai, accompanying the enthusiastic reception of Japanese colour woodblock prints.[1] In 1888, the magazine *Le Japon artistique* (published in English as *Artistic Japan*) was founded, and Parisian art dealers not only regularly had Japanese art on offer but organised exhibitions as well, including an 1893 show at Galerie Durand-Ruel dedicated to Kitagawa Utamaro and Utagawa Hiroshige. The Musée Guimet was opened in 1889, the Musée Cernuschi in 1898 and the Musée d'Ennery in 1908 – three museums devoted to Asian art and which held collections of Japanese colour woodblock prints. Lastly, there was the 1906 Parisian premiere of Puccini's opera *Madama Butterfly*, first performed in Milan and Brescia in 1904, which made an impression on artists as well.[2]

Depictions of Japanese women in kimonos, or rather European women in Japanese costume holding a fan as their key accessory, multiplied in the art of the latter half of the nineteenth century. Yet even then, "*Japonisme*" was understood to be more than the cyclical accumulation of certain visual motifs – in contrast to the term "Orientalism", which indeed remained closely tied to specific motifs. *Japonisme*, since defined according to the formal and technical characteristics of a work of art,[3] can be traced as a phenomenon into the twentieth century.

What fascinated Whistler, Manet, Degas, Van Gogh and Gauguin as well as such painters as Bonnard, Matisse, Marquet, Derain and Delaunay about Japanese colour woodblock prints were the often glowing colours, the use of line, the emphasis on surface, the staggered use of visual grounds, the strict steering of the gaze to favour certain perspectives and detail views, unusual dimensions, the concentration on a few details to sometimes make them seem "zoomed in on", and the – supposed – simplicity of the overall impression.

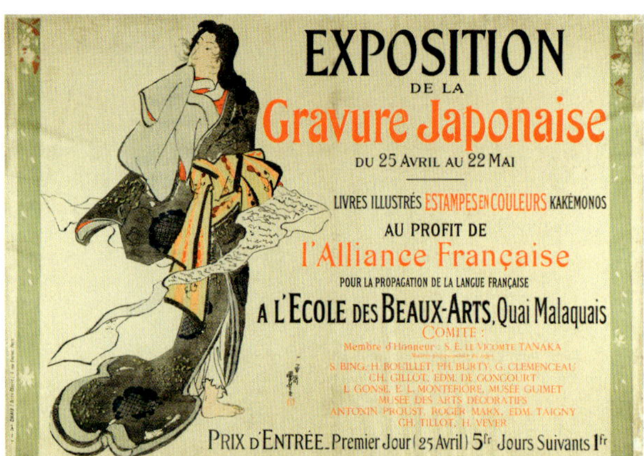

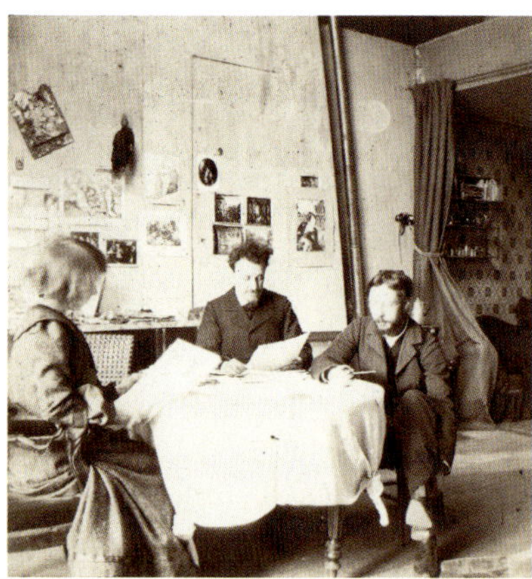

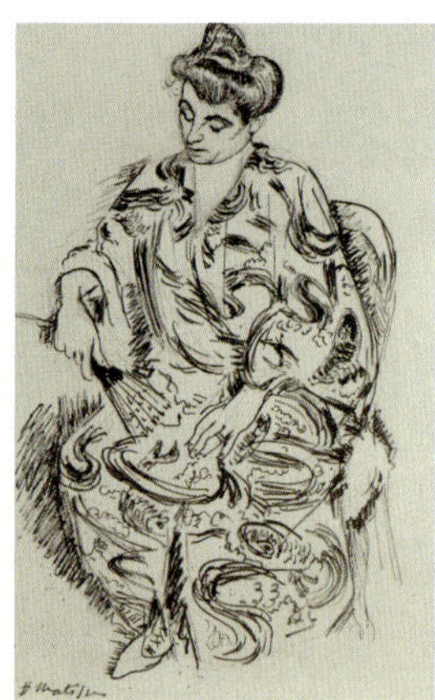

With Japan's participation in the Paris World Fair of 1900, providing for the first time a comprehensive look at Japanese culture on European soil, the purely motif-related fashion went into decline. The formal aspects specific to colour woodblock prints, however, continued to enjoy an audience and lost none of their effect. A third wave of *Japonisme* came in the years between 1909 and 1914, with the Musée des Arts décoratifs organising an annual exhibition that incorporated a variety of Japanese colour woodblock prints.[4]

The Japanese colour woodblock print had represented virgin territory for the artists of the 1860s and the 1870s – the pioneers, as it were, in Europe's discovery of the genre. By contrast, the younger generation grew up in a climate in which word had spread about how fevered the previous decades' artistic encounter with prints from Japan had been and why. The painters who, in the 1890s, stood at the outset of their careers simultaneously developed within a milieu in which *Japonisme* had already made a major impression on the – its own – present. To innovate, these painters had no choice but to react both to the art of Japan, on the one hand, and to French art as it had been changed by the influence of Japan, on the other. Late blossoming of *Japonisme* included Symbolist painting, containing at times *Japonisme*-inflected elements, and in particular the painting, architecture, interior design and decorative arts of art nouveau in France. *Japonisme* received a further boost from a group of artists who formed in the 1890s, the Nabi. They included Félix Vallotton, Édouard Vuillard and Pierre Bonnard, also known as "le Nabi très japonard".[5]

Naive imagery in screaming colours

After finishing his studies in law and gaining first experiences as a painter, Pierre Bonnard (1867–1947) may have come into contact with Japanese graphic art as early as 1889 at the Paris World Fair for which the Eiffel Tower was built. It is certain that he had, by this time, already made the acquaintance of multiple exponents of progressive painting, painters who were not only among those who were enthusiastic about Japanese art but who were practitioners of *Japonisme* as well: Maurice Denis, Paul Sérusier and Paul Ranson. In 1889, Bonnard attended an exhibition with works by Paul Gauguin, Émile Bernard and Louis Anquetin. In 1890, he saw an exceptionally comprehensive show of Japanese masters at the École des Beaux-Arts, comprising seven hundred works (fig. 1). One aspect among many that may have interested him there was the virtuosic treatment of figures, seemingly floating in space yet still anchored in the surface. Experimentation with simultaneous perspectives combining different points of view was another inspiration that Bonnard owed to this exhibition.[6] Lastly, he worked with extremely narrow and tall dimensions derived from kakemonos and folding screens, which had been used previously for tapestry curtains and posters but not paintings (p. 329). Bonnard's fascination was so great that he felt a need not only to acquire a collection of Japanese colour woodblock prints and keep them in sight to the greatest extent possible, but also to imitate them and then go further – to take their principles and appropriate them, develop them and bring them into harmony

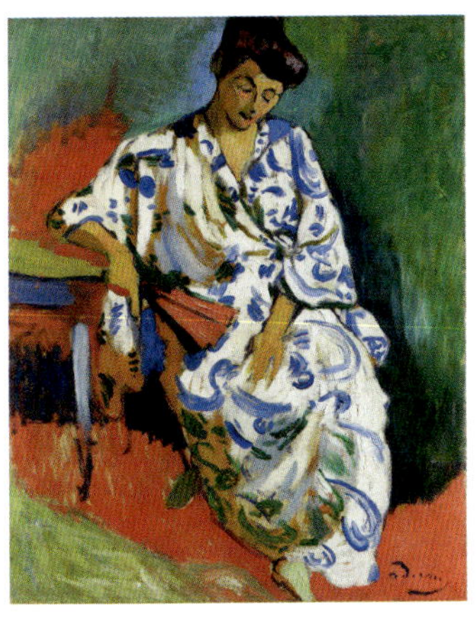

1 Jules Chéret, Poster for the *Exhibition of Japanese Prints* at the École des Beaux-Arts, Paris, 25.4–22.5.1890, Museum für Kunst und Gewerbe Hamburg
2 Anonymous, Marthe de Méligny (born Maria Boursin), Pierre Bonnard and a friend (Félicien Fagus?) in Bonnard's studio (65, rue de Douai, Paris), circa 1905–1910, Private Collection; on the wall are a palette, sketches and reproductions of works of art, including an engraving after Giorgione's *Concerto campestre* (also called *Pastorale*) from the Louvre and, to the left of the stove flue, a Japanese print
3 Henri Matisse, *Madame Matisse as a Japanese Woman*, 1905, Private Collection
4 André Derain, *Madame Matisse in a Kimono*, 1905, Private Collection, Courtesy of Nevill Keating Pictures, London

with ideas of his own (fig. 2 and p. 330).[7] Bonnard recalled later: "There (in the department stores) I found prints on crepe or rice paper with astonishing colours [...]. I covered the walls of my room with this naive imagery in screaming colours. [...] What I saw before me was something very alive, very sophisticated."[8]

Bonnard also became active as an amateur photographer in this period; his oldest extant photograph is from 1891. In this situation – a first acquaintance with the *Japonisme* of his contemporaries, discovery of the Japanese original works and first experiences with the medium of photography that remained off limits to wide segments of the population – can be seen a state of affairs that affected all other artists. Put another way, a more complex situation existed on the eve of the twentieth century than in Manet's and Whistler's era. The "pioneering period" was past, the presence and reception of Japanese graphic art had now become established, access to the "sources" had become significantly easier than it had been a few decades previously, and at the same time *Japonisme,* which was altering habits of seeing, had become so widespread that people had become almost unaware of it. There was also the fact that photography had entered into artists' studios, not only as a snapshot, an aid to memory and a means of gathering subject matter, but also as a medium with interesting formal and aesthetic characteristics of its own. To put it more pointedly, several factors had arisen in many artists' studios by the year 1900, making it difficult to clearly establish today whether certain works of painting and graphic art solely have their origins in the encounter with Japanese art, in the impact of *Japonisme*'s first and second generations or, indeed, in the influence of photography. In many cases, the individual impulses are mixed and blended in the result.

Henri Matisse (1869–1954) was a pupil at the Académie Julian and the École des Beaux-Arts in the 1890s, like Bonnard, although he was later to move in different circles and pursue paths of his own. Matisse nonetheless may have come across Japanese art early as well. He later claimed to remember first taking conscious note of Japanese colour woodblock prints in the Parisian quarter of Saint-Germain-des-Prés, in rue de Seine, where dealers sold graphic art out of boxes at shop entrances.[9] Matisse did not name a certain date or even a year. Even so, the landscapes that he painted between 1896 and 1906 on the Breton island of Belle-Île and in Collioure show a specific use of perspective more likely to have derived from an examination of Japanese art than from an interest in photography. Although Matisse started out living in cramped conditions typical of Paris, he adopted unusual points of view for his interiors as well, including vistas from an elevated perspective – views from a window, for instance, with the window jamb partly visible.

After painting his wife in a Japanese gown in 1901, Matisse drew and painted her as a Japanese woman again in 1905 (fig. 3 and p. 94).[10] The star witness to one of these sittings, at which Amélie Matisse posed as model, was André Derain (1880–1954), who also painted Madame Matisse as a Japanese woman (fig. 4). What is more, Derain showed his older colleague Matisse how he placed Amélie Matisse in this attire on the beach.[11]

The two painters thus revealed an interest in Japanese culture that was very much in the foreground. Many of their predecessors had harboured the same interest over the preceding four decades. Or is the

Japonisme manifest here a result of both the "superficial" subject matter of a woman in a kimono and the ornamental penetration of figure and ground, as in Japanese colour woodblock prints? Are Matisse and Derain here carrying forward the "ornamental" visual language not only of Japanese artists but also of Vuillard and Bonnard, who drew on Japanese sources before them? It is a difficult question to answer, not least because Matisse (who came from the north of France, famous for its textile industry) showed a weakness for fabric and fabric patterns early on, another source that should be taken seriously.[12] Whatever the case may be, many other works by Derain and Matisse show a thoroughgoing examination of Japanese art.

One impetus for Matisse to take an interest in Japanese colour woodblock prints may have come from Gustave Moreau, the teacher who was most important to him. The Symbolist Moreau kept his work as a painter in his studio in rue de La Rochefoucauld so separate and distinct from his work as a teacher at the École des Beaux-Arts that his pupils may hardly have seen – with their eyes – his bold and so-modernist-seeming colour experiments. Yet Moreau was regarded as a very open man and enjoyed sharing his experiences with his students. Japanese graphic art inspired Moreau to paint watercolours (fig. 5) in 1869, at the outset of the first major wave of *Japonisme*. He later gained further prominence as a connoisseur of Japanese art.[13]

Albert Marquet (1875–1947) was also a pupil of Moreau's. Unlike Bonnard and Matisse, who knew and appreciated one another early on but only entered into deeper dialogue as friends at an advanced age, Marquet and Matisse were already close friends before 1900. Both worked predominantly as painters at the time, but each produced numerous drawings as well, including sketches and caricatures. Although many early drawings by Matisse have been lost, a number of extant graphic works by Marquet can give an idea of what also interested Matisse at the time, including impressions of wandering through Parisian streets, fleeting scenes with passers-by captured with a few quickly placed strokes. Marquet's works recall depictions by Japanese graphic artists; their minimalist lines and swings of the brush have a calligraphic quality (fig. 6). Marquet appears to express such an interest in calligraphy when informing Matisse in 1899: "I am writing to you with an amazing Japanese brush." The accompanying drawing shows passers-by on a bridge, likely the Pont des Arts in Paris, and underneath them a figure who resembles a geisha.[14] When Marquet wanted to visit Berlin in 1909, Matisse recommended Hotel Deutscher Kaiser so that he could visit the two museums across the way, one devoted to the Far East – by which Matisse meant the Ethnological Museum.[15] Matisse knew only too well that Marquet would be interested in the museums' collections, and Marquet's widow Marcelle Marquet remembered later: "To reach the stage where every dot and every stroke I paint will be alive. How often I have heard this expression of Hokusai's quoted!"[16] Matisse himself went so far as to say: "When I see Hokusai I think of our Marquet – and vice versa. What I mean is not imitation of Hokusai, but similitude."[17]

Light, shapes and characters from colours

Derain intentionally followed Matisse to Collioure in 1905 to be able to work together with him. A portrait like Derain's of Madame Matisse, which can be seen as a homage to the two artists' shared passion for Japanese art, is an exception among the group of paintings that Derain created there on the Mediterranean. What really interested him above all else was landscape painting. Although landscape works find mention in every history of Fauvism on the strength of their colours alone, they are often equally distinguished by a use of perspective that clearly indicates Derain's *Japonisme*, which likely came down to him through the art of Van Gogh. A variety of Derain's works painted on the Seine and the Thames are conceived in this way, but his true epitome of *Japonisme* in the early twentieth century is *The Two Barges* (fig. 7 and p. 10). Before his stay in Collioure, Derain had begun to experiment with Chinese ink and to sketch chrysanthemums and figures. Yet his *Japonisme* fell by the wayside when he turned away from the colourism that he had pursued with Matisse and moved on – first to Cubism and then to a method of his own.

The early work of Robert Delaunay (1885–1941) reflects his encounter with the principles of neo-impressionism led by Georges Seurat and Paul Signac. Seurat and Signac had already found numerous younger imitators by 1900, many of whom swiftly moved beyond the dominance of individual dots and

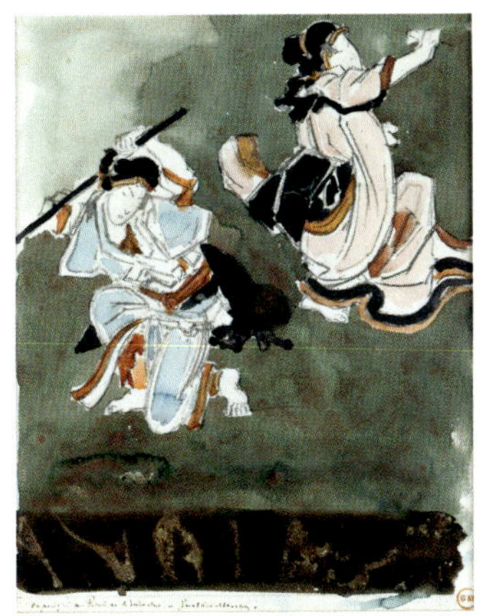

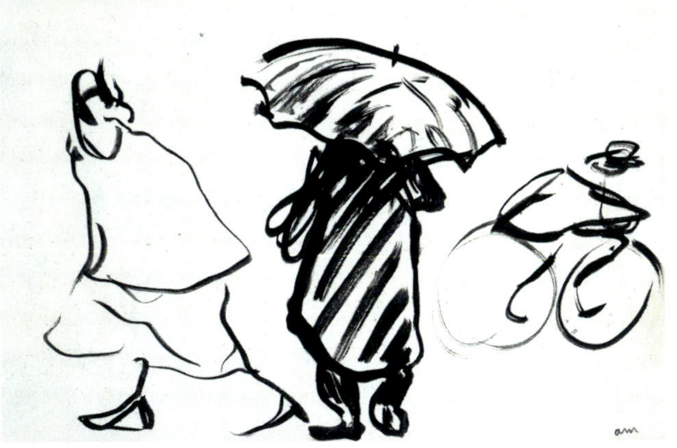

5 Gustave Moreau, *Two Japanese Kabuki Actors in Female Roles*, undated (before 1869), watercolour drawing after a triptych by Utagawa Kunikiyo II, Musée Gustave Moreau, Paris

6 Albert Marquet, *Woman, Figure with Umbrella, Bicycle*, 1904, Musée d'art moderne André Malraux, Le Havre

dabs of paint. Around 1905, Delaunay established that Derain and Matisse were exploring neo-impressionism through the use of energetic brushstrokes and small areas of colour. Delaunay took this up in 1906 when painting the portrait of his fellow painter Jean Metzinger, who was roughly his age, with a tulip in his buttonhole, using a solid, compact style seemingly based on the structure of Paul Cézanne (fig. 8). Delaunay also looked back on other visual experiences, including the art of Gauguin and Van Gogh. In a manner similar to those artists' explicit expressions of their passion for all things Japanese, Delaunay placed Metzinger in front of a portrait of a Japanese woman pinned to the wall, presumably referring not to an individual interest of Delaunay or Metzinger, but instead to a shared passion.[18]

By this time, Bonnard's interest in Japanese graphic art had long since become a settled part of his personality as an artist. Many works from this period and later years reflect the artist's study of certain aspects of the prints with which he, as a young painter and graphic artist, had "wallpapered" his room. Putting the narrow portrait formats of the sort represented by the painting from Cologne (p. 329) behind him, in *The Sunny Terrace* (1939–1945, Private Collection), he turned to extreme landscape dimensions related to the *emakimono* format.[19] More enduring, however, were his use of diagonality, overhead views, simultaneous perspectives and a penchant for simplification. What was clear for Bonnard himself was that the encounter with Japanese colour woodblock prints led to understanding the possibility of translating light, shapes and character only with the aid of colour and without falling back on tonal values (regulating light and dark).[20]

Bonnard created his painting *The Studio with Mimosa* (1939–1946) at his house in Le Cannet, near Cannes, with a magnificent mimosa shrub in front of the studio window (fig. 9). The window's grille structure and the diagonal rail of a platform built into the studio provide the painting with a structure behind which small, subtly nuanced areas and dabs of colour seem to float in space, evoking paradisiacal nature extending out to the sea and the Massif d'Esterel mountain range. The separation of and connection between interior and exterior, as well as the simultaneity of what is apparent on first glance and what opens up to the gaze only gradually, including the suggestion of a truncated figure at the lower left edge of the painting, go back to Bonnard's interest in mechanisms of visual perception – and, indeed, the attempt to translate light, shapes and character solely by means of colour. Although the painting paraphrases no specific Japanese inspiration in any way, Bonnard's internalisation of the stylistic principles of the colour woodblock print may be traced down to this late masterpiece all the same.

In 1946, Bonnard wrote that he had already been interested in the wonderful profusion of colour ("bariolage magnifique") in Japanese crepe prints back in his youth, emphasising that he only later came to understand the beauty of the great Japanese graphic artists, who were more restrained and explored the relationships of pure colour in a less obvious way.[21] Here, he was alluding to an – apparently highly productive – misunderstanding that Matisse also spoke of: "To tell the truth, these prints [the ones purchased in rue de Seine] were mediocre reproductions, and even so I was not moved in the same way when I had the opportunity to see the originals. They did not bring to me the same freshness of a revelation."[22]

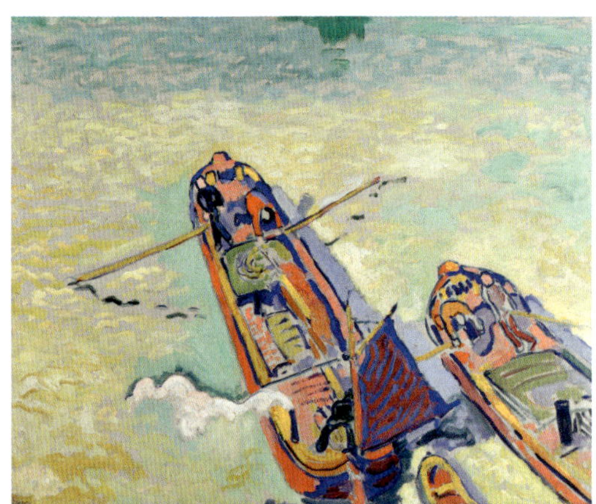

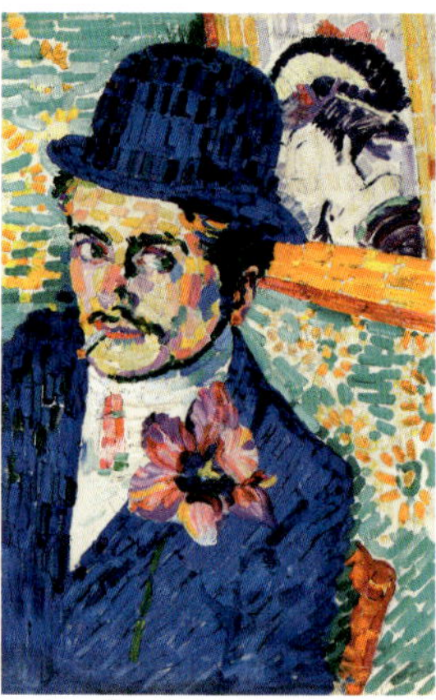

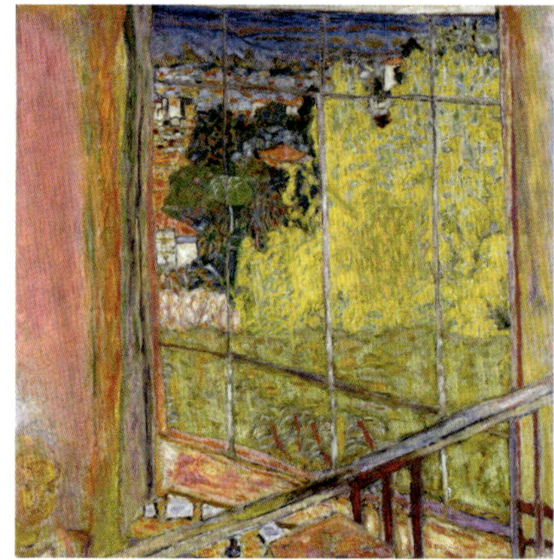

Matisse asserted elsewhere: "Bonnard told me the same thing and added that he was a bit disappointed by the originals. This was explained by the patina and a bit of discolouration of the old prints. If we had seen only the originals, we might not have been impressed to the same extent as we were by the reprints."[23]

The artistic generation that is at the centre of our examination here did not often speak of the significance of Japanese art for its own work. Thus, the influence of Japanese art on modernist artists has occasionally become a topic of debate – for example, in the assessment of Matisse's oeuvre. The latter left his mark, as has been mentioned, with a number of paintings and drawings with only superficial connections to *Japonisme.* Another example of these works is a drawing made in 1914 of his daughter Marguerite in Japanese dress, entitled *Utamaro*. Many years later, his sitter recalled that her father was an enthusiastic museum goer and went to the Musée Guimet and the Musée Cernuschi with particular frequency for a time. She also recounted that her father often saw important specimens of Japanese and Chinese art at the art dealer Charles Vignier's gallery between 1911 and 1914. But he never bought anything and, in her view, judging by his work, was not really influenced by the works he saw there.[24]

What Marguerite did not mention is the series of annual exhibitions at the Musée des Arts décoratifs organised by Charles Vignier and Raymond Koechlin between 1909 and 1914, showing the works of colour woodblock print artists including Suzuki Haronubu, Utagawa Hiroshige, Katsushika Hokusai, Torii Kiyonaga, Utagawa Toyokuni and Kitagawa Utamaro, and which Matisse, in spite of his extensive travelling, surely did not ignore entirely.[25] Matisse regarded the works from Japan as a "lesson in purity and harmony",[26] but did not go into further detail. We only know that he owned a small collection of art including paintings by Courbet, Gauguin and Cézanne and to which, sometime between 1912 and 1914, he added a Japanese colour woodblock print depicting a leaping carp.[27] It is telling that this was exactly the period in which Matisse repeatedly painted interiors with goldfish bowls, subject matter that had been quite uncommon in European painting until that time. Matisse may have been inspired to paint his depictions of goldfish in much the same way as Claude Debussy was inspired by a lacquer koi that he owned to write his 1907 composition *Poissons d'or*.

Matisse's biographer Pierre Schneider, an expert on the artist's work and less biased than his daughter, also strongly relativised Matisse's *Japonisme*. His pronounced interest in Byzantine, Islamic and Chinese art should certainly not be overlooked. However, such authors as Matisse's important collector Albert C. Barnes, Robert Reiff, and the biographers Alfred H. Barr, Jr. and Jack Flam, dedicate extensive discussions to possible connections between Matisse in France and the art of Japan.[28] In his creative approach to Japanese prints, Matisse was undoubtedly in pursuit of a synthesis, the roots of which were intertwined with other components into unrecognisability, including through generalisation and internalisation.[29] And Matisse undoubtedly also drew on "second-hand suggestions of Japanese prints" – in other words, to the *Japonisme* of Degas, Van Gogh or Vuillard.[30] Indeed, a series of works suggest connections to Japanese art through their use of perspective (cf. p. 327) and figures intersecting with the frame, as seen in paintings

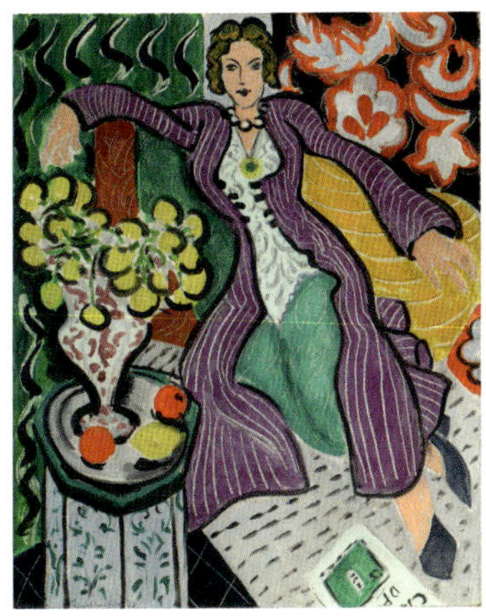

7 André Derain, *The Two Barges*, 1906, Musée National d'Art Moderne / Centre de Création Industrielle, Centre Pompidou, Paris
8 Robert Delaunay, *Man with a Tulip (Portrait of Jean Metzinger)*, 1906, Private Collection
9 Pierre Bonnard, *The Studio with Mimosa*, 1939–1946, Musée National d'Art Moderne / Centre de Création Industrielle, Centre Pompidou, Paris
10 Henri Matisse, *Woman in a Purple Coat*, 1937, The Museum of Fine Arts, Houston, Texas, USA / Gift of Audrey Jones Beck

from 1912 and after. In addition, later works – depicting visual levels and grounds in intense dialogue with one another and in which links between figures, flowers, fabrics, carpets and furniture are elevated to a principle of composition – call to mind Japanese works in which the collision of fabrics and decorative elements in different patterns are openly celebrated in the same vein. Matisse's paintings *Yellow Odalisque* (Philadelphia Museum of Art) and *Woman in a Purple Coat* (Museum of Fine Arts, Houston), both from 1937, bear elegant witness to this; the patterns of the blouse, skirt, coat, armchair upholstery, tile floor, carpet, wall, furniture and vase, at once lively and competing for our attention, are almost in competition with the figure and the bouquet of flowers (fig. 10).

Matisse's *Japonisme* is conveyed not so much by individual motifs as by numerous and diverse formal characteristics that endure from his early work until his maturity. Much like Bonnard, Matisse mentioned the Japanese influence only in the realm of his palette: "Colour exists in itself and possesses a beauty all its own. The Japanese crepe prints [...] revealed that to us. I understood then that one can work with expressive colours that are not necessarily descriptive colours. [...] With the eye purified, cleansed by the Japanese crepe prints, I was able to perceive colours truly through their emotive power."[31] And here, we can also recall Matisse's dictum: "The Orientals made use of black as a colour, notably the Japanese in their prints."[32]

What applied to outstanding painters, about whose relationship to Japanese graphic art at least a few words have been said, may also hold true for those artists of the early-twentieth-century avant-garde for whom less testimony has come down to us. The Japanese colour woodblock print was a veritable source of inspiration – not for imitation, but instead for sounding out similitude (to borrow the words of Matisse on Marquet) and for strengthening independent concepts; not only a model, but also a catalyst,[33] as the critic Ernest Chesneau wrote in 1878 of the first generation of *Japonistes*: "And they all found in it less an inspiration than a confirmation of their own ways of seeing, feeling, understanding and interpreting nature."[34]

Catalogue

"Japan in Paris" – Japanese objects in everyday life

Paintings by James Tissot, Alfred Stevens and Giuseppe De Nittis give us an idea of everyday life. Admittedly, it is an arranged life with a view into the private sphere, into opulently decorated ateliers, discreetly furnished boudoirs or staged living spaces. The interiors and collected objects in them are full of atmosphere and charged with connoisseurship; either hidden or clearly visible, these objects are part of the setting, as if it were the most natural thing. The focus is on artefacts of Japanese origin, works in ivory or enamel, faience and porcelain, metalwork, lacquerware, wooden sculptures, embroidered silk, painted screens, carved furniture and shrines – objects which arrived in Paris from the 1860s onwards and which, passing through the hands of dealers, directly found their way into collections or the studios of both artists and writers. The enthusiasm for Japanese art was advocated not least of all by artists who made recourse to it, sometimes subtly and other times more blatantly. Artists such as Manet, Monet, Tissot, Fantin-Latour, Degas and others sought to lend themselves a sophisticated air *en passant*, thus enhancing their art in the fashion of the day to attract and captivate potential collectors – "Japan in Paris", as Ernest Chesneau was to proclaim in an article in 1878.

Japanese art introduced new textures and provided fresh inspiration for the decor of the artists's studio – a gold-leaf screen, for instance, decorated with sparingly distributed white blossoms dividing the room and reflecting the light, as seen in the painting *Portrait of a Lady* by De Nittis (p. 111). The luminous screen serves as a backdrop for the model Léontine De Nittis dressed à la mode in pale-blue Japanese floral silk.

In no way comparable with Western art were the objects arriving from Japan, like the Noh mask, for example, which inspired Stevens's strange and enigmatic scene; in *The Japanese Mask* (p. 115) from 1874/1875, two young women dressed in expensive ball gowns sit closely together, viewing – both pensive and fascinated – a remarkable Japanese mask worn by a figure in matching costume who enters the loge on the left side in front of a background that has a faintly Far Eastern decor with red flowers. The mask corresponds to the *kotobide* type, a fox-like demon with bulging eyes, open mouth, two rows of teeth, moustache, tongue, flat nose and high-drawn eyebrows.

In 1869, in order to demonstrate his full understanding of the latest trends, Tissot used a pavilion in the style of a Japanese shrine equipped with Japanese furniture as the backdrop for his painting of two curious, interested ladies – a space that may well be a depiction of the Parisian house which the painter had moved to the year before. Tissot stages his *Young Women Looking at Japanese Articles* (p. 107) amidst a curiosity cabinet of diverse textures and new materials. The women are standing on a carpet, presumably of oriental origin, admiring Japanese objects: a lacquered table, a porcelain vase (possibly Chinese) with a fern, a draped piece of fabric and the model of a *fusutabune* (a combined rowing and sailing boat in the Portuguese shipbuilding tradition). Behind the back of the ladies in Parisian attire, Tissot paints half of a shrine the size of a cabinet: it is richly carved with ornaments, the door stands open revealing consoles piled one on top of the other with an integrated landscape picture, on which little dolls sit dressed in traditional Japanese costume. Such lacquerware is of legendary rarity, both elaborate and inexplicable in its manufacture, with an impact of hitherto-unknown intensity and depth of colour. Tissot takes a closer look at his model in *The Japanese Scroll* (p. 113), a painting produced in 1872 during his exile in London. Having taken part in the Franco-Prussian War of 1870/1871 and after the abolition of the Paris Commune, Tissot, of necessity, took refuge in the town on the Thames where he lived with his mistress Kathleen Newton until 1876. As Tissot's muse and model, she is shown in the picture pausing for a moment while reading a colourful scroll to meet the eyes of the viewer. The encounter of two cultures is effortlessly narrated in this setting – with other scrolls stored in a cylindrical receptacle lending further texture to the salon and boudoir, which is otherwise furnished in a contemporary fashion.

Japanese objects gradually became a more familiar sight and began to make their way into the impressionist style of painting. In *Still Life with Bouquet* (p. 58) – a homage to Manet – Auguste Renoir paints a traditional still life: Manet's framed etching *The Little Cavaliers* (after a painting attributed to Velázquez in the Louvre) hangs on the wall; below the painting and on a console is a still-wrapped bouquet of roses and baby's breath lying beside a vase with an undoubtedly Chinese decor and two small leather-bound volumes. A lush bamboo blossom (?) is stuck in the vase together with a delicately drawn leaf-shaped fan (*uchiwa*) with a butterfly framed by white and red poppies – as if all of this were the most common thing.

In 1880, Manet also consciously crossed the line between both cultures when a Japanese hanging scroll – the equivalent of an expansive wallpaper – forms the backdrop for his painting *Basket of Flowers* (p. 121), in which an eye-catching bouquet of peonies is painterly arranged on a distinctive round-bodied baroque wall console. The two still lifes with vase and flowers by Monet (1883) and Redon (1905), which the artists arranged in a more traditional manner, also belong to this category. In the case of Redon, it is various flowers in a contemporary Japanese vase with the motif of an opulently dressed demon-actor with a wild kind of wig. Monet, in contrast, arranges Far Eastern poppies in an Asian vase (pp. 120, 127).

Vincent Van Gogh came across such "new" motifs whilst still in Antwerp, according to a letter written to his brother Theo on 28 November 1885. After his arrival in Paris in the spring of 1886, he reacted all the more intensely to the woodblock prints from Japan, as is reflected in a number of landscapes, portraits and still lifes. His enthusiasm for the new medium not only led to a significant collection of Japanese prints but, in the spring of 1887, he also presented an exhibition of *ukiyo-e* woodblock prints in Café du Tambourin on Boulevard de Clichy in Paris. With their motifs and stories of simplicity in everyday life and of harmony with nature, the Japanese woodblock prints awakened in Van Gogh a longing for life in this mystical and peaceful Far Eastern land. In 1887, while still in Paris, he incorporates important motifs of Japanese woodblock prints into his paintings, such as in *The Courtesan (after Eisen)* (p. 123). The May 1887 issue of the illustrated magazine *Paris illustré* was dedicated to Japan and showed Keisai Eisen's courtesan from 1840 on its title page (p. 71). Van Gogh did not use the original woodblock print for his motif on a faux-golden undercoat, but instead used the reverse illustration for the title page and arranged the complete painting like the panel of a Japanese screen in a Japanese garden setting depicting a bamboo grove and cranes in a pond with flowering water lilies. Van Gogh took elements of other woodblock prints, such as those by Utagawa Yoshimaru II (p. 72), for his complex homage to the art of Japan.

In *Still Life with Onions and Japanese Woodcut,* Paul Gauguin also quickly emerges as an aficionado of *Japonisme*. Here, he casually places a Japanese woodblock print (most likely of the actor Utagawa Toyokuni I) next to a ceramic vessel and onions on the kitchen table (p. 125). Like Renoir, Manet, Tissot, De Nittis, Stevens and particularly Van Gogh, Gauguin collected Japanese objects and artefacts, incorporating them into his pictorial creations as *trouvailles* of an entirely novel aesthetic.

Mario-Andreas von Lüttichau

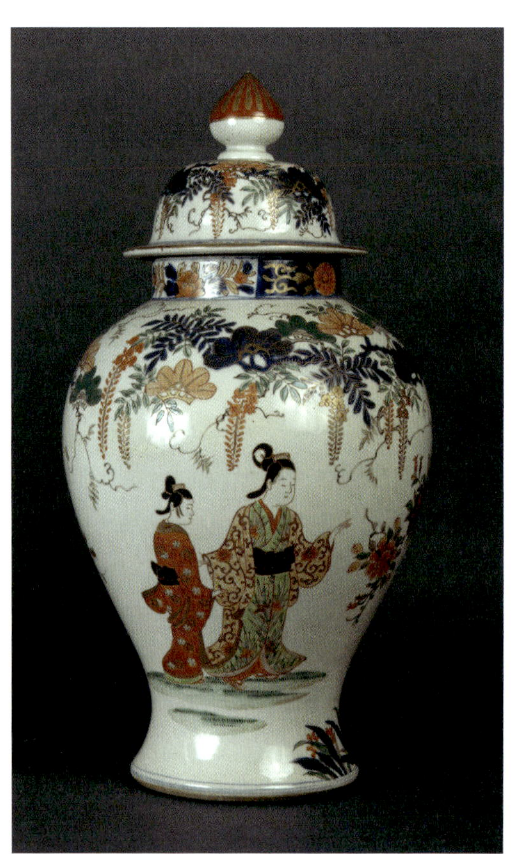
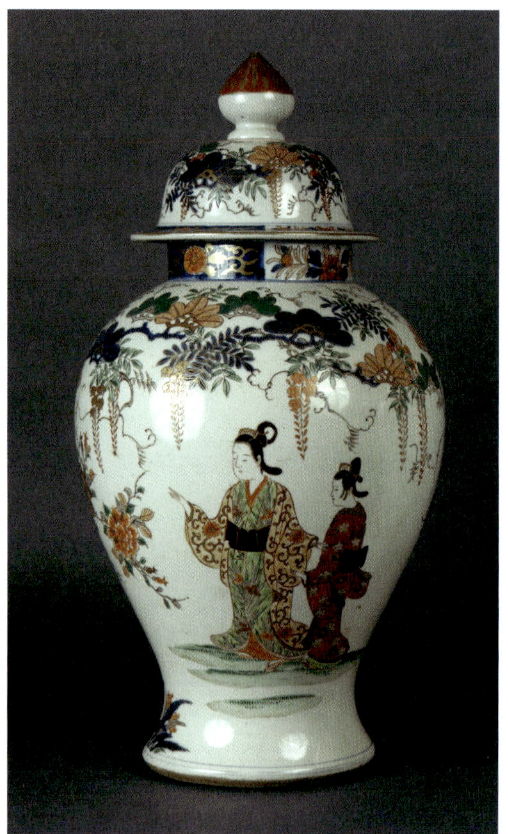

337 Japan, *Pair of Covered Vases*, Edo period, 18th c.

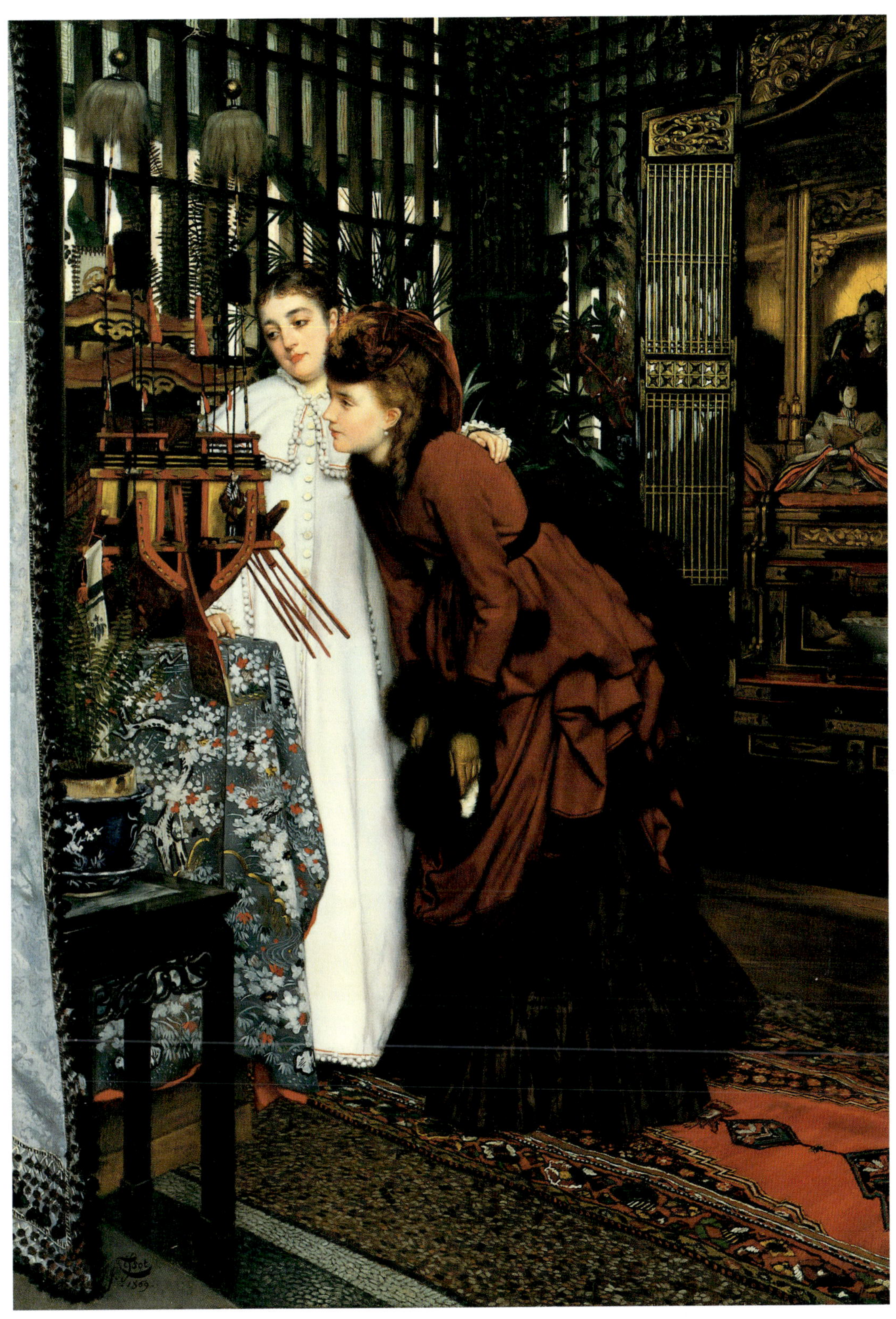

67 James Jacques Joseph Tissot, *Young Women Looking at Japanese Articles*, 1869

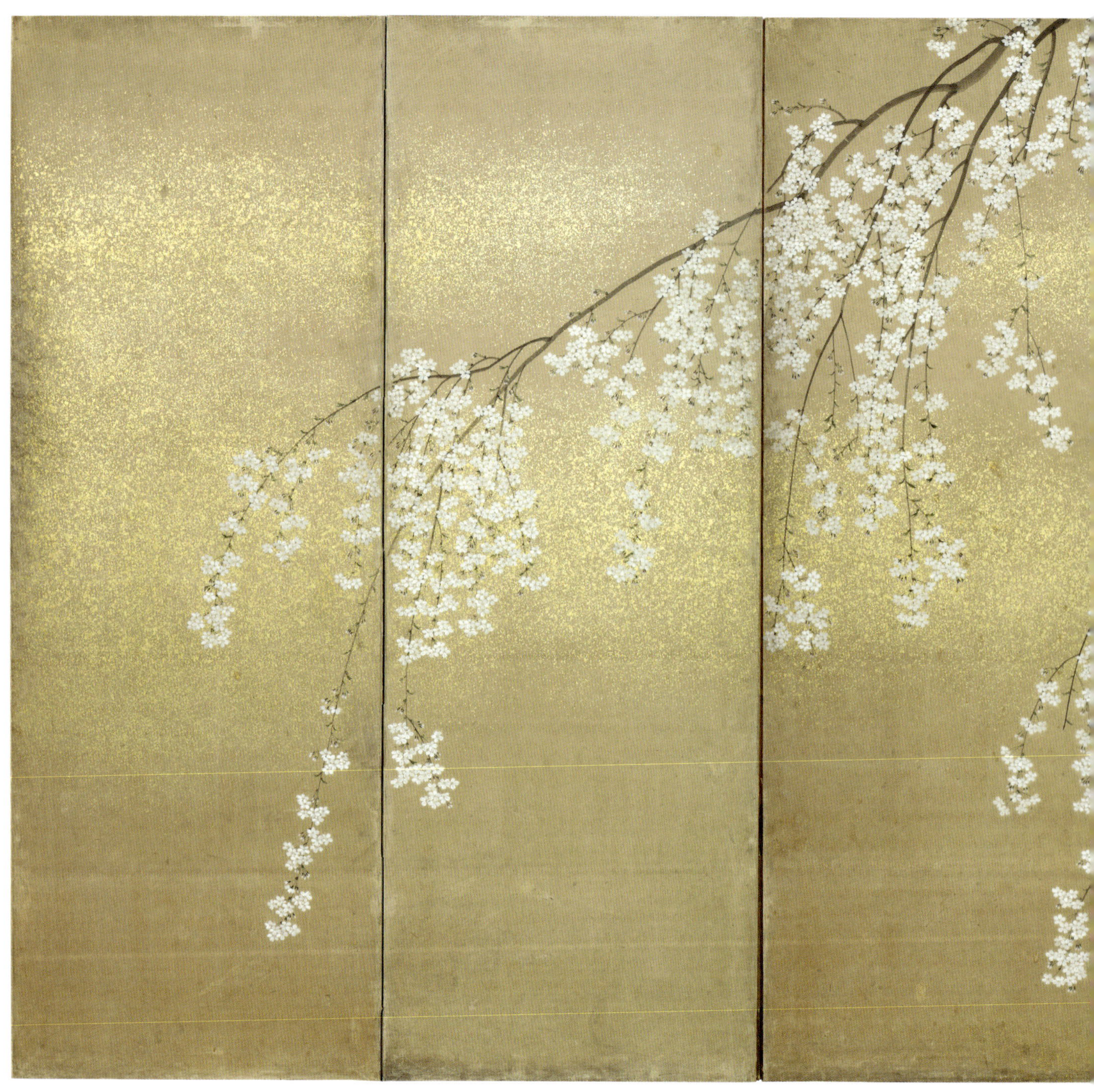

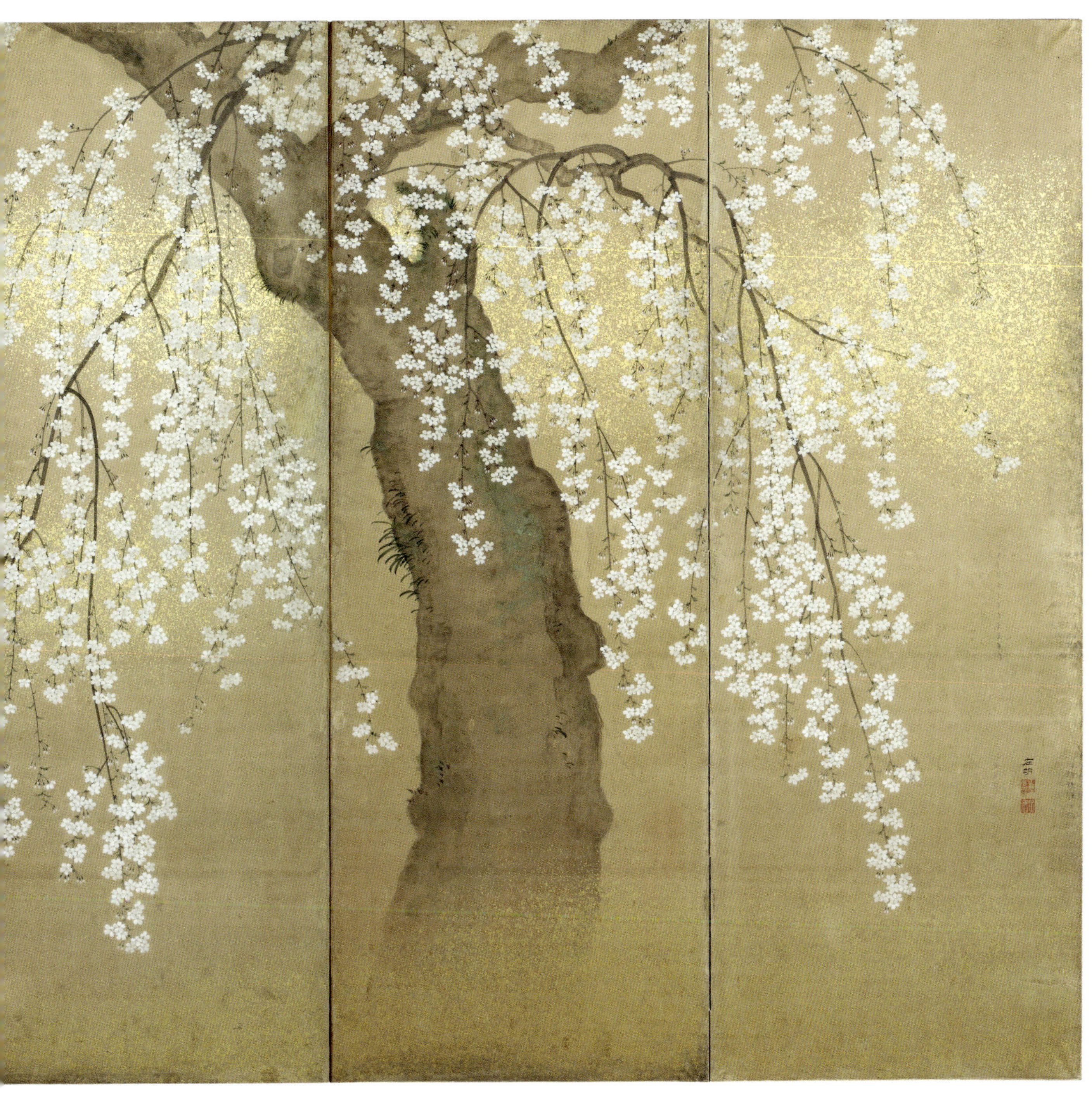

183 Hara Zaimei, *Blossoming Cherry Tree on Gold Ground*, late Edo period, early 19th c.

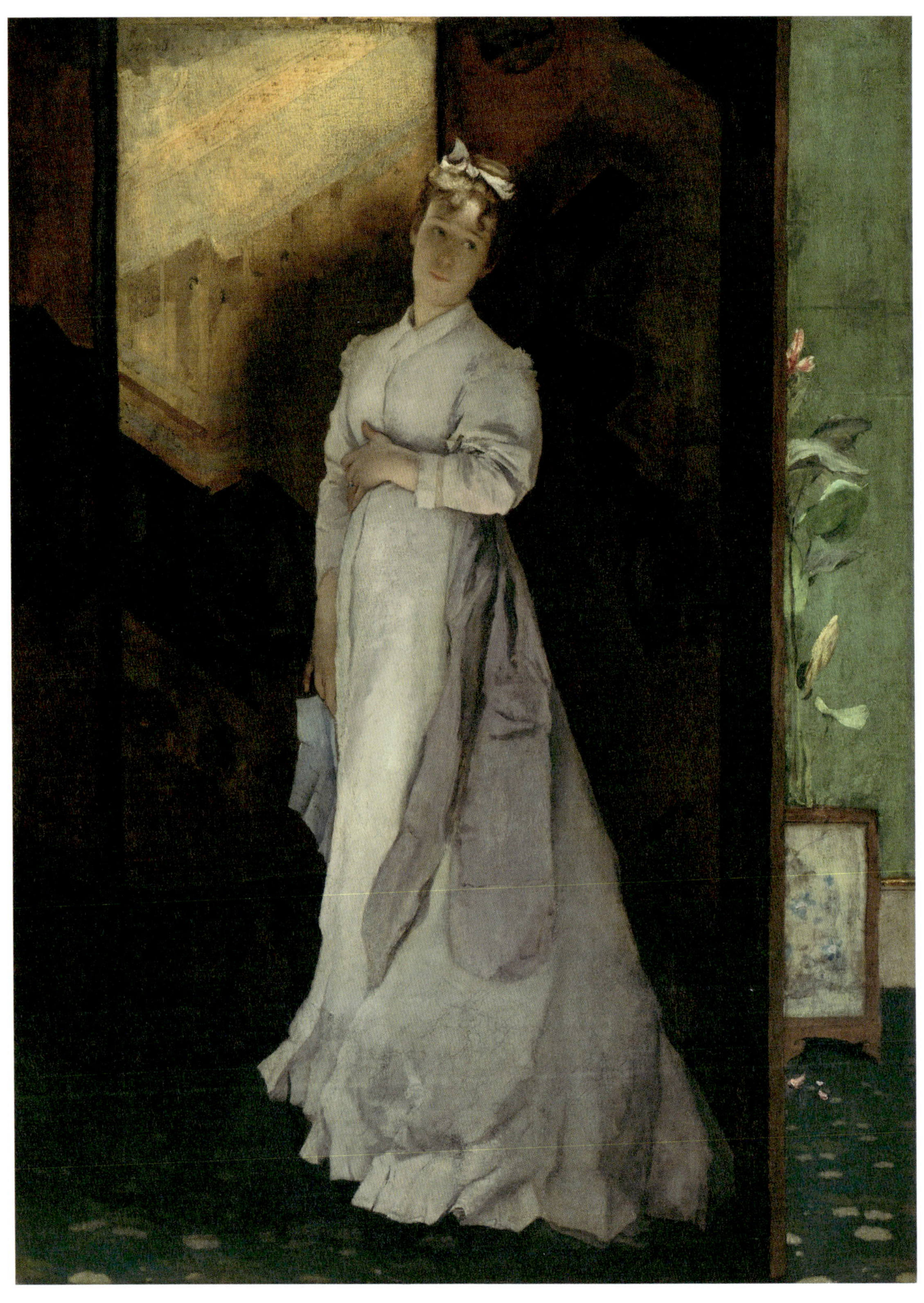

65 Alfred Stevens, *The Letter of Separation*, circa 1867

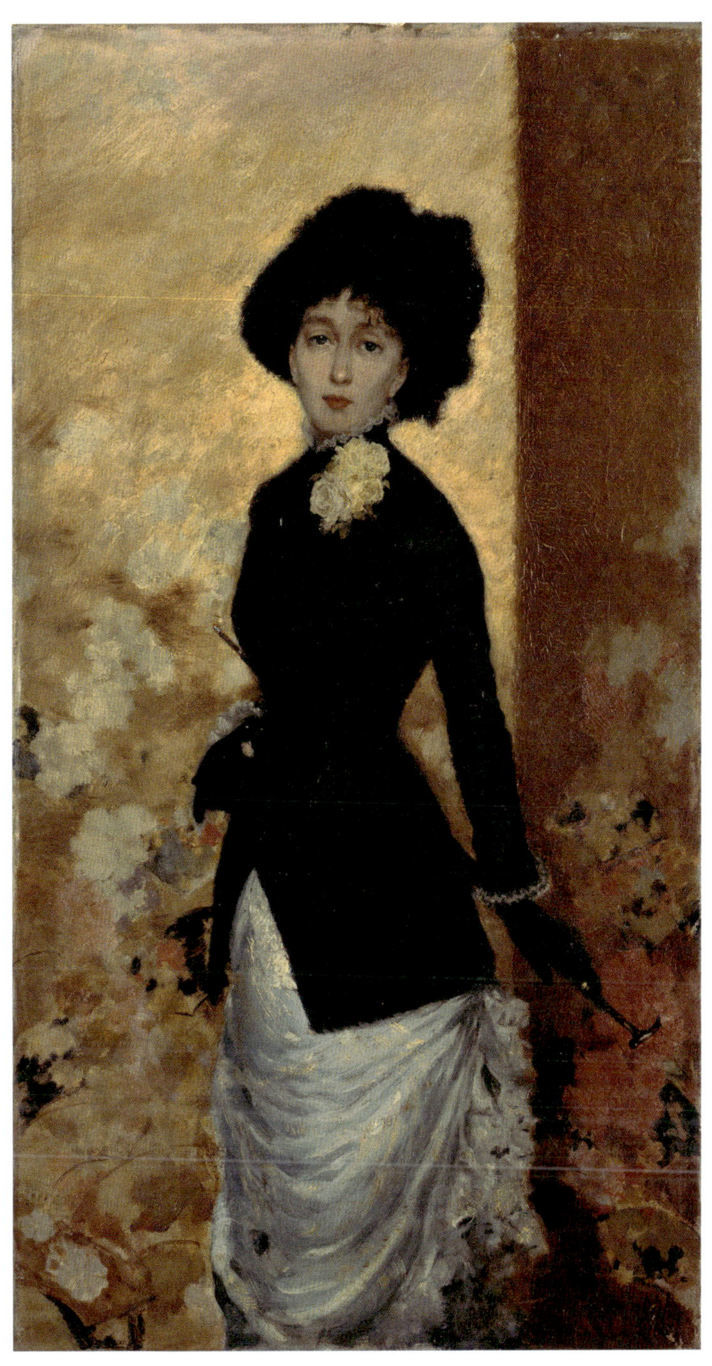

13 Giuseppe De Nittis, *Portrait of a Lady*, 1880

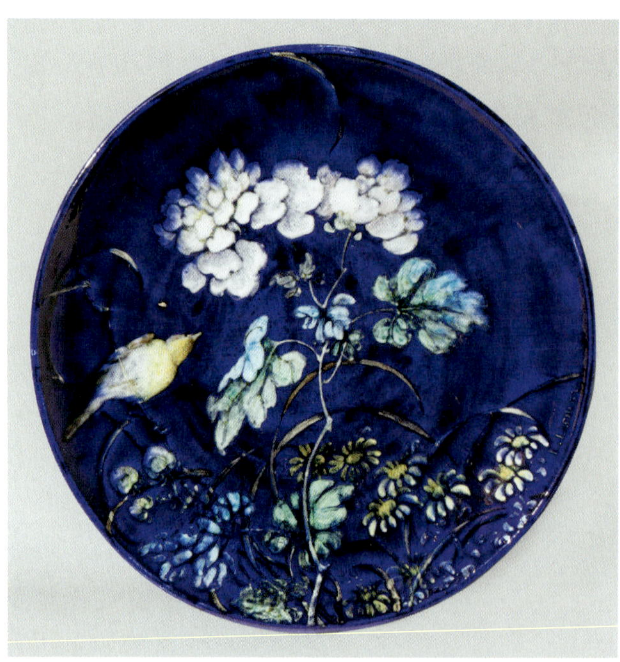

134 Joseph Théodore Deck and Edmond Lachenal, *Wall Plate with Branch of Peonies*, circa 1870–1880

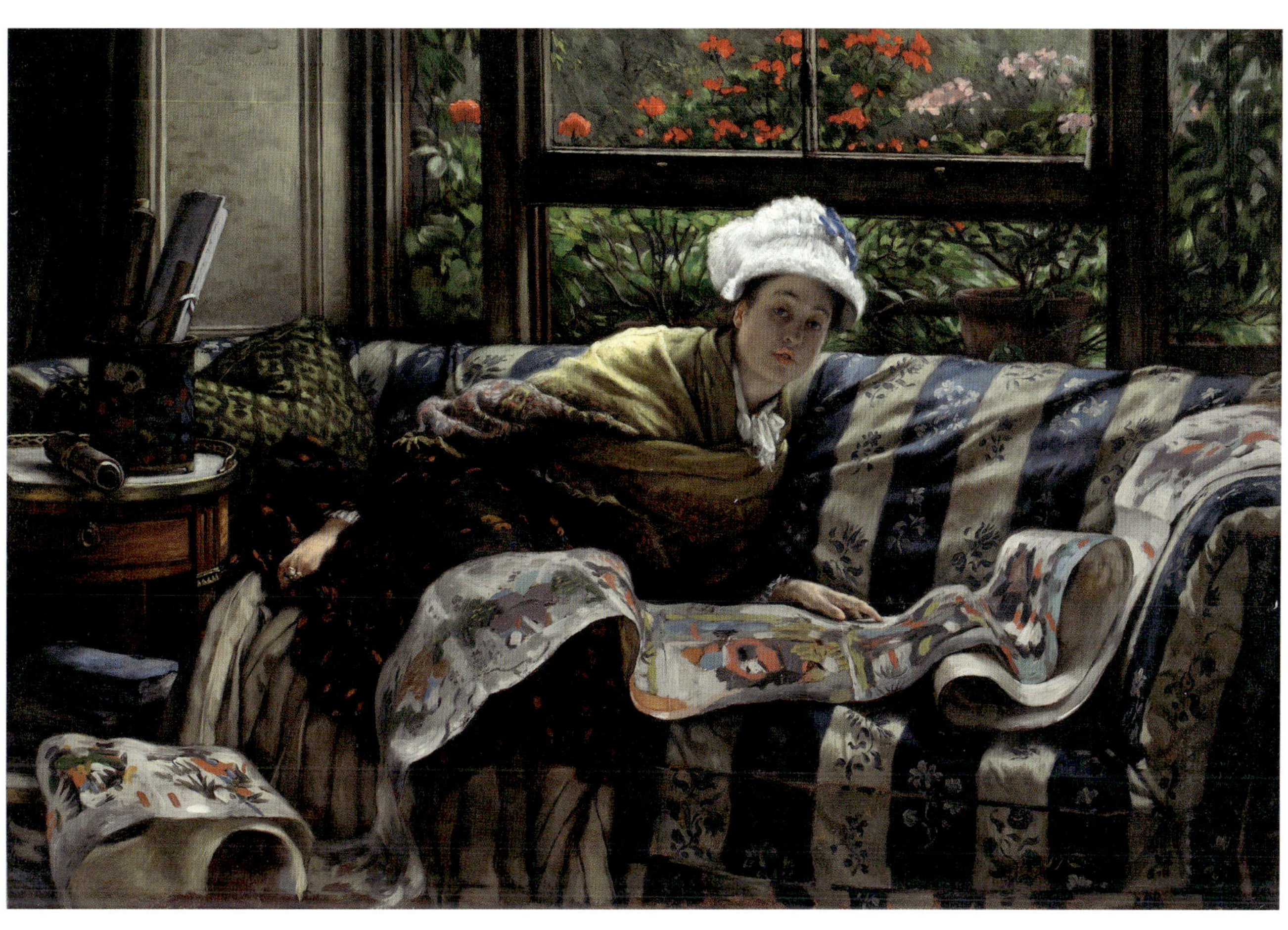

68 James Jacques Joseph Tissot, *The Japanese Scroll*, circa 1872

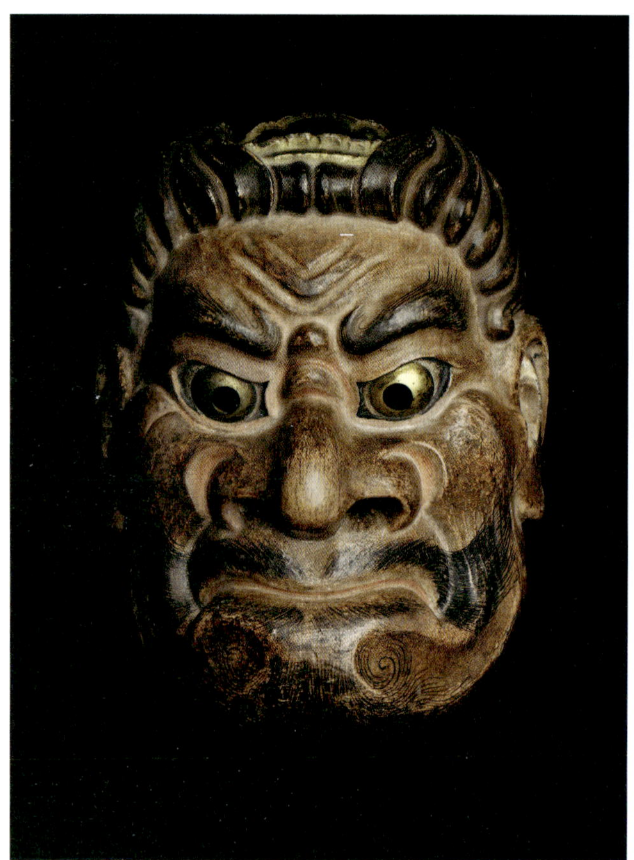

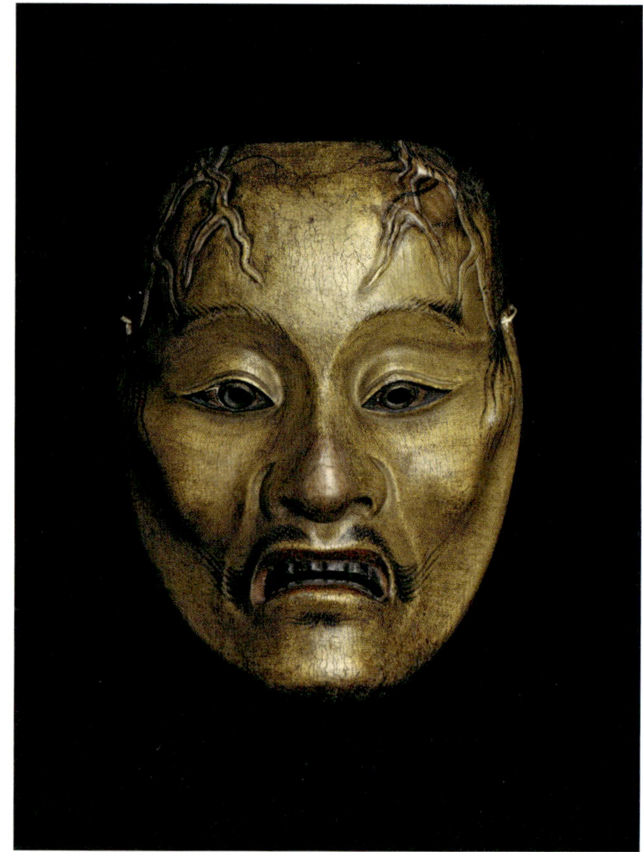

292 Ji'unin, *Fudō-myōō-Beshimi* (Noh theatre face mask), 15th/16th c.
293 Deme Mitsuteru, *Suji-otoko* (Noh theatre face mask), 16th c.

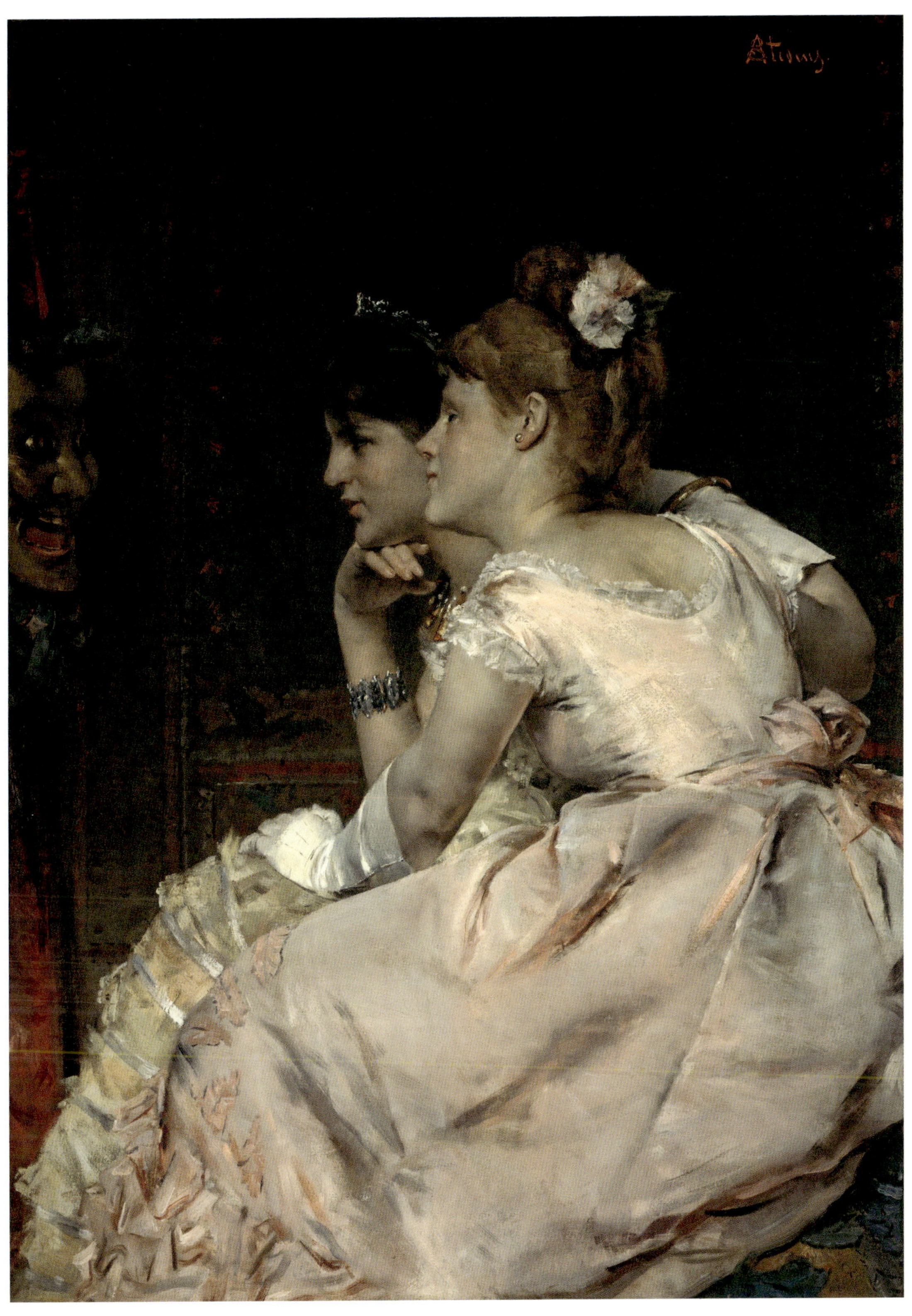

66 Alfred Stevens, *The Japanese Mask*, circa 1874/1875

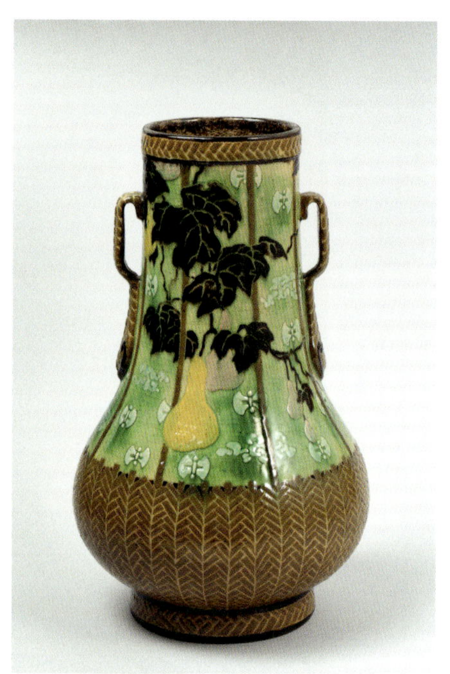

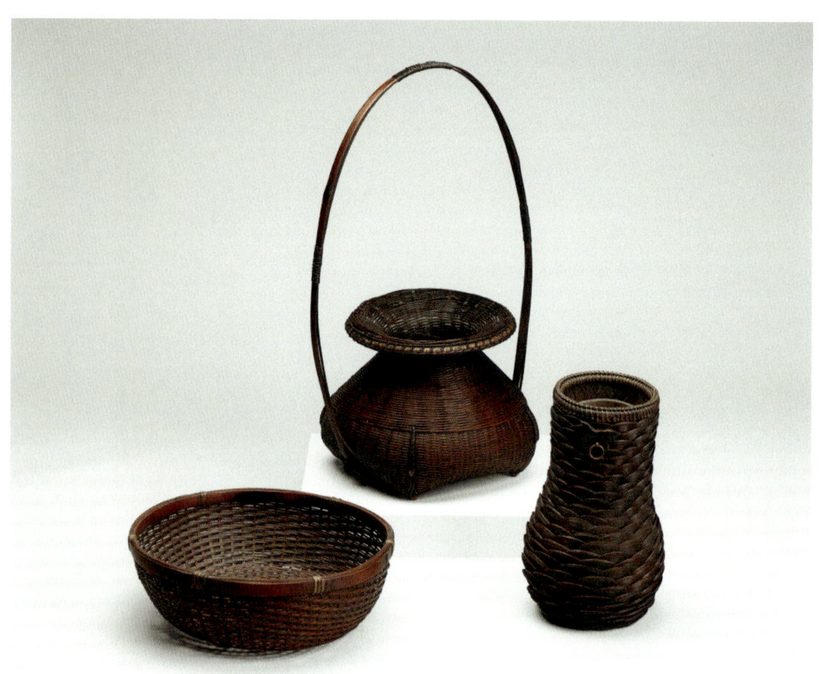

347 | 346 | 348 Japan, *Baskets*, late 19th c.
136 Camille Moreau-Nélaton, *Vase with Handles, with Basketwork Deco*, 1883

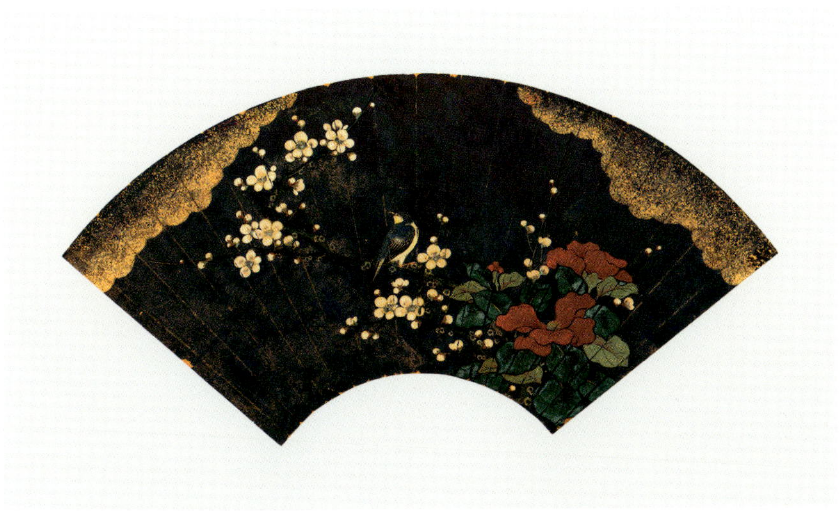

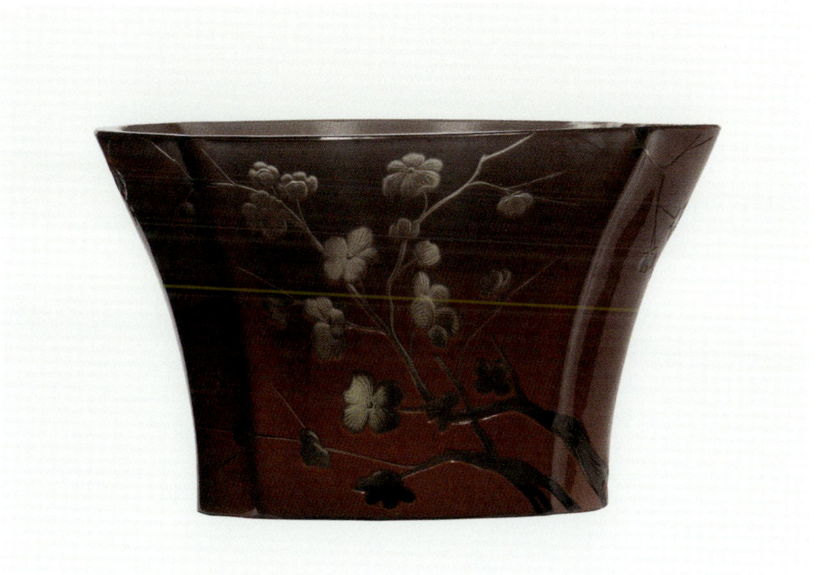

178 Japan, *Bird on Plum Blossom Branch,* probably 17th c.
148 François-Eugène Rousseau, *Jardiniere*, circa 1884

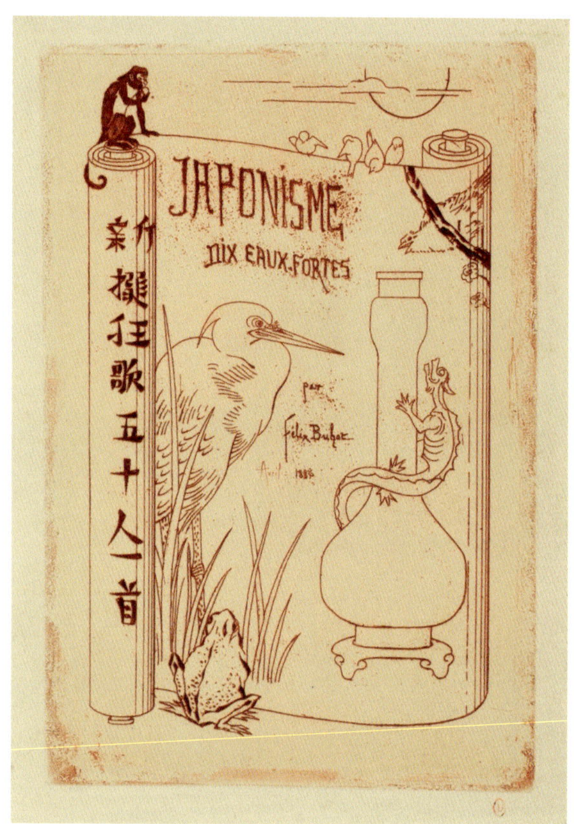

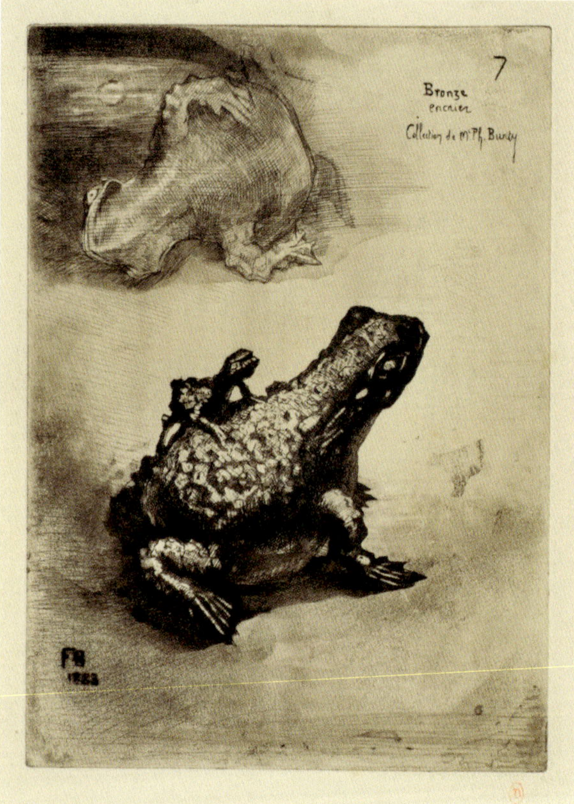

91b | 91l Félix Buhot, *Japonisme: Cover* | *Bronze Inkwell* or *Bronze Toad*, 1883

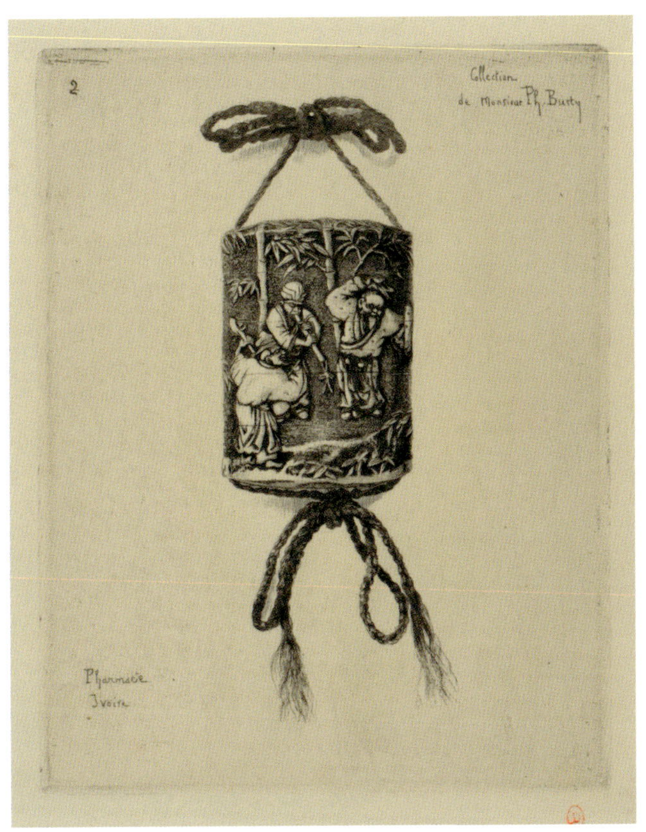

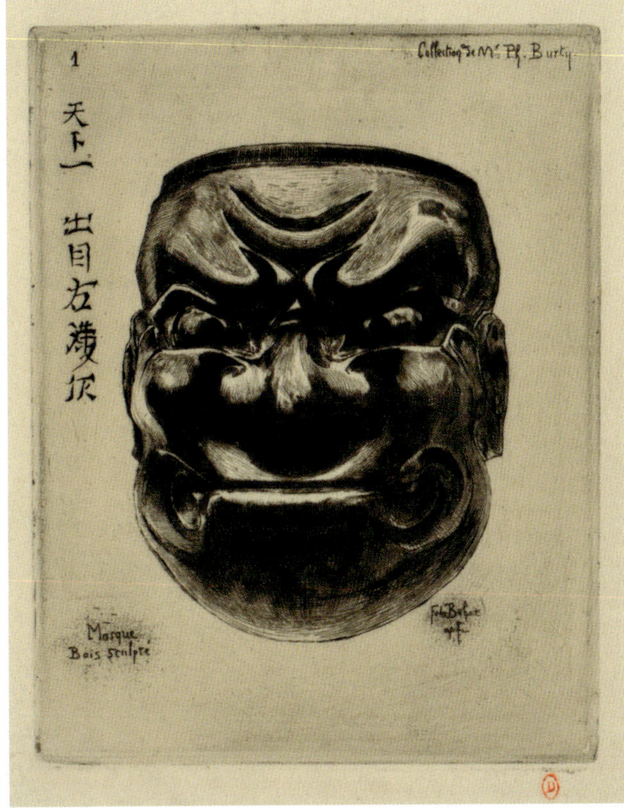

91f | 91d Félix Buhot, *Ivory Medicine Container* | *Carved Wooden Mask*, 1883

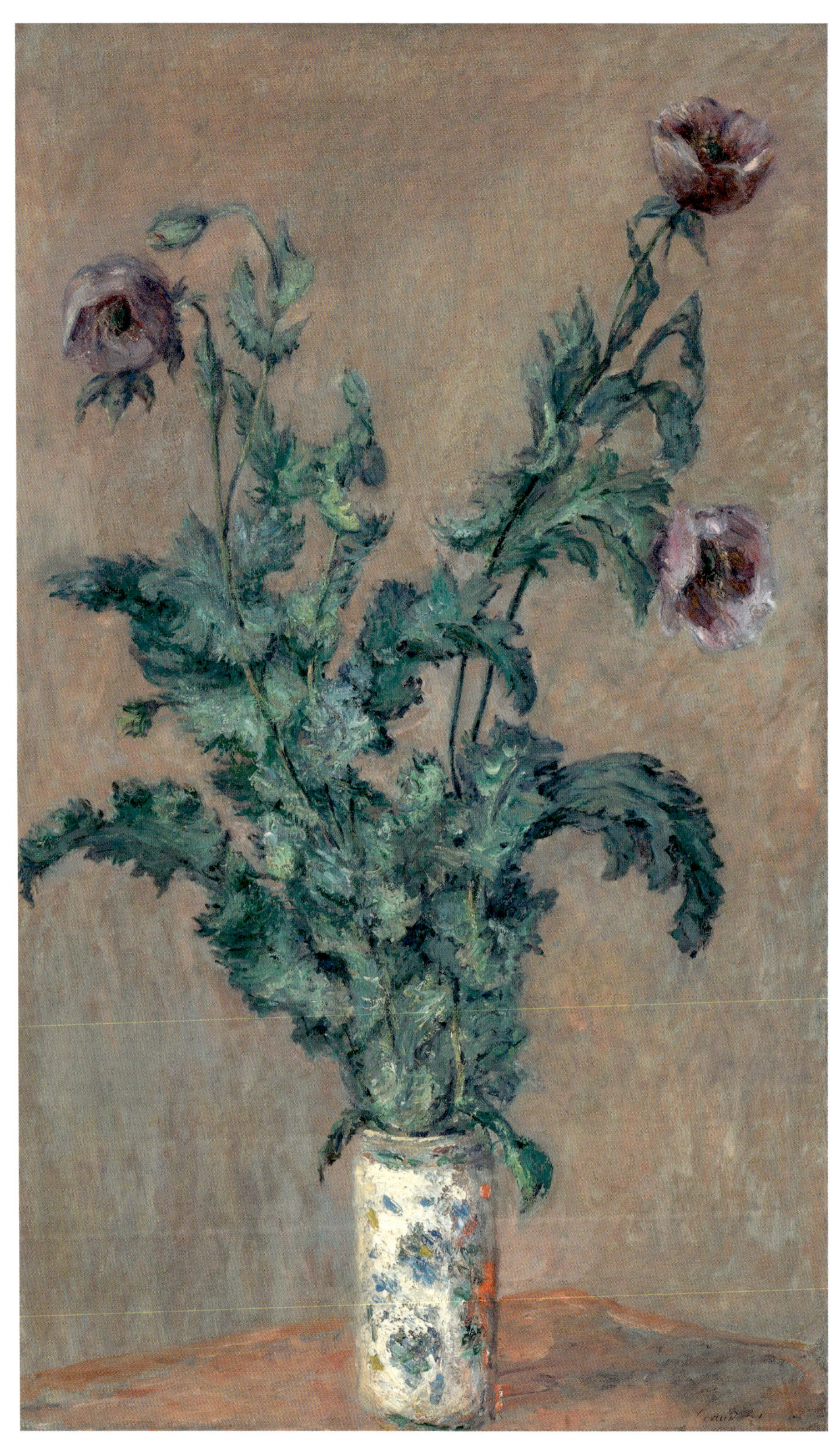

46 Claude Monet, *Vase of Poppies*, 1883

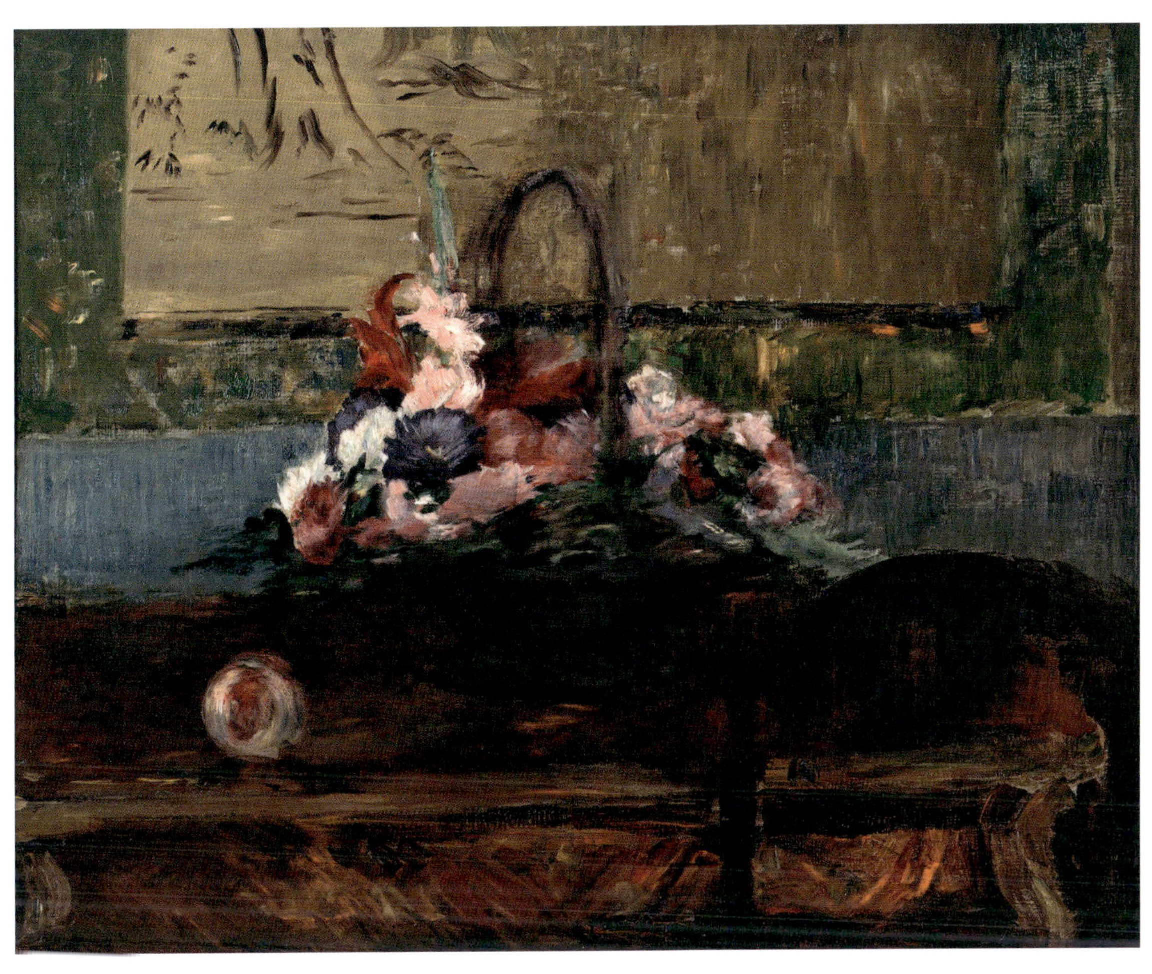

43 Édouard Manet, *Basket of Flowers*, 1880

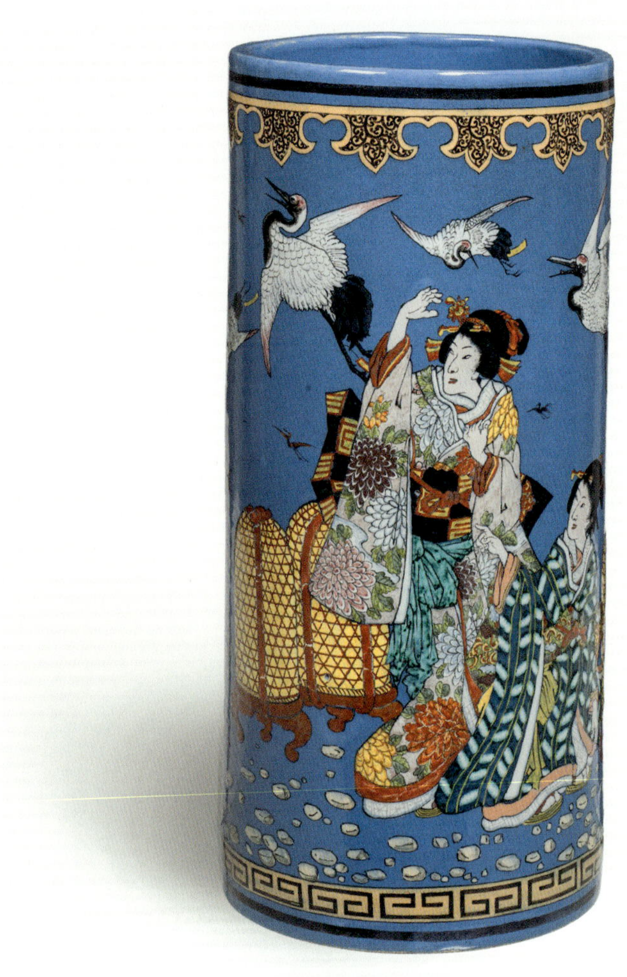

135 Genlis et Rudhard, *Vase*, 1865/1874

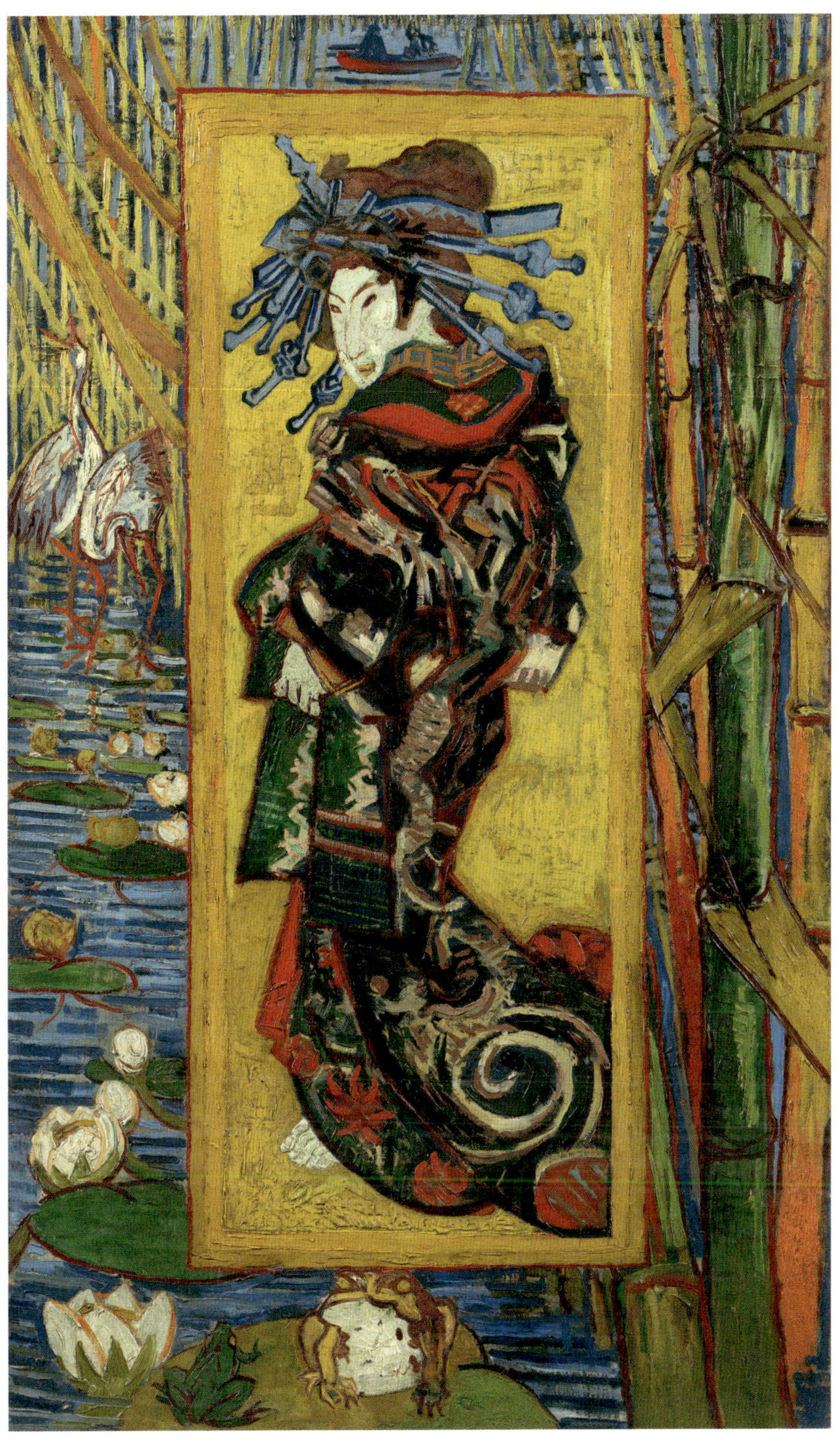

37 Vincent Van Gogh, *The Courtesan (after Eisen)*, 1887

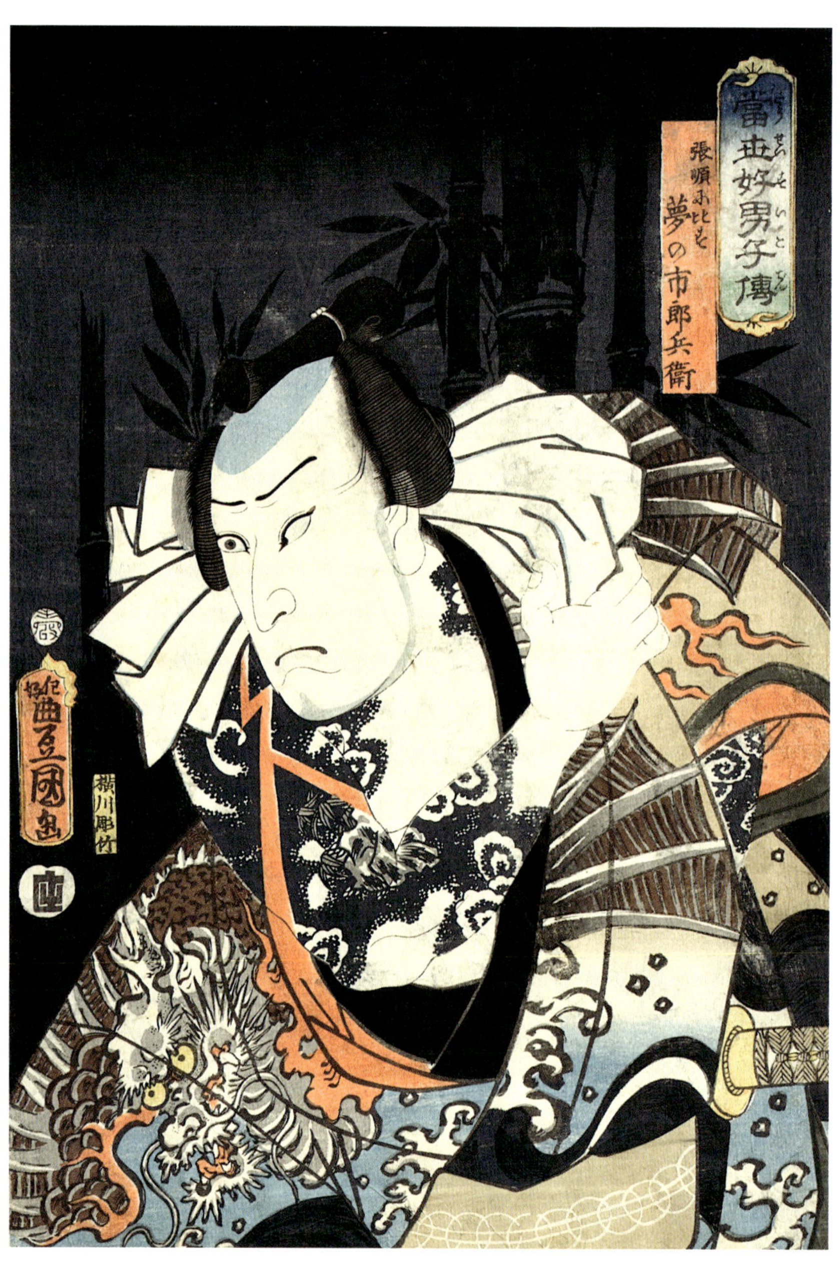

213 Utagawa Kunisada (Toyokuni III), *Yume no Ichirobei in the Manner of Zhang Shun (Chōjun)*, 1859

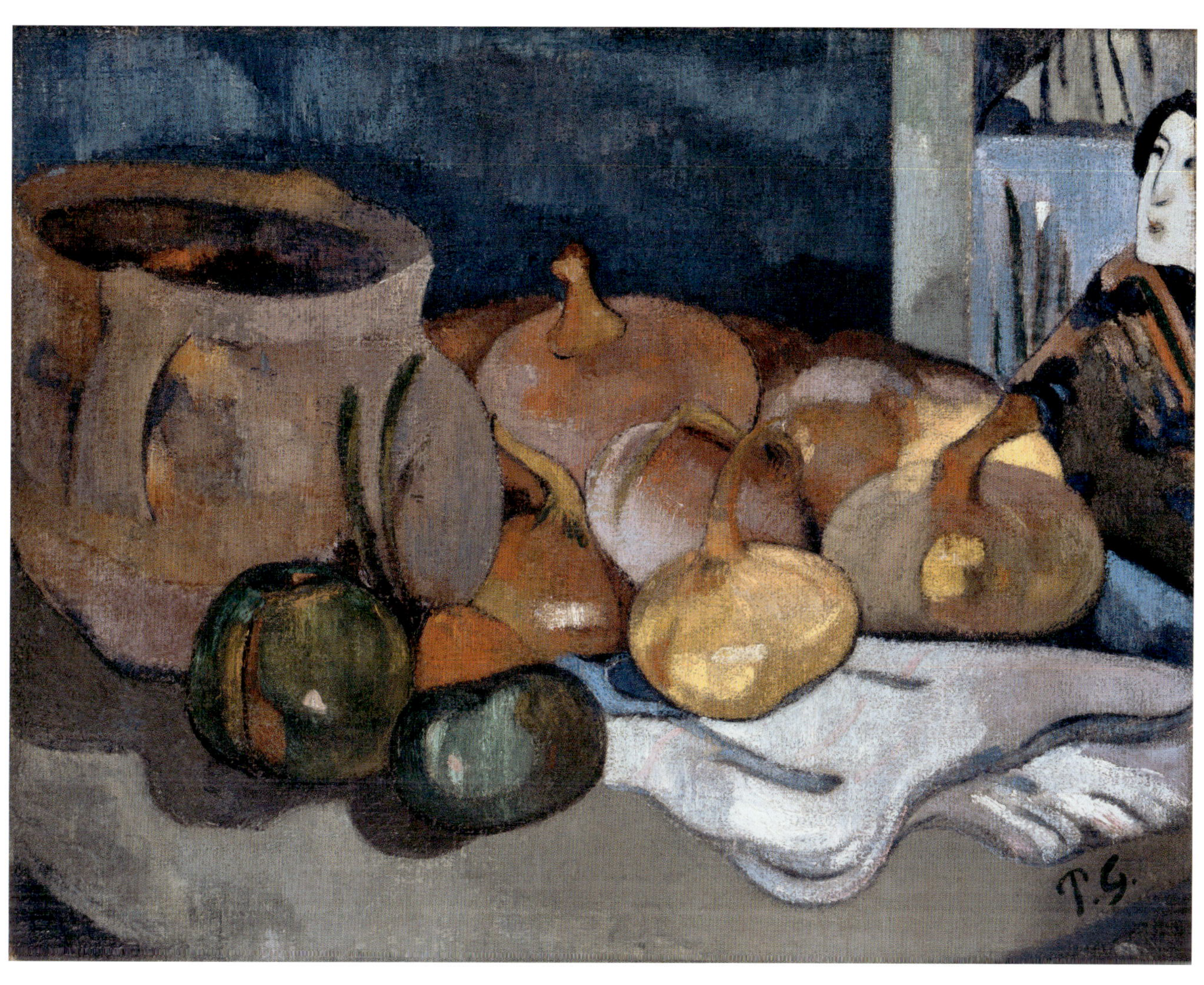

34 Paul Gauguin, *Still Life with Onions and Japanese Woodcut*, circa 1889

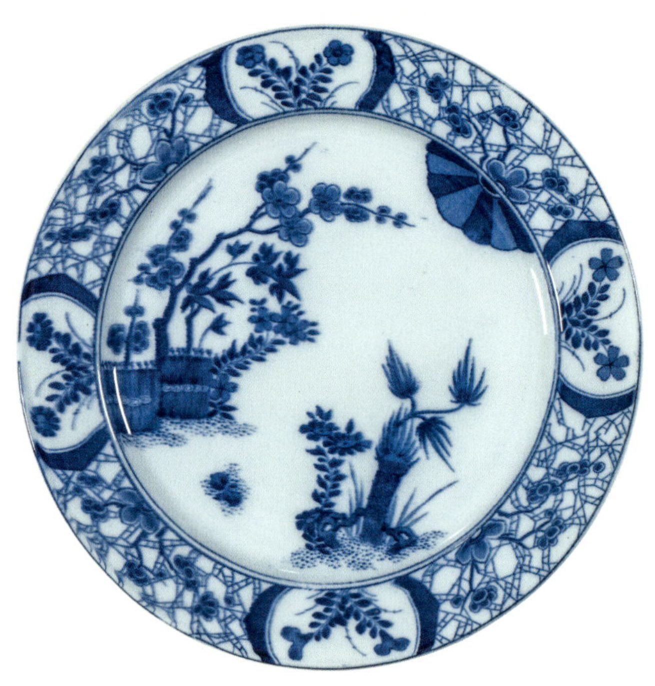

130 Barluet et Cie, *Plate*, circa 1879

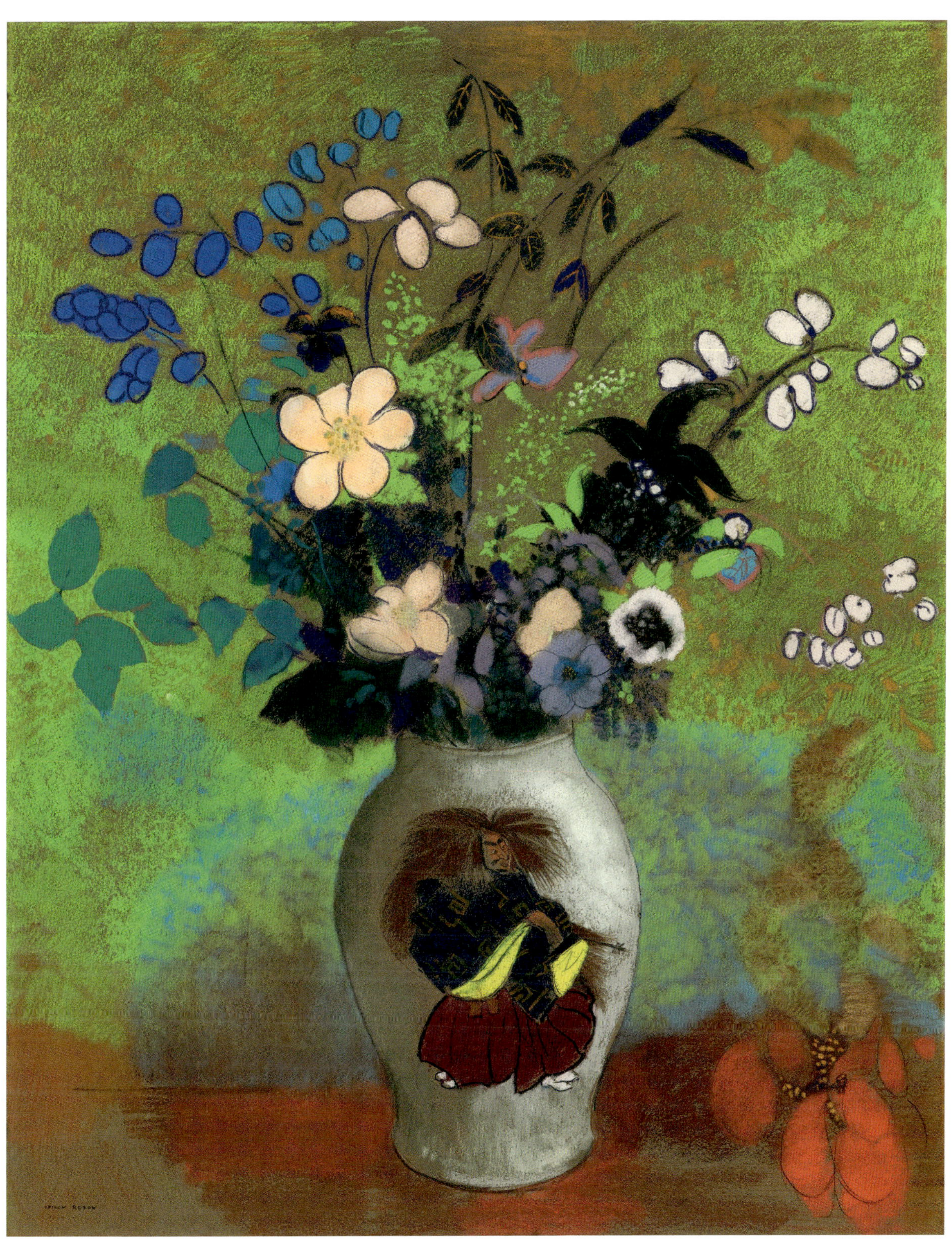

61 Odilon Redon, *The Japanese Warrior Vase*, circa 1905

Promenades japonaises – artists in Japan

Western diplomats, traders and engineers, but also journalists, artists and tourists – the number of those who set off for the unknown, and therefore enigmatic, land of Japan after its enforced opening in 1854 was large. The foreigners usually arrived in Yokohama, a harbour town that was set up to receive the newcomers. From there, the enterprising travellers could venture into the country's interior. They included the banker Henri Cernuschi, who was travelling with the art historian Théodore Duret; the industrialist Émile Guimet, accompanied by the artist Félix Régamey; and the writer and naval officer Pierre Loti, who was inspired by his stay in Japan to write his famous novel *Madame Chrysanthème* (1888). Like Régamey, some other writers, artists and photographers also made the journey. In their works, these artists captured a fascinating world presented to their curious eye.

One year after his arrival in Yokohama in 1863, Felice Beato, a photographer of Italian origin, opened a successful photo studio with Charles Wirgman, correspondent for the newspaper *The Illustrated London News,* and ran it until 1877. The new medium, which was first brought to Japan in 1848 as the daguerreotype, enabled the recording of a society in the midst of change, which transformed seamlessly from a feudal structure into a modern empire. Beato laid the foundations for an "exotic" – and, at the same time, poetic – snapshot of society, which would continue to exist throughout the rest of the nineteenth century. Many photographers, such as the Austrian Baron Raimund von Stillfried-Ratenicz or the Japanese Kusakabe Kimbei, drew their advantage from the flourishing business and opened their own photo studios in Yokohama – the former purchased Beato's negatives in 1877, before selling some of them to the latter in 1885.

Landscapes, everyday scenes and small craft workshops were the typical themes of this photographic production, which intensified from the 1860s onwards. In line with Katsushika Hokusai and Utagawa Hiroshige, photographers chose famous landscapes and places as motifs, such as Mount Fuji (p. 135) or the arched bridge and wisteria of the Kameido shrine (p. 134). Furthermore, they created a multifaceted picture of Japanese society by endeavouring to capture the variety of the small handcraft professions being practised at the time, such as that of the bearer of a traditional sedan chair made from bamboo (*kago)* or that of the umbrella maker (p. 136). The Japanese woman also inspired many pictorial compositions, often coloured by a diffuse eroticism that easily enchanted the West. Thus, for example, the Japanese woman was photographed at her toilette, playing music (p. 137) or in her kimono (p. 136). One of the photographs shows four dancers from behind in a pose that displays their kimono, the obi holding it together and their artful hairstyles particularly well. The black-and-white prints have been coloured carefully by hand and enhanced with delicate pastel paints. This artistic technique benefited from the skill of the Japanese, who were accustomed to colouring *ukiyo-e* prints. Although photos were certainly taken outdoors, many were shot in the studio, where accessories, decor and clothing formed part of a truly artistic staging.

The travellers were enchanted by these alleged snapshots that had, in truth, been cleverly staged to suit Western tastes (even by the Japanese themselves) and which often displayed an image of a traditional Japan that was threatening to disappear. Therefore, they rarely departed from the Japanese archipelago without taking some "photographic souvenirs" with them, usually bound in albums between lacquered covers decorated with ivory and mother-of-pearl.

In 1876, the French Ministry for Education and Art commissioned Émile Guimet to study the religions of the Far East in Japan, China and India. The industrialist from Lyon took Régamey with him on his journey. Of course, they visited Edo – the former main town of the Tokugawa shoguns and now the capital city of the Mikado – the shrine of Nikkō, the Tōkaido road and also the former imperial city of Kyoto. Guimet gathered information about the role of the Shinto and Buddhist religions, met monks and visited numerous temples.

The highest priest at the Shinto shrine of Ise even organised a religious dance especially for Guimet, which was sketched by Régamey (p. 132). But the two travellers were also fascinated by the theatre of everyday life: pedestrians, craftsmen, clothing and everyday utensils – nothing escaped Régamey's searching gaze, which was captivated by all that was new and picturesque. The portrait of Hyakutarō, on which he recorded the features of a rickshaw driver, groom or load carrier (p. 132) – recognisable by his indigo-blue jacket – demonstrates the artist's interest in the simple people of the street. With the spontaneity and freedom of sketching – pencil strokes applied with a light touch, accentuated by watercolours – Régamey also captured the landscapes that he discovered with relentless astonishment during the course of his travels, such as this view of the Arashiyama in Kyoto (p. 133). Back in France, Guimet presented the works and objects that he had acquired on his travels at the Paris World Fair of 1878, along with a series of paintings completed by Régamey based on the sketches he had made in Japan. From then on, the two men sought to make Japanese culture better known. In 1878 and 1880, Guimet published his travel stories *Promenades japonaises*, illustrated by Régamey. Moreover, the Lyon native founded a museum for ancient and Eastern religions, which opened its doors in his home town in 1879, before moving to Paris in 1889. Régamey became the author of several works on Japan, such as *Le Japon pratique* (1891), before he embarked on a second trip to the Japanese archipelago in 1899.

In 1888, the painter Louis Dumoulin travelled to Japan with the support of Jules Castagnary, the director of the Beaux-Arts at the time. Upon his arrival in Yokohama, the painter was captivated by the lively streets of the theatre quarter. He chose the facades of the theatre, with their colourful signs and banners displaying the name of the actors and the plays, as a motif for his work. With light and expressive brushstrokes and a bright and vibrant palette, the artist reproduced the raucous life of the street, the numerous passers-by who rush past either on foot or in rickshaws (p. 130). However, Dumoulin did not stay very long in Yokohama; as soon as he had arranged the formalities, he set off for the interior of the country. In Nikkō, he was smitten, like many artists, by the motif of the holy bridge made of red painted wood that spanned the little Daiya River (p. 131). The painter also depicted the Nikkō festival celebrating the former Tokugawa shogunate: clothed in costumes from an earlier age, a procession of Shinto priests, lords and armed Samurai warriors is seen passing the first Torii of the Shrine of Nikkō, not far from the five-storey pagoda (p. 130). Dumoulin provides us with picturesque and colourful snapshots of his travel impressions, which he painted very much according to Western stylistic principles. He eventually returned to Paris via China, Cochinchina and Malaysia, where he exhibited his – to use the words of Philippe Burty, the author of the preface to the catalogue – "painted travel notes" in 1889 at Galerie Georges Petit.

Beato, Régamey and Dumoulin were among the few artists who felt the urge to discover Japan with their own eyes. Although certainly interested in Japan and its art and culture, other artists did not visit the country. As Oscar Wilde noted in 1891, it was the powers of their imagination that often sufficed them: "In fact the whole of Japan is a pure invention. [...] And so, if you desire to see a Japanese effect, you will not behave like a tourist and go to Tokio. On the contrary, you will stay at home and steep yourself in the work of certain Japanese artists, and then [...] you will go some afternoon and sit in the Park or stroll down Piccadilly, and if you cannot see an absolutely Japanese effect there, you will not see it anywhere" (*The Decay of Lying*).

Claire Guitton

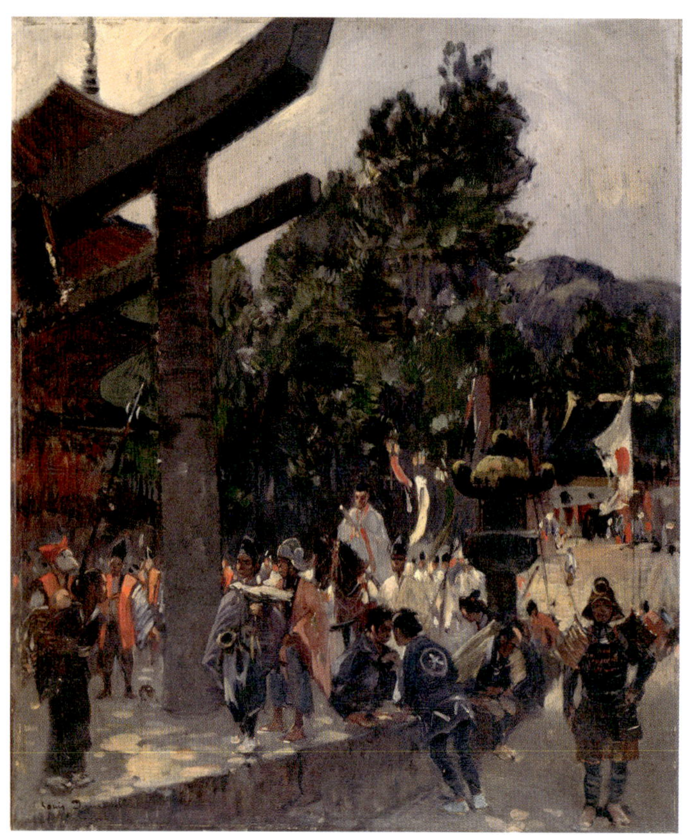

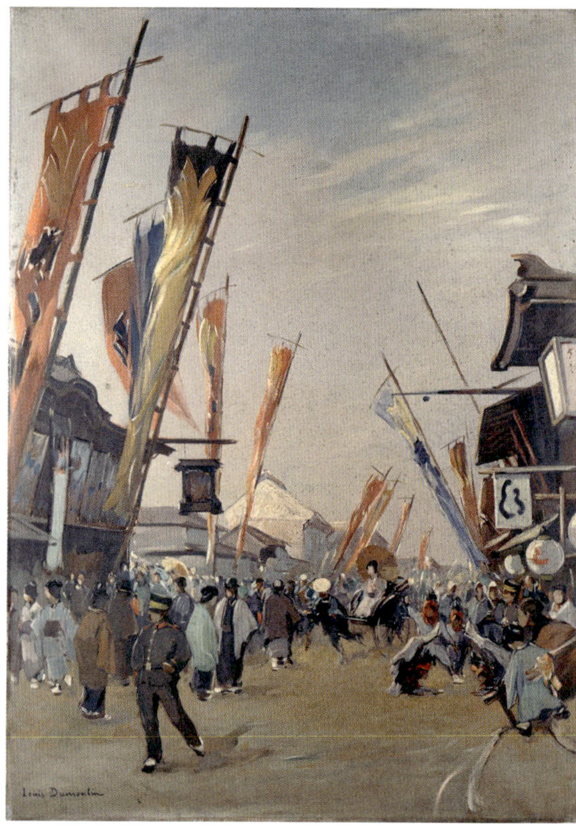

27 | 26 Louis Dumoulin, *Festival in Nikkō (Festival of Shōgun Ieyasu)*, 1888/89 | *Theatre District in Yokohama*, circa 1888

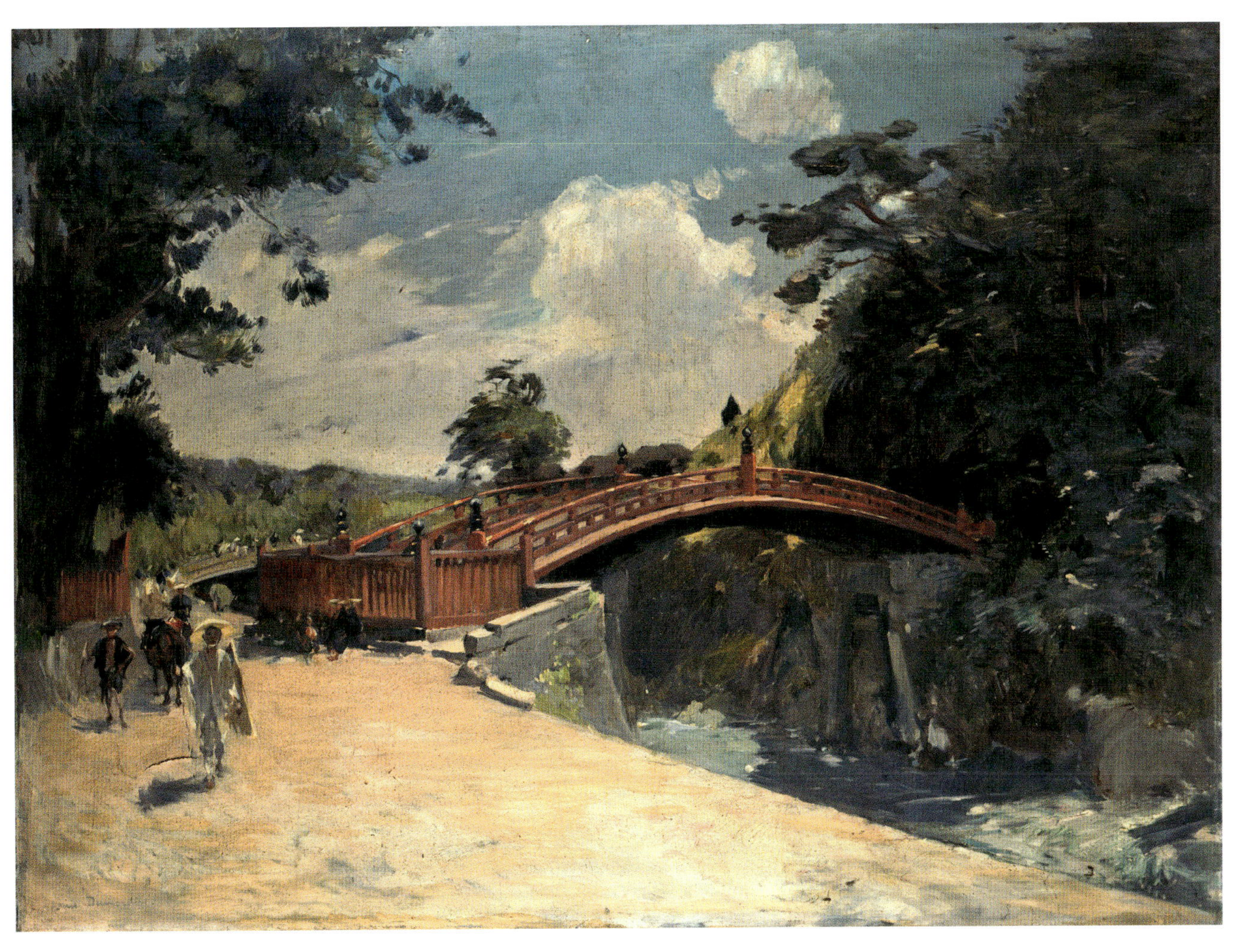

28 Louis Dumoulin, *The Sacred Bridge over the Daiya River in Nikkō*, 1888/89

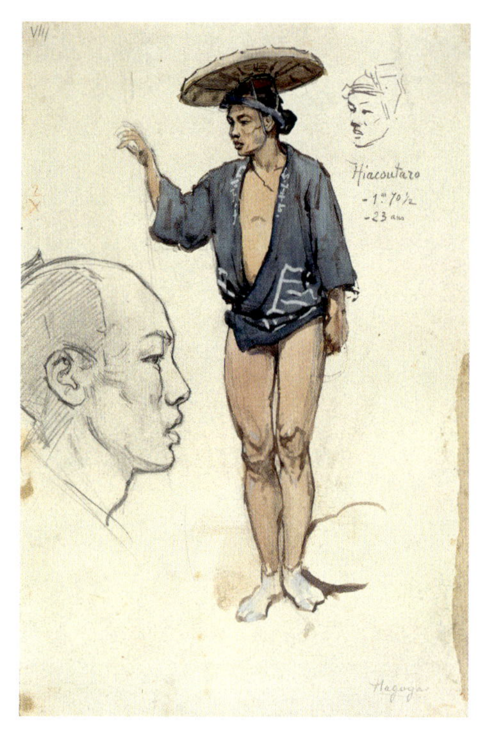

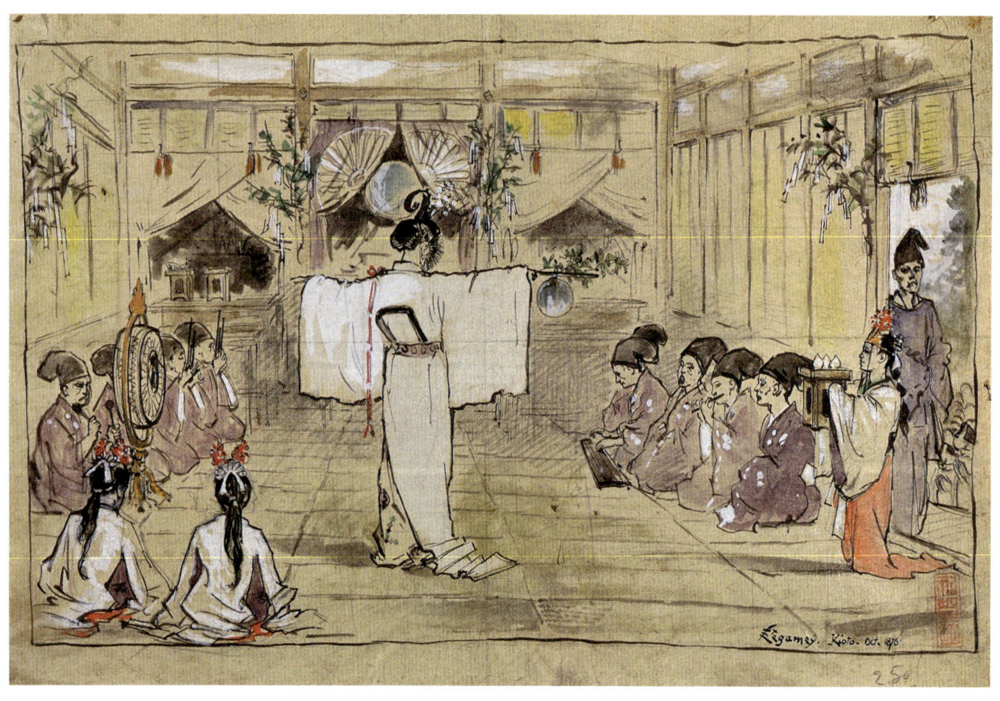

77 | 78 Félix Régamey, *Dance* | *Standing Figure*, 1876

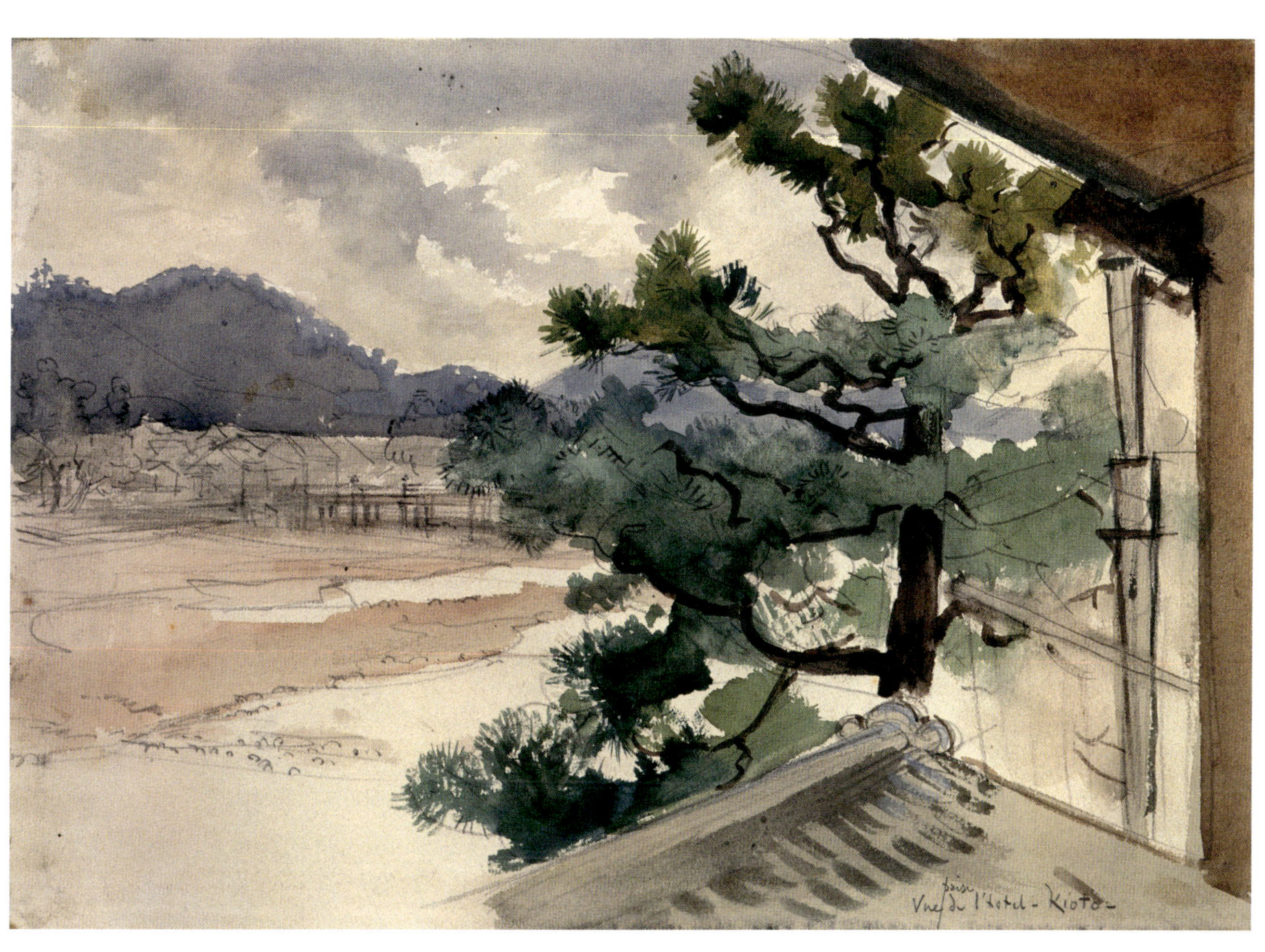

76 Félix Régamey, *View of Arashiyama in Kyoto*, 1876

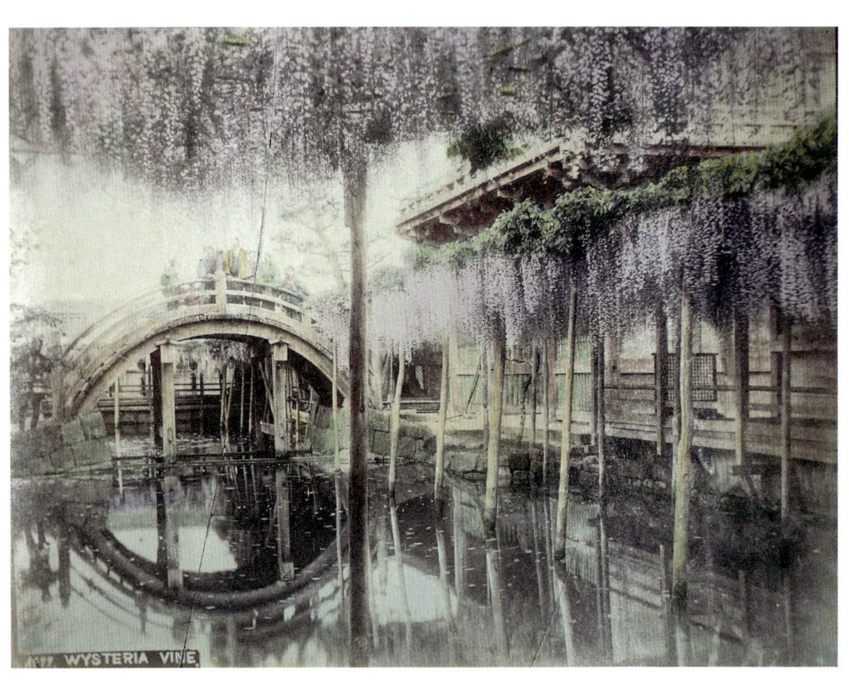

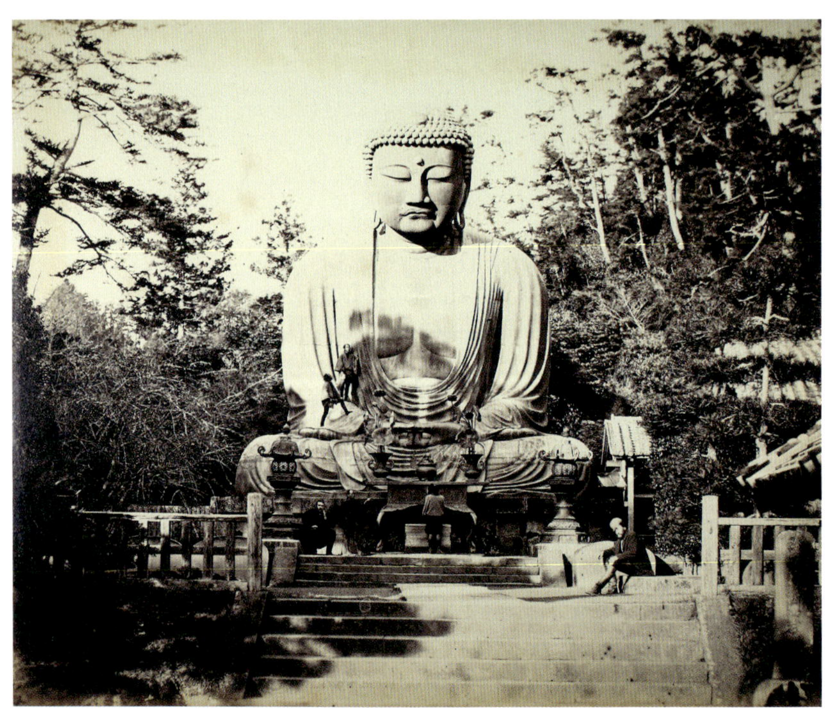

124 Tamamura Kōzaburō, *A Wisteria Trellis at Kameido Shrine in Tokyo*, 2nd half of 19th c.
113 Felice Beato, *The Bronze Statue of Dai-Bouts, Kamakura*, 1863

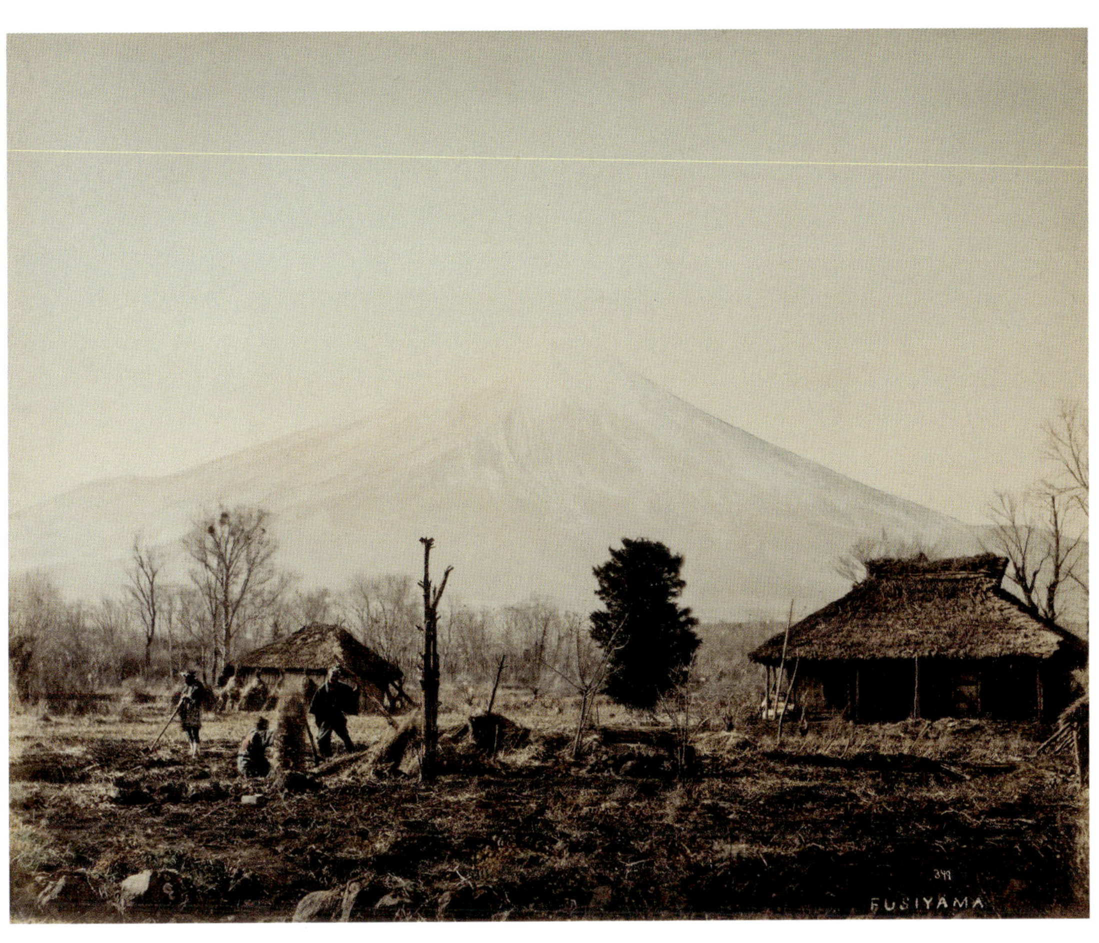

117 Felice Beato, *View of Mount Fuji*, 1867

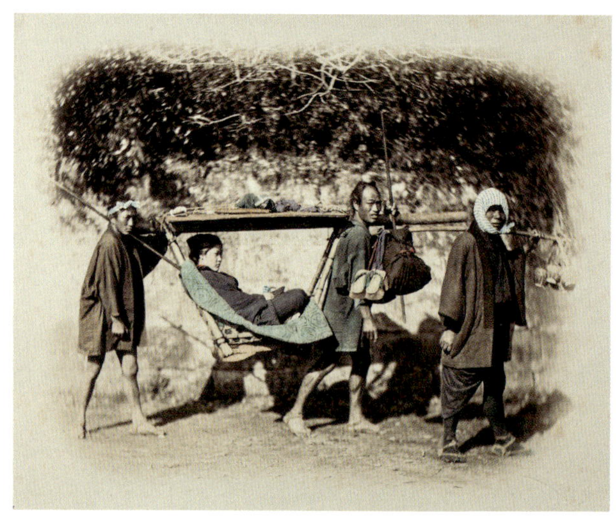

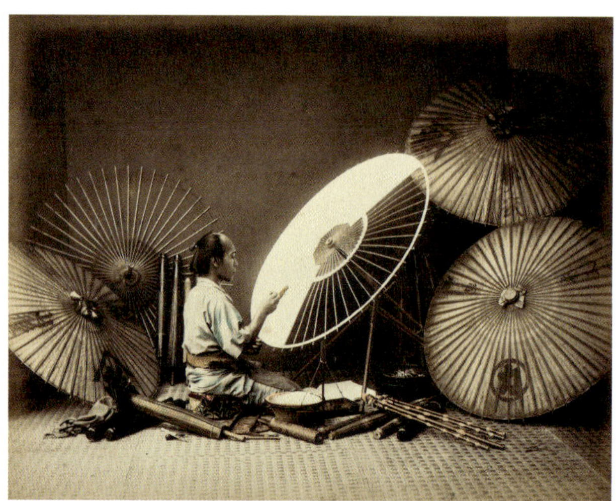

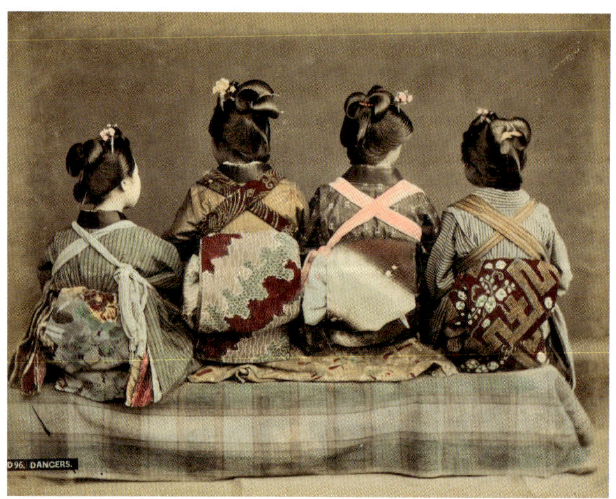

118 Felice Beato, *Litter Bearers*, circa 1868 | 122 Kusakabe Kimbei, *Umbrella Maker*, circa 1880
126 Unknown artist, *"D 96, Dancers"*, 2nd half of 19th c.

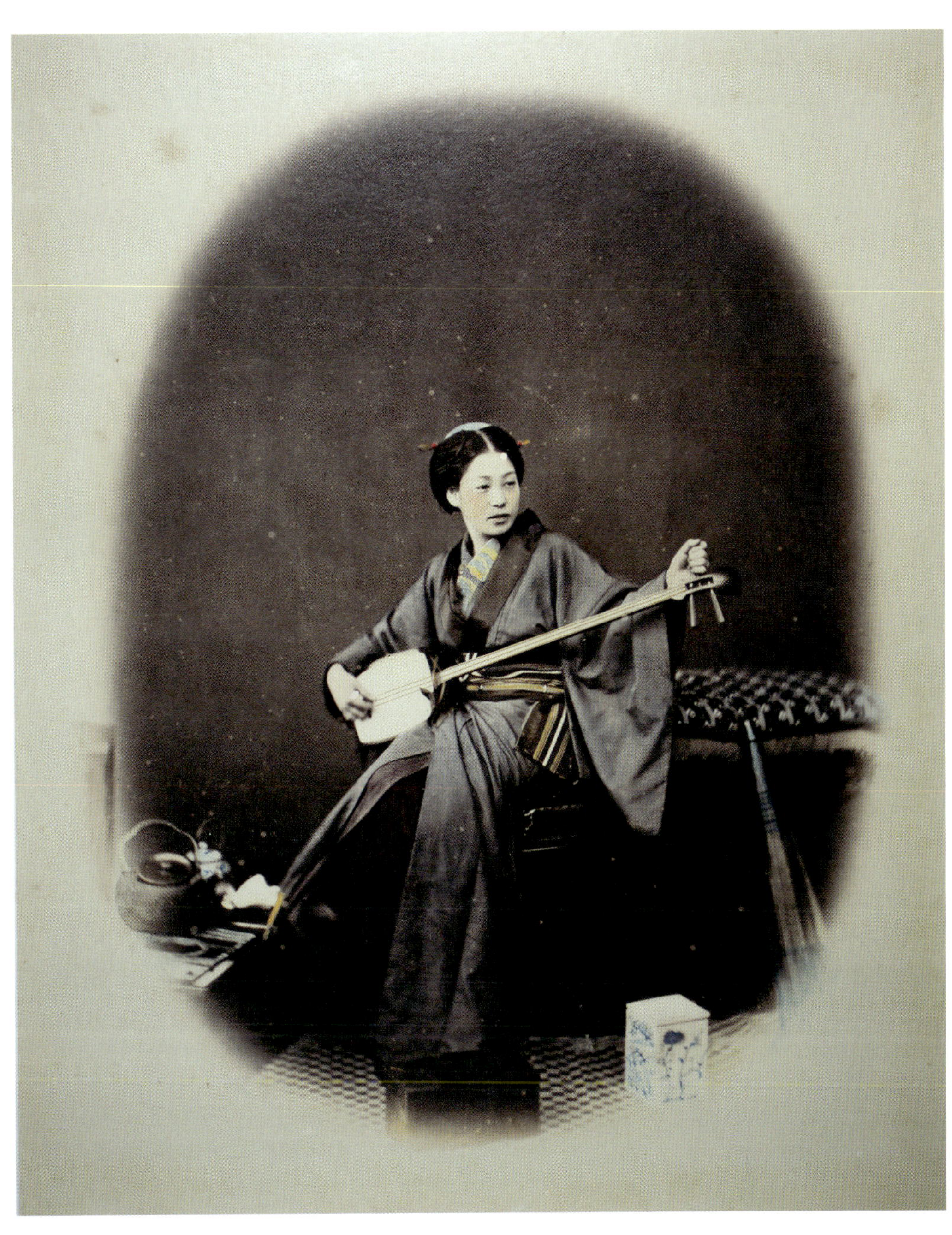

116 Felice Beato, *Woman Playing the Shamisen*, circa 1865

Of brocades and heroes – variations in Japanese colour woodblock prints

The success story of the popular Japanese woodblock prints known as *ukiyo-e* ("pictures of the floating world") got underway in the late seventeenth century. At the time, after a century of hostilities, the Tokugawa shogunate had transformed the country into a centralist feudal state and moved the political capital from Kyoto to Edo (present-day Tokyo). This era is accordingly referred to as the Edo or Tokugawa period (1603–1868). The relocation of the political apparatus of power to the new capital required the construction of paved trade routes, such as the East Sea Road (*Tōkaidō*), whose fifty-three stations linked Edo and Kyoto and whose sights would play a prominent role in the landscapes of Katsushika Hokusai (1760–1849) and Utagawa Hiroshige (1797–1858). Increasing economic stability prepared the ground for the development of a middle class with a culture of its own. The promenades of breathtaking beautiful courtesans and the sensational *kabuki* theatre performances represented the height of urban life. Ingenious writers such as Asai Ryōi (1612–1691) and Ihara Saikaku (1642–1693) recorded their impressions of town society, which they described as a "floating world" (*ukiyo*). This term has its origins in Buddhist terminology, where it stands for the ephemerally floating world of suffering. In keeping with the hedonist attitude in Edo, however, the two writers gave the expression a new twist to mean an evanescent realm in which, seemingly, nothing endures and all that remains is fleeting pleasure.

The depictions (*-e*) that conveyed this attitude were supplied by woodblock print illustrations – publishers and booksellers hired their own woodblock carvers and printers to transfer the artists' sketches to the medium of the woodblock print. Despite this division of labour, usually only the names of the publisher and the artist appear on the finished product. Hishikawa Moronobu (circa 1618–1694) was to become the most prominent of these early illustrators and is considered the founder of *ukiyo-e* in printmaking and painting. He created his style from a fusion of various media: as far as technique was concerned, he drew from books printed with the woodblock print method – in particular, prose, encyclopaedias and travel accounts furnished with line illustrations – especially from 1590 onwards.[1] With regard to content, however, he adhered to the painted genre depictions of bourgeois festivities (*rakuchū-rakugai-zu*) executed by members of the elitist painting schools and by anonymous town artists.[2] Especially worthy of note here are pictures of people dancing, making music or amusing themselves in other ways; as time went on, painters increasingly depicted them as individual figures before an empty background. Captured in the swirling movements of the revellers, the patterns on the vividly colourful kimono brocades likewise start to vibrate and, along with the black contour lines, condense to form the rhythmic arabesques typical of *ukiyo-e*.

When these images began to be reproduced on small-scale hanging scrolls for a less well-funded public, an independent art form for the bourgeoisie had been born. The first chief themes of *ukiyo-e* evolved in the process: depictions of dancing actors (*yakusha-e*) and beautiful women – above all, town belles, teahouse girls or courtesans (*bijin-ga*). Like their counterparts in earlier art forms, however, the faces of the figures in *ukiyo-e* were stylised ideal depictions, not realistic portraits.

In order to reach a broader public, artists and publishers began reproducing their pictures as single-sheet woodblock prints (*ichimai-e*) in the 1680s, rather than exclusively as book illustrations. As Moronobu became more and more popular, other artists also took an interest in the new art form and soon founded schools of their own specialising in certain motifs. Whereas the Torii school, for example, made a name for itself with its theatre depictions, the Kaigetsudō concentrated exclusively on beautiful ladies. In this initial phase of *ukiyo-e*, the images were printed as black-and-white linear depictions (*sumizuri-e*) and subsequently coloured in by hand. Colour combinations of red, yellow and green or indigo prevailed. Owing to the growing demand, advancements were made in the printing technique, and in the 1740s the first multicolour proofs were produced with one line block and three colour blocks (*benizuri-e*). The following decade saw the development of a register mark system (*kentō*) to ensure the precise adjustment of the paper to the printing blocks, leading in 1764/1765 to further improvements in multicolour printing of picture calendars (*e-goyomi*). The latter development came about through collaboration between the artist Suzuki Harunobu (1725–1770) and his rich patron; and with the aid of high-quality materials and skilled woodblock carvers, it resulted in a method of printing with more than eight colours. Owing to the high production costs involved, this revolution in the printing technique was initially limited to small-scale private commissions (*surimono*), but it was not long before it was adopted in commercial printing. The polychrome prints came to be called "brocade pictures" (*nishiki-e*) on account of the colourful kimono patterns in their compositions.

It was primarily prints from this second phase of *ukiyo-e* that found their way to Europe and North America, where – within the context of the phenomenon called *Japonisme* – they influenced several generations of artists and kindled a collecting passion that is still as much aflame as ever. In addition to Suzuki Harunobu, the artists Kitagawa Utamaro (1753–1806), Katsushika Hokusai and representatives of the Utagawa school, primarily Kunisada (Toyokuni III, 1786–1864), Kuniyoshi (1798–1861) and Hiroshige, are considered the most famous exponents of the brocade print. Whereas the two first-named artists depicted almost exclusively beautiful ladies, Hokusai and the artists of the Utagawa school were versed in several subjects. In the second half of the nineteenth century, Hokusai and Hiroshige moreover succeeded in enriching – and providing new impetus to – the *ukiyo-e* tradition stylistically and thematically with their landscapes (*fūkei-ga*) and views of famous sights (*meisho-e*). The Japanese woodblock prints of their time depicted countless other motifs as well and, thanks to their rapid reproducibility in large editions, they were also popular as advertising media and leaflets conveying all sorts of announcements and information.

Harunobu and Utamaro were among the great masters in the portrayal of beautiful women. As already mentioned, Harunobu was the first to profit from the precise production technique of the brocade print. Thanks to the large number of coloured printing blocks, he no longer had to avail himself of thick outlines in order to create a convincing pictorial dynamic, but could reduce the contours to thin but nonetheless literally pulsating lines. What is more, for the first time, artists now had a means of spreading their background compositions across the entire surface rather than having to confine them to just a few staffage elements. Under Harunobu's influence, the formerly corpulent women evolved into delicate fairy-like figures characterised by elegant movement, engaging in dialogue with one another and their surroundings. Harunobu's scenes of beautiful ladies are distinguished by the intimate tranquillity of domestic environments and accentuated by natural phenomena such as seasonal flowers, rain, wind or moonshine (p. 141). Rarely had an artist before Harunobu ever succeeded in combining such a wide diversity of subjects, and, even after his sudden death in 1770, his style continued to have an impact on the compositions of his fellow artists for nearly an entire decade. It was not until around 1790 that an artist came along who developed a new beautiful woman type: Utamaro. In his pictures, the bodily forms gain in size and the proportions in naturalism; the kimonos fall more softly and the hairstyles are more imposing (pp. 142, 143, 156). At the same time, Utamaro lends his portrayals of ladies a sensual aloofness.[3] However, his most important innovation, apart from the introduction of the bust portrait (*ōkubi-e*), was the attempt to depart from the idealised facial types and introduce physiognomic distinctions (*nigao-e*). In his compositions, he did in fact manage to make the women look different from one another by means of fine variations in the facial features. On account of the public's standardised tastes and the artists' dependence on the sale of their publications, however, these works were hardly more than a passing fad. Within the context of his portrait endeavours, Utamaro continued to depict customs and conventions (*fūzoku-ga*), a theme once pursued by Harunobu, and showed ladies engaging in everyday and intimate activities such as applying their make-up and dressing their hair. At the same time, he advanced the serialisation of single-sheet publications such as in the form of personifications of the *Six Crystal Rivers*, *Eight Views*, *Twelve Hours* as well as *Customs of Beauties Around the Clock* (pp. 142, 156).[4]

The second chief thematic complex of *ukiyo-e* was *kabuki* theatre. In addition to portraits of actors on or behind stage, this category also includes comprehensive scenic depictions of performances, illustrated theatre programmes (*banzuke*), posters (*kanban*) and theatre critique compilations (*hyōbanki*). As with the pictures of women, the artists were free to depict the actors on stage with props, accompanying musicians or the audience, or to embed them in an imaginary landscape corresponding to the scene in question (p. 150). Although their faces are likewise stylised, for the contemporary viewer the actors were always immediately identifiable by way of the family coat of arms (*mon*) depicted on the costume. In many of the vividly colourful works, the artist shows the hero of the play in the *mie* pose which the actor maintains for several seconds, tensing his body to an extreme degree in the process, and even rolling his eyes (p. 124). The play's emotional and tragic climax is expressed solely in this pose.

The Utagawa school was known for its tremendous production capacity – to the extent that, in the period of the brocade print, the Torii and Katsukawa schools (which were famous for their theatre prints) soon lagged behind it both qualitatively and quantitatively. Kunisada, who headed the Utagawa school from 1844 onwards, signing himself as "Toyokuni III" in deference to his master, was among the most prolific and versatile artists in this area. He owed his fame to his large series comprising more than a hundred compositions and, above all, to his grand-scale serial depictions of women.[5] Kuniyoshi, for his part, was also successful outside the theatrical field with his magnificent staging of great warriors of history and literature (*musha-e*) and his novel joke pictures (*giga*), with which he increased the school's fame and expanded its repertoire.[6]

In 1830, with his *36 Views of Mount Fuji*, Hokusai proved that landscape could be a profitable subject for large series and, building on this success, Hiroshige celebrated his own artistic breakthrough in 1832 with *53 Stations of the Tōkaidō*.[7] What the two artists shared in their approach to the depiction of nature was that they both availed themselves of the newly discovered stylistic influence of Western pictorial practices such as vanishing-point perspective, chiaroscuro and *sfumato*. Both artists also employed the intense Prussian blue that had come increasingly into use in woodblock prints from 1800 onwards and was largely responsible for the landscapes' characteristic aura (p. 146).[8] For all their similarities, however, a comparison of two pictures from the above-mentioned series – for example, Hokusai's *South Wind, Clear Sky* (p. 147) and Hiroshige's *Hakone, View of the Lake* (p. 149) – also sheds light on the differences in their working manners. Both prints feature a rocky mountain landscape distinguished by the contrasting shades of brownish red and blue and the technically achieved colour gradations (*bokashi*) typical of late woodblock prints. Another common feature is the division into three staggered diagonal stages of depth with a dark-green gradation at the foot of the mountain, the mountain peak as the main motif and a distant mountain range rounding out the composition at the upper left. On closer inspection, however, we notice Hokusai's more reduced palette, strong contrasts and the static zigzag of geometric forms. Hiroshige, on the other hand, employs a wider range of colours, softer forms and curved contours. His composition is enhanced by two tiny figures at the lower edge that serve to emphasise the vastness and calm elegance of the landscape. Hokusai often humorously caricatures human beings in interaction with their surroundings, as seen in his famous book series *Transmitting the Spirit, Revealing the Form of Things: Random Sketches by Hokusai* (*Hokusai Manga*). As mentioned above, he experimented with various themes and styles throughout his career, while Hiroshige specialised in landscape views, and in his last great series *One Hundred Famous Views of Edo*, he developed them further by working with unexpected angles of view and abrupt cut-offs (pp. 208, 209, 214, 220, 221).[9]

Sabine Bradel

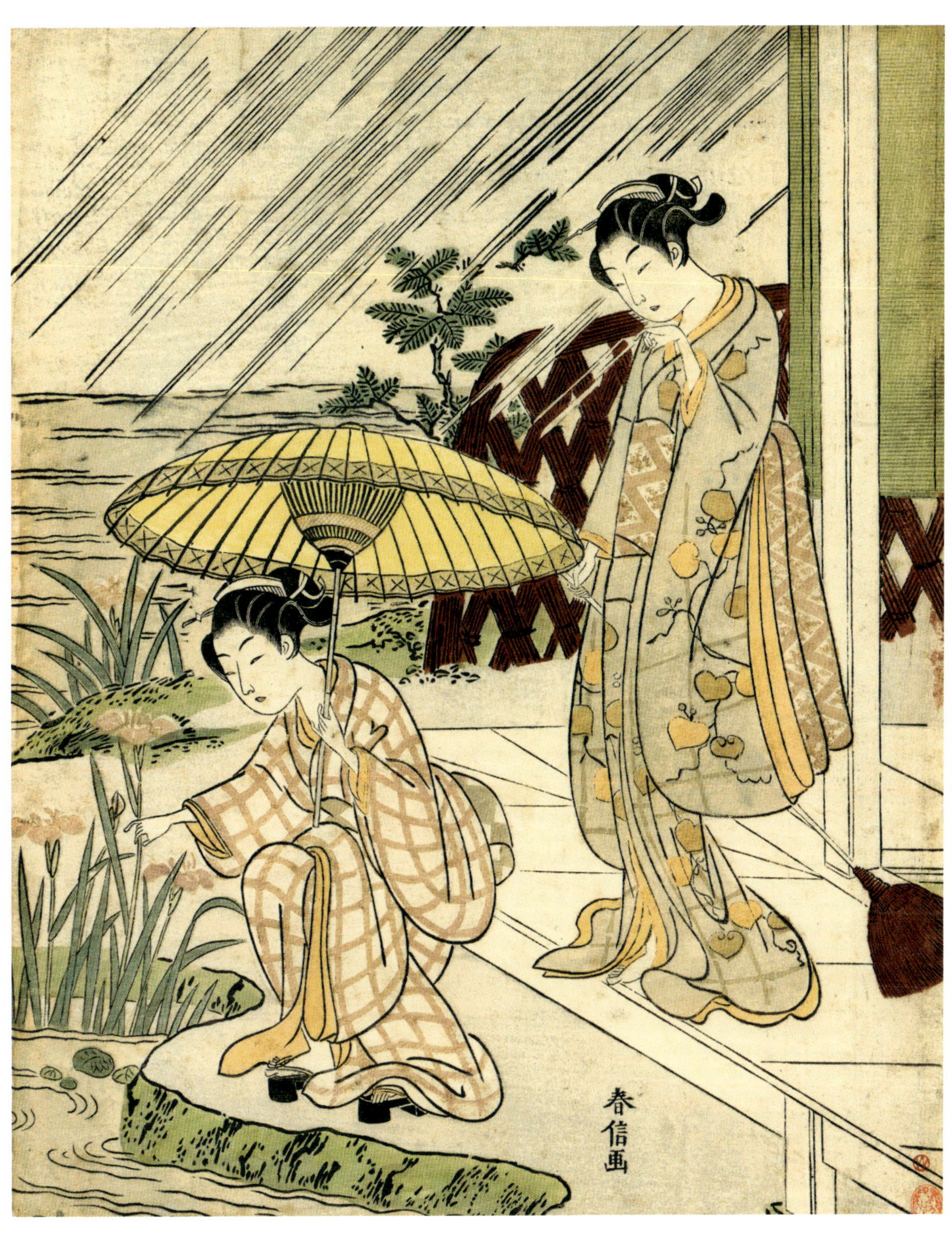

196 Suzuki Harunobu, *Picking Irises in the Rain*, circa 1767–1768

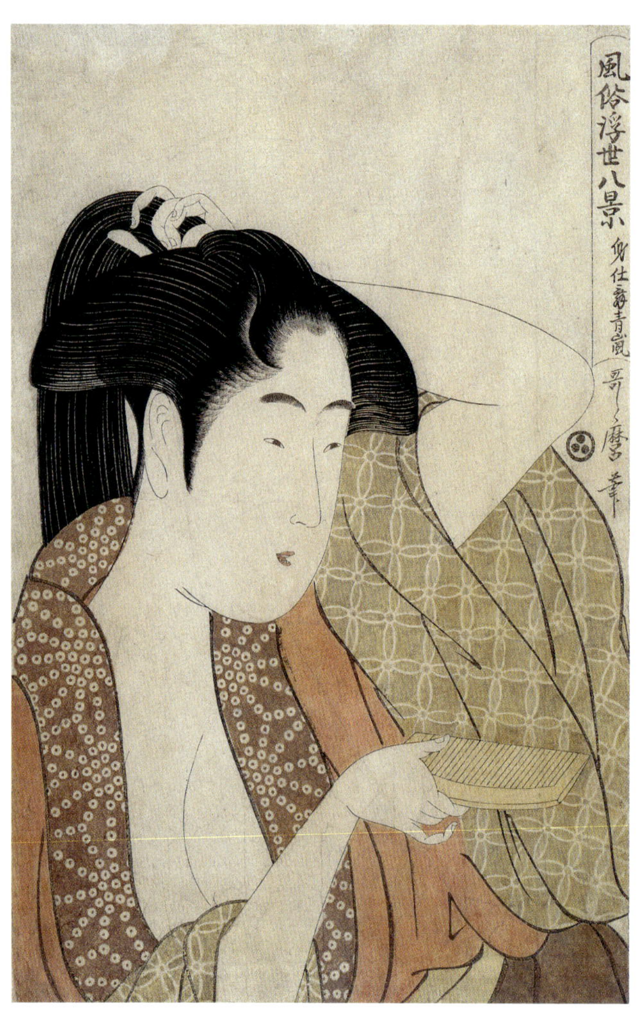

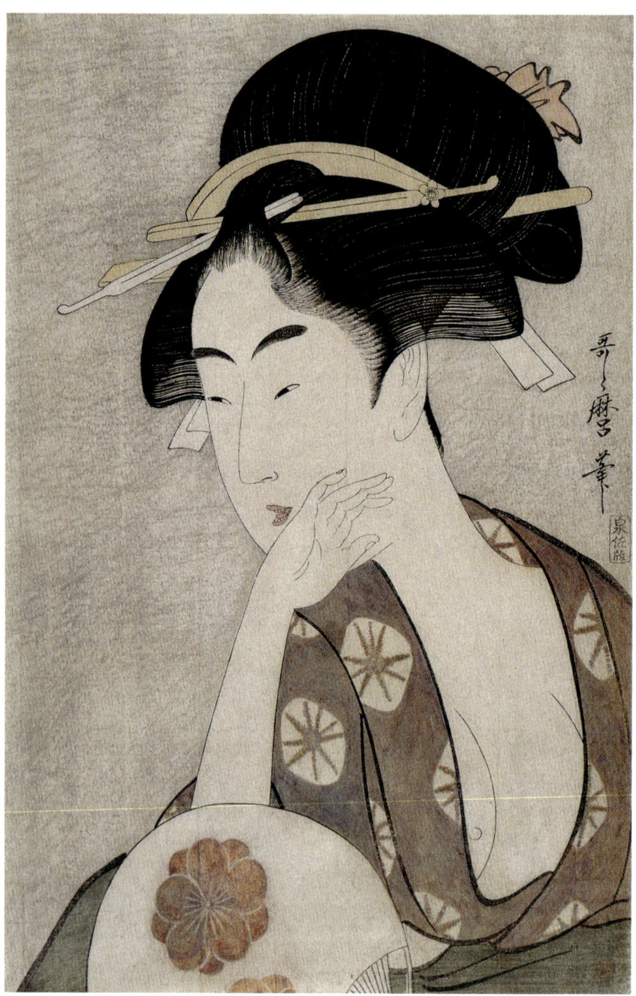

233b | 232 Kitagawa Utamaro, *Clearing Weather during the Toilette*, 1797 | *Lady with a Fan*, circa 1796

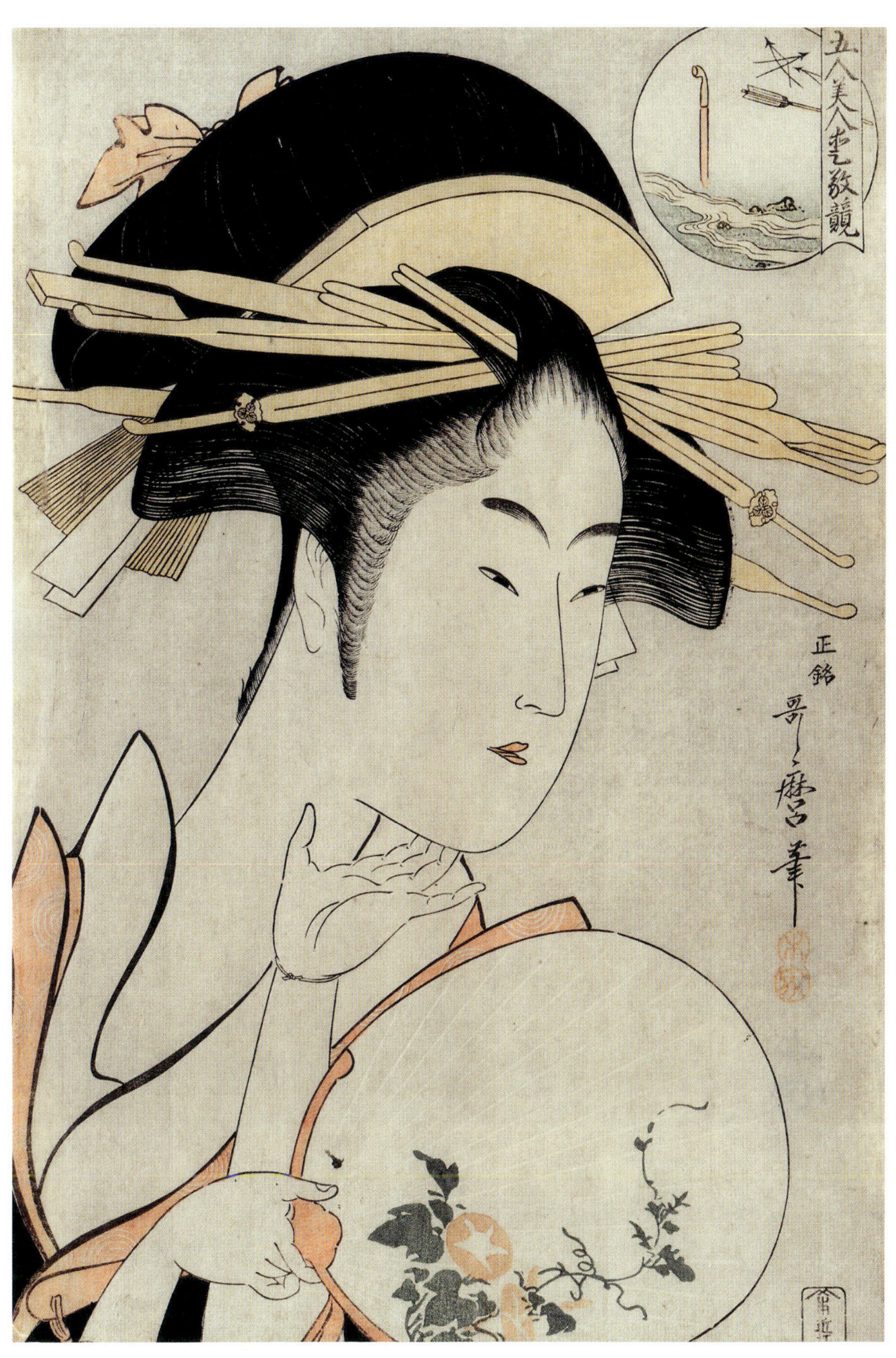

230a Kitagawa Utamaro, *Kisegawa of the Matsubaya*, 1795–1796

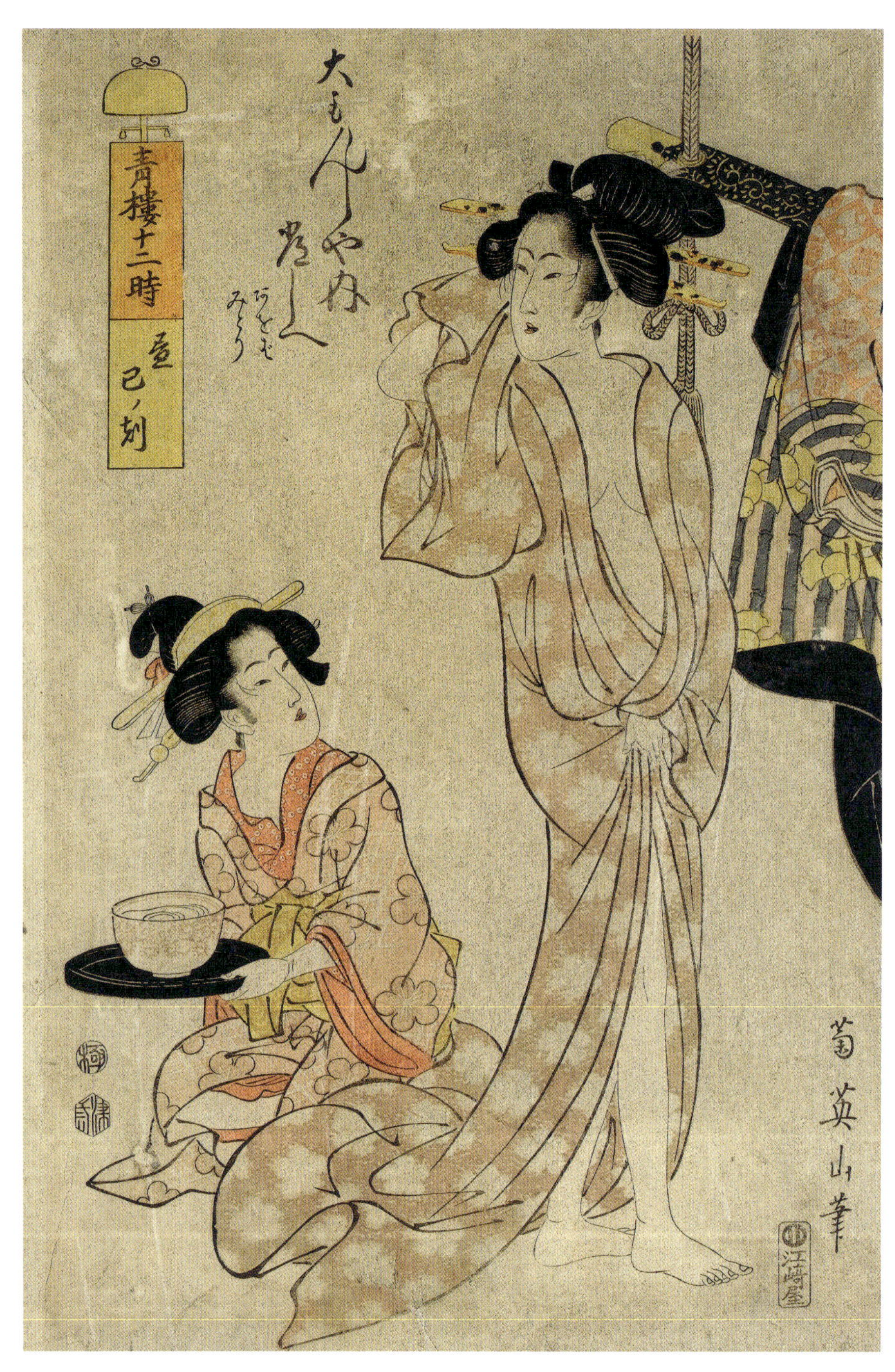

189 Kikugawa Eizan, *The Hour of the Snake: Toshie from the Daimonjiya House*, 1812–1820

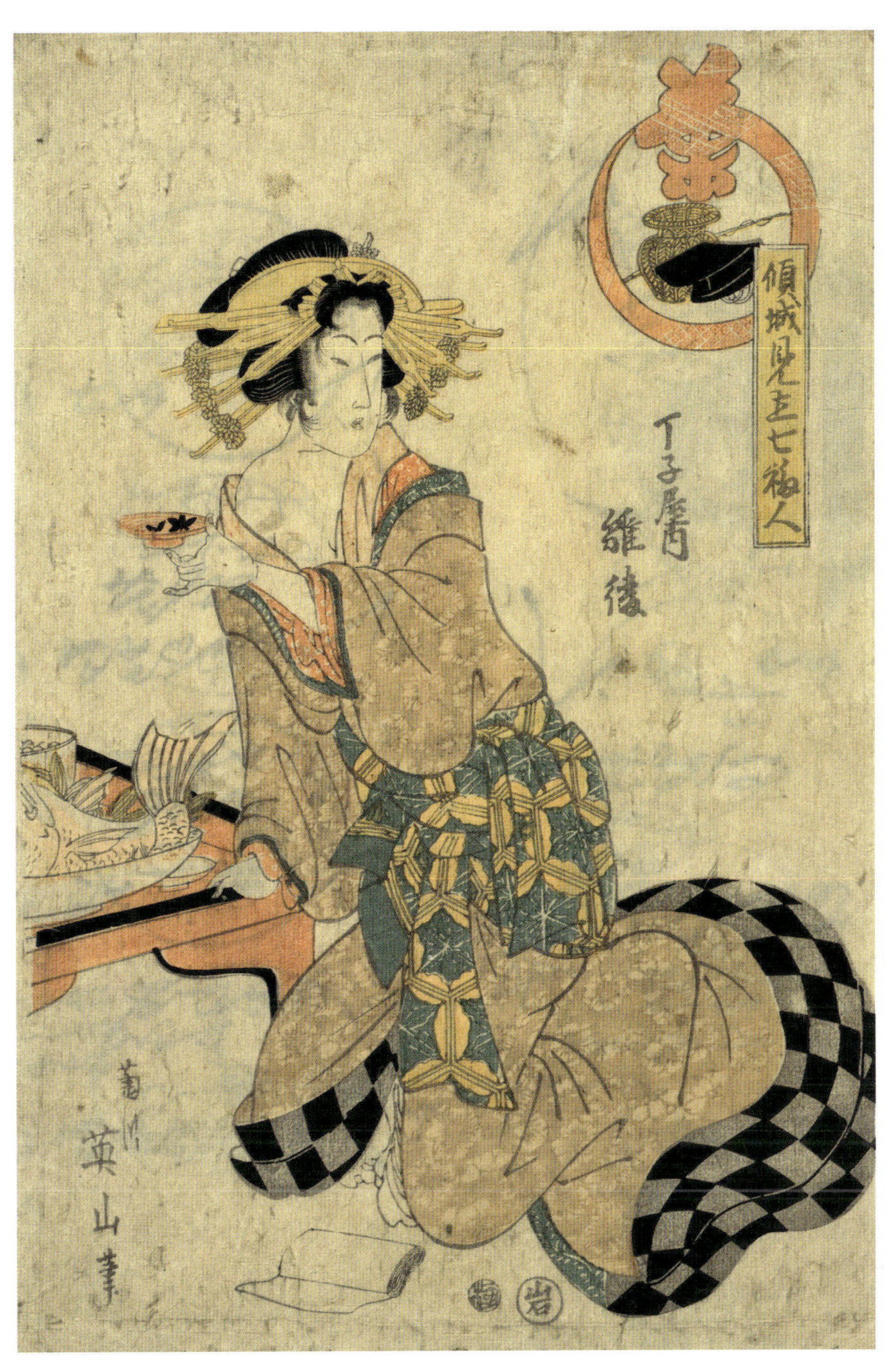

190a Kikugawa Eizan, *The Courtesan Hinaaya of the Chōjiya House*, 1814–1817

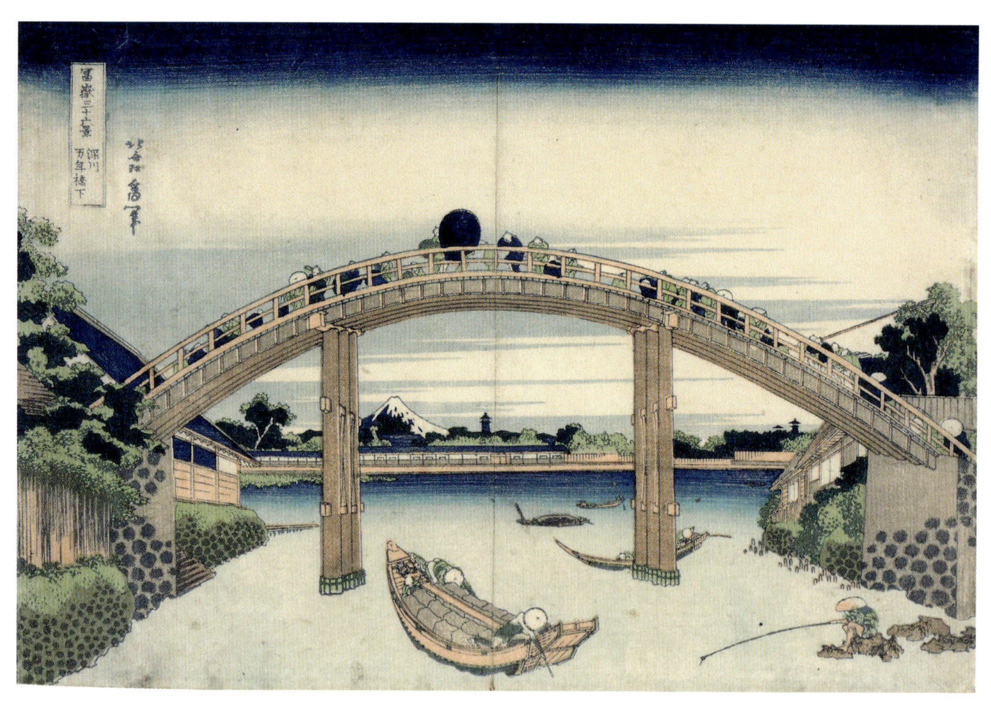

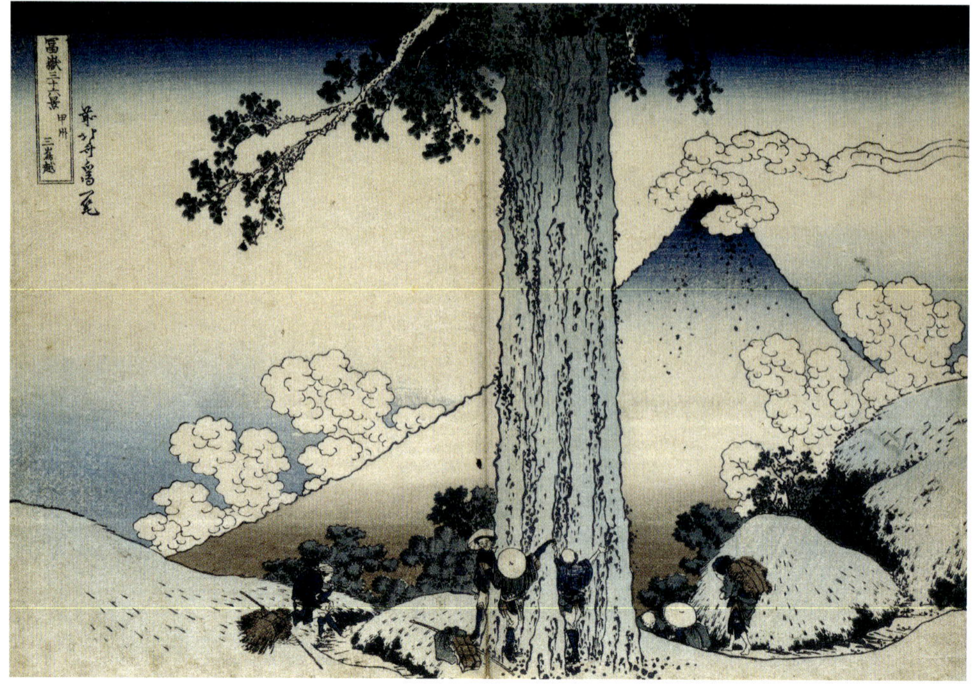

205r | 205c Katsushika Hokusai, *Under Mannen Bridge at Fukagawa* | *Mishima Pass in Kai Province*, 1830–1831

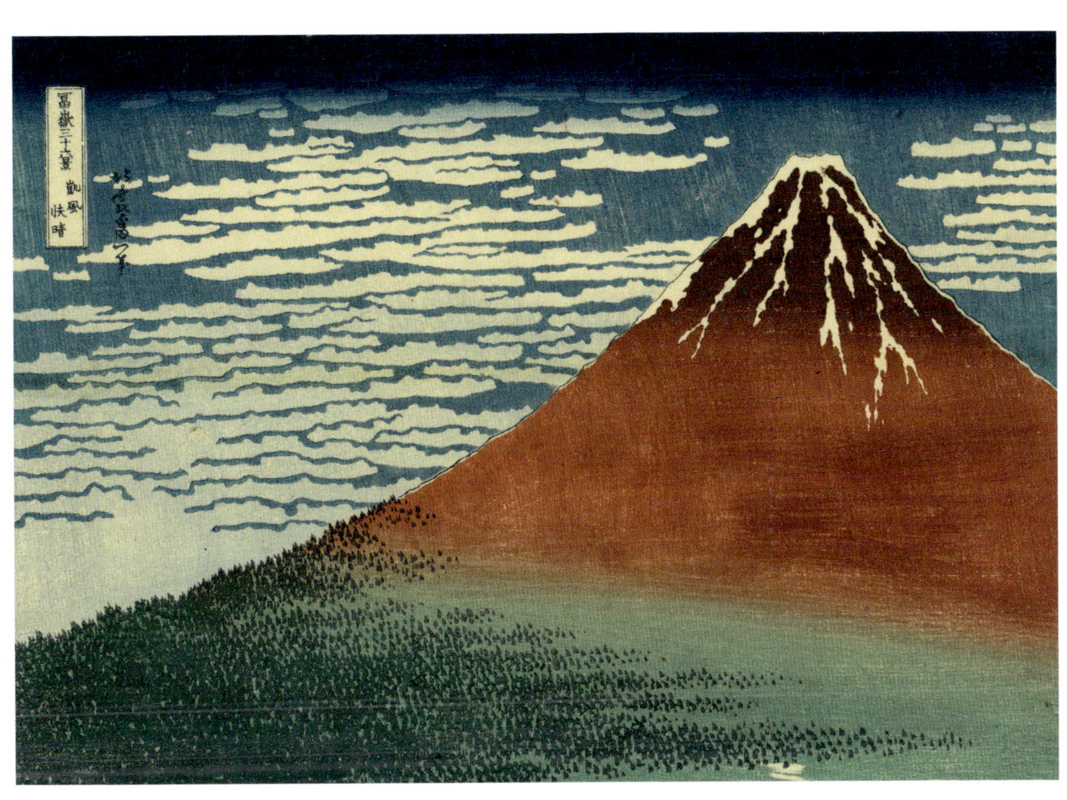

2050 Katsushika Hokusai, *South Wind, Clear Sky*, 1830–1831

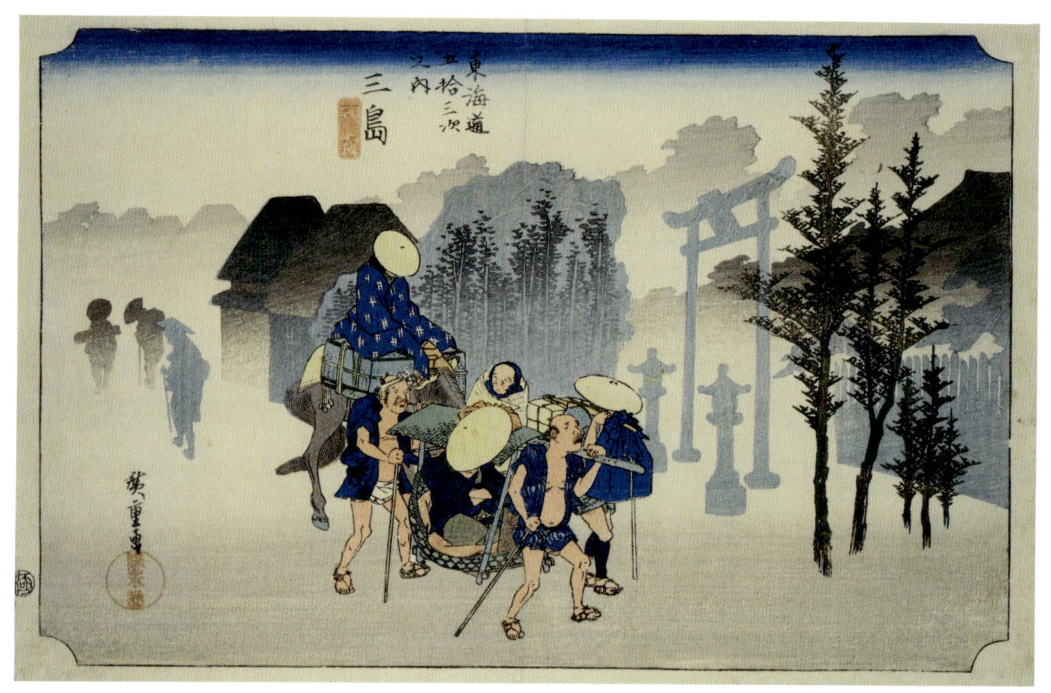

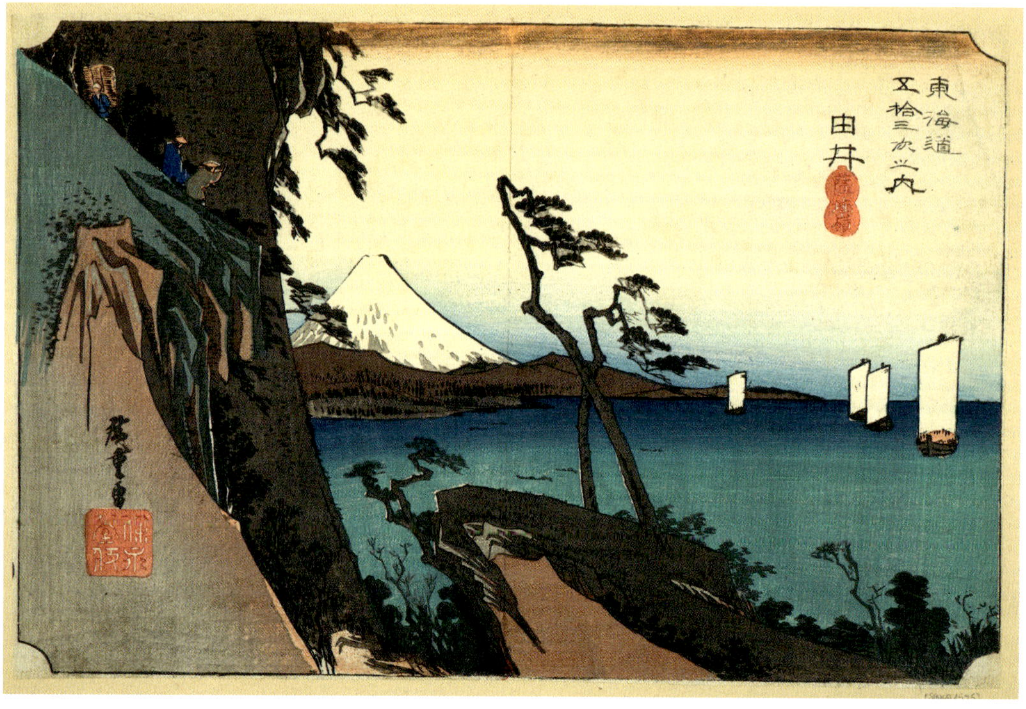

198d | 198e Utagawa Hiroshige, *Mishima, Morning Mist* | *Yūi: Satta Peak*, 1833–1834

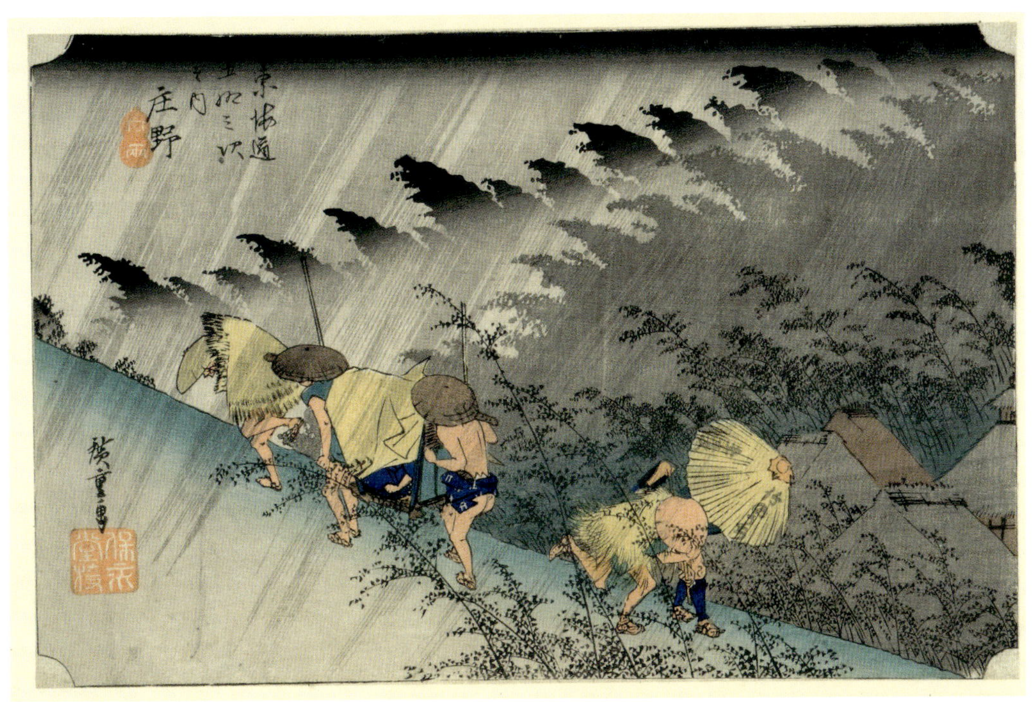

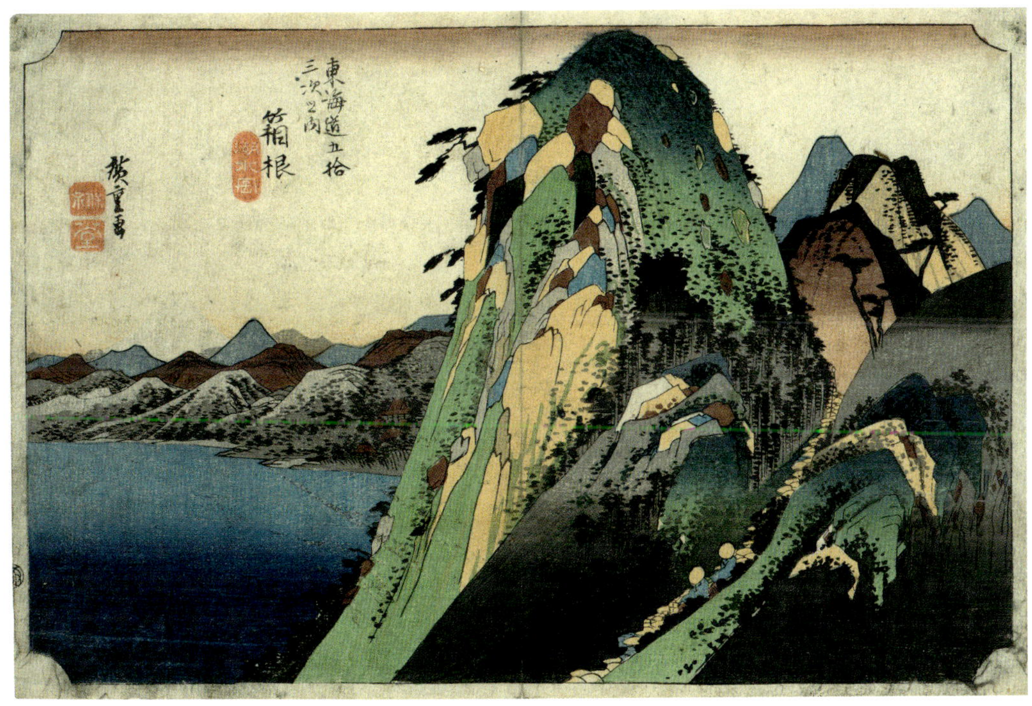

198h | 198b Utagawa Hiroshige, *Sudden Rain at Shōno* | *Hakone, View of the Lake*, 1833–1834

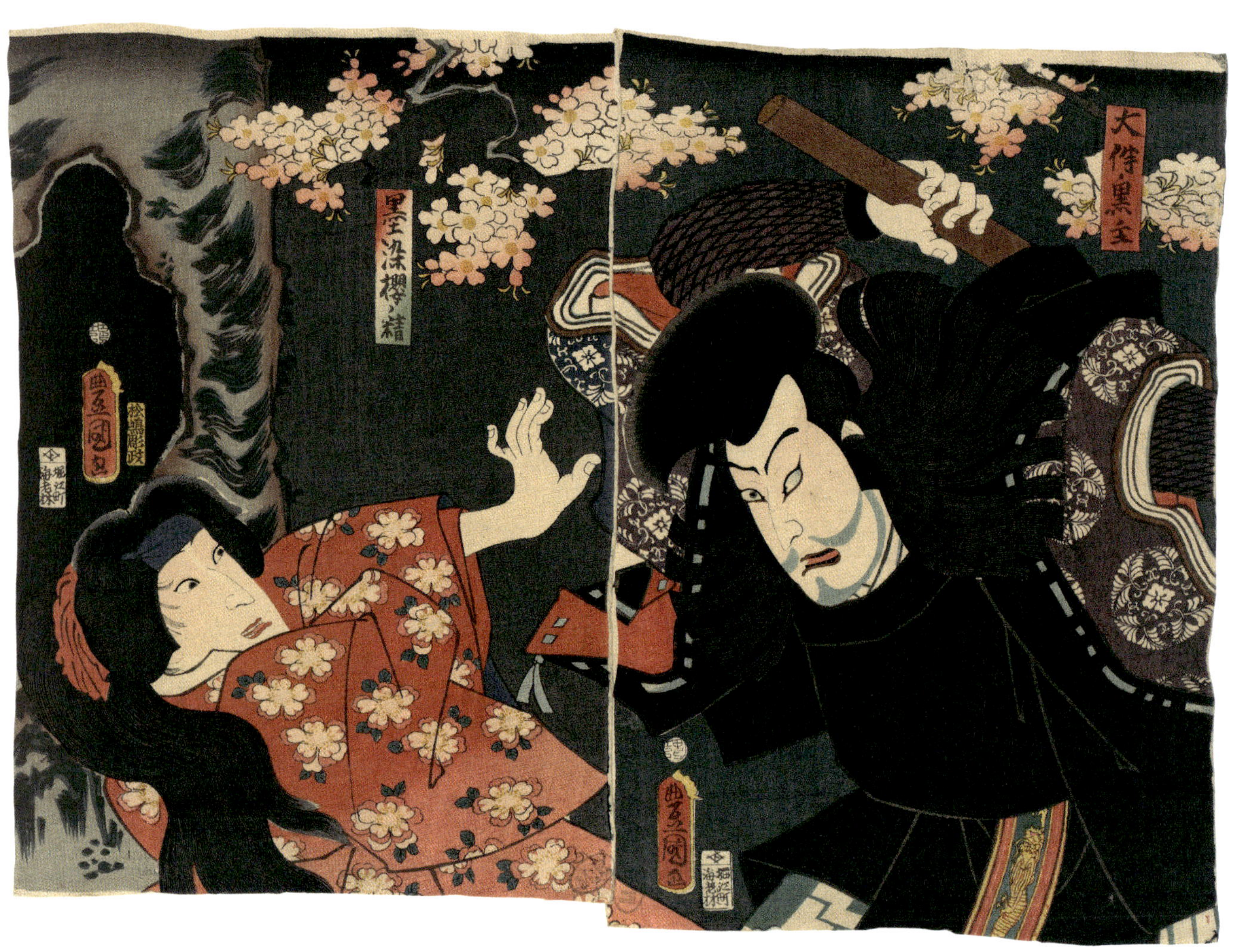

215 Utagawa Kunisada (Toyokuni III), *Ōtomo Kuronushi and the Cherry Blossom Spirit Sumizome*, 1860

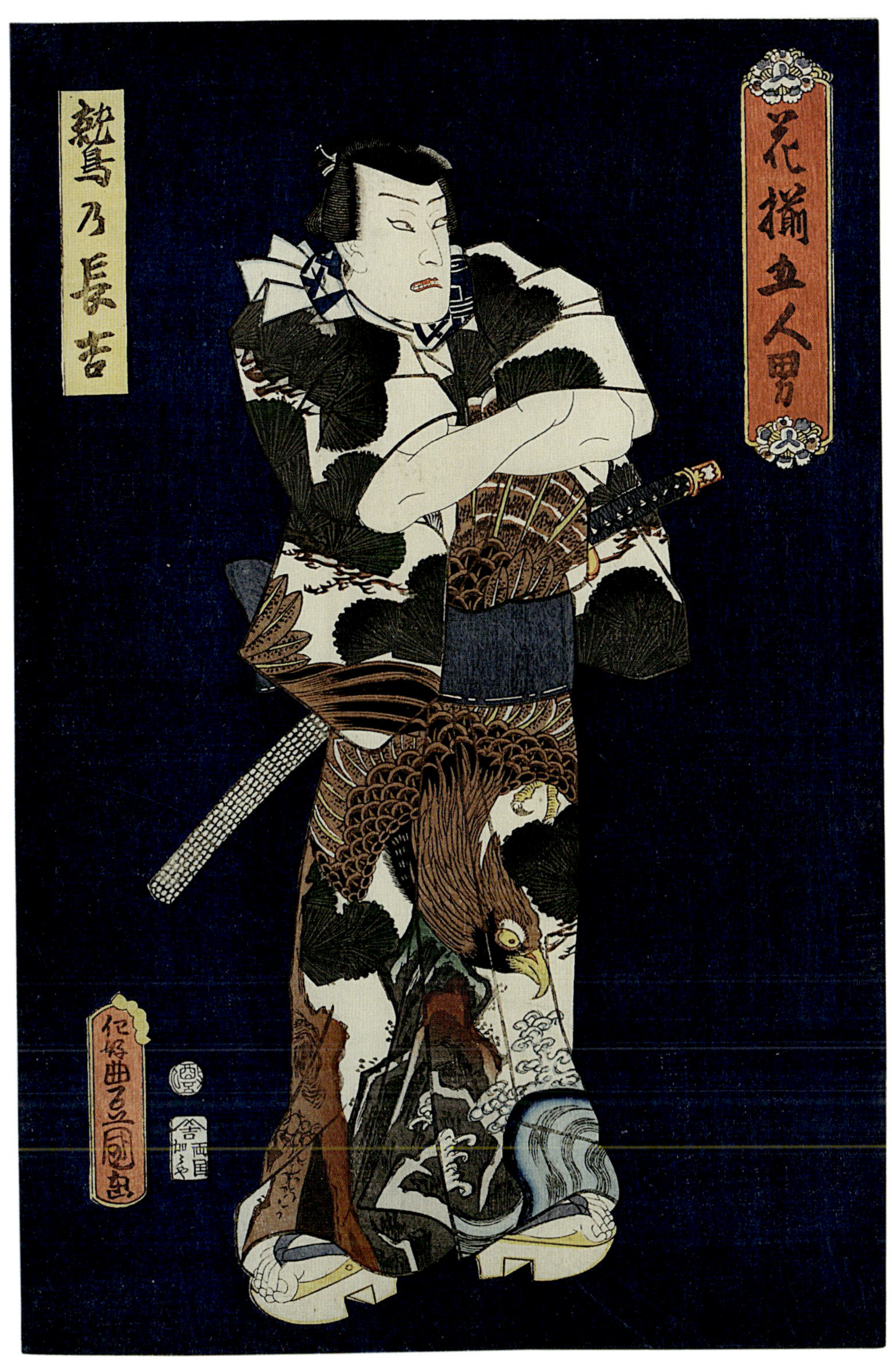

216 Utagawa Kunisada (Toyokuni III), *Nakamura Shikan VI in the Role of Washi no Chōkichi*, 1861

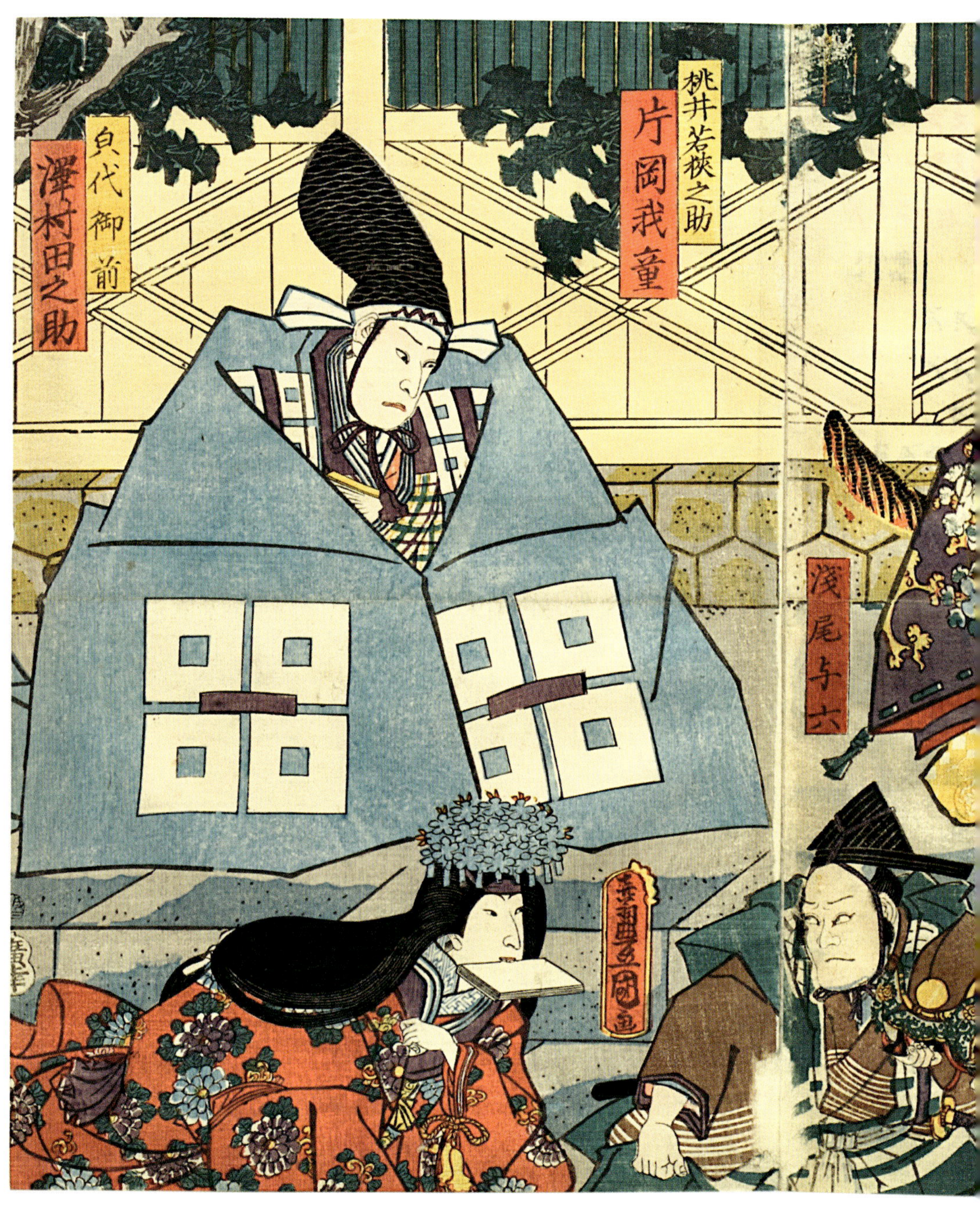
浅尾与六
桃井若狭之助
片岡我童
㒵代御前
澤村田之助

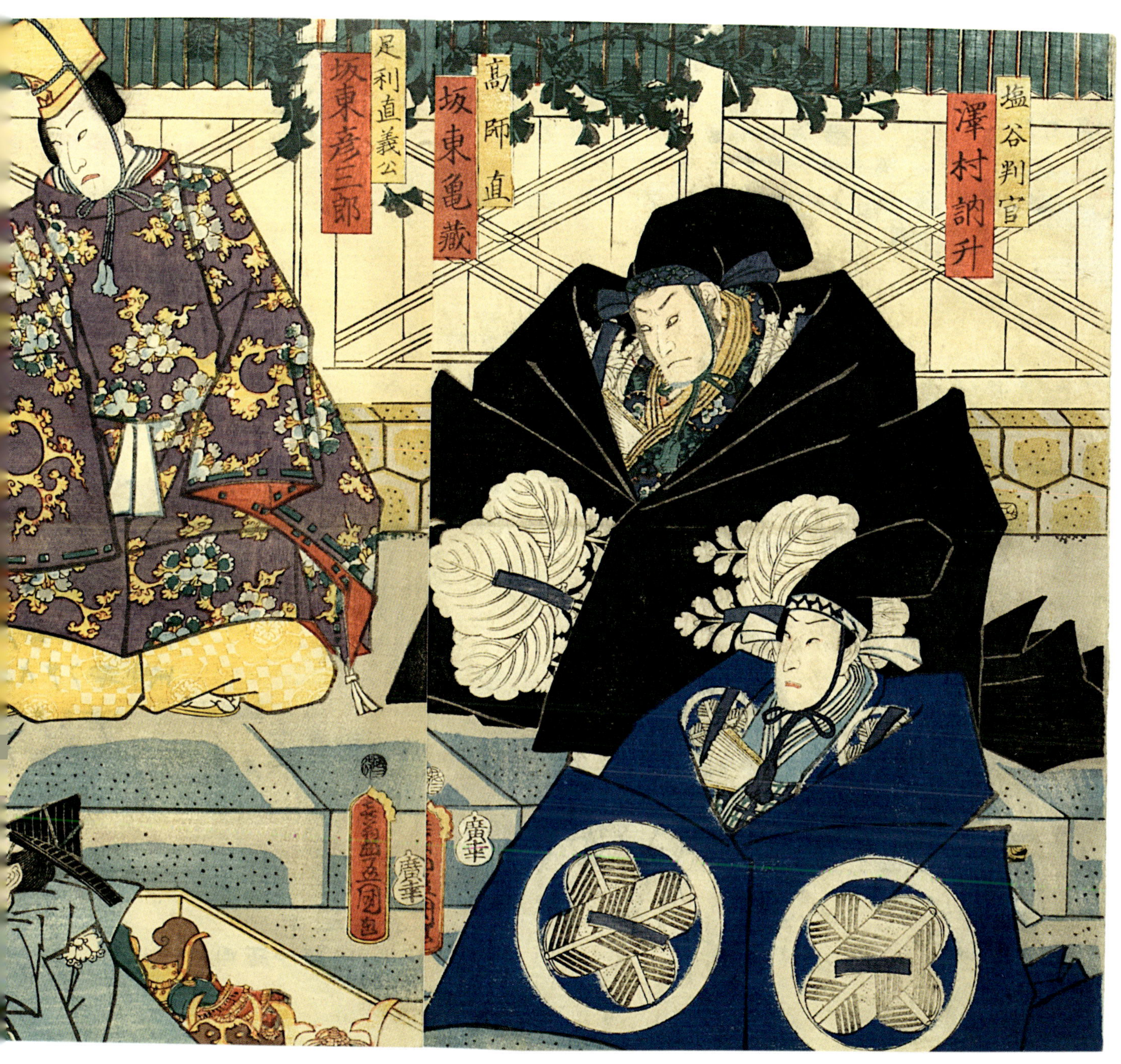

217 Utagawa Kunisada (Toyokuni III), *The Helmet: Duchess Kaoyo Recognises the Helmet of Yoshisada by his Scent*, 1862

The Japanese among us – motifs and series

Among Edgar Degas's most-loved subjects are young women washing themselves, getting dressed or combing their hair – a preference that became clear in his work from the mid-1870s onwards (pp. 157, 158, 159, 161). Before Degas, such motifs were only rarely found in European art, in contrast to the Japanese art of woodblock printing. Since Degas himself owned an extensive collection of Japanese woodblock prints, it can be assumed that he was inspired by such depictions. Imitating the Japanese form of narration, Degas placed his models in scenes "at their toilette", "getting their hair combed" or "after their bath" in a seemingly matter-of-fact manner. The scene in *Breakfast after the Bath* – a maid bringing a cup of tea (or rather chocolate?) to a woman who has just left the bath (p. 157) – reveals great thematic similarities to the scene depicted in Utamaro's *The Hour of the Snake* (p. 156).

Undoubtedly, the aesthetic sense of natural beauty, the accentuation of a lost perfection, is something typical of traditional Japanese art. Ikebana, the art of staging flowers, begins with "cutting" the flower, bringing the blossom to life by cutting it, and its effective presentation. Henri Fantin-Latour seems to imitate the "cutting" of a blooming rhododendron branch with his close-up composition from 1874, when he places the delicateness of the pink flowers next to the leathery, dark-green leaves with great dexterity (p. 163). The artist emphasises this delicately observed contrast of the two "beauties" – the leaf and the blossom – against a light-grey wall marked with delicate shadows in order to animate the space. The way in which the branch of the rhododendron, a plant imported from Asia, looms into the image as if from nothingness is reminiscent of Katsushika Hokusai's series of *Large Flowers* (p. 162).

Gustave Caillebotte was also interested in flowers imported from the Far East, as shown in his painting *Four Vases with Chrysanthemums* (p. 165) from 1893. White and yellow chrysanthemums, a plant that was originally grown in China and imported to Europe from Japan for the first time in the 1860s, are seen to grow in the delicate, greyish-pink visual space. With this floral still life, the artist seems to have internalised Japanese stylistic effects, with a gaze from above onto vases of Chinese origin, asymmetrically arranged, holding many different kinds of chrysanthemum flowers, the national symbol of Japan.

Besides the Far Eastern flora, French artists were especially fascinated by the motif of the sea, which appears particularly frequently in the work of artists such as Katsushika Hokusai or Utagawa Hiroshige. In his painting *The Violet Wave* (p. 171) from 1896/1897, for example, Georges Lacombe reinterprets the large wave from Hokusai's three-volume work *One Hundred Views of Mount Fuji* (p. 170) in his very own way. Lacombe himself owned the volume in question and engaged with the motif of the wave in his work several times.

For Monet's paintings of the pyramids of Port Coton (p. 177), woodblock prints by Hiroshige were most certainly an inspiration (pp. 172–173, 174, 175). At least it was the Japanese artist who directed Monet's interest to motifs that had always been present but never central to French art. With these paintings that emerged in Belle-Île, Monet began to paint in series, taking up the subject of the rock pyramids in the six versions known today that only differ slightly from one another (p. 176).

The motif of the sea and seriality also played a decisive role in the work of Gustave Courbet. During his stays in Étretat on the French coast, he insistently painted the wide expanse of the sea – and in 1869, for the first time, the motif of a powerfully surging, crashing wave, with an explosion of ocean spray, across the entire breadth of the canvas (p. 169). The wildness of his ocean is very immediate, and he applied the raw and dirty paint with great emotion using a kitchen knife. The threateningly crashing, spraying wave came to emblematise Courbet's efforts to create a new, realistic depiction of nature that differed markedly from the wealth of detail in Romantic painting.

The radically new and powerful way in which Courbet choreographs the motif of the crashing wave brings to mind another equally impressive and emblematic landscape: Hokusai's *Under the Wave off Kanagawa* from the series *36 Views of Mount Fuji* (p. 167), which in the West became symbolic for Japanese art, in general, and shaped the notion of Japan fostered by the West like hardly another image. And not only the motif of the wave is relevant here: the artist might well have found inspiration in Hokusai or Hiroshige in his serial approach. Both Japanese artists took various motifs – such as Mount Fuji, bridges or waterfalls – as the basis for their woodblock-printed series or books. At any event, Courbet painted the motif of the wave time and again between 1869 and 1872, resulting in around forty variations.

Paul Cézanne most likely took his inspiration for his repeating motif of Mont Sainte-Victoire from the Japanese artists. Since the end of the 1860s, he had been moving in a circle of artists, critics and writers from Café Guerbois in Paris who enthusiastically received the art of *ukiyo-e* popular in Japan: Édouard Manet, Auguste Renoir, Edgar Degas, Henri Fantin-Latour, Claude Monet, James McNeill Whistler, Zacharie Astruc and Émile Zola. We can exclude the possibility that Cézanne had no knowledge of the circulating volumes of *Manga* by an artist like Hokusai or the woodblock prints of other Japanese artists, whose forms of expression included the use of a decentred visual structure, partial motifs, a raised perspective, strong contrasts and flatness of colour, especially in landscapes. It remains an open question whether it was a coincidence that Cézanne painted the silhouette of Mont Sainte-Victoire, an emblem of his birthplace, at least 36 times over the years, varying the motif of the mountain and the landscape around it since the mid-1880s in a manner similar to the way Hokusai once honoured the sacred mountain of Fuji with 36 views characterised by an evocative choreography (pp. 146, 147, 178, 192). Unlike the Japanese artist, Cézanne felt committed to a certain natural verisimilitude. Yet, and this might have been borrowed from the woodblock prints of Hokusai that he was familiar with since the 1860s in Paris, he staged the landscape with the massif and its spatial arrangement in layers of paint as a highly atmospheric visual space, often horizontally structured, almost entirely without perspective. Cézanne achieved the effect of traditional perspective in an illusory space with the help of a stage-like arrangement – bushes, young trees, or even cut trees and branches that reach like scenery into the landscape, for instance, blocking the direct gaze of the beholder into the distance towards the mountain (p. 179). Still, in the landscape *Mont Sainte-Victoire Seen from Les Lauves*, Cézanne departs from these compositionally immanent techniques in favour of an almost free and vague allusion to the central motif (p. 180). Just as in a watercolour, the artist uses paint confidently and sparingly, accompanied by a few contouring lines horizontally filling the breadth of the landscape. It is unclear whether Cézanne failed to complete this painting or did not want to complete it, or whether, using the brightness of the neutral white of the canvas in contrast to the largely blue-to-green shades, he intended to ground the staggered effect of the landscape in depth. It is evident, however, that Cézanne, like Hokusai, reduced the depiction of what he saw to a few moments that clarify the motif, and with this landscape had internalised the requirements of the central compositional structure implemented in the Far East, far from any pre-existing reality.

Mario-Andreas von Lüttichau

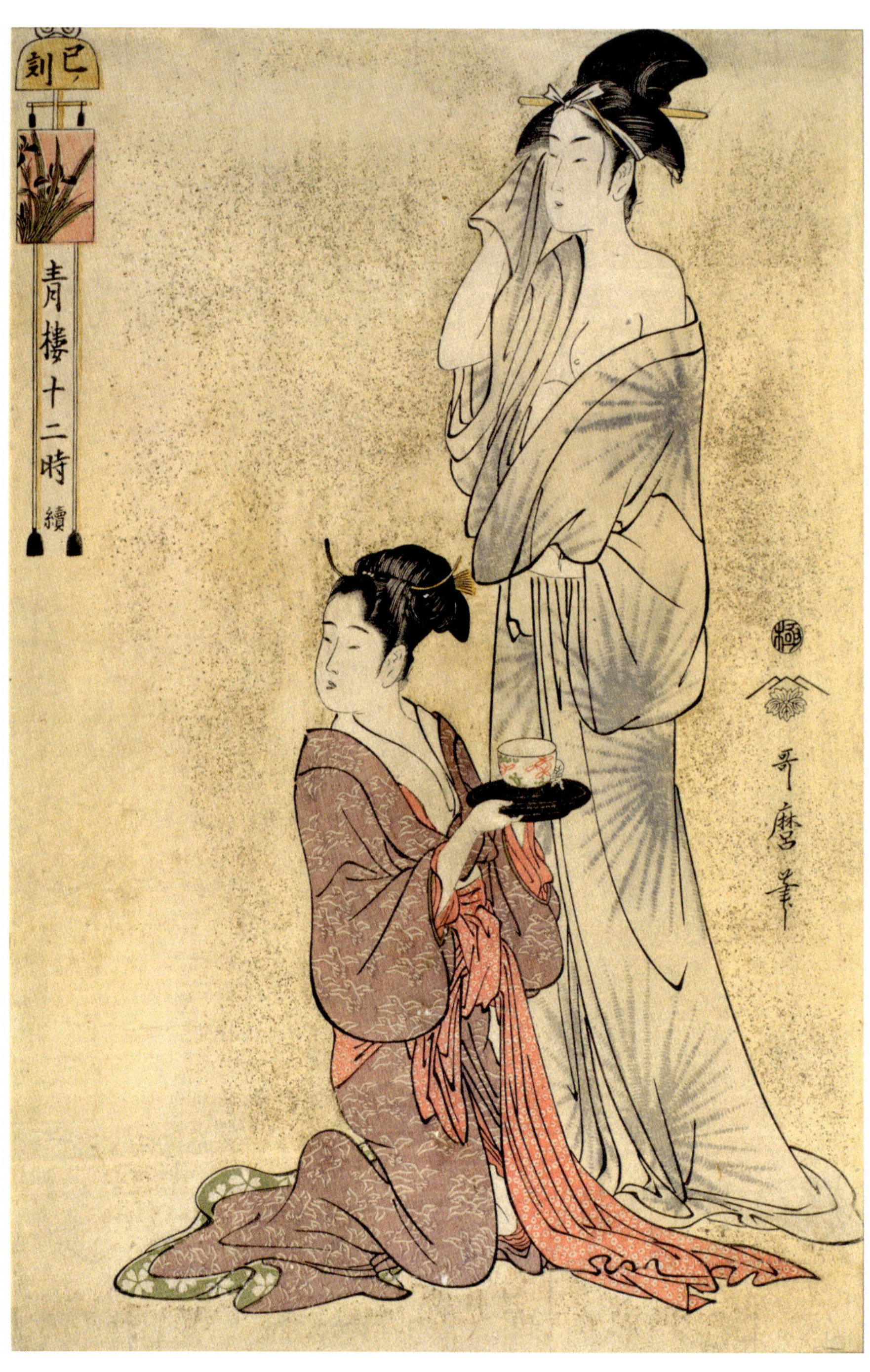

227 Kitagawa Utamaro, *The Hour of the Snake*, 1794–1795

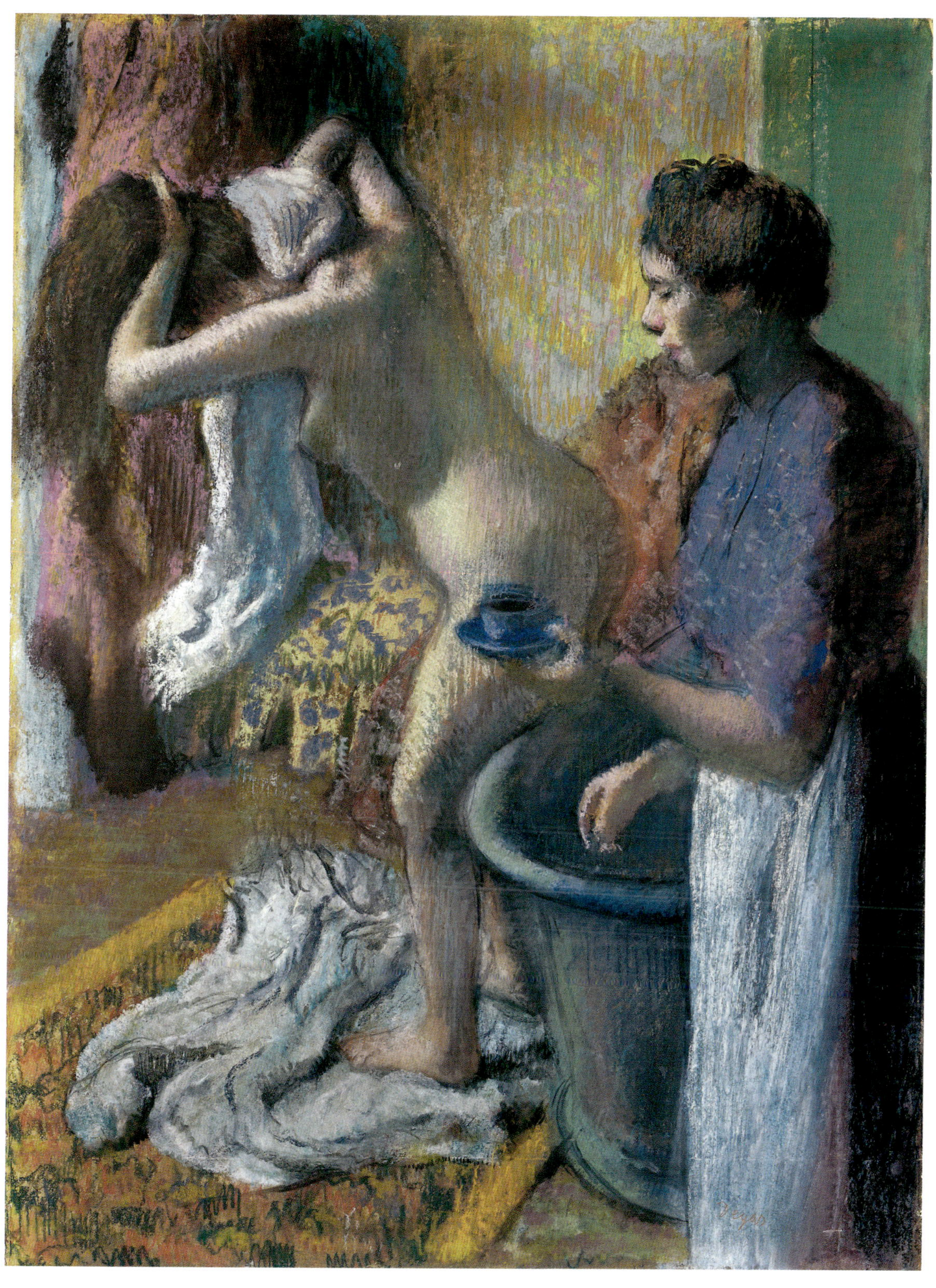

21 Edgar Degas, *Breakfast after the Bath*, circa 1895/1898

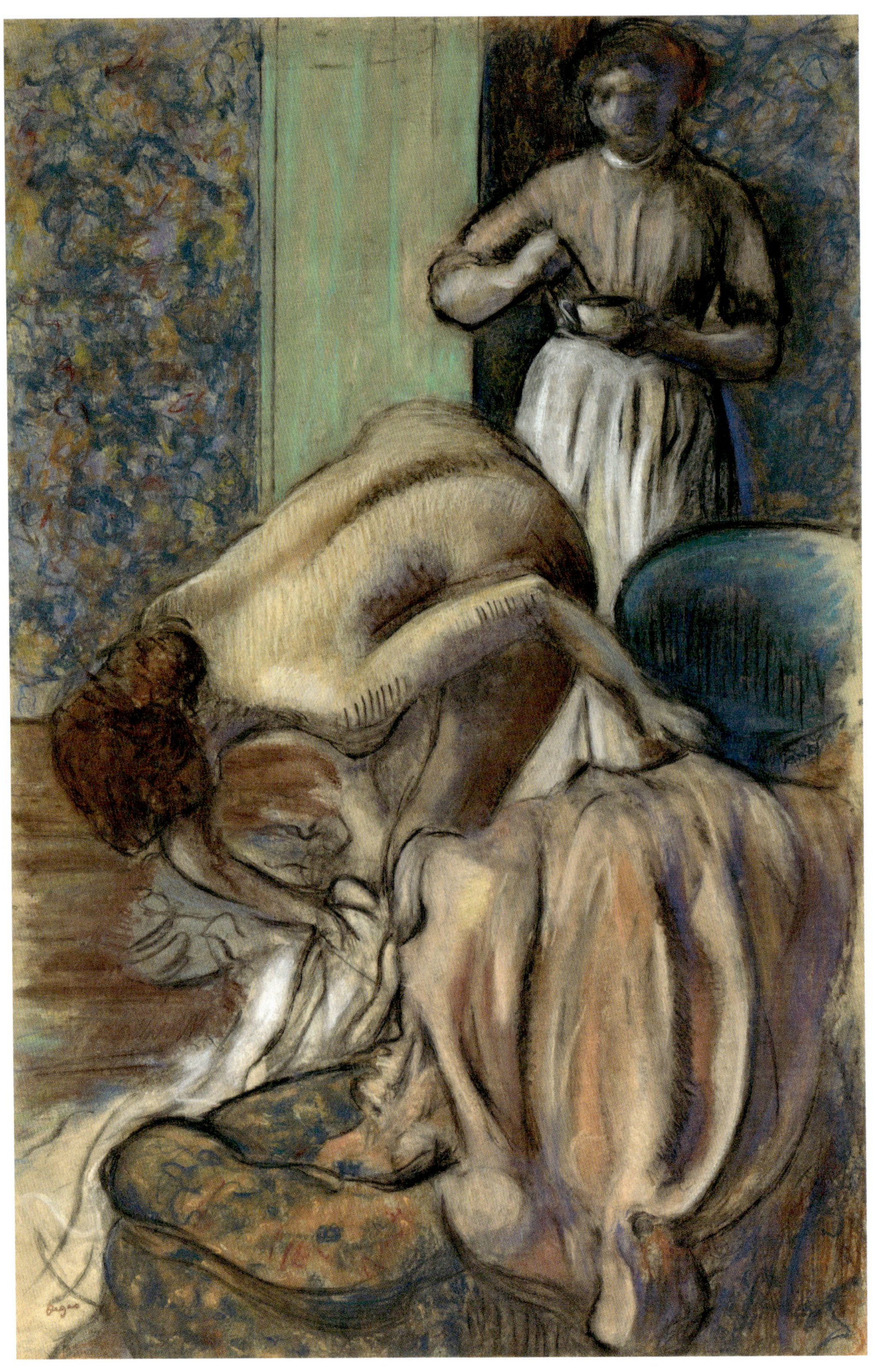

19 Edgar Degas, *Breakfast after the Bath*, circa 1894

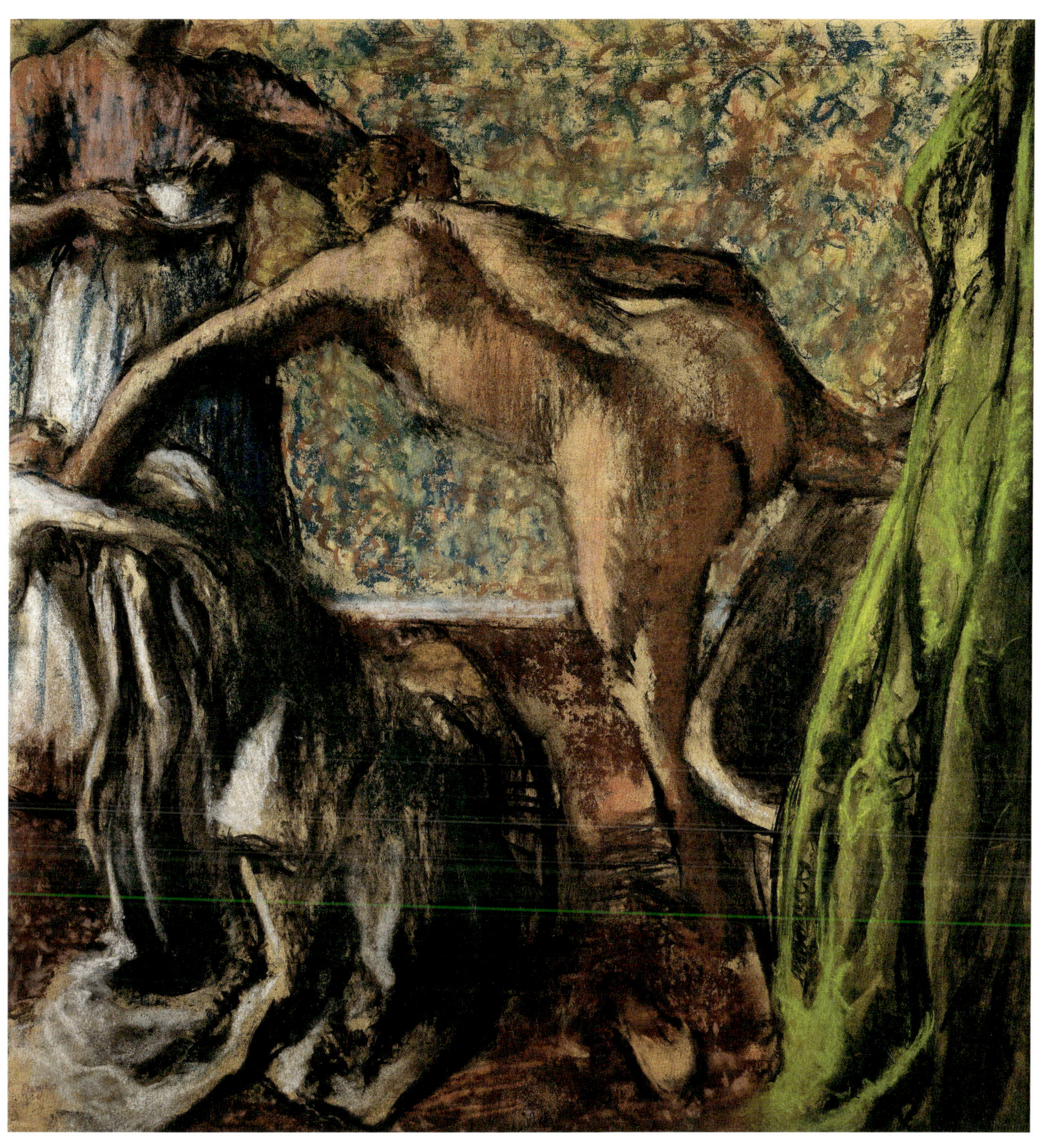

20 Edgar Degas, *Breakfast after the Bath (The Bath)*, circa 1895/1898

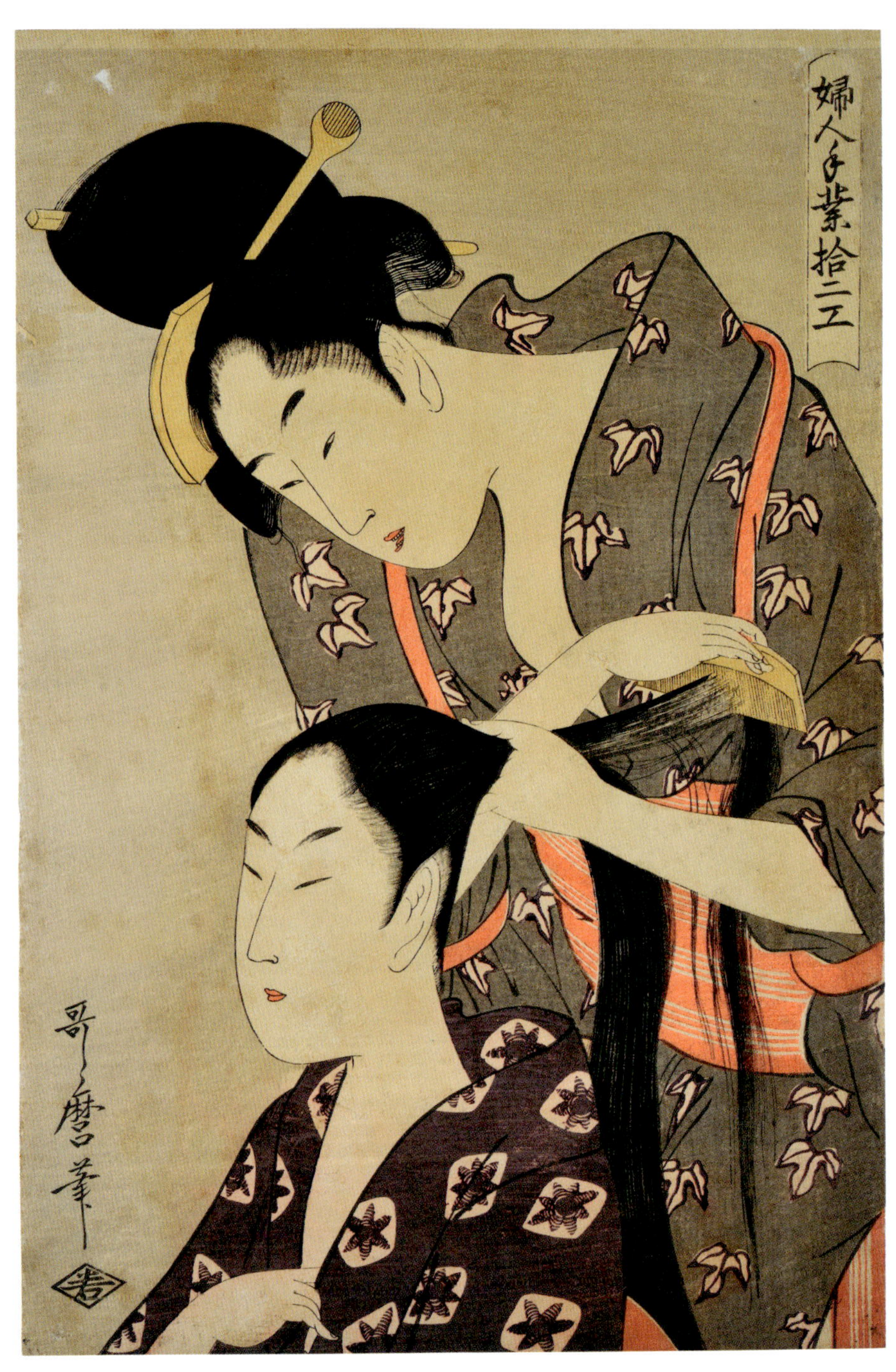

234 Kitagawa Utamaro, *Hairdresser*, 1798–1799

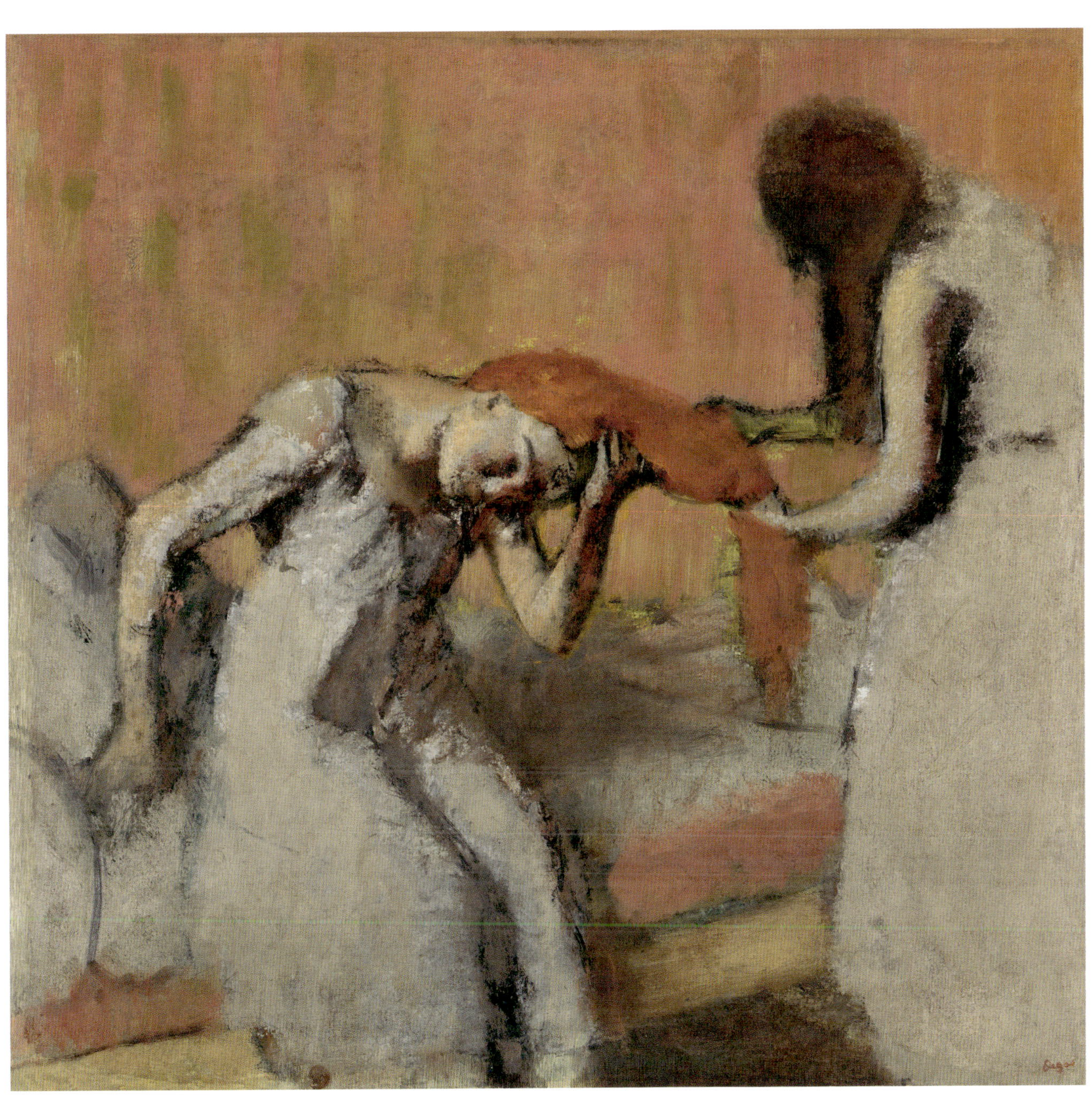

18 Edgar Degas, *Morning Toilette*, 1892/1895

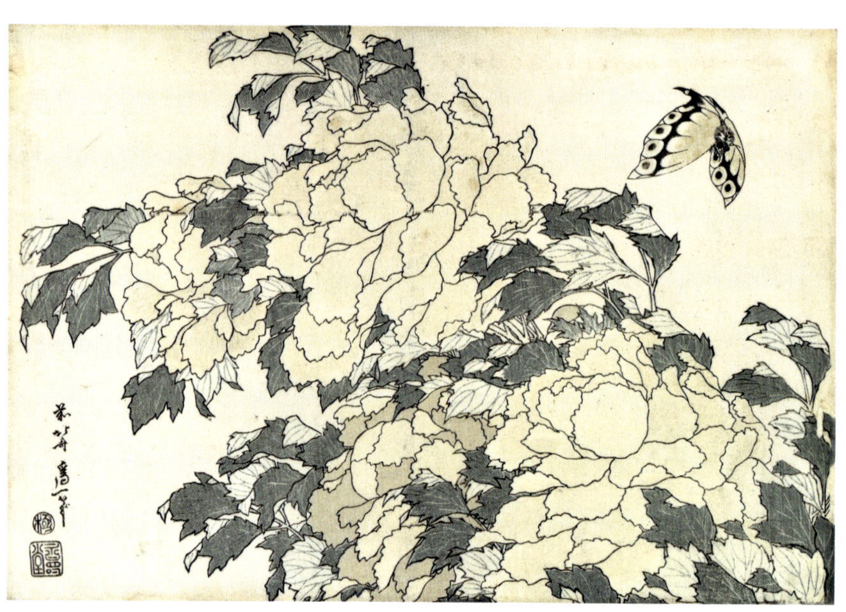

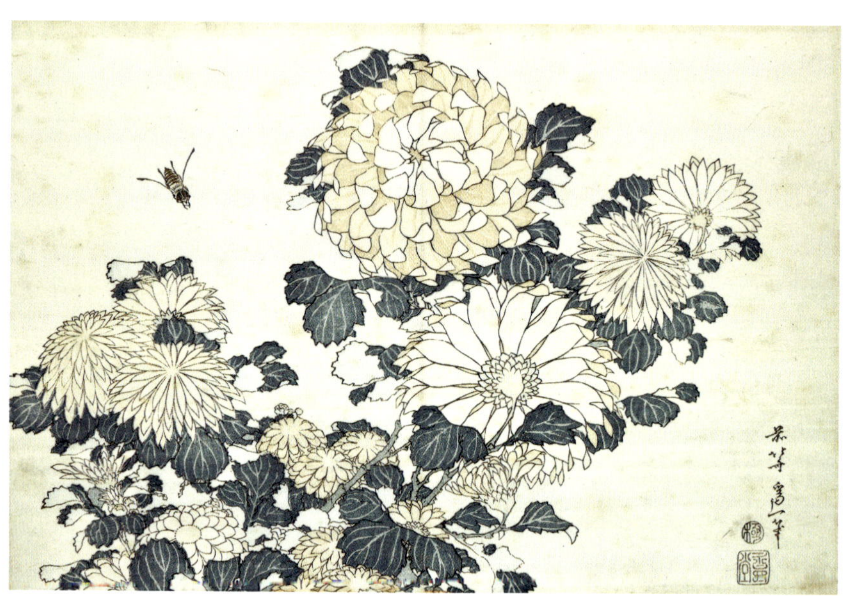

206b | 206a Katsushika Hokusai, *Peonies and Butterfly* | *Chrysanthemums and Horsefly*, 1833–1834

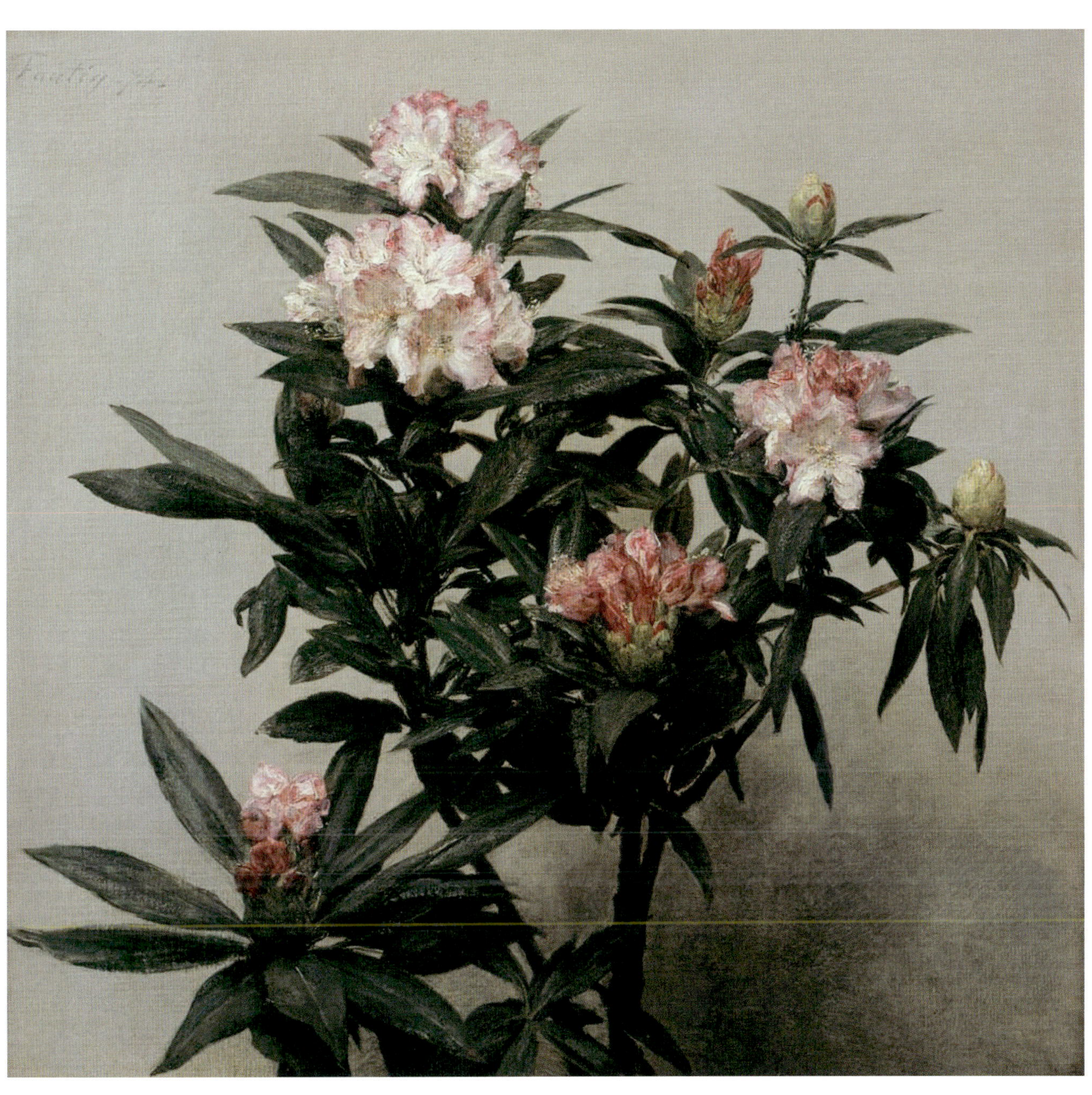

30 Henri Fantin-Latour, *Blossoming Rhododendron Branch*, 1874

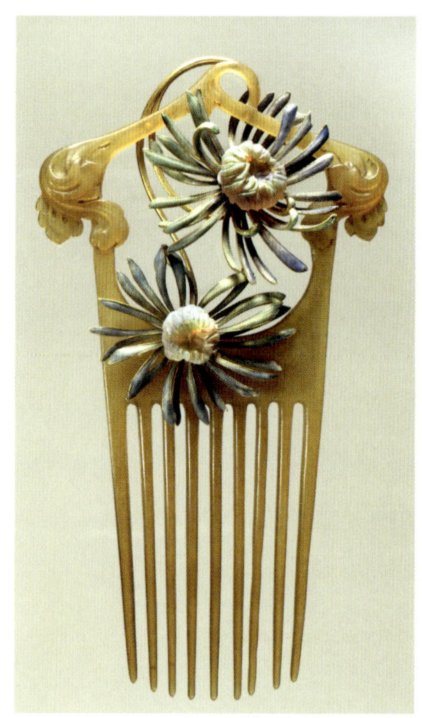

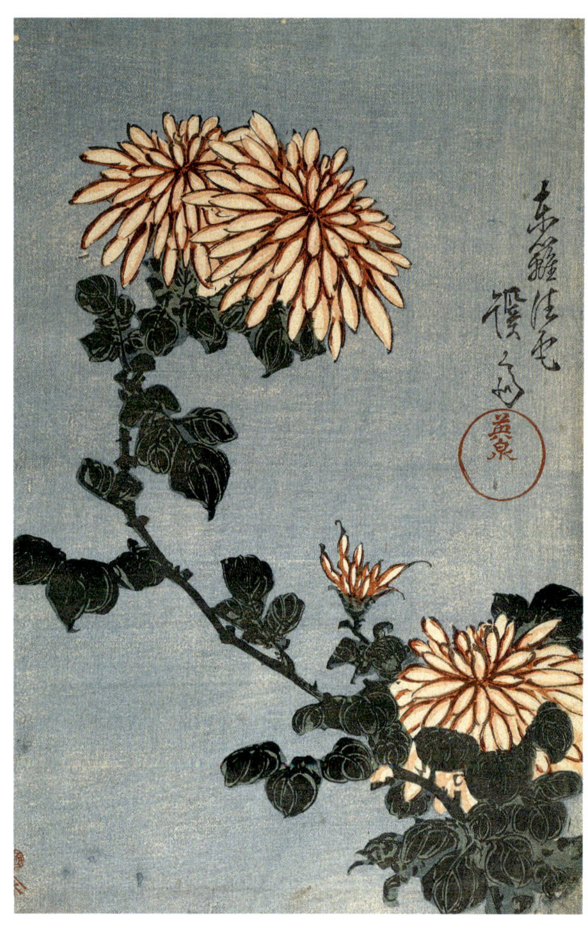

184 Keisai (Ikeda) Eisen, *Chrysanthemums*, 1830s
169 René Lalique, *Comb with Chrysanthemum Decor*, 1899–1900

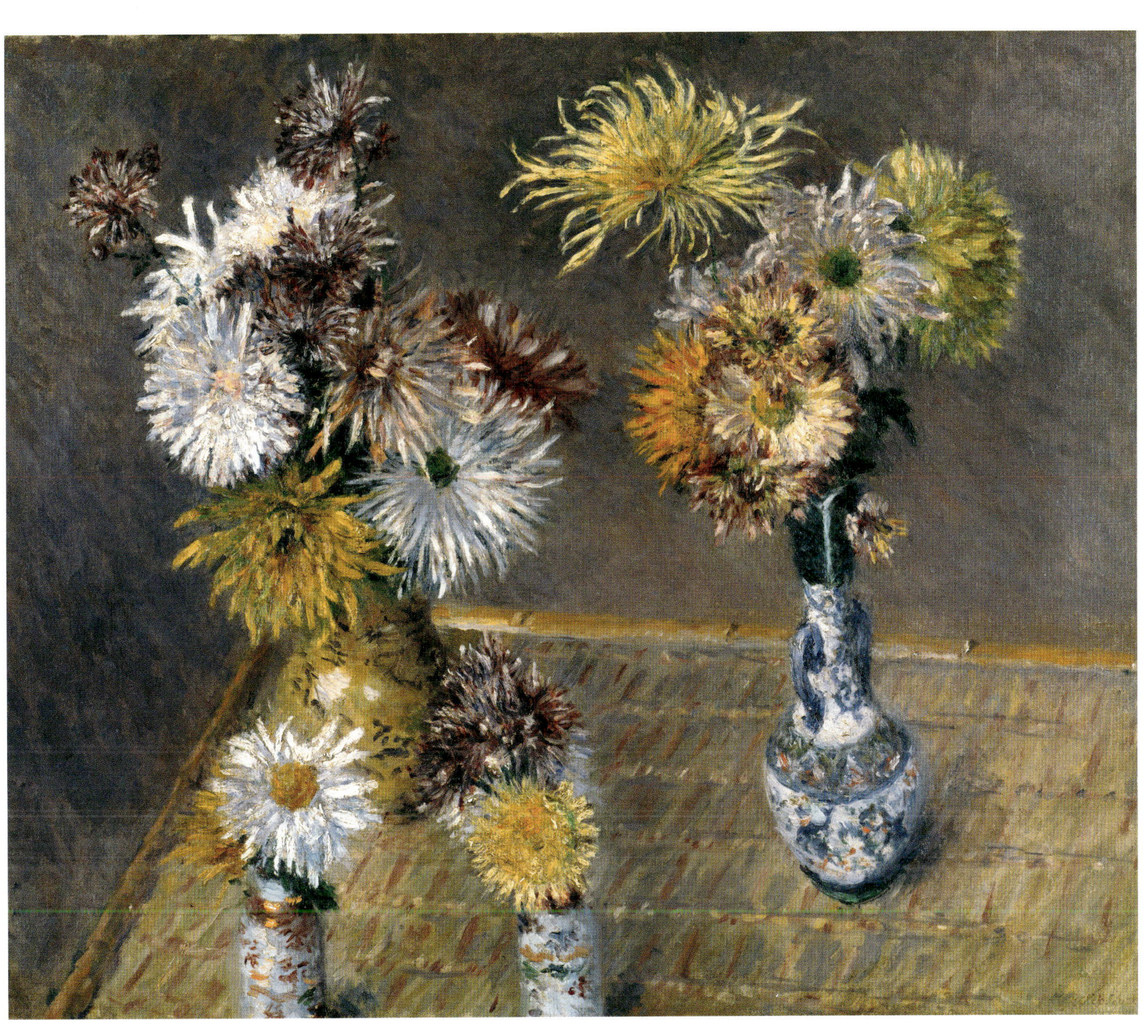

6 Gustave Caillebotte, *Four Vases with Chrysanthemums*, circa 1893

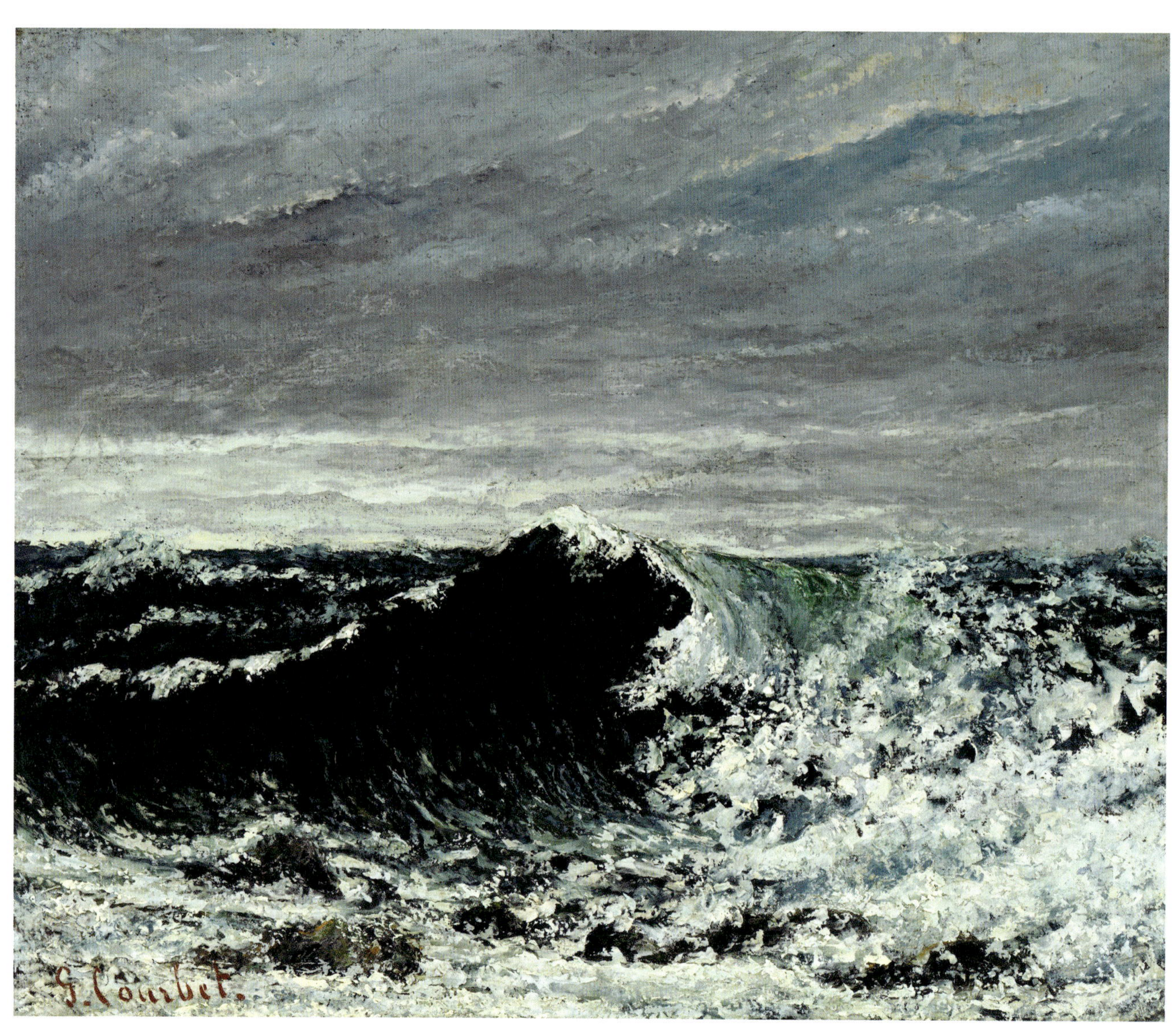

11 Gustave Courbet, *The Wave*, circa 1869

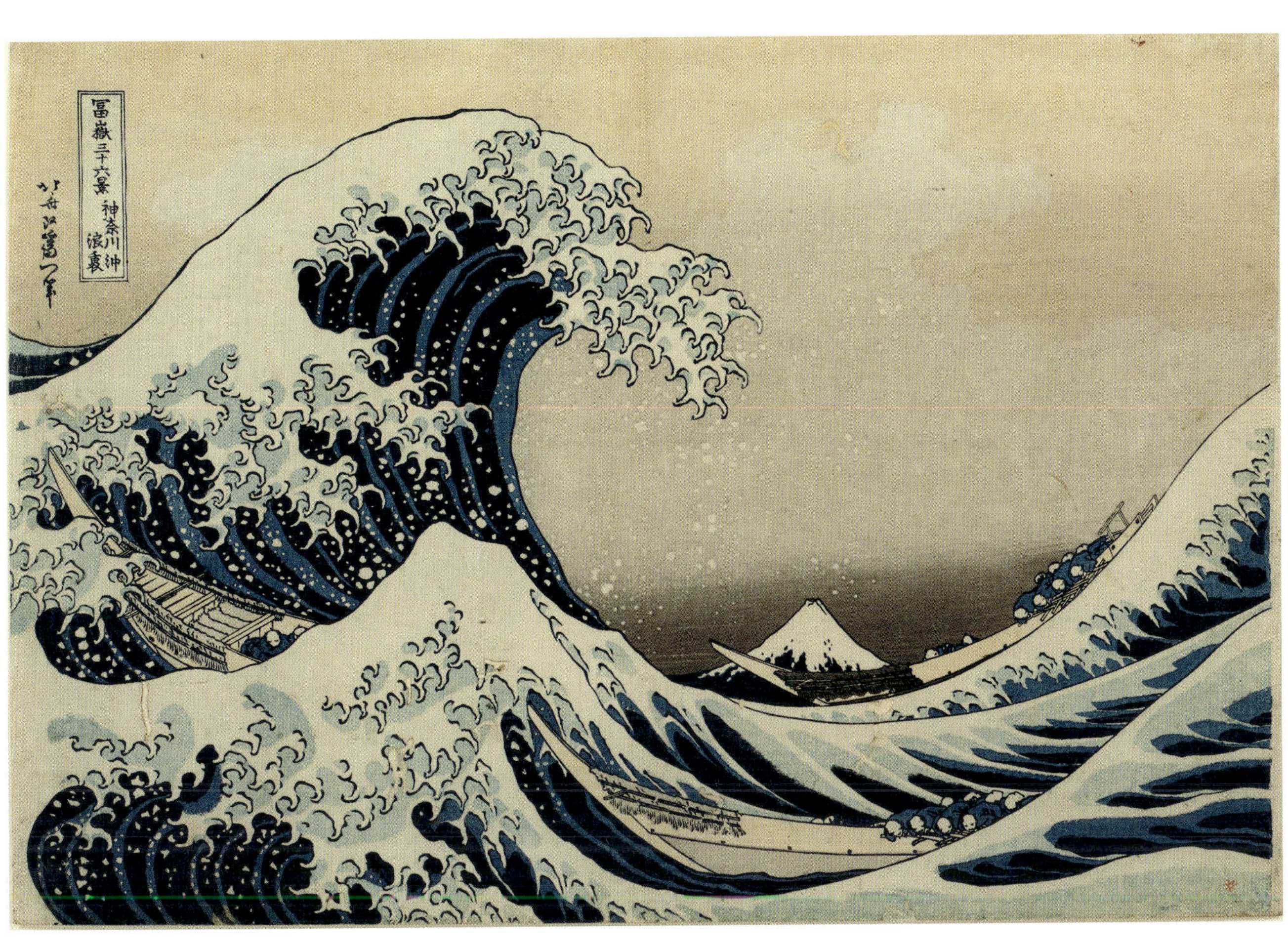

205d Katsushika Hokusai, *Under the Wave off Kanagawa*, 1830–1831

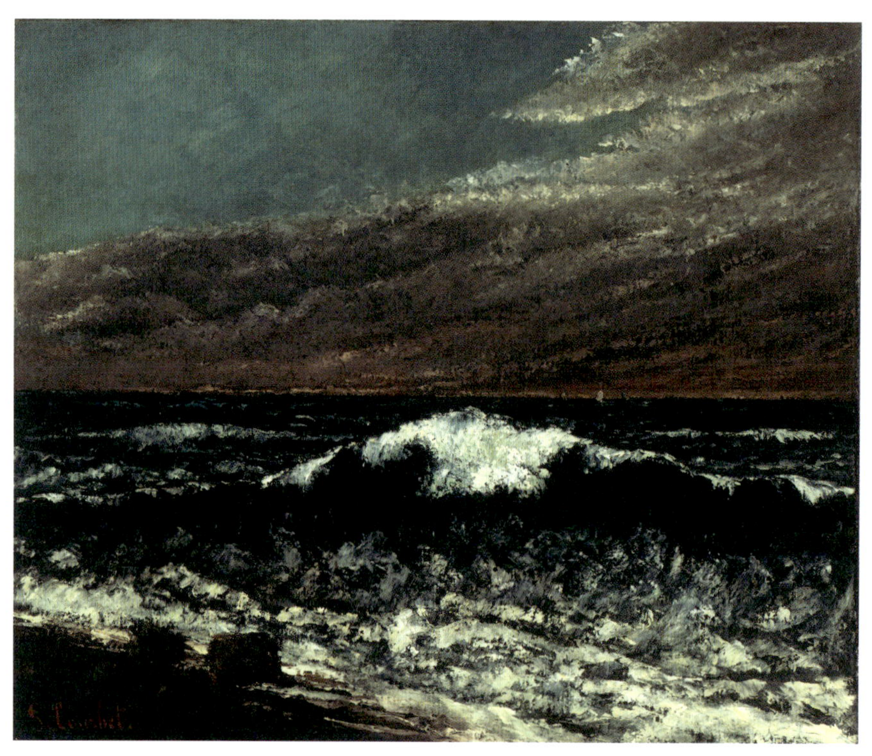

12 Gustave Courbet, *The Wave*, 1870

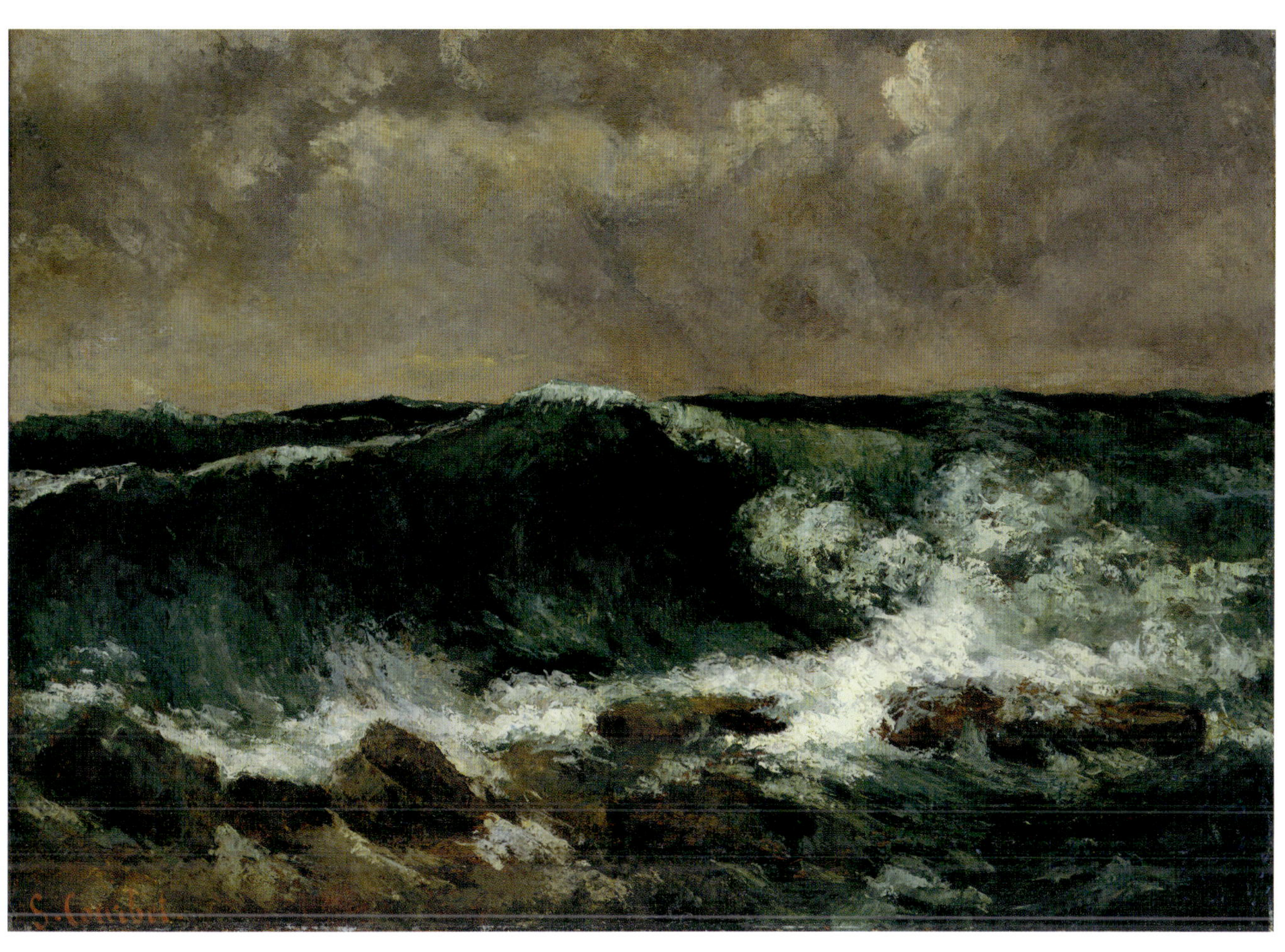

10 Gustave Courbet, *The Wave*, 1869

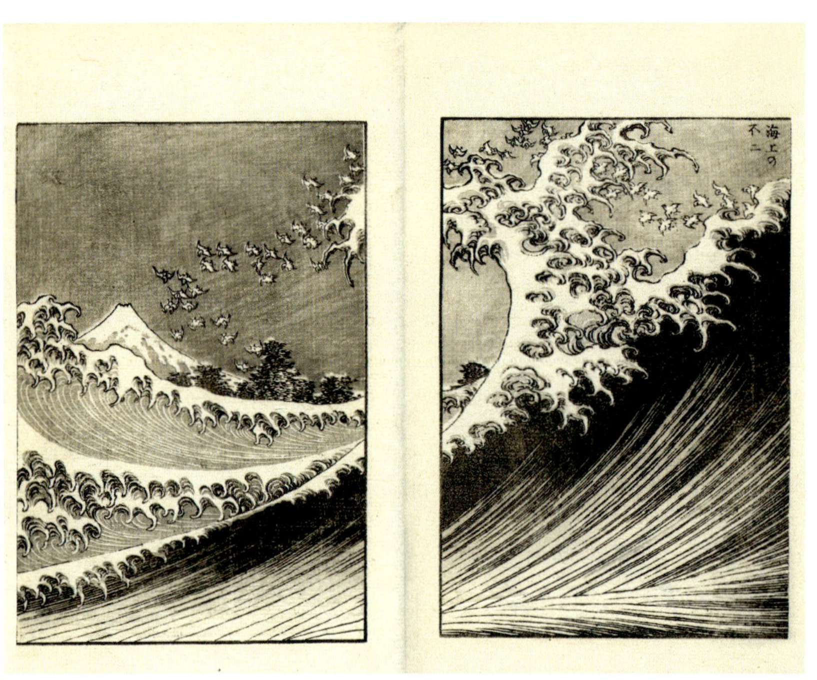

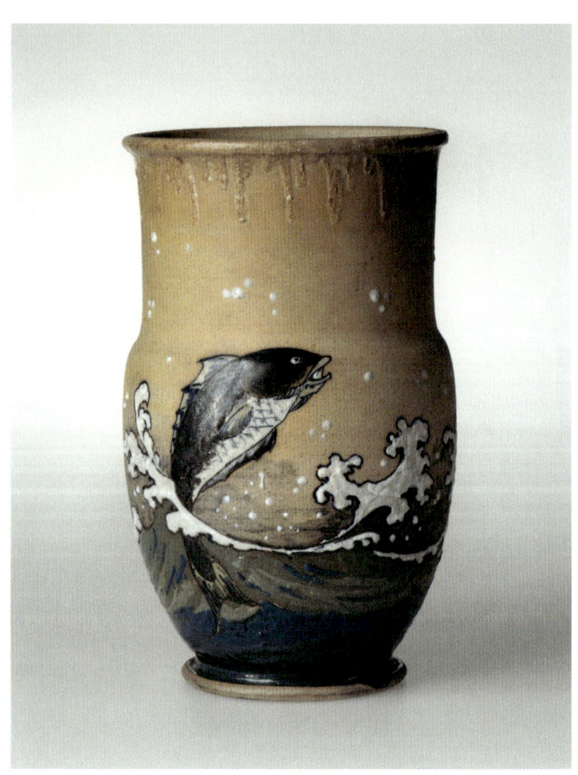

247 Katsushika Hokusai, *Mount Fuji at Sea* from vol. 2 of *One Hundred Views of Mount Fuji*, 1835
156 Ernest Chaplet, *Vase with Wave Decor*, 1886/1887

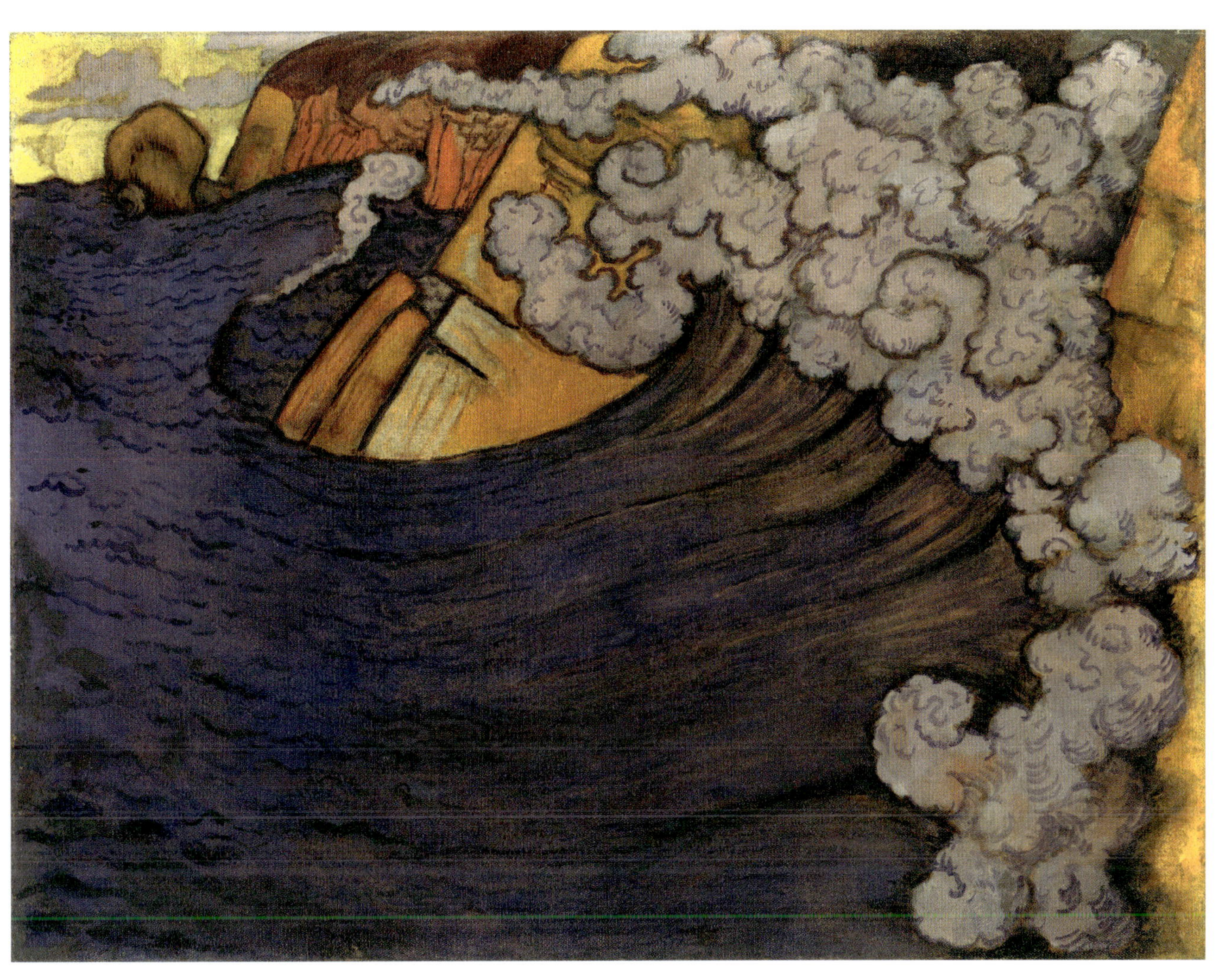

42 Georges Lacombe, *The Violet Wave*, 1896–1897

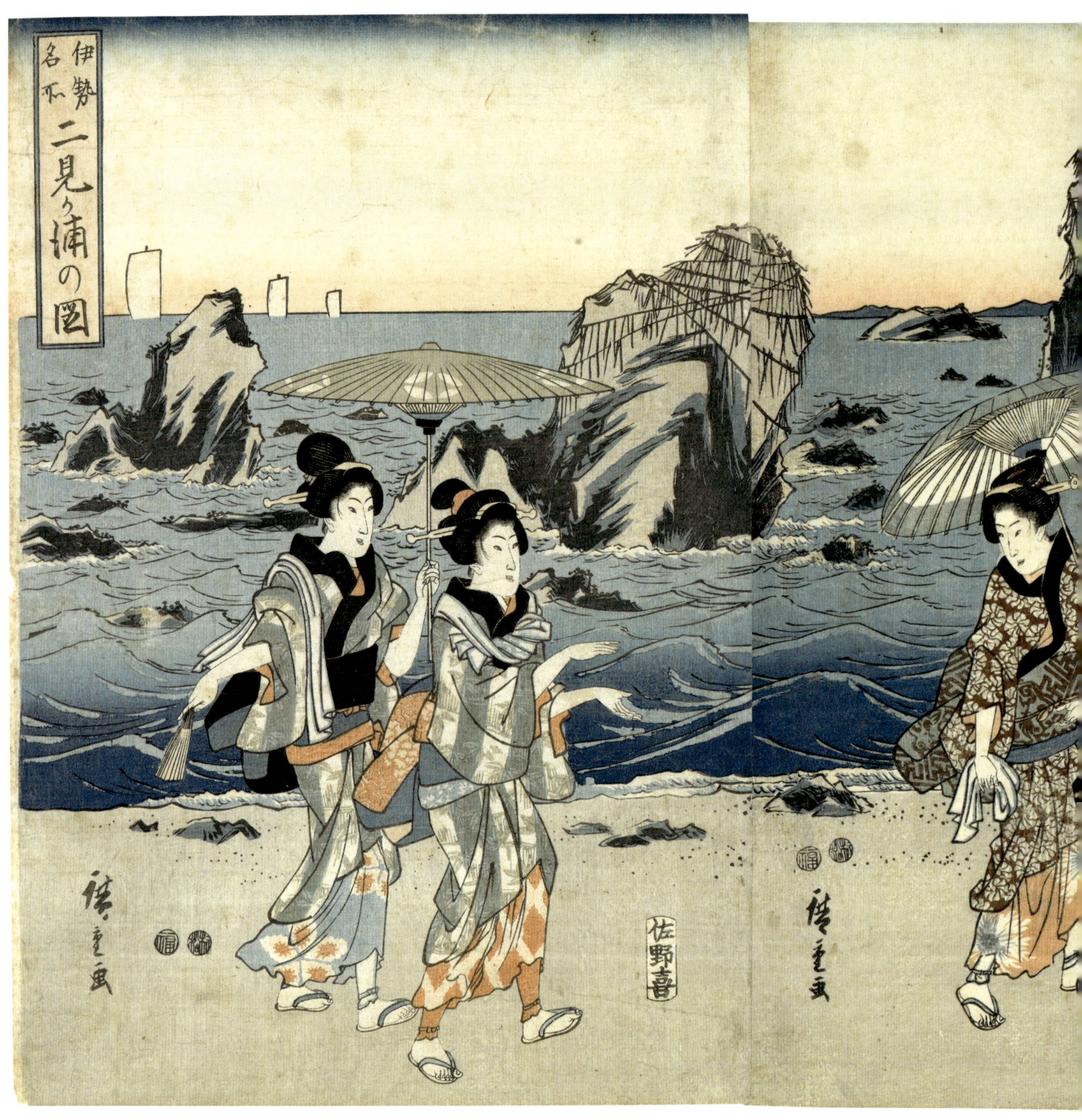
伊勢名所
二見ヶ浦の図
廣重画
佐野喜
廣重画

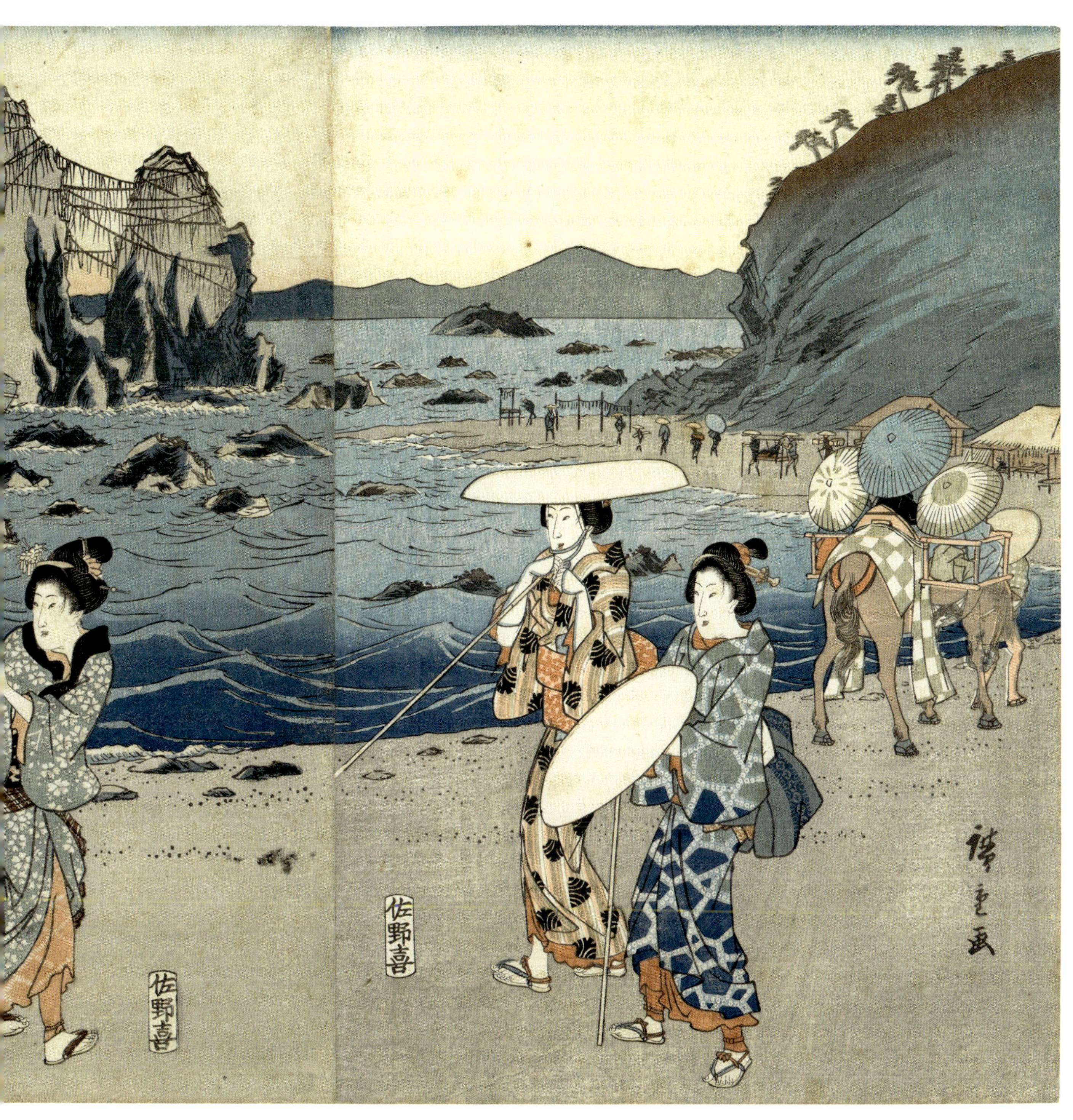

201 Utagawa Hiroshige, *View of Futamigaura*, 1847–1852

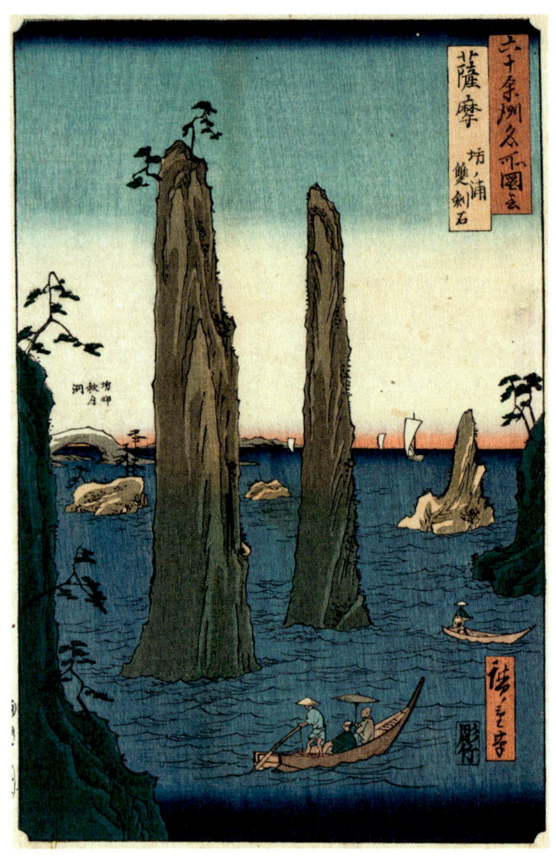

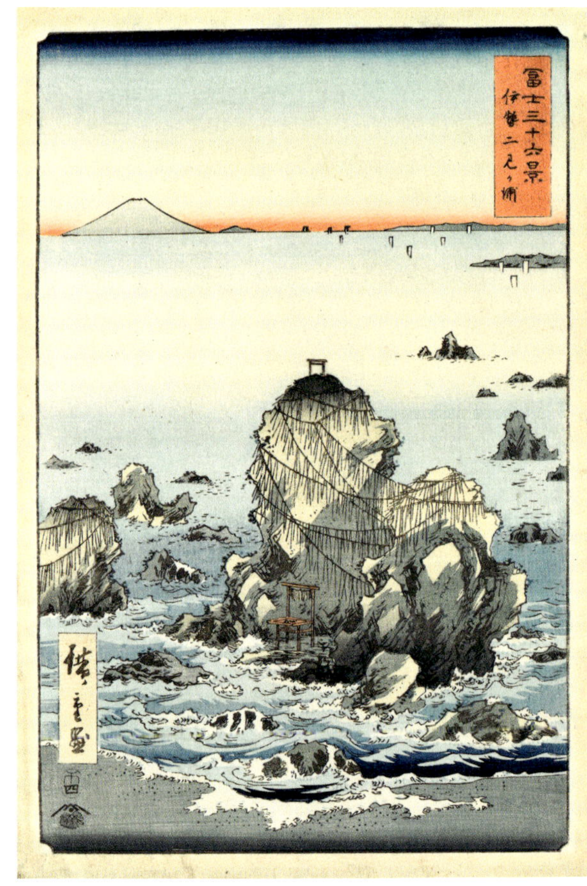

202f | 204c Utagawa Hiroshige, *Satsuma Province: Bō Bay, The Two-Sword Rocks*, 1856 | *Futamigaura in Ise Province*, 1858

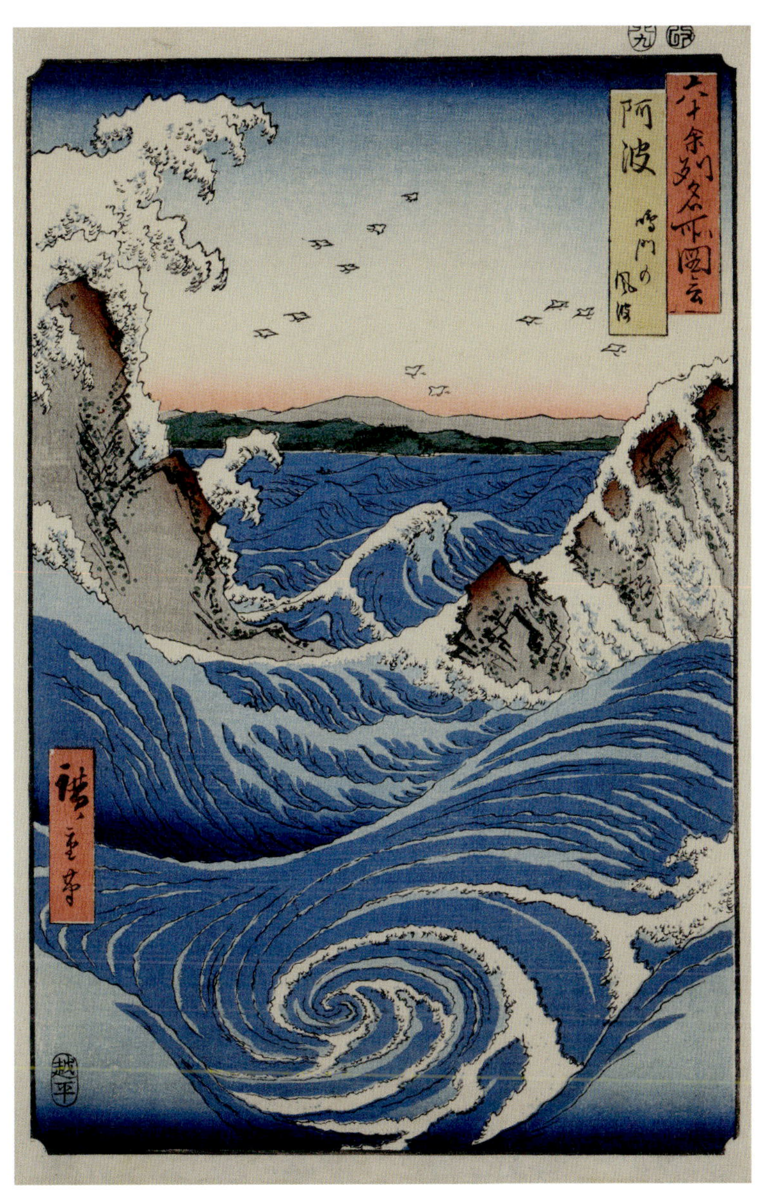

202d Utagawa Hiroshige, *Awa Province: Naruto Whirlpools*, 1855

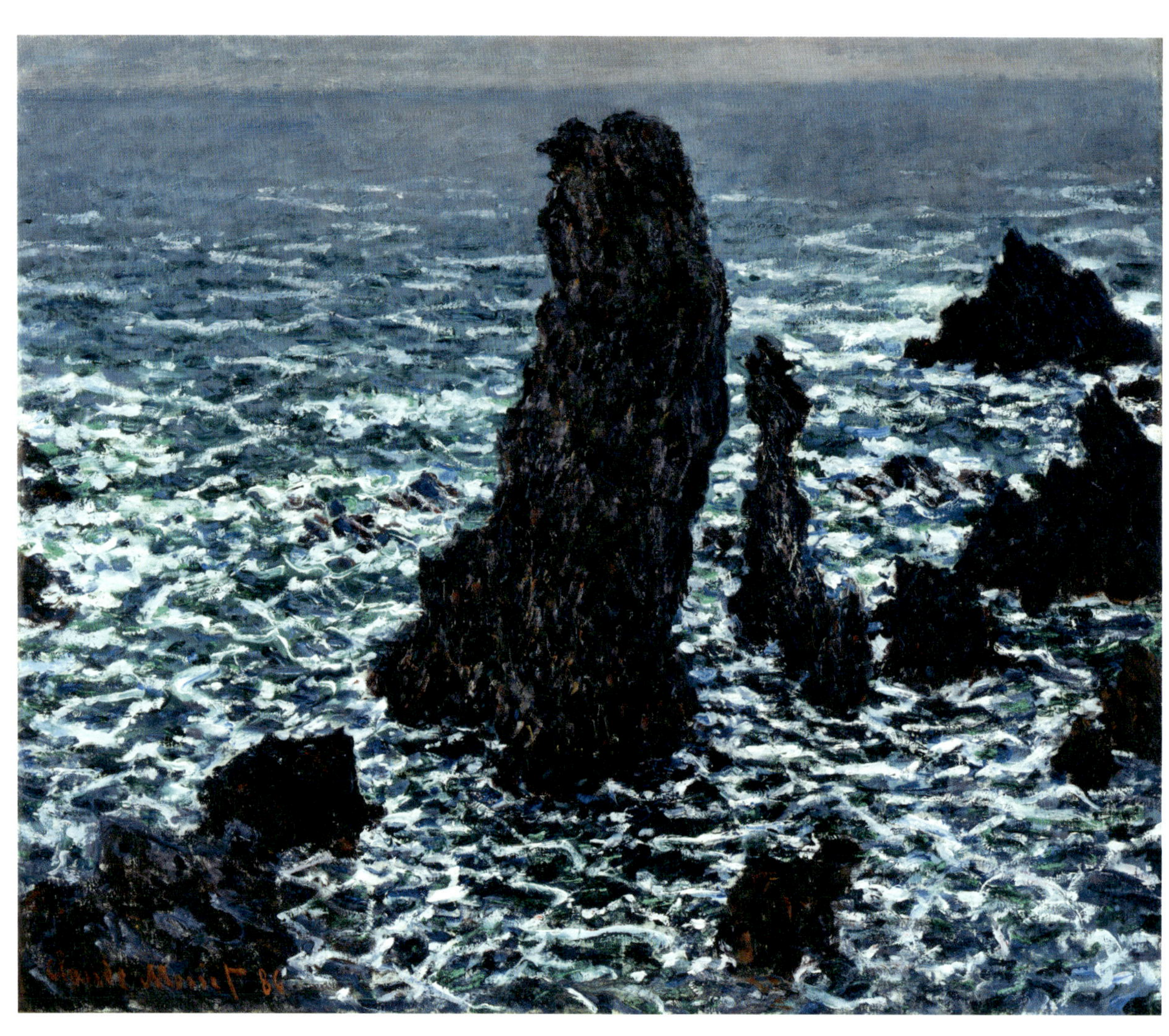

47 Claude Monet, *Rocks at Belle-Île*, 1886

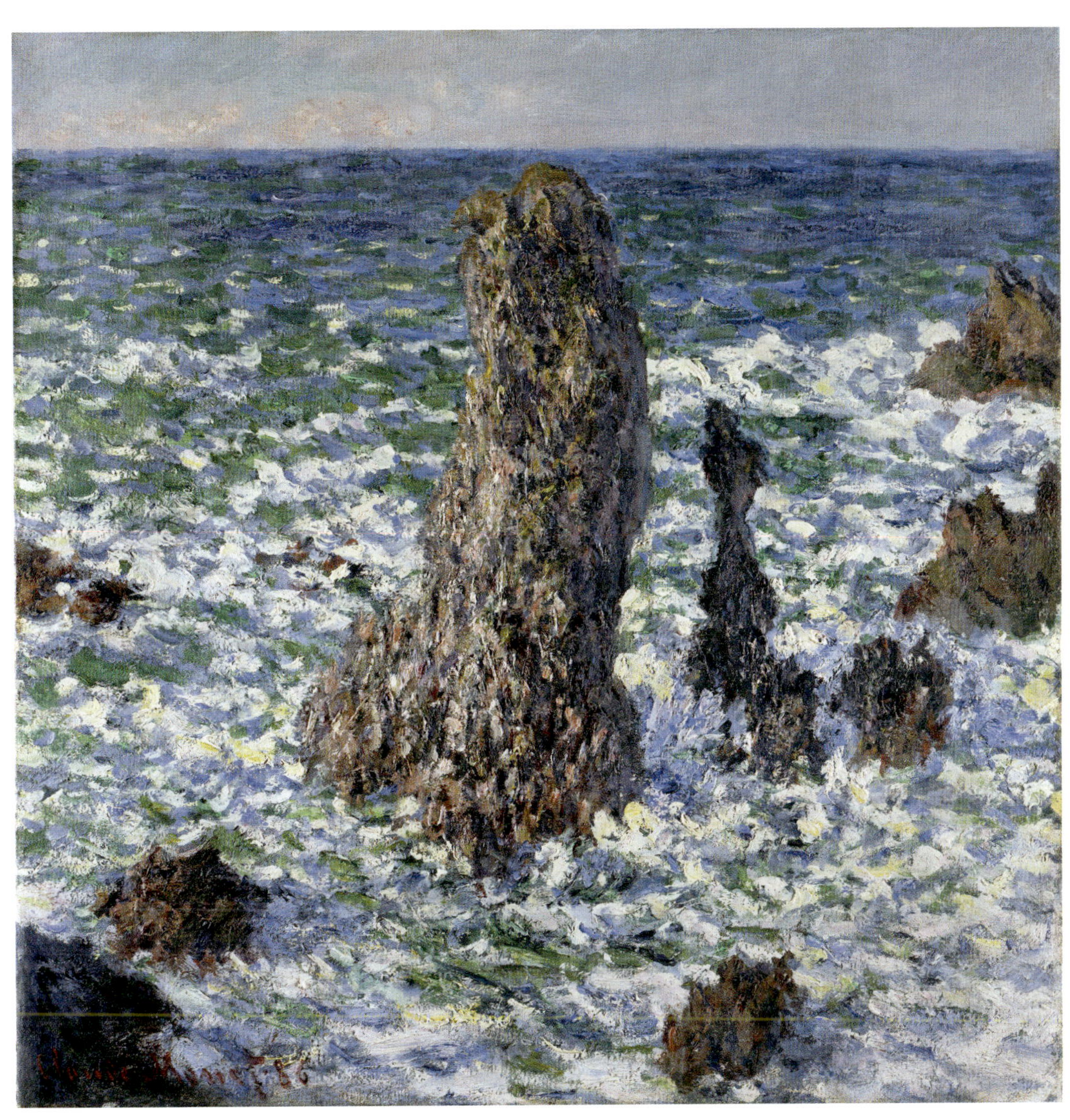

48 Claude Monet, *The Rock Pyramids at Port-Coton in the Sun*, 1886

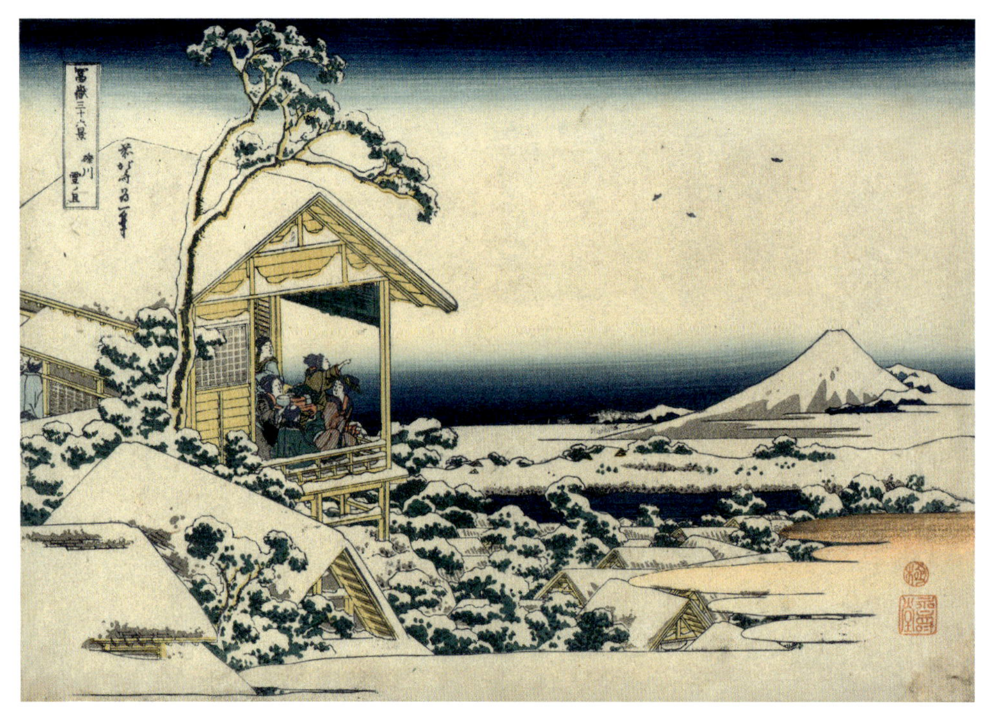

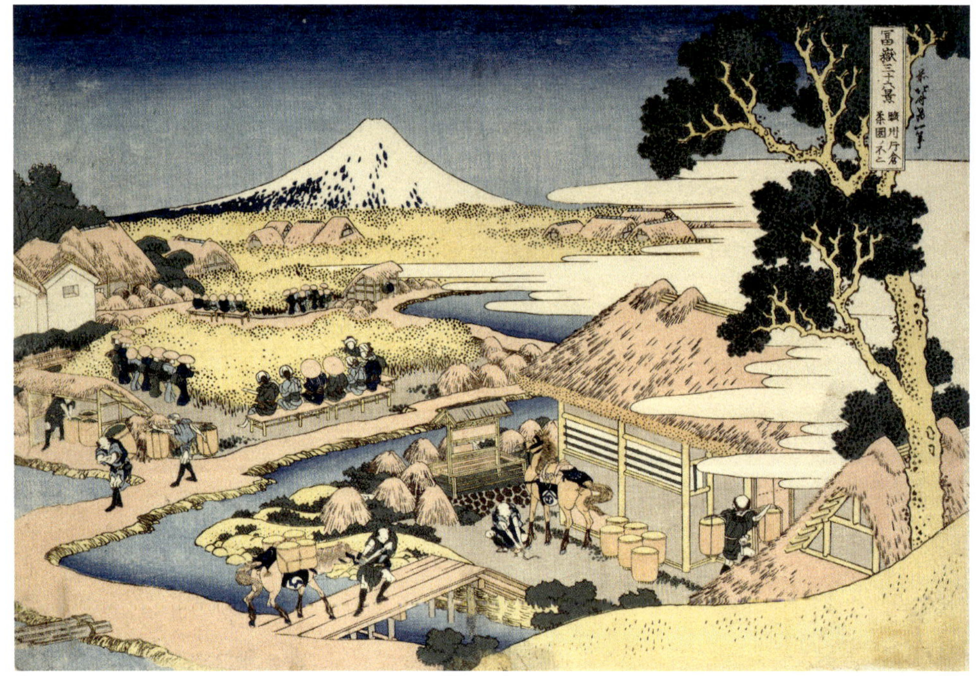

205n | 205b Katsushika Hokusai, *Snowy Morning at Koishikawa* | *Fuji from the Tea Plantation of Katakura in Suruga Province*, 1830–1831

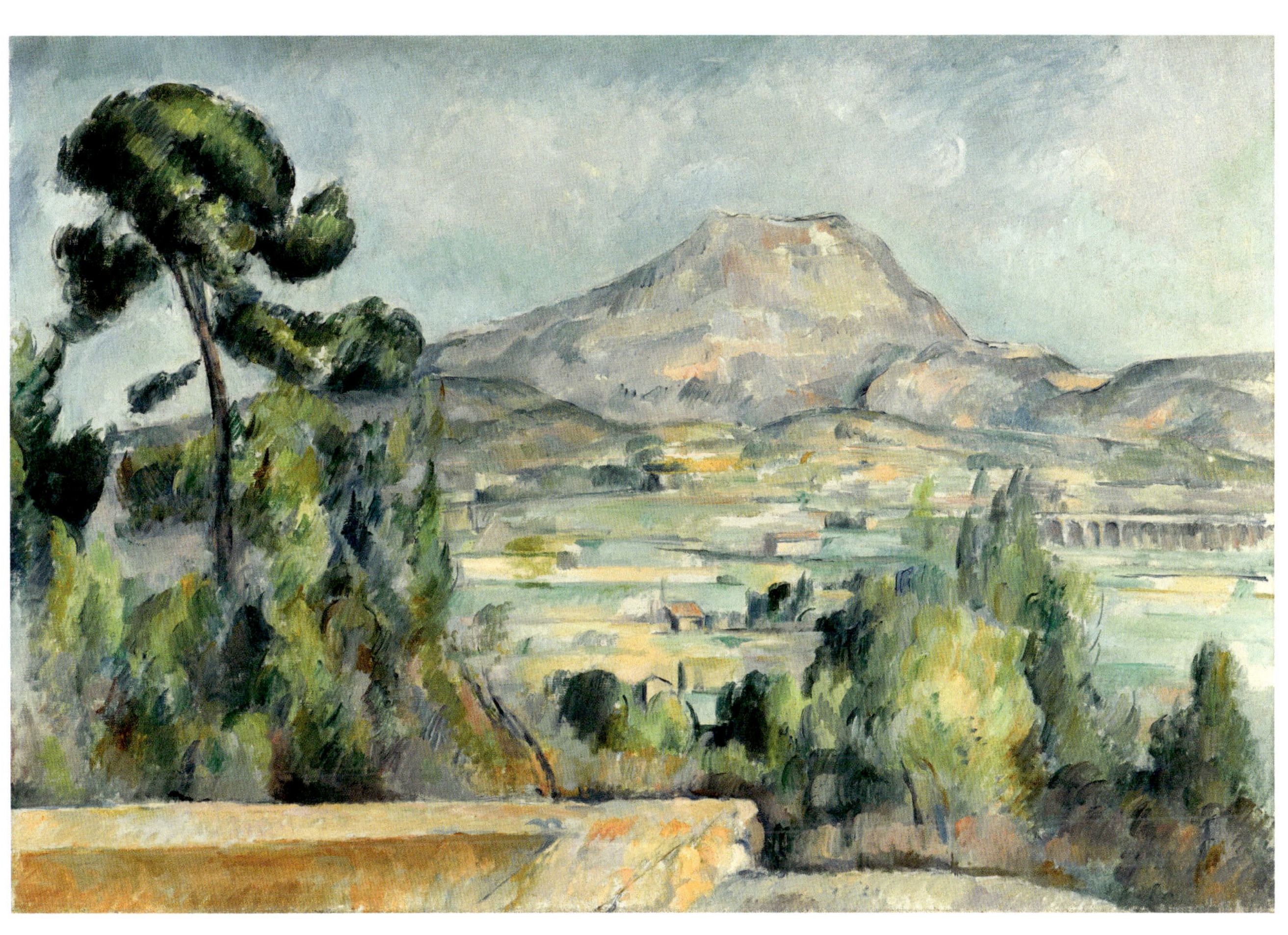

7 Paul Cézanne, *Mont Sainte-Victoire*, circa 1890

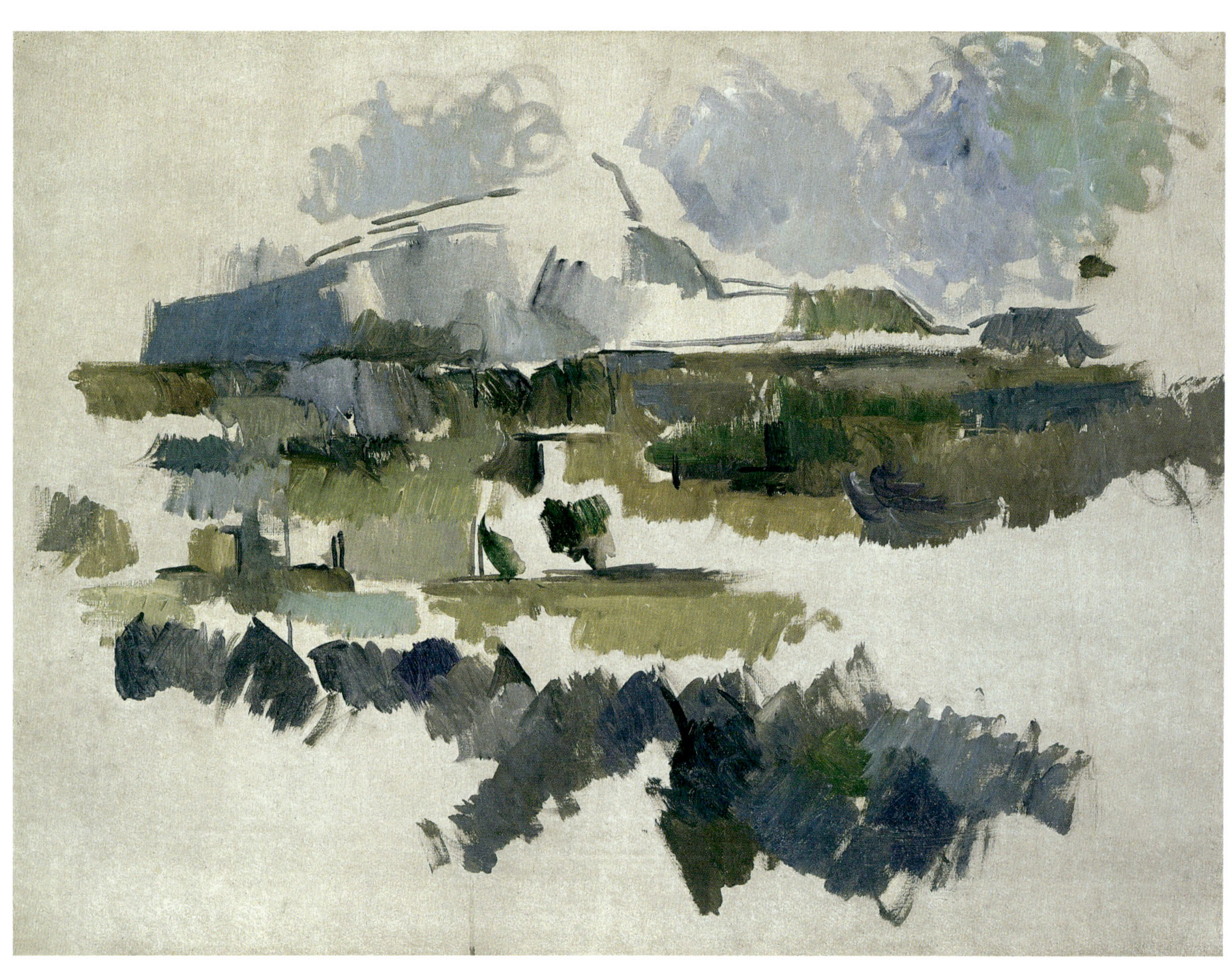

9 Paul Cézanne, *View of Mont Sainte-Victoire Seen from Les Lauves*, 1904/1906

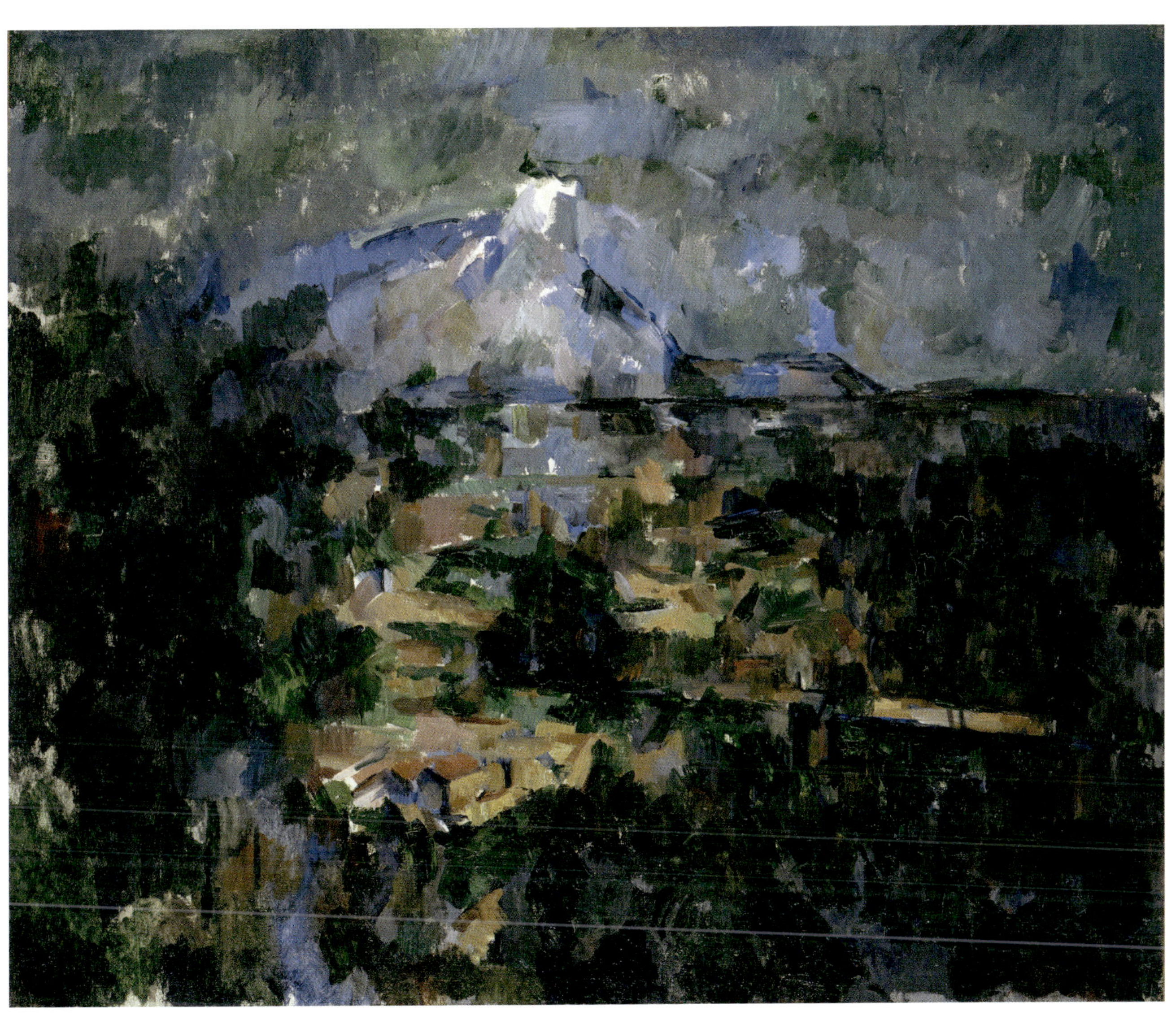

8 Paul Cézanne, *View of Mont Sainte-Victoire Seen from Les Lauves*, 1904/1906

Japonisme on paper

Three figures playing different instruments in semi-relief, with bamboo in the background: this motif decorates a Japanese medicine case carved out of ivory, an inro that Félix Buhot depicts in one of his etchings (p. 119). The sheet belongs to a ten-part series bearing the title *Japonisme*, in which Buhot explores objects from the collection of his friend, the art critic Philippe Burty (pp. 118, 119). Burty was a passionate collector of Japanese woodblock prints and objects, including inros, netsukes and masks. His collection of over 2,500 items was open for viewing to all those interested – be it artists, writers and connoisseurs. Burty had been the one to coin the term *Japonisme*, first using it in a series of articles published from 1872 to 1873 in the journal *La Renaissance littéraire et artistique*. For him, the term referred to the study and understanding of Japanese art and its unique aesthetic, which he sought to encourage.

Besides Japanese objects, colour woodblock prints were the primary focus of the French reception of Japanese art. Engaging with these works played a decisive role in a turn in Paris towards colour in printing and the development of the modern colour poster. And important in this process was Henri Rivière, who introduced the Japanese techniques of printing with several colours to France between 1889 and 1894. He was a great lover of Japanese woodblock prints and objects, which he studied and acquired on visits to prominent dealers in East Asian art such as Siegfried Bing, Hayashi Tadamasa and Florine Langweil. With the title of the colour lithographs *36 Views of the Eiffel Tower* that appeared in book form in 1902, Rivière was alluding to the series *36 Views of Mount Fuji* by Katsushika Hokusai, which he also owned. From the latter's work, he adopted the principle of the serial repetition of the main motif: in the same way that Hokusai used Mount Fuji, Rivière shows the Eiffel Tower in the process of being built during different seasons and in various weather conditions, in diagonal visual compositions and asymmetric, decentred sectional views (pp. 192, 193). In terms of style and landscape composition, borrowings from Utagawa Hiroshige can be recognised too – for example, the in part extremely closely cut motifs in the foreground (pp. 220, 221). Rivière created this series partially using photographs as a basis, pictures he took while viewing the construction site. In an additional series showing scenes of Brittany, *The Magic Hours*, Rivière imitates his Japanese models not just in borrowing the narrow visual format of Japanese scrolls, but also in the subtle depiction of various times of day like the morning and evening twilight, the illustration of fog and the use of bold cuts of prominent visual motifs (pp. 194, 195). The emphasis on silhouettes is an additional specialty that Rivière saw in the Japanese woodblock prints and also made a subject in his works (pp. 148, 286).

Visits to collectors and dealers of Japanese art as well as exhibitions were important for the artists' engagement with the subject of Japan. For example, Mary Cassatt, an American artist who joined the group of the impressionists, visited the show of Japanese woodblock prints organised in 1890 by Siegfried Bing at the École des Beaux-Arts in Paris several times (p. 96). In a letter to her friend Berthe Morisot from April 1890, she euphorically reports of her visit to the exhibition: "Seriously, *you must not* miss that. You who want to make color prints you couldn't dream of anything more beautiful. I dream of it and don't think of anything but color on copper. […] You *must* see the Japanese – *come as soon as you can*."

Cassatt had engaged with Japanese models in her art for some ten years already, but most intensely in a series of ten colour etchings created in the twelve months after her visits to the exhibition. With a special sensitivity, she describes intimate scenes from female domestic life, including representations of the close relationship between mothers and children or toilette scenes. In the process, she was translating motifs from Japanese woodblock prints – for example, those by Suzuki Harunobu and Kitagawa Utamaro, artists whose work Cassatt also collected – to the reality of French everyday life. In the print *The Bath*, Cassatt comes closest to her model Utamaro.

Like he, she largely refuses all modelling of the body, defining it solely with dark, simple outlines, giving the depiction a generally flat and stylised appearance. The scene between mother and child is reduced to the essential. As in Utamaro, the space surrounding the figures is not elaborated in any way (pp. 187, 189) – in other sheets from the same series, it is filled with ornaments of kimono materials, floral motifs and patterns of Persian miniatures from Cassatt's own collection (p. 191). Cassatt also adopted the mirror motif with the doubling of the figures viewing themselves in the mirror from Utamaro (pp. 186, 190). She used the Japanese paper format of the *ōban* and produced the series herself working jointly with a professional printer, whereby she tried to recreate the special qualities of the Japanese colour woodblock prints – for example, an especially luscious colour – with the help of techniques familiar to her of dry point, aquatint and soft-ground etching.

Edgar Degas, a friend of Cassatt's, also engaged intensely with Japanese art. In one etching, for example, he depicts Cassatt while visiting the Louvre in a Japanese-inspired vertical format (p. 185). He shows her as a strikingly outlined rear figure together with another female figure, probably her sister. Not only the special emphasis placed on the silhouette recalls Japanese models, but also the cropping of the scene depicted.

Another admirer of Japanese art, culture and lifestyle was Henri de Toulouse-Lautrec. Not only did he have himself portrayed in a kimono and had ink and brushes imported from Japan, but he had wanted to travel to Japan his whole life, a wish that nonetheless remained unfulfilled. In his art, he treated themes from Parisian places of public entertainment, music halls, cafes and brothels, for which both Japanese woodblock prints and his much-admired Degas served as important models. Toulouse-Lautrec regularly spent his evenings at cafe concerts in Montmartre, attentively sketching the expressions and gestures of the protagonists appearing there. These motifs found their way into his posters, in which he also masterfully uses Japanese stylistic techniques. He refrains from a traditional modelling of the body and combines the contouring of strong stylised colour surfaces with a simplification and reduction of the visual motifs (p. 199). The poster *Divan Japonais* (p. 198) depicts a scene from the at the time highly popular establishment of the same name. The furnishings and decor of this cafe concert, featuring lanterns and bamboo, evoked the Far East, and the staff wore kimonos. Borrowing from Japanese models, Toulouse-Lautrec shows the can-can dancer Jane Avril as a striking silhouette in the foreground, whilst disrespectfully severing the head of the singer Yvette Guilbert, who is standing stage left. In turn, the reduced way in which the arms of the conductor and the scrolls of the contrabasses emerge from the orchestra pit recall similar depictions by Degas, who himself had picked up certain aspects of Japanese woodblock prints (p. 204).

Engaging with the Japanese aesthetic thus confirmed many Western artists – from Buhot to Toulouse-Lautrec – in their striving towards artistic renewal and supported their emancipation from the European visual tradition. They all experimented with *Japonisme* on paper.

Ulrike Hofer

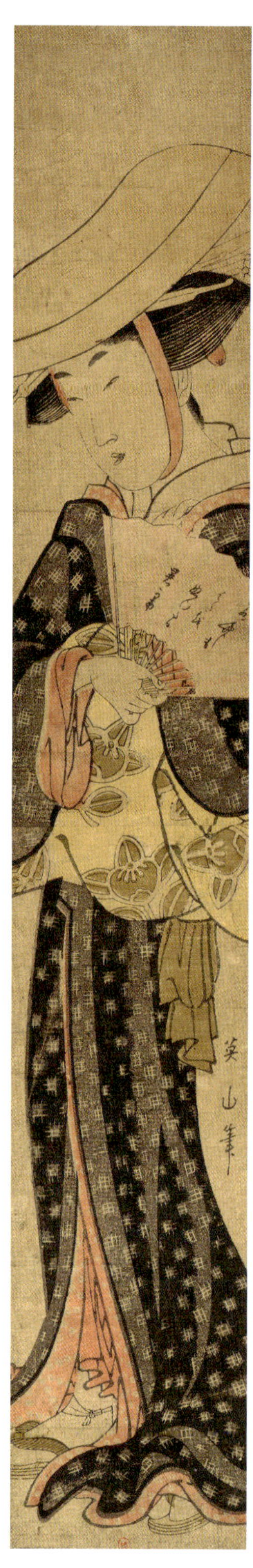

188 Kikugawa Eizan, *Woman Dressed for Travelling and Holding an Inscribed Fan*, 1804–1817

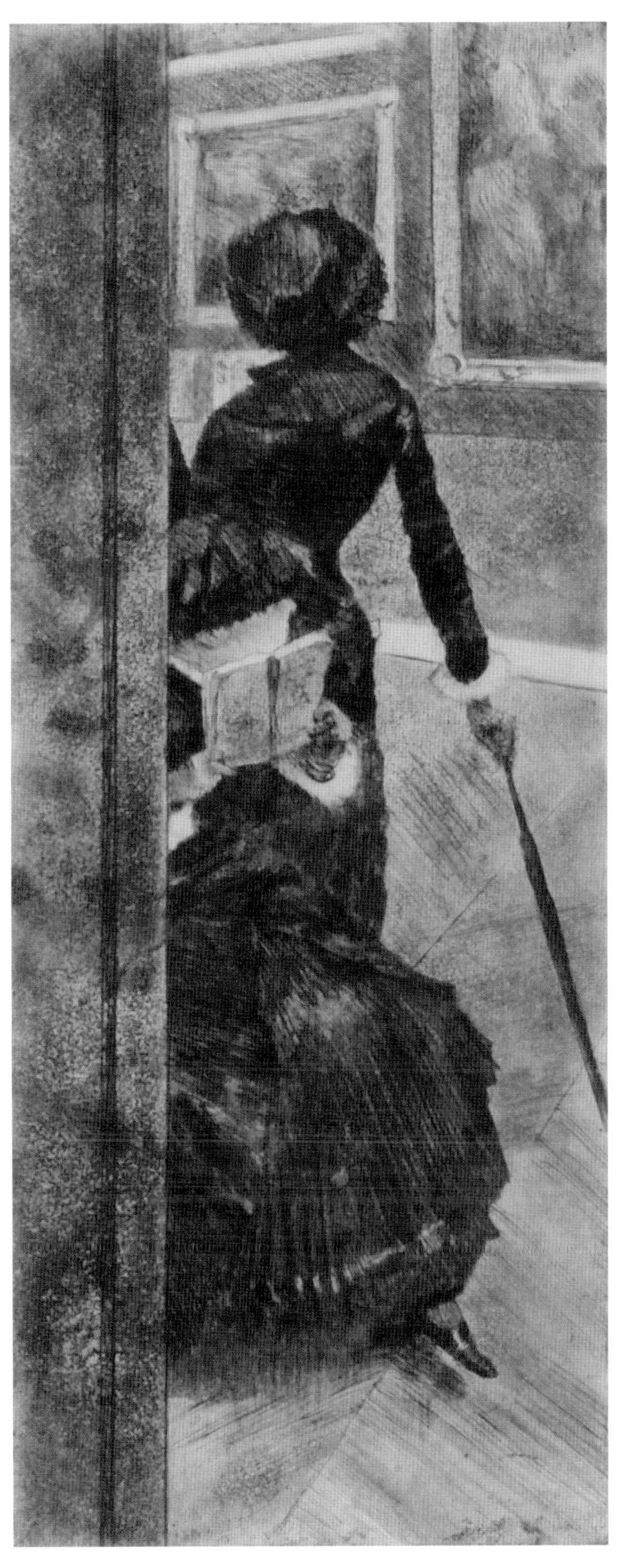

94a Edgar Degas, *Mary Cassatt at the Louvre: The Paintings Gallery*, 1879–1880

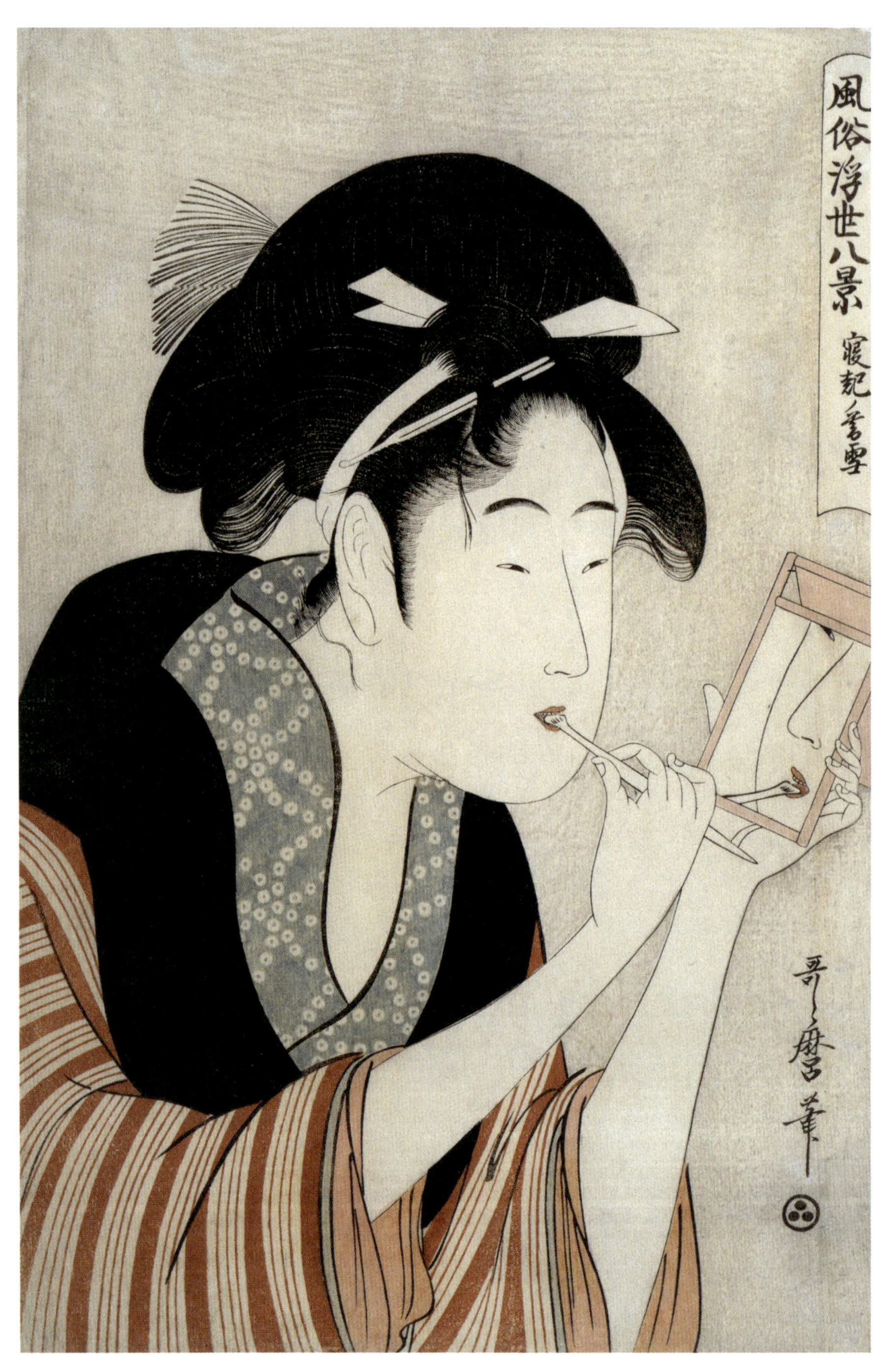

233a Kitagawa Utamaro, *Evening Snow in the Mood of Awakening*, 1797

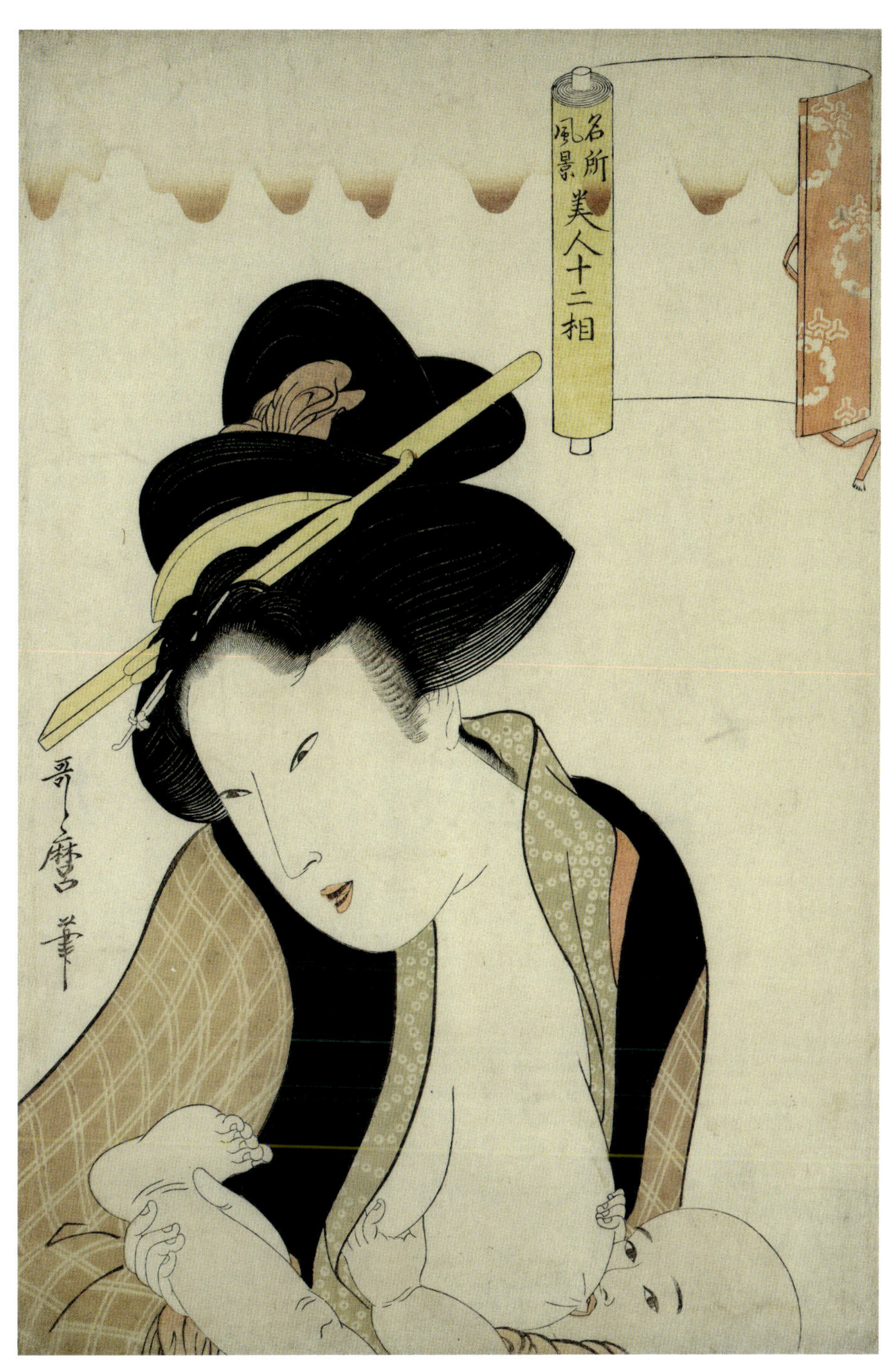

241 Kitagawa Utamaro, *Mother and Child*, circa 1804

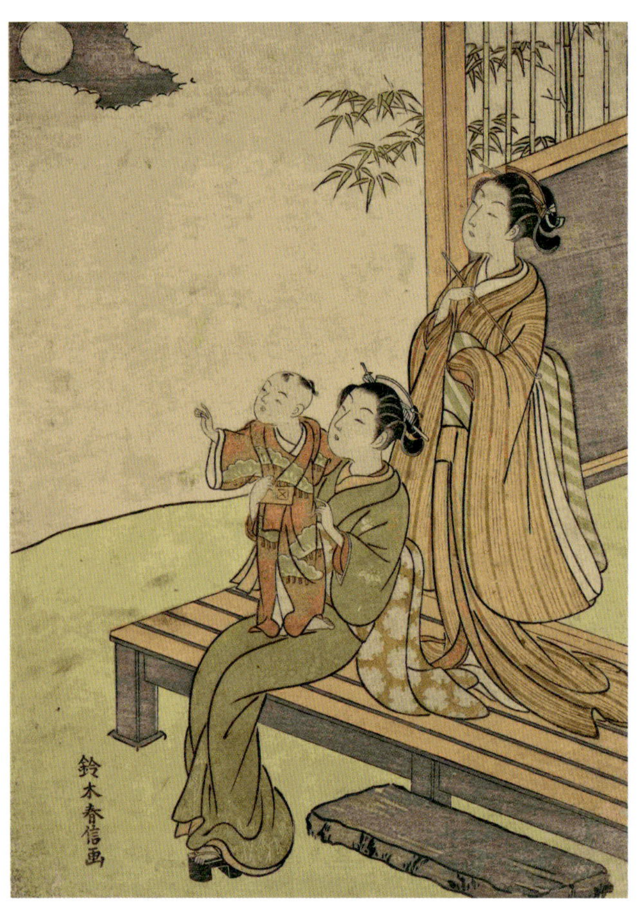

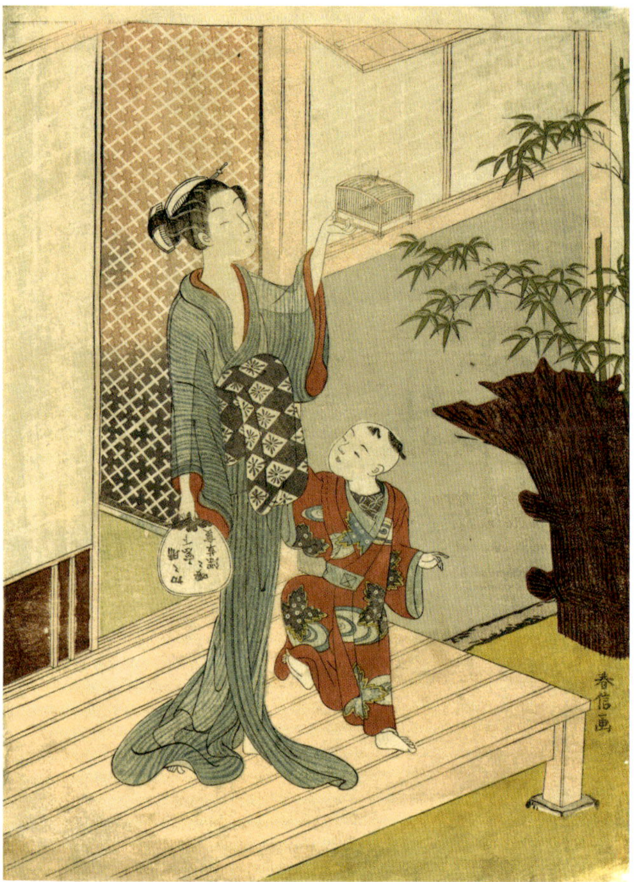

194 | 195 Suzuki Harunobu, *Viewing the Moon* | *Woman Holding Insect Cage, and Small Boy*, circa 1767–1768

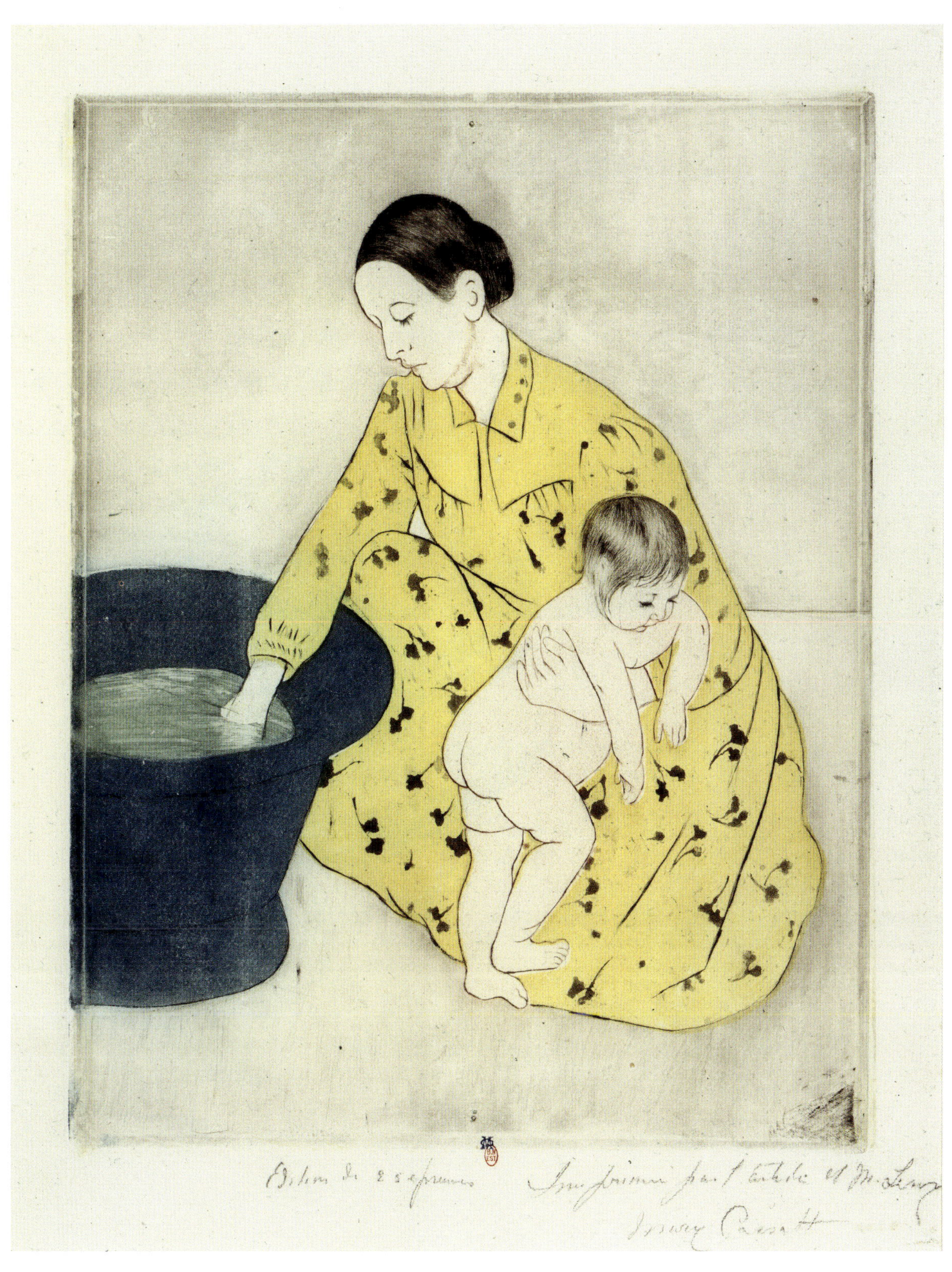

92a Mary Cassatt, *The Bath (also The Tub)*, 1890–1891

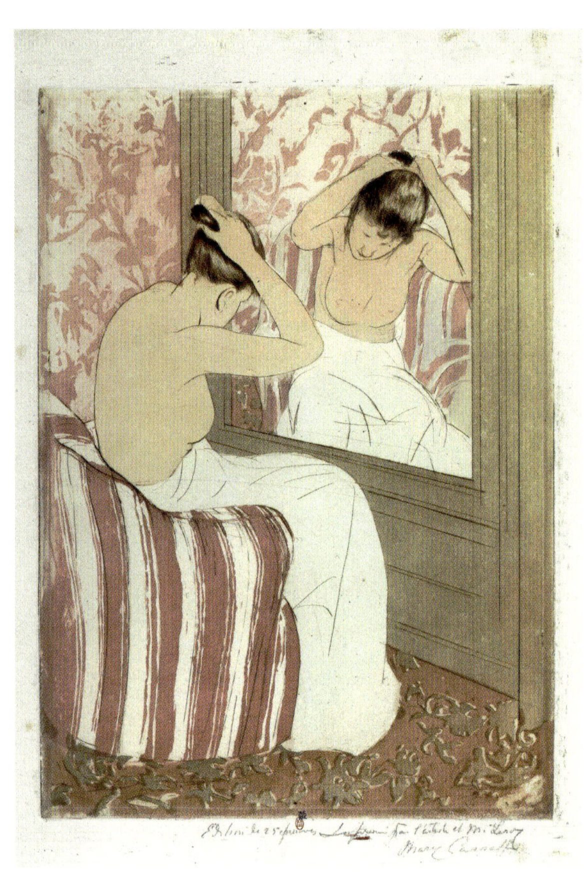

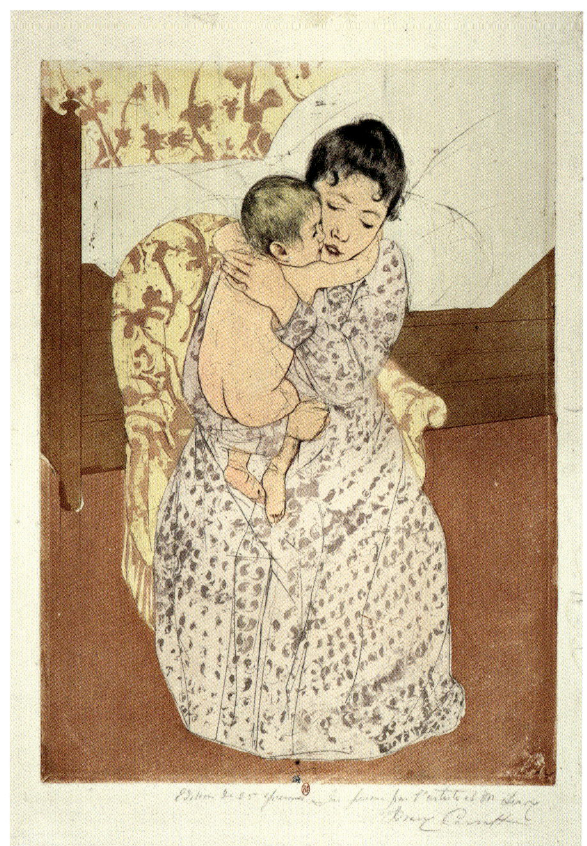

92j | 92g Mary Cassatt, *The Coiffure* | *Maternal Caress*, 1890–1891

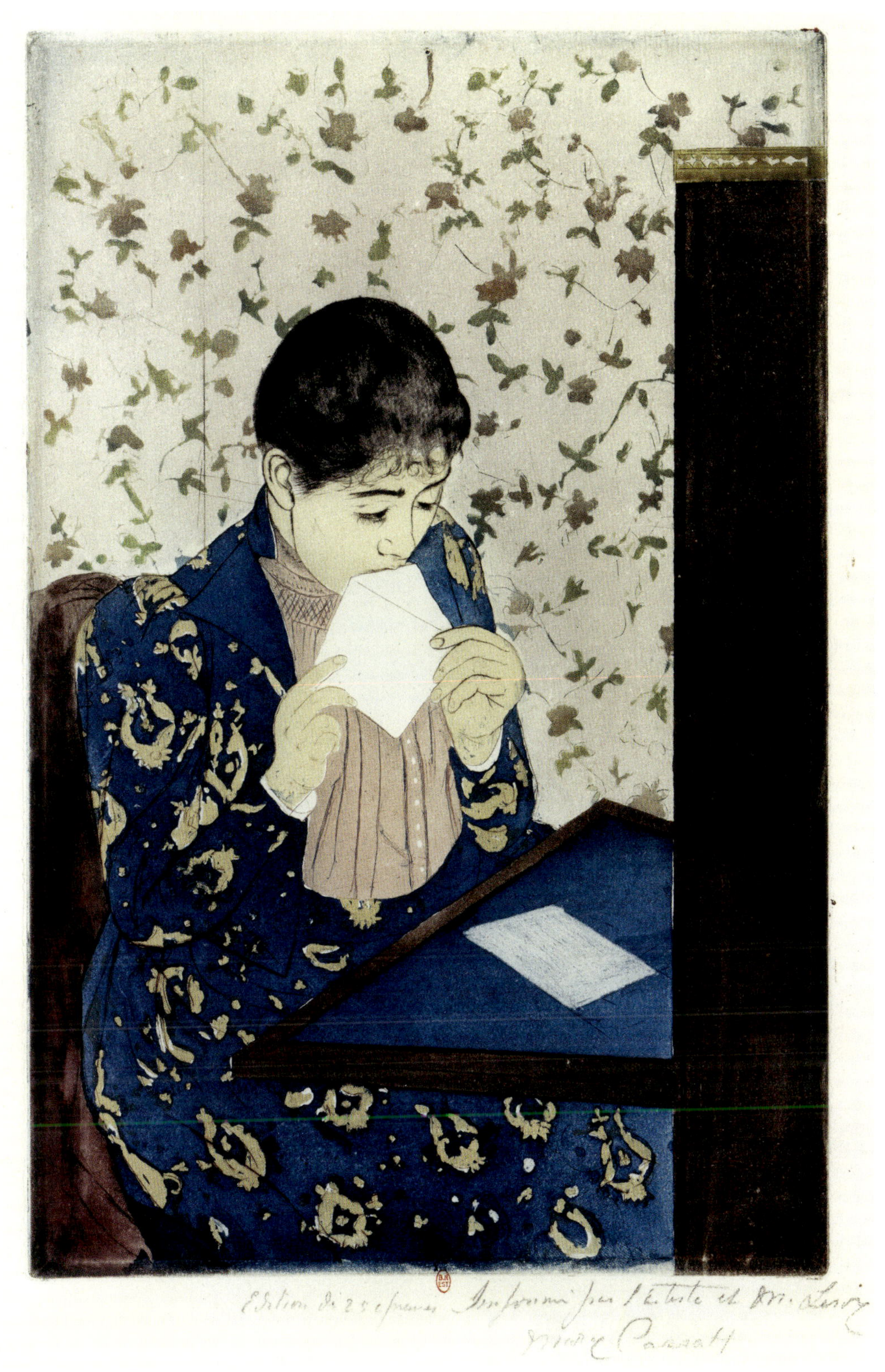

92d Mary Cassatt, *The Letter*, 1890–1891

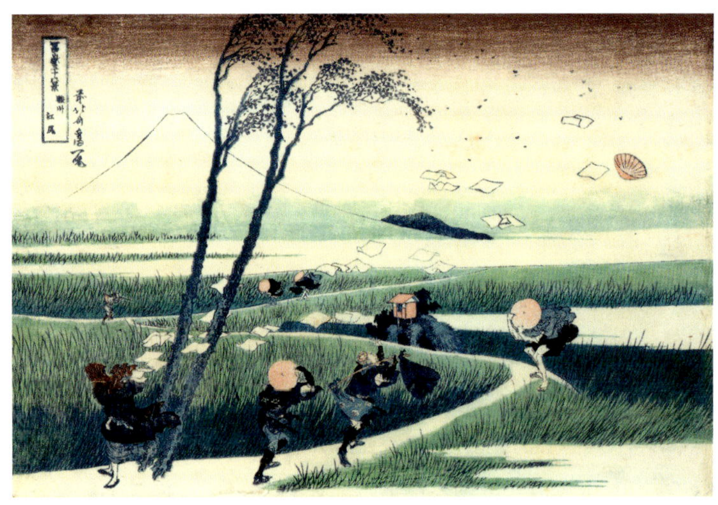

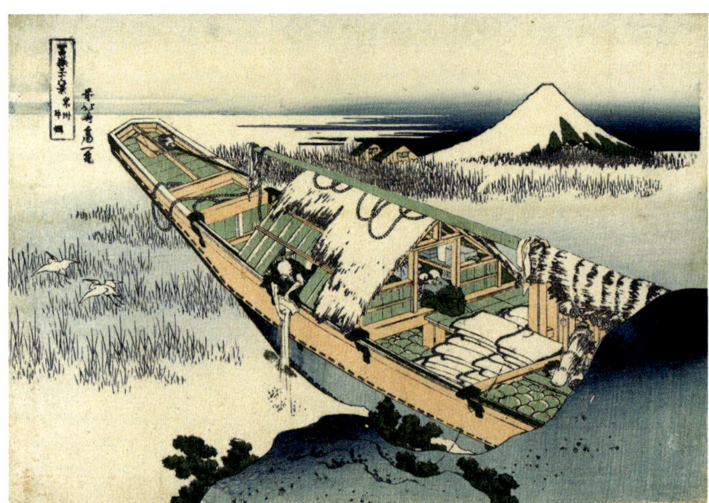

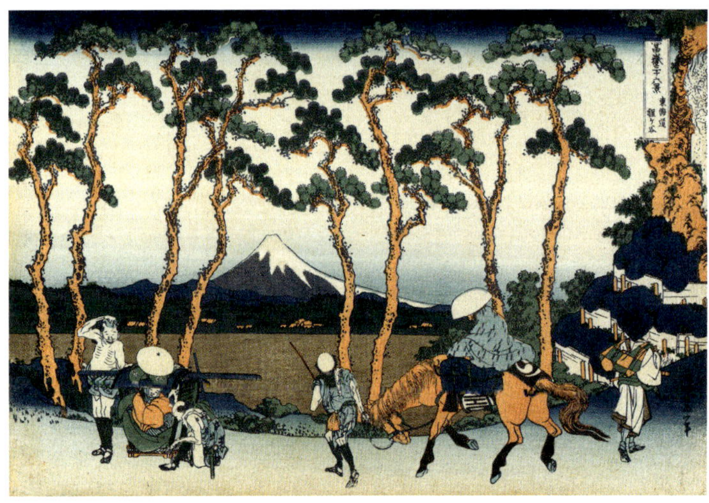

205f | 205s | 205h Katsushika Hokusai, *Ejiri in Suruga Province* | *Ushibori in Jōshū Province* | *Hodogaya on the Tōkaidō*, 1830–1831

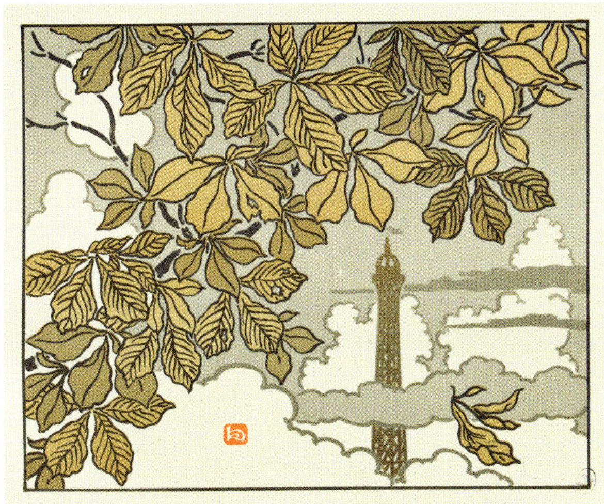

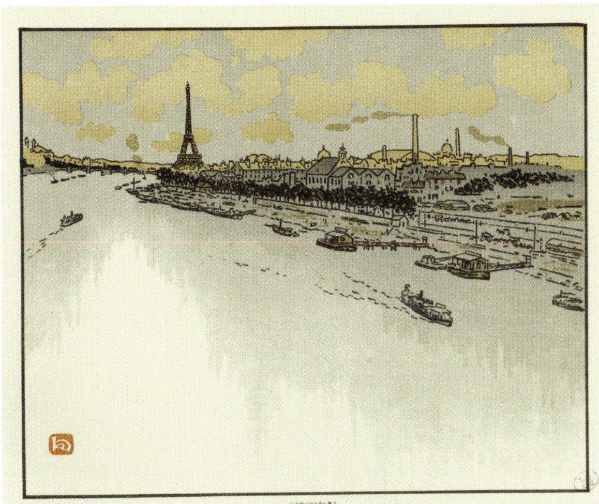

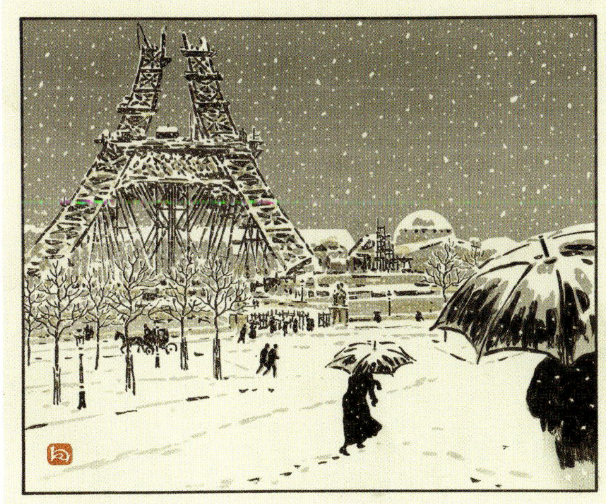

99b | 99f | 99c Henri Rivière, *36 Views of the Eiffel Tower: Frontispiece | View from the Point-du-Jour | The Tower under Construction, View from the Trocadéro*, 1902

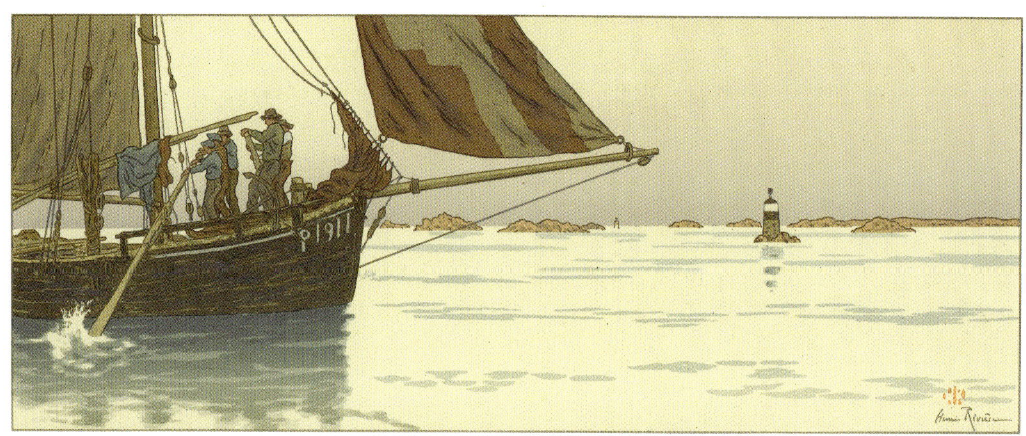

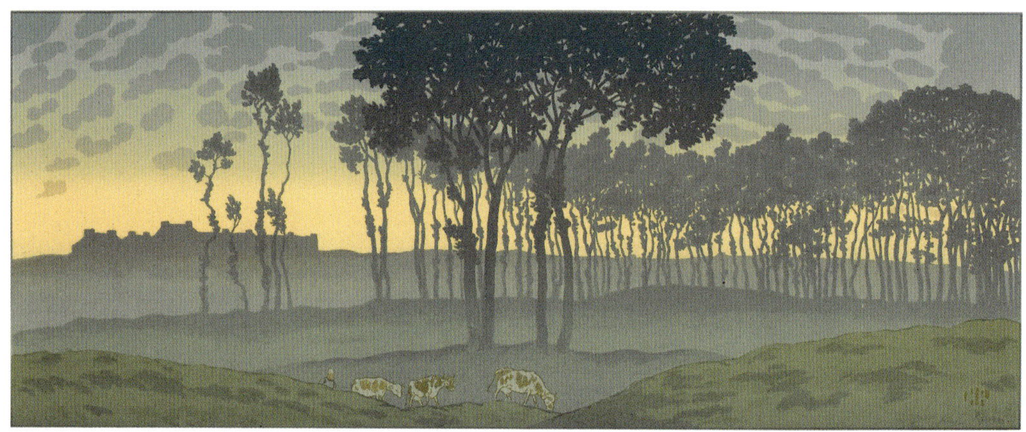

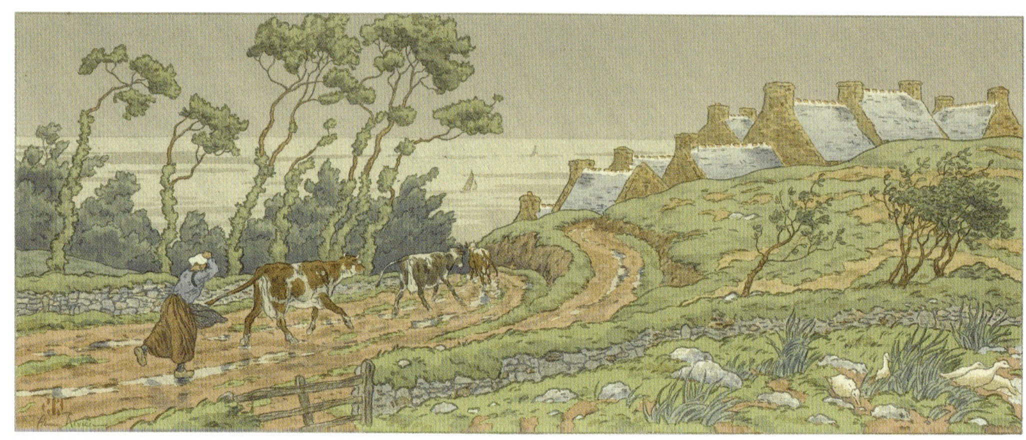

98e | 98a | 98d Henri Rivière, *Quiet Sea*, 1902 | *Dawn*, 1901 | *The Shower*, 1901

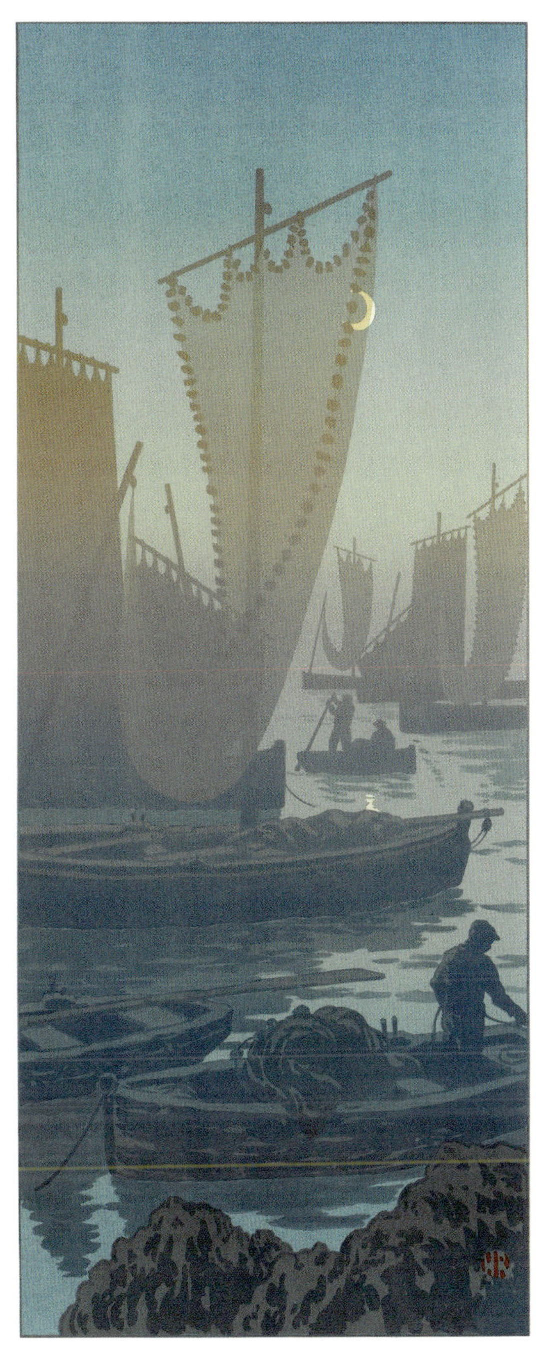

98c Henri Rivière, *Crescent*, 1901

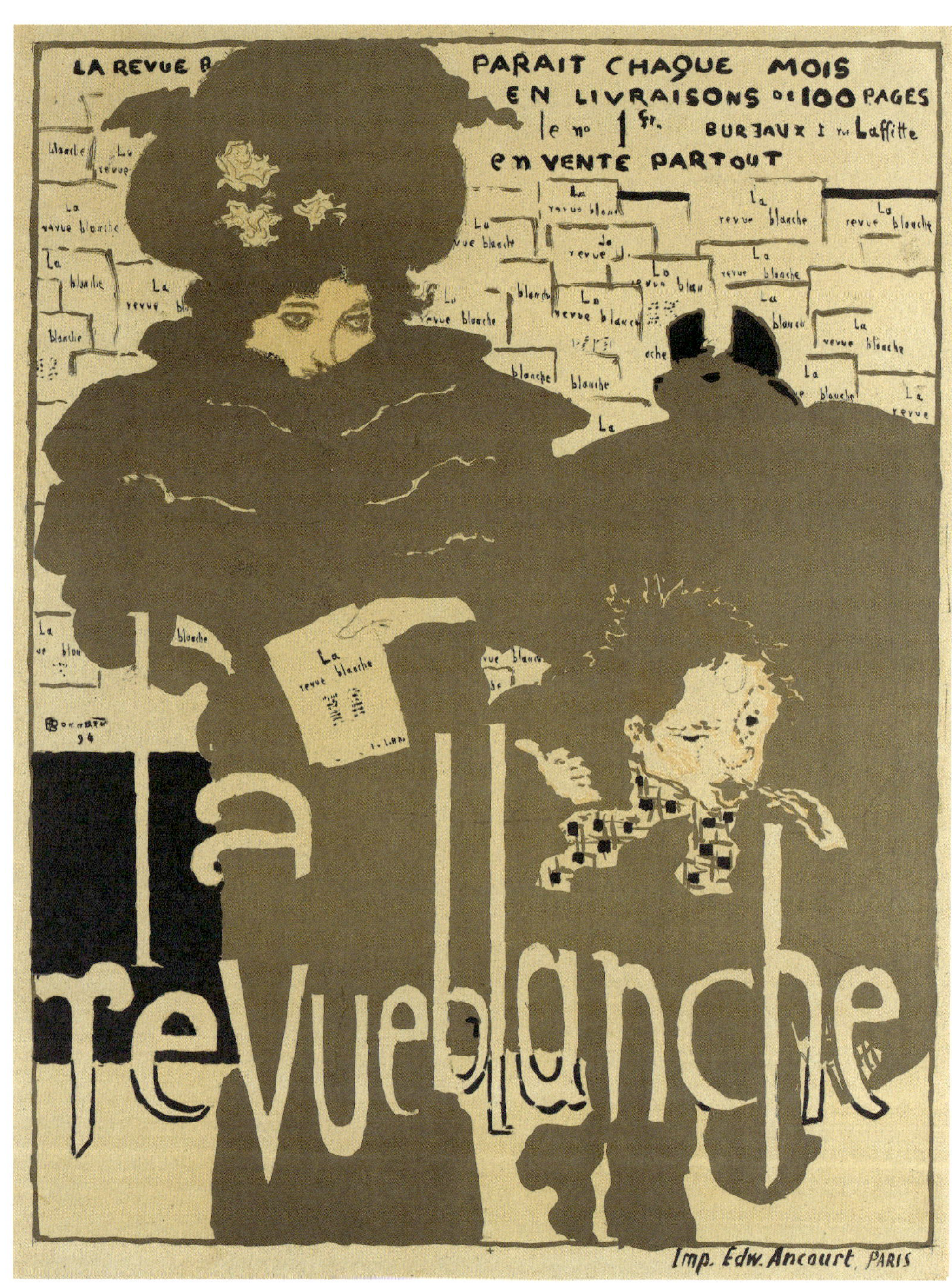

90a Pierre Bonnard, *La Revue blanche*, 1894

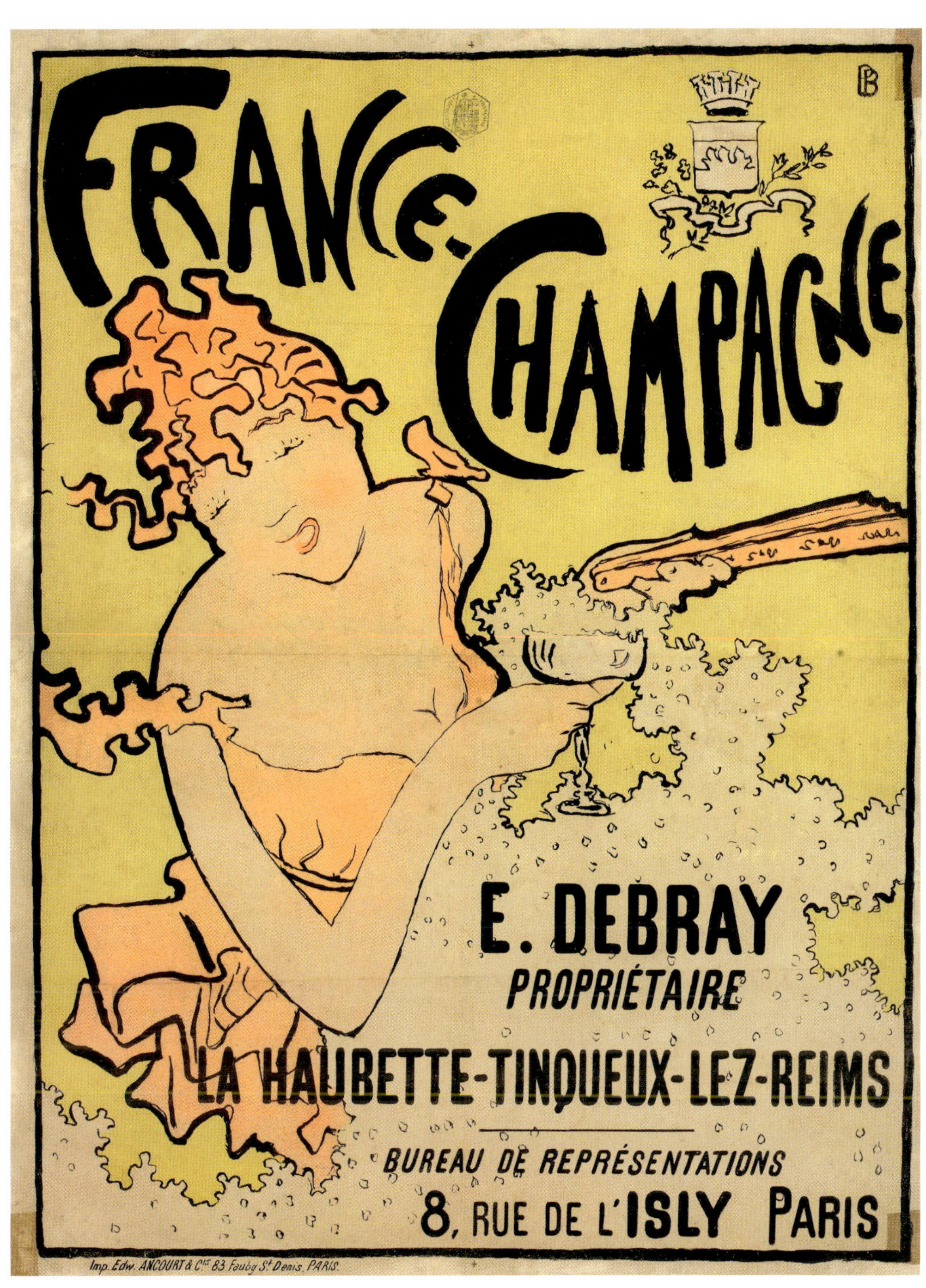

89 Pierre Bonnard, *France-Champagne*, 1891

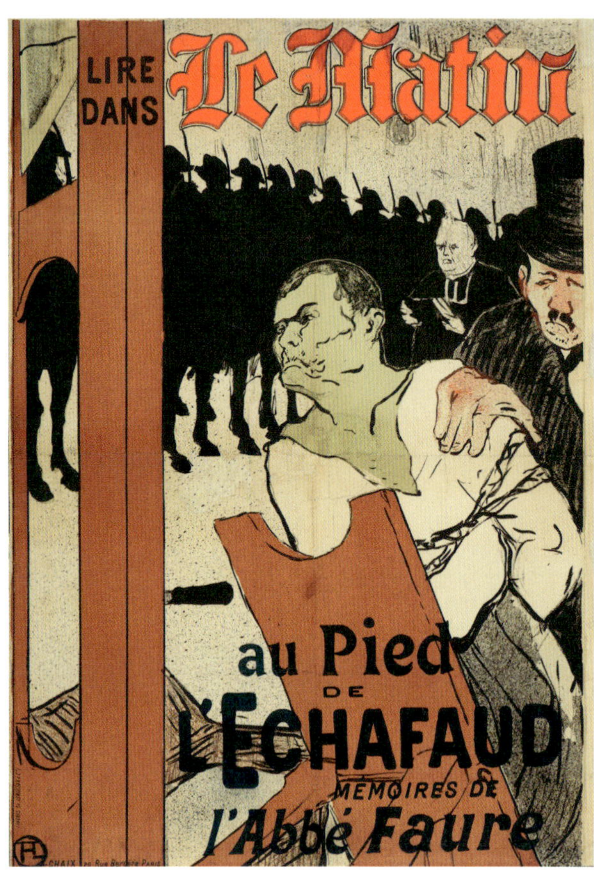

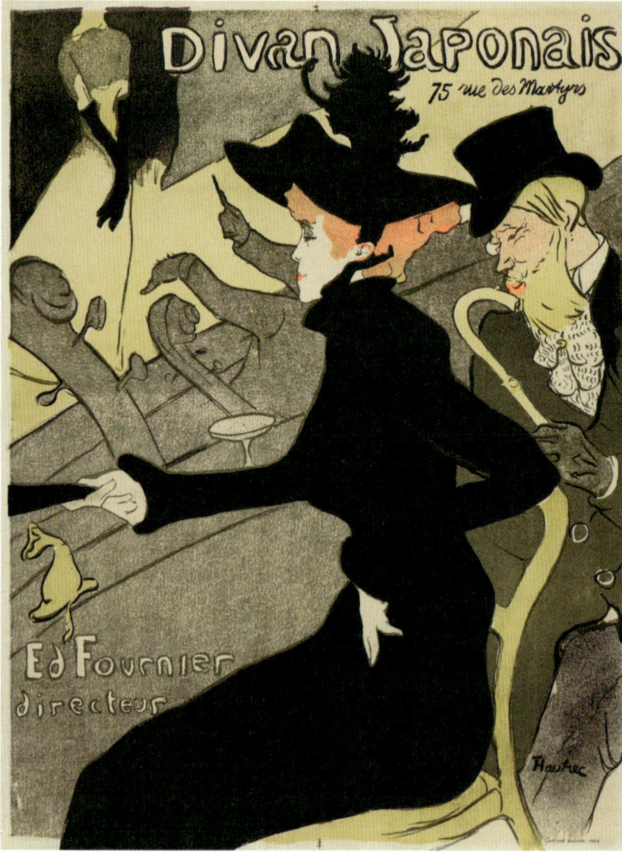

104 | 102a Henri de Toulouse-Lautrec, *Le Matin* | *Divan Japonais*, 1893

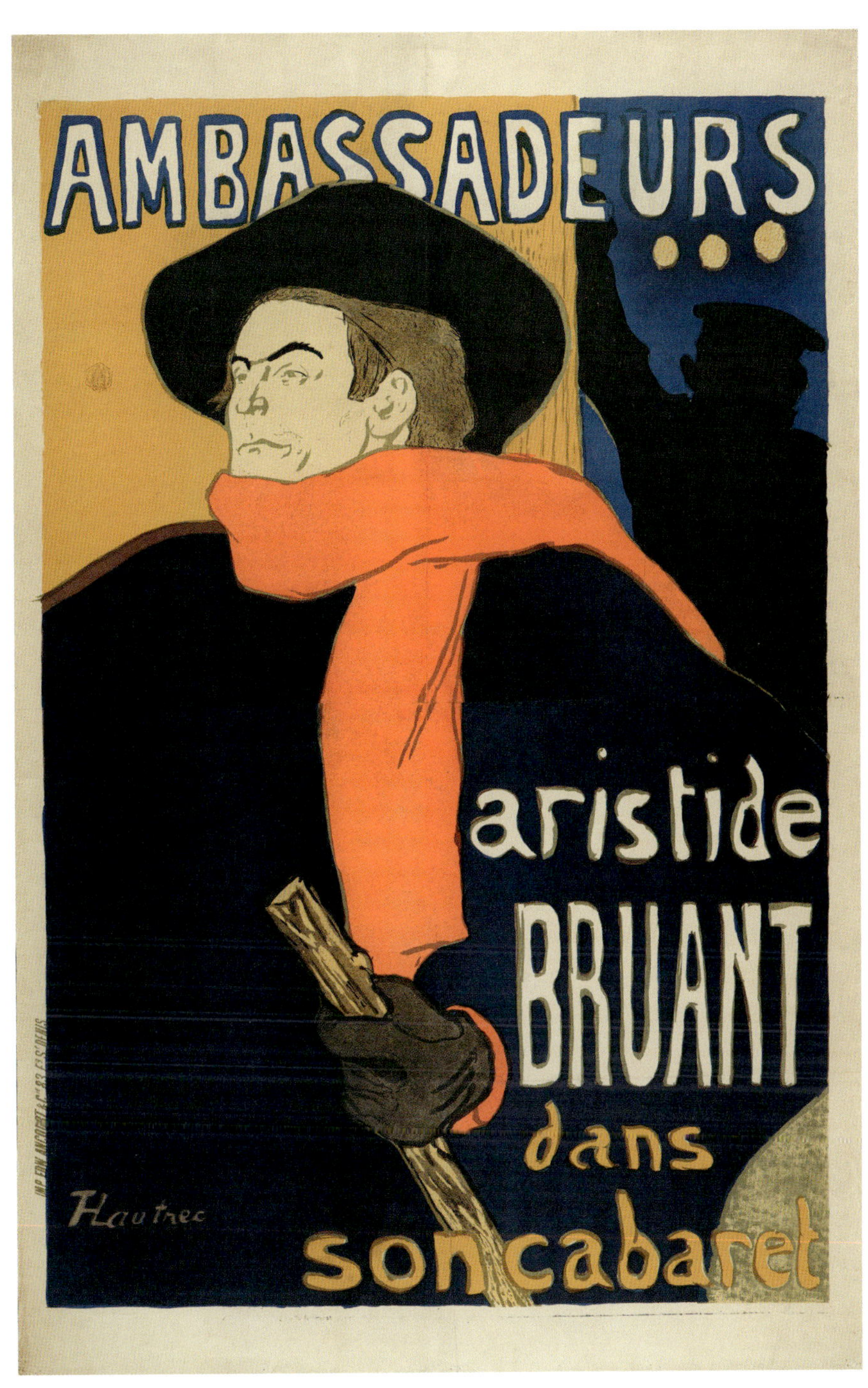

101 Henri de Toulouse-Lautrec, *Ambassadeurs, Aristide Bruant in His Cabaret*, 1892

Japan internalised

During the second half of the nineteenth century, French artists – alongside depicting Japanese objects and engaging with Japanese motifs – adopted compositional solutions and stylistic techniques from Japanese art, making them fruitful for their own artistic production. Japanese models can be detected in various works to the extent that Japanese aesthetic approaches were internalised and reinterpreted by artists in Europe. This was already visible in the work of the first generation of *Japonistes* such as James McNeill Whistler and Edgar Degas.

Around 1860, Whistler began collecting both Chinese and Japanese artefacts and woodblock prints, which can often be seen in his paintings (p. 60). In a series of landscapes, he also referred to these models in compositional and stylistic terms. For example, in his vertical representation of the Thames, *Variations in Violet and Green* from 1871 (p. 203), the line of the horizon is placed high in the image, as in works by Utagawa Hiroshige, who sometimes omitted the horizon entirely (pp. 208, 209). We know that Whistler engaged with woodblock prints by Hiroshige, quoting several of them in his painting *Caprice in Purple and Gold: The Golden Screen* from 1864 (Freer Art Gallery, Washington DC). His respect for Japan is also reflected in the Japanese-inspired motif of the butterfly that Whistler used to sign his works, as seen in his 1872 depiction of a lone boat on the nocturnal Thames, *Nocturne: Blue and Silver – Cremorne Lights* (p. 202). With its atmospheric character and the harmoniously unified colours, the painting recalls examples of East Asian ink painting, whereas the Far Eastern atmosphere of the London river landscape is additionally emphasised by inserting bamboo branches in the image foreground.

In his depictions of ballerinas, Whistler's friend Degas also used stylistic means borrowed from Japanese woodblock prints. As in Hiroshige's visual compositions (p. 209), in Degas's 1872 painting *Orchestra Musicians* (p. 205), the figures – which are shown in close-up at the viewer's eye level in the image foreground – are radically severed by the edge of the picture. In a painting of a ballerina twenty years later (p. 204), Degas radicalised this principle of severing motifs, lending the scene a particularly modern aspect. Only two scrolls on string instruments indicate the musicians found in the orchestra pit, directing the gaze to the stage where the ballerina moves gracefully. Other paintings by Degas showing several dancers in various poses and unconventional framings (pp. 206, 207) might well have emerged as a result of engaging with Katsushika Hokusai's *Manga* movement studies or the practice of chronophotography that developed in the late 1870s (p. 66).

Japanese art was also an important source of inspiration for the artists of the Brittany-based school of Pont-Aven. Alongside Louis Anquetin and Paul Sérusier, these included Émile Bernard und Paul Gauguin, who both stayed in the small northern French village of Pont-Aven in 1888. Based on an interest in medieval glass painting and enamel works using the cloisonné technique, folk art, the so-called *images d'Épinal* and, above all, Japanese woodblock prints, they developed a "cloisonnesque" and synthetic style characterised by the simplification of form, on the one hand, and the use of pure, interlinking colour surfaces in dark contours, on the other. In his *Bretonneries*, a portfolio of hand-coloured zincographs, Bernard depicts scenes of peasant life in Brittany, some of which are highly stylised (pp. 212, 213). Darkly contoured surfaces are combined with severed motifs in the foreground, recalling Hiroshige's works. The parallel arrangement of tree trunks in the title zincograph from the portfolio can also be found in Japanese prints (pp. 192, 208). Bernard chose similar compositional devices in his painting *The Wave* from 1892 (p. 215); all that is visible in the foreground is the head of a Breton woman wearing a white bonnet, whilst in the background various visual elements are spread out as powerful surfaces of colour, in part darkly contoured.

Bernard and Gauguin were invited by their friend Vincent Van Gogh to the southern French town of Arles to live out the ideal of an artists' commune there in the Yellow House, based on Van Gogh's conception of the peaceful cohabitation among Japanese artists. But Gauguin arrived alone in October 1888. In Arles, the works that then emerged were decidedly shaped by Japanese stylistic techniques. In Gauguin's *Arlésiennes (Mistral)* (p. 217), the figures and the landscapes are stylised as simple geometric forms in lush, monochromatic fields of colour. As dark silhouettes, the two women from Arles in the foreground are set apart from the fields of colour where the path and the grass are painted. The artificiality of the scene is additionally amplified by the strongly upward view of the horizonless landscape that appears as if springing out towards the viewer; the rules of European central perspective are utterly ignored here. A similarly high degree of stylisation is evident in the painting *Blue Trees* (p. 68). The large, yellow-and-green surfaces of the landscape, outlined in blue, and the yellow sky form a clear contrast against the strong blue of the tree trunks organised in a decorative, parallel arrangement. Here, too, the line of the horizon is placed very high up in the image. That same year, Gauguin created the work *Little Cat Eating out of Bowl* (p. 216) in the form of a fan – a format that enjoyed great popularity at the time in line with Japanese fashion. In this work, the unusually narrow image detail brings the cat and the objects arranged on the table surprisingly close to the eye of the beholder.

In a letter written to his sister Willemien in September 1888, Van Gogh reports from Arles, where he had been staying since February: "For myself, I don't need Japanese prints here, because I'm always saying to myself *that I'm in Japan here*. That as a result I only have to open my eyes and paint right in front of me what makes an impression on me." The artist, who together with his brother Theo was a passionate collector of Japanese woodblock prints, now envisioned Japan in the south of France, associating the Far Eastern country with utopian visions. This was a highlight in terms of artistic identification with the country. For example, Van Gogh related a scene that he had observed at the Arles harbour to a Japanese artist. In July, he reported to his brother in a letter: "I saw a magnificent and very strange effect this evening. A very large boat laden with coal on the Rhône, moored to the quay. Seen from above it was all glistening and wet from a shower; the water was a white yellow and clouded pearl-grey, the sky lilac and an orange strip in the west, the town violet. On the boat, small workmen, blue and dirty white, were coming and going, carrying the cargo ashore. It was pure Hokusai." Van Gogh processed this observation in the painting *Quay with Men Unloading Sand Barges* (p. 10). The striking use of colour, the strong contours and the dramatic upward gaze as well as omission of the horizon recall Japanese woodblock prints by artists such as Hokusai or Hiroshige. He created the painting *Sower with Setting Sun* (p. 223) in Arles as well. In the front part of the painting, there are the strongly cut, schematic outlines of the sower at work along with a fragment of a tree. The diagonal division of the image, the close-up perspective and the flatness are very similar to a print by Hiroshige, *Plum Estate, Kameido* (p. 221), of which Van Gogh owned a copy. In the background, the landscape spreads out – a field in purple and yellow in lively lines and a sky in yellow. Dominant here is the motif of the yellow disc of the sun – for Van Gogh, a virtual symbol of his utopia in the south as his paradise.

Ulrike Hofer

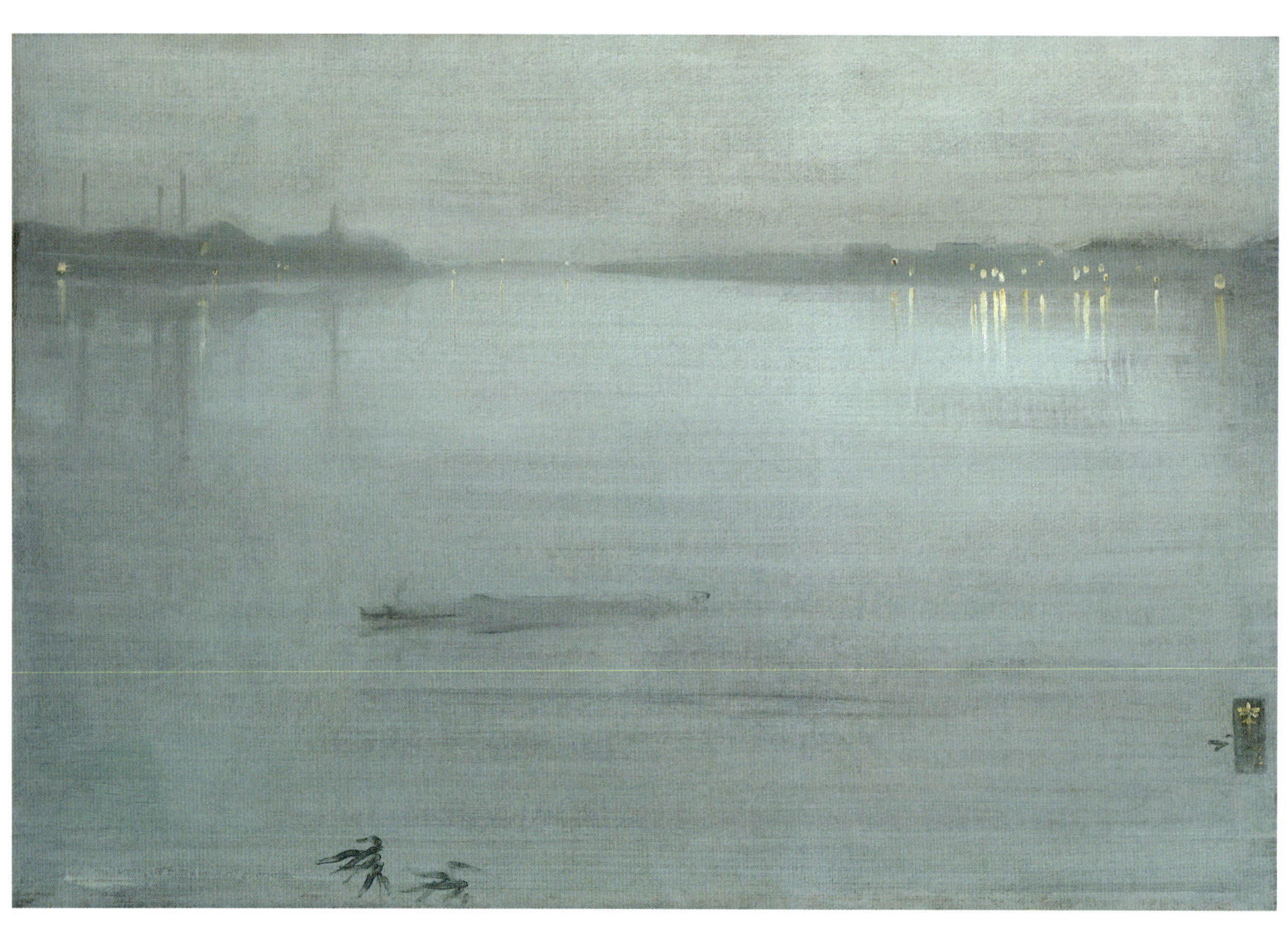

74 James Abbott McNeill Whistler, *Nocturne: Blue and Silver – Cremorne Lights*, 1872

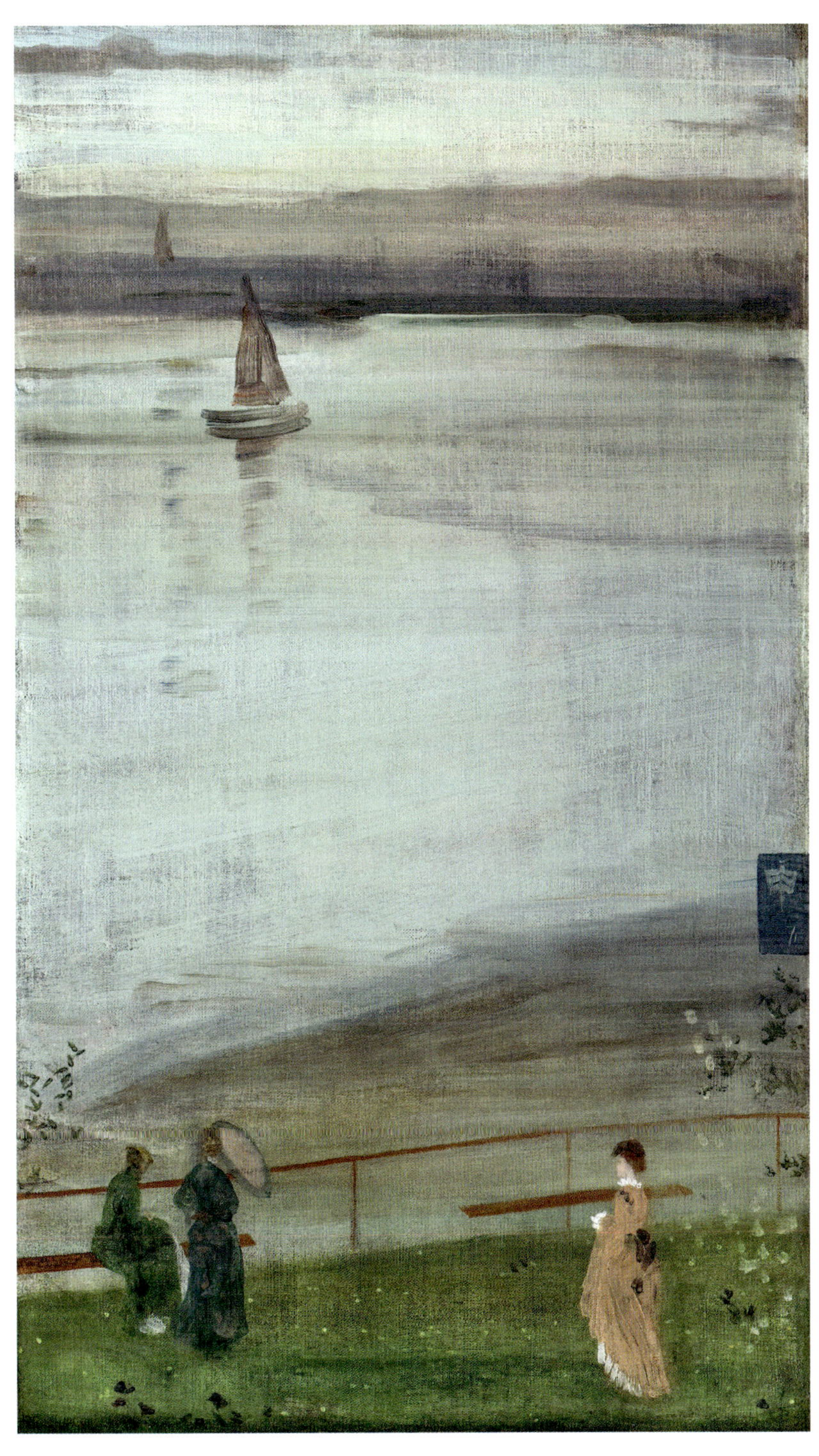

73 James Abbott McNeill Whistler, *Variations in Violet and Green*, 1871

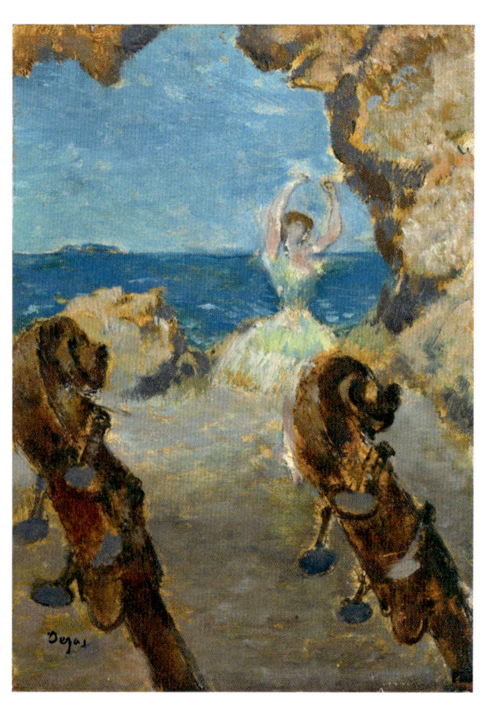

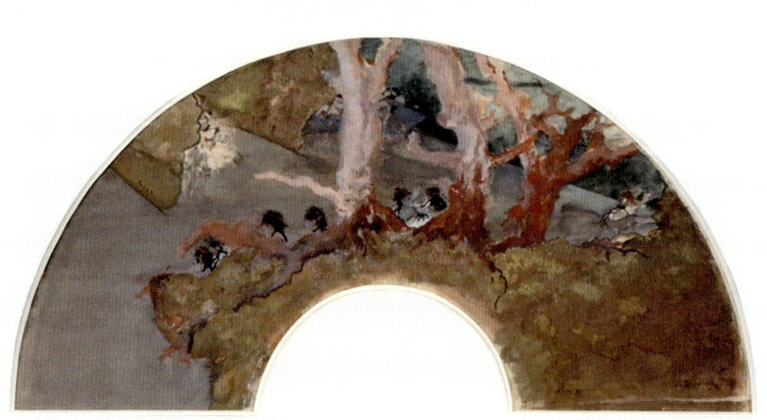

17 | 84 Edgar Degas, *Ballet Dancer*, 1891 | *Dancers Behind the Scenes*, circa 1878/1879

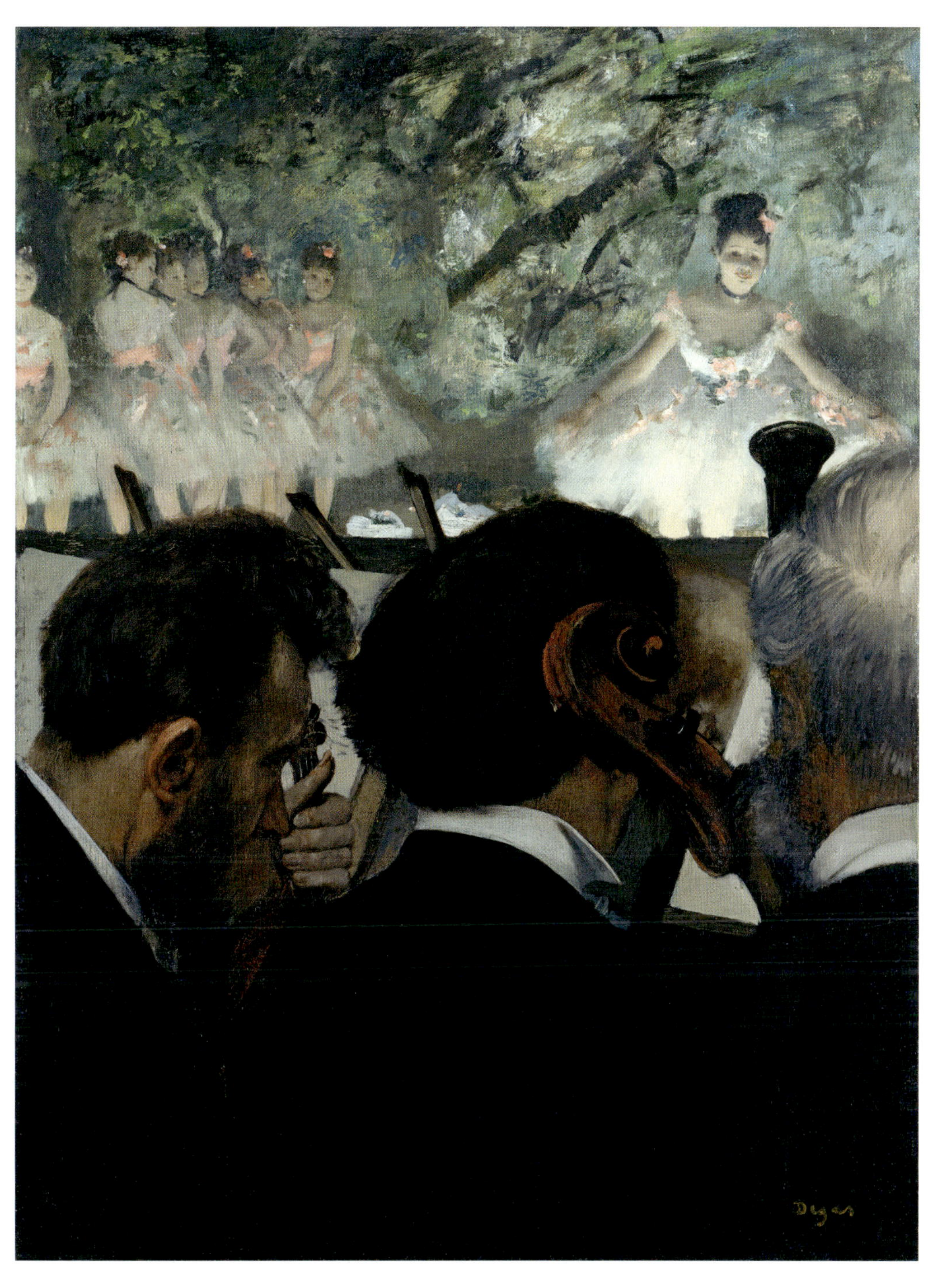

14 Edgar Degas, *Orchestra Musicians*, 1872 (reworked 1874–1876)

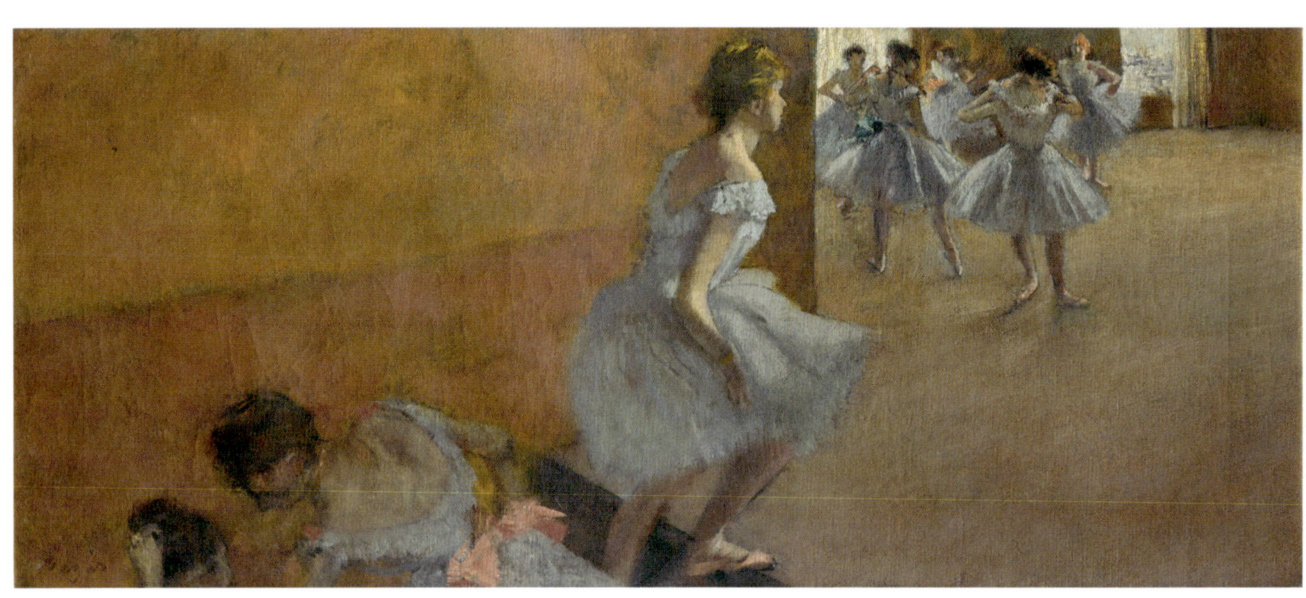

15 Edgar Degas, *Dancers Mounting the Stairs*, 1886/1890

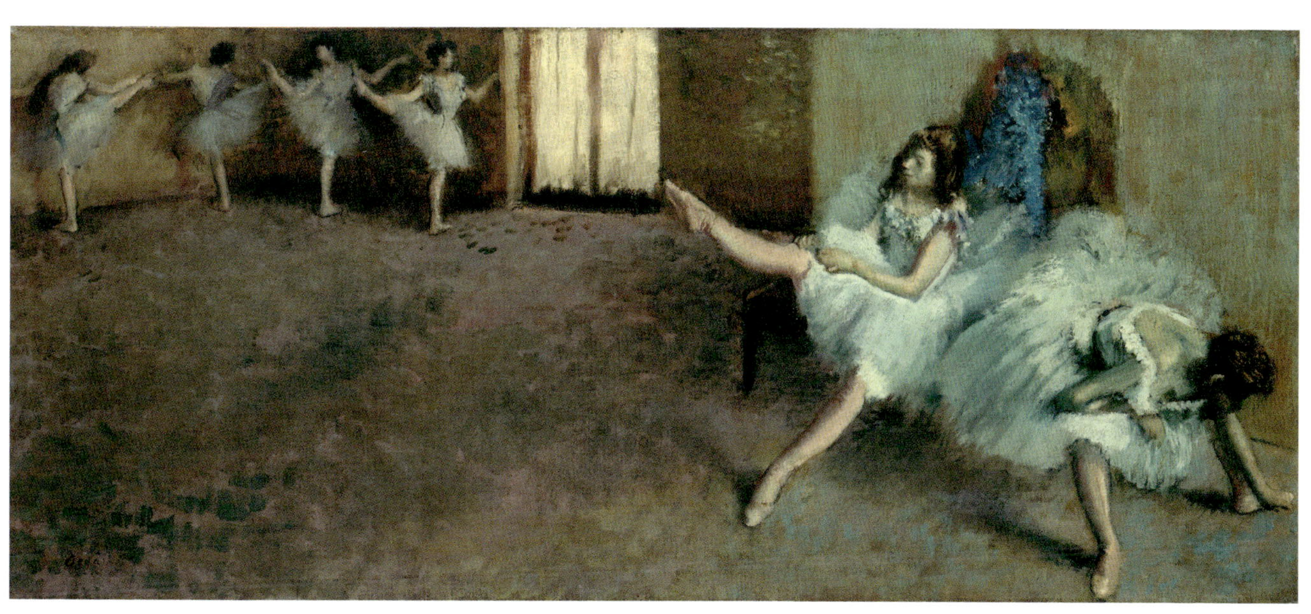

16 Edgar Degas, *Before the Ballet*, 1890/1892

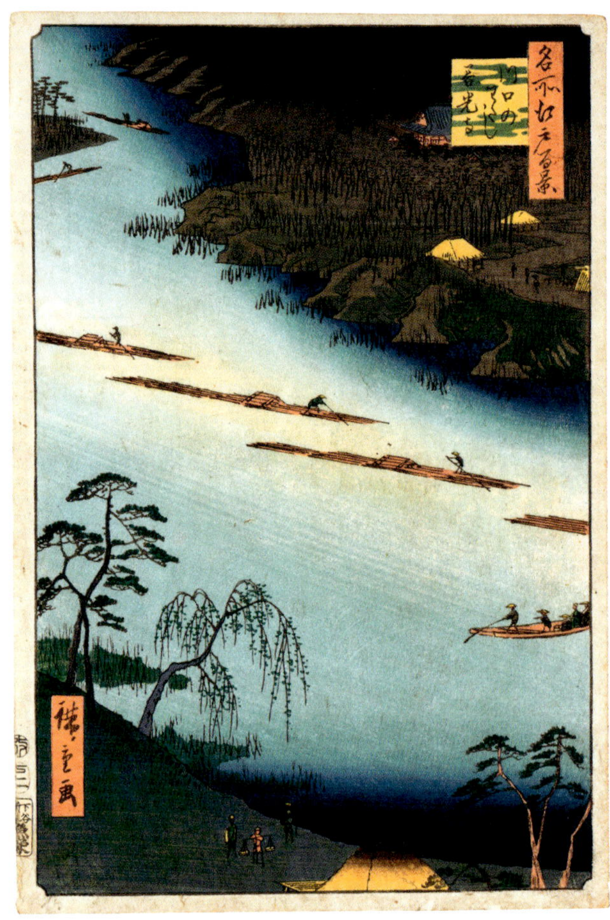

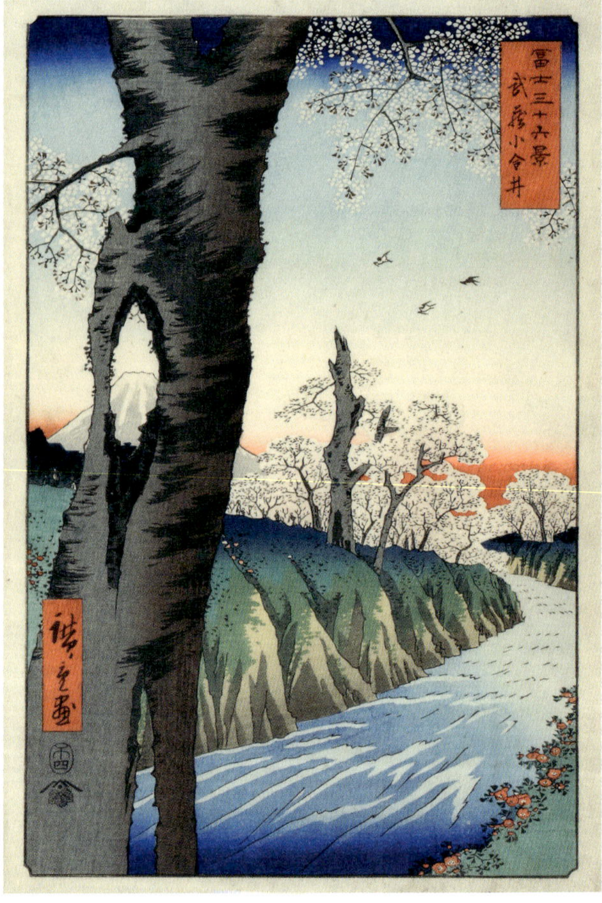

203a | 204e Utagawa Hiroshige, *The Kawaguchi Ferry and Zenkōji Temple*, 1857 | *Koganei in Musashi Province*, 1858

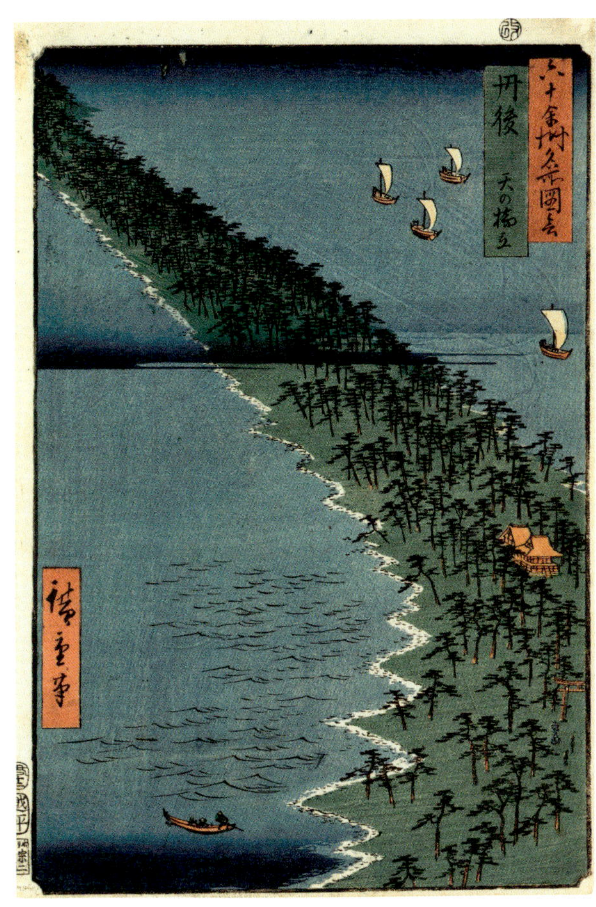

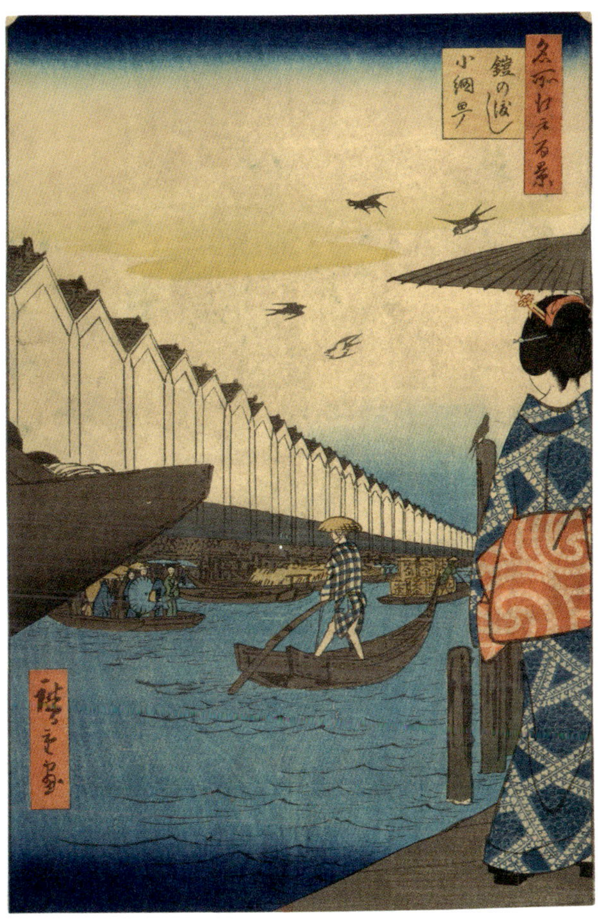

203e | 202a Utagawa Hiroshige, *Yoroi Ferry, Koami-chō*, 1857 | *Tango Province: Ama no hashidate*, 1853

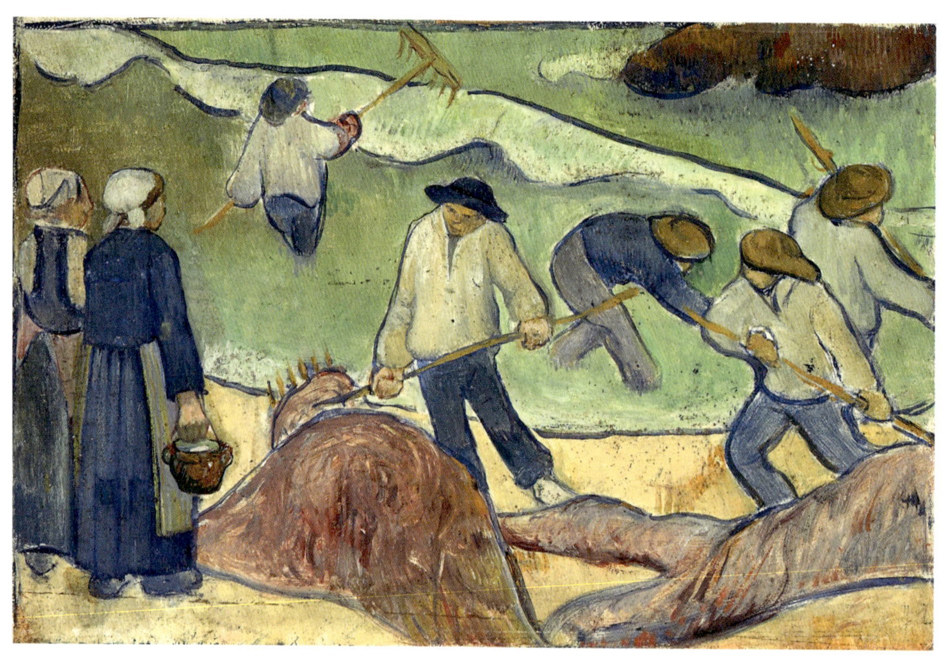

63 Paul Sérusier, *Small Landscape with Seaweed Gatherers*, circa 1889

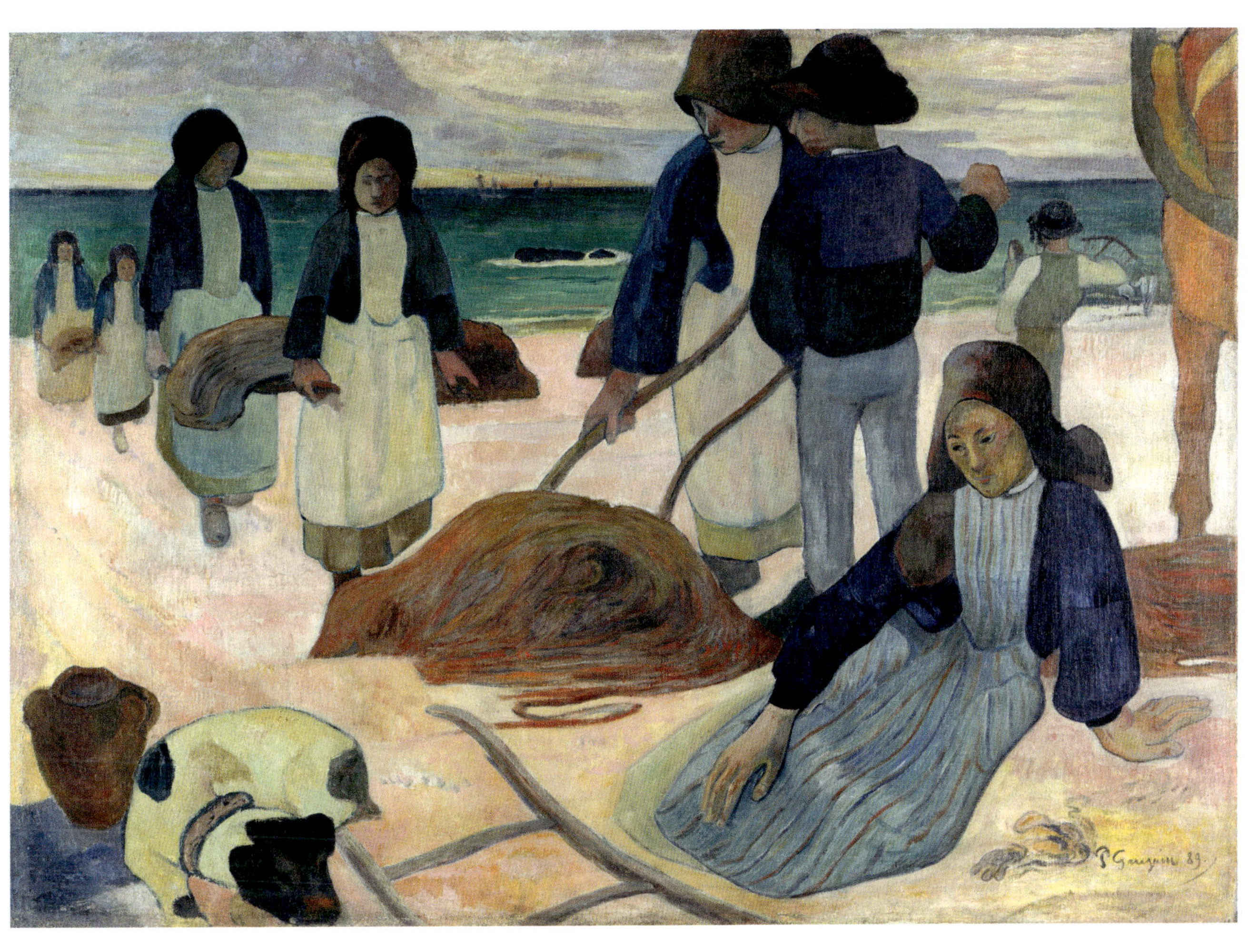

33 Paul Gauguin, *The Kelp Gatherers (II)*, 1889

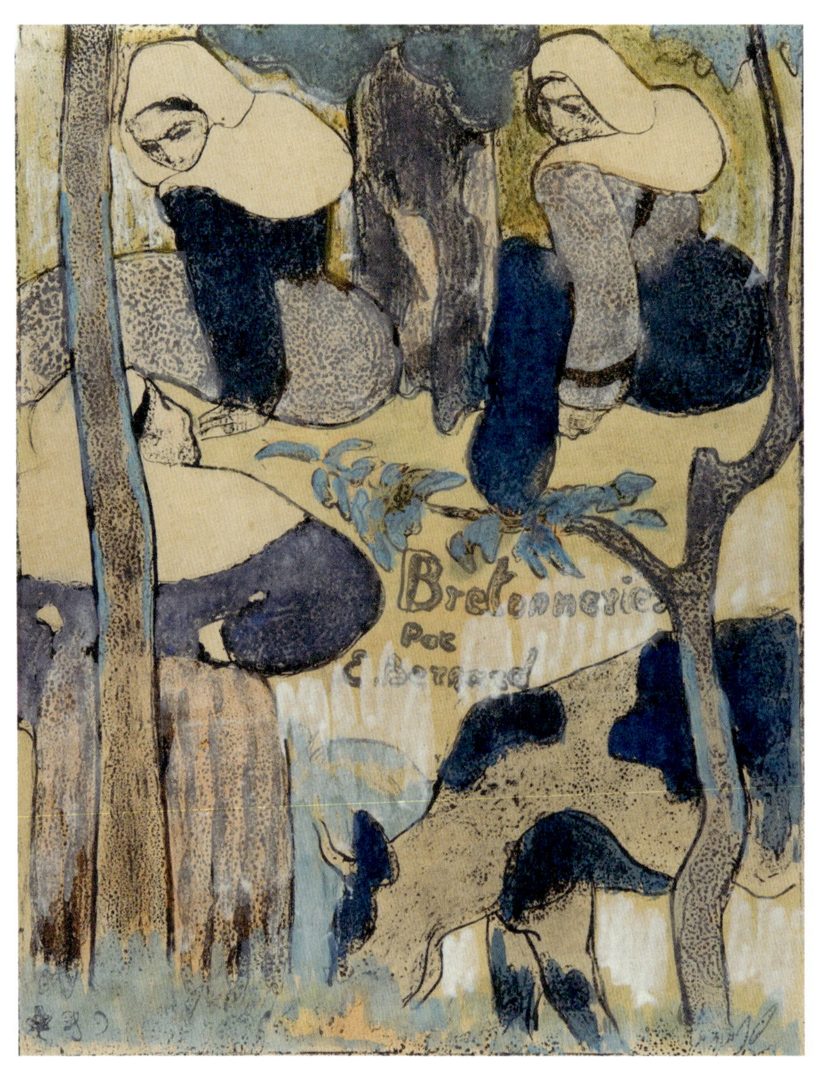

88a Émile Bernard, *Bretonneries (Title Page)*, 1889

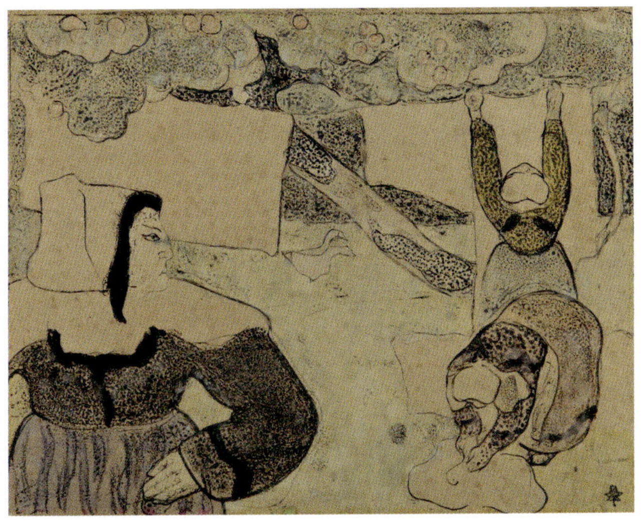

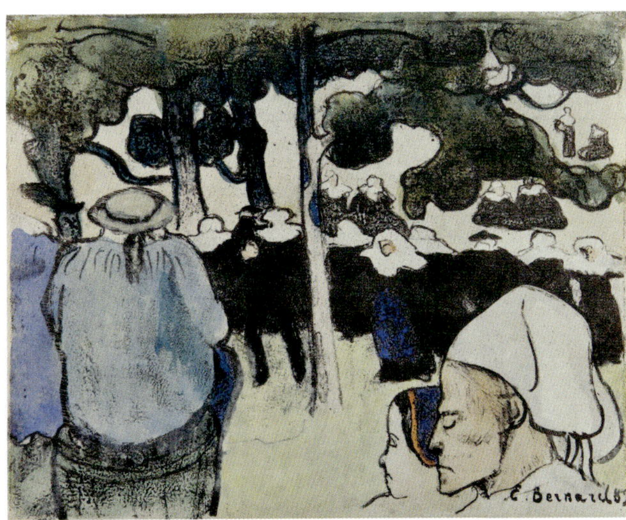

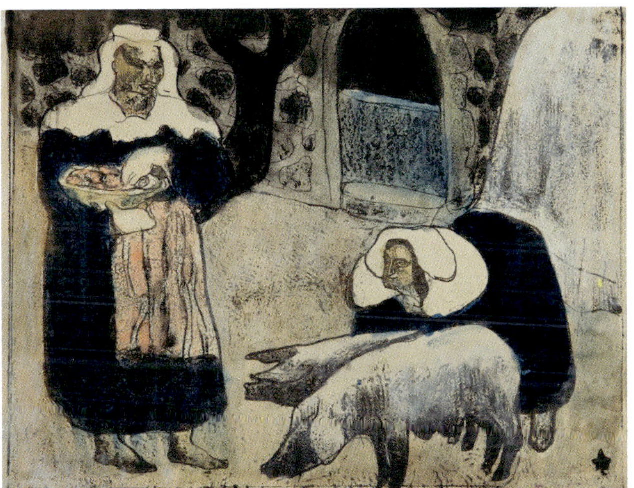

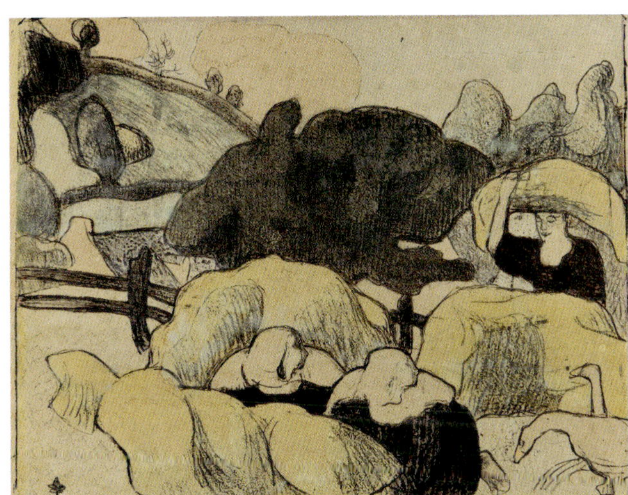

88c | 88f | 88e | 88d Émile Bernard, *Breton Women Hanging Washing* | *Breton Wedding* | *Breton Women Feeding the Pigs* | *Breton Women Making Haystacks*, 1889

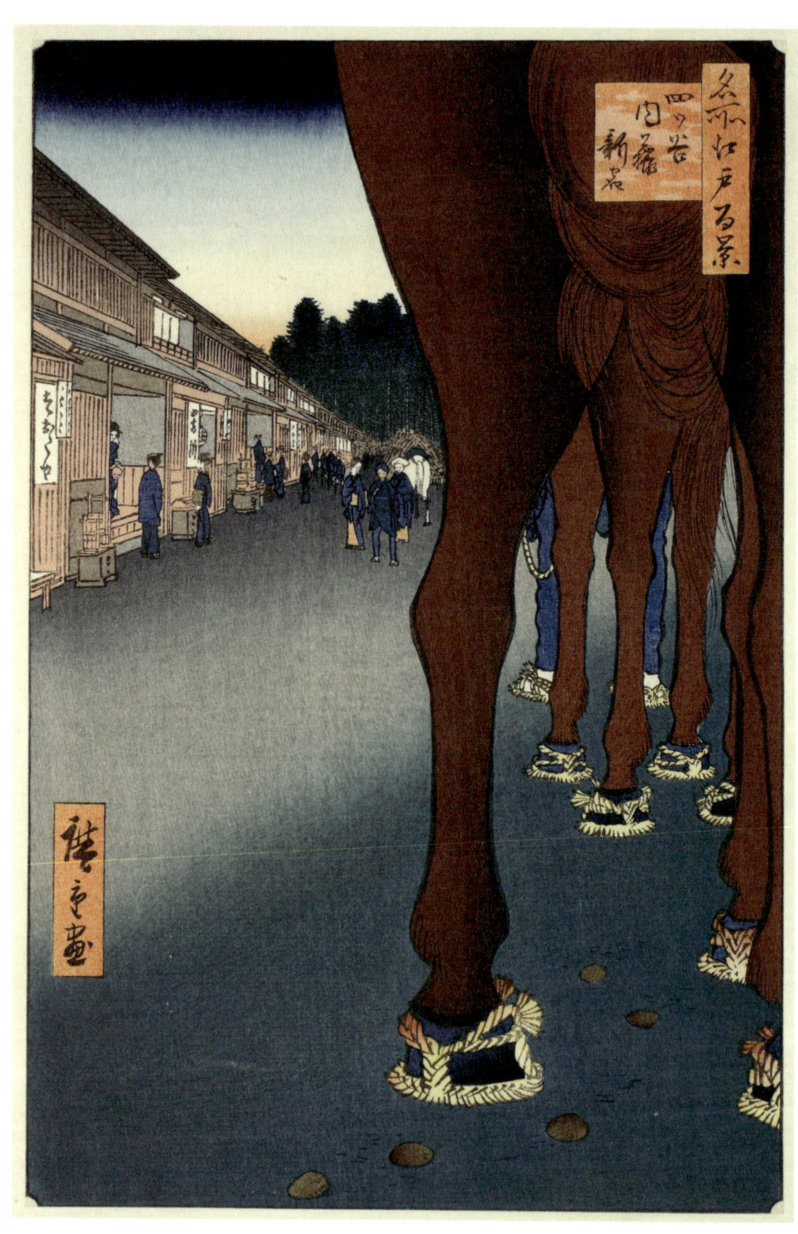

203n Utagawa Hiroshige, *Naitō Shinjuku at Yotsuya*, 1857

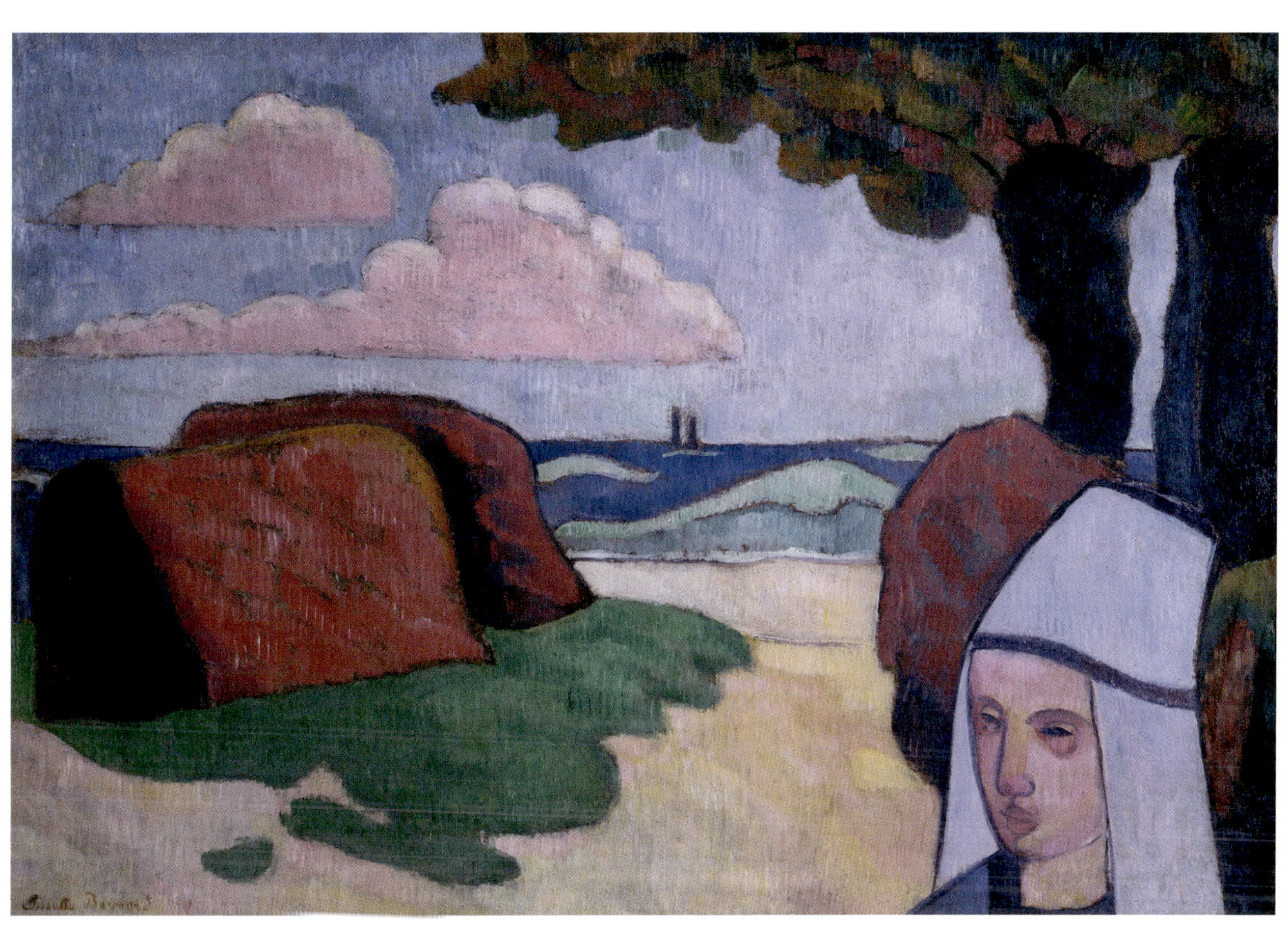

1 Émile Bernard, *The Wave*, 1892

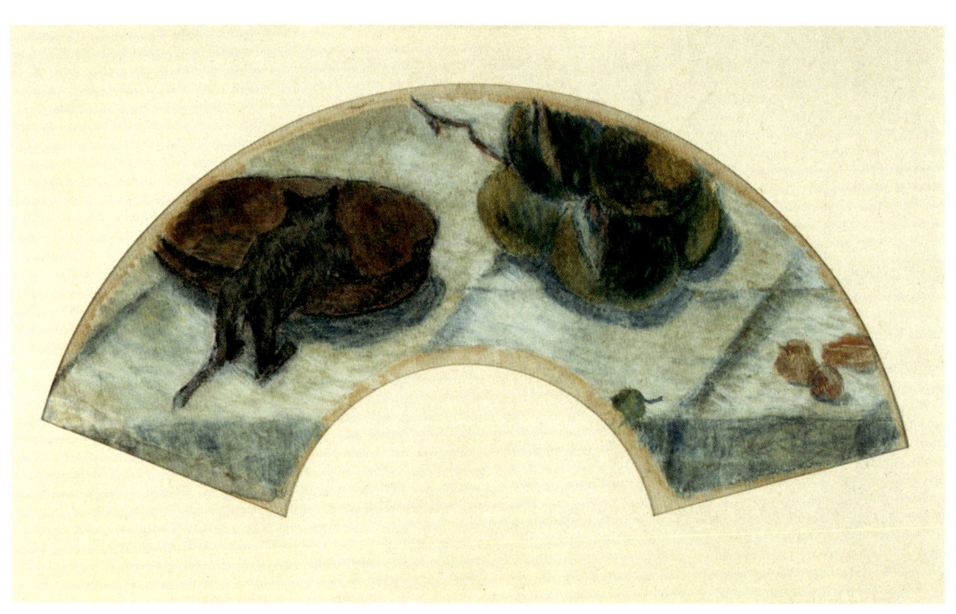

85 Paul Gauguin, *Little Cat Eating out of Bowl*, 1888

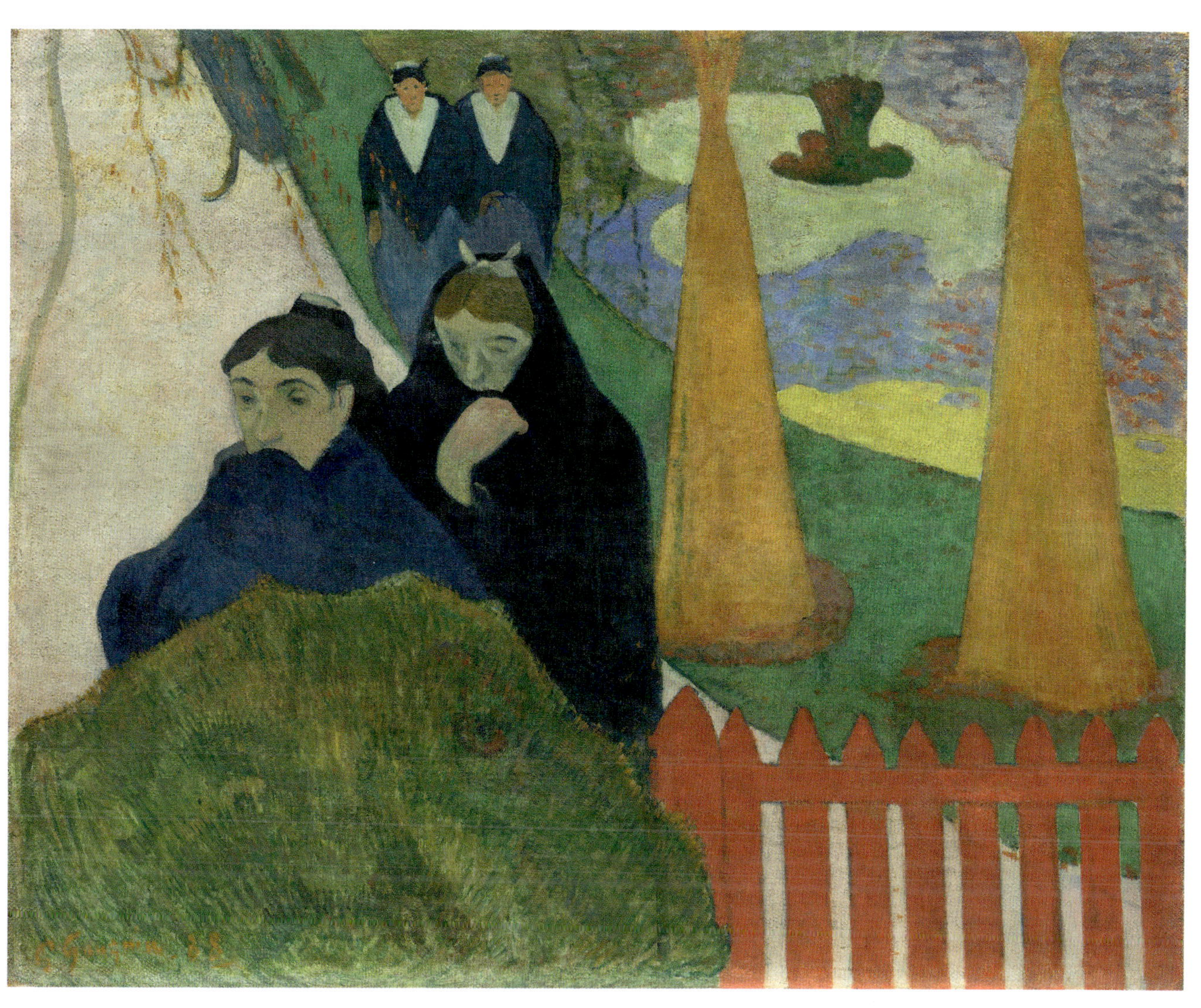

31 Paul Gauguin, *Arlésiennes (Mistral)*, 1888

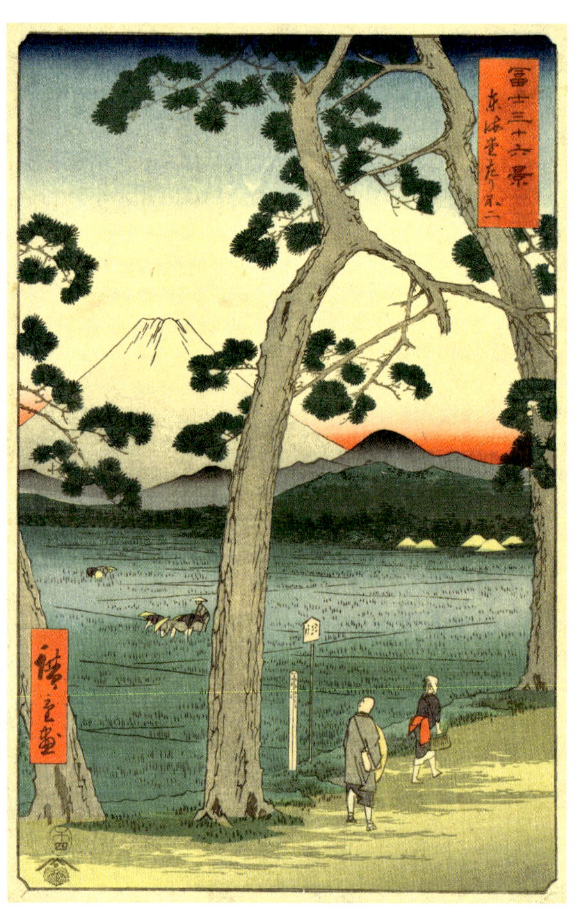

204a Utagawa Hiroshige, *Fuji at Left from the Tōkaidō,* 1858

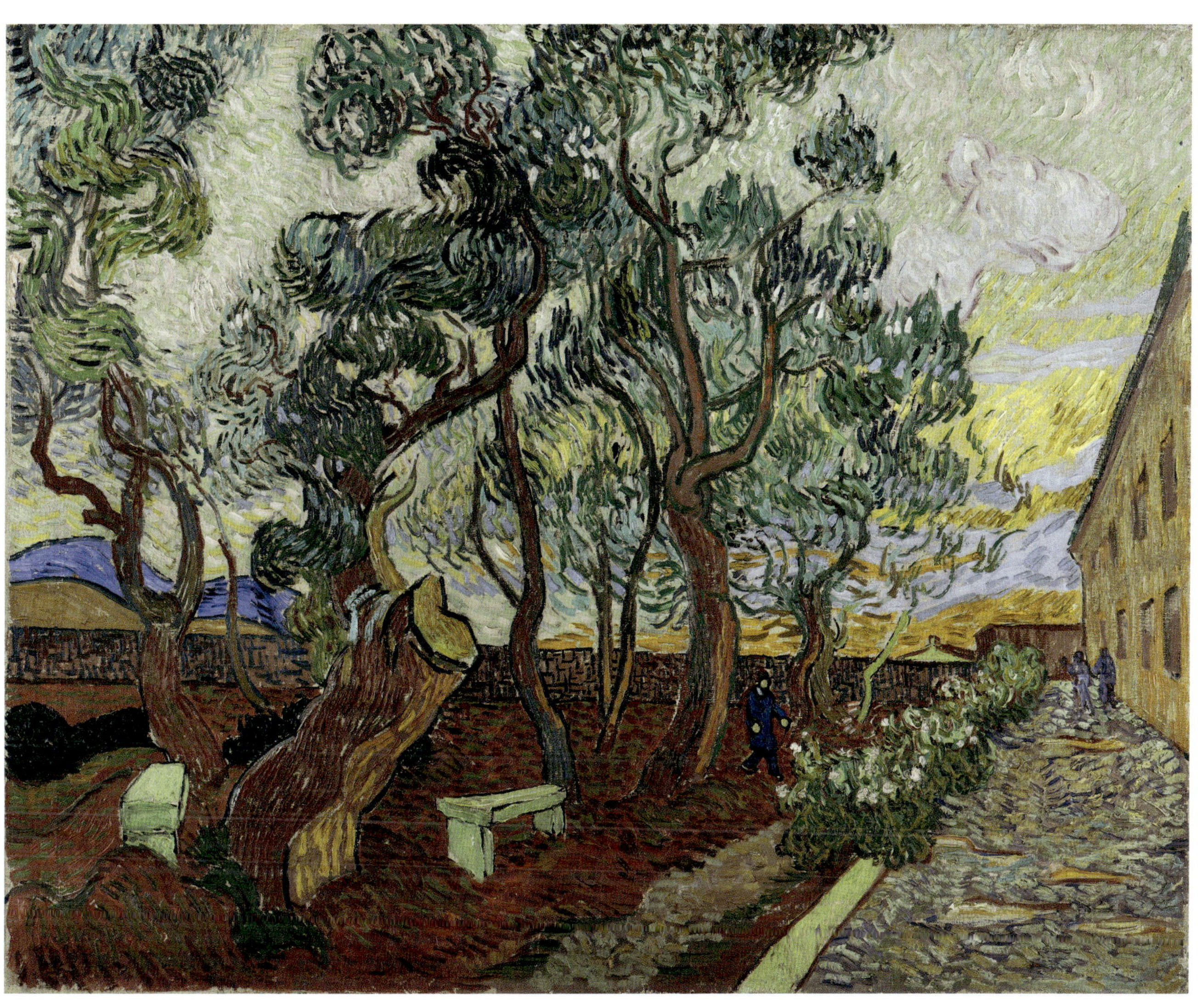

41 Vincent Van Gogh, *A Corner of the Asylum and the Garden with a Heavy, Sawed-Off Tree*, 1889

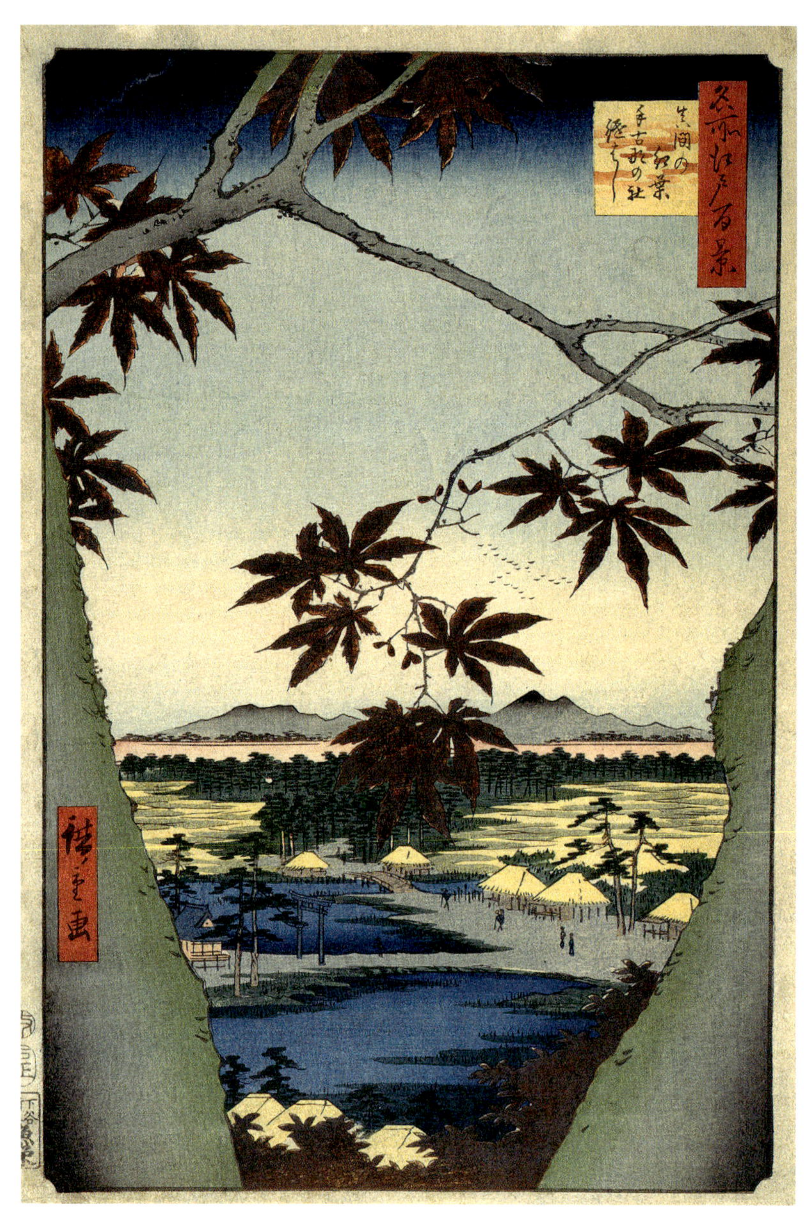

203p Utagawa Hiroshige, *Maples, Tekona Shrine and Bridge at Mama*, 1857

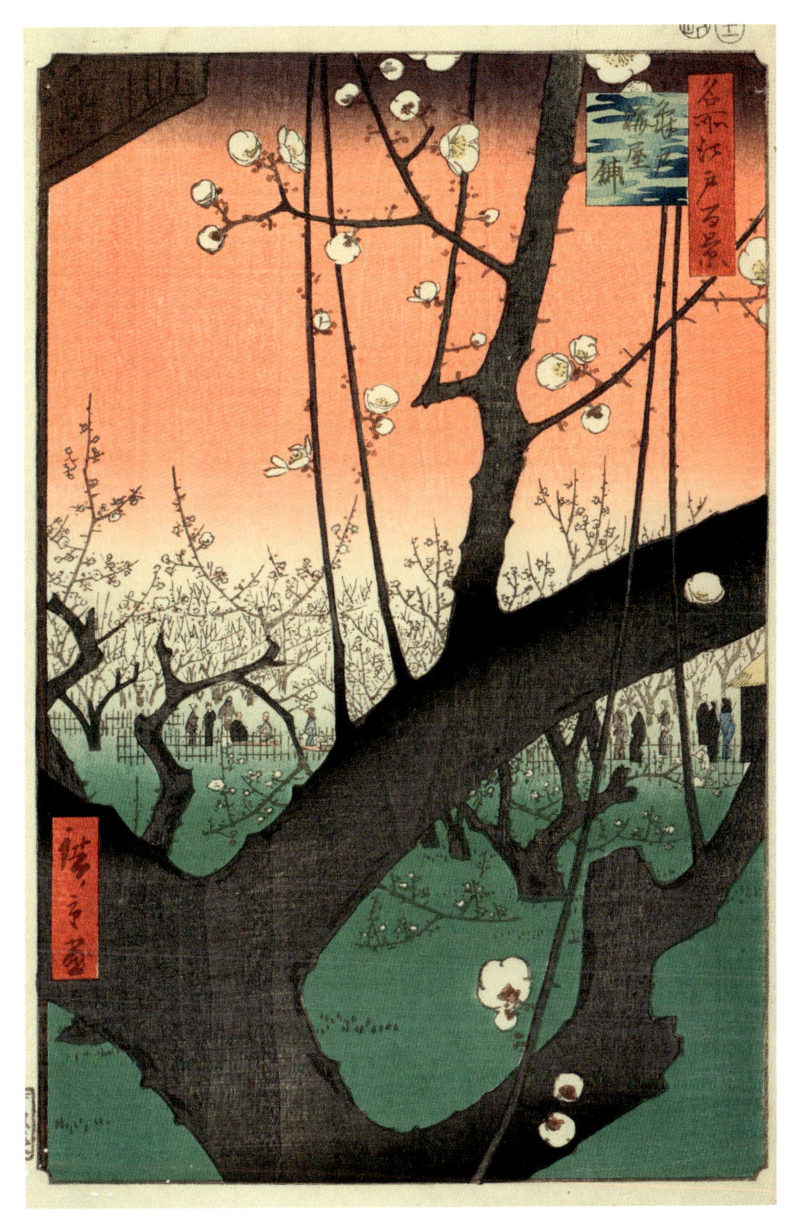

203d Utagawa Hiroshige, *Plum Estate, Kameido*, 1857

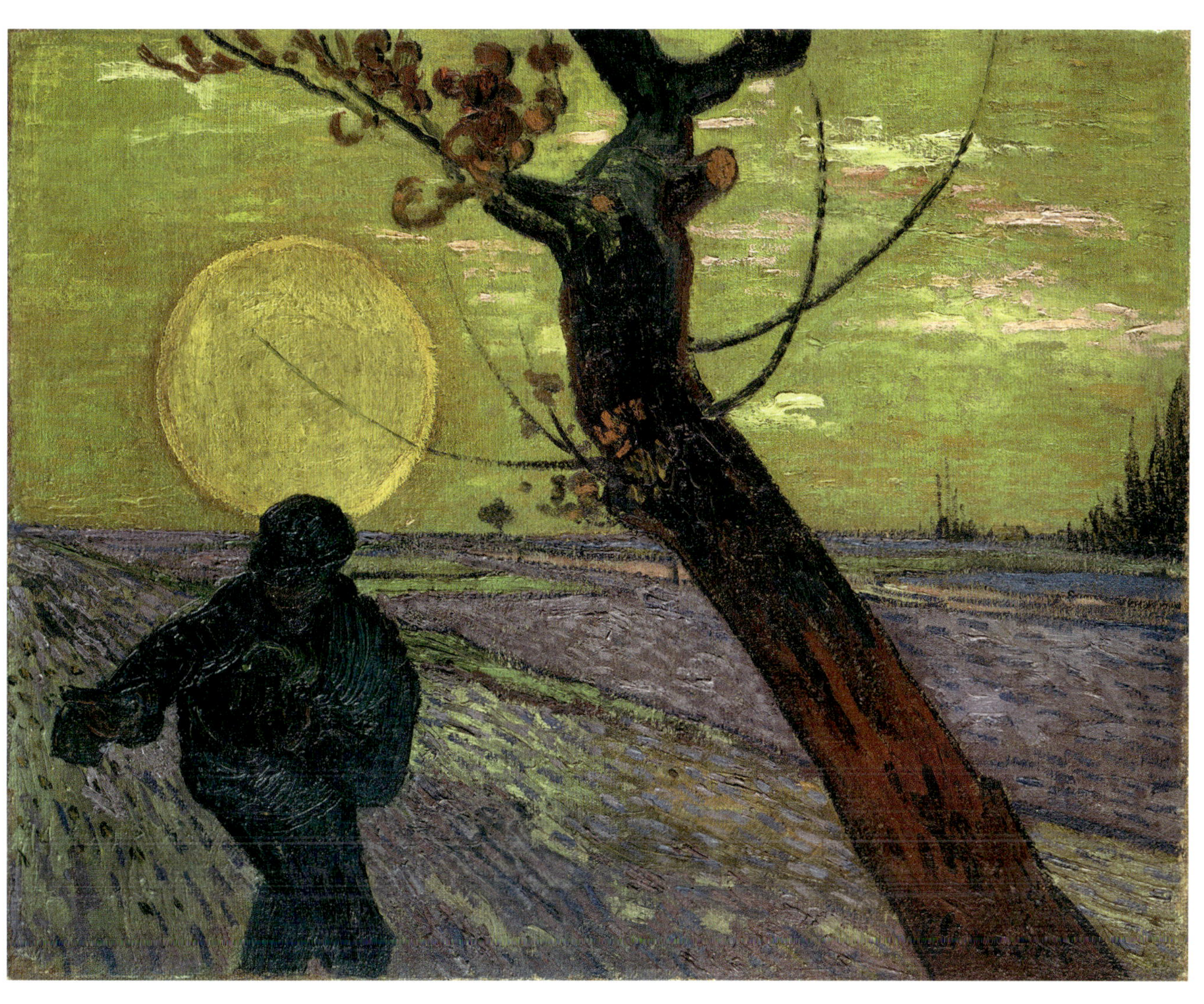

40 Vincent Van Gogh, *Sower with Setting Sun*, 1888

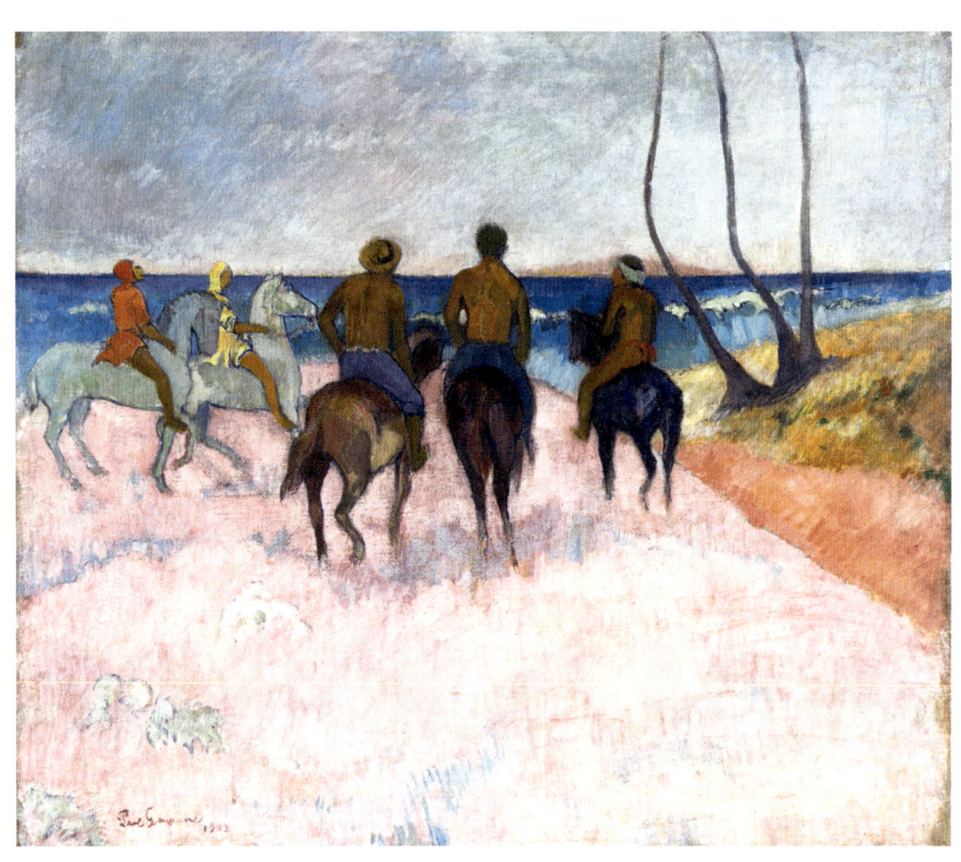

36 Paul Gauguin, *Riders on the Beach (I)*, 1902

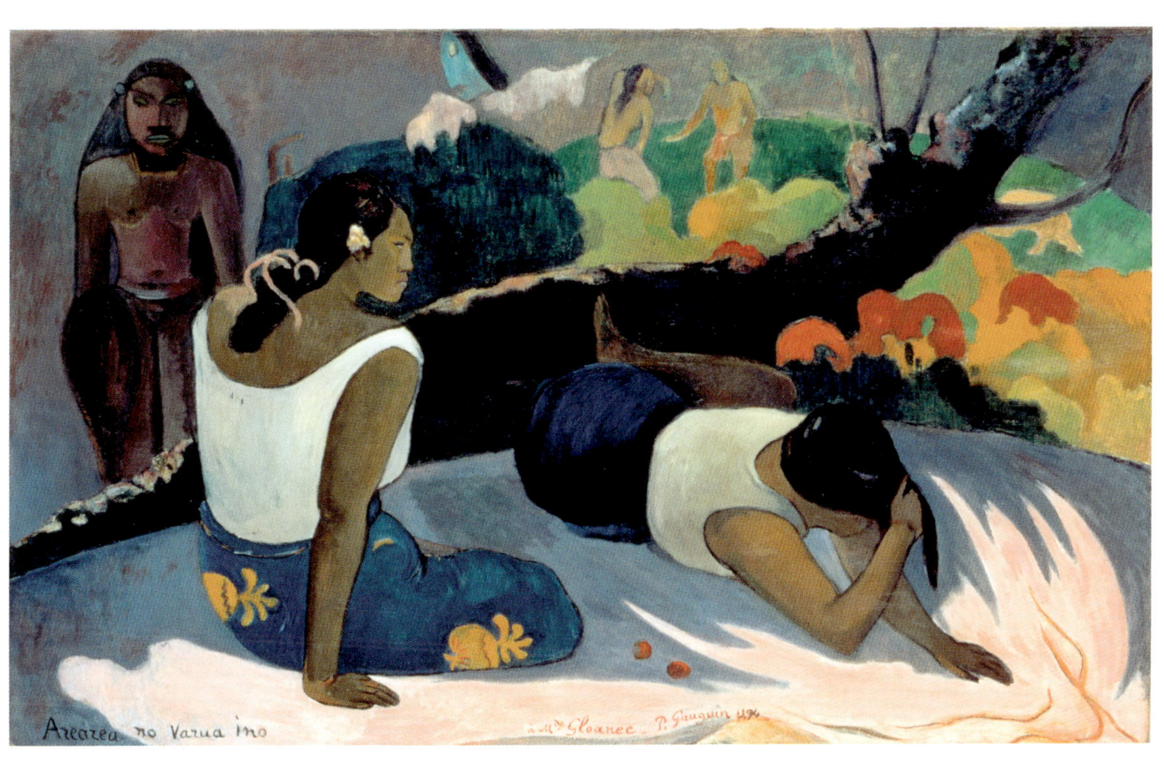

35 Paul Gauguin, *Reclining Tahitian Women*, 1894

Japanese art at Museum Folkwang

Museum Folkwang features a substantial inventory of Japanese artefacts of very diverse genres, all of them acquired at an early date when Museum Folkwang was still located in Hagen.

Contained in the collection are a number of paintings in the form of hanging scrolls dating from the nineteenth century. The India ink painting *Herons on a Meadow in the Snow* (p. 231) is signed by Kano Yōsen-in Korenobu (1753–1808), a well-known professional Edo painter of the Kanō school working for the shogunate. The use of the Buddhist honorary title *hōin* in the signature is an indication that the work was executed after 1794. In addition, the collection held by Museum Folkwang includes (Buddhist) sculptures (p. 232), masks and a Noh theatre robe as well as lacquerware and numerous tea bowls. Other categories of objects comprise bamboo baskets (p. 116) and some textile dyeing stencils (*katagami*; pp. 236, 237). They were exported in large quantities to Europe in the nineteenth century. Their graphically expressive and, at the same time, stylised ornaments and designs particularly catered to late-nineteenth-century European artists who were in search of new modes of artistic expression (pp. 282, 283). The focus of Museum Folkwang's Japanese Collection is on artefacts of an altogether high quality – this is especially true for the tea cere-mony equipment and the vast collection of wooden masks for the Japanese Noh dance theatre and the Kyōgen intermission play. Finally, there are high-quality small objects such as inros (portable medicine containers), netsukes (belt toggles) and tsubas (sword hand guards).

Noh robe and masks

All the twenty-nine masks for the Noh theatre and the comic intermission of the Kyōgen are carved in wood and coloured on a base consisting of a mixture of lime and glue. Ideally, the expression of the elaborately carved mask and the actor's personality are to merge into one, as the masks do not completely cover the actors' faces. Stamps on the back of the masks provide information about the professional mask-carving schools that emerged in the sixteenth century. The demon mask of the Fudō Myōō-Beshimi type (p. 114), stemming from the Muromachi period (1392–1573), combines the mask style of the folkloric demon Beshimi with the mask of the wrathful king of wisdom Fudō Myōō ("the immovable wisdom king"), a deity against evil spirits especially venerated in Japanese esoteric Buddhism. The back of the mask carries a large seal that refers to Ji'unin, a carver monk who lived in the fifteenth century and who, in the tradition of the Japanese mask carvers, belongs to the *chūsaku*, the masters of the middle period. The physiognomic features of the Sujiotoko mask type ("man with veins"; p. 114) are carved in a very fine and clean manner, lending the mask a magnificently intense expression. Two small inlaid metal rings suggest the eyes. The carver's stamp on the back of the mask assigns it to Deme Mitsuteru of the sixteenth century, the first master among the Deme school of mask carvers. Masks of the *ko-omote* type ("small face"; p. 234) were made to present graceful young female figures in the Noh dance theatre. It is the standard female mask in the Noh. The face, more rounded than oval, reflects the female ideal of the Heian period (794–1185). The existing mask is the work of Kodama Ōmi Mitsunaga (died in 1704) and testifies immense carving and pictorial qualities. The Noh robe (p. 235) is a so-called *karaori*, an opulent brocade robe with shuttle-woven patterns in coloured silk and gilt paper bands in the shape of a kimono. A distinctive feature of the Noh robes is the lengthened front hem. The robes for the Noh theatre often combine contradictory aspects of audaciousness, elegance, refinement and aesthetics. The robes themselves were made of exquisite fabrics with an impressive brightness and clarity of colours due to the natural dyes used. The dyed threads were woven into opulent patterns and designs. The patterns of the female robes primarily represent plants, blossoms and flowers of the four seasons, whereas male robes are graced with powerful, often exotic patterns. The design of the robe on hand bears a variation of dance fans on a golden background, and it is particularly suited for the role of young women such as the *ko-omote.*

Lacquerware

Lacquerware is a typical Japanese handicraft and is as highly regarded in East Asia as it is in the West. Due to the intrinsic characteristics of Japanese lacquer (*urushi*), a great number of finishing and decorative techniques were developed in Japan as early as antiquity. The quality of the lacquer that can be used in its liquid state, but likewise hardened, is perfectly suited to transpose literary and pictorial subjects. The material offers an ideal surface for manifold, historically significant aesthetic ideas. By far the most important lacquer technique is the so-called "sprinkled picture" (*makie)*, a distinguished artistic style that already developed as early as the Heian period (794–1185). In principle, the *makie* technique entails the sprinkling of gold and silver powder onto a design sketched into the lacquer; the powder can be applied both on a flat or raised surface. In addition, graded colourings and sprinklings of the powder, varying in density, enable a large range of expressive possibilities. Objects from the Tokugawa period (1603–1868, also known as the Edo period) form the core collection of Japanese lacquerware at Museum Folkwang, and they are characterised by a multitude of lacquer trends. The Tokugawa period had a penchant for precious gold sprinklings and detailed designs that followed existing practices known from the courtly lacquer art of the Japanese Middle Ages. The style of lacquerware of the Tokugawa period also produced daring technical, formal and decorative innovations, including the combination of divergent materials such as mother-of-pearl, stone, coral or lead with gold sprinklings.

Among the oldest Japanese lacquer objects in the museum collection is a flat square box (p. 242) dating from the early seventeenth century, documented and identified in terms of its formal elements as an incense container (*kōgō*). From the Kamakura period (1185–1333) onwards, a great number of small boxes and containers with gold lacquer turned up in the lacquerware of Japan, and these objects were more often than not parts of a bigger set of cosmetic boxes *(tebako)*. Traditionally, the square boxes were used for powder, the rectangular ones for the black tooth-colouring paste, and the round ones for scents and perfumes. However, with the widespread acceptance of the tea ceremony in society, this rather theoretical classification lost importance by the end of the fifteenth century at the very latest. The tea lovers' passion for collecting old artefacts led to a change in the use of small divided boxes and containers including lacquerware; now the objects were more frequently used as *kōgō* in the tea ceremony. The lid and bottom edges of the square box shown are slightly rounded; the edges are set in lead. The flat lid features a so-called dust border (*chirii*) sprinkled with gold dust. The surface, a black lacquer base of plain gold sprinkling, displays the motif of a grazing doe in a landscape only vaguely suggested by a few waves. The animal, portrayed in a naturalistic and lively manner, with careful detail to its hide and the eye accentuated with red lacquer, is a typical example of the early Tokuwaga period, which preferred a simple yet stylised expression. A close-up view reveals the enormous emphasis given to the animal body depicted in front of an empty background. And the original literary motif of the bellowing stag in a forlorn autumnal scenery ever so much favoured since the fifteenth century is shown, together with the pattern of two flowering sweet-clover twigs in gold sprinkling on the inside of box and on the underside of the lid, executed on a lacquer base of loosely sprinkled gold flakes in different golden hues (*nashiji*). Here, the initial melancholic connotation of the pattern is almost absent, but it made the *kōgō* an ideal object for the tea ceremony. Apparently, the top of the box's lid is part of another lacquer object, since the motif touches the lower right edge of the picture as if it were cut.

Alongside other small boxes and larger containers, Museum Folkwang has a respectable stock of calligraphy boxes (*suzuribako*). Of particular interest are two writing boxes, both bearing the seal of the famous lacquer artist Ritsuō (Ogawa Haritsu, 1663–1747). The flat, oval writing box with a hooded lid (*inrōbuta*; p. 243) consists of braided bamboo covered in dark lacquer. The motif of the *enkō sokugetsu* ("monkey reaches for the moon") adorns the top of the lid, referring to a parable about the illusions of the phenomenological world in Zen Buddhism. The underside of the lid shows the illustration of a naturalistic crab sitting at the edge of a slope overgrown with reed grass. The typical Ritsuō seal of a white clay plate with the character "Kan" is visible in the lower left of the picture. Ritsuō tended to craft an inlay of contrasting materials on a black base that was typical of him. The inlaid version of carved lacquer, ceramic, coloured glass, ivory and lead is named after Ritsuō and called *Haritsu zaiku* ("handicraft after Haritsu"). The writing box at hand shows a combination of diverse materials – such as the ceramic crab covered in an iridescent green-white glaze. The eyes of the animal are of mother-of-pearl, and its claws are made of lead. The texture of the slope is an imitation of slate; mother-of-pearl stones are set on it. Like calligraphy boxes and inros, Ritsuō lacquerware is clearly inspired by Chinese handicrafts of the late Ming period (1368–1644) and Qing period (1644–1911), and it reflects the contemporary Chinese influence on Japan. At times bizarre, the colour spectrum of Ritsuō lacquers sets itself distinctly apart from the customary elegant gold lacquers of the Tokugawa period, something that made Ritsuō artefacts (including ceramics) even more popular. Although the seal of the box at hand carries a minor spelling error, the writing box as such is of extremely good quality. The seal is found in an identical spelling on other objects in the Ritsuō style, thus it can be assumed that it is a studio work directly following the Ritsuō tradition. Hence, the lacquer artist Mochizuki Hanzan (exact dates unknown, presumably 1743–1790) repeatedly used Ritsuō's (incorrect) seal. During the nineteenth century and pursuant to the world fairs in the West, the demand for Ritsuō lacquerware was enormous – above all, since his name was mentioned as the only representative of Japanese handicrafts in the influential article "Ritsuo et son école" penned by Ernest Hart in volume 12 of the magazine *Le Japon artistique* of 1889. At that time, the artist's typical ceramic seal sufficed in the West as proof for a genuine object by Ritsuō. On another virtually square writing box with a fitted lid (p. 245), the image of the renowned poet Saigyō Hōshi (1118–1190) contemplating Mount Fuji, and framed by a pine grove, is depicted on the lid top with a black lacquer base. Again, various inlay materials grace the box (glazed ceramic, ivory, mother-of-pearl, lead) – in this case, combined with different sprinkled lacquer techniques (*hiramakie, hirame, togidashi*) in gold and silver. This mix of materials indicates that the box originates from the nineteenth century, a time when objects in the typical Ritsuō aesthetic with complicated, partly precious sprinkled lacquer techniques became popular. This is apparent in the elaborate gold and silver sprinklings on the underside of the lid depicting a clouded mountain landscape with pines. The red "kan" seal on a white ceramic plate is found in the lower right half of the picture. The object is undoubtedly an excellent studio work in the tradition of Ritsuō. A writing box with a slightly curved fitted lid (p. 244) is found amongst other lacquerware in the museum collection; the top of the lid shows the martial tools of a samurai and, on the underside, an ornate rocky island scenery under a full moon and waves around it, as well as a low desk (*bundai*) with a design of feathers (p. 38), the latter once belonging to Siegfried Bing in Paris. The desk, in particular, suggests that the brightly coloured and delicately executed *togidashi makie* ("polished sprinkled picture") used for the illustration of feathers, in combination with finest mother-of-pearl dust on a brilliant black lacquer base, was developed for export in the late nineteenth century.

Inros

Inros (boxes for seals) constitute a very popular genre of Japanese artefacts which, from the sixteenth century onwards, contained seals, seal lacquer and, from the seventeenth century, medicines as well. Men who wore kimonos without pockets carried inros suspended from the waist by a cord and attached to the sash by a toggle or netsuke (literally: "root-fix") and held in place by a small stopper (*ojime*). The preferred material for the majority of these containers, often decorated with luxurious lacquer designs, was Japanese cypress. However, inros were also made of materials such as ceramic, metal or horn. Their popularity culminated in the nineteenth century. At that time, scores of lacquer masters and workshops had specialised their production in this field – also for the European export market – and signed their objects. The self-assured passing on of workshop traditions can be traced over several generations of artists by the identical signatures continually used. The decorative designs on the inros are infinitely vast, depicting – alongside landscapes, animals and plants – Taoist, Buddhist, traditional and literary themes as well. During the late Tokugawa period, the urban population often preferred grotesque, humorous everyday scenes as subjects for inros. Frequently, pictorial elements were transferred from contemporary paintings and woodblock prints. The group of high-quality inros found in the museum collection beautifully reflects the great variety of techniques and styles for medicine containers dating from the eighteenth and nineteenth centuries.

Distinguished lacquer masters of that period were members of the Kajikawa family based in Edo (Tokyo). The five-part inro (p. 239) with an offset cord guide is clearly fashioned in the tradition of this school, with its two-sided depiction of a lush peony in full flower – its design painstakingly worked in radiant gold and silver tones on a pear base (*nashiji*). Its origin surely dates back to the eighteenth century. The rounded four-part inro with a curved base and lid and a covered cord guide (p. 239) is adorned with the motif of two hares on both sides, each on a brightly polished black lacquered base. While the front side, with its gold and silver sprinkling, depicts the hares sitting amongst grasses, the rear side shows them from behind in an opaque white inlay of mother-of-pearl with a sprinkled pattern simulating copper (*shakudō takamakie*). The base carries the signature "Kajikawa" in gold lacquer with the red Kajikawa lacquer seal in the *tsubō* form. It is difficult to assign this object to one particular artist of the family; stylistically and technically, it belongs to the nineteenth century.

Bearing the design on both sides of a sailboat in the waves (p. 238), the six-part inro has an offset cord guide as well as a curved base and lid. The technically elaborate decor consists of silver and gold sprinkling, tin inlays and a little bit of red lacquer on a bright black lacquered base. The diagonal composition is based on motifs and styles of the Rimpa school tradition. The inro has no signature, but it can be regarded as a follow-up of (Yamada) Jōka(sai) (1681–1704). Again, the artist had several successors with an identical signature. Size and dimensions suggest that it dates from the nineteenth century; noticeable is the absence of mother-of-pearl inlays typical for this design. The small five-part inro with a base of finest gold dust (*ikakeji*), adorned with a design of irises in inlay of mother-of-pearl, lead and gold (p. 238), refers to pictorial traditions of a classical literary theme, *The Tales of Ise* (*Ise monogatari*), compiled in the ninth century. In them, the irises represent images of longing for a faraway home. In the early eighteenth century, the painter and designer Ogata Kōrin (1658–1716) created a pair of screens exclusively decorated with irises from the *Ise*. These paintings became iconic patterns for numerous adaptations of the theme, such as in lacquerware. The little inro shown is also part of this development and dates from the early nineteenth century.

Netsukes

The small group of netsukes at Museum Folkwang is of a consistently excellent quality. With the exception of a few figurative eighteenth-century netsukes in ivory, the collection also contains motifs of animals and plants in boxwood and ivory (pp. 240, 241) and figurative designs that superbly represent the naturalistic style of the Tokugawa period in the nineteenth century. Although the function of the netsukes was an inseparable part of the inros, the former became a highly coveted collector's item in Europe from the nineteenth century onwards. The Japanese passion for netsukes today can be seen as a reaction to their European acceptance. The netsuke with the design of a little devil (*ōni*) impersonating Raiden, the god of thunder who beats a head-high drum with his drum-stick (p. 241), is an excellent example of the combination of different materials found in nineteenth-century netsukes. Boxwood, ivory, horn, mother-of-pearl and silver (?) – today, unfortunately rubbed off or oxidised – were used to create impressive miniature scenes full of life and humour. The cord eyes are of ivory. The signature "Chikusai" is scratched on an ivory cartouche at the bottom of the object. Several net-suke carvers of this name have been passed on; a certain Chikusai of the early nineteenth century is known for his use of boxwood together with ivory and mother-of-pearl.

Tea bowls

Tea bowls used in the tea ceremony (*sadō*) with powdered tea (*matcha*) represent another group of Japanese artefacts at Museum Folkwang. They constitute the most important element in the equipment used for a tea ceremony. Following the Song Chinese ritual, the tea ceremony primarily found its followers in Zen monasteries in Japan. Here, guests were served frothed-up tea in black glazed bowls with conically shaped sides and a high footing called *temmoku* bowls, the term being a derivation of the type of Chinese Jian ceramic ware that took its name after Mount Tianmu in the province of Fujian. The so-called yellow *temmoku* ceramic (*kitenmoku*; p. 246) is a good example for the Japanese variations that developed over time. Bowls like this one were displayed on lacquered bowl stands (p. 246) in a tea ceremony. These stands are very similar in form and design to Chinese models of the Song period (960–1279) executed in a monochrome lacquer. The petal-shaped bowl stand shown is lacquered in the so-called Negoro manner – whereby the upper vermillion lacquer layer has worn off through use, revealing the layer of black lacquer underneath. These traces of age are considered visual aesthetic proof of a profound beauty that lies hidden behind things – the ideal embodiment of the essence of the Way of Tea. Along with an increasing popularity of the tea ceremony in the sixteenth century came the demand for locally produced glazed ceramic ware. Large ceramic centres like Seto and Mino, but Kyoto likewise, met the requirements. The tea bowl with straight walls and pronounced grooves (p. 248) is in the Mino style. Covered by a white dipped glaze, it is a fine example of the reintroduced Mino ceramic ware in the second half of the eighteenth century. Repairs carried out in gold lacquer are an expression of the high esteem that this object enjoyed in the past. The so-called Raku ware of Kyoto ranks among the most important types of Japanese tea ceremony ceramics produced by the Raku family from its beginnings in the sixteenth century with Chōjirō right up to the present day. A particularly beautiful piece is the stoneware tea bowl with straight wall (p. 268) covered with a low-fired reddish lead glaze. It carries the "Raku" stamp on its base. Along with red Raku ware (*akaraku*), there also exists black Raku ware (*kuroraku*). The small tea bowl with a shining glaze that picks up the formal Raku style comes from the Aka-hada kiln in Nara (p. 249), as shown by the stamp on the base. Akahada ceramic ware, which often displays underglaze paint-ings, and masterpieces of the Seven Kilns were highly valued by Kobori Enshū (1579–1647), one of the famous tea masters of the Tokugawa period. The powdered tea was kept in small stoneware tea containers (*chaire*) with lids of ivory. Here, too, different forms developed such as the oval tea container with two little decorative handles from Takatori (p. 264). The small round-bodied tea container from Seto shows the popular *kata-suki* type withstraight shoulder (p. 247).

Antje Papist-Matsuo

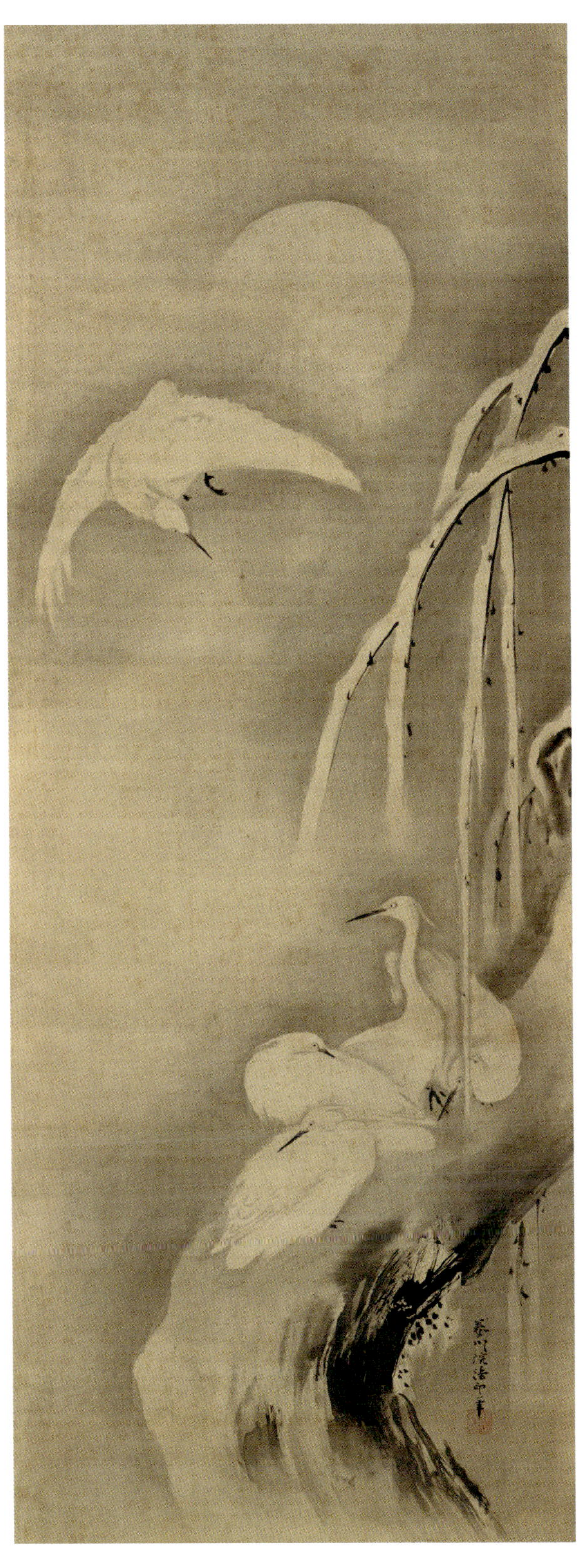

173 Kano Yōsen-in Korenobu, *Herons on a Meadow in the Snow*, after 1794

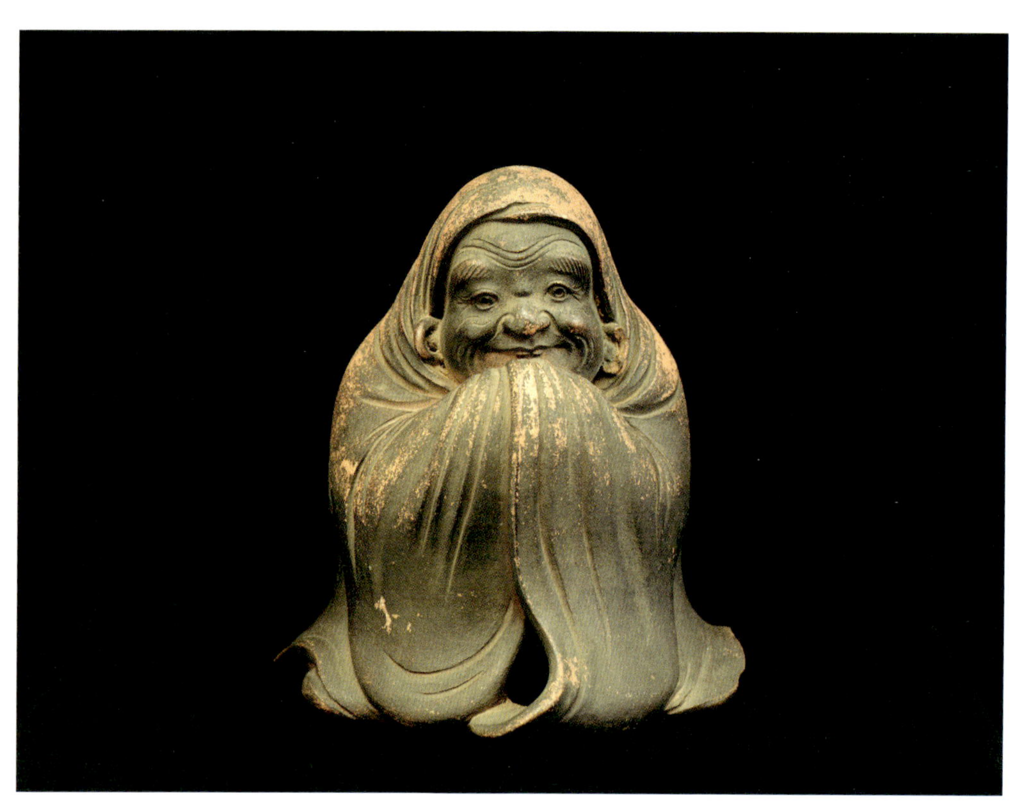

298 Japan, *Daruma (or Bodai Daruma?)*, 19th c.

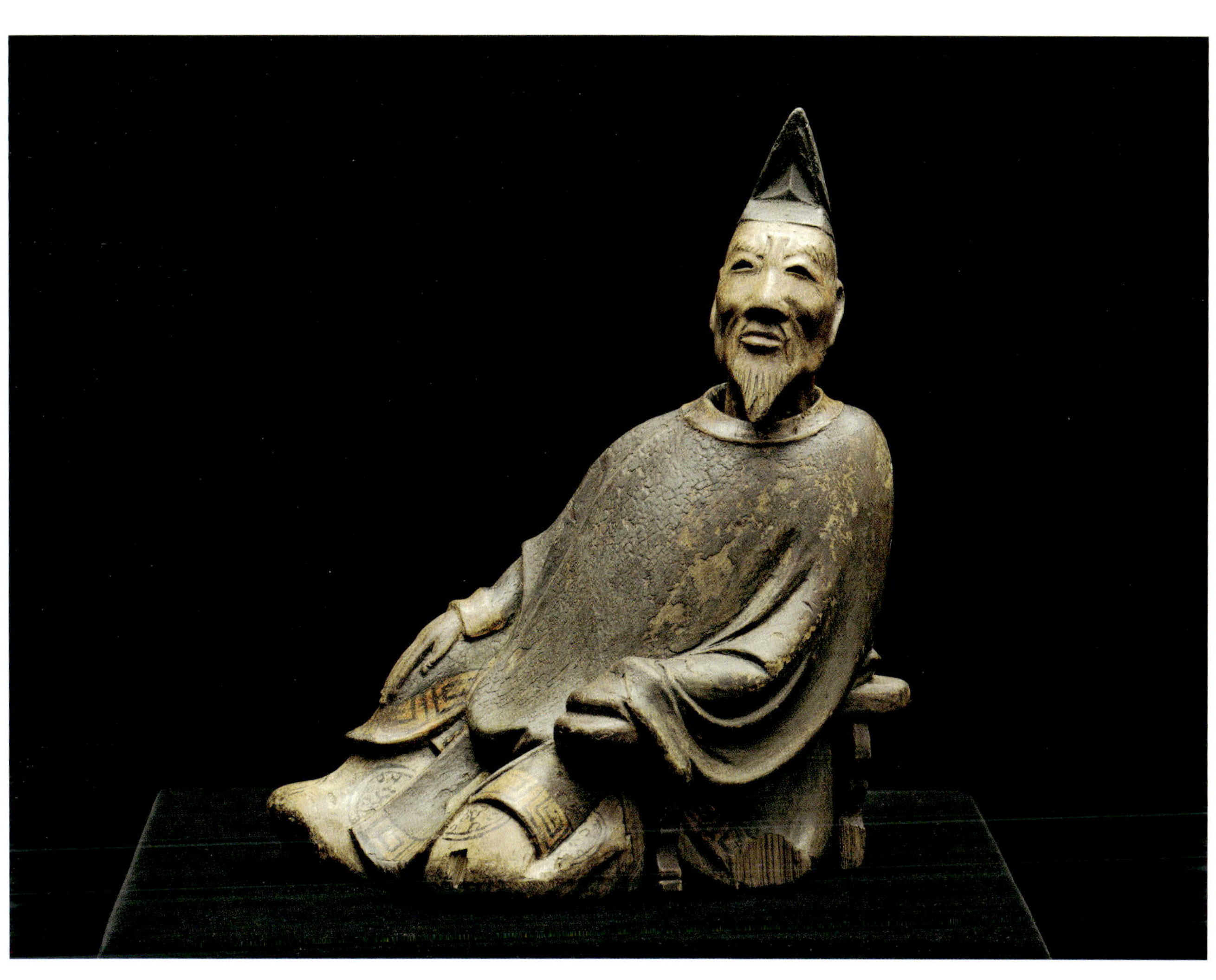

299 Japan, *Hitomaro*, probably 19th c.

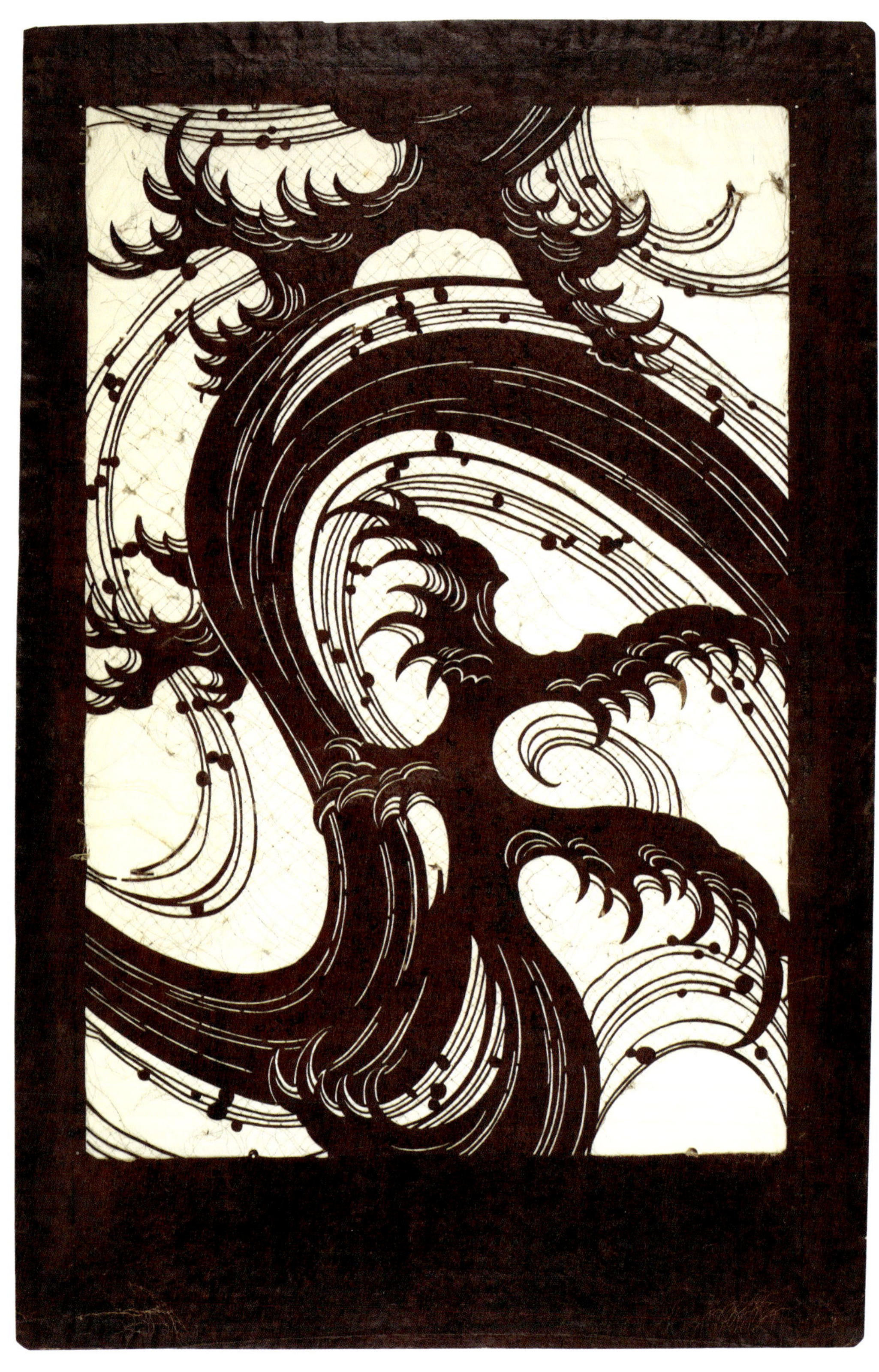

279 Japan, *Katagami*, 2nd half of 19th c.

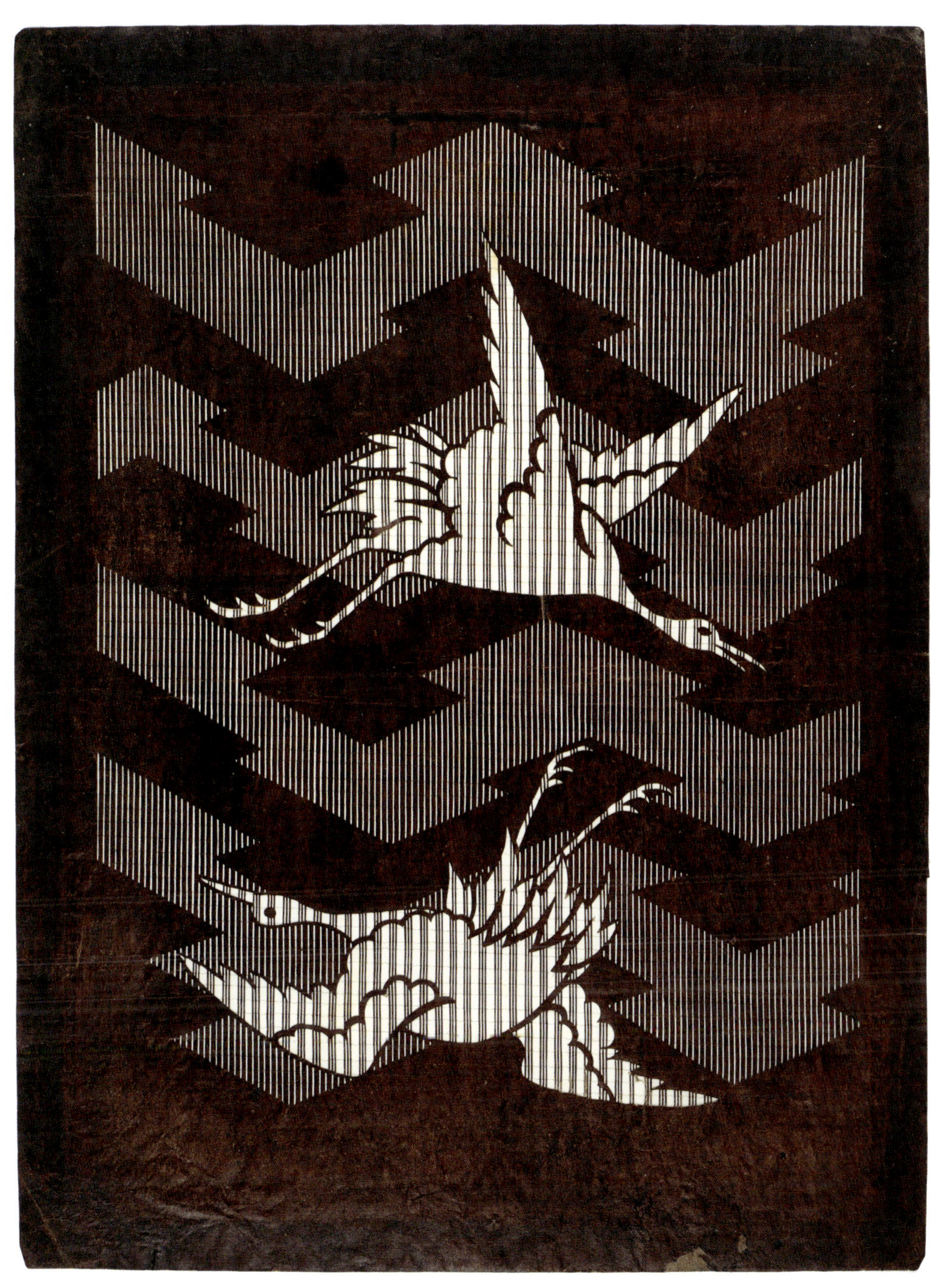

280 Japan, *Katagami*, 2nd half of 19th c.

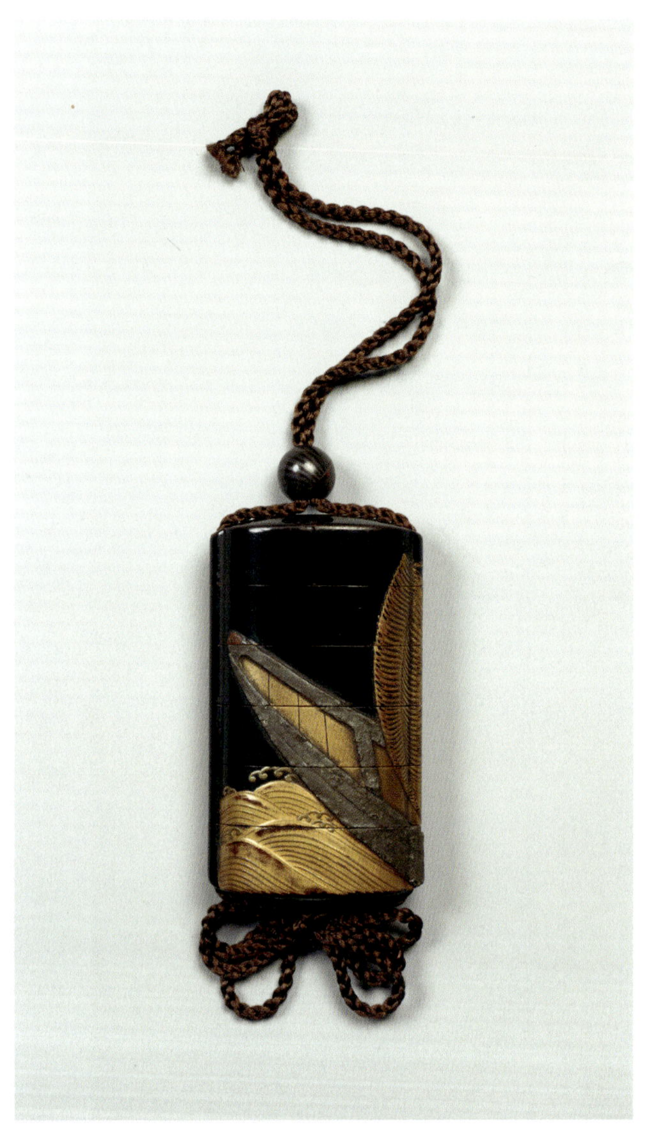

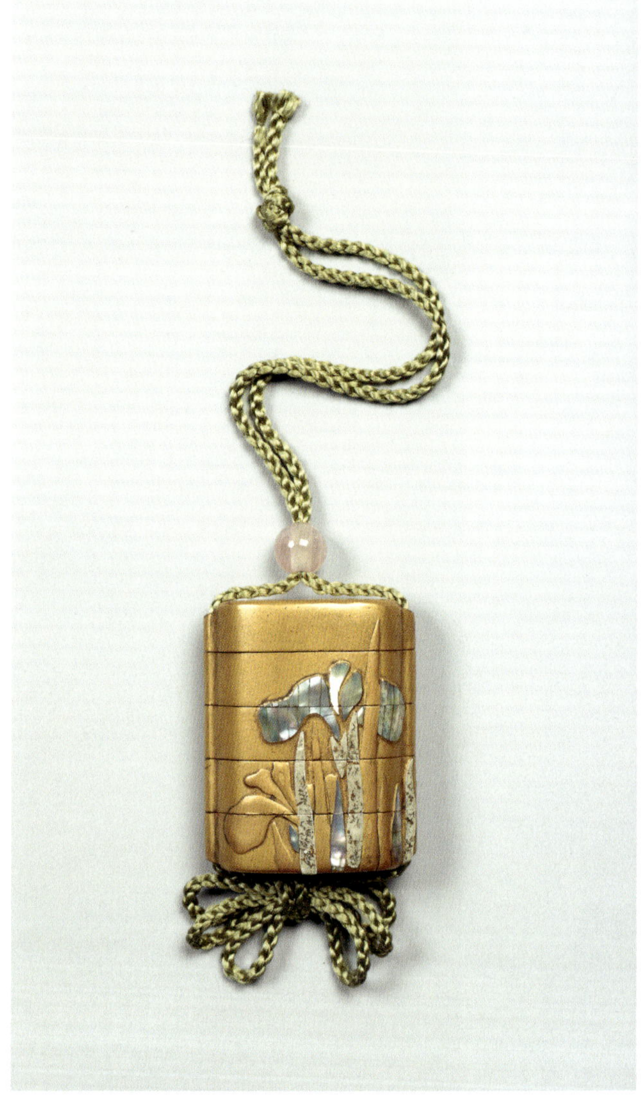

314 | 313 Japan, *Inros*, late Edo period, early 19th c.

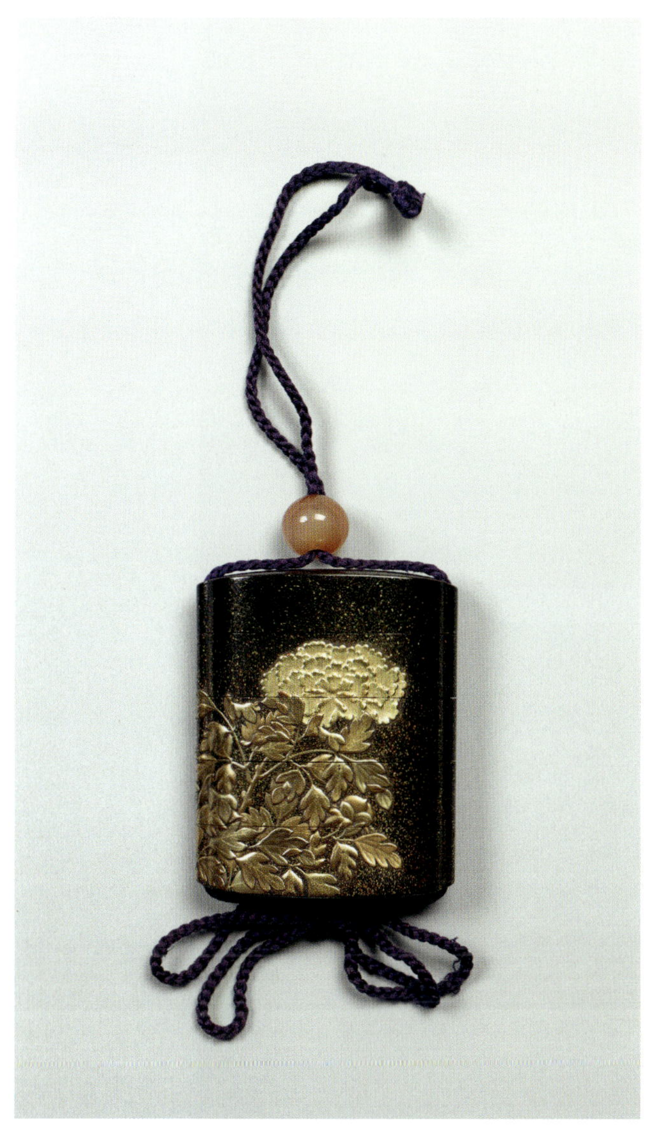

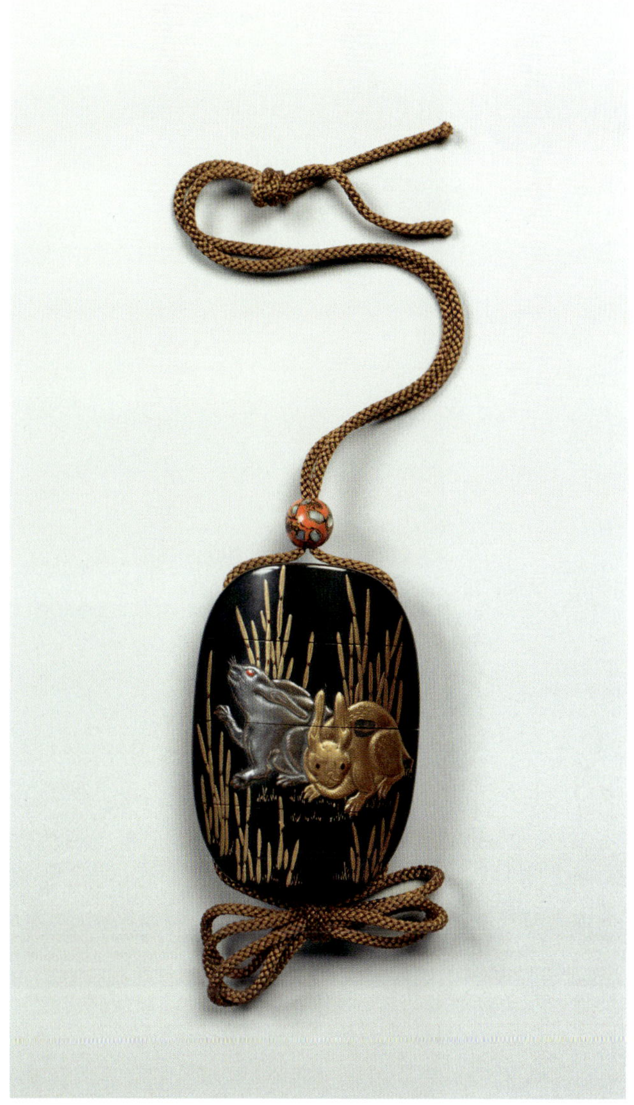

311 | 315 Japan, *Inros*, Edo period, late 18th c. and 19th c.

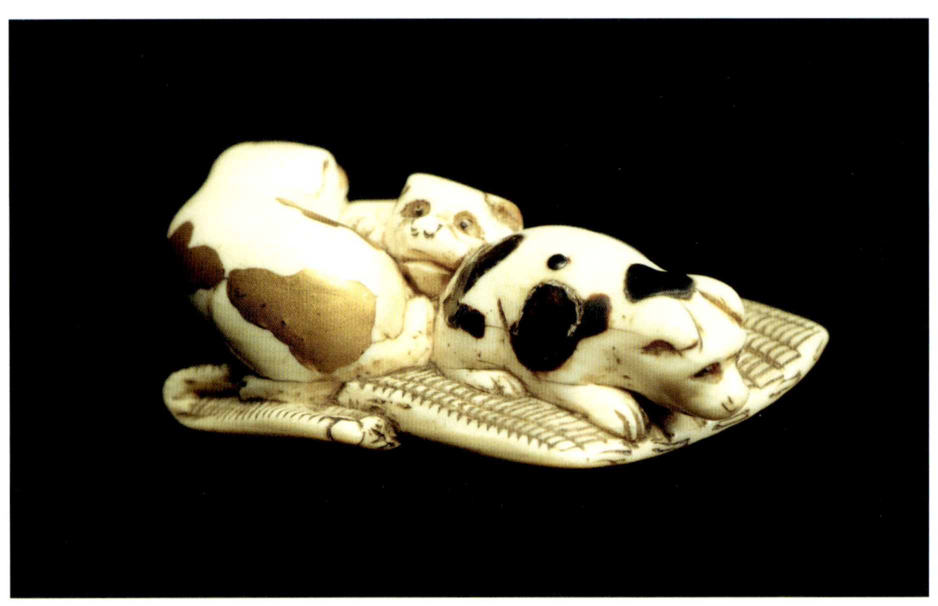

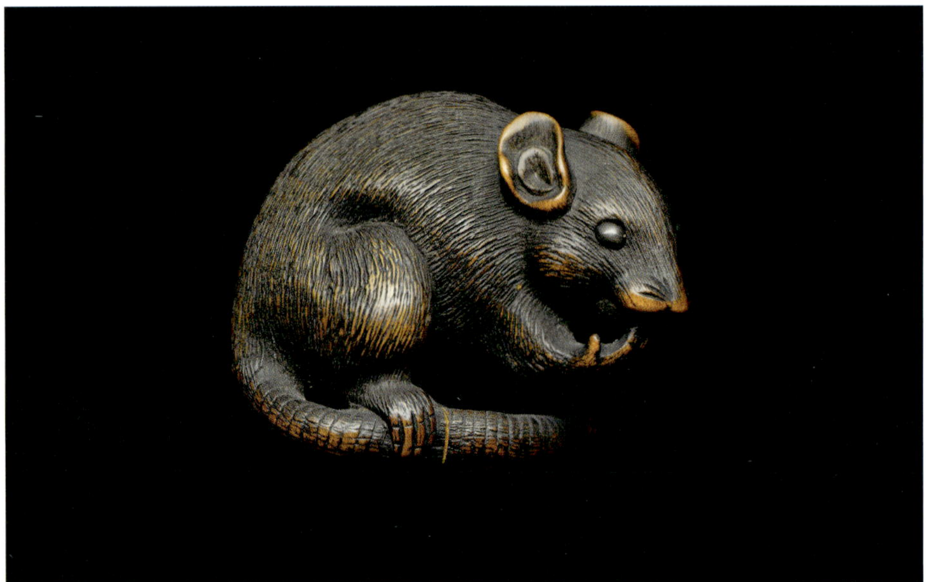

327 | 326 Japan, *Netsukes*, 19th c.

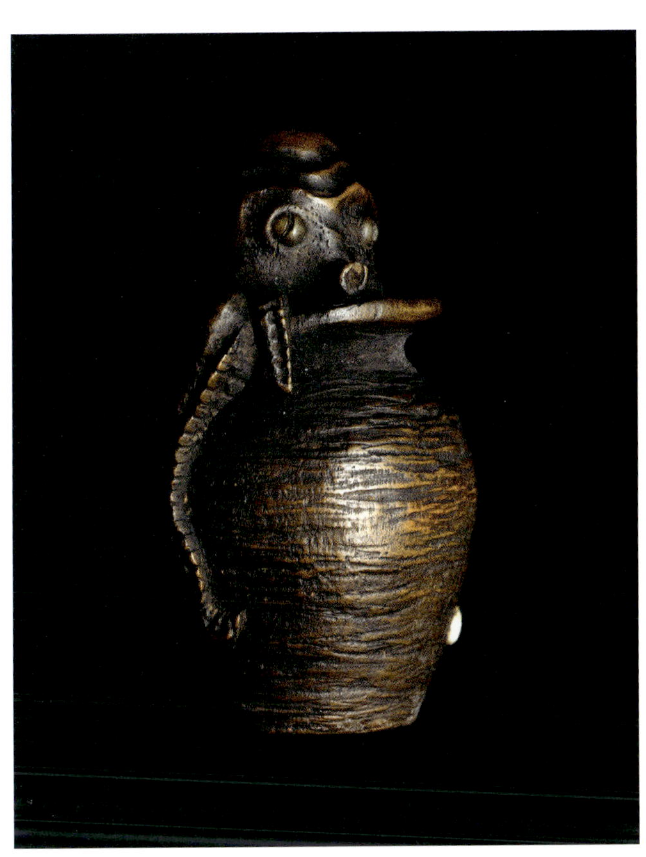

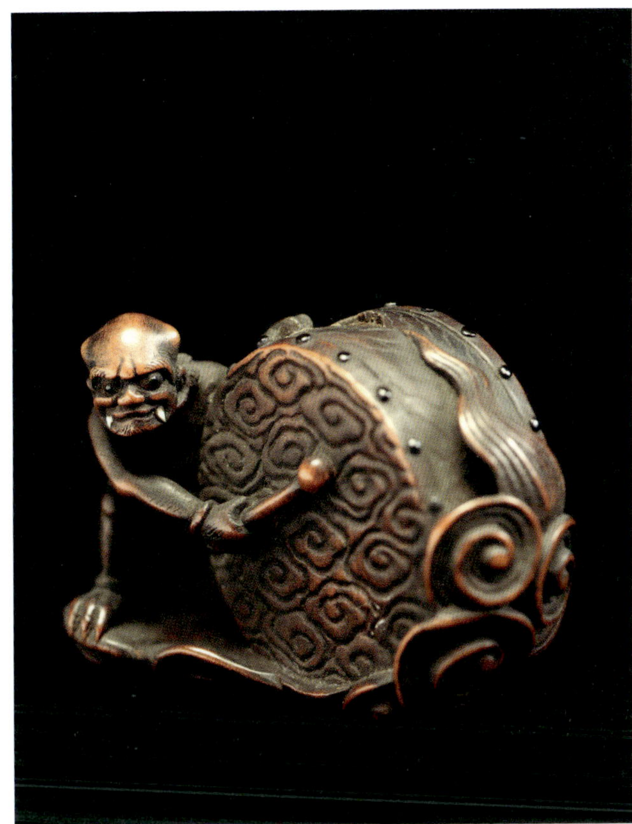

322 | 328 Japan, *Netsukes*, 19th c.

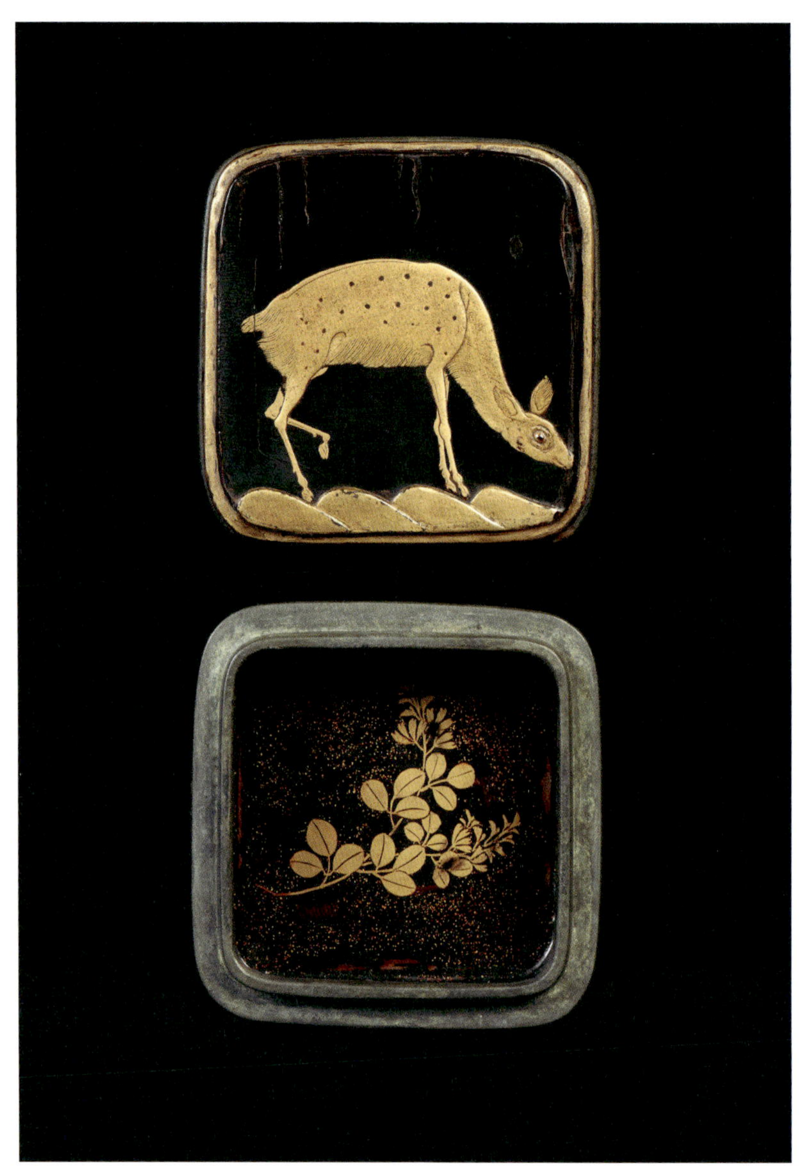

303 Japan, *Incense Box (kōgō)*, early Edo period, early 17th c.

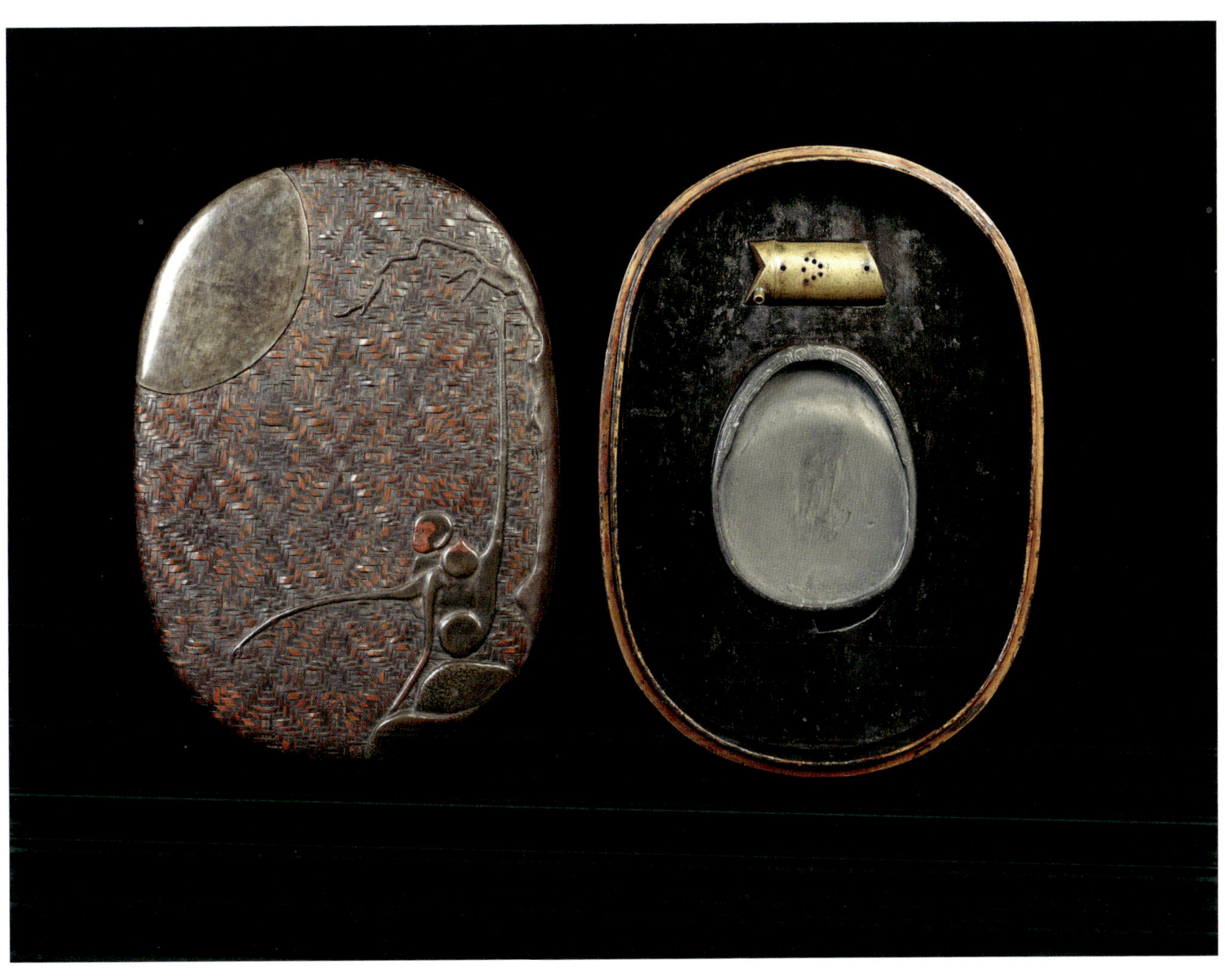

306 Japan, *Writing Box (suzuribako)*, late Edo period, late 18th/early 19th c.

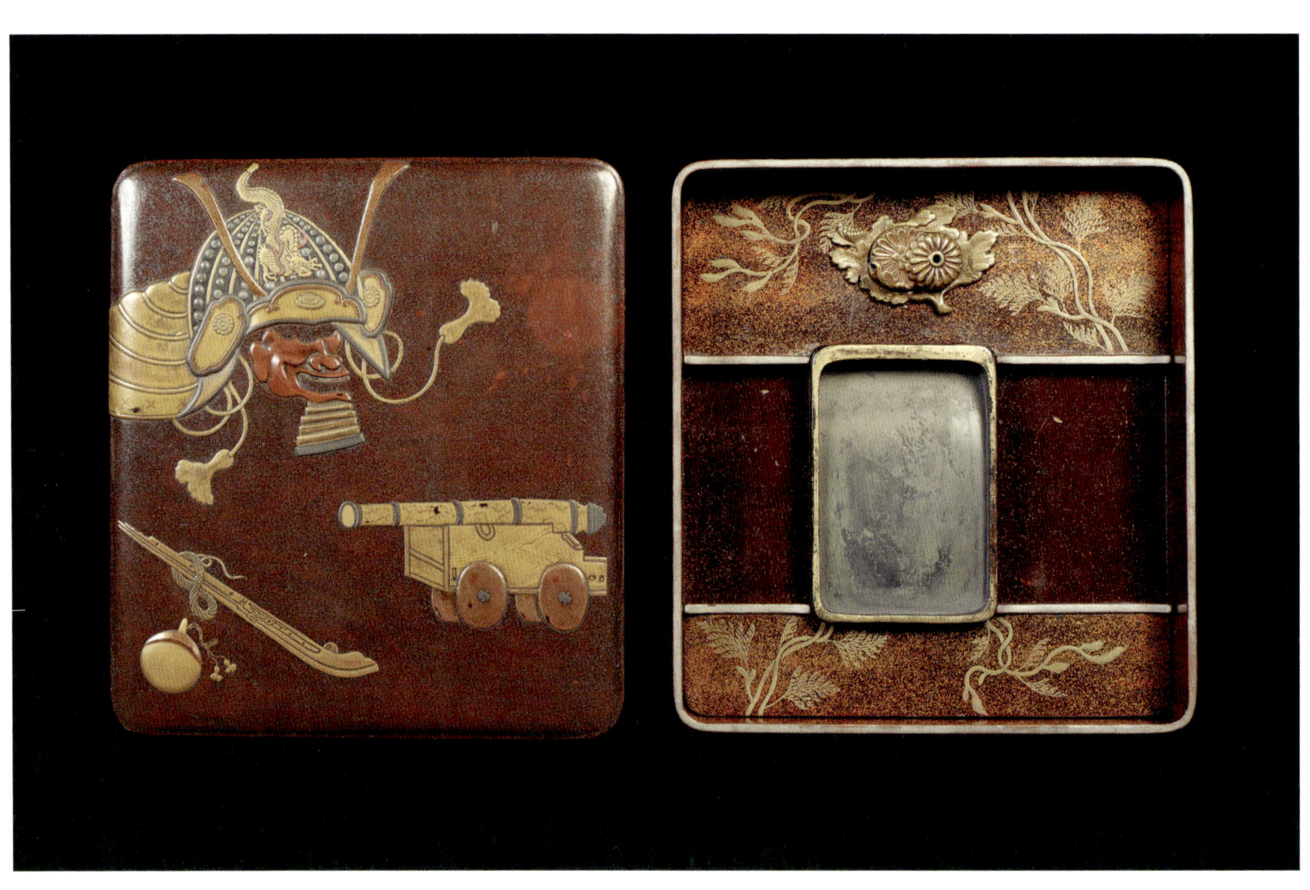

308 Japan, *Writing Box (suzuribako)*, Meiji period, late 19th c.

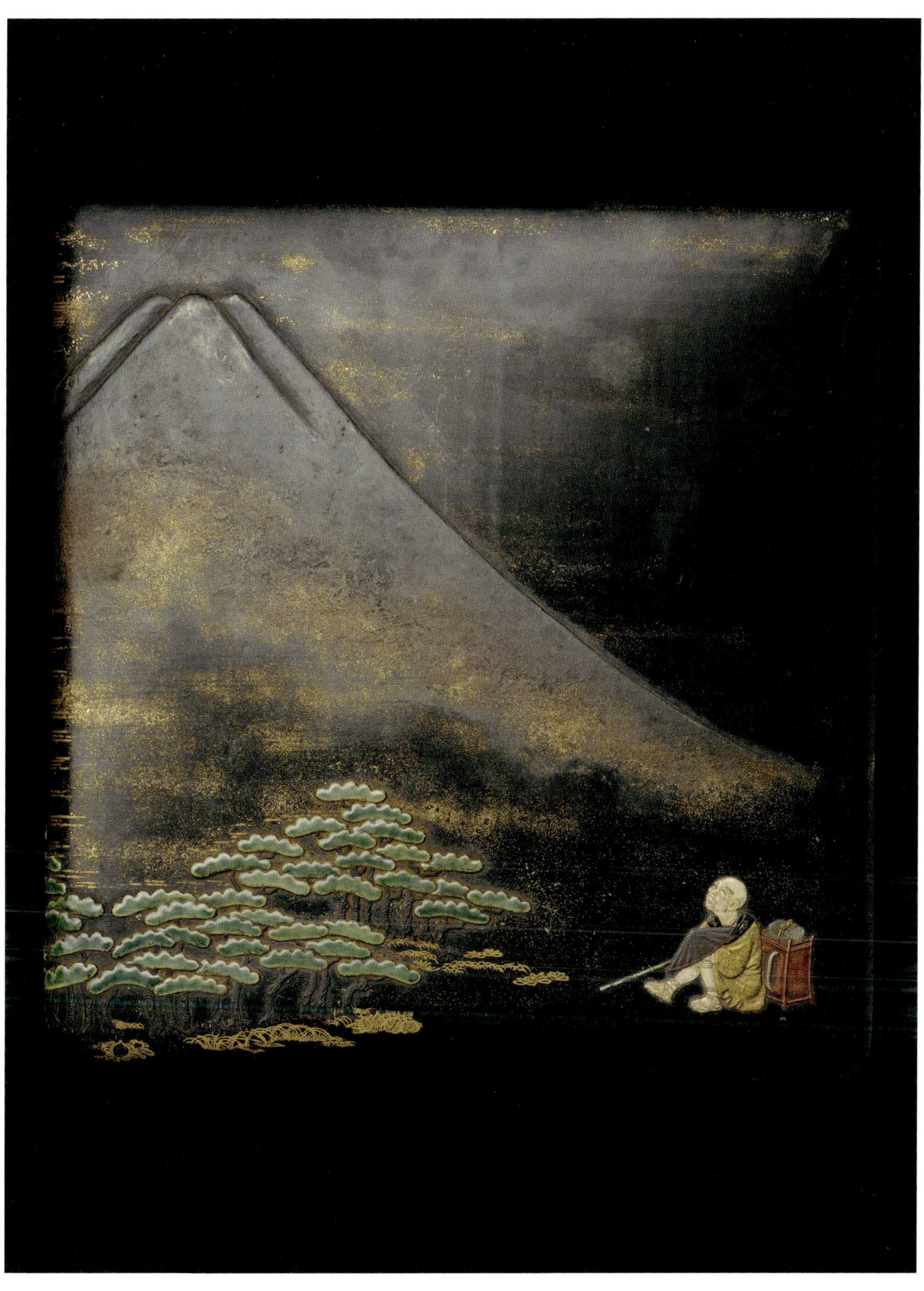

307 Japan, *Writing Box (suzuribako)*, 19th c.

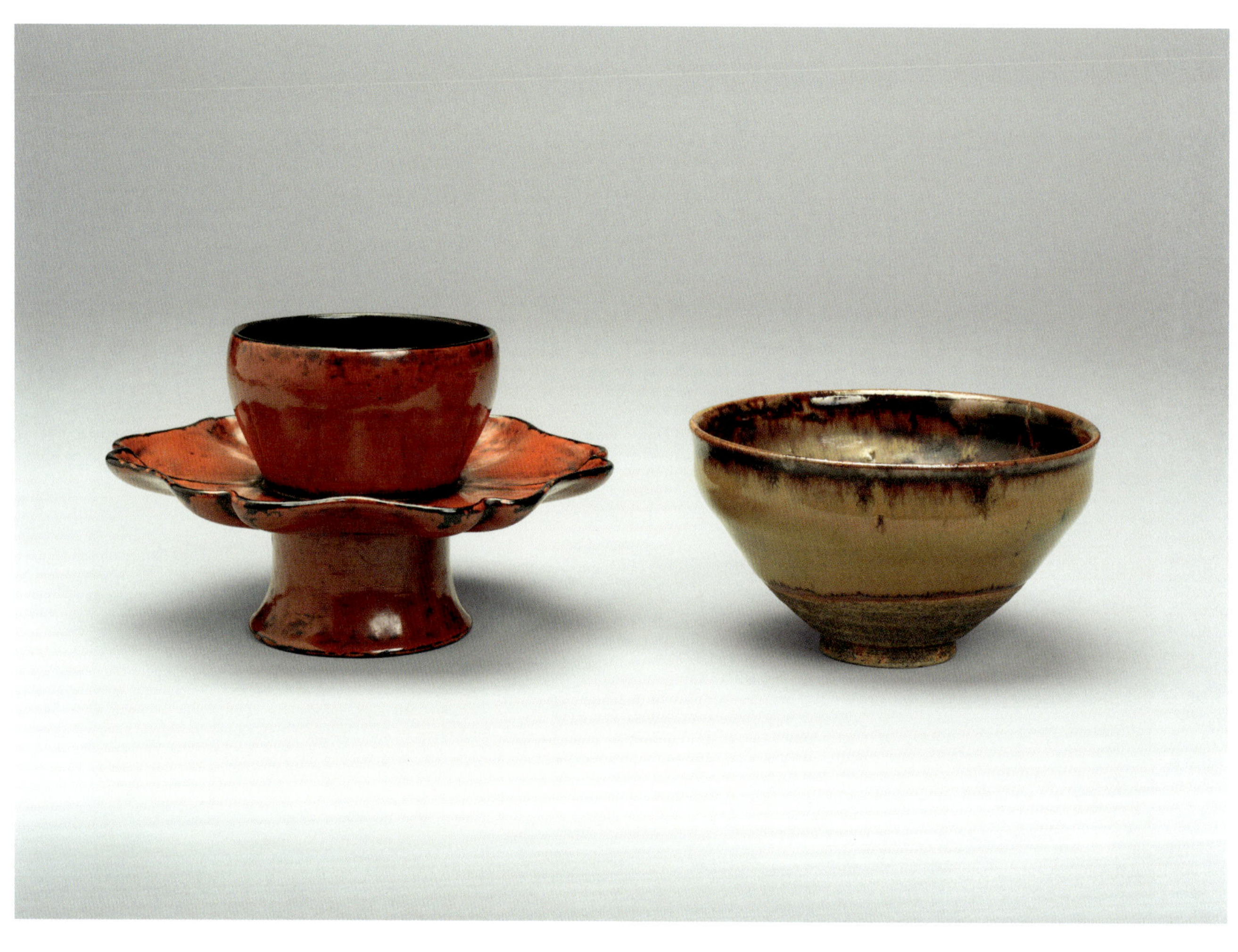

300 | 330 Japan, *Bowl Stand (temmoku-dai)*, Muromachi period, 15th/16th c. | *Tea Bowl (chawan) of the temmoku type*, Edo period, 17th c.

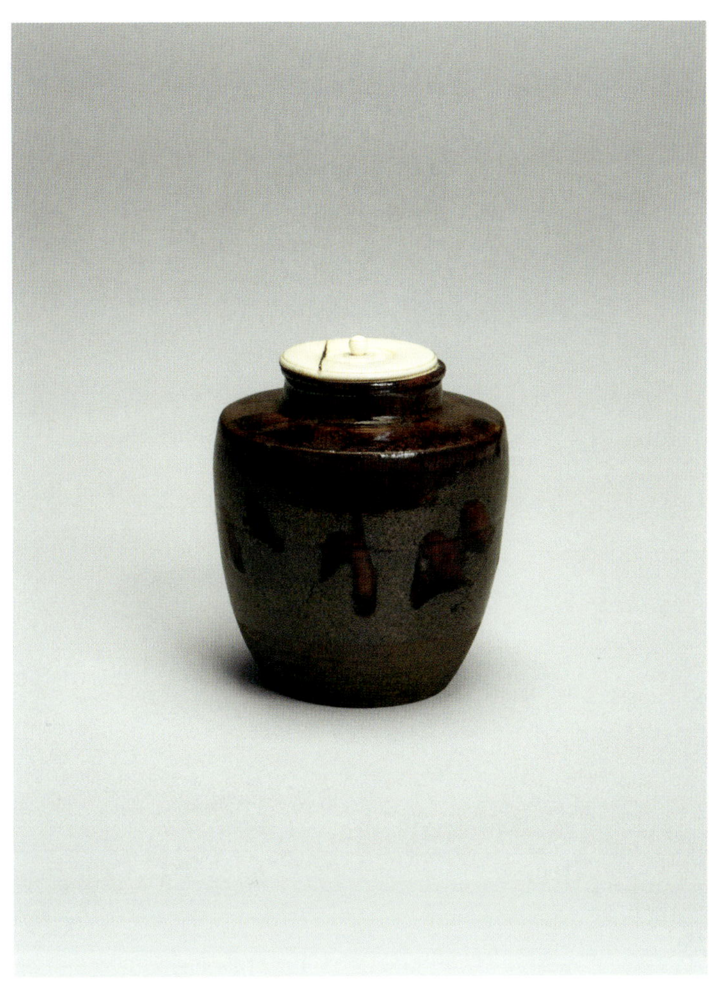

336 Japan, *Tea Jar (chaire) with Straight Shoulder*, Edo period, late 17th/18th c.

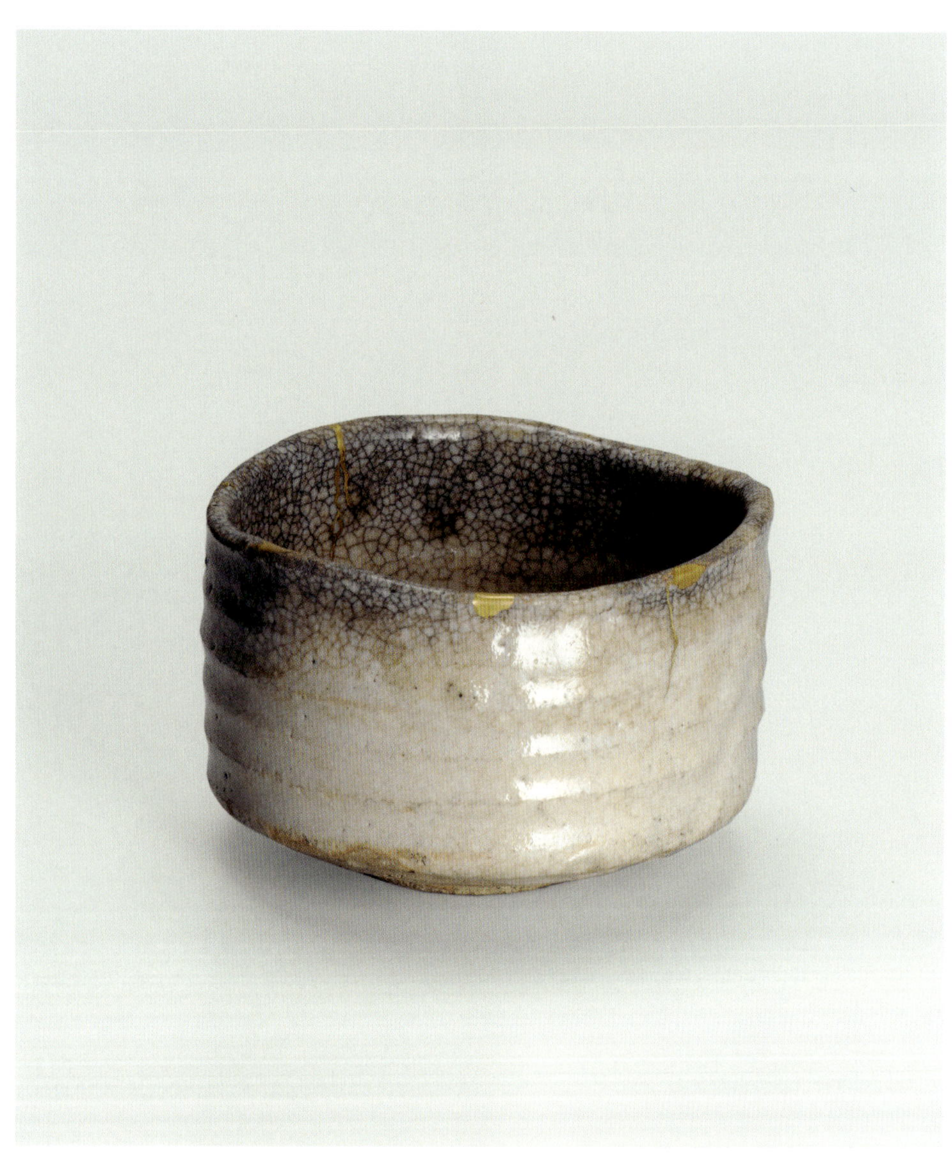

341 Japan, *Tea Bowl (chawan)*, Edo period, 18th c.

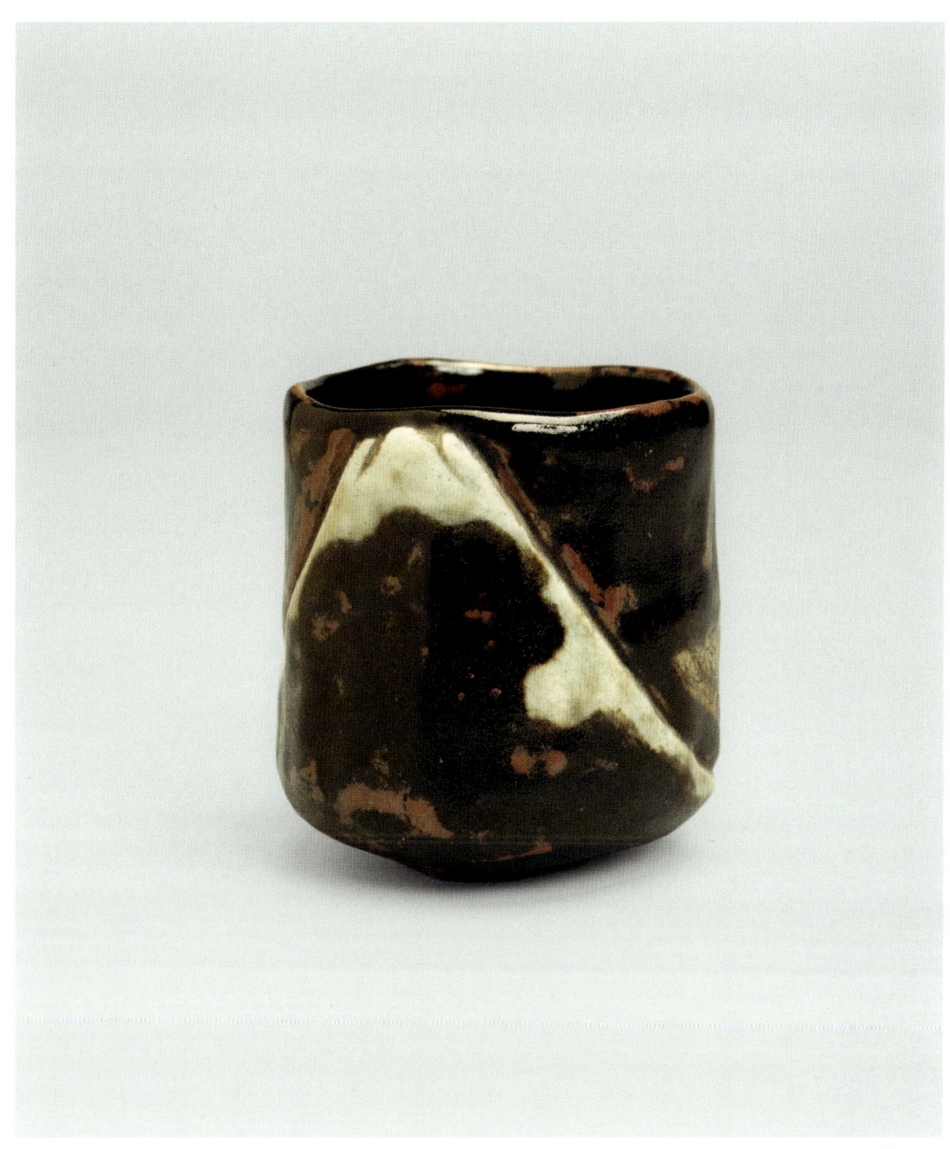

343 Japan, *Tea Bowl (chawan)*, 19th c.

Decorative arts in France

The enthusiasm for Japanese art dating from the mid-nineteenth century was reserved not only for woodblock prints, but also applied to sculptures, ceramics, lacquerware, tsubas, netsukes, textiles and the like. The beauty, novelty, radical nature and technical excellence of these objects held much fascination – characteristics that represented a true "treasure" in the eyes of artists of the Western world.

The *Service Rousseau* is one of the first pieces of evidence of *Japonisme* in the decorative arts. It is the result of a cooperation between the entrepreneur and designer (*marchand-éditeur*) François-Eugène Rousseau and the painter and engraver Félix Bracquemond, who designed the motifs for this service. Bracquemond was one of the first collectors of Japanese colour woodblock prints. Legend has it that he was the first to discover the *Manga* by Katsushika Hokusai in 1856. Bracquemond drew widely from the repertoire of Japanese woodblock prints and books for this earthenware table service with over two hundred pieces. He adopted motifs directly from Katsushika Hokusai and Utagawa Hiroshige, but also from lesser-known artists such as Katsushika Taito II, Katsushika Isai and Nakayama Sūgakudō. For example, the lobster and aubergine motifs that decorate one of the platters in the service (p. 252) were inspired by two woodblock prints from the *Large Series of Fish* by Hiroshige (p. 253). Alongside the iconographic aspect, the asymmetry, a certain liberty in arranging the motifs and the audacious use of empty space are fundamental elements that testify to a profound understanding of the basic principles of Japanese art. The *Service Rousseau* (p. 252) was shown for the first time on the occasion of the Paris World Fair of 1867 and met with great success there.

Yet Bracquemond was not the only one to draw from the repertoire of Japanese woodblock prints. The carp motif on the vase by Émile Gallé, which was shown at the Paris World Fair of 1878, was taken from the thirteenth volume of the *Manga* by Hokusai (p. 256). Rousseau also made use of a carp motif stemming from a woodblock print by Taito II (pp. 254, 255), which was used in 1889 by Siegfried Bing for the cover of the twentieth issue of his magazine *Le Japon artistique*. The carp is a frequent motif in Japanese art, a symbol of strength and courage. And while the fish leaping over a wave, which decorates the vase by Ernest Chaplet (p. 170), does not seem to have been taken directly from a Japanese woodblock print, the motif of the rolling wave still appears to have a certain similarity to Hokusai's famous colour woodblock print *The Great Wave off Kanagawa* (p. 167) as well as *Mount Fuji at Sea* from his album *One Hundred Views of Mount Fuji* (p. 170). When designing their vase, the painter Julien Genlis and the ceramic artist and painter Charles Rudhard drew on a motif from a triptych by Utagawa Kunisada II (p. 122).

Designed by Édouard Lièvre and then cast in bronze by Ferdinand Barbedienne, the *Jardiniere* (p. 78) is in itself a manifesto of *Japonisme*. It combines original Japanese elements with motifs in the Japanese style. The foot of the actual Japanese vase probably dates from the beginning of the nineteenth century. The upper piece, however, most likely goes back to the second half of the nineteenth century and corresponds more with the Japanese models that were intended for export. As far as the dragon is concerned, it is very similar to a censer that had been brought back from Japan in 1873 by the collector Henri Cernuschi. This ensemble is completed by the small round Japanese-looking table designed by Lièvre, with a base that resembles a bamboo stem, decorated with dragons and turtles.

The artists also liked to take inspiration from Japanese objects, which they would then imaginatively transfer to other materials. The ceramic artist Camille Moreau-Nélaton, for instance, imitated the shape of Japanese baskets made from woven bamboo (p. 116). By transferring it to ceramic, a vase was created from which an ornamental pumpkin tendril sprouted, a common motif in Japanese art. Émile Gallé for his part was inspired by tsubas, Japanese sword hand guards, which were very much appreciated in Europe because of the radical synthesis in their ornamentation. Three tsuba motifs decorate his vase (p. 261); upon exposure to light, their silhouettes appear as in a Chinese shadow play.

Japanese flora and fauna were also a source of fascination and fantasy for those in the West. The advent of imports of Japanese plants to Europe triggered a downright craze. Like Monet, Gallé was one of the principal devotees of these flowers. He had a great passion for botany and built up an important collection of Japanese plants. By the time of his death, the collection held more than four hundred different species. French artists were fascinated by this exotic flora, which was also reflected in Japanese woodblock prints, and soon absorbed it into their repertoire of motifs. The most frequently represented flowers included chrysanthemums, peonies, poppies, irises, water lilies, wisteria and orchids (pp. 164, 306, 312). The motif of the blossoming branch, often that of a cherry or plum tree, which is so typical of Japanese art, was also adopted with great enthusiasm by French artists (pp. 112, 117).

At the Paris World Fair of 1878, the French public discovered Japanese ceramics used for the tea ceremony. The somewhat coarse and robust appearance of these items, mostly stoneware, bemused the visitors, who were more accustomed to the fine, multicoloured porcelain ware that had been made for export. Yet for a small group of connoisseurs and artists, these objects represented nothing less than a revelation. This was certainly the case with the sculptor Jean Carriès, who some years later – haunted by the memory of these Japanese ceramics – decided to work with stoneware. By now, Carriès was not the only one to work with this material in the Japanese spirit. Adrien Dalpayrat, Auguste Delaherche and Alexandre Bigot, as well as Paul Jeanneney and Georges Hoentschel, distinguished themselves in this discipline. The simple, clear forms of the Japanese bowls and pots that were made for the tea ceremony served as their inspiration. For example, they adopted the outline of a sake calabash (pp. 266, 267) or that of a *chaire*, a container for tea powder (pp. 247, 269). The fine ivory lids that gently sealed the jars were also borrowed from Japanese art (p. 264). French potters, too, were fascinated by Japanese ceramics with traces of gold on the surface, indications of earlier restoration. The Japanese did in fact use gold to restore valuable ceramics (p. 262). Fascinated by these flecks of light, Carriès adopted the method – albeit for purely aesthetic purposes (p. 263).

The unpolished and primitive nature of the stoneware enthralled French ceramicists, and they took pleasure in the direct confrontation with the material. Random and irregular distortions, drops and cracks were often direct and intrinsic effects of the material itself. These artists also studied Japanese firing processes with great interest. This was true of Jeanneney, for example, who developed a glaze for the conversion of Auguste Rodin's *Monumental Head of Balzac* to stoneware (p. 271), which was very similar to that of stoneware from Tanba or Bizen. As for Jeanneney, he obtained a dark-brown glaze with yellow specks. The Japanese achieved this effect with the help of burning pine ash that randomly fell onto the pieces whilst in the kiln.

Claire Guitton

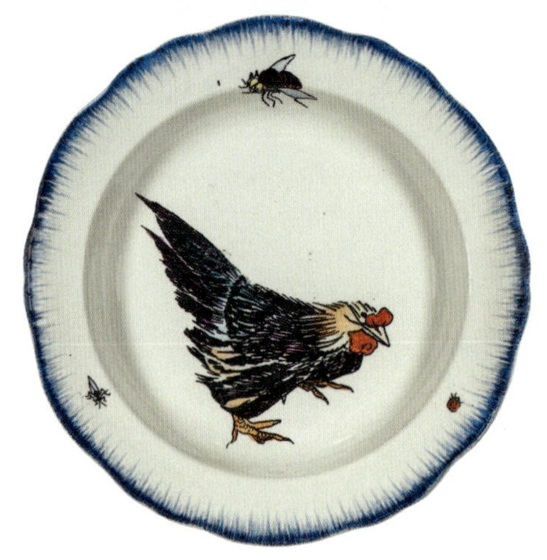

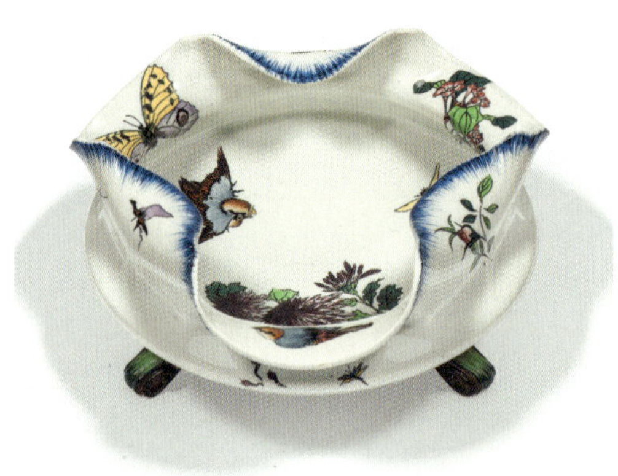

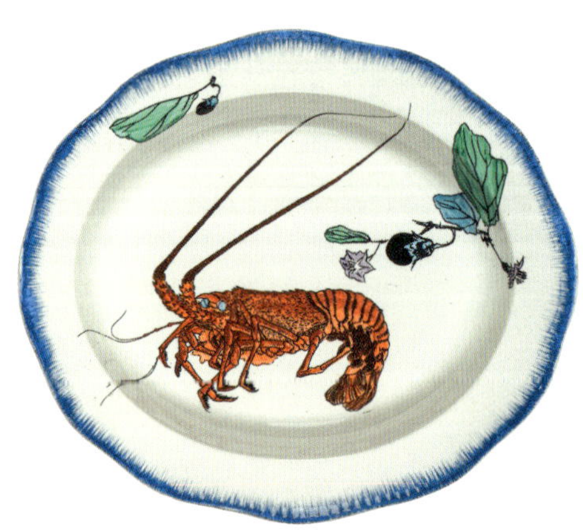

132 | 133 | 131 Félix Bracquemond, François-Eugène Rousseau, Lebeuf Milliet & Cie, *Deep Plate | Vegetable Bowl (triangular) | Platter,* 1866/1876

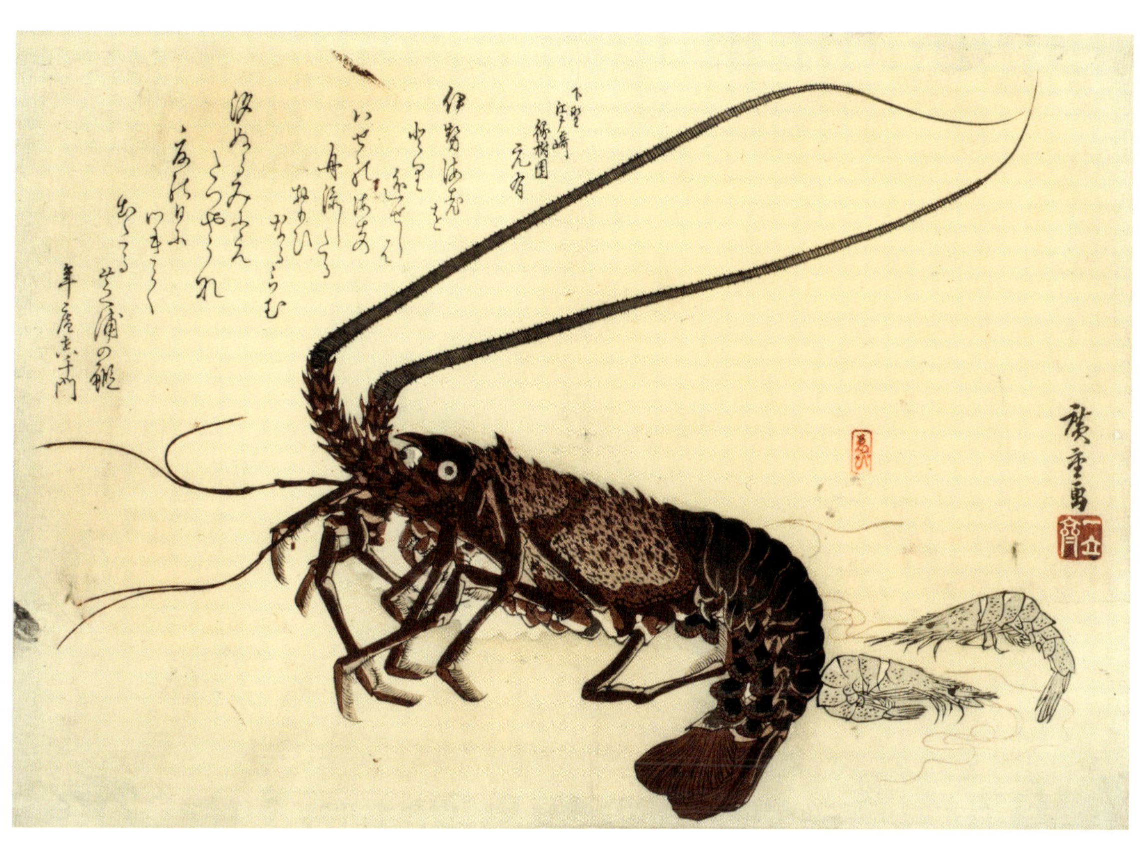

197 Utagawa Hiroshige, *Lobster and Shrimp*, circa 1832–1833

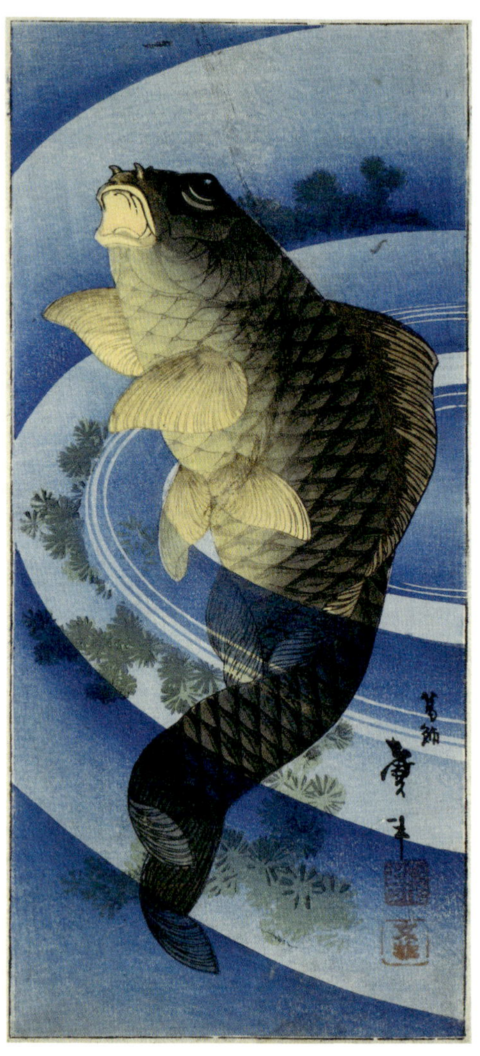

224b Katsushika Taito II, *Carp (Koi)*, circa 1830–1844

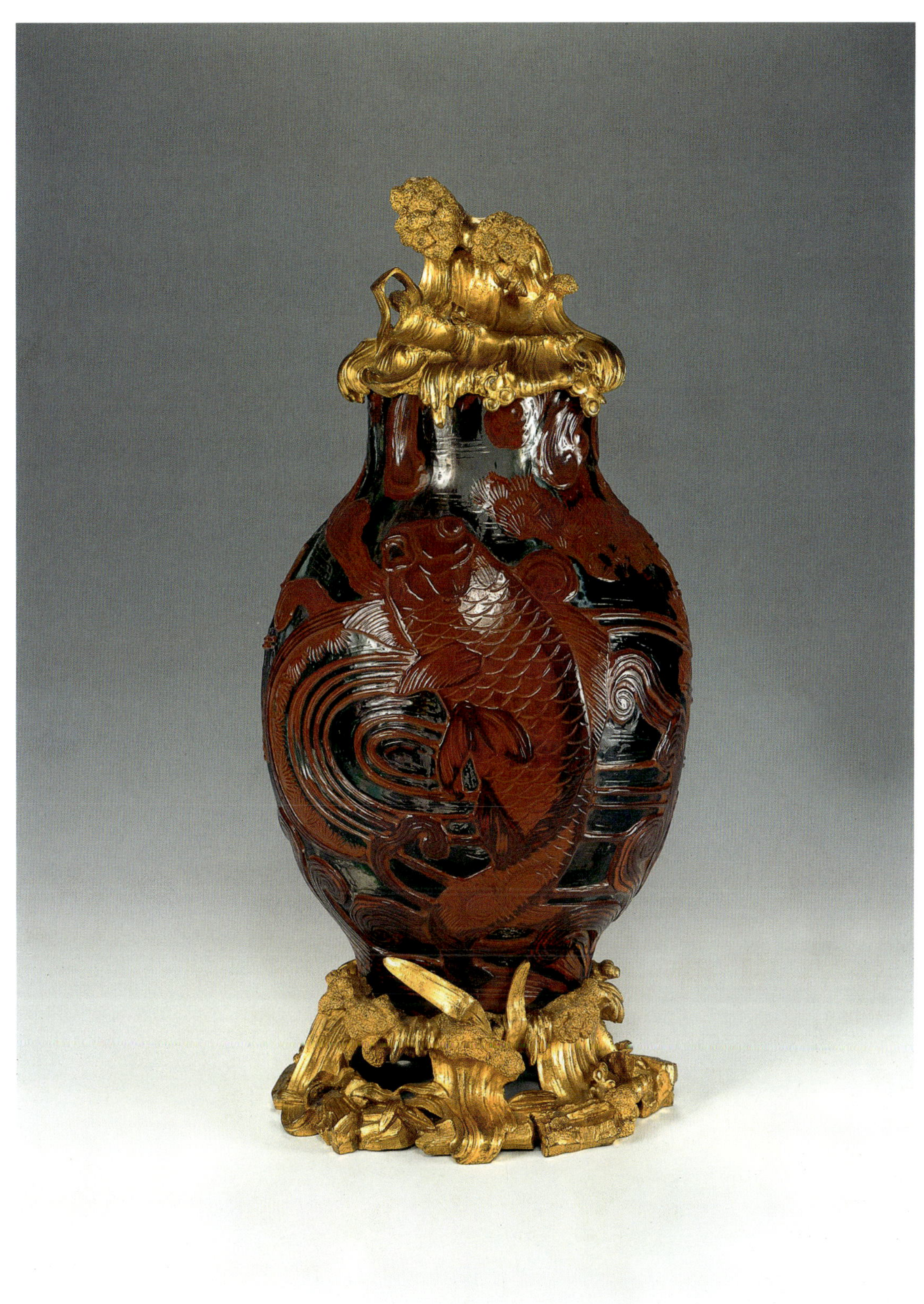

149 François-Eugène Rousseau and/or Ernest-Baptiste Léveillé, *Covered Vase with Base*, circa 1888–1890

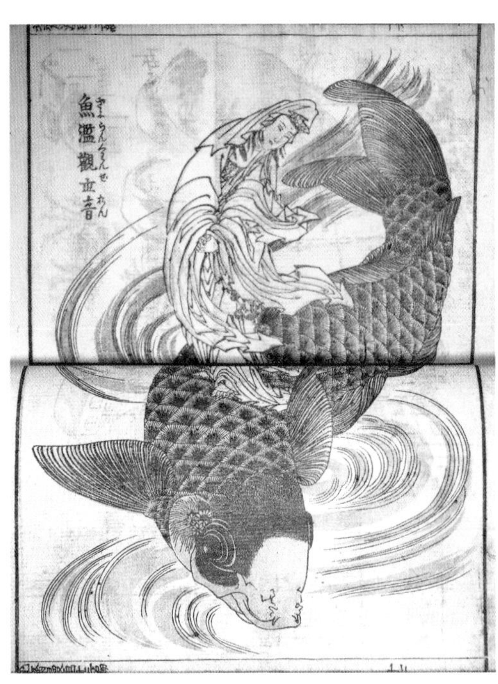

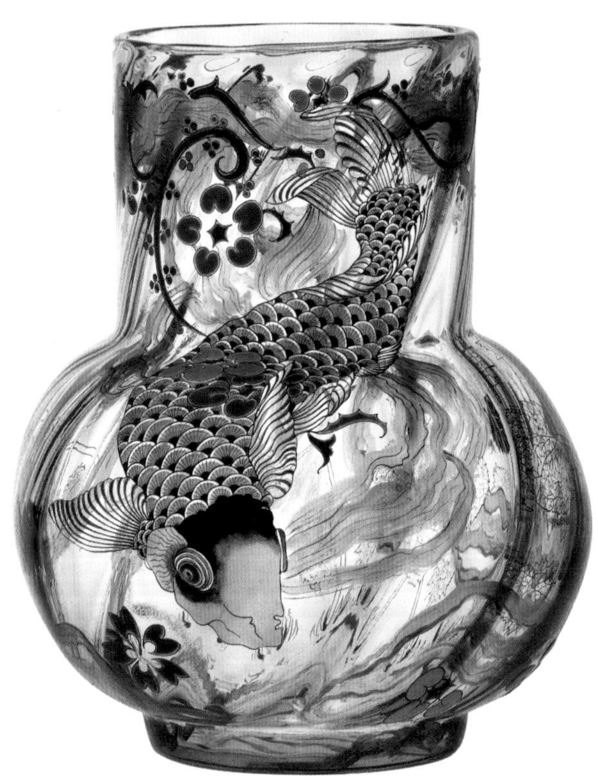

140 Émile Gallé, *Vase with Carp Motif*, 1878
248n Katsushika Hokusai, *Manga*, vol. 13, 19th c. (1st ed. 1849)

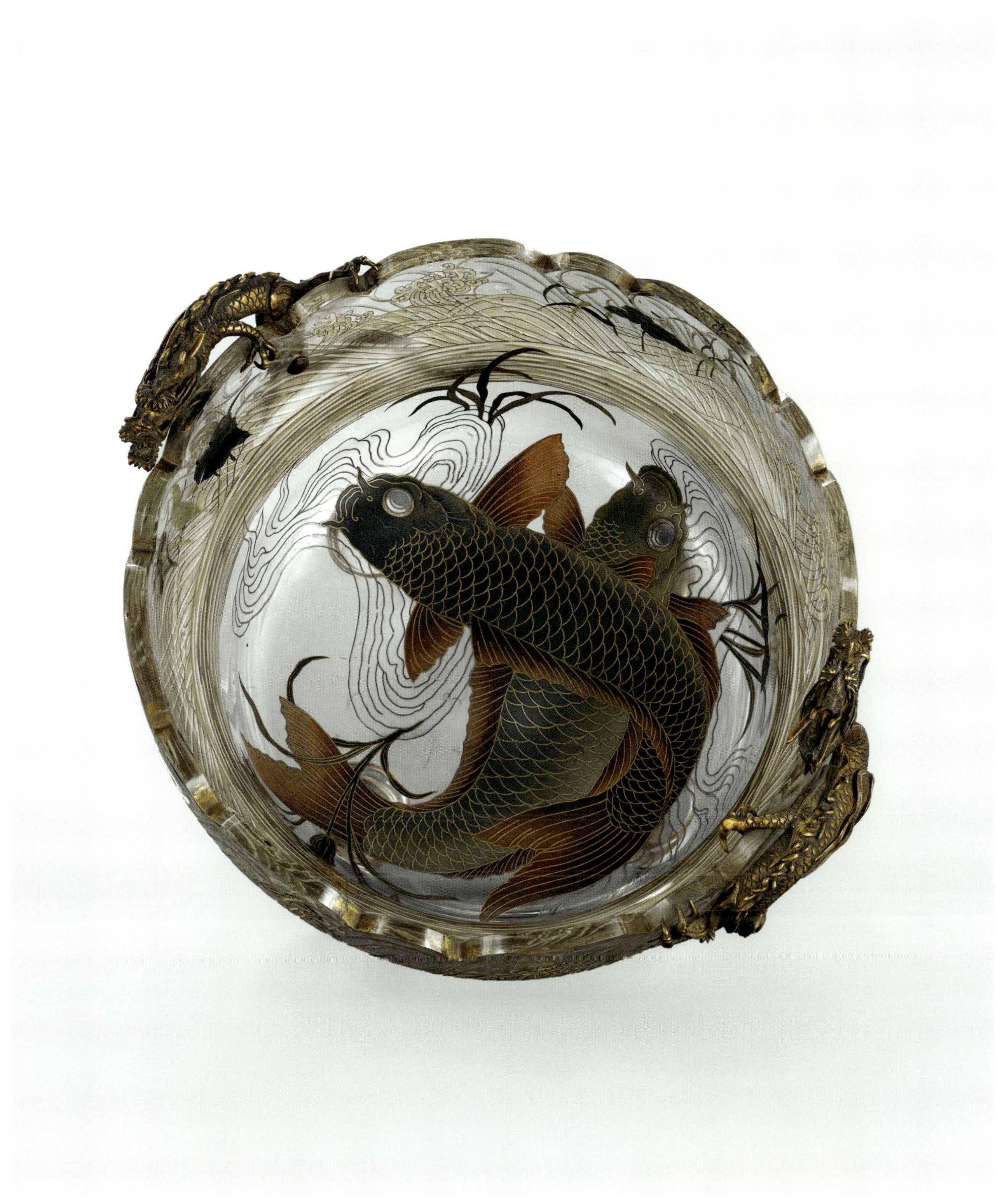

138 Escalier de Cristal, *Bowl with Mounted Dragon*, circa 1875

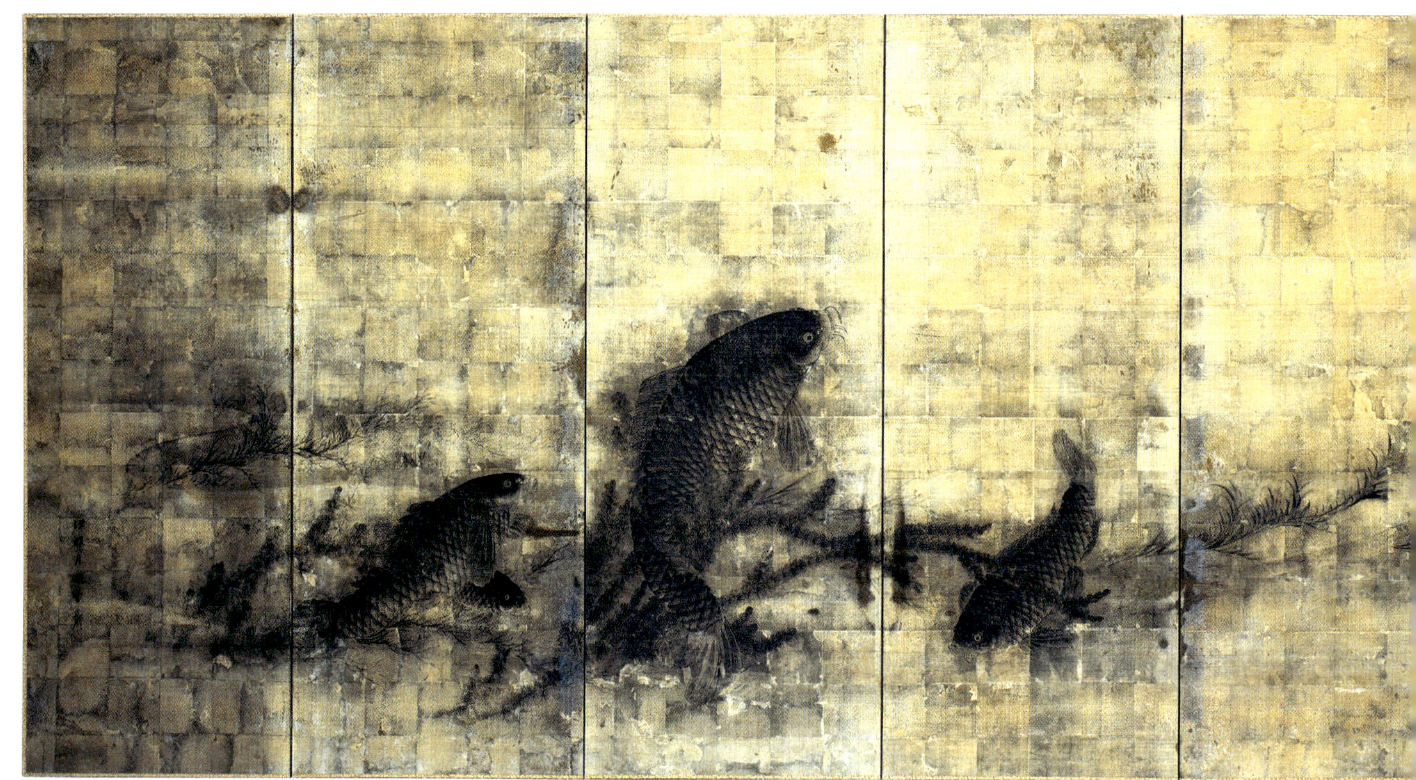

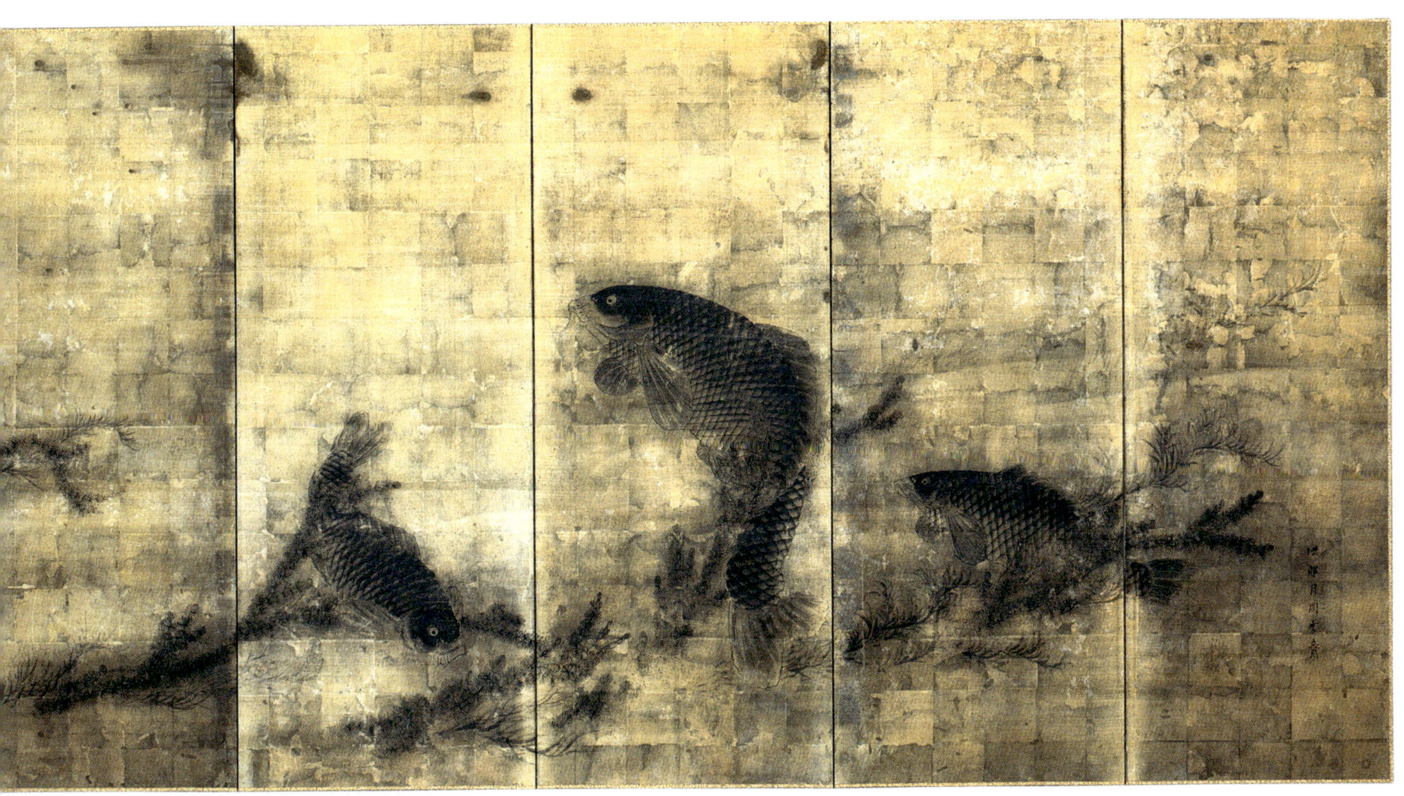

182 Tsukioka Sessai, *Carps*, late Edo period, 1839 or before

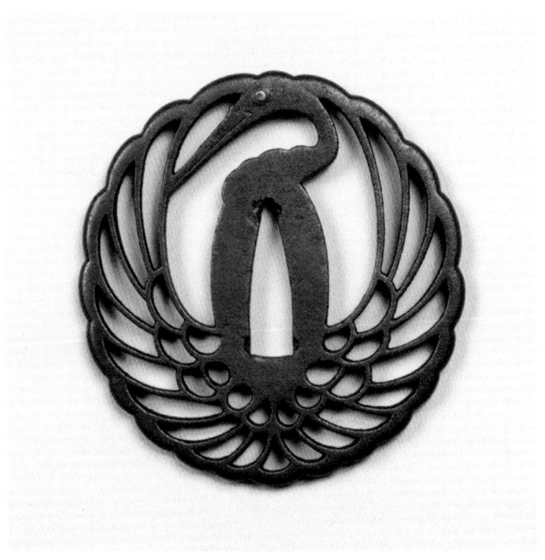

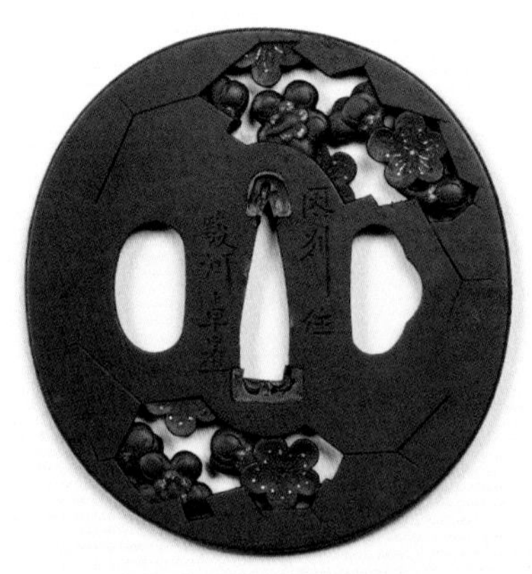

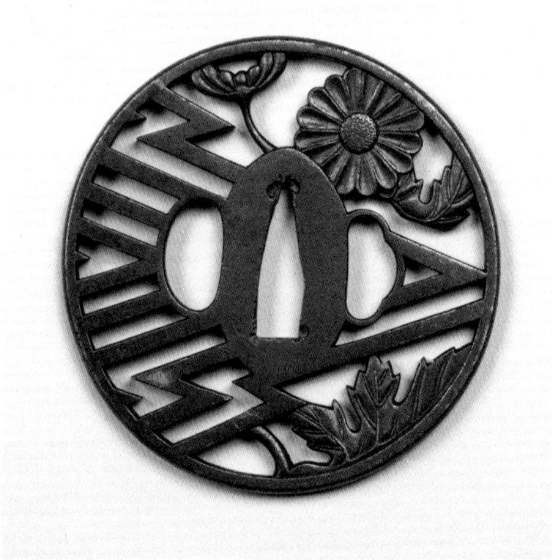

352 | 357 | 351 Japan, *Tsubas*, circa 1750–1800 and circa 1800–1850

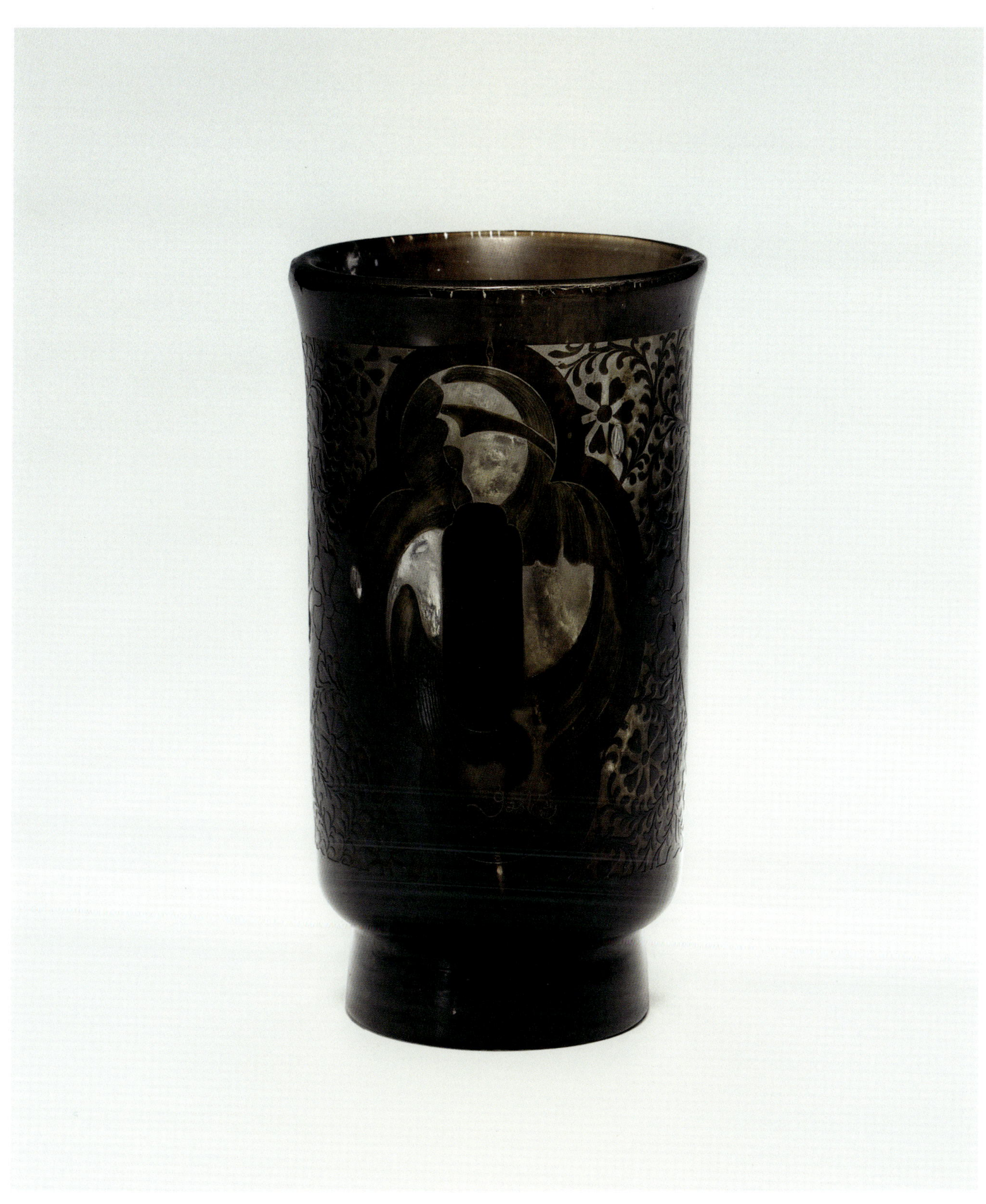

144 Émile Gallé, *Vase with Flower and Vine Decor*, 1900

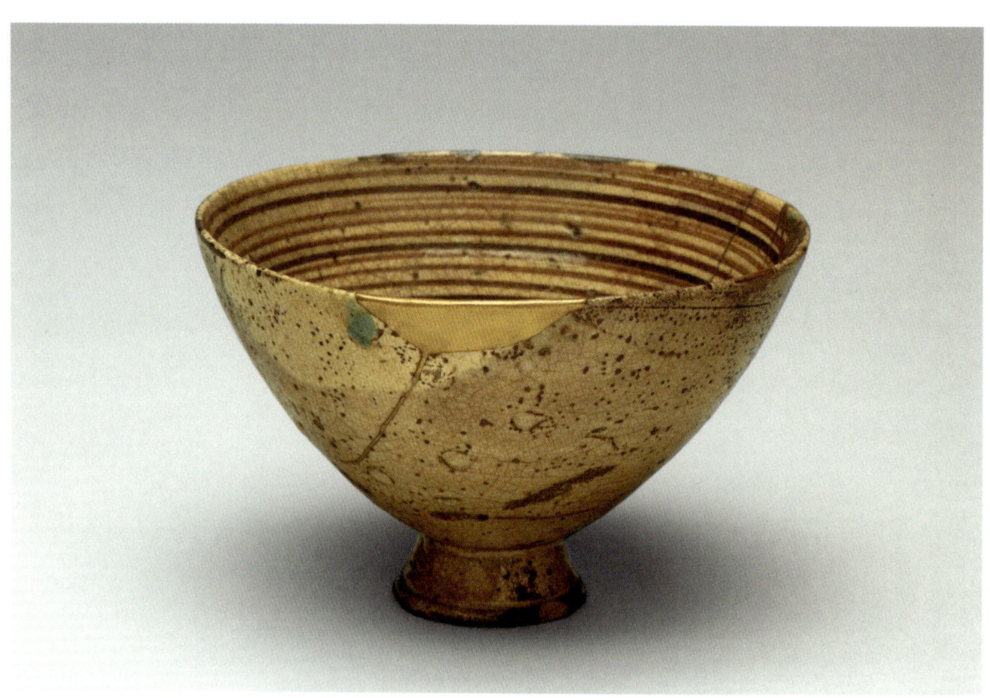

339 Japan, *Food or Tea Bowl (chawan)*, Edo period, 18th c.

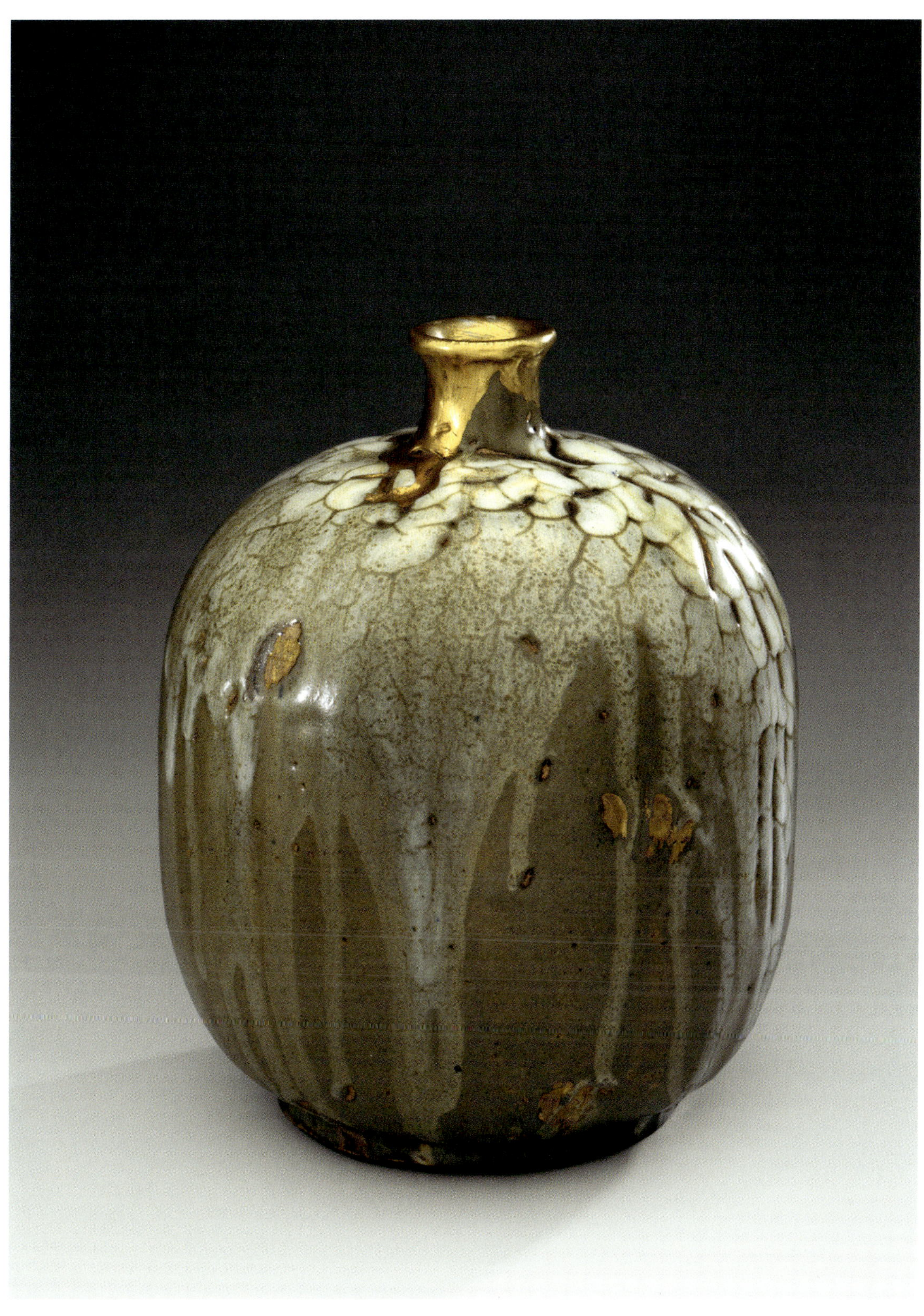

154 Jean Carriès, *Elongated Spherical Vase*, circa 1890

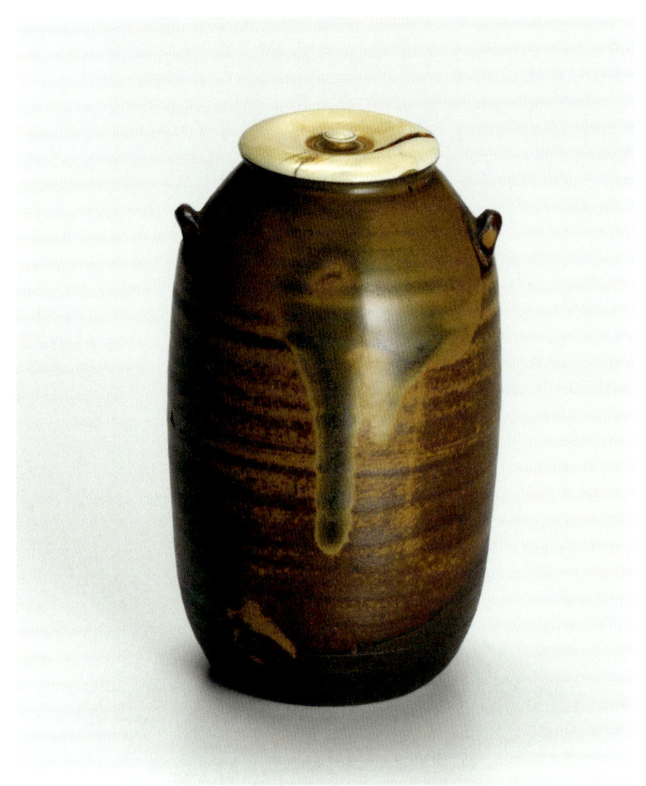

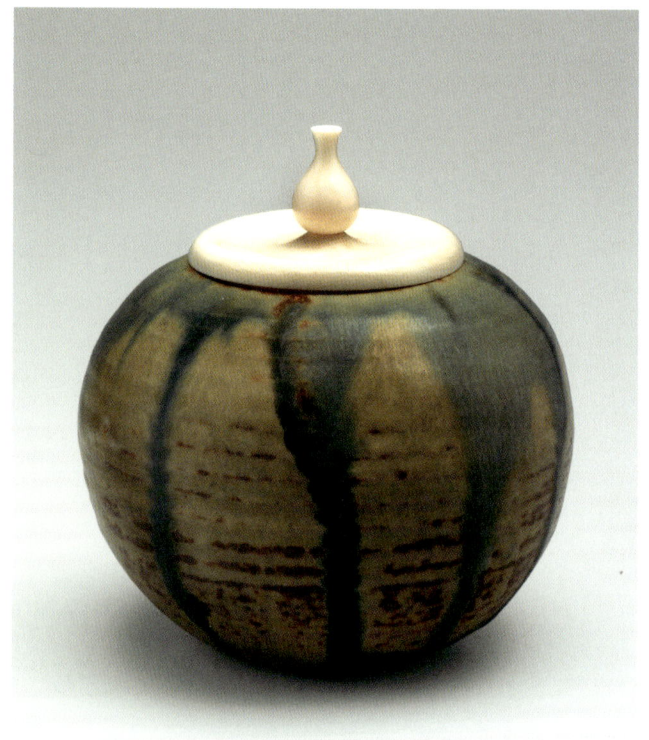

340 Japan, *Tea Jar (chaire)*, Edo period, 18th c.
162 Paul Jeanneney, *Jar with Grooved Sides*, circa 1898

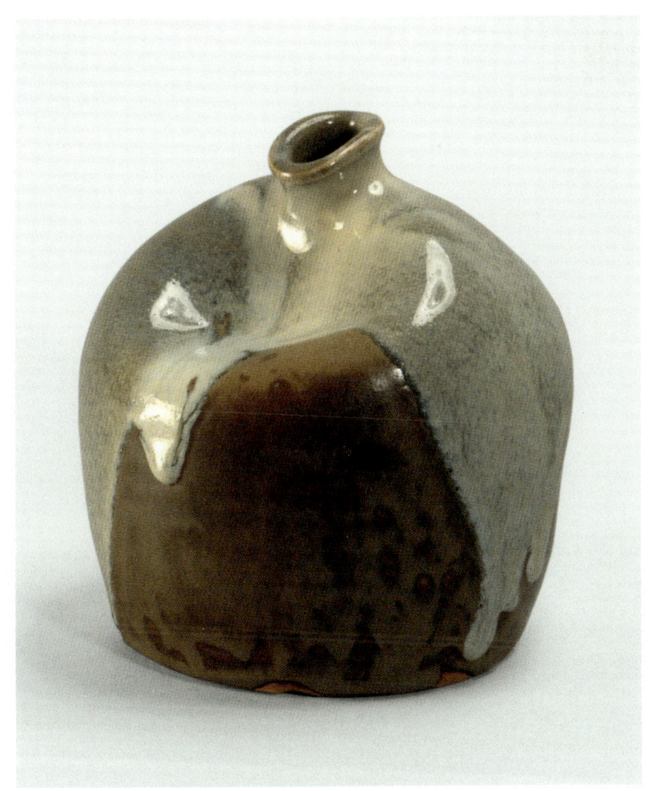

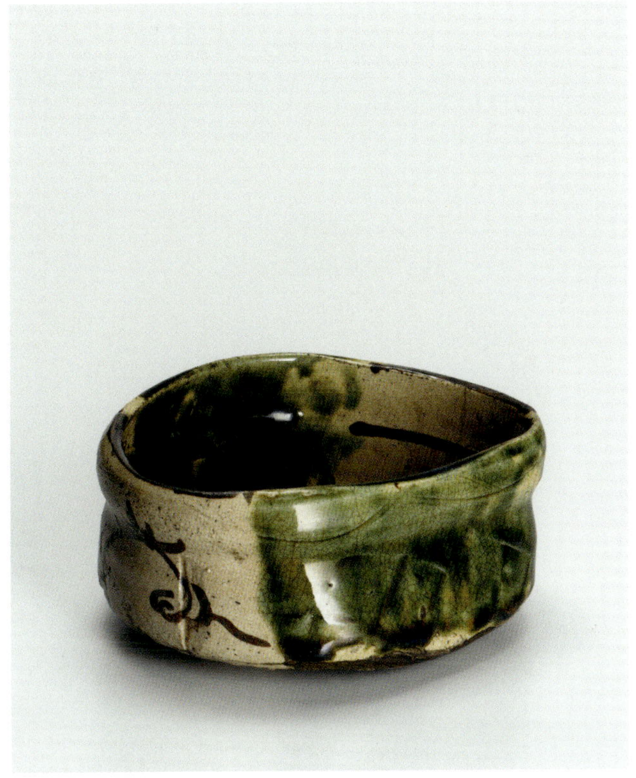

152 Jean Carriès, *Dented Vase*, 1888–1894
338 Japan, *Tea Bowl (chawan) in the Shape of a Shoe (kutsugata)*, Edo period, 18th c.

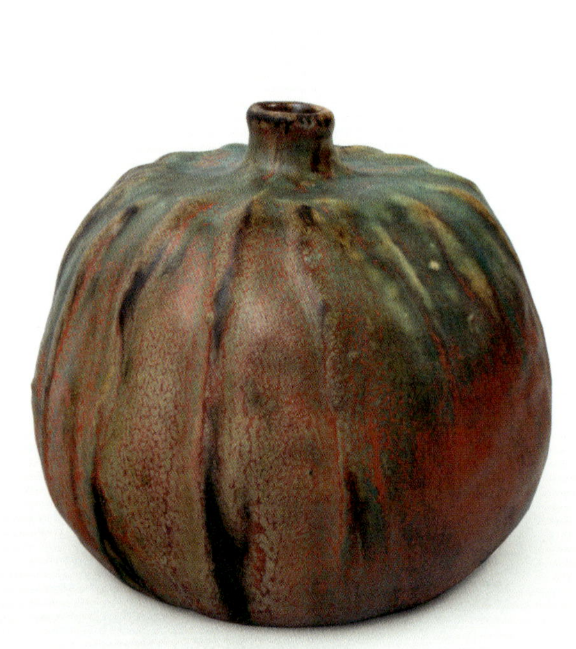

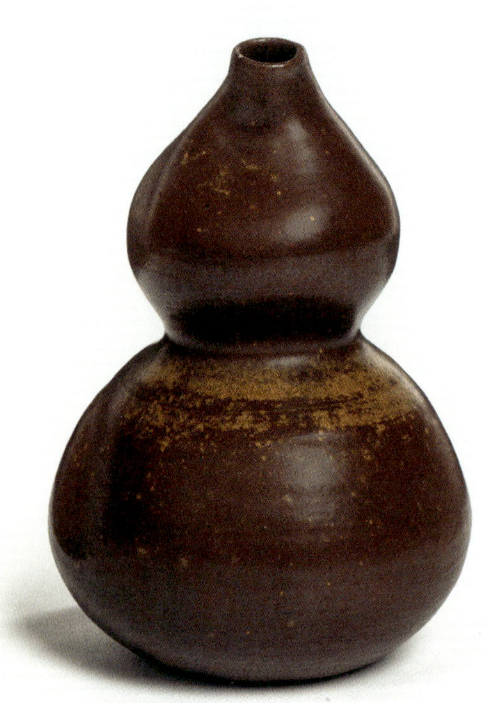

158 Pierre Adrien Dalpayrat, *Gourd Vase*, circa 1895
166 Paul Jeanneney, *Vase*, circa 1900

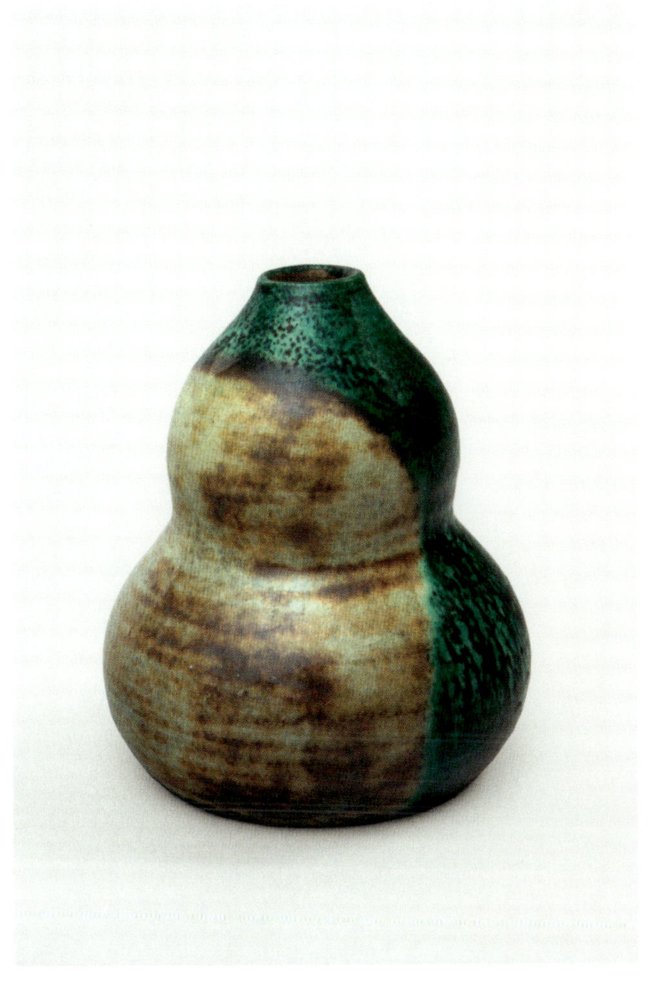

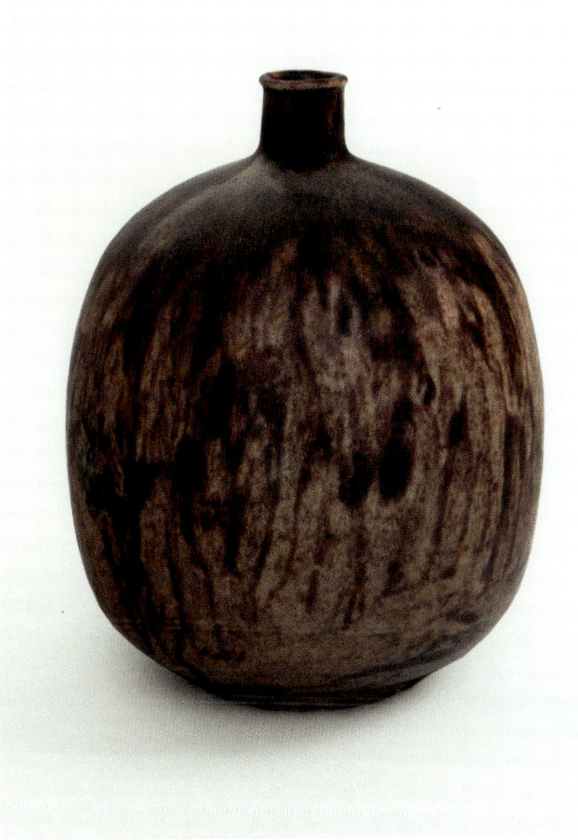

345 | 344 Japan, *Double Gourd Vase* | *Vase*, 19th c.

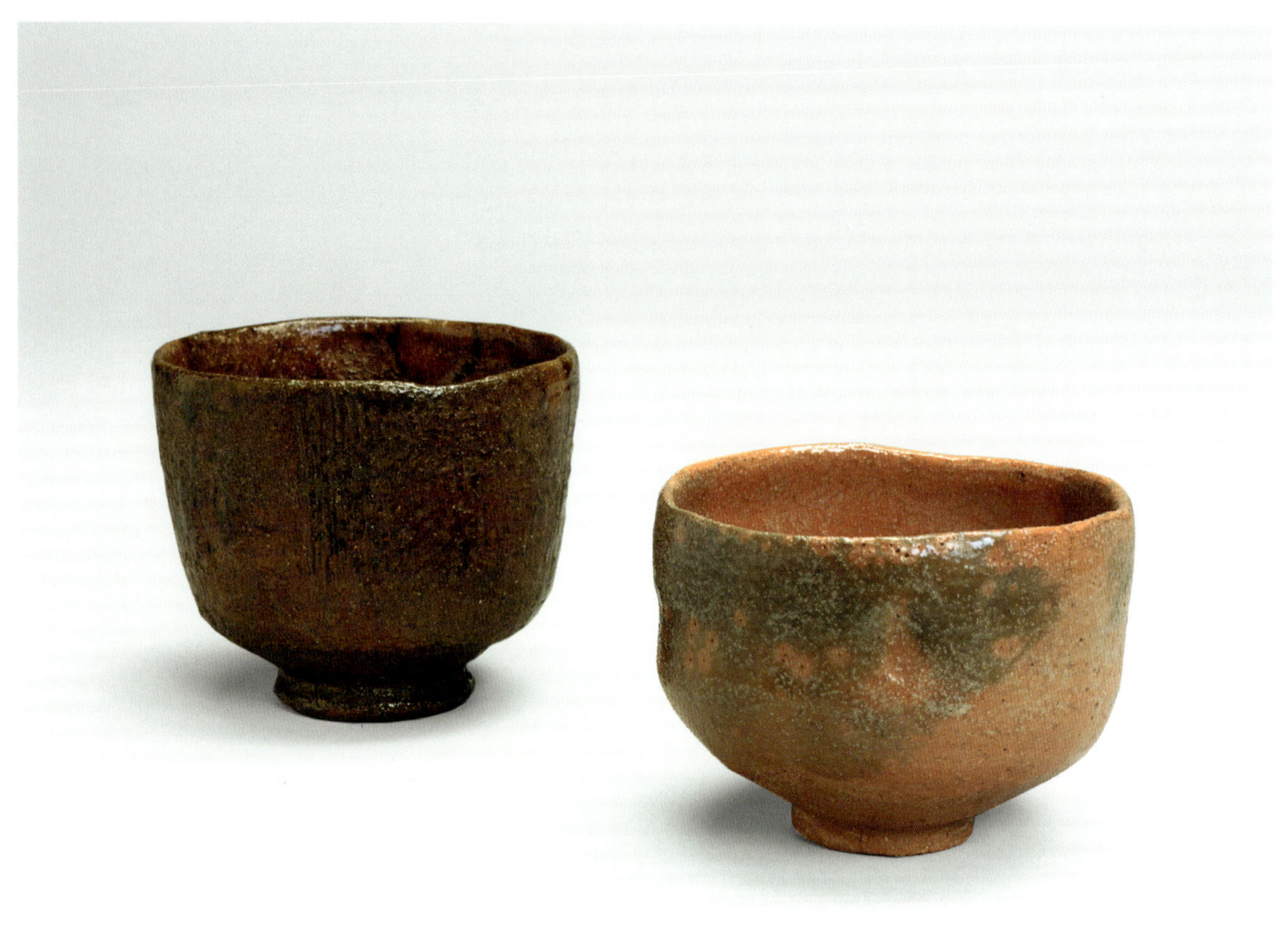

334 | 331 Japan, *Tea Bowls (chawan)*, Edo period, 17th/18th c.

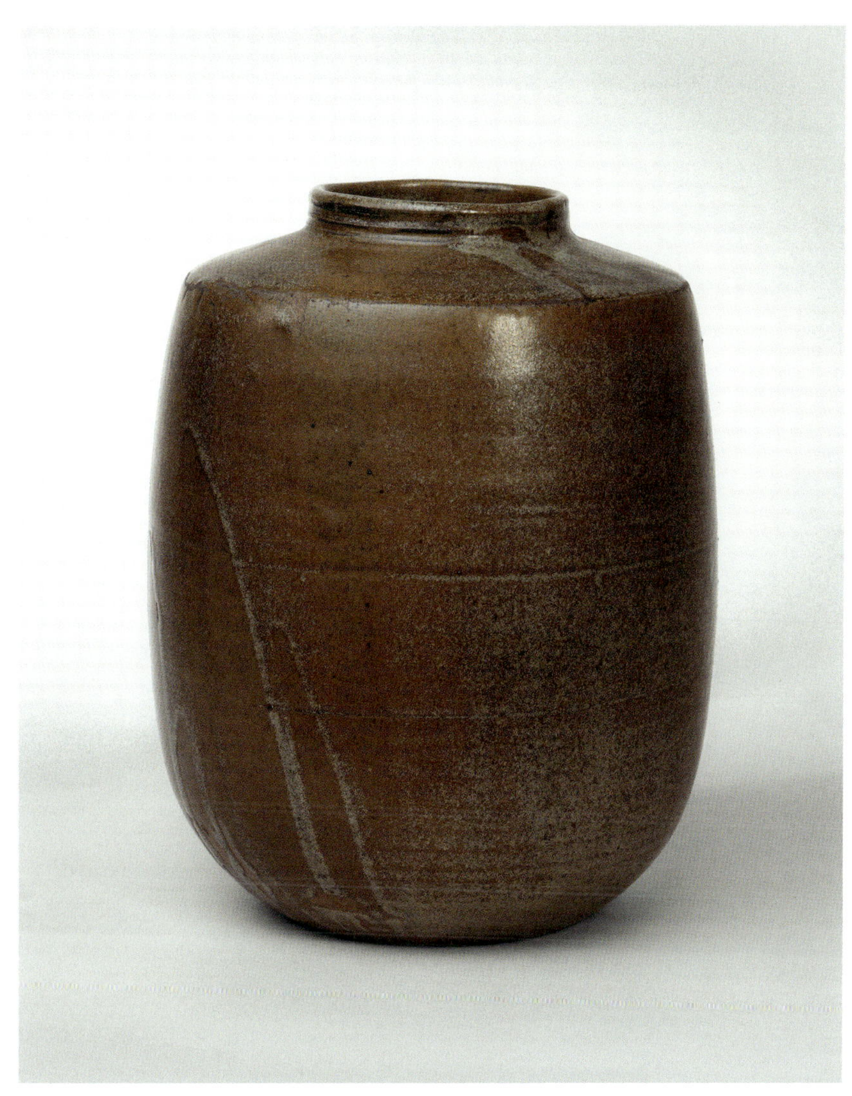

155 Jean Carriès, *Vase*, 1892

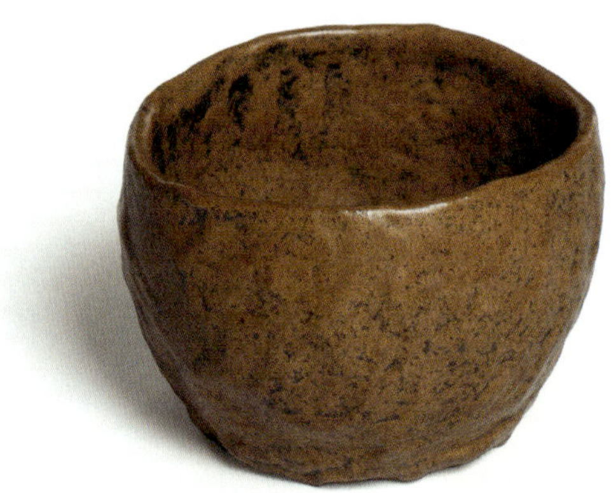

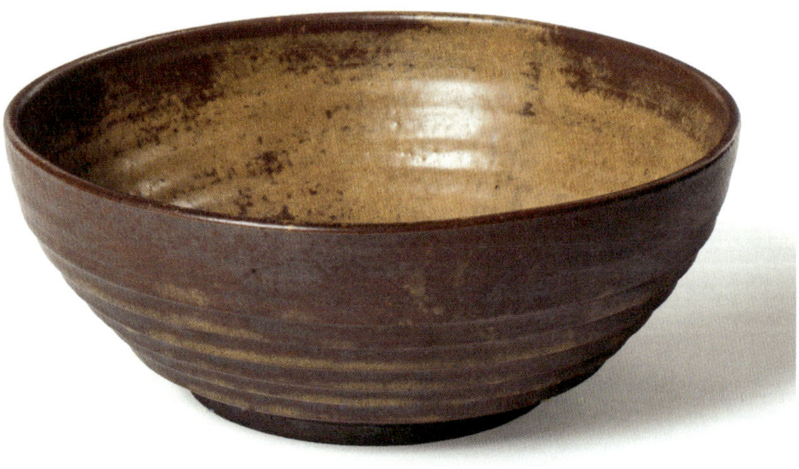

165 | 164 Paul Jeanneney, *Bowls*, circa 1900

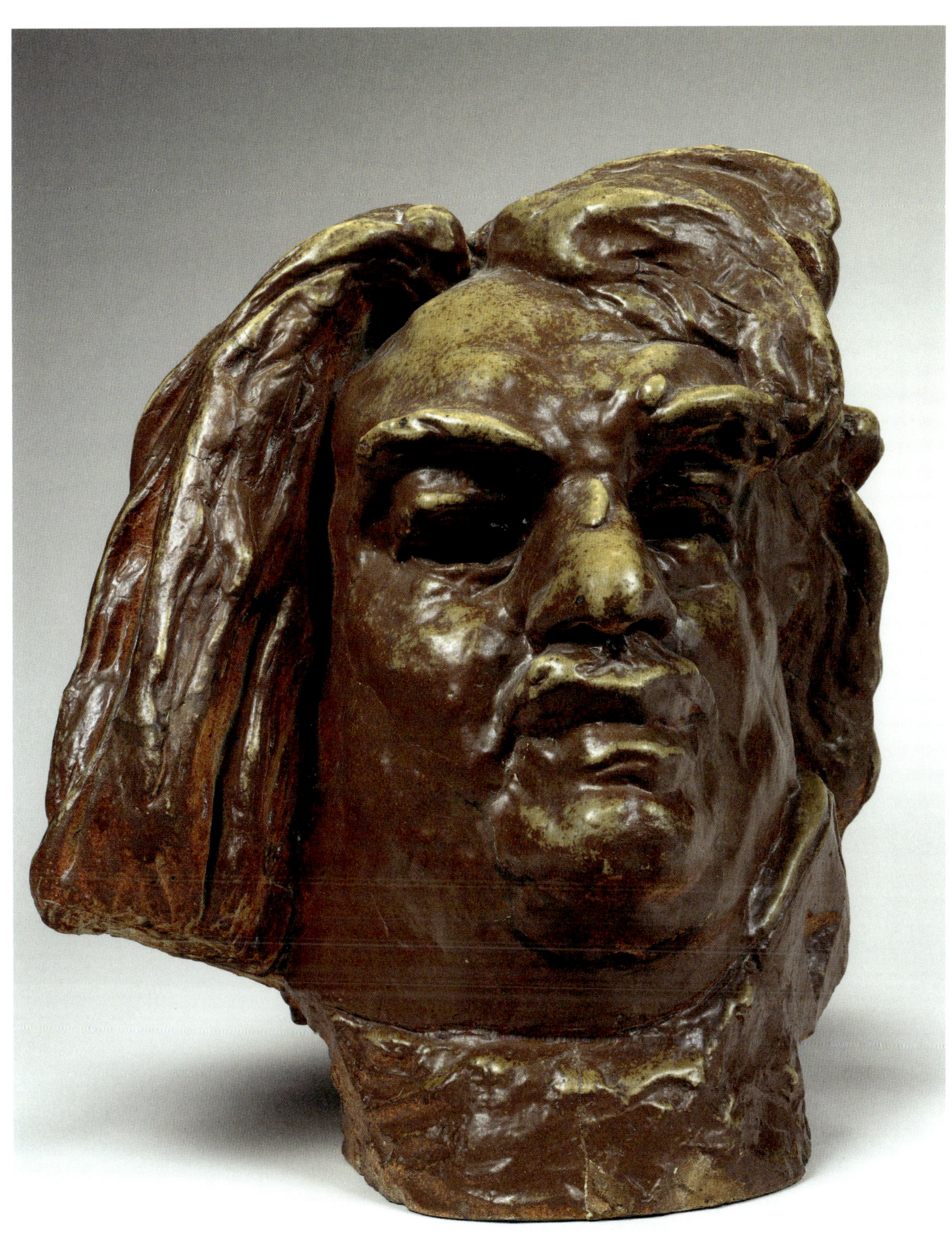

167 Auguste Rodin and Paul Jeanneney, *Balzac, Monumental Head*, probably 1899

The Nabi and the decorative

In 1888, Paul Sérusier founded the group "Les Nabis" at the Académie Julian in Paris. Adapting the Hebrew word *nebiim*, he and his fellow artists defined themselves as "prophets" of sorts – not without a bit of humour. In such a spirit of youthful self-confidence, this "enlightened circle" including Pierre Bonnard, Maurice Denis, Paul Ranson and somewhat later Édouard Vuillard, Félix Vallotton and Georges Lacombe demanded nothing less than the renewal of art and a turn away from established academic traditions. With a special eye for the role of the decorative arts, they called for the equal treatment of all artistic genres and, thus, a non-hierarchical approach to their works. Alongside Paul Gauguin and the Pont-Aven school, the primitives of the quattrocento and images of popular art, it was an engagement with East Asian art – and particularly Japanese woodblock prints – which substantially inspired this undertaking. The Nabi themselves collected works from Japan, using them to decorate their studios and homes. Above all, they treasured Japanese art for qualities such as its flatness and its decorative aspects: in 1888, the historian Louis Gonse called the Japanese "the foremost decorators in the world" in the magazine *Le Japon artistique (Artistic Japan).*

The works of the Nabi included designs for lampshades, wallpaper and furniture as well as folding screens and fans, the two latter of which enjoyed increasing popularity with the rise of the Japanese fashion in France. Bonnard's four vertical panels *Decorative Panneaux – Women in the Garden* from 1890/1891 (p. 279) were originally conceived as a single folding screen. Several characteristics refer to Japanese wood-block prints as a point of reference, such as the markedly flat depiction of the four stylised female figures dressed in con-spicuously patterned clothing and the flat garden landscapes suggested by decorative floral elements. The distinctive curves of the woman in a red dress on the far-left panel recall Japanese depictions of women, for example, by Kitagawa Utamaro (p. 278). In his folding screen, *Nannies' Promenade, Frieze of Carriages* (p. 86), Bonnard presents a scene that takes place across several panels, customary for East Asian folding screens: a woman in a reduced, planar and dark silhouette is shown taking a stroll across the Parisian Place de la Concorde with children and dogs. While the entire group of figures placed at the front is depicted from above, Bonnard changes the perspective according to East Asian style, placing the governesses and the hackney carriages in the background frontally vis-à-vis the beholder. The tendency towards an exaggerated, slightly deformed pose of the woman on the third panel can be similarly found in Japanese woodblock prints – for example, on a print by Utagawa Kuniyoshi (p. 278) owned by Bonnard's friend Denis. Like the figures in East Asian ink paintings, Bonnard's forms float against the empty background, lacking any additional detail.

Bonnard, whom the art critic Félix Fénéon called "the very Japanese Nabi", applied the principle of combining several points of view in his painting *Women with a Dog* of 1891 (p. 289). As in Japanese portraits of actors, the viewer is brought very close to the group of women with a dog, painted from above, severed as if by accident by the edge of the painting – giving the impression of a scene witnessed coincidentally. In the background, other figures are shown, who are in turn depicted from below. Denis also owned a similar theatrical scene by Utagawa Kuniyoshi (p. 287) that his friend was surely familiar with. As Bonnard himself insisted, the chequered flat pattern of the dress was inspired by Japanese models.

Portrait of Madame Ranson, in Green painted by Denis in 1893 (p. 277) reveals striking patterns and various perspectives as well. While the blouse of Ranson's wife is depicted in a view slightly from below, the skirt and the decorative rug on which she stands are shown in the image as if dramatically seen from above, seemingly robbing the figure of her stability. Other conspicuous elements include the narrow vertical format of the painting, which recalls Japanese scrolls and screens, and the vertical signature in a cartouche. Denis owned more than ninety Japanese woodblock prints. In the figures of his religious and Symbolist paintings, he combined the model of idealised Japanese female figures, whose bodies are not modelled with light and shadow, but by using curved arabesque outlines – as in Suzuki Harunobu and Kitagawa Utamaro (p. 156) – combined with the disincorporated figurative ideal of Italian quattrocento primitives such as Fra Angelico. In contrast to Japanese figures shown undertaking everyday activities, Denis presents unreal dreamlike scenes. In his painting *July* from 1892 (p. 295), the flat figures – outlined by delicate and continuous contours only – wander through an ornamental landscape. The figures in *Virginal Spring* (p. 298) from 1894 are stylised into unified white silhouettes. Taking a dramatic view from above, Denis has placed them in a landscape far away from reality on a pink surface ornamented with depictions of trees.

In Vuillard's painting *Family in the Garden* (p. 274), the figures in the front are cut off, as in Japanese models; and the narrow horizontal format recalls that of Japanese scrolls. The tendency in Japanese woodblock prints to use special ornamentation is also strongly emulated in *Madame Vuillard Arranging Her Hair* from 1900 (p. 292). Here, Vuillard's mother is shown arranging her hair in the mirror, whereby the pattern of her dress, the floor and the wallpaper are given equal pride of place. All visual elements seem placed on a single plane, giving the entire scene a very flat, artistic and highly decorative character. In many Japanese woodblock prints from the second half of the nineteenth century, figures are often similarly placed in colourfully patterned clothes against various designs, such as against a folding screen. Vuillard himself possessed a triptych by Utagawa Kunisada that illustrated this pleasure in combining various structures and forms of ornamentation.

In his woodblock prints with strong black-and-white contrasts, Vallotton also reflects Japanese visual solutions – for example, by choosing a narrow framing that brings the viewer close to the scene depicted or by severing the motifs, as in Utagawa Hiroshige. This also includes the combination of various viewpoints within a single print, as in the works *The Shower* and *The 1st of January* (p. 285). The subjects chosen by Vallotton, like that of the gust of wind (p. 284) or low-lying clouds in mountain landscapes, were also often treated in Japanese art (pp. 147, 192). In the patterns on the blanket upon which a nude woman stretches, the print *Laziness* also reveals Vallotton's preoccupation with *katagami*, Japanese paper stencils (pp. 282, 283). An important characteristic of his woodblock prints is the contrast between the black printed and white areas of the image, where the paper itself becomes an integral part of the image. Valloton's fans depicting children chasing a cat also borrow from Japanese models, as does his bonbonnière fashioned in the manner of a Japanese lacquer chest (pp. 242, 280, 281).

Ranson, another close member of the Nabi, shows his engagement with Japan in combining compact fields of colour with delicate contours. In his painting *Coastline* (p. 296), he presents a landscape in which a woman with a Japanese-looking silhouette strolls by. In his *Washerwomen at the Laïta River* (p. 297), Sérusier similarly takes up a relevant principle of Japanese woodblock prints in his landscape comprising simplified, connected fields of colour.

Ulrike Hofer

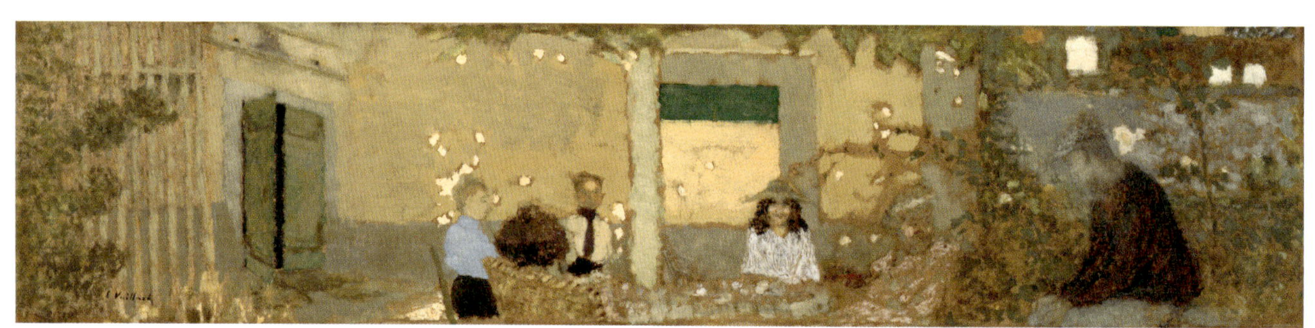

71 Édouard Vuillard, *Family in the Garden*, 1898

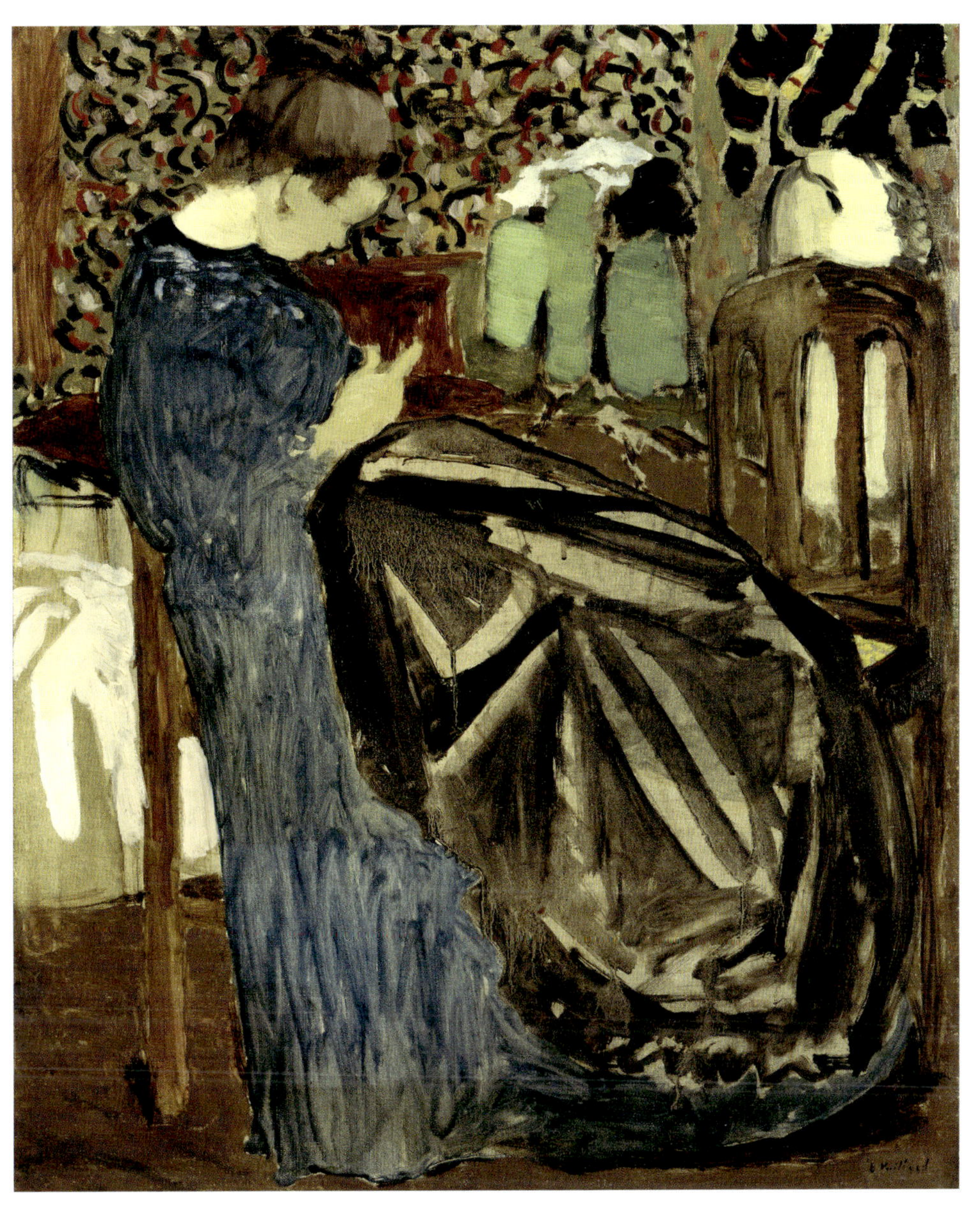

69 Édouard Vuillard, *A Seamstress*, 1892

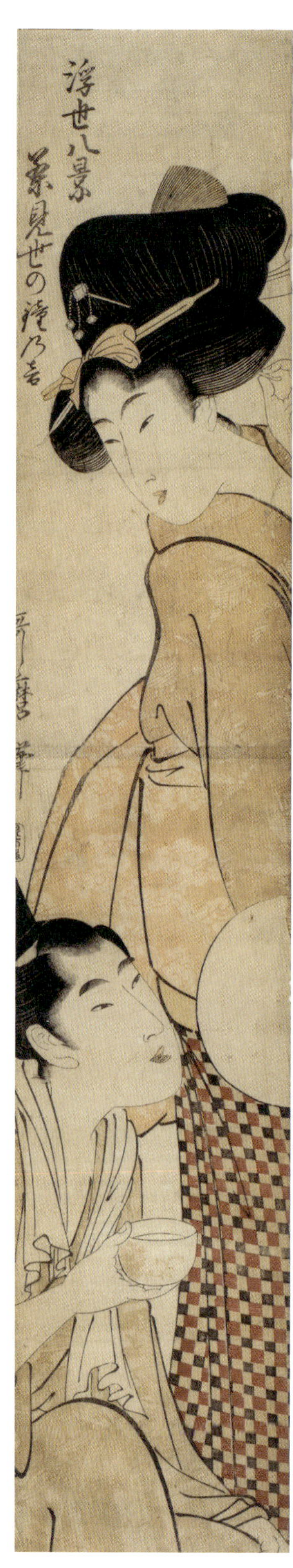

238 Kitagawa Utamaro, *The Sound of the Teahouse Bell*, 1802

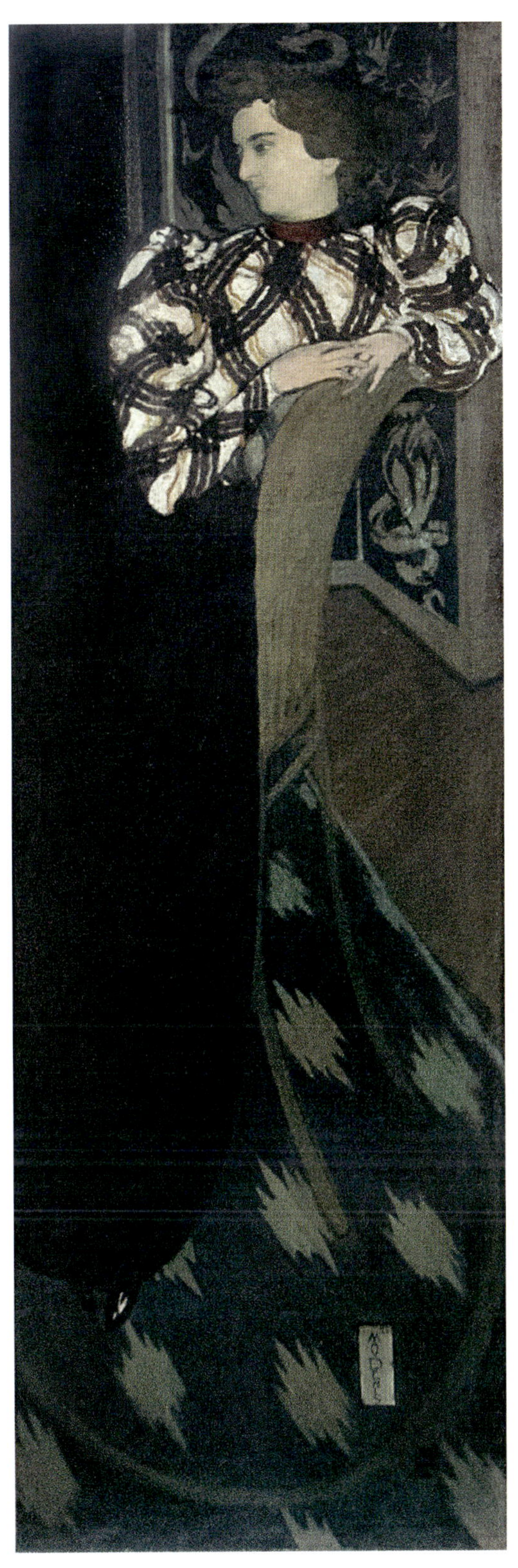

24 Maurice Denis, *Portrait of Madame Ranson, in Green*, 1893

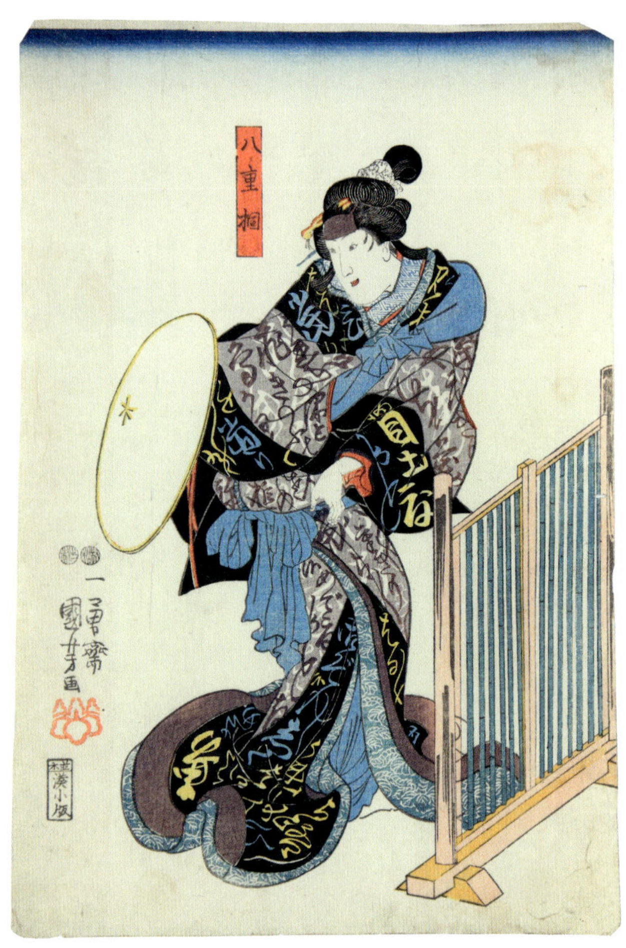

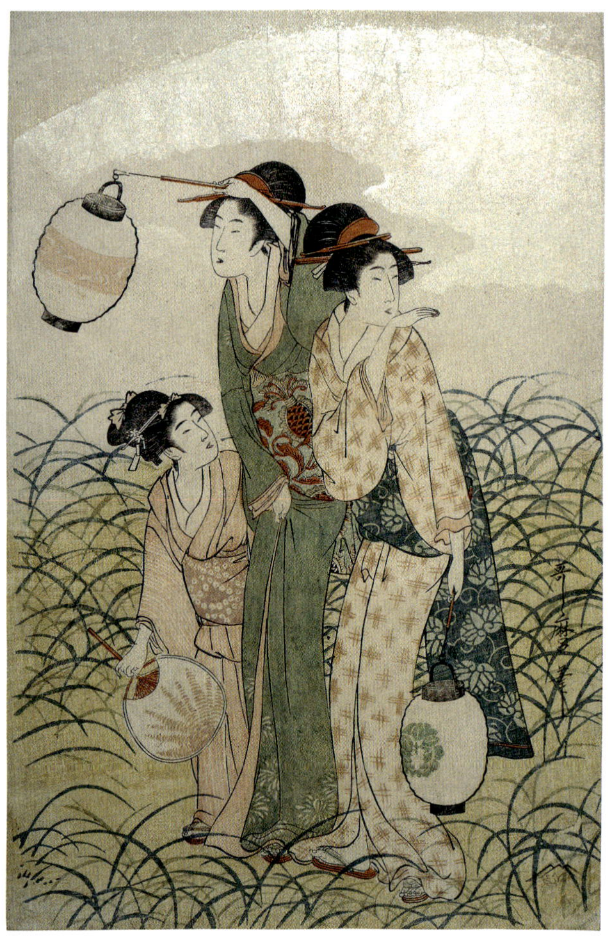

220 Utagawa Kuniyoshi, *The Actor Ichimura Uzaemon XII in the Role of the Princess Yaegaki*, 1848
231 Kitagawa Utamaro, *Episode in Musashino of the "Tales of Ise"*, 1796

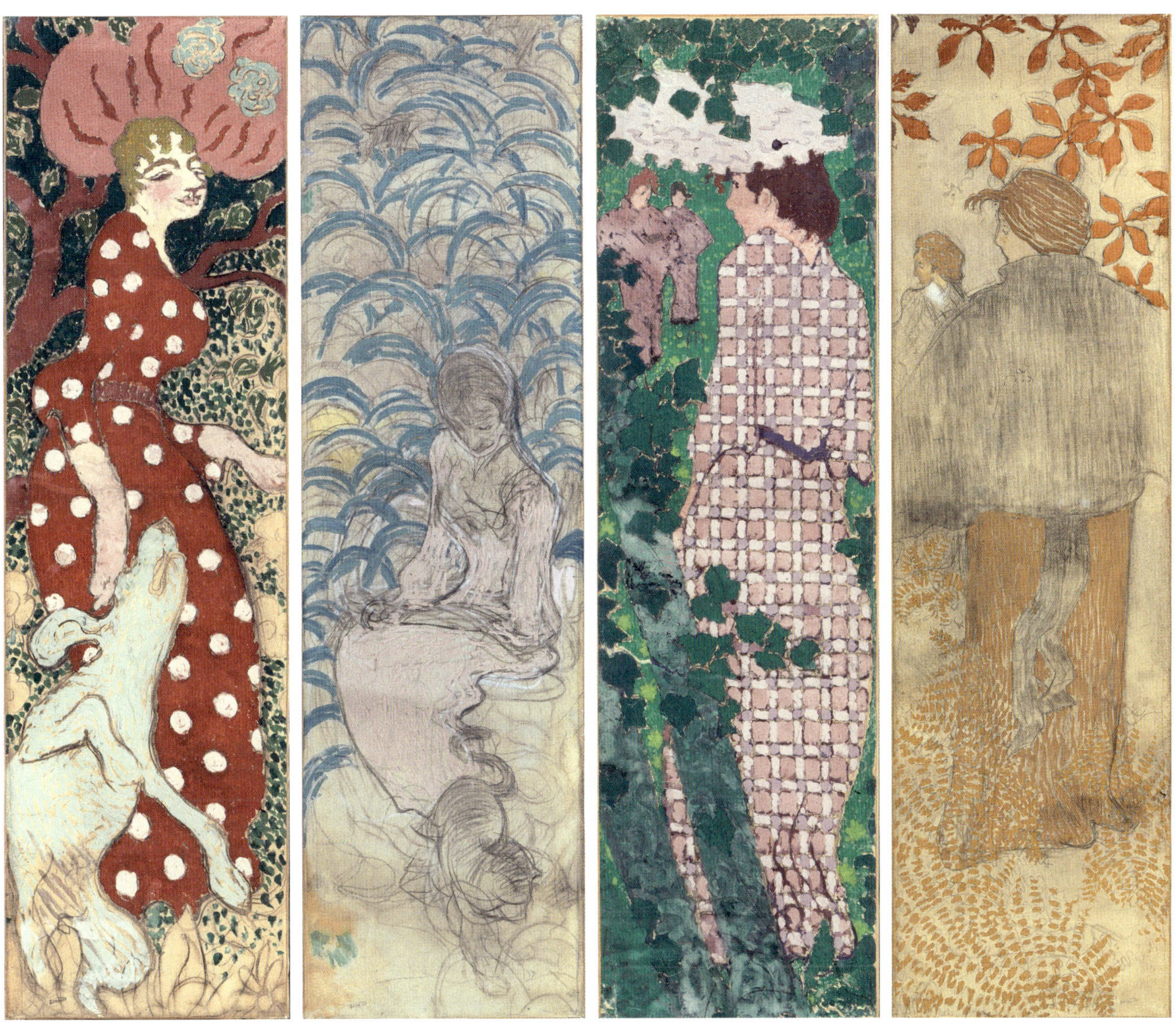

2 Pierre Bonnard, *Decorative Panneaux – Women in the Garden*, 1890/1891

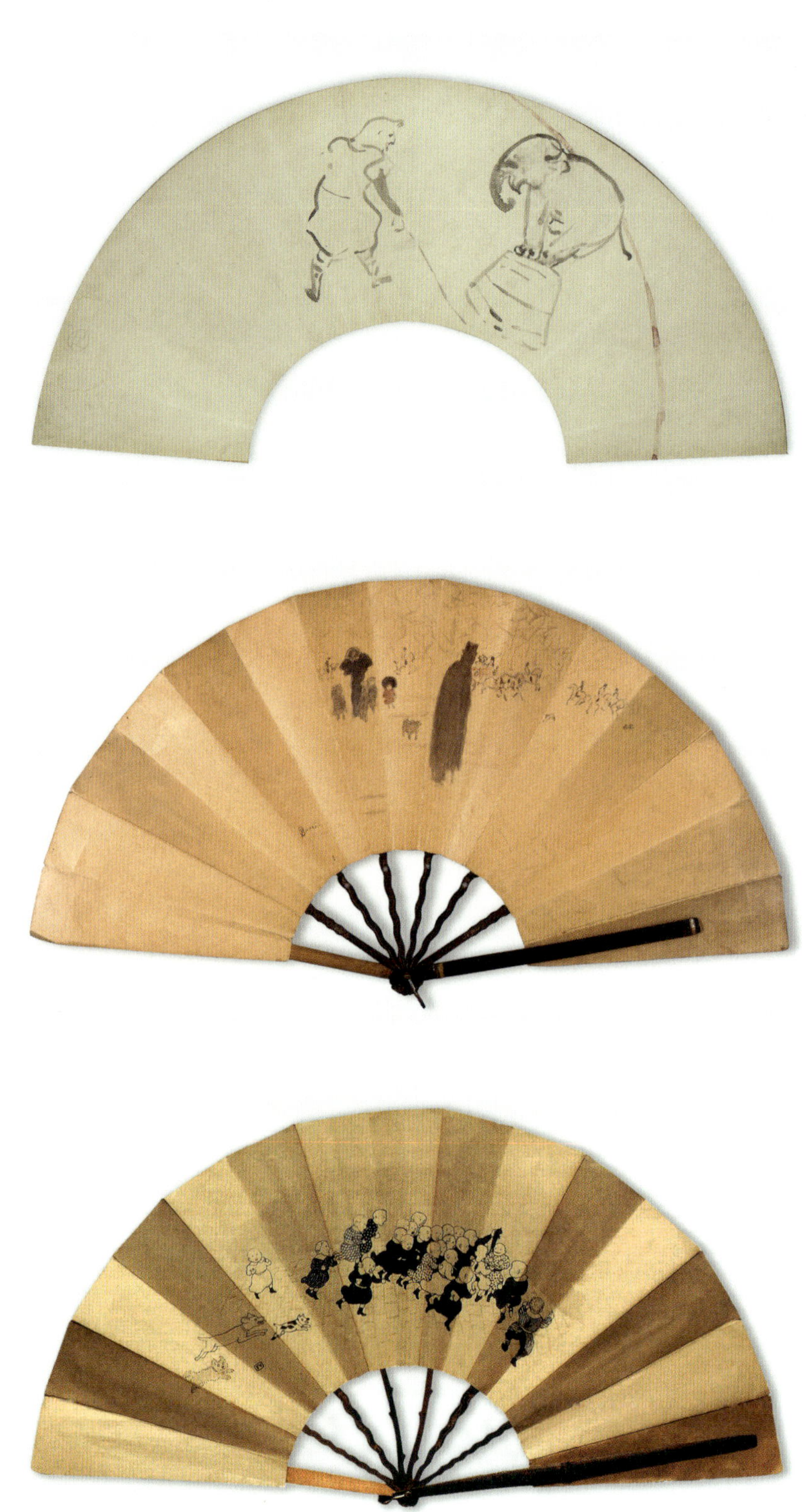

86 Henri de Toulouse-Lautrec, *At Circus Fernando*, 1888
82 Pierre Bonnard, *Promenaders and Riders in the Avenue du Bois*, 1894
87 Félix Vallotton, *Fan*, circa 1896–1898

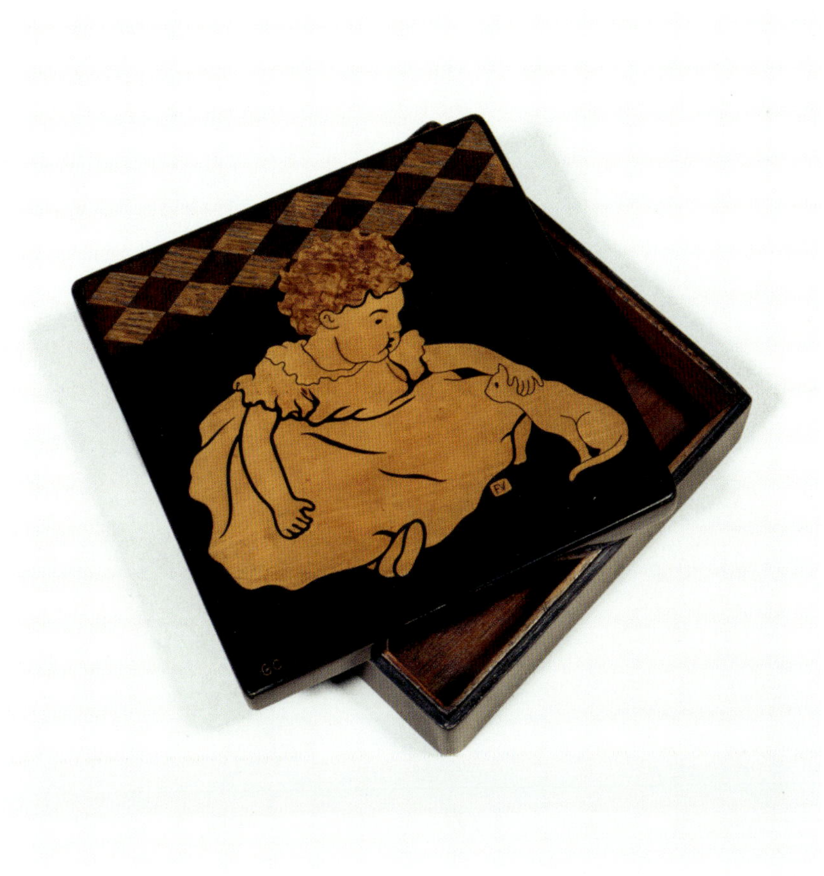

170 Félix Vallotton, *The Girl with the Little Cat (Bonbonniere)*, circa 1896

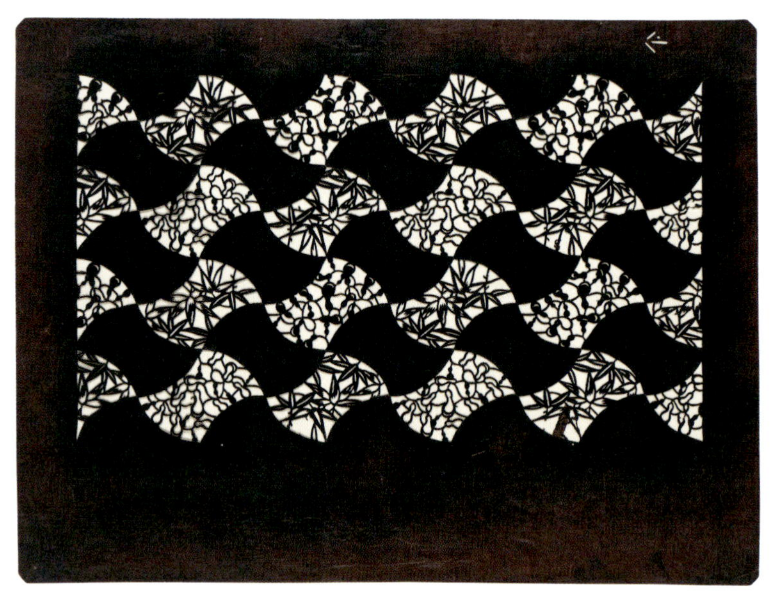

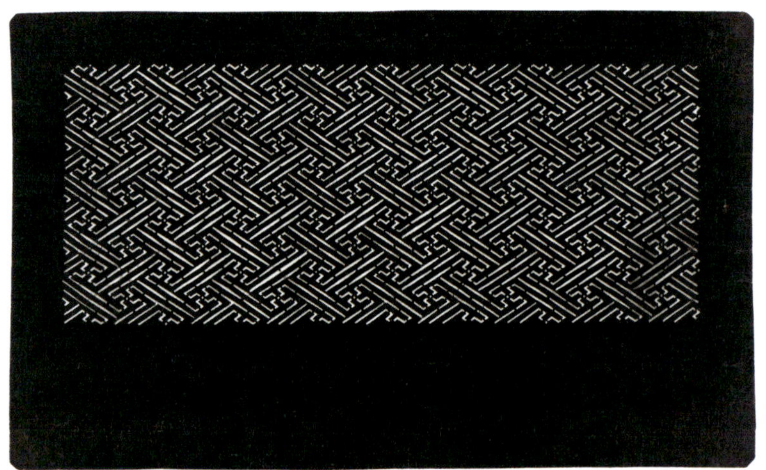

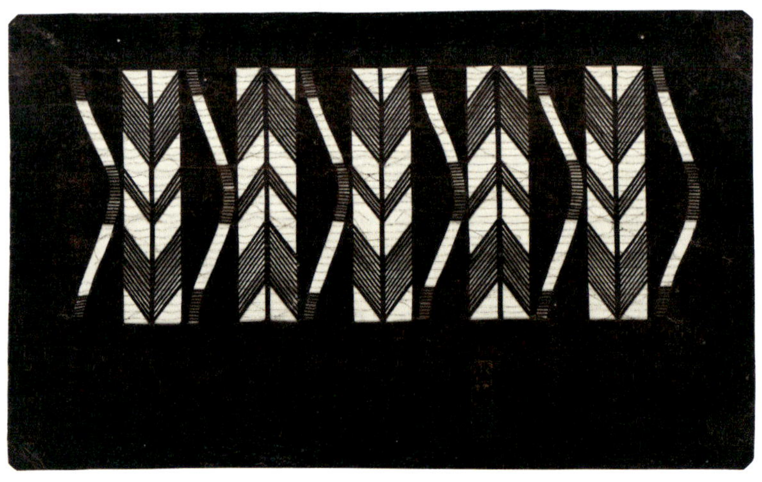

288 | 287 | 284 Japan, *Katagami*, circa 1900

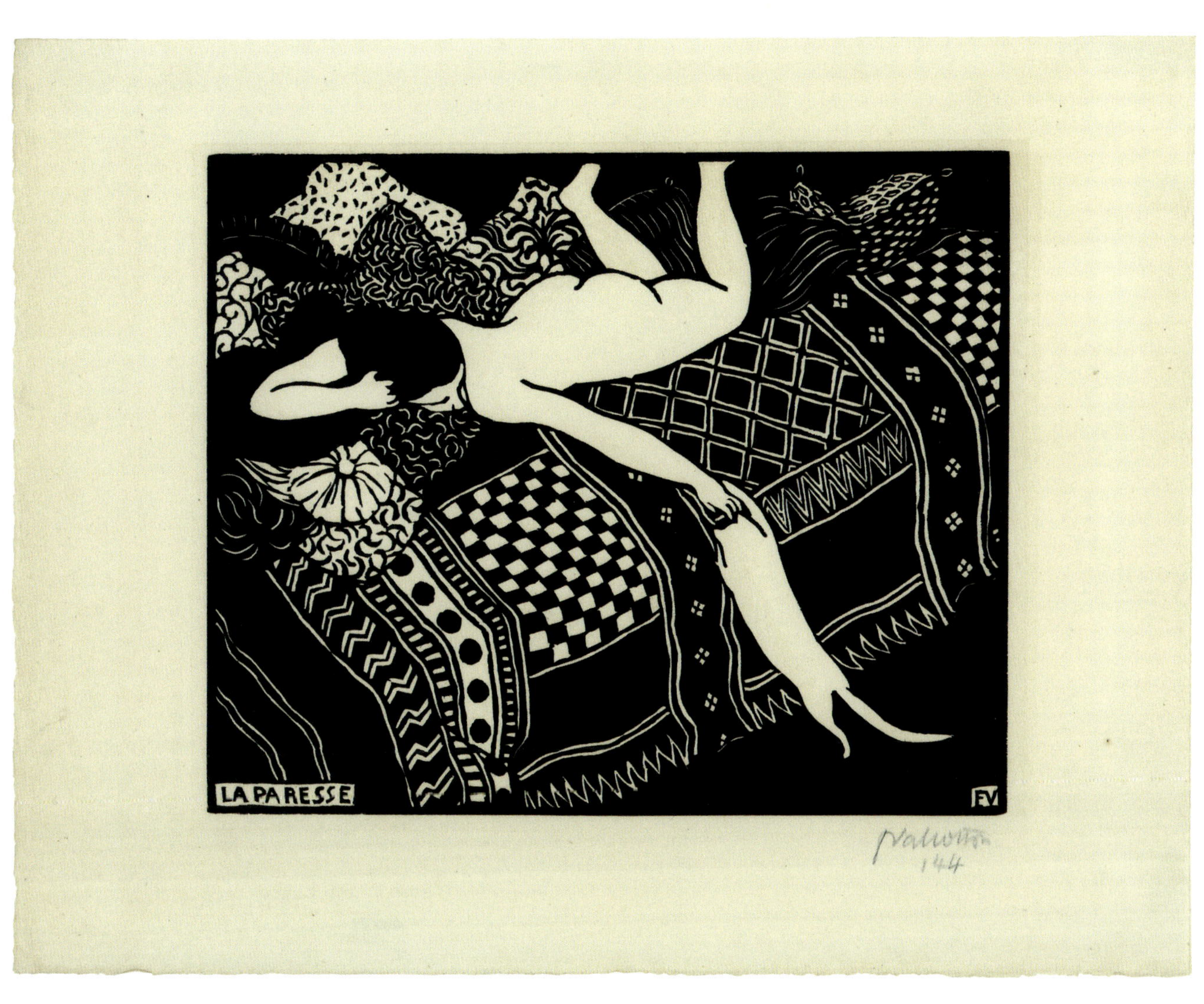

112 Félix Vallotton, *Laziness*, 1896

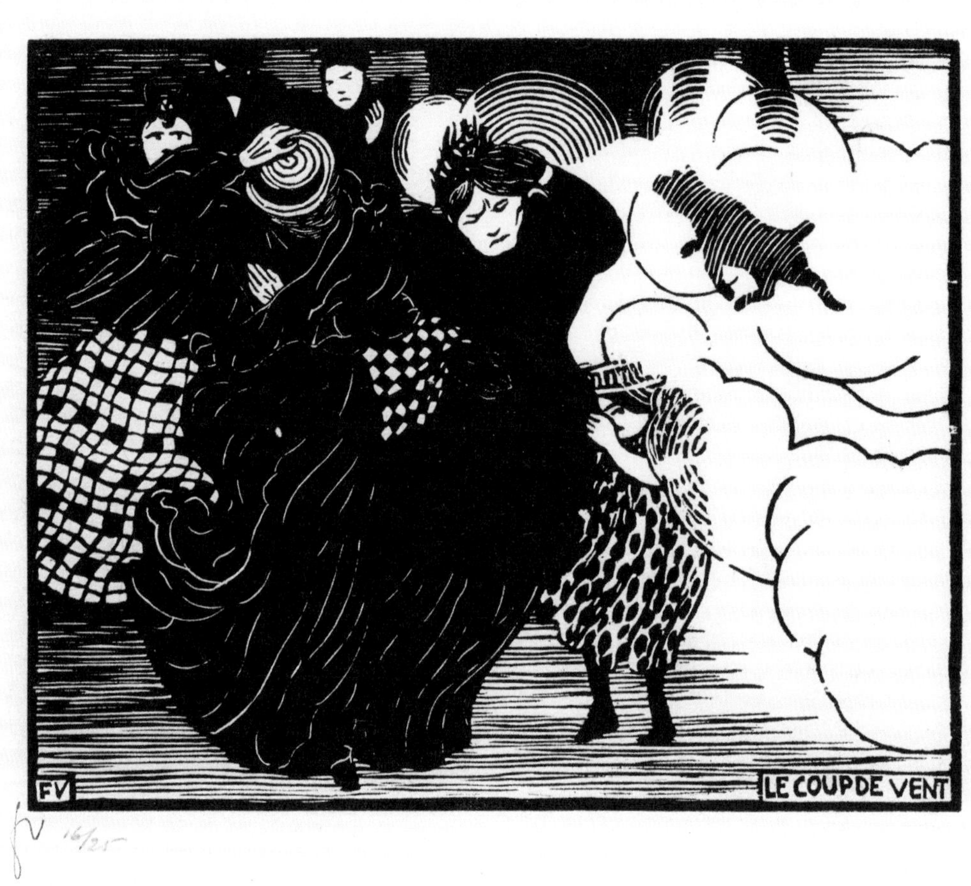

108 Félix Vallotton, *The Gust of Wind*, 1894

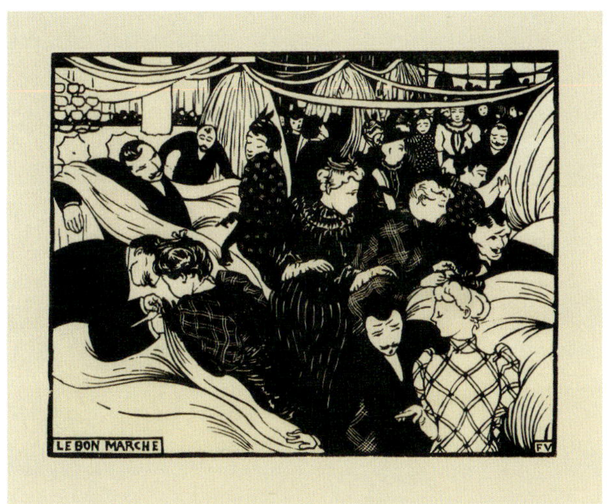

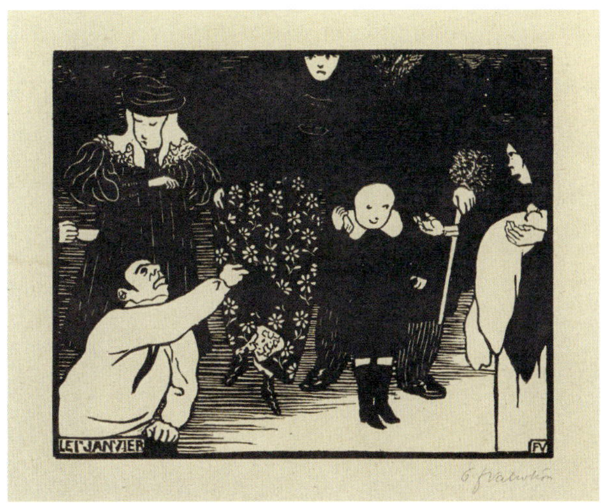

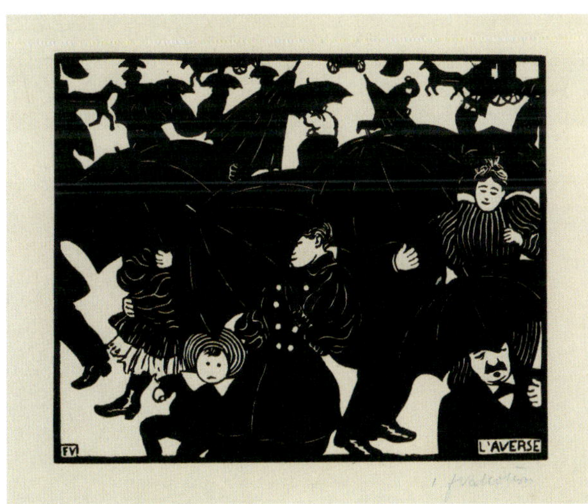

107 | 111 | 110 Félix Vallotton, *The "Bon Marché" Department Store*, 1893 | *The 1st of January*, 1896 | *The Shower*, 1894

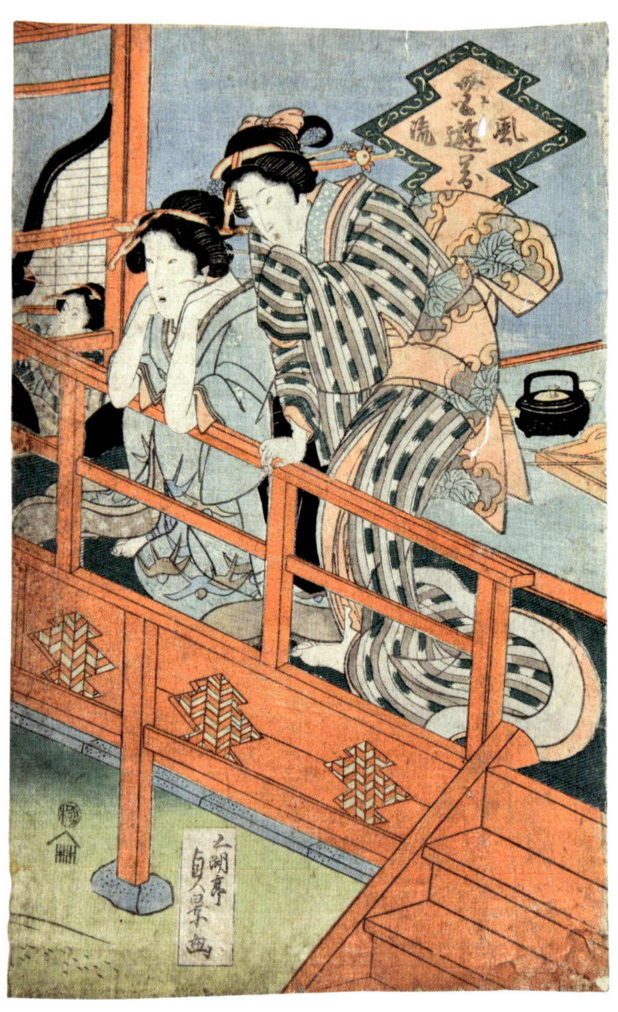

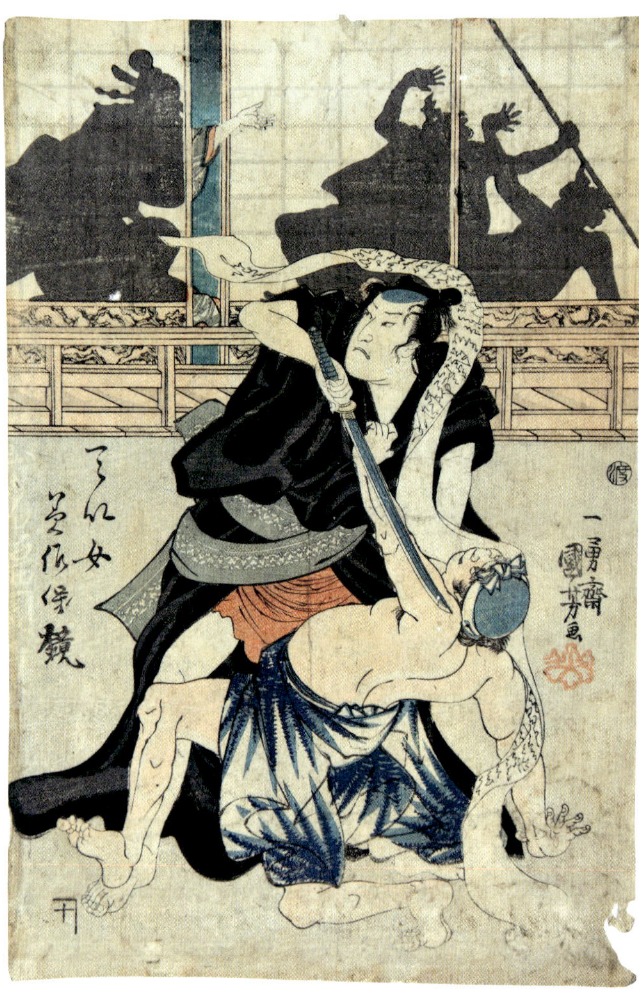

223 Utagawa Sadakage, *Elegant Play of Flowers*, 1818–1830
219 Utagawa Kuniyoshi, *Okon's Lover Fukuoka Mitsugu*, 1843–1847

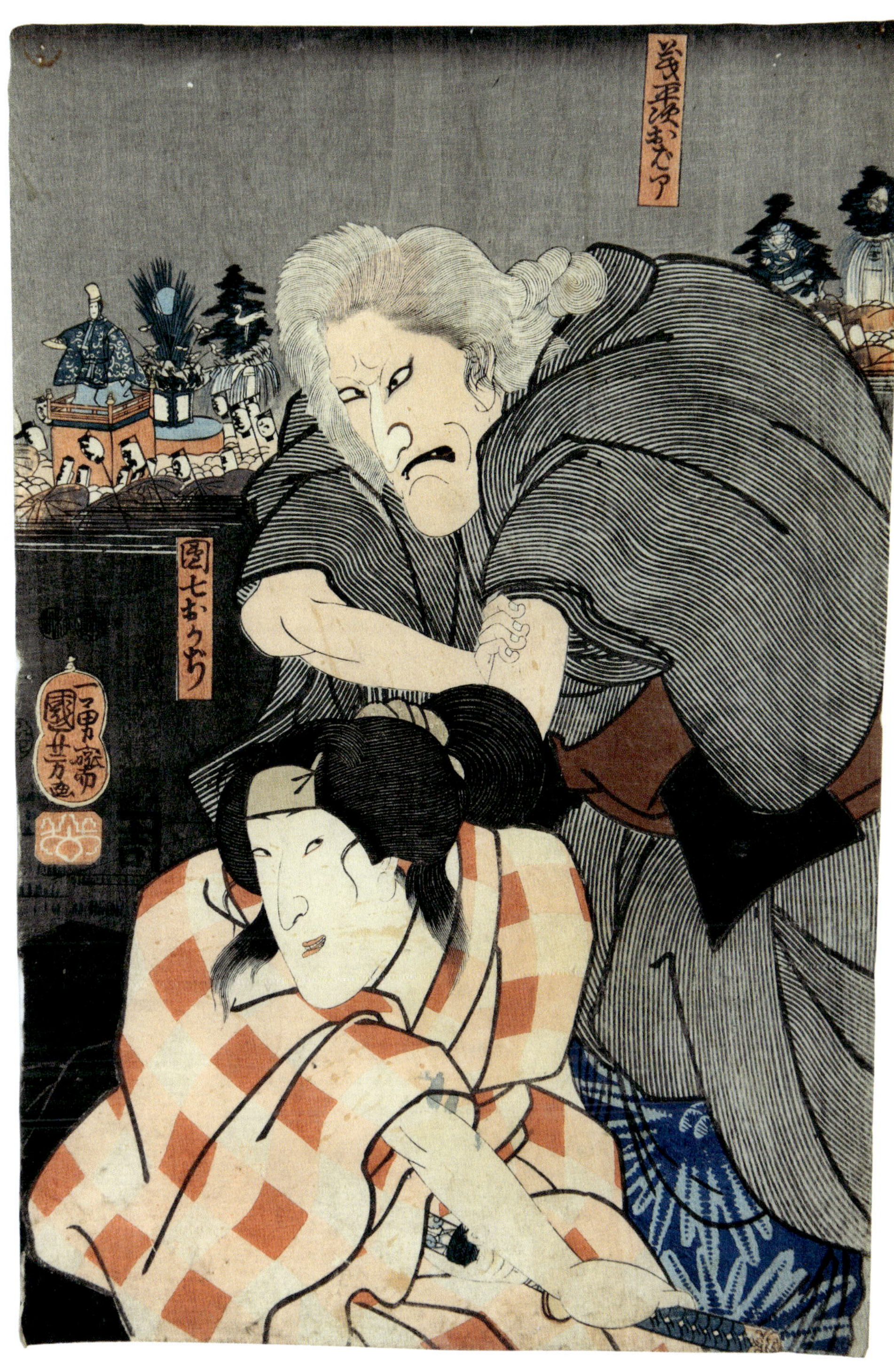

221 Utagawa Kuniyoshi, *The Actor Seki Sanjūro III in the Role of Giheiji Obaba and the Actor Bandō Shūka in the Role of Danshichi Okaji*, 1852

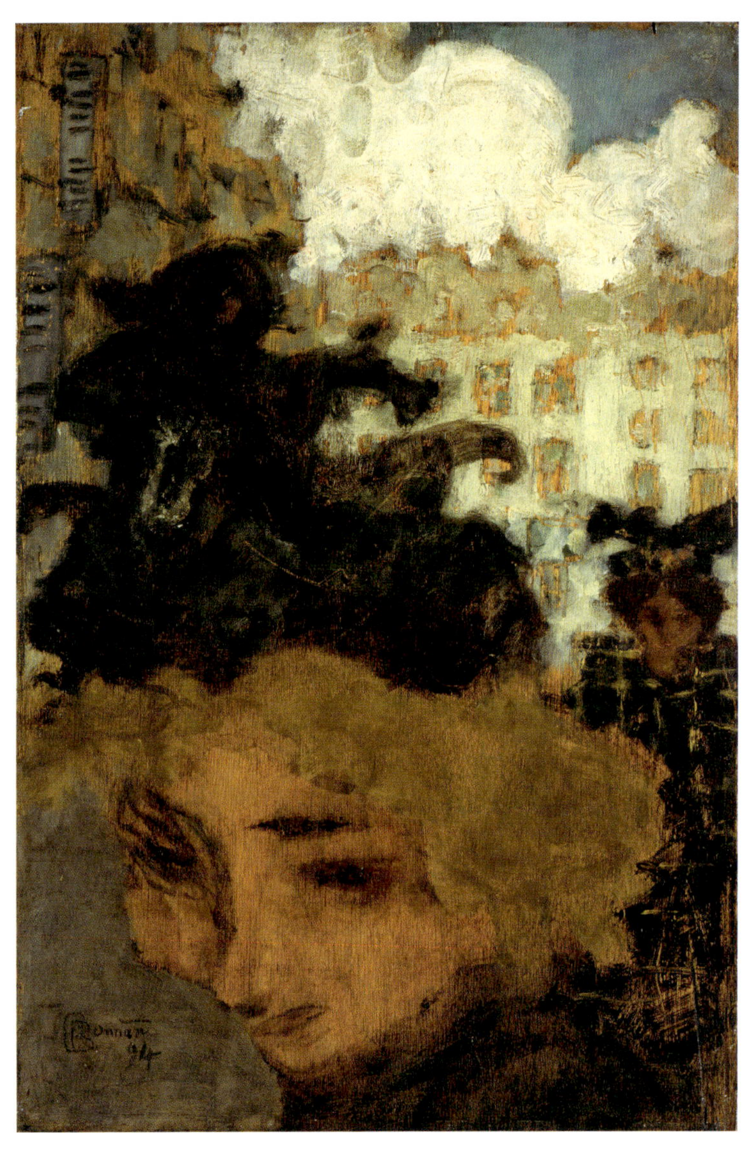

4 Pierre Bonnard, *The Passerby*, 1894

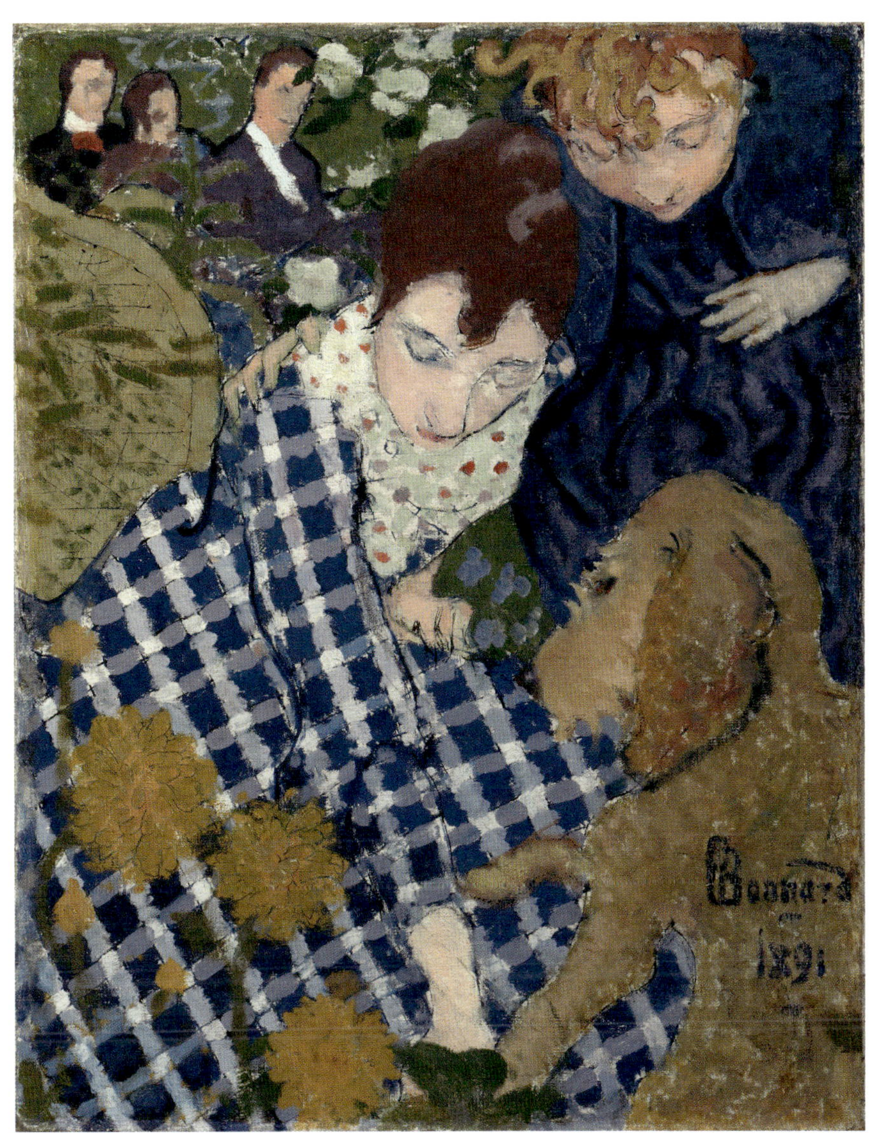

3 Pierre Bonnard, *Women with a Dog*, 1891

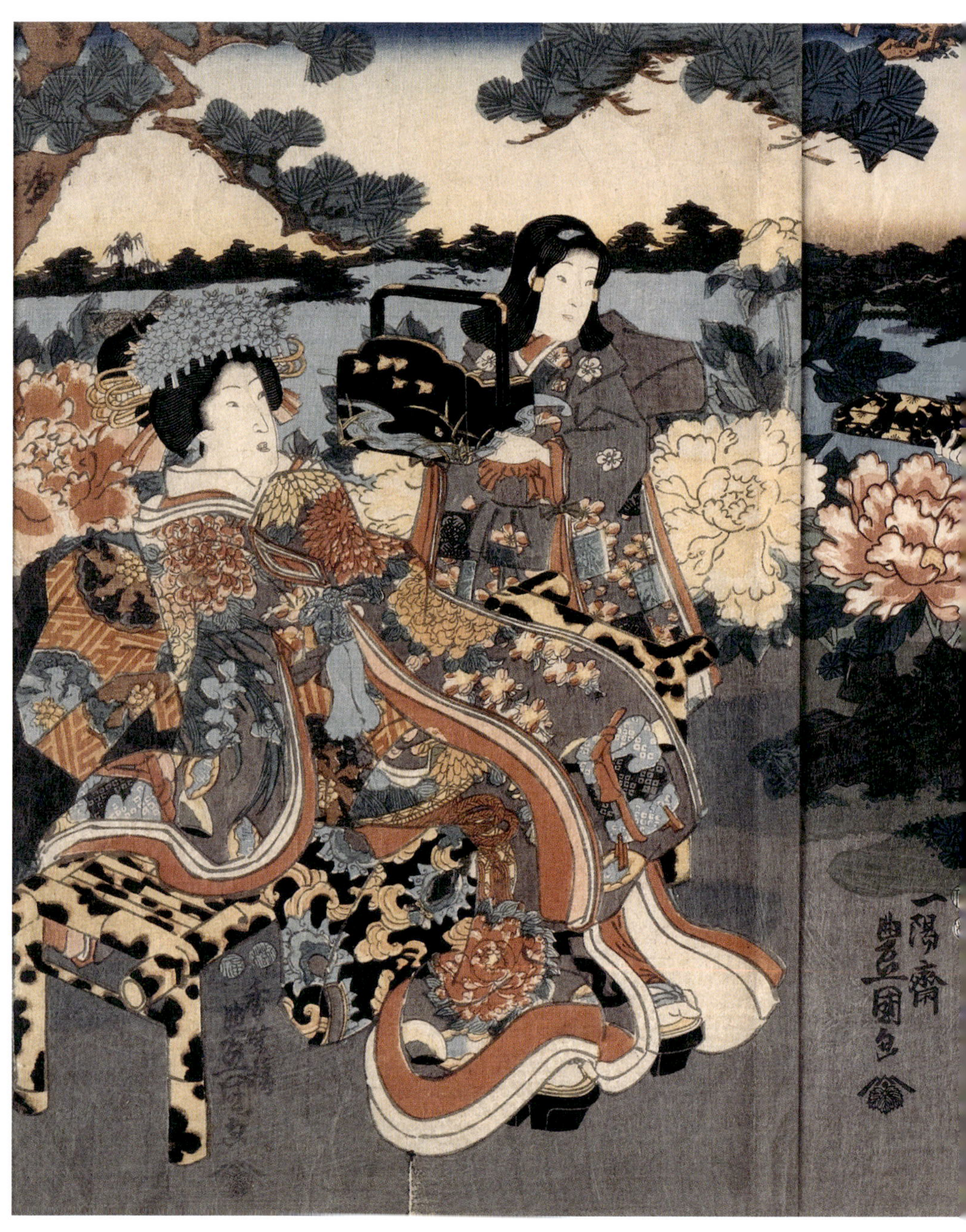

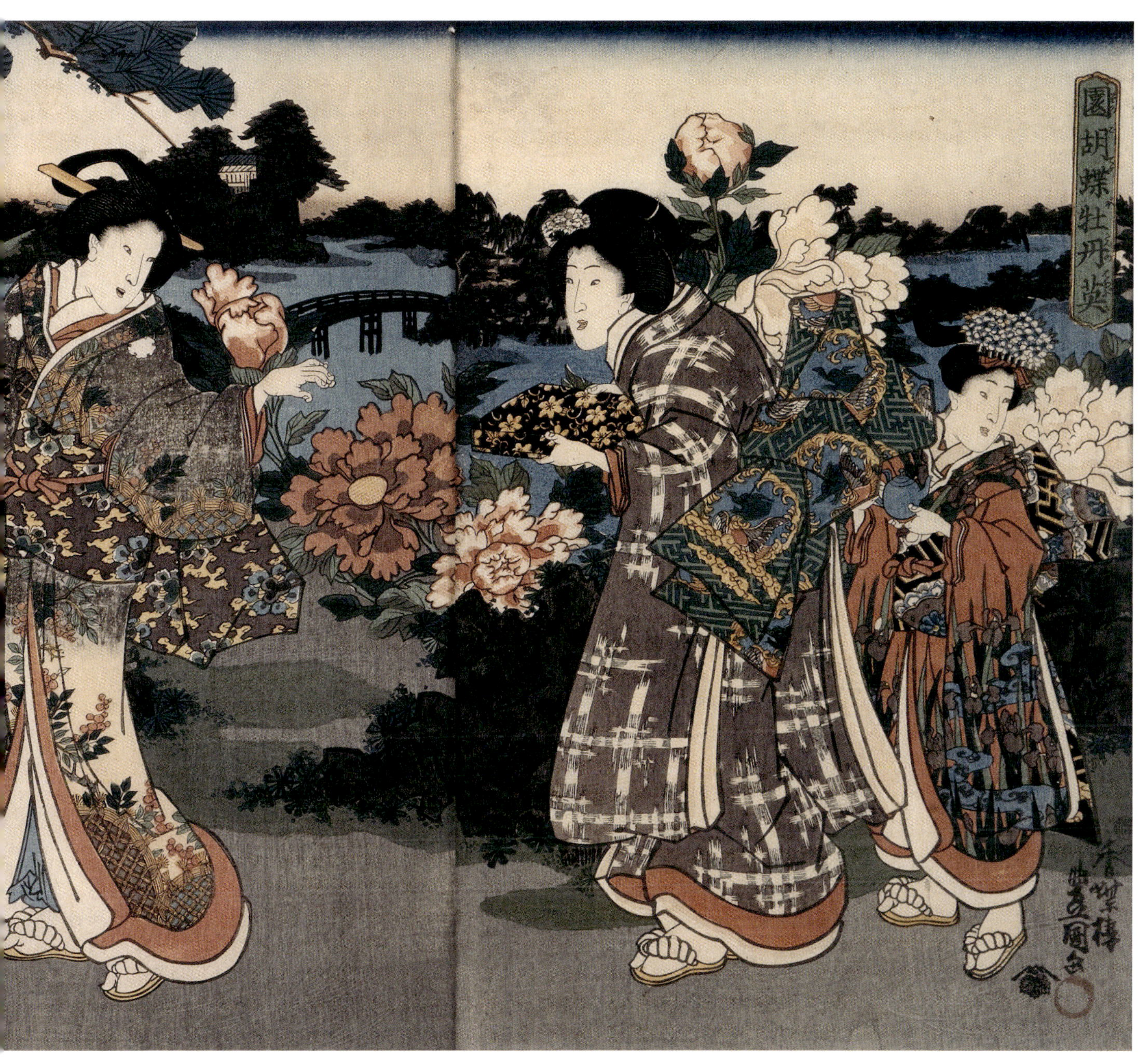

210 Utagawa Kunisada (Toyokuni III), *The Splendour of Butterflies and Peonies in the Garden*, 1849

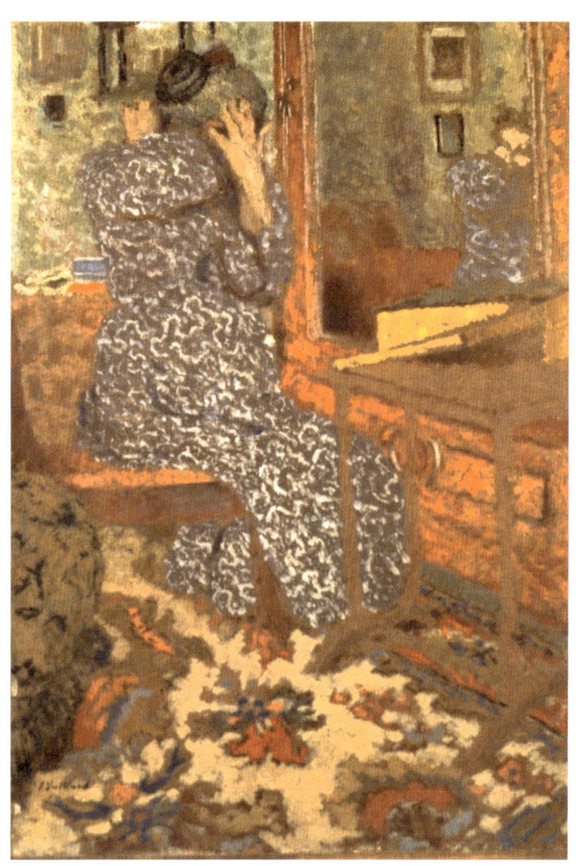

72 Édouard Vuillard, *Madame Vuillard Arranging Her Hair*, 1900

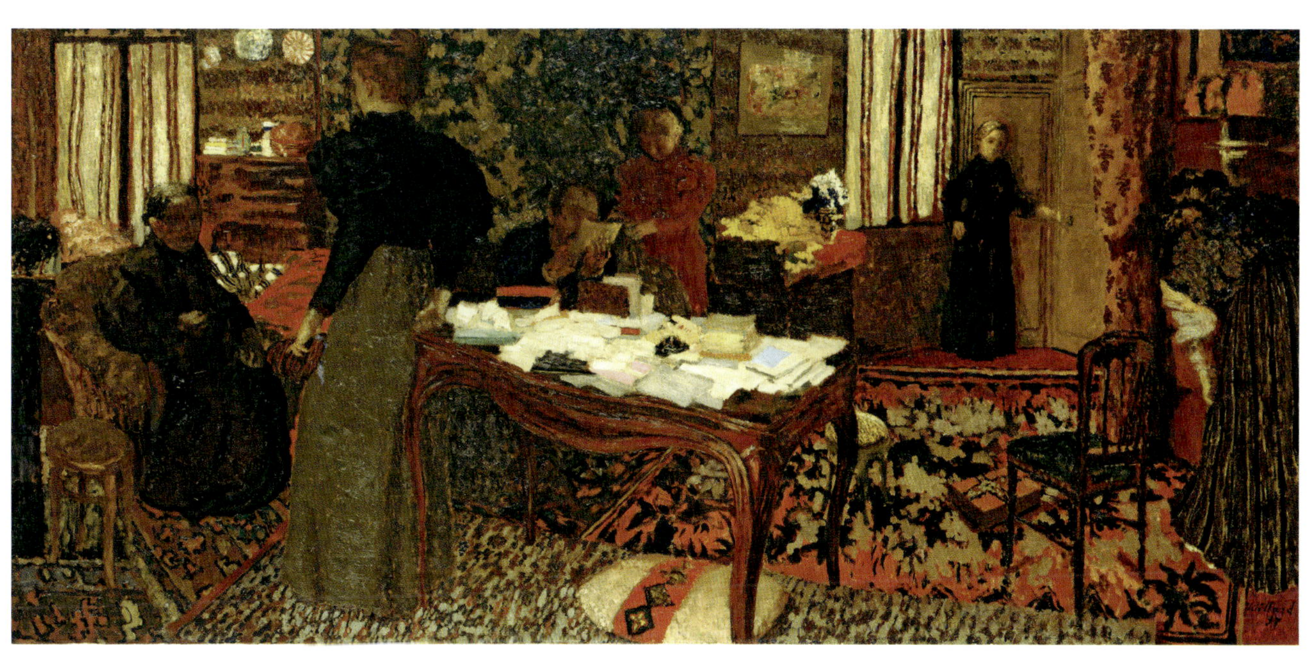

70 Édouard Vuillard, *Large Interior with Six Persons*, 1897

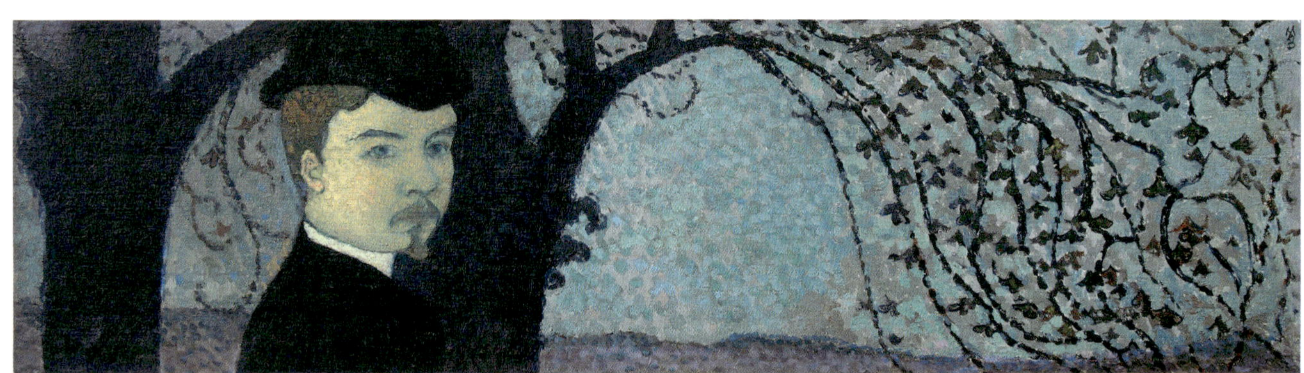

22 Maurice Denis, *Self-Portrait beneath Trees*, circa 1891

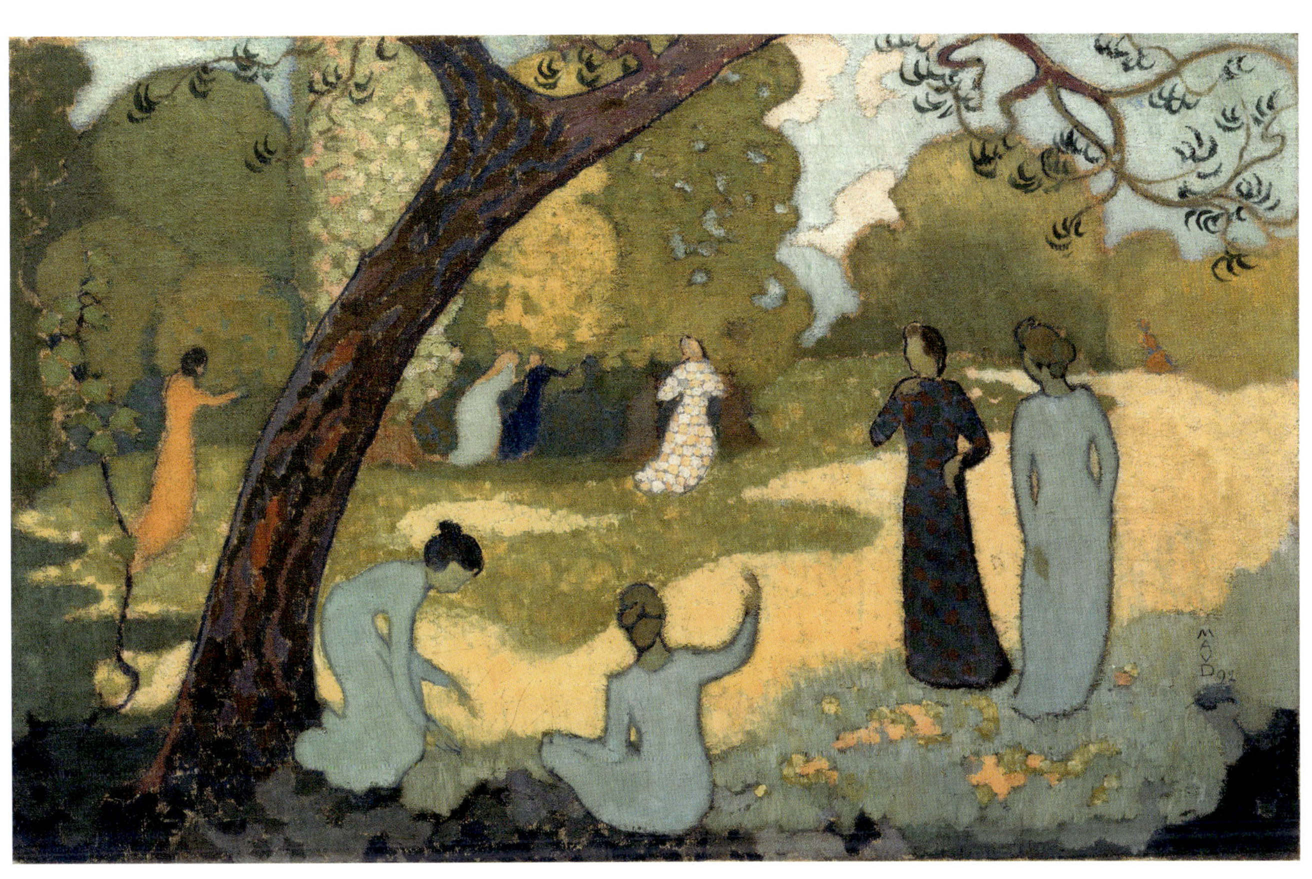

23 Maurice Denis, *July*, 1892

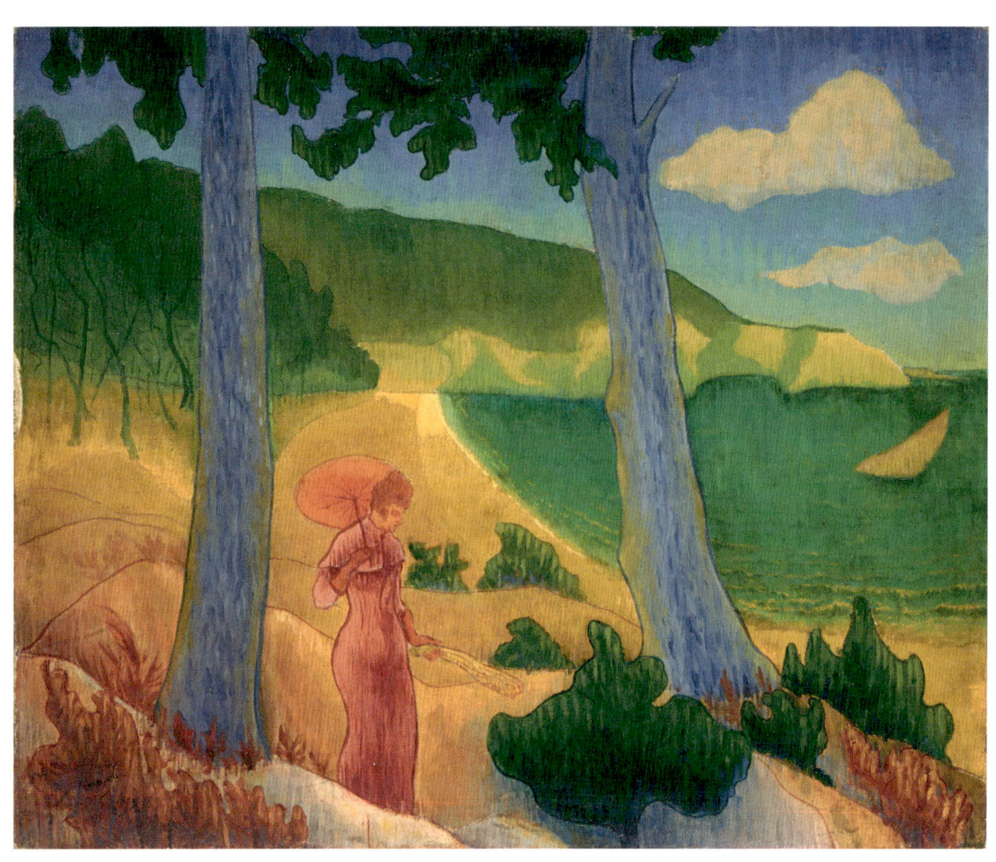

59 Paul Ranson, *Coastline*, 1889

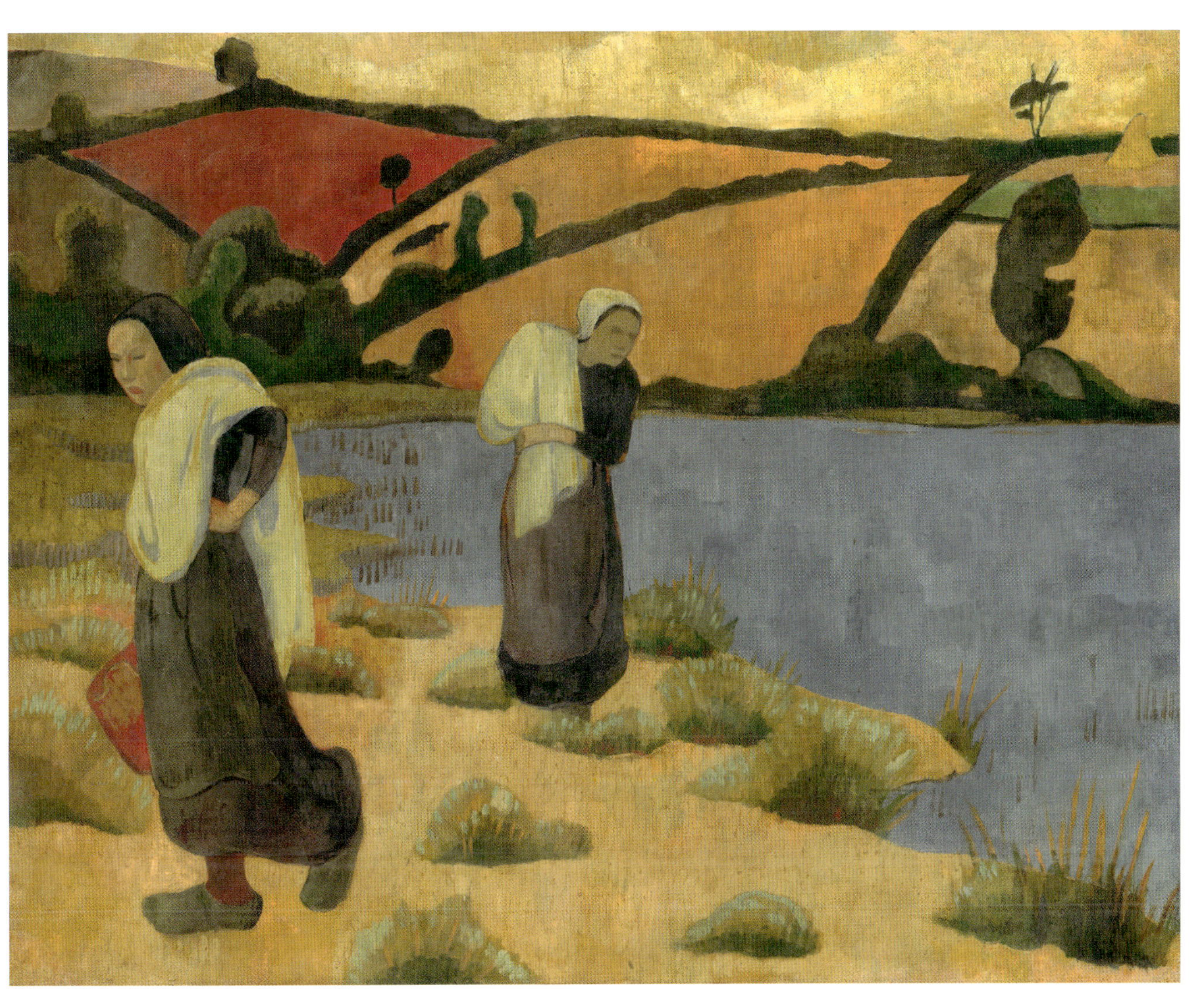

64 Paul Sérusier, *Washerwomen at the Laïta River*, 1892

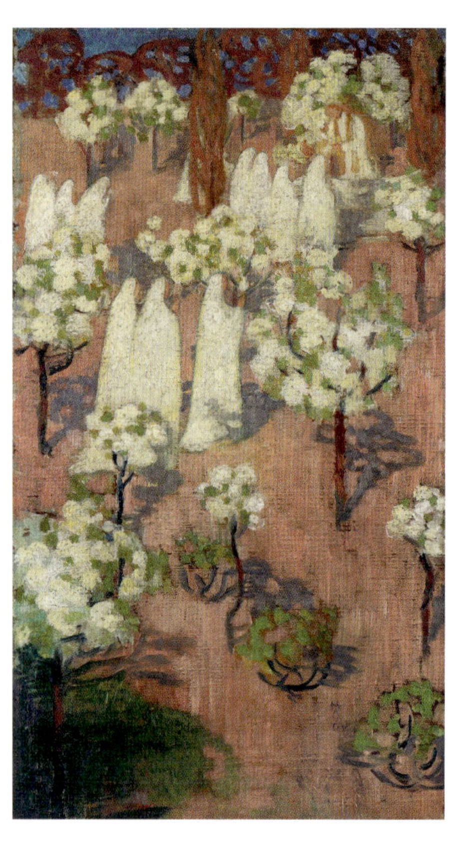

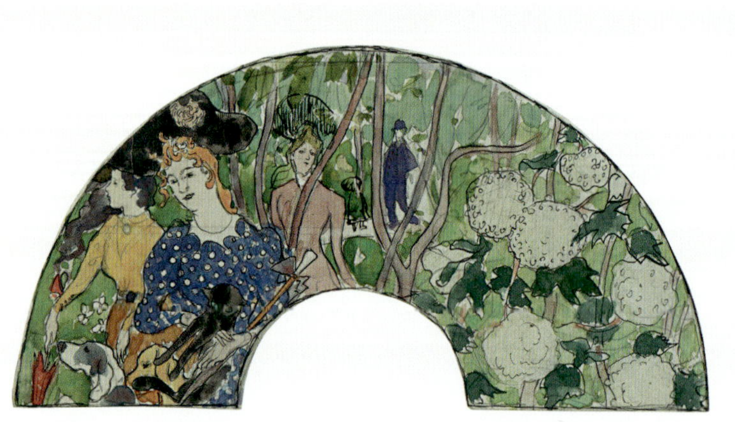

25 Maurice Denis, *Virginal Spring*, 1894
81 Pierre Bonnard, *Women and Flowers*, circa 1891

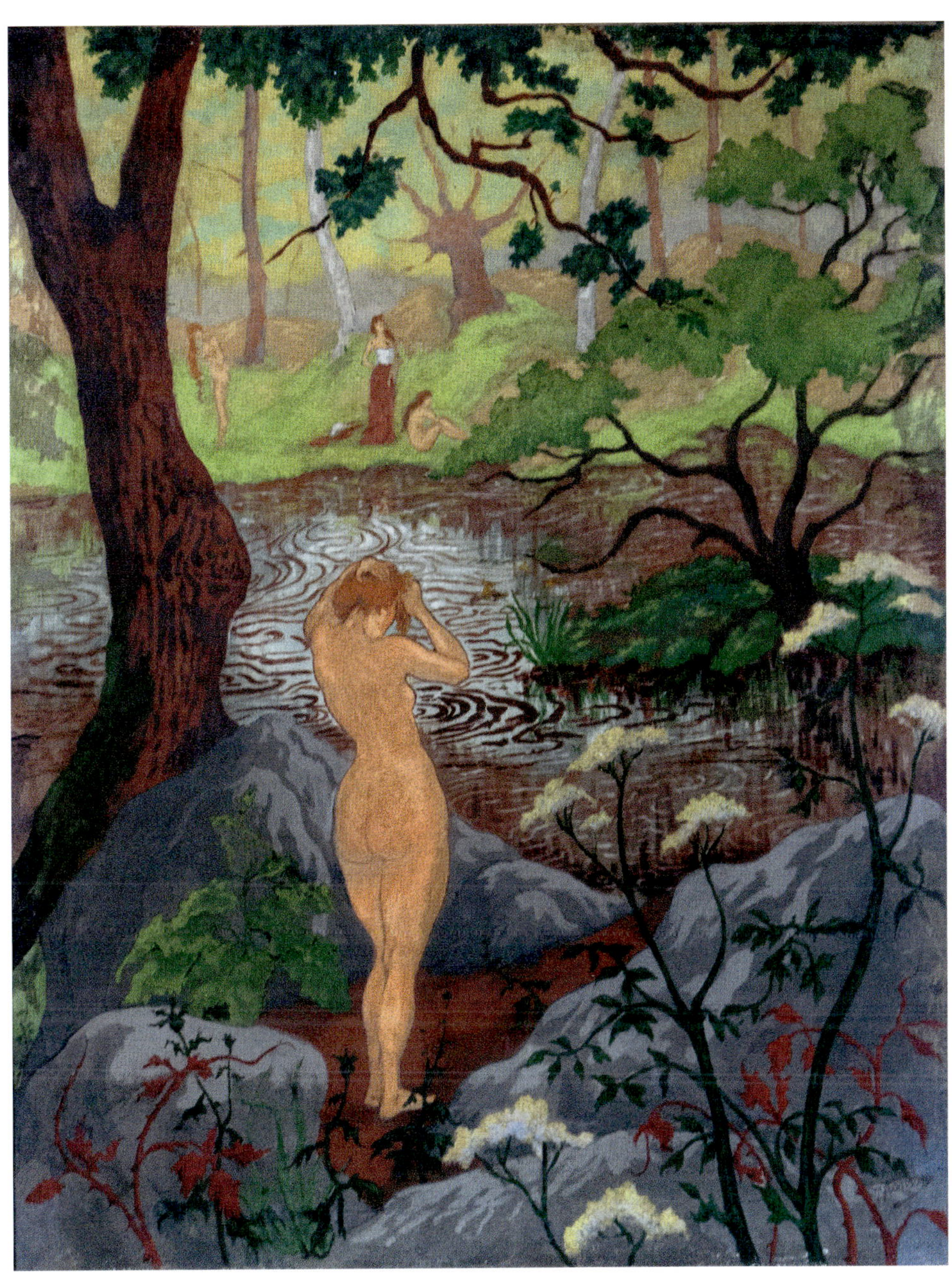

60 Paul Ranson, *Female Nude Arranging Her Hair at the Edge of a Pond*, circa 1897

"A dream of the farthest east" – Monet's garden in Giverny

In 1883, Claude Monet left Poissy in order to settle in the village of Giverny in Normandy about seventy kilometres from Paris. After becoming the owner of his Giverny estate in 1890, he had a water-lily pond built from 1893 onwards. This "water garden" – which Monet had designed as a "treat for the eyes" but also "for use as a painting motif" – was an inexhaustible source of inspiration for the artist, together with the flower garden (p. 302) that spread out in front of the long pink-plastered building.

"As soon as the Japanese peonies arrive, plant them straight away in the right place if the weather allows [...] In March start cultivating the chrysanthemums [...]," wrote Monet to his gardener around 1900. He shared his enthusiasm for the plants and trees from Japan, whose splendour was gradually being discovered by the West, with his friends – the painter Gustave Caillebotte, the writer Octave Mirbeau and the politician Georges Clemenceau. Along with the native plants, there bloomed anemones, peonies and cherry and maple trees from Japan along the paths of his garden. Monet bred chrysanthemums as well, a plant especially revered in the Land of the Rising Sun.

The painter's interest in Japanese flora can also be seen in his *ukiyo-e* collection decorating the walls of his dining room and the small blue salon in his house (p. 54). In particular, Monet owned four Japanese woodblock prints from the series of *Large Flowers* by Katsushika Hokusai (p. 162). In 1924, the writer and art historian Marc Elder reported what Monet is said to have called out in admiration when viewing the print *Peonies and Butterfly* from his collection: "Hokusai ... how powerful his work is! Just look at the butterfly, how it struggles against the wind, and how the flowers bend ... nothing is useless ... life in all its simplicity ..." Indeed, the painter was fascinated by Hokusai's attentive observations of nature, by the sense of vitality flowing out of his woodblock prints and by the conciseness of the imagery. Undoubtedly, Monet's studies of the Japanese masters encouraged him to observe nature in detail. In 1897, Monet chose a chrysanthemum bed in his garden as a motif (p. 307). The painter decided on a close-up view from above, in which the flowers – in luminous red, yellow and orange – stand out against a green background of leaves. Just as Hokusai's flowers "bend", the painter suggests that the petals and leaves are trembling from the delicate movement caused by a breath of wind. The vibrating, saturated surface of the painting gives the impression of vitality and atmosphere, which was so important to Monet.

The "water garden" was bordered by irises, reeds, Japanese peonies, poplars and weeping willows. The water lilies blossomed on the surface of the water and spread out their large leaves. A small bridge, which would later be decorated with wisteria, arched over the pond. This "bridge in the Japanese style", to use Monet's words, is certainly reminiscent of some woodblock prints by Hokusai or Hiroshige (pp. 146, 303). In 1905, the art critic Louis Vauxcelles spoke of a "dream of the farthest east". And the gardener Georges Truffaut even imagined he was "in a suburb of Yokohama". Although Monet by no means wished to imitate the Japanese, some elements certainly did resemble Japanese garden design: the asymmetrical pond, the countless vantage points and the play of reflections of light upon the water.

Between 1899 and 1900, Monet created an ensemble of paintings with the motif of the Japanese bridge (pp. 304, 305), only a section of which is shown, surrounded by luxuriant nature reflected in the surface of the water covered in luminously coloured water lilies. The painter trimmed his motif very deliberately – a very widespread method in Japanese art (pp. 46, 214), the effects of which Monet studied very closely. Thus, for example, the Duc de Trévise reported the following remark by Monet in 1927: "What we appreciated above all in the West was the bold fashion of designing their subjects: those people [the Japanese] have taught us to compose differently, there is no doubt about that."

From 1903, Monet gradually abandoned the motif of the Japanese bridge in order to devote himself solely to the subject of the water lilies and the reflecting surface of his pond. In 1909, the artist exhibited a novel ensemble of paintings that he called "water landscapes" at Galerie Durand-Ruel. From 1914, he took even more radical paths with his studies by selecting a larger format for his pictures and taking a much closer approach to his motifs.

In the course of an increasingly radical development of impressionism, Monet attempted to record the fleeting moment. He wanted to capture the reflections of light, the moods and metamorphoses. And he frequently depicted the effects perceived on the water: the blue reflection of a sky dotted with white clouds (p. 309), the green harmony of the weeping willows, the reflections of which merge with the leaves of the water lilies (p. 308), a golden atmosphere that immerses the picture in a diffuse light (p. 313), or the pink and violet colouring of the sky and the air, spreading out in iridescence (pp. 310–311). The study of the Japanese aesthetic, in which the wind, the rain and storms were common motifs (pp. 149, 192), served to reinforce Monet in his subtle observation of nature and its metamorphoses.

By concentrating on one single motif and teasing out its endlessly fine variations, Monet continued the serial work that he had already carried out intensively in the 1890s. Japanese woodblock prints are also likely to have influenced the painter then, as the creation of series was a common method for *ukiyo-e* colour woodblock prints. Some of the most famous examples include Hokusai's series *36 Views of Mount Fuji* (pp. 147, 167, 192), of which Monet owned nine prints.

While concentrating on the reflecting surface of his pond, Monet dispensed with all reference points; the bridge, the river bank and the trees disappeared. He even omitted the horizon so that the water occupied the entire area of his painting. This means that the surface appears to reach out towards the viewer in a manner similar to some Japanese woodblock prints (pp. 208, 209). The extreme spatial construction was joined by an extraordinarily free arrangement of water lilies. Monet did not try to place them at the centre or to arrange them symmetrically – quite the contrary: without hesitation, he positioned them off-centre or in isolation in the picture, sometimes even trimming them when they ended up at the edges of the composition. This freedom in arranging pictorial motifs is also found in Japanese art, as the art critic Roger Marx emphasised. In an article published in *Gazette des Beaux-Arts* in 1909, he compared Monet's arbitrary arrangement with that of the decorative motifs on Japanese textiles (*fukusa*).

In 1914, the painter embarked on a massive project that would ultimately lead to the *Grandes Décorations* of Musée de l'Orangerie in Paris, an ensemble of twenty-two panels hung in two oval rooms, which had been designed especially for them. The painting held by Kunsthaus Zürich is one of those pictures that Monet excluded from the final project (pp. 310–311). It shows the radical change in scale very clearly. The reflecting surface of the pond, from which some blossoming water lilies emerge, stretches across an area that is two metres high and six metres wide – only a few irises and willow branches suggest the water's edge. The viewer is physically surrounded by a piece of nature, an effect that can also be found in Japanese art. Life-sized illustrations of landscapes were brought into Japanese interiors by folding screens (*byōbu*) and, even more so, by movable partition walls (*fusuma*) that were frequently decorated with paintings on paper or silk.

Claire Guitton

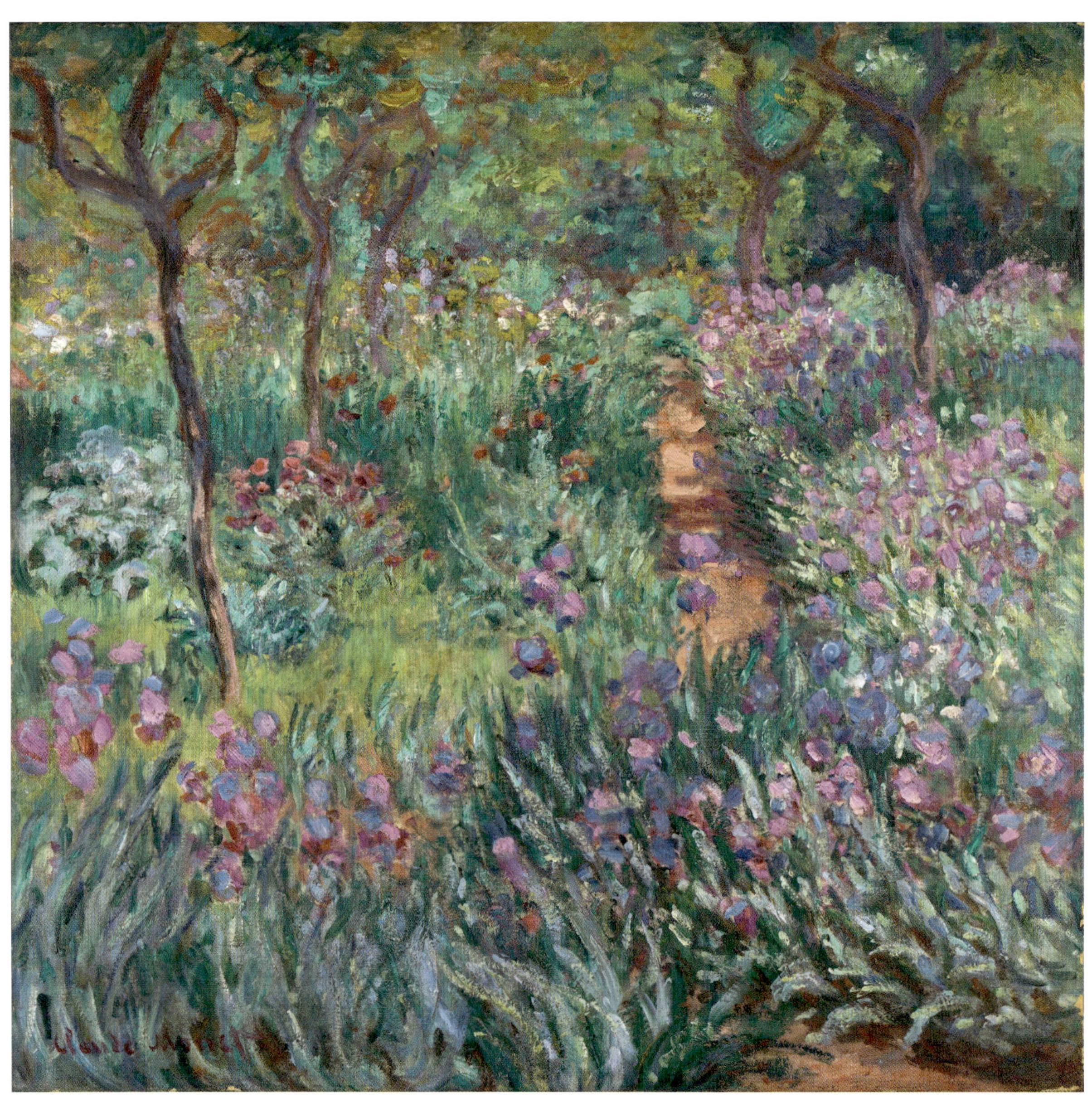

52 Claude Monet, *The Artist's Garden in Giverny*, 1900

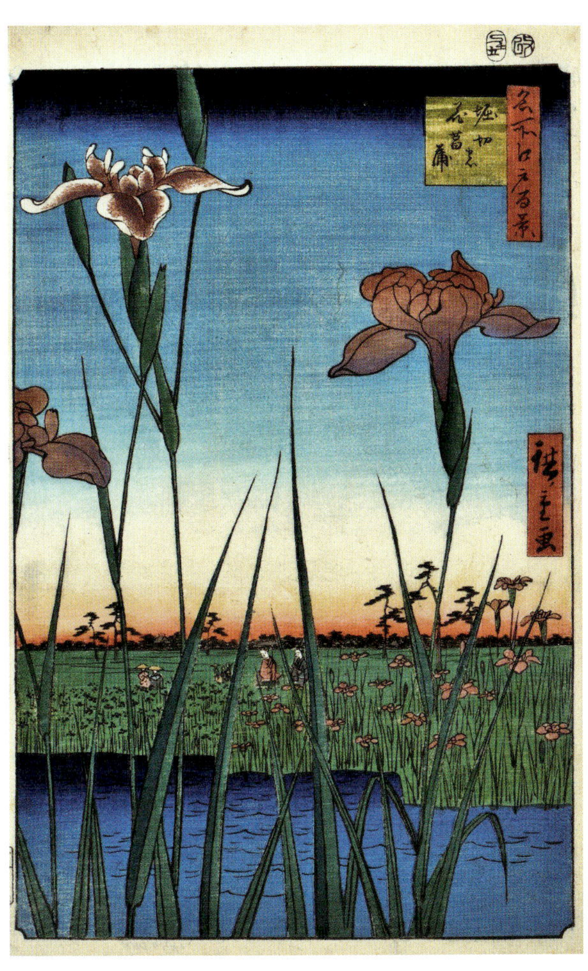

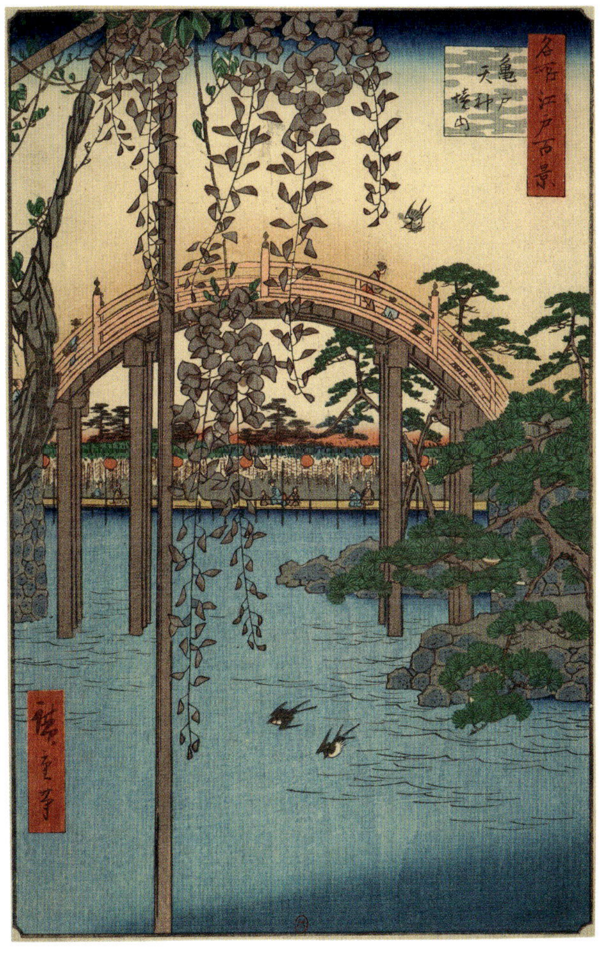

203j | 203k Utagawa Hiroshige, *Horikiri Iris Garden*, 1857 | *Inside Kameido Tenjin Shrine*, 1856

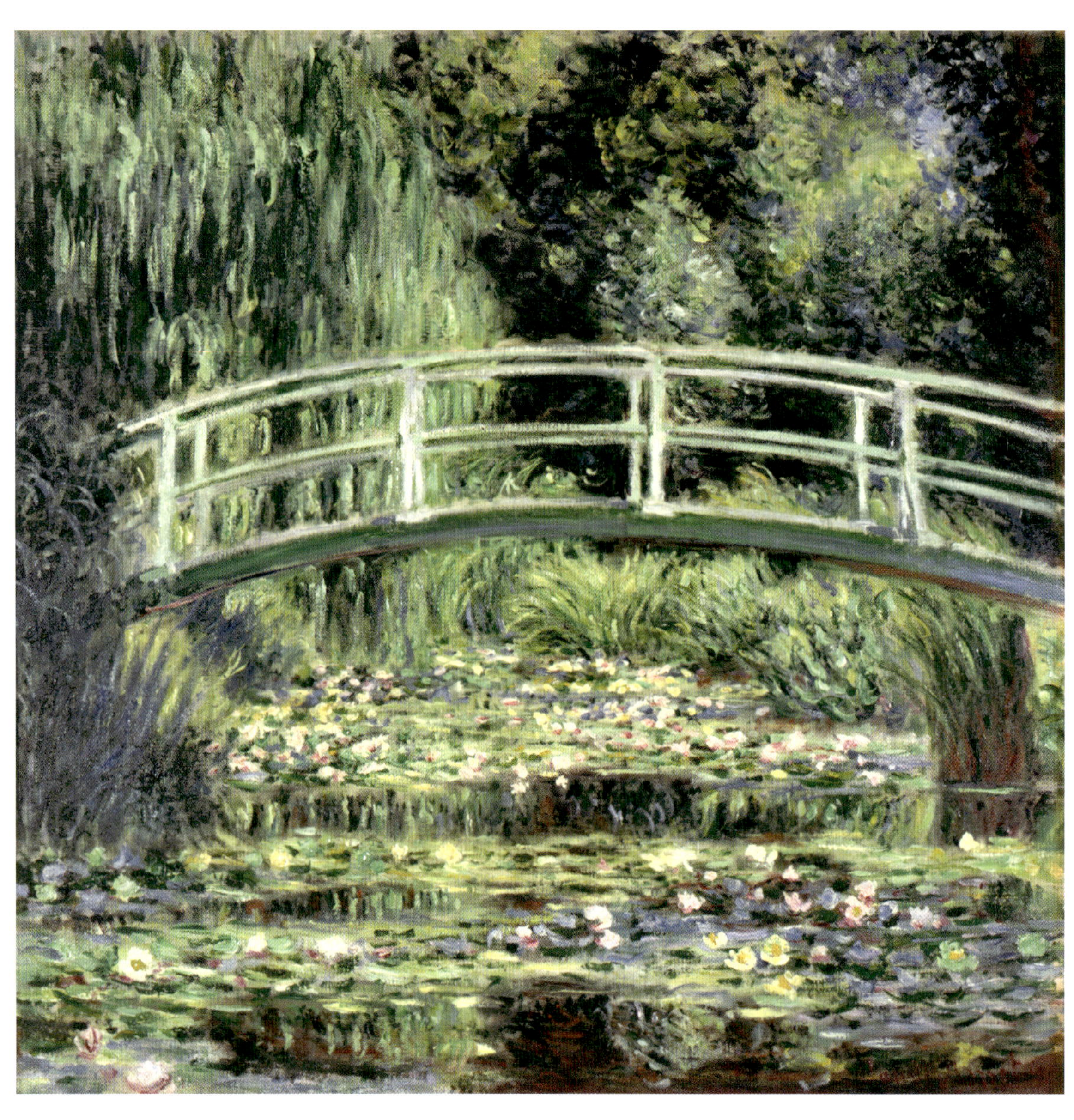

50 Claude Monet, *Water-Lily Pond*, 1899

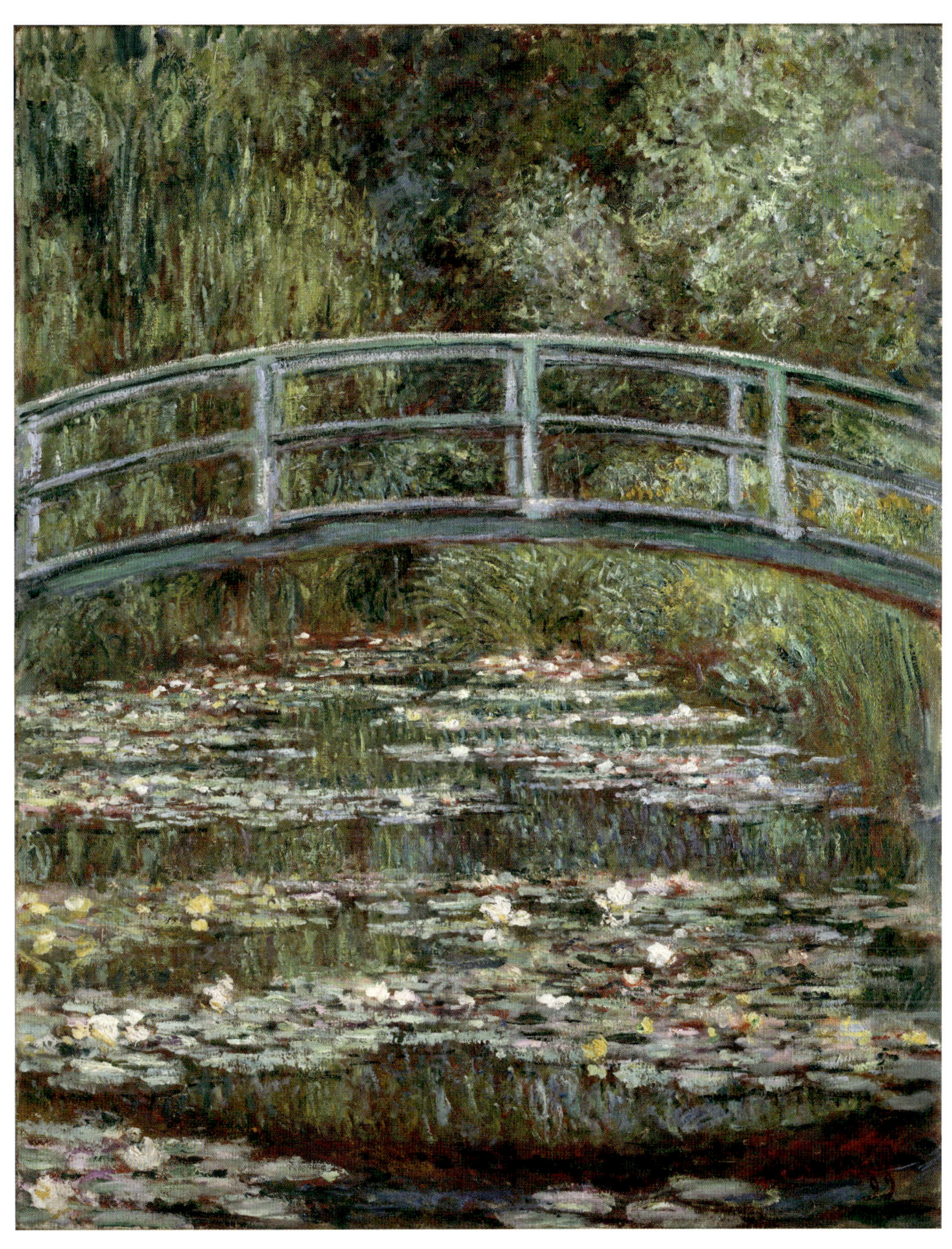

51 Claude Monet, *Bridge over a Pond of Water Lilies*, 1899

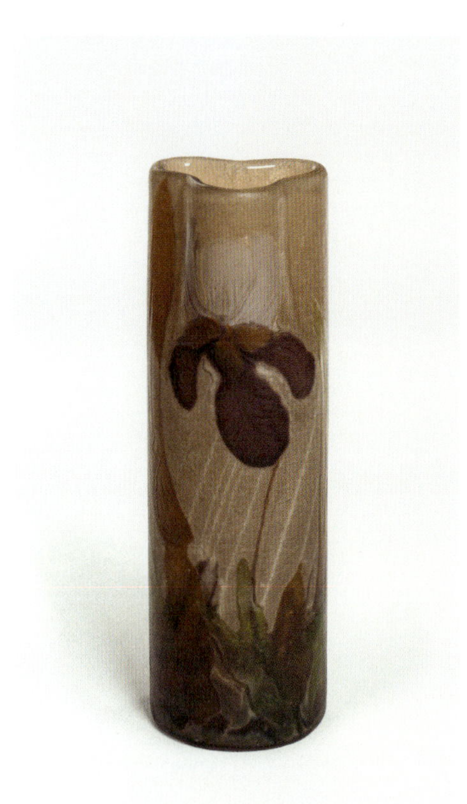

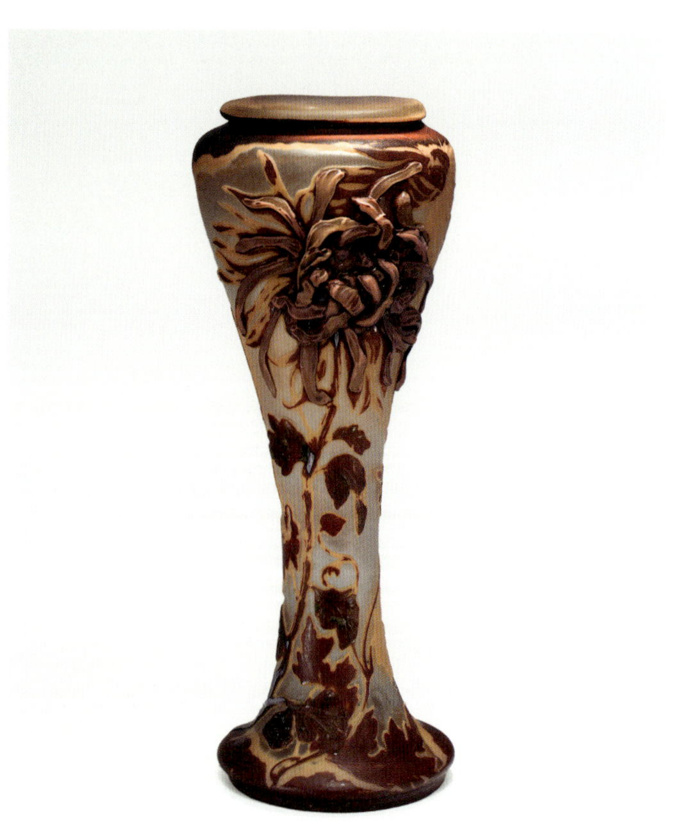

142 | 145 Émile Gallé, *Vase*, 1898/1900 | *Vase*, circa 1901–1903

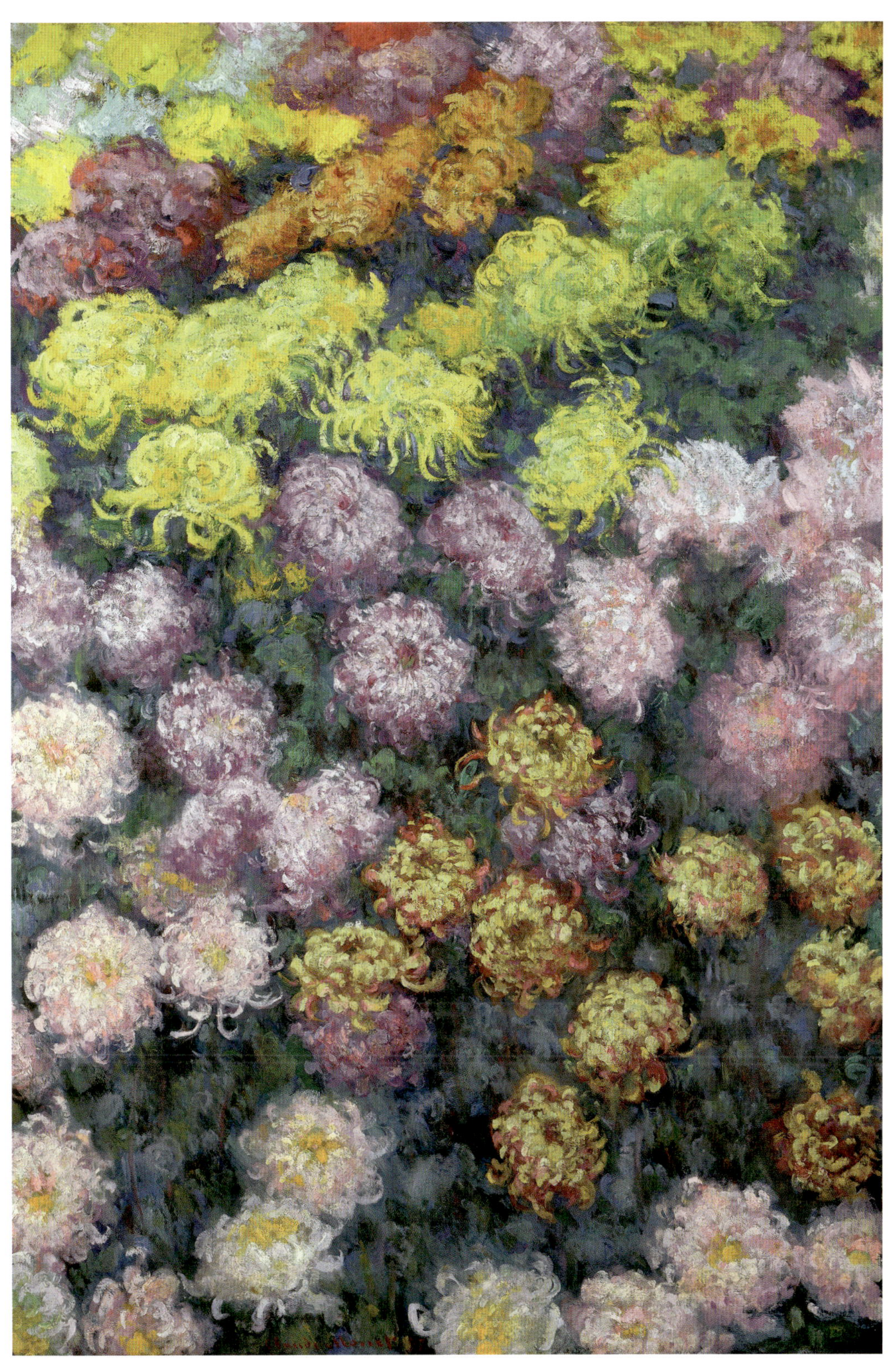

49 Claude Monet, *Bed of Chrysanthemums*, 1897

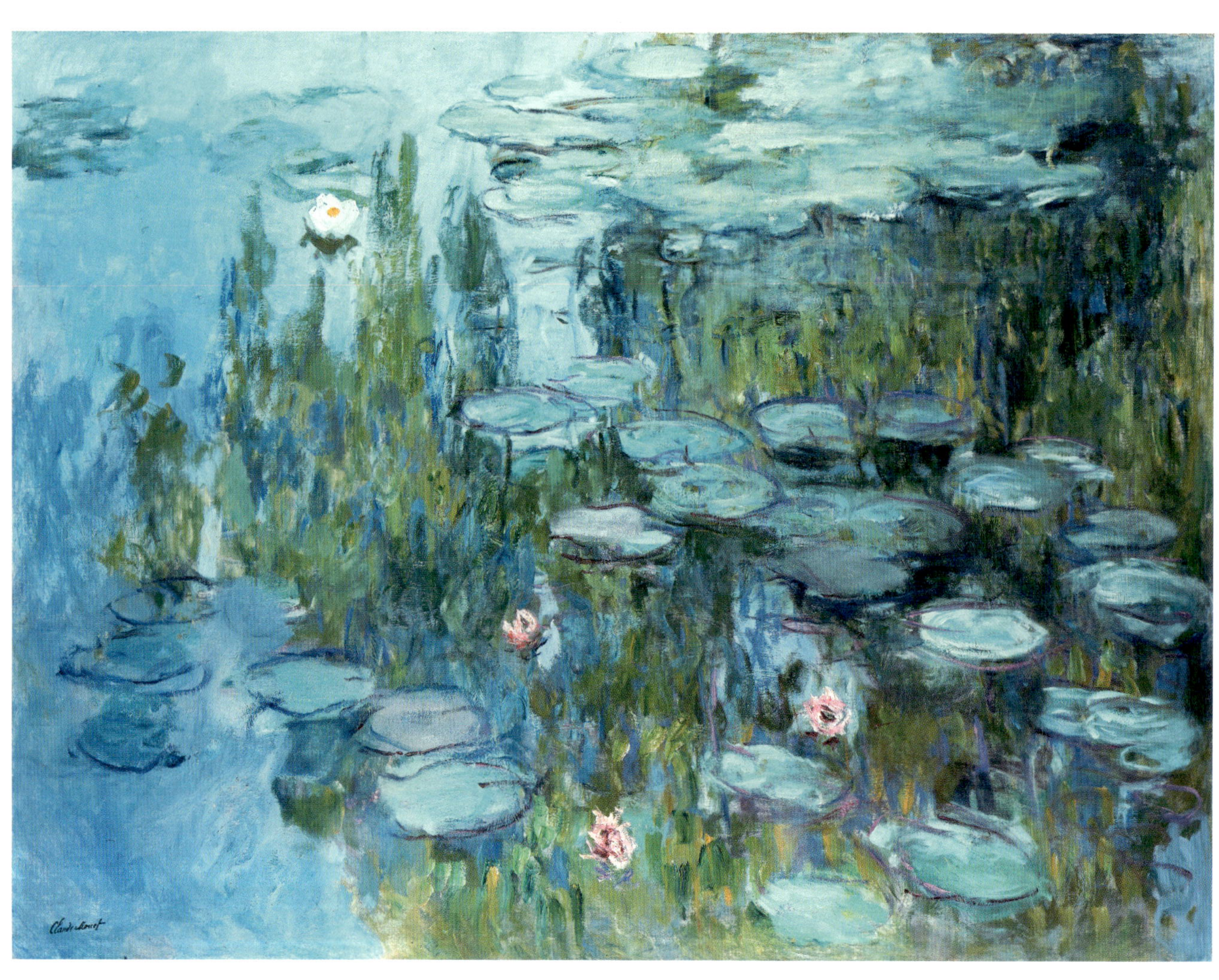

54 Claude Monet, *Water-Lilies*, circa 1915

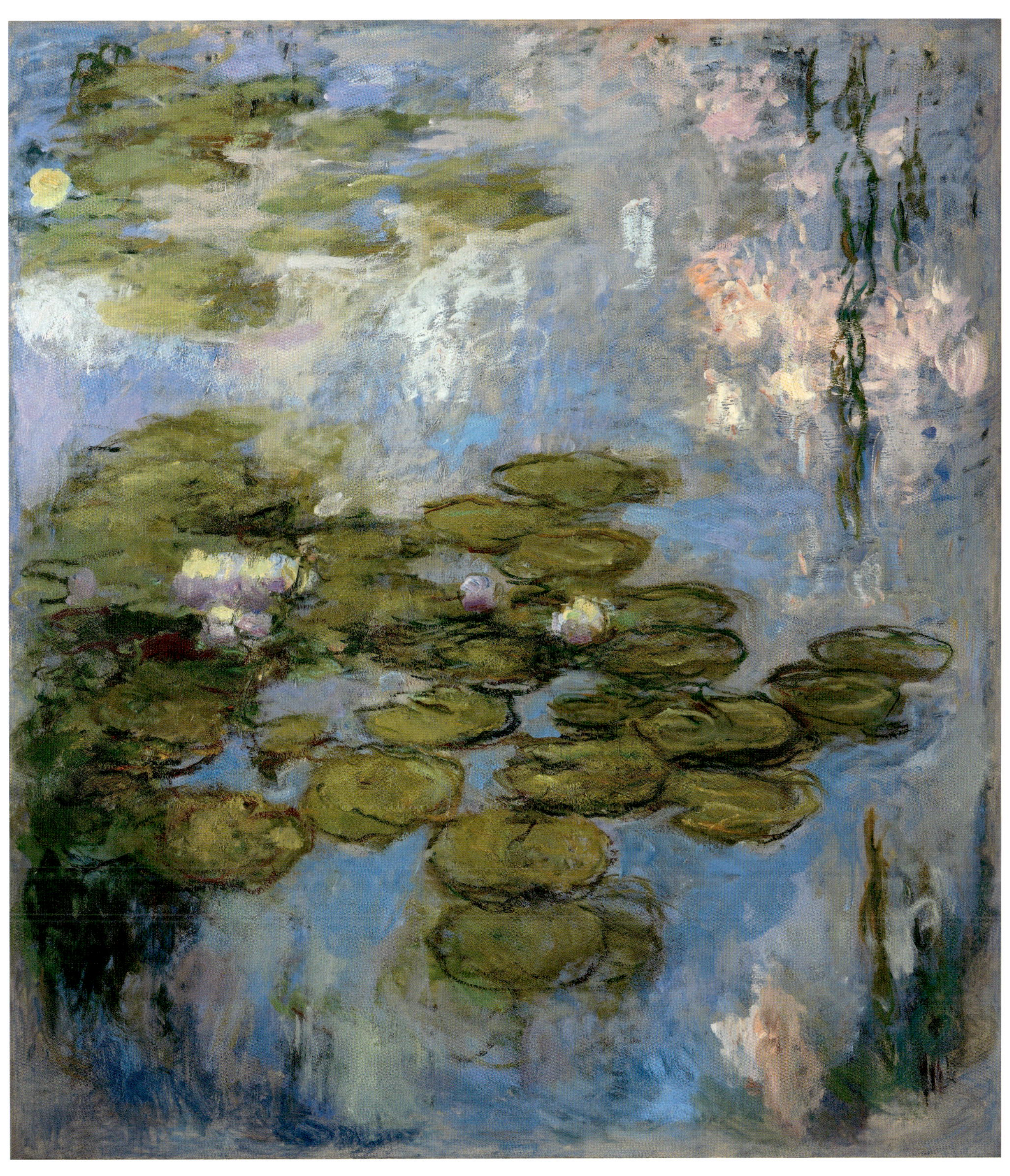

56 Claude Monet, *Water-Lilies*, 1916/1919

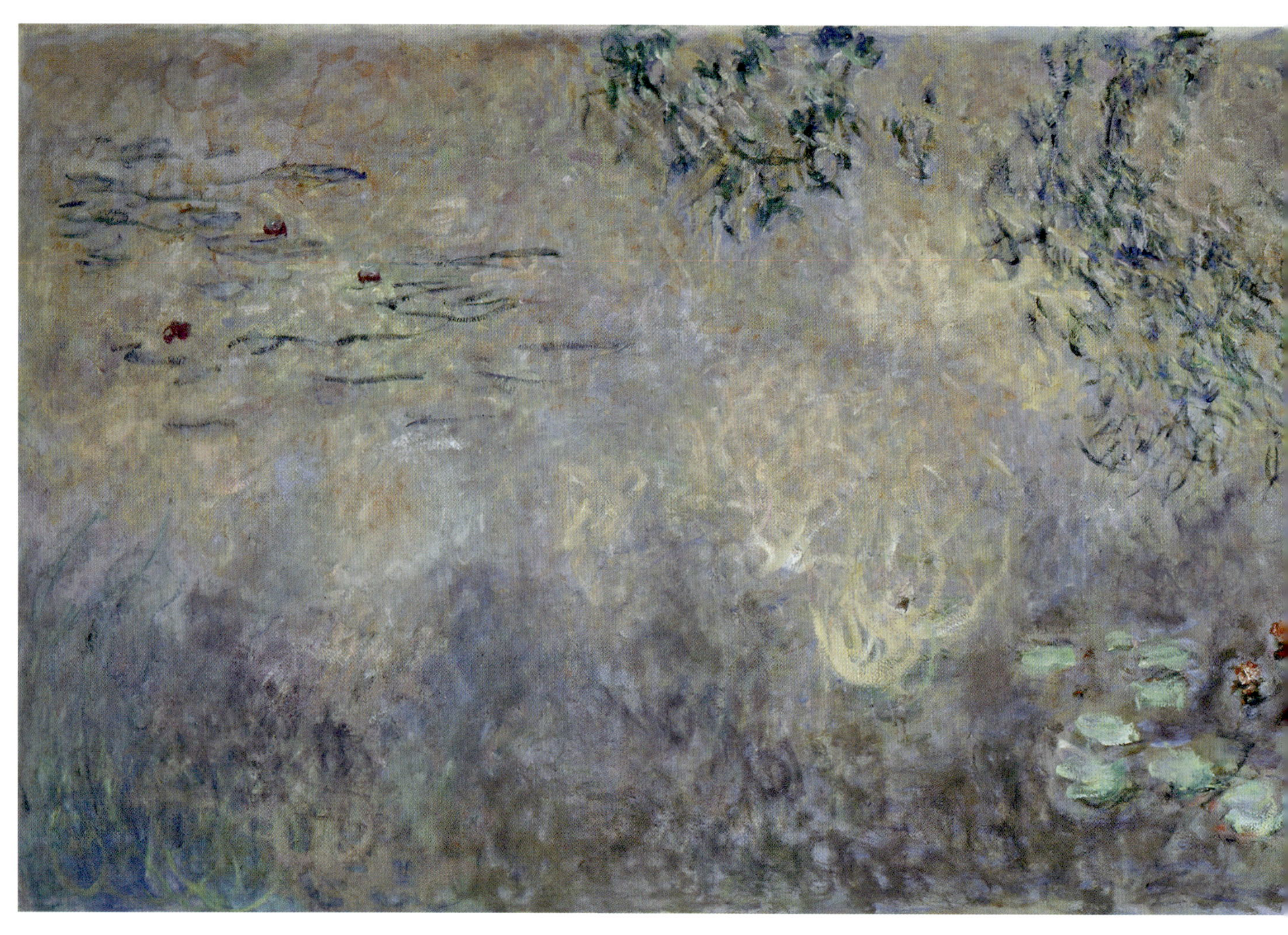

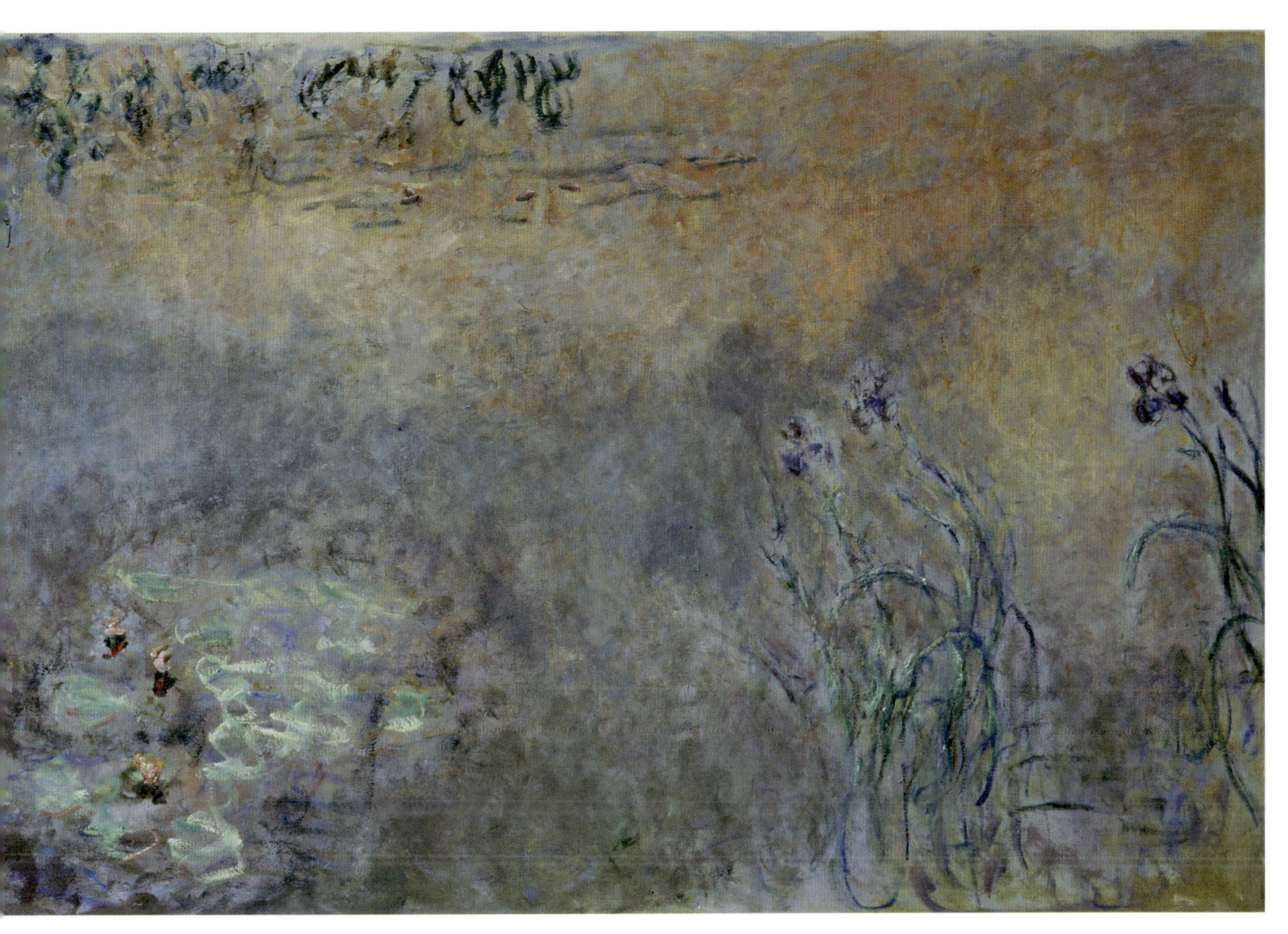

53 Claude Monet, *Water-Lily Pond with Irises*, 1914/1922

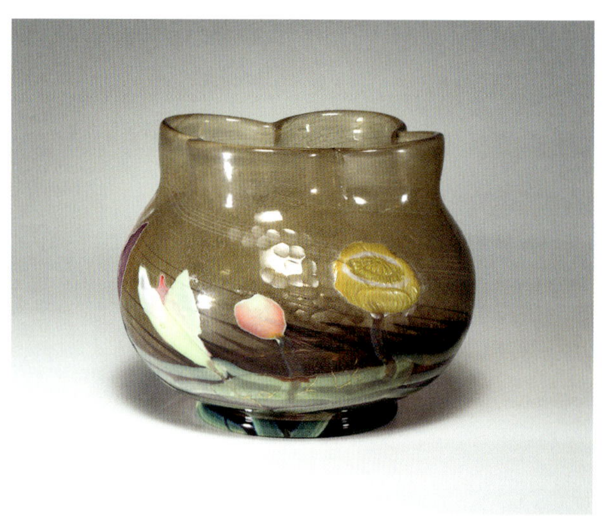

143 Émile Gallé, *Vase*, circa 1898–1900

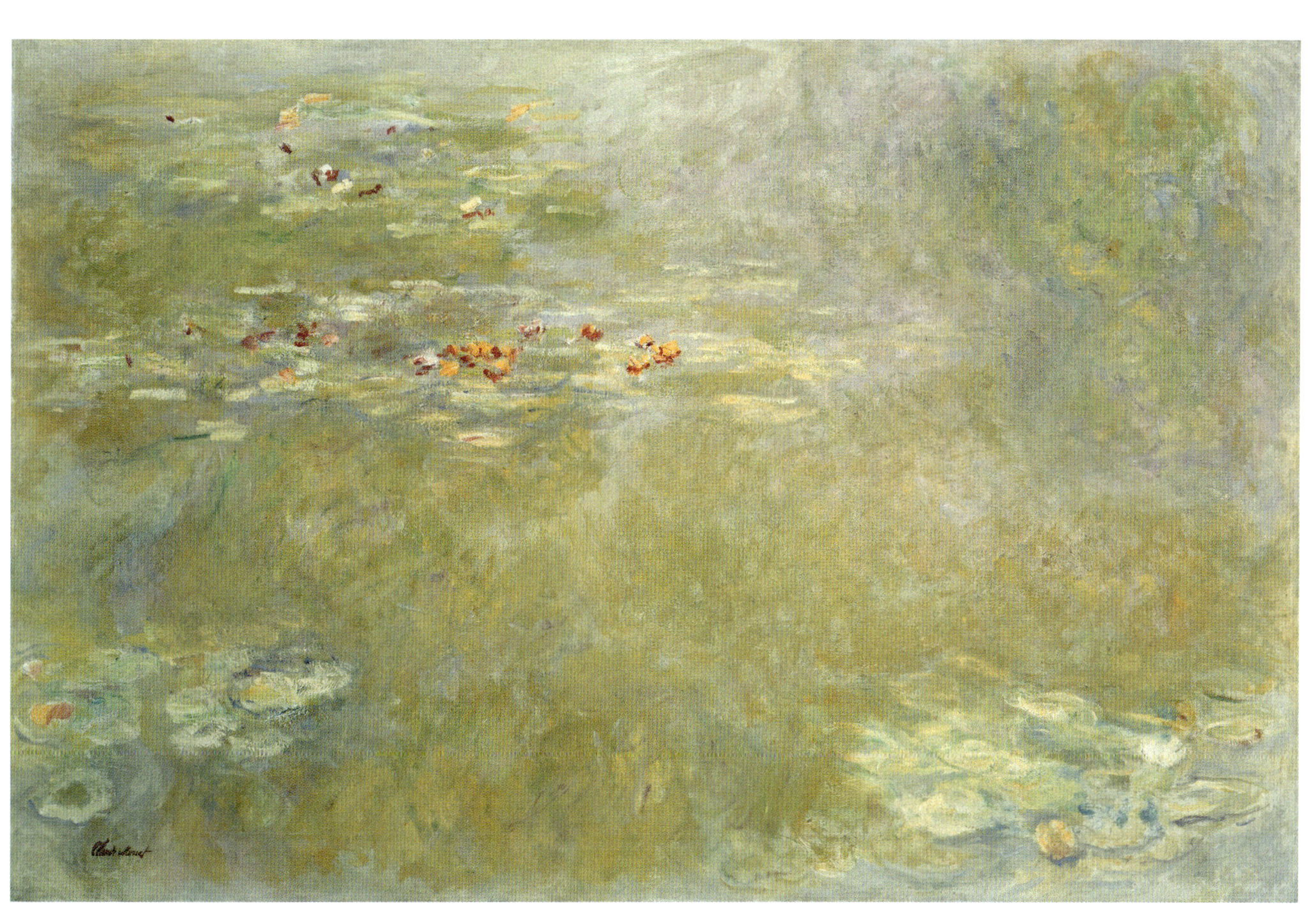

55 Claude Monet, *The Water-Lily Pond*, circa 1916

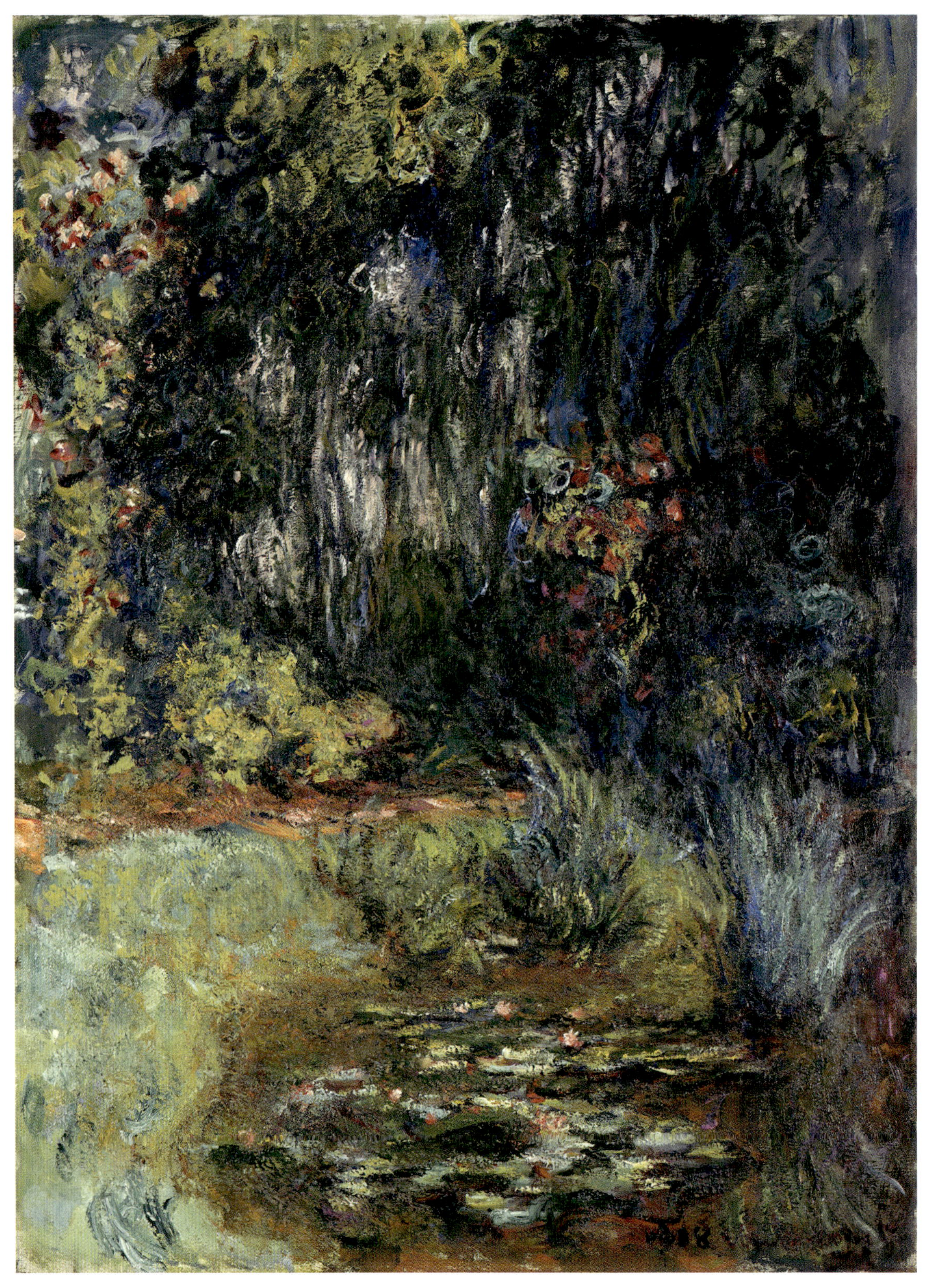

58 Claude Monet, *The Water-Lily Pond*, 1918

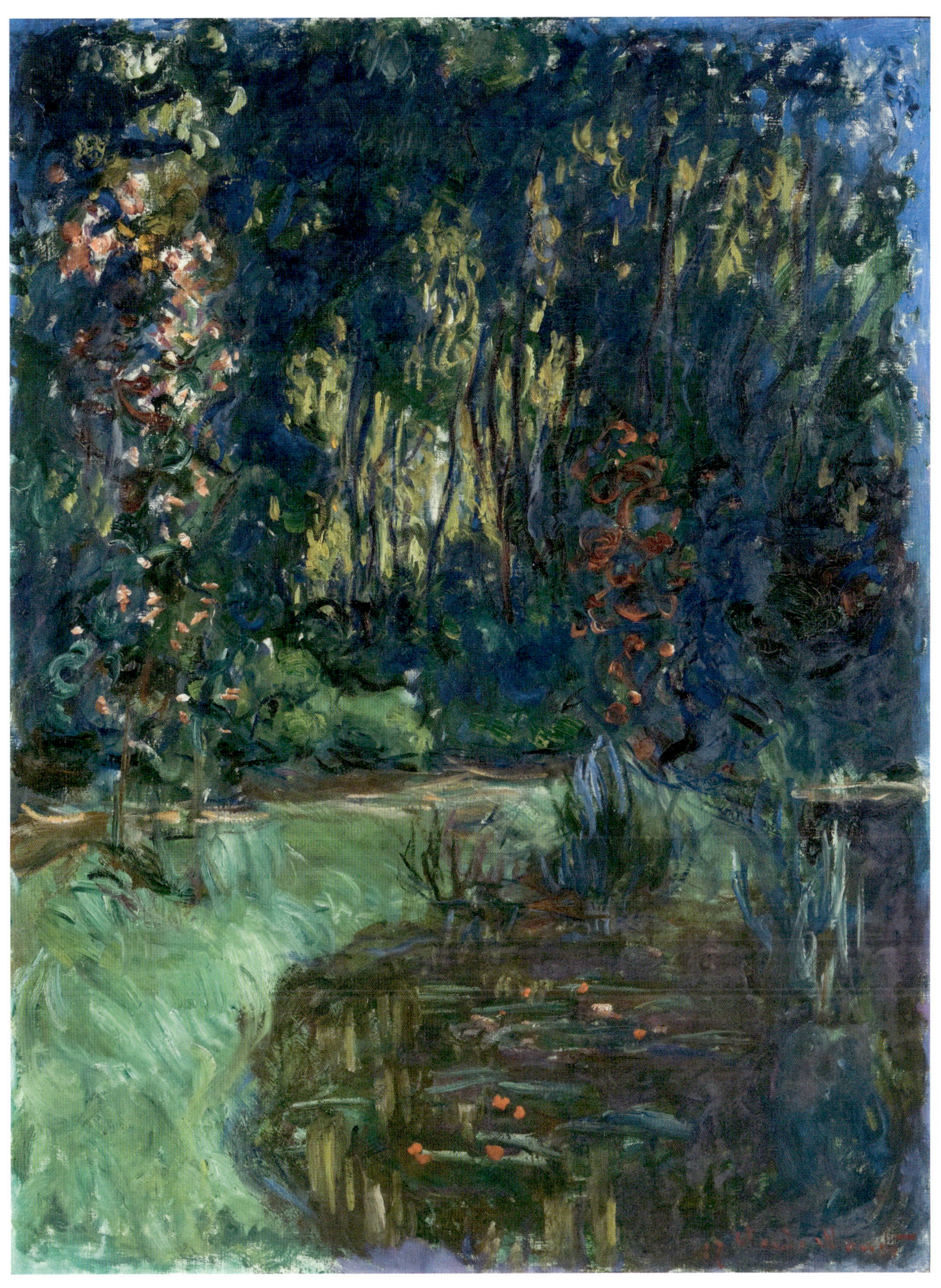

57 Claude Monet, *The Water-Lily Pond at Giverny*, 1917

"Art is never chaste" – Picasso and erotic *Japonisme*

The interest in Japanese art among European artists during the second half of the nineteenth century has been a topic of frequent discussion, and the present exhibition is yet another magnificent example of this. Degas, Monet, Fortuny, Van Gogh and numerous other artists felt attracted to previously unknown artistic forms, which destabilised the old European artistic tradition. Nonetheless, the significant interest in Japanese erotic art among these very same artists, ranging from Rodin to Picasso, is less well known. The *shunga* – Japanese prints, books, albums and erotic paintings from the Edo period – exuded a great attraction for these artists, serving as an inspiration and model for new artistic approaches to the representation of sexuality.

One example of this little-known aspect of *Japonisme* can be seen in the celebrated portrait of Émile Zola painted by Édouard Manet in 1868 and first shown at the Salon that same year (p. 61).[1] This work has frequently been declared an example of the initial wave of *Japonisme* surfacing in the French capital around the time of the Paris World Fair of 1867 – on the one hand, due to its use of flat colours almost without shadows, the fruit of an interest in the recently discovered Japanese prints. On the other hand, the image also includes objects that had recently arrived from Japan, which would become one of the principal points of artistic reference in the work of Manet, besides the oeuvre of Velázquez and the painting of the Golden Age. In his portrait of Zola, Manet included a Japanese folding screen as well as a *ukiyo-e* print by Utagawa Kuniaki II placed alongside reproductions of his own *Olympia* and Velázquez's engraving *The Triumph of Bacchus*. Nonetheless, what the painting does not reveal is another reality that Manet must have been very familiar with: the interest that erotic prints from Japan had already awakened among various critics and avant-garde artists. We must only think of historian James Laver's reminiscences of Émile Zola's home: "Zola was so far bitten by the craze for Japanese prints that he had the staircase of his house hung with some of the less reticent examples of furious fornication."[2] Zola collected Japanese erotic prints enthusiastically, as did critics and writers like Jules and Edmond de Goncourt, Zacharie Astruc and Philippe Burty, and artists such as Marià Fortuny, Edgar Degas, Auguste Rodin, Henri de Toulouse-Lautrec, Armand Rassenfosse, Anders Zorn, Adolphe Crespin, Aubrey Beardsley, John S. Sargent, Egon Schiele, Gustav Klimt and Pablo Picasso.[3] To what can this interest be attributed? Just as Utagawa Hiroshige's landscapes showed new perspectives, views and framings, and the work of Utamaro, Torii Kiyonaga, Katsushika Hokusai or Keisai Eisen presented new subjects and distinct ways of approaching everyday life, erotic prints from Japan also offered a plethora of artistic approaches that were innovative and surprising for European eyes. In fact, *shunga* went beyond the elements shown in most *ukiyo-e* prints with their new perspectives and flat use of colour: breaking with many conventions, they seduced the viewer with their more natural, fresh, original and expressive approach to the representation of sex, free of taboos or prejudice.

Interwoven bodies with emphasised genitalia, even close-up depictions that might well have had an impact in paintings as emblematic as Gustave Courbet's celebrated *The Origin of the World* (1866, Musée d'Orsay, Paris), now appeared coupled with explicit sex scenes or unusual iconographies full of vitality and fantasy. As Jules de Goncourt noted in his diary as early as 1863: "The other day I bought some albums of Japanese obscenities. They delight me, amuse me and charm my eyes. I look on them as being beyond obscenity, which is there, yet seems not to be there, and which I do not see, so completely does it disappear into fantasy. The violence of the lines, the unexpectedness of the conjunctions, the arrangement of the accessories, the caprice in the poses and the objects, the picturesqueness, and, so to speak, the landscape of genital parts."[4]

Beginning in the 1860s and especially during the period of the greatest development of *Japonisme* in the last third of the nineteenth century, Japanese erotic art achieved a surprising spread all across Europe – to the point that the expression "come see my Japanese prints" became a popular euphemism among the French middle classes for an invitation to have sex. Goncourt's praise in his respective monographs for Utamaro (*Outamaro*, 1891) and Hokusai (*Hokousaï*, 1896) was accompanied by a growing circulation of works amongst dealers in Japanese art, such as Hayashi Tadamasa in Paris or Ernst Fritzsche in Berlin. The first studies especially dedicated to the subject were published in 1907: *Das Geschlechtleben* (sic) *in Glauben, Sitte und Brauch der Japaner* by Friedrich Solomon Krauss and *Japanische Erotik,* presumably by Julius Kurth. Alongside volumes on Hokusai's *Manga*, Hiroshige's landscapes and Utamaro's portraits of courtesans, erotic works therefore also became widespread: the series *Sode no maki* (circa 1785) by Kiyonaga (p. 320), the album *Utamakura* (1788) by Utamaro and the three volumes of *Kinoe de Komatsu* (1814) by Hokusai, as well as countless prints by Harunobu, Eisen or Kunisada. And so it is no surprise that traces of Japanese art can be found in works with erotic themes as varied as the watercolours of Edgar Degas, the illustrations of Aubrey Beardsley, the engravings of Ernst Ludwig Kirchner, the sculptures and drawings of Auguste Rodin or the paintings of Egon Schiele.

Surely one of the most significant examples of an interest taken in *shunga* is Pablo Picasso, due both to his links to the *Japonisme* around 1900 and his representative status in the context of twentieth-century art as a whole. Picasso discovered Japanese art in Barcelona during the late 1890s, so that elements of the *Japonesque* can be found in several works he created in the art nouveau style. For instance, around 1903 as a young man in Barcelona, he created several small-format drawings on the verso of postcards advertising the yarn and stocking shop of his friends Sebastià and Carles Junyer Vidal. These drawings include typical elements of an imagined Japanese sexual visuality – for example, one of the many versions of tentacular iconography that became widespread in erotic books like Hokusai's *Kinoe no Komatsu*. After moving to Paris in the early 1910s – despite his adamant assertion to Apollinaire that he had no interest whatsoever in oriental, Chinese, Persian or Japanese art[5] – he began collecting *ukiyo-e* and realised several of his first approaches to monochromatic painting using India ink. Although various links can be traced between Picasso's work and Japanese art throughout the course of his lifetime, his interest in Japanese art and particularly *shunga* becomes most pronounced after the 1930s, when he acquired a portfolio of erotic prints that came primarily from the former collection of the French diplomat Philippe Berthelot.[6]

Although art historians have denied Picasso's interest in Japanese art, there can be no doubt that he indeed engaged with this imagery – from *shōdo* calligraphy, *sumi-e* painting and in particular erotic *shunga* prints (of which he owned a collection that included representative works from the seventeenth, eighteenth and nineteenth centuries) or prints from albums by Furuyama Moroshige and Nishikawa Sukenobu to prints from the series *Sode no maki* (circa 1785) by Torii Kiyonaga (p. 320) or *Kōshoku zue jūnikō* (circa 1788) by Katsukawa Shunchō. On several occasions, Picasso enthusiastically showed these works to friends and companions like Brassaï, Joan Miró, Josep Llorens Artigas, Ikeda Masuda or André Verdet, and on one of these occasions Picasso claimed, as noted by the Japanese artist Okamoto Tarō: "There is a type of old Japanese prints made of red sumi ink alone and painted by hand. I love them and I have many of them. They are erotic, they are magnificent. The later *ukiyo-e* are complex and I do not like them so much. How fantastic are the works from the primitive period!"[7]

"Art is never chaste", as Picasso asserted.[8] In this sense, eroticism and sexuality appeared throughout his artistic career in his drawings, paintings and engravings, from the turn of the century to the end of his life, and this fruitful body of work repeatedly reveals a surprising dialogue with his collection of *shunga*. Perhaps the most direct parallels to the erotic prints in his collections can be found in the series of engravings *The Embrace* (1963) and those dedicated to *Raphael and the Fornarina* (1968), the latter of which was included in *Suite 347* (pp. 319–325).

Picasso created the prints dedicated to *Raphael and the Fornarina* at his villa Mas de Notre-Dame-de-Vie in Mougins between the months of March and October in 1968. They were exhibited in December of the same year, together with the other prints from *Serie 347* at the Parisian gallery of Louise Leiris. In the same way that various bath scenes included in the *Serie 347* were created as a tribute to Ingres and his celebrated painting *The Turkish Bath* (1862, Musée du Louvre), the scenes of *Raphael and the Fornarina* are inspired by two other paintings by Ingres dedicated to the Renaissance painter and, as claimed by Vasari, his supposed lover. In this way – based on Ingres – the works ingeniously depict the purported encounters between the painter and the model, several meetings full of passion and eroticism, before the eyes of various voyeurs, from Michelangelo to the Pope. And while scenes of the same series, such as *By the Turkish Bath: Women Sunbathing by the Pool* (1968), enter into dialogue with the eroticism of both Ingres and Koryūsai, the individual scenes of *Raphael and the Fornarina* can be seen in relation to other works by Kiyonaga or Shunchō (pp. 319, 320), due to their explicit representation of sex, their composition, the positioning of the figures, enacting almost contortionist gestures, and their meticulousness in the representation of pubic hair and out-of-proportion genitals. In addition, the way Picasso frames the genitals, emphasising them together with the faces of the figures depicted, is something that can also often be seen in *shunga*.

There are many artists who, apparently with no relation to *shunga*, nonetheless felt fascinated by these erotic prints, and collections like those housed in the Musée Rodin in Paris and the Historisches Museum in Regensburg are examples of this. In other words, there is no doubt that the phenomenon of *Japonisme* also extends to Japanese erotic art, which left a strong impression on many artists at the turn of the century. The fresh and vital approach to sexuality present in the *shunga* was understood as another source of inspiration and played an important role on the path to modernism. Intimate and almost secret, this *Japonisme* was experienced by each of these artists in a distinct, unique and highly personal form.

Ricard Bru

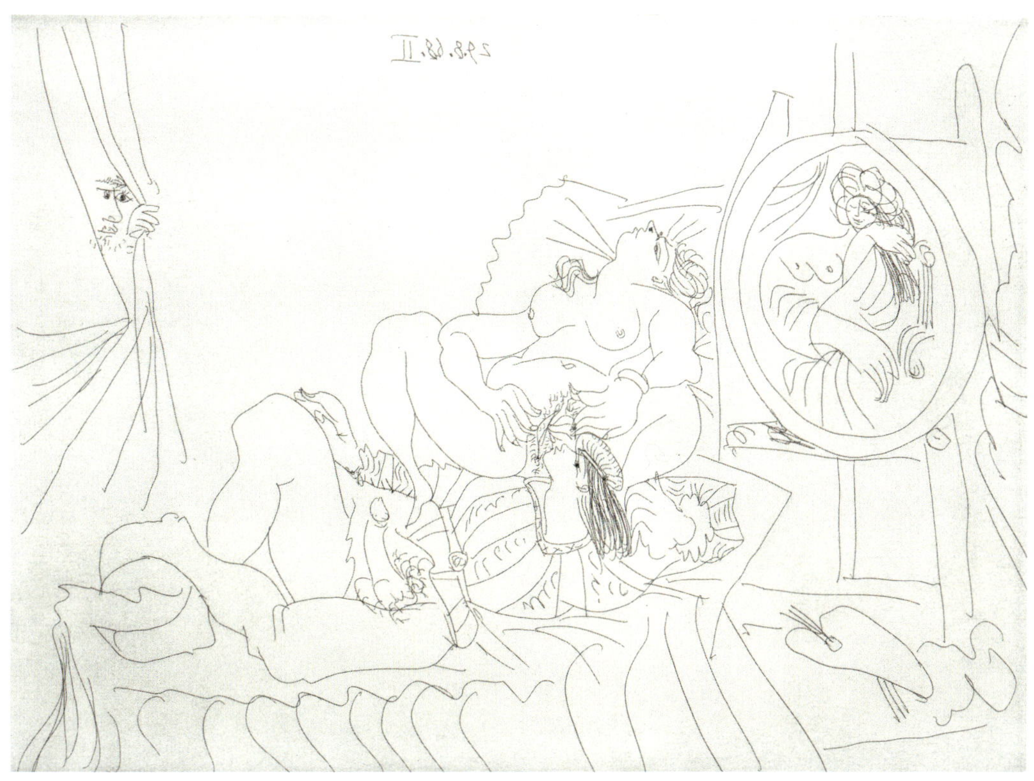

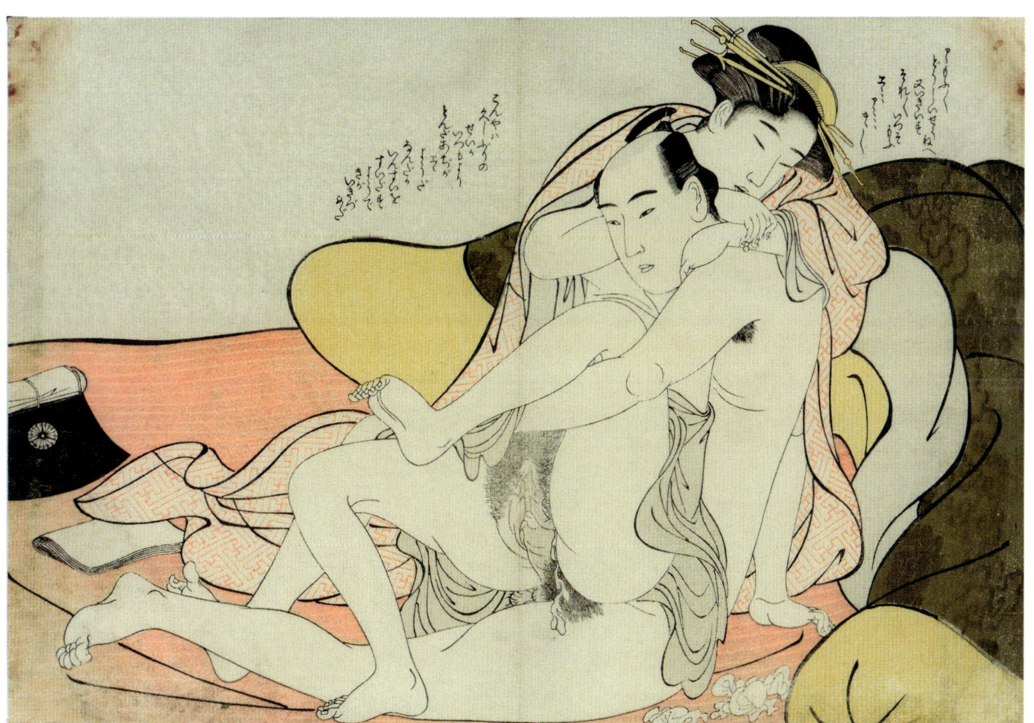

95a Pablo Picasso, *Raphael and the Fornarina II*, 29.8.1968
265 Katsukawa Shunchō, *A Pair of Lovers*, circa 1783–1895

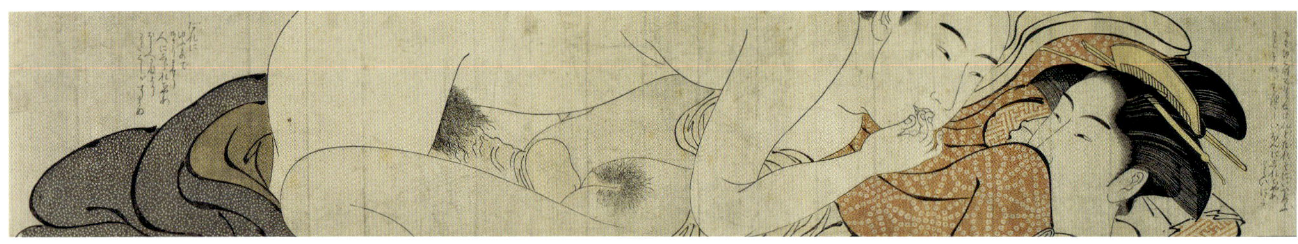

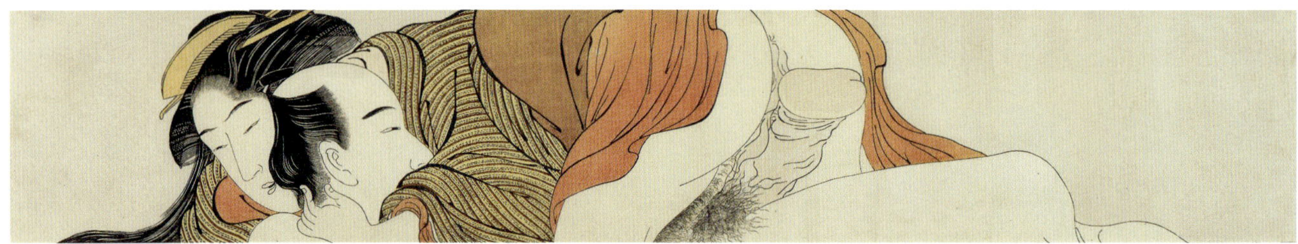

261a | 261b Torii Kiyonaga, *Secret Encounter* | *A Middle-Aged Couple*, circa 1785

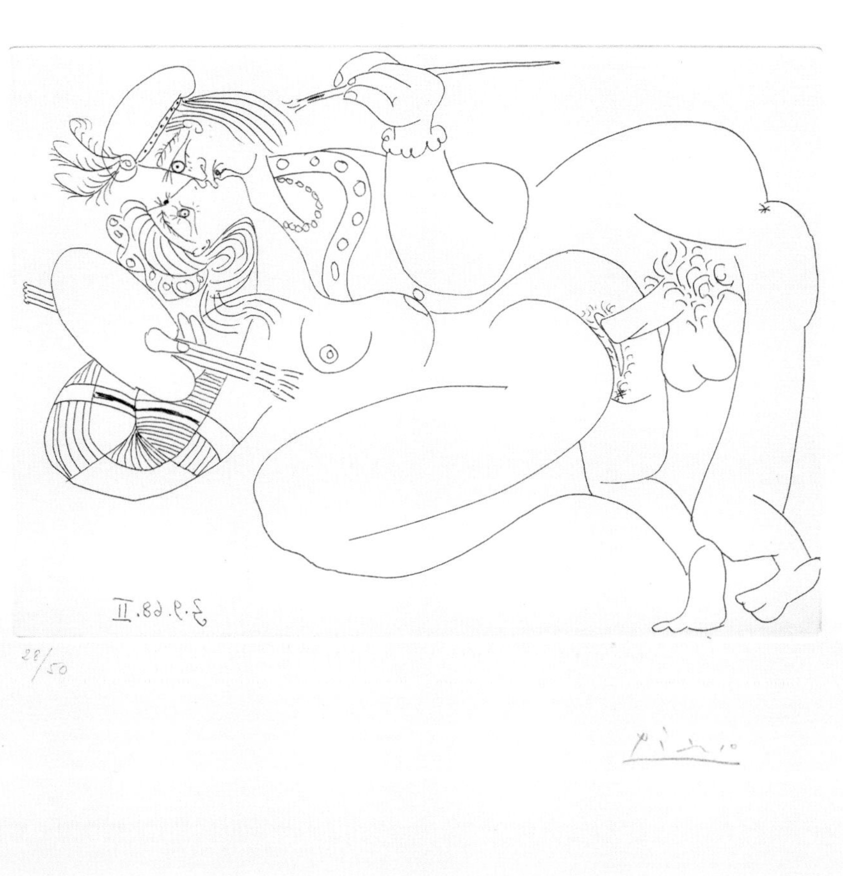

95j Pablo Picasso, *Raphael and the Fornarina XIV*, 3.9.1968

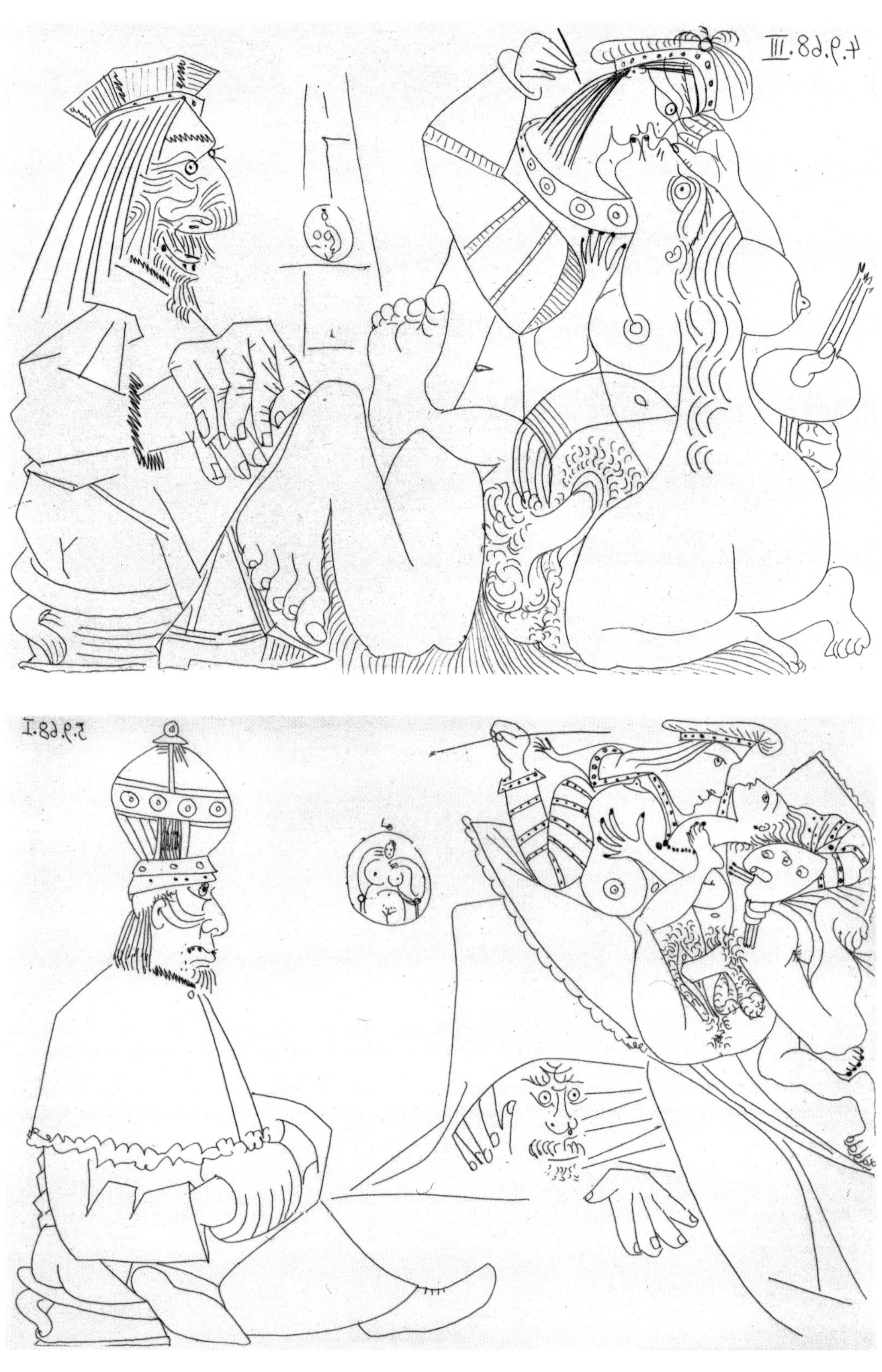

95m | 95o Pablo Picasso, *Raphael and the Fornarina XVII*, 4.9.1968 | *Raphael and the Fornarina XIX*, 5.9.1968

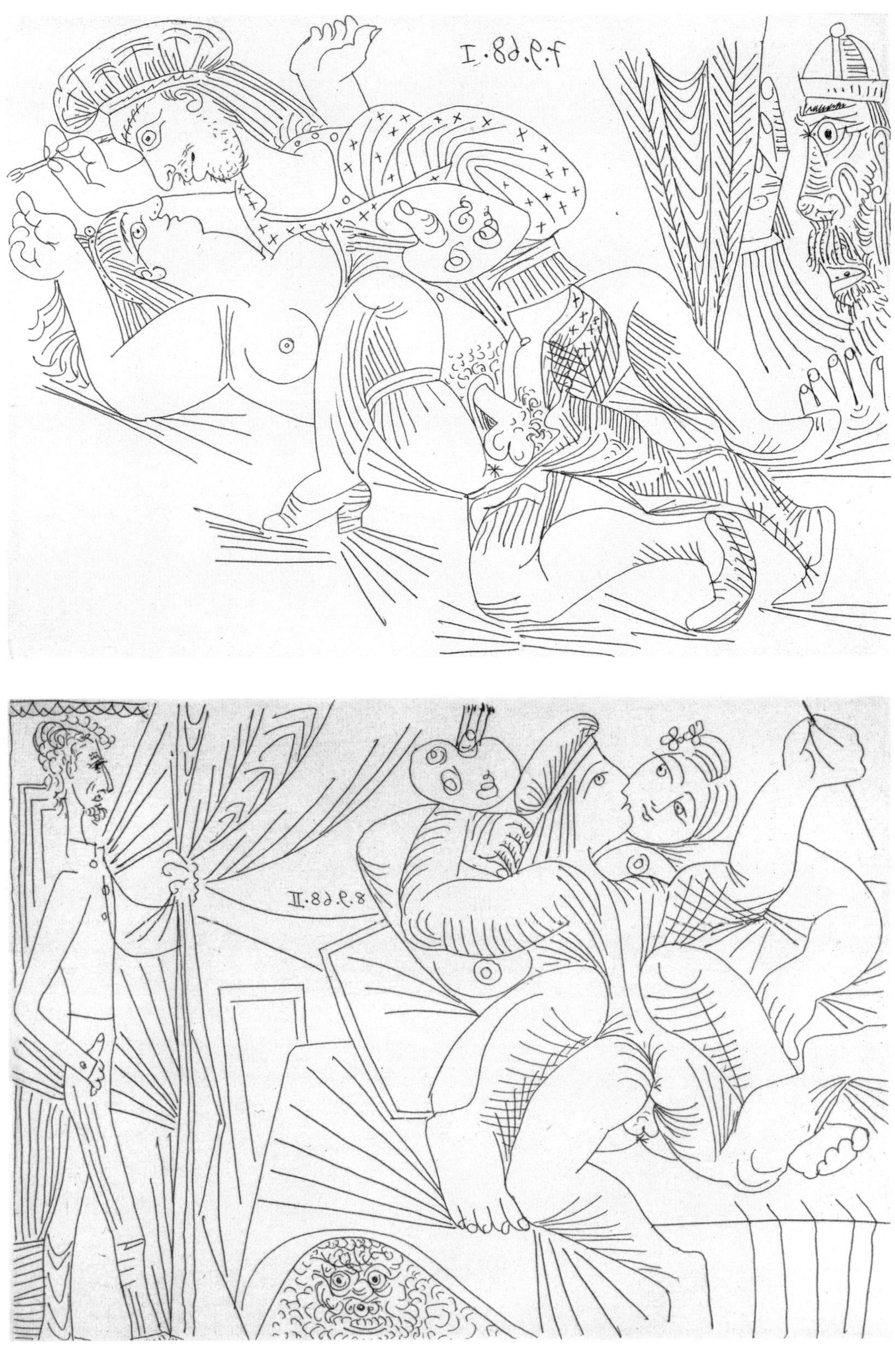

95q | 95s Pablo Picasso, *Raphael and the Fornarina XX*, 7.9.1968 | *Raphael and the Fornarina XXII*, 8.9.1968

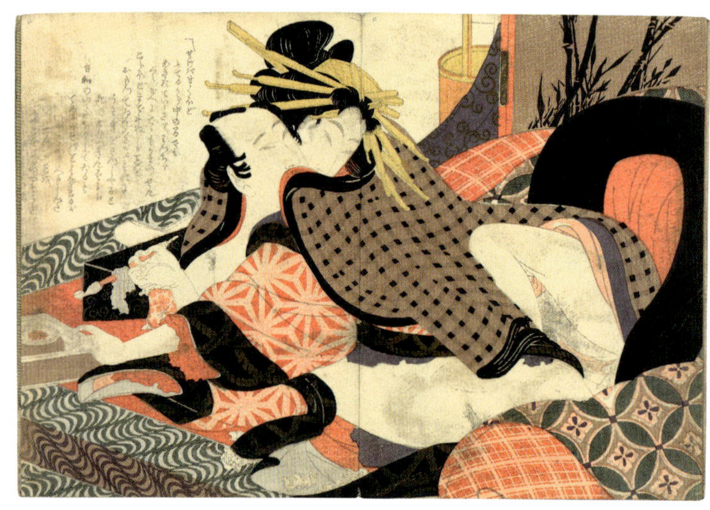

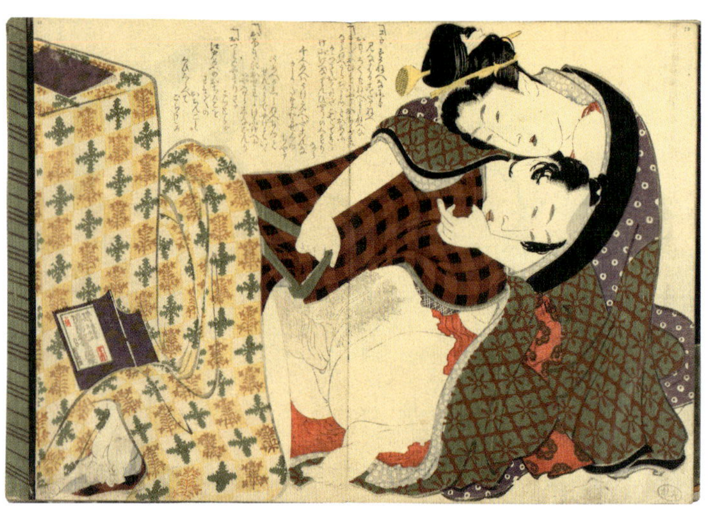

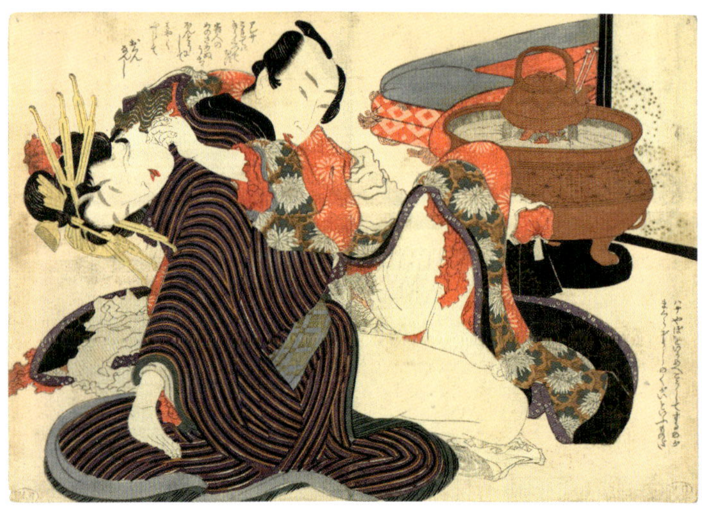

259 Katsushika Hokusū, attributed to, two sheets from the album *A Dyer's Saffron*, circa 1830 (top and bottom)

258 Katsushika Hokusai, sheet from the album *Models of Couples*, 1812

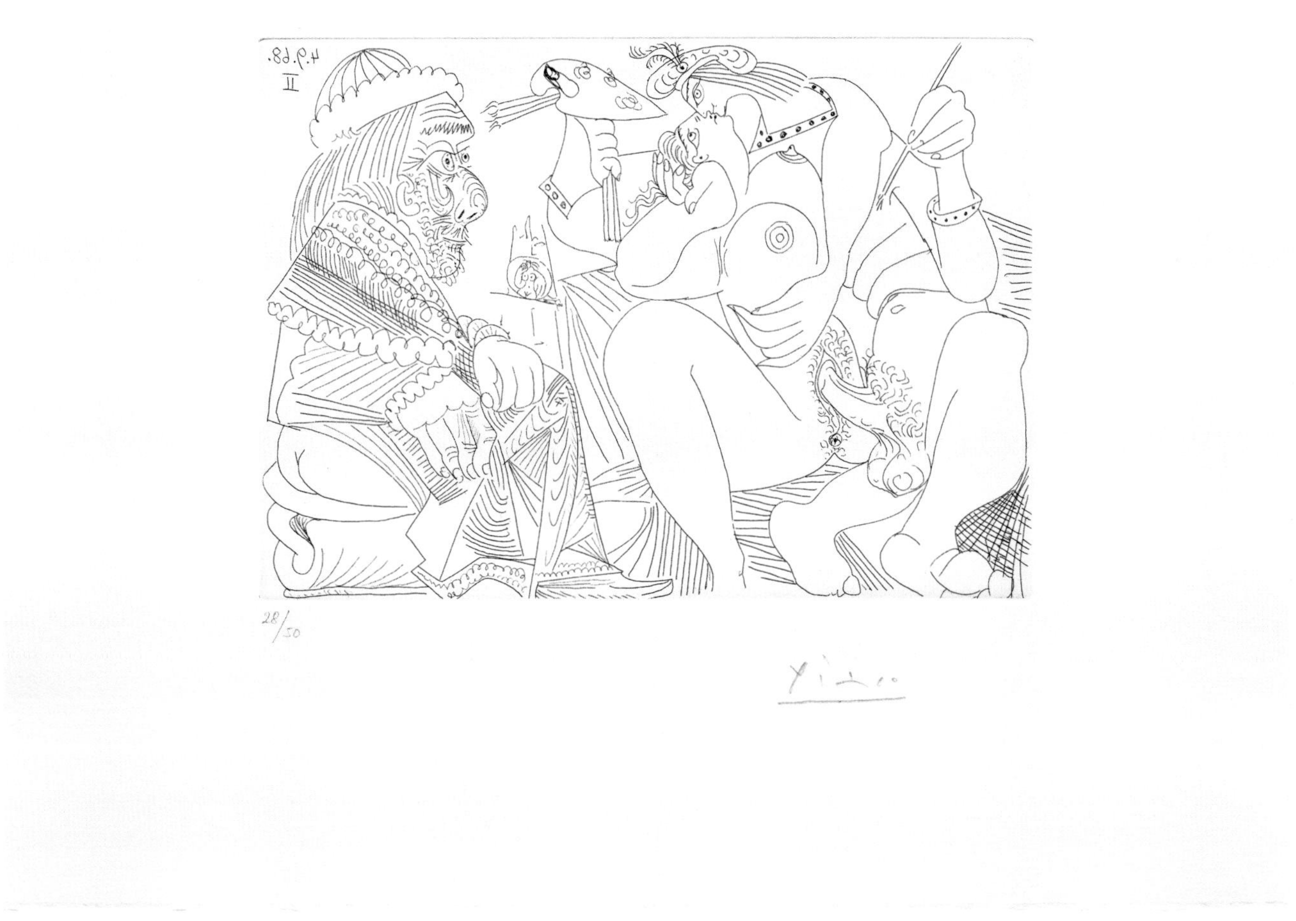

951 Pablo Picasso, *Raphael and the Fornarina XVI*, 4.9.1968

And Japan remains with us – a glimpse into the twentieth century

Brassaï's photograph (p. 330) of a wall in Pierre Bonnard's studio take a year before his death in Le Cannet in 1947 seems virtually like an archive of his life's work. In the form of an assemblage, astonishing things have been pinned to the wall by the artist – certainly in part to place his work in the tradition of "the greats". There are postcards of paintings by Vermeer, Seurat, Gauguin, Monet, Cézanne or Guillaumin, drawings and sketches of several of his own works, a larger print from Picasso's *Seated Woman on Wooden Chair* (1941), a nude typical of Renoir's late period, with dedication, and more – including a reproduction of a woodblock print showing an everyday Japanese scene.

For Pierre Bonnard, who was born in 1867, and Henri Matisse, born in 1869, an interest in Japanese art and culture can be presumed to be an everyday matter: in the work of both artists, the *Japonesque* manifested itself far into the twentieth century, albeit in often slightly hidden ways. A not-so-subtle example of this is Matisse's hastily painted portrait of his wife Amélie standing by the water, wearing a kimono with her hair put up in typical Japanese style (p. 94). Taking the narrative realism of Tissot, Stevens or De Nittis around 1870 as a point of departure, a form of colour painting developed in Matisse's work in which the figure and background interact independent of subject and form, and which later, following Édouard Vuillard, also became motif-defining for French Fauvism, using both striking and common accessories. Years later, Matisse pursued another Japanese technique of composition in his painting of a view of the beach promenade from his room in the Hôtel Méditerranée, Nice. Except for the black notebook that gave the picture its very title, all the visual motifs in this painting are only partially visible and subject to changing perspective (p. 327).

The coincidental status of Japanese objects is also manifest in the work of James Ensor, whose well-known penchant for the strange, macabre and grotesque in his family found sustenance in the shape of Asian objects early on. His aunt Mimi and his mother ran souvenir shops in Ostende, peddling a mixture of European, Japanese and Chinese curiosities and knick-knacks. Ensor was interested in the secretive, intimate and somewhat stuffy atmosphere exuded by them. For example, he composed his painting *Fans and Fabrics* of 1906 (p. 328) by individually arranging various fans for the viewer's perspective, displayed flat in the image. The Japanese models among them, which had become a fashionable accessory ever since the Paris World Fair of 1867, seem to surpass the "typically" French ones.

Bonnard and Matisse would later increasingly make use of Japanese techniques of composition, lending their paintings a touch of Far Eastern subtlety despite their formal radicalness. It is no accident that Bonnard – as in his painting *Female Nude in the Mirror* from 1910 (p. 329) – used an extremely narrow vertical format common for folding screens and hanging scrolls; here, in line with the format, he included striking and enticing partial views of the motif. But not just the uncompromising viewpoint, the extremely narrow format and the striking perspective suggest an intense dialogue with Japanese models. In viewing landscapes like Bonnard's painting *In a Southern Garden* from 1914 (p. 331), we are indirectly reminded of formal structures based on the balanced composition of Japanese colour woodblock prints, like those hanging on the artist's studio wall. It is not necessarily the individual motifs that recall a Japanese spirit, but rather the overall picture and the Far Eastern aesthetic that it generally reveals, along with the coincidence of Japanese objects with a European mentality, which can be seen to resonate in French painting from the 1860s onwards. It was to continue for three generations and "seemed to rehearse the meaning of the world differently" (Edmund de Waal, *The Hare with Amber Eyes: A Hidden Inheritance*, 2010).

Mario-Andreas von Lüttichau

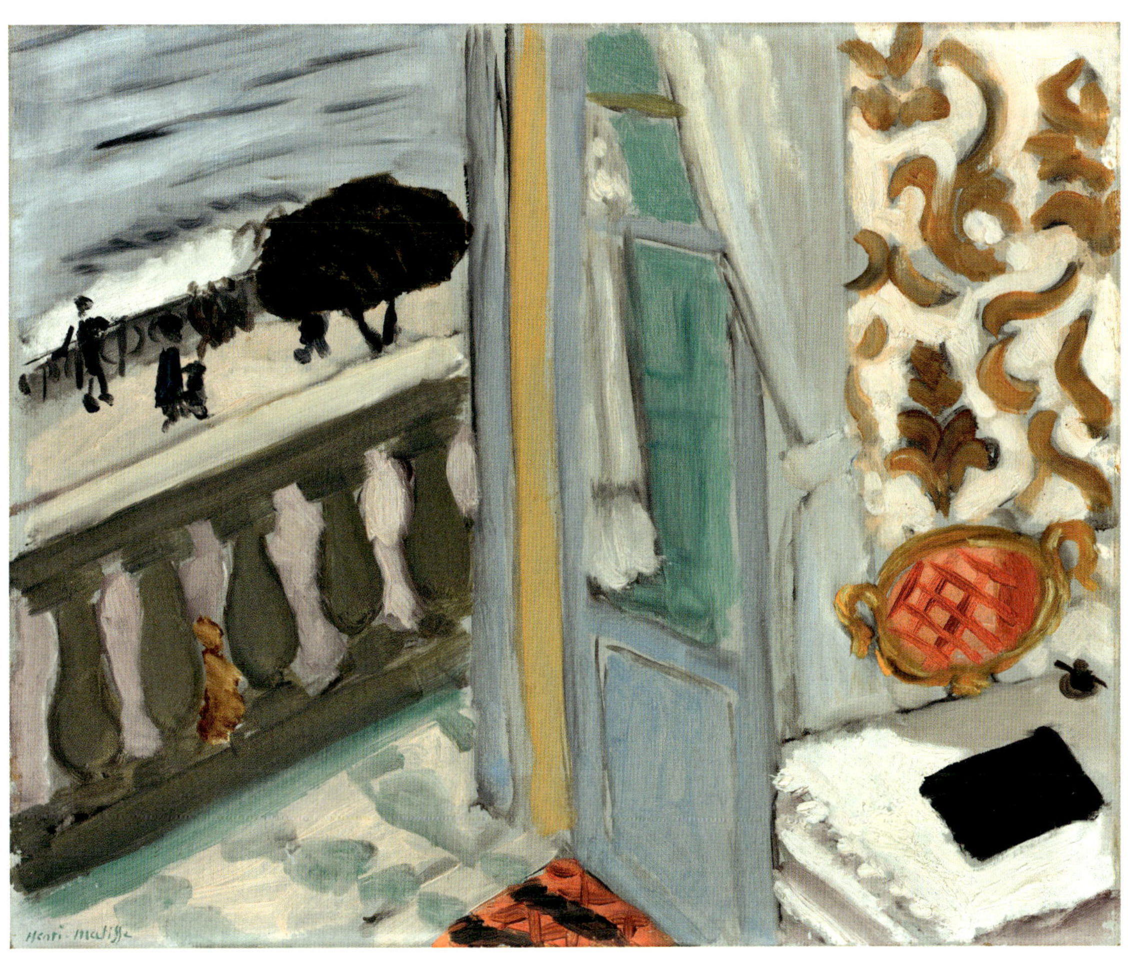

45 Henri Matisse, *Interior with Black Notebook*, 1918

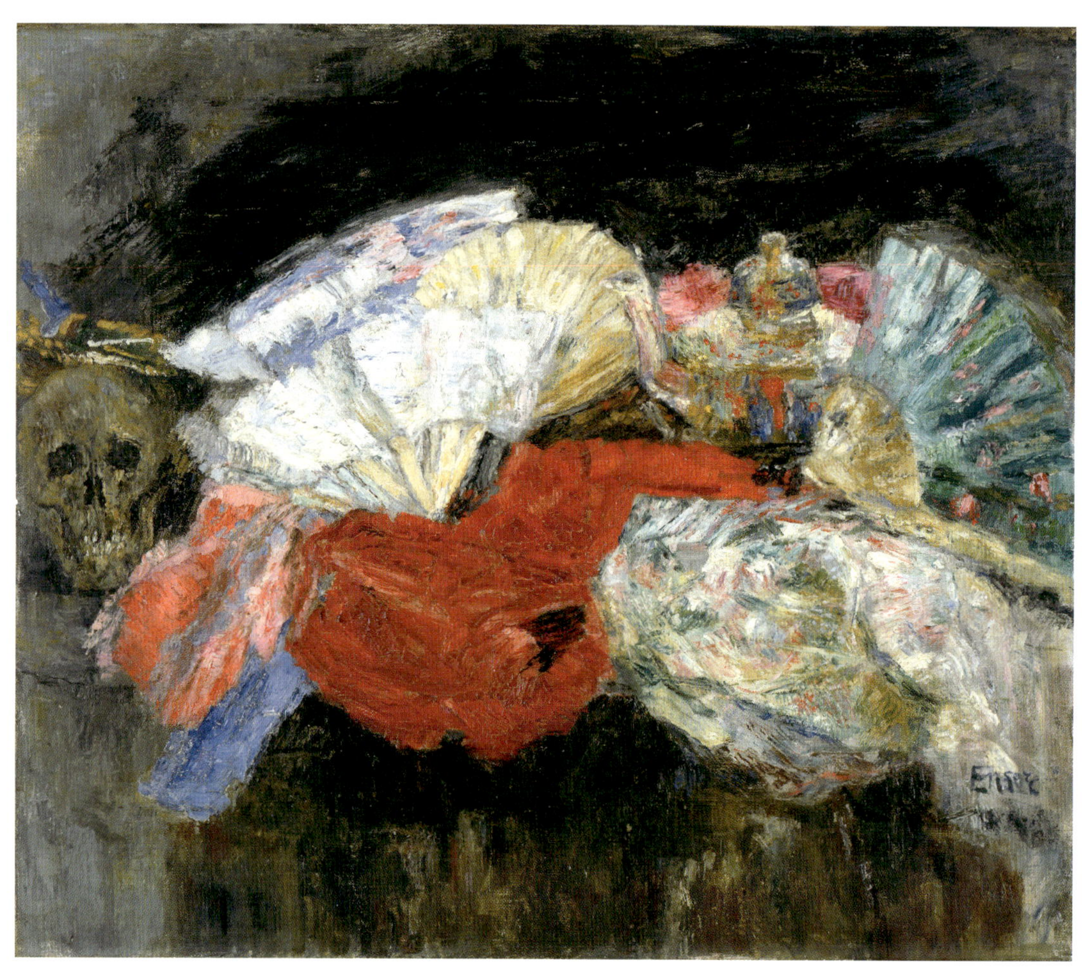

29 James Ensor, *Fans and Fabrics*, circa 1906

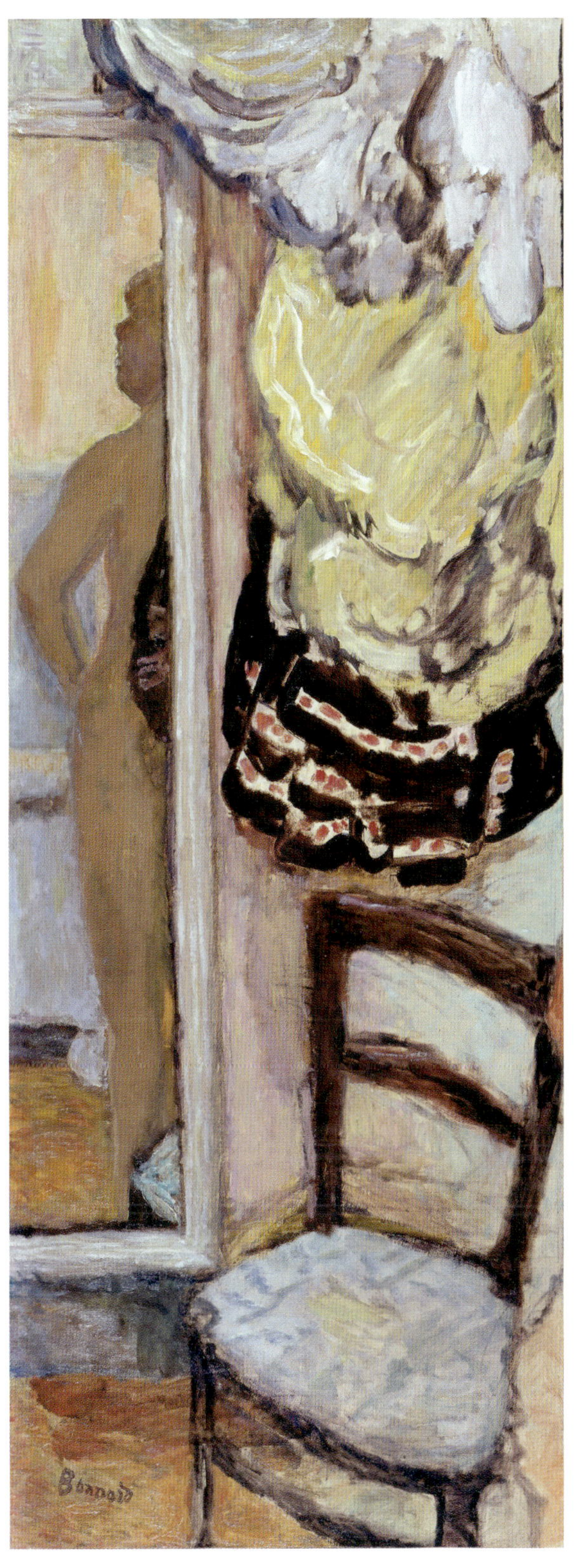

5 Pierre Bonnard, *Female Nude in the Mirror*, 1910

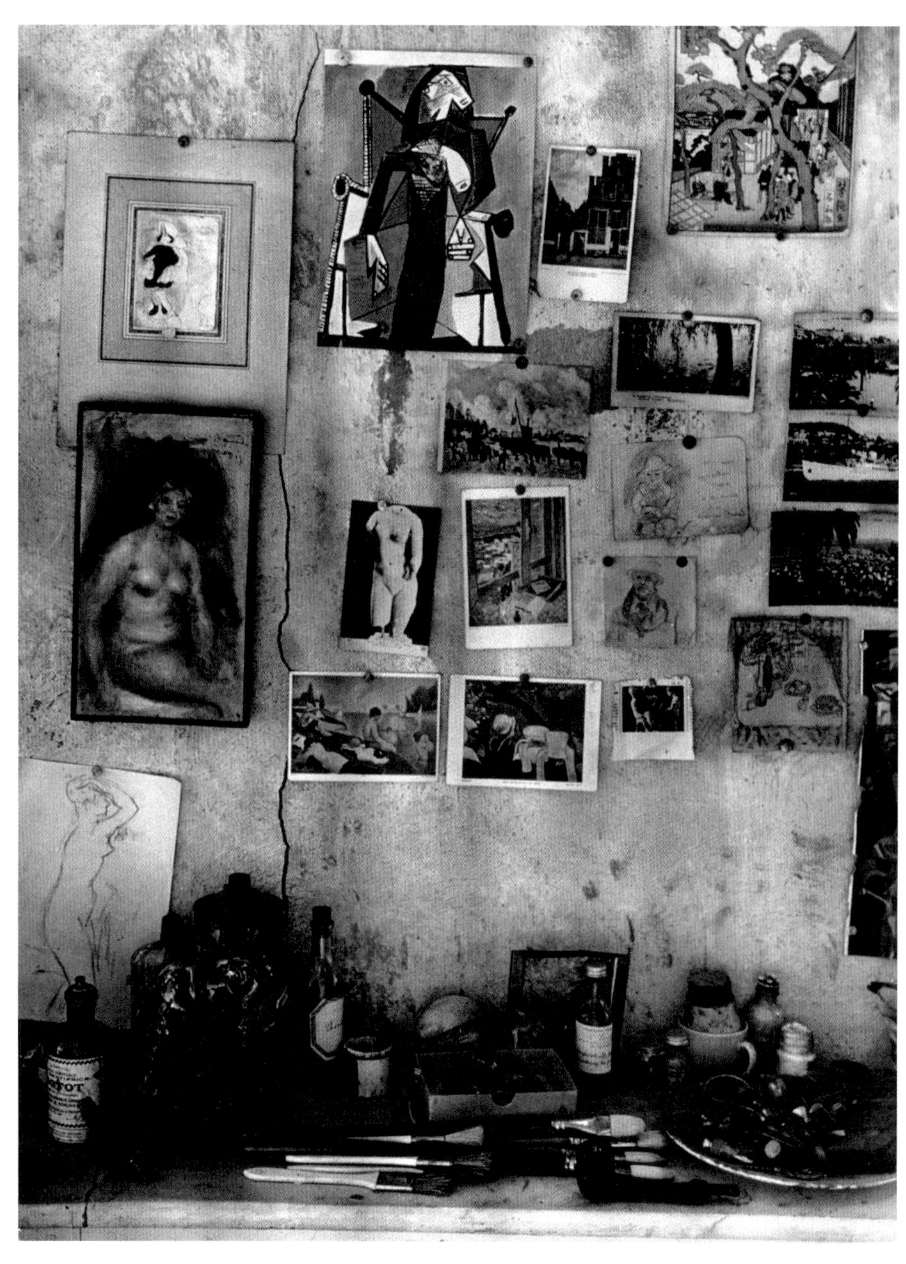

Brassaï, *Wall in Pierre Bonnard's Studio with Japanese Woodblock Print / Mur chez Bonnard (estampe japonaise)*, 1946, gelatin silver print, Private Collection (not included in the exhibition)

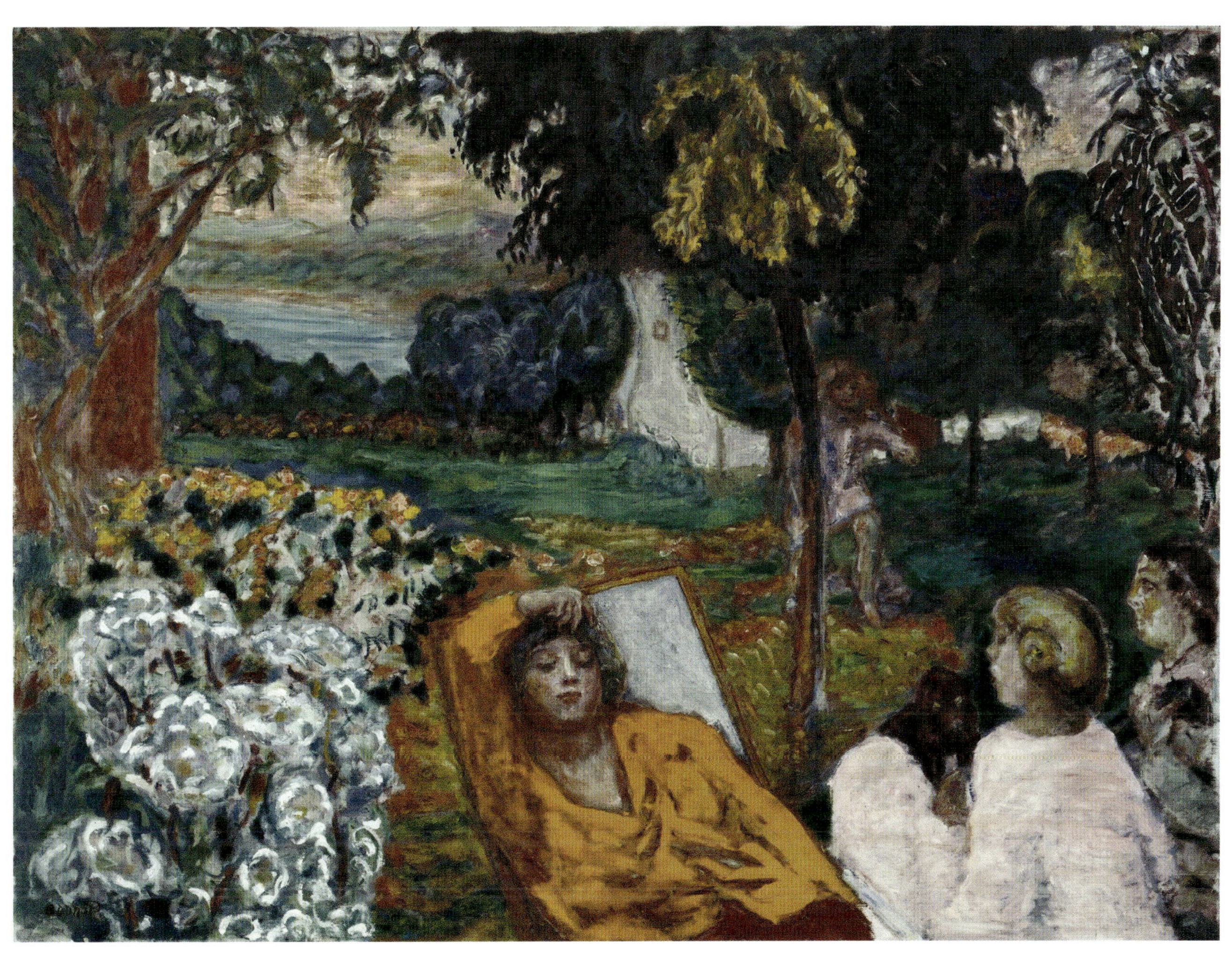

Pierre Bonnard, *In a Southern Garden / Dans un jardin méridional*, circa 1914,
oil on canvas, 84 x 113 cm, Kunstmuseum Bern,
Geschenk des Staates Bern, inv. no. G 1430 (not included in the exhibition)

Appendix

For Japanese names, as in the entire catalogue, we have adhered to the Japanese way of writing names – i.e. surname followed by first name.

Notes

Sandra Gianfreda, *Introduction*

► 1 "Japonisme! Attraction de l'époque, rage désordonnée qui a tout envahi, tout commandé, tout désorganisé dans notre art, nos modes, nos goûts, même notre raison", Adrien Dubouché, "La céramique contemporaine à l'Exposition universelle", in: *L'Art*, 20.10.1878, p. 57. Unless otherwise specified, all quotations in English have been translated by the translator of this essay. ► 2 "Et quand je disais que le japonisme était en train de révolutionner l'optique des peuples occidentaux, j'affirmais que le japonisme apportait une *coloration* nouvelle, un *système décoratoire* nouveau, enfin si l'on veut une *fantaisie poétique* dans la création de l'objet d'art, qui n'existait jamais dans les bibelots les plus parfaits du moyen âge et de la renaissance", Edmond and Jules de Goncourt, *Journal des Goncourt – Mémoires de la vie littéraire*, vol. 6, Paris, 1892, p. 308 (revised edition by Robert Ricatte, vol. 2, Paris, 1989, p. 1065). ► 3 The article appeared in the editions of 18.5.1872, pp. 25–26, 15.6.1872, pp. 59–60, 16.7.1872, pp. 83–84, 27.7.1872, pp. 106–107, 10.8.1872, pp. 122–123, and 8.2.1873, pp. 3–5. ► 4 In: *The Academy*, 7.8.1875, p. 150; cf. Gabriel P. Weisberg, "Philippe Burty and a Critical Assessment of Early 'Japonisme'", in: *Japonisme in Art: An international Symposium*, The Society for the Study of Japonisme (ed.), Tokyo, 1980, pp. 107–125, esp. pp. 116–119. ► 5 Vol. 2, pp. 214–218, esp. p. 218. In 1883, Claretie likewise ascribed the invention of the term to Chesneau (in: *La vie à Paris 1883*, Paris, 1884, p. 181). ► 6 The letter was published in 1877 in the weekly magazine *Musée universel*, vol. 9, p. 374, and in Philippe Burty, *Maîtres et petits maîtres*, Paris, 1877, p. 274. ► 7 "Le goût de la chinoiserie et de la japonaiserie, ce goût, nous l'avons eu des premiers. Ce goût aujourd'hui descendu aux bourgeois, qui plus que nous l'a senti, prêché, progagé? Qui s'est passionné pour les premiers albums japonais, a eu le courage d'en acheter?", Goncourt, *Journal* (see note 2), vol. 3, Paris, 1888, p. 238 (revised edition by Robert Ricatte, vol. 2, Paris, 1989, pp. 178–179, with slightly different wording); Klaus Berger, *Japonismus in der westlichen Malerei 1860–1920*, Munich, 1980, p. 16. English version of Berger: *Japonisme in Western Painting from Whistler to Matisse*, Cambridge, 1992. ► 8 Edmond de Goncourt, *La Maison d'un artiste*, Paris, 1881, vol. 1, pp. 208–209. ► 9 Goncourt, *Journal*, Robert Ricatte (ed.) (see note 2), vol. 1, p. 730 (14.9.1861; this passage does not appear in the first edition of 1887). ► 10 Léonce Bénédite, "Félix Bracquemond: l'animalier", in: *Art et Décoration*, 1905, vol. 17, pp. 37–47, esp. p. 39; and idem, "Artistes contemporain: Whistler", in: *Gazette des Beaux-Arts*, 1905, vol. 34, p. 142. ► 11 Marc Elder, *À Giverny, chez Claude Monet*, Paris, 1924, pp. 63–64. ► 12 *Jean-François Millet*, exh. cat., Grand Palais, Paris, Paris, 1975, p. 27; Robert L. Herbert, *Barbizon Revisited*, New York, 1962, p. 81. ► 13 On the *Recueil:* Geneviève Lacambre, "Hokusai and the French diplomats. Some remarks on the collection of Baron de Chassiron", in: *The Documented Image. Visions in Art History*, Gabriel P. Weisberg and Laurinda S. Dixon (eds.), Syracuse, 1987, p. 73. ► 14 Elisa Evett, *The Critical Reception of Japanese Art in Late Nineteenth-Century Europe*, doctoral dissertation 1980, Ann Arbor, 1982, pp. 108–114 (on the difference between Japan and China); Diane N. Towle, *Spaces of Japonisme and the Art of Whistler, Van Gogh and Monet: Collecting, Decoration and the Japanese Other*, doctoral dissertation 2013, pp. 104–106 (PDF available online). ► 15 Mae Michiko, "Nipponspiration als transkulturelle Grenzüberschreitung in der Kunst – Japonismus und japanische Populärkultur", in: *Nipponspiration: Japonismus und japanische Populärkultur im deutschsprachigen Raum*, Mae Michiko and Elisabeth Scherer (eds.), Cologne, Weimar and Vienna, 2013, pp. 21–48. Also see the essay by Mae Michiko in this publication. Cf. also Franziska Ehmcke, "Westliche kulturtheoretische Konzepte und die Frage, ob Japan noch seinen Weg zwischen Tradition und Moderne sucht", in: *Reisen im Zwischenraum – Zur Interkulturalität von Kulturwissenschaften: Festschrift für Helmolt Vittinghoff zum 65. Geburtstag*, Franziska Ehmcke and Martin Müller (eds.), Würzburg, 2012, pp. 31–44. ► 16 "L'enthousiasme gagna tous les ateliers avec la rapidité d'une flamme courant sur une piste de poudre. On ne pouvait se lasser d'admirer l'imprévu des compositions, la science de la forme, la richesse du ton, l'originalité de l'effet pittoresque, en même temps que la simplicité des moyens employés pour obtenir de tels résultats", *Gazette des Beaux-Arts*, 1878, vol. 18, p. 387. ► 17 Berger, *Japonisme* (see note 7), p. 169. ► 18 "Chacun d'eux s'assimila de l'art japonais les qualités qui recélaient les affinités les plus voisines avec ses propres dons. [...] Et tous y trouvèrent une confirmation plutôt qu'une inspiration à leurs façons personnelles de voir, de sentir, de comprendre et d'interpréter la nature. De là un redoublement de l'originalité individuelle au lieu d'une lâche soumission à l'art japonais", Ernest Chesneau, "Exposition universelle. Le Japon à Paris", in: *Gazette des Beaux-Arts*, vol. 18, 1.9.1878, p. 396. ► 19 For example, Josse (=Lucien Falize), "L'art japonais à propos de l'Exposition organisée par M. Gonse – Lettres de M. Josse à M. Louis Gonse, directeur de la Gazette des Beaux-Arts", in: *Revue des arts décoratifs*, 1882–1883, pp. 354, 359, 361; Louis Gonse, *L'Art japonais*, Paris, 1883, vol. 1, p. 2. ► 20 Tsuji Nobuo, "De l'influence des illustrations des livres occidentaux sur les dessins d'Hokusaï. La clé de son originalité", in: *Gazette des Beaux-Arts*, 1989, vol. 113, pp. 187–200; Timon Screech, "Rezeption und Interpretation der westlichen Perspektive im Japan des 18. Jahrhunderts", in: *Japan und Europa 1543–1929*, exh. cat., Martin-Gropius-Bau, Berlin, Berlin, 1993, pp. 128–137; Gary Hickey, "Waves of Influence", in *Monet & Japan*, exh. cat., National Gallery of Australia, Canberra, Virginia Spate et al. (ed.), Melbourne, 2001, pp. 174–185. Also see the essay by Mae Michiko in this publication. ► 21 See the essay by Mae Michiko in this publication. ► 22 See his letters to Émile Bernard, 18.3.1888, to Theo Van Gogh, 5.6.1888 and 29.9.1888, to Willemien Van Gogh, 9/14.9.1888, and to Paul Gauguin, 17.10.1888. Vincent Van Gogh, *The Letters*. All references to and quotations from Van Gogh's letters cite the online edition of Leo Jansen, Hans Luijten and Nienke Bakker: www.vangoghletters.org. Also see Kōdera Tsukasa , "Van Gogh's Utopian Japonisme", in: *Japanese prints. Catalogue of the Van Gogh Museum's Collection*, Charlotte van Rappard-Boon et al. (ed.), revised edition, Zwolle, 2006, pp. 11–45, esp. pp. 25–30. ► 23 Berger, *Japonisme* (see note 7), p. 87. ► 24 In: *Japonisme in Art. An international Symposium*, The Society for the Study of Japonisme (ed.), Tokyo, 1980, p. 43. ► 25 "J'ai vu un effet magnifique et tres étrange ce soir. Un très grand bateau chargé de charbon sur le Rhône ammaré au quai. Vu d'en haut il etait tout luisant et humide d'une averse, l'eau était d'un blanc jaune et gris perle trouble, le ciel lilas et bande orangé au couchant, la ville violette. Sur le bateau de petits ouvriers bleus et blancs sales allaient et venaient portant la cargaison à terre. C'etait de l'Hokoussaï pur." Van Gogh, *Letters* (see note 22), letter no. 652, 31.7.1888. ► 26 "Il a fallu l'arrivée parmi nous des albums japonais pour que quelqu'un osât s'asseoir sur le bord d'une rivière, pour juxtaposer sur une toile un toit qui fût hardiment rouge, une muraille qui fût blanche, un peuplier vert, une route jaune et de l'eau bleue. Avant l'exemple donné par les japonais c'était impossible", cited in: Théodore Duret, *Les peintres impressionnistes*, Paris, 1878, p. 13. English translation cited in: Paul Wood, *Western Art and the Wider World*, Chichester, West Sussex, 2014, p. 146. ► 27 *Secret Images: Picasso and the Japanese Erotic Print*, exh. cat., Museu Picasso, Barcelona, Ricard Bru and Malén Gual (eds.), London, 2009; Ricard Bru, *Erotic Japonisme: The Influence of Japanese Sexual Imagery on Western Art*, Leiden, 2013. ► 28 Susan J. Napier, *From Impressionism to Anime. Japan as Fantasy and Fan Cult in the Mind of the West*, New York, 2007; Mae Michiko, *Nipponspiration* (see note 15).

Mae Michiko, Japonisme *as a transcultural process – Odano Naotake, Katsushika Hokusai and Vincent Van Gogh*

► 1 "Révolutionner l'optique", Edmond and Jules de Goncourt, *Journal des Goncourt: Mémoires de la vie littéraire*, vol. 6, Paris, 1892, p. 308 (revised edition by Robert Ricatte, vol. 2, Paris, 1989, p. 1065). Unless otherwise specified, all quotations in English have been translated by the translator of this essay. ► 2 Klaus Berger, *Japonisme in Western Painting from Whistler to Matisse*, trans. by David Britt, Cambridge, 1992, p. 334.► 3 Ibid., p. 337. ► 4 Ibid., p. 3. ► 5 Ibid., p. 4. ► 6 Franz Wickhoff, "Die Zukunft der Kunstgewerbemuseen", in: *Kunst und Kunsthandwerk*, vol. 1, 1898, p. 17. ► 7 Claudia Delank, *Das imaginäre Japan in der Kunst. "Japanbilder" vom Jugendstil bis zum Bauhaus*, Munich, 1996, p. 15. ► 8 Vincent Van Gogh, letter no. 585 to Theo Van Gogh, Arles, on or around 16.3.1888, Leo Jansen, Hans Luijten and Nienke Bakker (eds.), *Vincent Van Gogh: The Letters*, Van Gogh Museum/Huygens Institute (KNAW), http://vangoghletters.org/vg/letters.html. ► 9 Douglas W. Druick and Peter K. Zegers, *Van Gogh and Gauguin: The Studio of the South*, exh. cat., The Art Institute of Chicago and Van Gogh Museum, London and New York, 2001, p. 98. ► 10 Hans Jaffé, "Vincent van Goghs Suche nach dem heiteren Leben im japanischen Holzschnitt", in: *Weltkulturen und moderne Kunst*, Siegfried Wichmann (ed.), Munich, 1972, p. 169. ► 11 Vincent Van Gogh, letter no. 686 to Theo Van Gogh, Arles, 23/24.9.1888 (see note 8). ► 12 Siegfried Bing, "Programme", in: *Le Japon artistique, Documents d'Art et d'Industrie*, issue 1, 1888, p. 7. ► 13 Foreword to: Katsushika Hokusai, *Fugaku Hyakkei* (with comments by Suzuki Jūzō), Tokyo, 1986. ► 14 Vincent Van Gogh, letter no. 686 to Theo Van Gogh, Arles, 23/24.9.1888 (see note 8). ► 15 Kōdera Tsukasa, *Gohho. Nihon no yume ni kaketa geijutsuka*, Tokyo, 2010, p. 363. ► 16 Vincent Van Gogh, letter no. 686 to Theo Van Gogh, Arles, 23/24.9.1888 (see note 8). ► 17 Théodore Duret,

Van Gogh, Paris, 1924, p. 103, cited in: Inaga Shigemi, "Fan Gohho to Nihon, soshite Chūgoku", in: *Jinbungaku Fōramu*, Atomi Gakuen Joshi Daigaku, no. 2, 2004, p. 104. ► 18 Vincent Van Gogh, letter no. 685 to Theo Van Gogh, Arles, 21.9.1888 (see note 8). ► 19 Inaga, "Fan Gohho" (see note 17), p. 107. ► 20 Kobayashi Hideo, *Gohho no tegami*, vol. 20, Tokyo, 2004, pp. 11–12. ► 21 Cf. Inaga, "Fan Gohho" (see note 17), pp. 106–107. ► 22 Gary Hickey, "Waves of Influence: Japan and the West", in: *Monet & Japan*, exh. cat., National Gallery of Australia, Canberra, Virginia Spate et al. (ed.), Melbourne, 2001, p. 175. ► 23 Ibid., p. 174. ► 24 Kōno Motoaki, "Edo kaiga to kyakkanshugi", in: *Edo no naka no kindai*, Takashina Shūji, Tokyo, 1996, p. 268. ► 25 Ibid., pp. 268–269. ► 26 Hans Belting, *Florence and Baghdad. Renaissance Art and Arab Science*, trans. Deborah Lucas Schneider, Cambridge, Mass., 2011, p. 1. ► 27 Ibid., p. 19. ► 28 Ibid., p. 23. ► 29 Timon Screech, "Rezeption und Interpretation der westlichen Perspektive im Japan des 18. Jahrhunderts", in: *Japan und Europa 1543–1929*, exh. cat., Martin-Gropius-Bau, Berlin, Berlin, 1993, p. 136. ► 30 Belting, *Florence* (see note 26), p. 43. ► 31 Screech, "Rezeption" (see note 29), p. 128. ► 32 Inaga Shigemi, "Seiyō hakurai no shosekijōhō to Tokugawa Nihon no shikakubunka no henbō – 1730 nen kara 1830 nen ni kakete", in: *Nihon kenkyū*, no. 31, 2005, p. 21. ► 33 Hickey, "Waves" (see note 22), p. 175. ► 34 Inaga, "Seiyō hakurai" (see note 32), p. 29. ► 35 Belting, *Florence* (see note 26), p. 15. ► 36 Ibid. ► 37 Cf. Mabuchi Akiko, *Japonizumu. Gensō no Nihon*, Tokyo, 2008, pp. 113–114. ► 38 Berger, *Japonisme* (see note 2), p. 6.

Gregory Irvine, *The presentation, perception and collection of Japanese art in nineteenth-century France*

► 1 R. H. P. Mason and J. G. Caiger, *A History of Japan*, revised edition, Rutland and Tokyo, 1997; Marius B. Jansen, *The Making of Modern Japan*, Cambridge, Mass., 2000. ► 2 *Illustrated London News*, 20.9.1862, p. 320. ► 3 Hannah Sigur, *The Influence of Japanese Art on Design*, Utah, 2008, p. 36. ► 4 W. Burges, "The International Exhibition", in: *Gentleman's Magazine*, July 1862, pp. 3–12, cited in: Anna Jackson, "Art and Design: East Asia", in: *The Victorian Vision: Inventing New Britain*, London, 2001, p. 303. ► 5 *Illustrated London News*, 20.9.1862, pp. 318–319. ► 6 Léonce Bénédite, "Félix Bracquemond, l'animalier", in: *Art et Décoration*, 17.2.1905, pp. 39–40. ► 7 Baron Charles de Chassiron, *Notes sur le Japon, la Chine et l'Inde, 1858, 1859, 1860*, Paris, 1861, pp. 213–233. ► 8 *Japanese Collections in European Museums. Reports from the Toyota-Foundation-Symposium Königswinter 2003*, Josef Kreiner (ed.), Bonn, 2005, vol. 1, p. 15. ► 9 For further images of the Vienna displays, see Doi Kumiko, Ito Yoshiaki and Ogawa Mikio, "Expositions of the Early Meiji Period: Encounter East and West", in: *Japan Goes to the World's Fairs: Japanese Art at the Great Expositions in Europe and the United States 1867–1904*, exh. cat., Los Angeles County Museum, Los Angeles, 2005, pp. 24–26. ► 10 For further reading on Japan's official involvement in the international exhibitions, see Yokomizo Hiroko, "The Presentation and Reception of Japanese Art in Europe during the Meiji Period", in: *Japonisme and the Rise of the Modern Art Movement: the Arts of the Meiji Period*, Gregory Irvine (ed.), London, 2013, pp. 54–90. ► 11 Ibid, p. 68. ► 12 Kawakami Akane, *Travellers' Visions: French Literary Encounters with Japan, 1881–2004*, Liverpool University Press, 2005, p. 18. ► 13 *The Origins of L'Art Nouveau: The Bing Empire*, exh. cat., Van Gogh Museum, Amsterdam et al., Ithaca (NY), 2004. ► 14 V&A Registry, Nominal File, "Bing, Mons. S." (unpaged). ► 15 *Les origines de L'Art Nouveau. La maison Bing*, exh. cat., Musée des Arts décoratifs, Paris et al., Gabriel P. Weisberg et al. (ed.), Paris, 2004, p. 16. ► 16 *Japanese Collections* (see note 8), vol. 1, p. 23. ► 17 V&A Registry (see note 14). ► 18 Ibid. ► 19 Ibid. ► 20 Hannah Sigur, *The Influence of Japanese Art on Design*, Utah, 2008, p. 77. ► 21 *Japanese Collections* (see note 8), vol. 1, p. 23. ► 22 *The Paris Exhibition of 1878: An Illustrated Weekly Review of Trade, Industrial, Agriculture and Art*, London, 14.9.1878, p. 435. ► 23 V&A Archives (see note 14). The eagle referred to is another major piece of Meiji-period metalwork in the V&A's collection acquired from Algernon B. Mitford (later Lord Redesdale), who had served in the diplomatic service in Japan in 1875 (museum no. 603-1875). ► 24 See Rupert Faulkner and Anna Jackson, "The Meiji Period in South Kensington: The Representation of Japan at the Victoria and Albert Museum 1852–1912", in: *Meiji No Takara: Treasures of Imperial Japan* (The Nasser D. Khalili Collection of Japanese Art; 5 vols), vol. 1, *Selected Essays*, Oliver Impey and Malcolm Fairley (eds.), London, 1995, pp. 152–195. ► 25 For further discussion of the Japanese art sales in Paris, see Manuela Moscatiello, "A craze for auctions: Japanese art on sale in 19th century Paris", in: *Andon* 2011, no. 90, pp. 22–45. ► 26 *Japanese Collections* (see note 8), vol. 1, p. 15. ► 27 *The Academy*, 7.8.1875, pp. 150–151. ► 28 For an extensive study of Philippe Burty, see Gabriel P. Weisberg, *The Independent Critic: Philippe Burty and the Visual Arts of Mid-Nineteenth Century France*, New York et al., 1993.

Christoph Dorsz, *The museum as a school of vision – Karl Ernst Osthaus and Museum Folkwang's Japanese Collection*

► 1 Karl Purgold to Karl Ernst Osthaus (= KEO), letter 23.8.1898, Archive Museum Folkwang (= Archiv MF), A1/297. At least two of the baskets remain in the collection: inv. nos K 677 and 678. ► 2 KEO to Brinckmann, letter 13.7.1899, a copy of the original from the archive of the Museum für Kunst und Gewerbe Hamburg, Karl Ernst Osthaus-Archiv, Osthaus Museum Hagen (= KEO-Archiv), unsigned. ► 3 Max Liebermann's small collection – consisting largely of woodblock prints, tea ceramics and lacquerware – mainly entailed purchases from R. Wagner; see Herbert Butz, "'Ça m'intéresse énormément': Liebermanns Ostasiatika", in: *Max Liebermann: Die Kunstsammlung von Rembrandt bis Manet*, Bärbel Hedinger, Michael Diers and Jürgen Müller (eds.), Munich, 2013, pp. 55–64. ► 4 R. Wagner to KEO, invoice 30.4.1901, KEO-Archiv, F1 106/7. Of the five netsukes, four remain extant: inv. nos KPL 85, 90, 96 and 98. ► 5 Julius Meier-Graefe, *Pächter und Bing* (1929), cited in: *Julius Meier-Graefe. Kunstschreiberei. Essays und Kunstkritik*, Henry Schumann (ed.), Leipzig and Weimar, 1987, pp. 228–240, here p. 239. ► 6 KEO, *Van de Velde. Leben und Schaffen des Künstlers*, Hagen, 1920 (Die Neue Baukunst 1), p. 27. ► 7 Gabriel P. Weisberg, "Jugendstil und Japonismus. Zur *katagami* Rezeption im Frühwerk van de Veldes", in: *Prophet des Neuen Stil. Der Architekt und Designer Henry van de Velde*, Helmut Th. Seemann and Thorsten Valk (eds.), Göttingen, 2013 (Klassik Stiftung Weimar Jahrbuch 2013), pp. 33–48, here p. 36. The artist primarily used colour woodblock prints and paper stencils in frames of his own design to decorate his home. ► 8 KEO, *Van de Velde* (see note 6), p. 17. ► 9 *Objets d'art ancien de la Chine et du Japon provenant en majeure partie de la Collection Edmond Taigny*, auc. cat., Hôtel Drouot, Paris, 1903. The collection still includes: lots 18bis (inv. no. K 132), 34 (inv. no. KPL 165), 75 (inv. no. K 274), 109 (inv. no. K 254), 110 (inv. no. K 270), 139 (inv. no. KPL 159), 148 (inv. no. KPL 163), 254 (inv. no. KPL 138a–f), 308 (inv. nos K 902, 903, 905, 908). ► 10 *Objets d'art de la Chine et du Japon. Porcelaines, bronzes, laques, émaux cloisonnés, gardes de sabre, étoffes, etc. formant la collection de Feu M. Paul Brenot*, auc. cat., Hôtel Drouot, Paris, 1903. The collection still includes lots 145 (inv. no. KPL 118), 387 (inv. no. KPL 123), 397 (inv. no. KPL 122), 518 (inv. no. K 756?), 521 (inv. no. K 767), 522 (inv. no. K 762), 528 (inv. no. K 756?, inv. no. K 765), 543 (inv. no. K 757), 544 (inv. no. K 760), 590 (inv. no. 758). ► 11 KEO, *Folkwang. Jahresbericht*, offprint *Hagener Zeitung* 19.10.1904, KEO-Archiv, V 289/7. *Collection Ch. Gillot. Objets d'art et Peintures d'Extrême-Orient*, auc. cat., Galeries Durand-Ruel, Paris, 1904. Among Japanese objects, KEO acquired lots 73 (sold in 1912), 90 (inv. no. KPL 58), 97 (inv. no. KPL 78) and 1961 (inv. no. TS 06 92). ► 12 "Karl With's 'Buddhistische Plastik' in Japan" Eine Würdigung (1919), cited in: *Karl Ernst Osthaus. Reden und Schriften. Folkwang, Werkbund, Arbeitsrat*, Rainer Stamm (ed.), with a contribution by Rainer K. Wick, Cologne, 2001 (Kontext 3), pp. 237–238, here p. 237. ► 13 Josef Kreiner, "Some Remarks on Japanese Collections in Europe", in: *Japanese Collections in European Museums: Reports from the Toyota Foundation-Symposium Königswinter, vol. I: General Prospects*, idem (ed.), Bonn, 2005 (Japan Archiv, vol. 5), pp. 3–52, here p. 31. For a contemporary perspective, see the essay by Robert Breuer, "Zur Revision des Japonismus", in: *Deutsche Kunst und Dekoration*, vol. 11 (7), 1906, pp. 445–448. ► 14 KEO, "Karl Withs 'Buddhistische Plastik in Japan'", in: *Kunst und Kunsthandwerk*, vol. 22 (11–12), 1919, pp. 386–390, here p. 387. ► 15 KEO to Carl Grund, draft of a letter 1.8.1919, KEO-Archiv, F2 93/2. ► 16 KEO, "Karl Withs 'Buddhistische Plastik'" (see note 12), p. 237. ► 17 Paul Vautier, Foreword, in: *Japanische Stichblätter und Schwertzieraten. Sammlung Georg Oeder. Beschreibendes Verzeichnis von P. Vautier*, Otto Kümmel (ed.), Berlin, 1916, p. IX. The pieces not acquired by Oeder or KEO were purchased by the painter Friedhelm Haniel. The collection was dissolved in 1977; see *Auktion 74. Sammlung Friedhelm Haniel, vorm. Paul Vautier*, auc. cat., Kunsthaus am Museum Carola van Ham, Cologne, 1977. ► 18 Karl With, *Autobiography of Ideas: Lebenserinnerungen eines außergewöhnlichen Kunstgelehrten*, Roland Jaeger (ed.), Berlin, 1997, pp. 48–81. ► 19 MF to Norddeutsches Lloyd, draft of a letter 16.1.1914, KEO-Archiv, F2 789/2. ► 20 Ernst Lorenzen, "Der deutsche Werkbund in Hagen", in: *Rheinisch-Westfälische Zeitung*, 9.7.1914, no. 820 (evening edition); idem, "Kunstausstellungen in Hagen", in: *Westfälisches Tageblatt*, 10.7.1914, no. 159, p. 3; M-S. (Fritz Meyer-Schönbrunn), Hagen i. W., in: *Der Cicerone*, vol. 6, 1914, p. 516. Of the acquisitions mentioned, only two fans can be clearly identified (inv. no. C 658 and inv. no. C 659). The sculpture bears the inv. no. P 276. ► 21 Karl With, *Buddhistische Plastik in Japan bis in den Beginn des 8. Jahrhunderts n. Chr.*, Vienna, 1919, pp. 22–23 and p. 118; figs 4–5. It was only after the death of KEO that With allowed loans from the East Asian collection for the first time, including *Shōtoku Taishi*; see *Ostasiatische Kunst*, exh. cat., Kestner-Gesellschaft e. V., Hanover, 1921, no. 281 with illustrations. ► 22 The objects acquired in 1920 – a lacquer box and two paintings from the Muromachi period – are no longer in the collection. *Ostasiatische Kunst. Dubletten* *aus den staatlichen Museen in Berlin (cat. no. 1846)*, auc. cat., Rudolphe Lepke's Kunst-Auctions-Haus, Berlin, 1920, nos 275, 664 and 667. ► 23 The first three paintings and the two sculptures have been part of the Museum Folkwang Collection up until today: inv. no. K 905 (Kanō Yōsen-in Korenobu), inv. no. G 54 (Gauguin), inv. no. G 115 (Maillol), inv. no. P 46 (Minne), inv. no. P 36 (Maillol). Hodler's painting, today in a private collection, was auctioned by Paul Cassirer on 8.3.1917. Despite what the catalogue raisonné states, the picture does not come from Alfred Walter Heymel's Collection; cf. Oskar Bätschmann, Paul Müller, *Hodler. Catalogue raisonné der Gemälde*, vol. 1: *Die Landschaften*, Zurich, 2008, no. 315. Neither the vase nor the *katagami* illustrated remain in the collection. ► 24 KEO, "Das Folkwang-Gebäude und sein Schöpfer", in: *Die Rheinlande*, vol. 5, no. 3, 1905, p. 88. ► 25 KEO, "Zur Einrichtung von Museen" (22.9.1903), in: *Die Museen als Volksbildungsstätten. Ergebnisse der 12. Konferenz der Centralstelle für Arbeiter-Wohlfahrtseinrichtungen*, Berlin, 1904, p. 140. ► 26 Alexis Joachimides, *Die Museumsreformbewegung in Deutschland und die Entstehung des modernen Museums 1880–1940*, Dresden, 2001, pp. 116–117. ► 27 KEO, *Van de Velde* (see note 6), p. 24. ► 28 KEO, "Der Folkwang in Hagen", undated, unpublished manuscript, KEO-Archiv, NAC2 12/15. ► 29 One important lot was auctioned off in 1919 at Rudolph Lepke's auction house in Berlin; see *Antiquitäten und alte Gemälde aus verschiedenem Privatbesitz (cat. no. 1827)*, auc. cat., Rudolphe Lepke's Kunst-Auctions-Haus, Berlin, 1919. ► 30 Maurice Denis, *Madonna with Child (The Kiss)*, 1902, MF, inv. no. G 38; Paul Gauguin, *The Kelp Gatherers (II)*, 1889, MF, inv. no. G 51; Paul Gauguin, *Riders on the Beach (I)*, 1902, MF, inv. no. G 52; Edvard Munch, *Winter at Nordstrand*, 1900/1901, Private Collection; Gerd Woll, *Edvard Munch. Complete Paintings*, London and New York, 2009, no. 473; Henri Rousseau, *A Centennial of Independence*, 1892, The Getty Center Los Angeles, inv. no. 88.PA.58; Dora Vallier, *Tout l'œuvre peint de Henri Rousseau*, Paris, 1982, no. 54. ► 31 R. Wagner to KEO, invoice from 12.10.1900, KEO-Archiv, F1 106/2. Of these *katagami*, four remain extant: inv. nos C 660–C 664. ► 32 KEO-Archiv, F1 144/1–3. Karl W. Hiersemann, *Katalog 288. Japanische Farbenholzschnitte. Ein-, Zwei- Drei- und Fünf-teilige Darstellungen sowie illustrierte Bücher, Kakemonos, Albums und einige japanische Original-Malereien*, Leipzig, 1903, p. 1. ► 33 Bing to KEO, invoice 7.5.1903, Archiv MF, A1/135–136. *Objets d'art* (see note 9), no. 295 (*Promenade sous les arbres fleuris*). Candidates include nos 341, 508, 797, 850, 892, 934, 964, in: Hirano Chie, *Kiyonaga. A Study of his Life and Work*, Boston, 1939. ► 34 Hiersemann, *Katalog 288* (see note 32), no. 165. Timothy Clark and Asano Shūgo, *The Passionate Art of Kitagawa Utamaro*, London, 1995, no. 202. ► 35 Hiersemann, *Katalog 288* (see note 32), no. 174 (*Sitzende junge Frau, sich in zwei Spiegeln betrachtend; neben ihr steht ein Mädchen*); not listed in Klaus-Joachim Brandt, *Hosoda Eishi 1756–1829. Der japanische Maler und Holzschnittmeister und seine* Schüler, Stuttgart, 1977. For purposes of comparison, see *Seki Temple (Sekidera)* now on the New York art market; see http://www.scholten-japanese-art.com/printsV.php?printID=847 (last accessed 1.3.2014). ► 36 KEO acquired at least one sheet from Toyokuni I; see Hiersemann, *Katalog 288* (see note 32), no. 133 (*Schauspieler in Rolle, in der Linken eine Falle [?] haltend*). ► 37 Bing to KEO, invoice 7.5.1903, Archiv MF, A1/135–136. *Objets d'art* (see note 9), no. 296 (*La Halte du palanquin*). This work is perhaps identical to *The Actor Iwai Hanshiro IV in Female Role, Standing Beside a Litter*, The Metropolitan Museum of Art, New York, inv. no. JP2783. ► 38 Hiersemann, *Katalog 288* (see note 32), no. 41 (*Meeresstrand mit sechs Fischerinnen und zwei Booten. Aus der Folge: "Hiakunin Jsshu Uba ga Yetoki", d. h. Erklärung der 100 Gedichte für Kinder*). ► 39 MF, inv. no. P 300; see Algemeene Kunsthandel D. Komter to KEO, invoice 7.9.1910, KEO-Archiv, R/F.DM.P 139/9. ► 40 MF, inv. no. P 301 (*Shō Kannon*) and MF, inv. no. P 316 (Maillol), KEO acquired both sculptures in Paris in 1904; see KEO, *Folkwang. Jahresbericht* (see note 11). ► 41 MF, inv. no. KPL 163 (*Beggar* or *Monk*) and MF, inv. no. KPL 159 (*Daruma*) (see note 9). It can be assumed that Taigny acquired a large number of the objects directly from Bing; see Raymond Koechlin, *Souvenirs d'un vieil amateur de l'art de l'Extrême-Orient*, Chalon-sur-Saône, 1930, p. 12. ► 42 MF, inv. no. KPL 118 (see note 10). ► 43 The picture, acquired in 1908, was lost due to wartime destruction at Museum Folkwang in 1945. ► 44 Curt Glaser, "Ausstellung alter ostasiatischer Kunst in der Königlichen Akademie der Künste zu Berlin", in: *Ostasiatische Zeitschrift*, vol. 1, 1912/1913, pp. 335–359, here p. 358. ► 45 Imai Yūko, "Changes in French Tastes for Japanese Ceramics", in: *Japan Review*, vol. 16, 2004, pp. 101–127. ► 46 Paul Westheim, *Ostasiatische Kunst. Zur Ausstellung der Berliner Akademie der Künste* (1912), cited in: *Die Ostasienausstellung Berlin 1912 und die Presse. Eine Dokumentation zur Rezeptionsgeschichte*, Hartmut Walravens (ed.), Hamburg, 1984 (Bibliographien zur ostasiatischen Kunstgeschichte in Deutschland 4), no. 68, pp. 92–94, here p. 93. ► 47 "Folkwang", in: *Westfälisches Tageblatt*, 5.1.1903, no. 3, MF, inv. no. KPL 144, acquired in 1900 by R. Wagner, Berlin; see Archiv MF, A1/99, and KEO-Archiv, F1 106/2. ► 48 MF, inv. no. KPL 139 a–e; see Archiv MF, A1/137. ► 49 MF, inv. no. KPL 140, ibid. ► 50 The printmaker Montefiore's Collection was sold in 1894; see *Objets d'Art Japonais provenant du Cabinet de Monsieur E.-L. M****, auc. cat., Hôtel des Commissaires-priseurs, Paris, 1894. ► 51 Ernst Große, "Über den Ausbau und die Aufstellung öffentlicher Sammlungen von ostasiatischen Kunstwerken", in: *Museumskunde*, vol. 1, 1905, pp. 123–139, here pp. 131–132. ► 52 Franz Wickhoff, "Die Zukunft der Kunstgewerbemuseen", in: *Kunst und Kunsthandwerk*, vol. 1, 1898, pp. 15–20, here p. 15. ► 53 Heinrich Wölfflin, *Kunstgeschichtliche Grundbegriffe*, Munich, 1915, p. 249. ► 54 Fritz Meyer-Schönbrunn, "Karl Ernst Osthaus und sein Werk", in: *Westermanns Monatshefte*, vol. 61 (726), 1916/1917, pp. 797–810, here p. 801. ► 55 Karl With, "Das Museum Folkwang und die ägyptischen Neuerwerbungen", in: *Die Rheinlande*, vol. 19, 1919, pp. 97–106, here p. 100. ► 56 Ernst Gosebruch, "Zur Neuordnung des Museums Folkwang in Essen", in: *Das Kunstblatt*, vol. 13 (2), 1929, p. 51.

Geneviève Aitken, *Claude Monet, Vincent Van Gogh, Henri Rivière and Auguste Rodin as collectors of Japanese woodblock prints*

► 1 The Franco-Japanese Treaty of Peace, Friendship and Commerce was concluded in Edo on 9.10.1858. Cf. Les Cinq climats, *Le Japon et la France, images d'une découverte*, René Sieffert (ed.), Paris, 1974, p. 35. ► 2 The subjects of these woodblock prints are women from different social classes, as well as around fifty views of Edo; cf. Madeleine David, "L'art japonais à l'Exposition universelle de 1867", in: *Le Japon et la France* (see note 1), p. 118. ► 3 *The Harvesters* (P. 7304), *The Viaduct at Arles* (P. 7303) and one of the three portraits of *Père Tanguy* (P. 7302) held in Musée Rodin, Paris. ► 4 Henri Rivière, *Les détours du chemin, souvenirs, notes et croquis, 1864–1951*, Barbentane, 2004, pp. 108–109. ► 5 In June/July 1888, Theo Van Gogh organised an exhibition with ten pictures painted by Monet in Antibes, presenting himself as their buyer. Vincent Van Gogh, *The Letters*, letter no. 625, 15–16.6.1888. All references to and quotations from Van Gogh's letters cite the online edition of Leo Jansen, Hans Luijten and Nienke Bakker: www.vangoghletters.org. ► 6 Theo Van Gogh in a letter to his brother: "Monet dit que tes tableaux étaient les meilleurs de l'exposition" ("Monet said that your paintings were the best in the exhibition."), Van Gogh, *Letters* (see note 5), letter no. 862, 23.4.1890. ► 7 Rodin gave Monet two sculptures as a gift: a *Minotaur* (plaster) and *Young Mother in the Grotto* (bronze), now held in Musée Marmottan (Paris, Musée Marmottan, MM. 5180 and MM. 5127). From Monet, Rodin received *Belle-Île*, painted in 1886 (Paris, Musée Rodin, P. 7329), and the pastel *Young Man with a Cap* (D. 7694). ► 8 Gustave Geffroy and Octave Mirbeau, *Claude Monet et A. Rodin*, Paris, 1889. ► 9 This album carries the inscription: "Depuis 1890 j'ai conservé ces estampes en feuilles détachées telles qu'elles se trouvaient dans le carton de Vincent Van Gogh à Auvers-sur-Oise me proposant de les monter à la manière des Japonais [...] en souvenir de Vincent Van Gogh et de mon père. Son ami. Paul Gachet, Auvers, octobre 1921" ("Since 1890, I have kept the woodblock prints on loose pages, just as they were found in Vincent Van Gogh's carton in Auvers-sur-Oise, and I undertook to bind them in the Japanese manner [...], in memory of Vincent Van Gogh and my father. His friend. Paul Gachet, Auvers, October, 1921"), Paris, Musée Guimet, MA 2107. ► 10 A sale of Japanese woodblock prints owned by Rivière from the 16th, 17th and 18th centuries took place on 26–28.10.1953 in the Hôtel Drouot in Paris; Musée Guimet also holds around twenty illustrated books that had been owned by Rivière. ► 11 Geneviève Aitken and Marianne Delafond, *La collection d'estampes japonaises de Claude Monet*, Paris, 1983 (new edition: Lausanne, 2003); *Catalogue of the Van Gogh Museum's Collection of Japanese prints*, Amsterdam, 1991. ► 12 *Rodin et le Japon*, exh. cat., Shizuoka Prefectural Museum of Art and Aichi Prefectural Museum of Art, Shizuoka, 2001 (2 volumes in Japanese, vol. 1 in French); *Henri Rivière*, exh. cat., Ishikawa Prefectural Museum of Art, Kanagawa Prefectural Museum of Modern Art Hayama and Yamaguchi Prefectural Hagi Uragami Museum, Tokyo, 2009. ► 13 Two kinds of calculation are used to evaluate each collection: piece by piece or as a whole when it concerns diptychs, triptychs or works with even more parts. It is important to bear this in mind, as they are not divided and presented in this manner. ► 14 Of which there were 200 individual pages, 26 triptychs, 1 diptych, 15 illustrated books, 3 albums containing different artists and 13 pages taken from albums. ► 15 The Collection comprises Vincent's and Theo's woodblock prints, plus those of Theo's son Vincent Willem Van Gogh (in which proportion is unknown). For the purpose of completion, the newspaper *Tokyo Shimbun* has since donated 35 woodblock prints by Hiroshige to the Collection. Cf. *Catalogue of the Van Gogh Museum's Collection* (see note 11), p. 8. ► 16 The woodblock prints generally bear a censorship stamp ("*kiwame*" – approved – or "*aratame*" – verified), with the exception of erotic woodblock prints (*shunga*), calendars and *surimono* (greeting cards). ► 17 "[...] où l'on brocantait les curiosités rapportées par les longs-courriers", in: Marc Elder, *À Giverny chez Claude*

Monet, Paris, 1924, pp. 63–64. ► 18 Edmond and Jules de Goncourt, *Journal des Goncourt – Mémoires de la vie littéraire*, vol. 6, Paris, 1892, p. 308, 17.2.1892. Unless otherwise specified, all quotations in English have been translated by the translator of this essay. ► 19 Van Gogh visited the Antwerp World Fair, where Japanese woodblock prints were presented; cf. Van Gogh, *Letters* (see note 5), note on letter no. 545, 28.11.1885. ► 20 "On nous laissait feuilleter pendant de longues après-midi, albums et estampes pour notre seule initiation, – on savait bien que nous n'étions pas des acheteurs – mais c'étaient de nouveaux adeptes qu'on formait", Rivière, *Les détours* (see note 4), p. 89. ► 21 "Si on disait à un amateur SÉRIEUX de japonaiserie [...] – monsieur je ne peux pas m'empêcher de trouver admirables ces crepons à 5 sous – Il est plus que probable que l'autre serait un peu choqué et aurait pitié de mon ignorance et de mon mauvais gout." ("Supposing one were to say to a SERIOUS collector of Japanese art [...] sir, I cannot help finding these 5-sous Japanese prints admirable – It's more than likely that that person would be a bit shocked and would pity my ignorance and my bad taste."), Van Gogh, *Letters* (see note 5), letter no. 686, 23 or 24.9.1888. ► 22 "Il n'y a pas beaucoup à y gagner, voilà pourquoi personne ne s'en occupe. Néanmoins au bout de quelques années tout cela deviendra bien rare, se vendra plus cher", Van Gogh, *Letters* (see note 5), letter no. 642, 15.7.1888. ► 23 "[...] cela te procurera un Claude Monet et d'autres tableaux car si toi tu prends le mal pour dénicher les crepons tu as bien le droit de faire des échanges avec, aux peintres contre des tableaux", ibid. ► 24 The collection set up in 1880 by Hayashi Tadamasa comprises between five hundred and six hundred paintings, acquired through purchase or exchange, including some pictures by Monet such as *Belle-Île*, which is kept in the Bridgestone Museum of Art, Ishibashi Foundation; further information on Hayashi Tadamasa in Brigitte Koyama-Richard, *Japon rêvé, Edmond de Goncourt et Hayashi Tadamasa*, Paris, 2001. ► 25 Today, the collection still contains six works by Toyokuni, four by Hiroshige, three by Eisen, one by Taigaku, one by Hokuju, one by Hokusai and one by Toyokuni II. In return, the members of *Shirakaba* expected a dispatch with some sculptures by the master, which they planned to exhibit in the near future. ► 26 Edmond de Goncourt, *La Maison d'un artiste*, Paris, 1881; also worth mention here is the novel *À Rebours*, published by Joris-Karl Huysmans in 1884. ► 27 "Mijn werkplaats is nog al dragelijk. vooral omdat ik een partij japansche prentjes tegen de muren heb gespeld die mij erg amuseeren", Van Gogh, *Letters* (see note 5), letter no. 545, 28.11.1885. ► 28 Arnost Hofbauer, "Quelques heures chez Rodin", in: *Volne Smery*, Prague, 1901, no. 5, pp. 135–142, cited in: Bénédicte Garnier, "Une collection de rêve", in: *Rodin. Le rêve japonais*, exh. cat., Musée Rodin, Paris, Paris, 2007, pp. 14–15. ► 29 "[...] profusion d'estampes japonaises, simplement mises sous verre, les plus belles, les plus rares", Gustave Geffroy, *Monet, sa vie, son œuvre*, Paris, 1980, pp. 448–449. ► 30 *Estampes japonaises primitives tirées des collections de MM. Bing, Blondeau, Bullier... [et al.]*, exh. cat., Musée des Arts décoratifs, Paris, M. Vignier and M. Inada (eds.), Paris, 1909: three items on loan from Rivière (Kiyonobu, Kiyomasu and unknown artists). *Harunobu, Koriusai, Shunsho. Estampes japonaises tirées des collections de MM. Bing, Bouasse-Lebel, Bullier ... [et al.]*, exh. cat., Musée des Arts décoratifs, M. Vignier and M. Inada (eds.), Paris, 1910: fifteen items on loan from Rivière (all by Harunobu). *Kiyonaga, Buncho, Sharaku, estampes japonaises ...*, exh. cat., Musée des Arts décoratifs, Paris, M. Vignier and M. Inada (eds.), Paris, 1911: two items on loan from Rivière (Shuncho, Sharaku). *Utamaro. Estampes Japonaises exposées*, exh. cat., Musée des Arts décoratifs, M. Vignier and M. Inada (eds.), Paris, 1912: four items on loan from Rivière. *Toyokuni [et] Hiroshigé. Estampes japonaises tirées de collections de MM. Bing ...*, exh. cat., Musée des Arts décoratifs, Paris, M. Vignier and M. Inada (eds.), Paris, 1914: one item on loan from Rivière (Hiroshige). ► 31 Henri Rivière lived in this house with his wife from December 1895 until 1913: "C'est ainsi que nous avions baptisé notre domaine: l'iris une de mes fleurs préférées, me servait de marque de cachet, j'en timbrais mes aquarelles" ("This is what we called our country house: the iris, one of my favourite plants, which served me as a seal motif, which I imprinted on my watercolours"), Rivière, *Les détours* (see note 4), p. 79. ► 32 "[...] je vous remercie d'avoir pensé à moi pour les fleurs d'Hokusai [...]. Vous ne me parlez pas des coquelicots et c'est là l'important, car j'ai déjà les iris, les chrysanthèmes, les pivoines et les volubilis", Daniel Wildenstein, *Claude Monet*, Lausanne, 1979, vol. III, letter no. 1322, 8.2.1896, p. 289. ► 33 *Le Jardin de Monet à Giverny: l'invention d'un paysage*, exh. cat., Musée des Impressionnistes, Giverny, Giverny and Milan, 2009. ► 34 During a tour of Norway in 1895, Monet wrote to Blanche Hoschedé: "J'ai là un motif délicieux des petites îles au ras de l'eau, toutes couvertes de neige et au fond une montagne. On dirait le Japon, ce qui du reste bien fréquent en ce pays. J'ai en train une vue de Sandviken qui ressemble à un village japonais, puis je fais une montagne que l'on voit de partout ici et qui me fait songer au Fuji-Yama." ("I have here a delicious motif of small islands covered completely in snow, lying just above the surface of the water, and in the background a mountain. It is like Japan, which is often the case in this country. I'm working on a view of Sandviken, which is similar to a Japanese village, and then I shall paint a mountain that can be seen everywhere here and which makes me dream of Fuji-Yama"), Wildenstein, *Claude Monet* (see note 32), vol. III, letter no. 1276, 1.3.1895, p. 282. ► 35 "[...] la loire fait des ornements japonais", Auguste Rodin, Carnet de dessin no. 23, D.6497bis, Musée Rodin, Paris. ► 36 "Le salon est en boiseries violettes, beaucoup de gravures japonaises y sont accrochées, ainsi que dans la salle à manger qui est toute jaune", Julie Manet, *Journal 1893–1899*, Paris, 1987, p. 45.

Sandra Gianfreda, *The early* Japonistes

► 1 The terms "Japoniste" and "Japonisant" were used synonymously in the nineteenth century to refer to a person with a declared interest in Japan; cf. Niiro Keiko, *L'image du Japon en France entre 1860 et 1915*, doctoral dissertation 1997, Villeneuve-d'Ascq (book on demand), pp. 284, 288, 344, 348. ► 2 Bracquemond may have come into contact with Whistler through his printer Auguste Delâtre; Whistler is thought to have introduced Tissot, a close confidant of Degas, to Japanese art; Whistler, Degas and Fantin-Latour, in turn, were close friends; De Nittis was a friend of Degas and Manet; Stevens and Fantin-Latour were friends of Manet as well. Fantin-Latour, who introduced Manet to Whistler, also socialised with Monet and Renoir. At the same time, many artists had contacts to art critics and writers too – for example, Manet to Zola, Baudelaire, Astruc and Théodore Duret, Whistler to Duret and Stéphane Mallarmé, Monet and Fantin-Latour to Astruc and Bracquemond, and Degas and De Nittis to the Goncourt brothers. On the *Société du Jing-lar*, see Bernard Bumpus, "The 'Jing-lar' and republican politics: drinking, dining and japonisme", in: *Apollo*, vol. 143, no. 409, March 1996, pp. 13–16. ► 3 In the multi-volume *Recueil de dessins pour l'art et l'industrie* by Adalbert de Beaumont and Eugène Collinot (appearing from 1859 to 1873), Delâtre printed motifs from Hokusai's *Manga* volumes – presumably for the first time – as artistic models (from 1861); see Geneviève Lacambre, "Hokusai and the French diplomats. Some remarks on the collection of Baron de Chassiron", in: *The Documented Image: Visions in Art History*, Gabriel P. Weisberg and Laurinda S. Dixon (eds.), Syracuse, 1987, p. 73. ► 4 Deanna Marohn Bendix, *Diabolical Designs. Paintings, Interiors, and Exhibitions of James McNeill Whistler*, Washington DC, 1995), pp. 65–67. ► 5 The model's father refused to purchase the painting at his daughter's request because he did not recognise her in it; see Andrew McLaren Young et al., *The Paintings of James McNeill Whistler*, text volume, Glasgow, 1980, pp. 26–27. ► 6 Library of Congress, Washington DC, Manuscript Division, Pennell-Whistler Collection, PWC 1/33/21; see http://www.whistler.arts.gla.ac.uk, letter no. 08040 (last accessed 23.2.2014). ► 7 On Whistler and *Japonisme*: *James McNeill Whistler*, exh. cat., Tate Gallery, London, Richard Dorment and Margaret F. MacDonald (eds.), London, 1994, pp. 85–97; Robin Spencer, "Whistler and Japan: Work in Progress", in: *Japonisme in Art: An International Symposium*, Society for the Study of Japonisme (ed.), Tokyo, 1980, pp. 57–81; Diane N. Towle, *Spaces of Japonisme and the Art of Whistler, Van Gogh, and Monet: Collecting, Decoration, and the Japanese Other*, doctoral dissertation 2013, Saint Louis, pp. 67–78 and pp. 130–179. ► 8 Michael Justin Wentworth, "Tissot and Japonisme", in: *Japonisme in Art* (see note 7), p. 128; Oswald Doughty and John Robert Wahl (eds.), *Letters of Dante Gabriel Rossetti*, vol. 2, Oxford, 1965, pp. 526–527. ► 9 Ibid. ► 10 A reviewer of the Paris Salon of 1865, however, dismissed Whistler's *Princess* as "pure caprice and fantasy" ("que du caprice et de la fantaisie"); see Gustave Vattier, "Le Salon de 1865: Cinquième et dernier article", in: *Le courrier du dimanche*, no. 27, 2.7.1865, p. 6. ► 11 Another explanation could be that he painted the work for reasons of financial difficulties, as such motifs were very popular. At any rate, when it was presented to the public with the title *Japonnerie* on the occasion of the second impressionist exhibition, it immediately found a well-funded buyer; see Virgina Spate and David Bromfield, "A New and Strange Beauty: Monet and Japanese Art", in: *Monet & Japan*, exh. cat., National Gallery of Australia, Canberra, Virginia Spate et al. (ed.), Melbourne, 2001, p. 23; also cf. Ruth Butler, "Money and *La Japonaise*", in: idem, *Hidden in the Shadow of the Master: The Model-Wives of Cézanne, Monet and Rodin*, New Haven, 2008, pp. 173–185; on the *Japonaise* as a parody, Vincenzo Farinella, "'Le bionde allegrie della natura': qualche verifica sul giapponismo di Monet", in: *Monet. Atti del convegno*, Treviso, 16–17.1.2002, Rodolphe Rapetti et al. (eds.), Conegliano, 2003, pp. 227–228. ► 12 René Gimpel, *Journal d'un collectionneur*, Paris, 1963, 19.8.1918, p. 68. Here, Monet also said that he had executed the painting just to earn money. ► 13 With *The Japanese Vase*, circa 1865, Private Collection. ► 14 Jules Champfleury devoted an article to the atelier house decorated in the Japanese style: "La mode des japoniaiseries", in: *La Vie parisienne*, 21.11.1869, reprinted in Geneviève and Jean Lacambre, *Champfleury: Son regard et celui de Baudelaire*, Paris, 1990, pp. 143–145. ► 15 Michael Wentworth, *James Tissot*, Oxford, 1984, p. 71. ► 16 "puissant élément de modernité", Alfred Stevens, *Impressions sur la peinture*, Paris, 1886, p. 30 (CI). ► 17 "Déjà même de prétendus peintres de la vie élégante nous fatiguent de leurs cabinets japonais, de leurs fleurs japonaises, de leurs laques et de leurs bronzes japonais qui prennent la place principale sur la toile et jouent un rôle bien autrement considérable que les personnages", Champfleury, "La mode" (see note 14); other painters who painted ladies in Japanese-style interiors in the 1870s and 1880s were Beyle, Croegart, Firmin-Girard, Lefebvre and Villa; see: author unknown, "Firmin-Girard et le Japonisme", in: *Bijutsushi-Ronsō (Studies in Art History)*, no. 6, Département d'Histoire de l'Art, Faculté des Lettres, Université de Tokyo, 1990, pp. 193–209 (http://utcp.c.u-tokyo.ac.jp/publications/pdf/CollectionUTCP7_Miura_06.pdf; last accessed 24.2.2014). ► 18 Colta Feller Ives, *The Great Wave: The Influence of Japanese Woodcuts on French Prints*, New York, 1974, p. 23; Theodore Reff, "Manet's Portrait of Zola", in: *The Burlington Magazine*, vol. 117, no. 862, Jan. 1975, pp. 34–44; Katharina Schmidt, "Zu Édouard Manets 'Porträt Émile Zola'", in: *Manet, Zola, Cézanne. Das Porträt des modernen Literaten*, exh. cat., Kunstmuseum Basel, Katharina Schmidt (ed.), Ostfildern-Ruit, 1999, pp. 21–47; Barbara Wittmann, *Gesichter geben. Édouard Manet und die Poetik des Porträts*, Munich, 2004, pp. 89–95. ► 19 In 1868, Astruc ranked Manet among the early collectors of Japanese art; see Zacharie Astruc, "Le Japon chez nous", in: *L'Étendard*, 26.5.1868, pp. 1–2; list reprinted in Sharon Flescher, *Zacharie Astruc, Critic, Artist and Japoniste*, doctoral dissertation 1977, New York and London, 1978, p. 360. Also cf. Manuela Moscatiello, *Le japonisme de Giuseppe de Nittis: Un peintre italien en France à la fin du XIXe siècle*, Berne et al., 2011, pp. 106–107; on Zola: Ernest Chesneau, "Exposition Universelle. Le Japon à Paris", in: *Gazette des Beaux-Arts*, vol. 18, 1.9.1878, p. 387. ► 20 Lane S. Faison, "Renoir's Hommage à Manet", in: *Intuition und Kunstwissenschaft. Festschrift für Hanns Swarzenski*, Peter Bloch et al. (eds.), Berlin, 1973, pp. 571–578. ► 21 Alain de Leiris, *The Drawings of Édouard Manet*, Berkeley and Los Angeles, 1969, no. 399; *Manet and the Sea*, exh. cat., The Art Institute of Chicago, Juliet Wilson-Bareau and David Degener (eds.), Chicago, 2003, p. 114. ► 22 One of his sketchbooks, for example, contains three motifs which he copied down to the detail from the second volume of Hokusai's *Manga*; see Anne Coffin Hanson, "Alain de Leiris, The Drawings of Édouard Manet", review in: *The Art Bulletin*, vol. 53, no. 4 (Dec. 1971), pp. 544–545. ► 23 Colta Ives, "Degas, Japanese Prints, and *Japonisme*", in: *The Private Collection of Edgar Degas*, exh. cat., The Metropolitan Museum of Art, New York, Anne Dumas et al. (ed.), New York, 1997, pp. 247–260. ► 24 Chesneau, "Le Japon" (see note 19), pp. 387 and 396. ► 25 *Degas and the Art of Japan*, exh. cat., Reading Public Museum, Reading (PA), Jill DeVonyar and Richard Kendall (eds.), New Haven and London, 2007. ► 26 Ibid., p. 21. The exchange cannot have come about before 1878, the year in which Hayashi and Degas presumably met at a demonstration of Japanese ink painting by Watanabe Seitei in the home of Philippe Burty. ► 27 Ibid., p. 68; Paul André Lemoisne, *Degas et son œuvre*, Paris, 1946–1949, vol. 1, p. 176. ► 28 For example, Pierre Guerre and Max Imdahl, in: *Wege zu Edgar Degas*, Wilhelm Schmid (ed.), Munich, 1988, pp. 207 and 298–309. ► 29 Françoise Heilbrun, "Sur les photographies de Degas", in: *Degas inédit. Actes du Colloque Degas*, Musée d'Orsay, Paris, 18–21.4.1988, Paris, 1989, pp. 159–180. ► 30 On the relationship between photography and painting: Aaron Scharf, *Art and Photography*, London, 1968; *Malerei und Photographie*, exh. cat., Kunsthaus Zürich, Erika Billeter (ed.), Zurich, 1977; Kirk Varnedoe, "The Artifice of Candor: Impressionism and Photography Reconsidered", in: *Art in America*, Jan. 1980, pp. 66–78; *Snapshot: Painters and Photography, Bonnard to Vuillard*, exh. cat., Van Gogh Museum, Amsterdam et al., Elizabeth W. Easton (ed.), New Haven and London, 2012. Also see: André Dombrowski, "History, Memory, and Instantaneity in Edgar Degas's Place de la Concorde", in: *The Art Bulletin*, vol. 93, no. 2, 2011, pp. 195–219. ► 31 Henri Loyrette, "Edgar Degas. Orchestermusiker", in: *Impressionisten. 6 Französische Meisterwerke*, published in conjunction with the exhibition *Six chefs-d'œuvre français prêtés par Francfort*, Musée d'Orsay, Paris, Frankfurt am Main, 1999, pp. 63–64. ► 32 *The Opera Orchestra*, circa 1870, Musée d'Orsay, Paris, *The Ballet from Robert le Diable*, 1871, The Metropolitan Museum of Art, New York; *The Ballet Scene from Meyerbeer's Opera Robert Le Diable*, 1876, Victoria and Albert Museum, London. ► 33 Theodore Reff, *Degas: The Artist's Mind*, London, 1976, pp. 77–78; John House, "Impressionism and Japan", in: *Japonisme and the Rise of the Modern Art Movement – The Arts of the Meiji Period: The Khalili Collection*, Gregory Irvine (ed.), London, 2013, pp. 110–111. ► 34 Shinoda Yūjirō, *Degas. Der Einzug des Japanischen in die französische Malerei*, doctoral dissertation 1957, Cologne, 1957, pp. 59–61; idem, "Der Einzug des Japanischen in die Französische Malerei: Hokusai und Degas", in: *Wege zu Edgar Degas* (see note 28), pp. 288–297; Siegfried Wichmann, "Bewegung als Eigenexistenz im Werk Hokusais und in den Pastellen und Zeichnungen von Edgar Degas", in: ibid., pp. 281–287. ► 35 For example, *Frieze of Dancers*, circa 1895, The Cleveland Museum of Art. ► 36 *Degas and the Ballet. Picturing Movement*, exh. cat., The Royal Academy, London, Richard Kendall and Jill DeVonyar (eds.), London, 2011, p. 150. ► 37 Also see: David Park Curry, *James McNeill Whistler: Uneasy Pieces*, New York, 2004, pp. 177–192. ► 38 There is a reference to this in: Jacques Dufwa, *Winds from the East: A Study in the Art of Manet, Degas, Monet and Whistler 1856–86*, Stockholm, 1981, p. 172; *Japan and Britain: An Aesthetic Dialogue 1850–1930*, exh. cat., Barbican Art Gallery, London et al., Satō Tomoko and Watanabe Toshio (eds.), London, 1991, p. 106; Ono Ayako, *Japonisme in Britain. Whistler, Menpes, Henry, Hornel and Nineteenth-Century Japan*, doctoral dissertation 2001, Abingdon, 2003, p. 79. ► 39 As early as 1868, he wrote to his friend Fantin-Latour, who had sent him two still lifes: "[…] et voici comment d'abord il me semble que la toile donnée, les couleurs doivent être pour ainsi dire brodées là dessus – c'est à dire la même couleur reparaitre continuellement ça et là comme le même fil dans une broderie – et ainsi avec les autres – plus ou moins selon leur importance – le tout formant de cette façon un patron harmonieux – Regardes les Japonais comme ils comprennent ça! – Ce n'est jamais le contraste qu'ils cherchent, mais au contraire la repetition" ("[…] and this is how it seems to me first of all that, with the canvas as given, the colours should be so to speak embroidered on it – in other words the same colour reappearing continually here and there like the same thread in an embroidery – and so on with the others – more or less according to their importance – the whole forming in this way an harmonious pattern – Look how the Japanese understand this! – They never search for contrast, but on the contrary for repetition"), 30.9.1868, Library of Congress, Washington DC, Manuscript Division, Pennell-Whistler Collection, PWC 1/33/28; see http://www.whistler.arts.gla.ac.uk, letter no. 11983 (last accessed 16.5.2014). ► 40 Elizabeth Robins Pennell and Joseph Pennell, *The Life of James McNeill Whistler*, 2 vols, Philadelphia, 1908, vol. 1, p. 234. ► 41 It is not possible to identify all seven of the paintings shown with certainty. In his scathing review of the exhibition, Ernest Chesneau cites the titles: *Le japonisme dans les arts*, in: *Musée universel*, 1873, 2nd semester, pp. 214–217. ► 42 Charles Stuckey, "The Predications and Implications of Monet's Series", in: *The Repeating Image. Multiples in French Painting from David to Matisse*, exh. cat., The Walters Art Museum, Baltimore, Eik Kahng (ed.), New Haven and London, 2007, pp. 99–100. ► 43 Mary Morton and Charlotte Eyerman, *Courbet and the Modern Landscape*, exh. cat., J. Paul Getty Museum, Los Angeles, et al., Los Angeles, 2006, p. 104. Also cf. Klaus Herding, "Gustave Courbet. Die Woge", in: *Impressionisten* (see note 31), p. 17. ► 44 Paul Huet, *Breakers at Granville Point*, 1853, Musée du Louvre, Paris; Whistler, *The Blue Wave, Biarritz*, 1862, Hill-Stead Museum, Farmington (CT); but also see examples of German art such as Carl Gustav Carus, *Surf at Rügen*, 1819, Staatliche Kunstsammlungen, Dresden. The most well-known photograph is undoubtedly that by Gustave Le Gray, *The Great Wave, Sète*, 1856/1857. ► 45 On this subject, see above all Joseph J. Rishel, "Gustave Courbet", in: *Manet and the Sea* (see note 21), pp. 159–164. ► 46 Linda Nochlin, *Courbet*, New York, 2007, p. 202; Jocelyn Bouquillard, "Vagues japonaises: l'influence des 'images du monde flottant'", in: *Vagues: Autour des* Paysage de mer *de Courbet*, exh. cat., Le Havre, 2004, pp. 40–41. ► 47 On Champfleury: Lacambre, *Champfleury. Son regard et celui de Baudelaire* (see note 14); Inaga Shigemi, "The Making of Hokusai's Reputation in the Context of Japonism", in: *Japan Review*, 2003, 15, pp. 78–79; when Champfleury's print collection was auctioned off on 26.1.1891, it included four Hokusai volumes, presumably *Manga*; see *Catalogue des eaux-fortes, lithographies, caricatures (…) formant la collection Champfleury*, with a foreword by Paul Eudel, Paris, 1891, p. 117 (no. 526). On Duret: Marie-Chantal Nessler and Françoise Royer, *Théodore Duret. Entre négoce de cognac et critique d'art*, Saintes, 2010, esp. chapters 4 and 6. ► 48 "Le Japon chez nous", in: *L'Étendard*, 26.5.1868; cf. *Le Japonisme*, exh. cat., Paris, 1988, p. 80. ► 49 Jacques de Caso, "1861: Hokusai rue Jacob", in: *The Burlington Magazine*, vol. 111, no. 798, Sept. 1969, p. 565; Lacambre, "Hokusai" (see note 3), p. 80; Henry B. Smith II, *Hokusai: One Hundred Views of Mount Fuji*, London, 1988, p. 22. Motifs from *One Hundred Views of Mount Fuji* were also reproduced in 1861 in the multi-volume work *Recueil de dessins pour l'art et l'industrie* by Adalbert de Beaumont and Eugène V. Collinot; see Lacambre, "Hokusai" (see note 3), p. 73, and Martin Eidelberg, "Bracquemond, Delâtre and the discovery of Japanese prints", in: *The Burlington Magazine*, vol. 123, no. 937, April 1981, p. 227. Astruc also had knowledge of the series by 1867 at the latest; see Flescher, *Zacharie Astruc* (see note 19), p. 504. ► 50 See especially Spate and Bromfield, "A New and Strange Beauty" (see note 11), pp. 15–16. The fact that Monet's painting was inspired by Japanese art can be deduced from statements by Monet and Renoir; see ibid., p. 201. ► 51 Matthi Forrer, *Hokusai*, Munich, 2010. ► 52 Stuckey, "The Predications" (see note 42); also see Sylvie Patin, "Les 'séries' dans l'œuvre de Monet", in: *Quarante-huit/Quatorze: La revue du Musée d'Orsay*, no. 4, 1992, pp. 51–60; Paul Hayes Tucker, *Monet in the '90s. The Series Paintings*, exh. cat., Museum of Fine Arts, Boston, New Haven and London, 1989. ► 53 Stuckey, "The Predications" (see note 42), p. 83. ► 54 "Je pioche beaucoup, je m'entête en une série d'effets différents (des meules) mais, à cette époque, le soleil décline si vite que je ne peux le suivre. Je deviens d'une lenteur à travailler qui me désespère mais plus que je vais, plus je vois ce que je cherche : 'instantanéité', surtout l'enveloppe, la même lumière répandue partout, et plus que jamais les choses faciles venues d'un jet me dégoûtent", in: Gustave Geoffroy, *Claude Monet, sa vie, son temps, son œuvre*, Paris, 1922, p. 189. English translation: Tucker, *Monet in the '90s* (see note 52), p. 3. ► 55 The idea that the Japanese series was the impulse for Monet's series is postulated particularly by David Bromfield, "Japanese Art, Monet and the Formation of Impressionism: Cultural Exchange and Appropriation in Later Nineteenth-Century European Art", in: *Recovering the Orient*, Andrew Gerstle and Anthony Milner (eds.), Chur et al., 1994, pp. 40–41, as well as in Spate and Bromfield, "A New and Strange Beauty" (see note 11), p. 39, and Towle, *Spaces of Japonisme* (see note 7), pp. 254–258; Stuckey, "The Predications" (see note 42), pp. 90–91, makes only marginal reference to this matter. ► 56 Marianne Delafond and Geneviève Aitken, *La collection d'estampes japonaises de Claude Monet*, Paris, 1983 (new edition: Lausanne, 2007), p. 12, pp. 61–64, p. 150. ► 57 Smith II, Hokusai (see note 49), p. 11; cf. Wolfgang Kemp, *Von Gestalt gesteigert zu Gestalt. Hokusais 100 Ansichten des Fuji*, Berlin, 2006, p. 10. ► 58 Gary Hickey, "Waves of Influence", in: *Monet & Japan* (see note 11), p. 178. ► 59 Stuckey, "The Predications" (see note 42), p. 83. ► 60 Gottfried Boehm, *Paul Cézanne. Montagne Sainte-Victoire*, Frankfurt am Main, 1988; *Sainte-Victoire, Cézanne 1990*, exh. cat., Musée Granet, Aix-en-Provence, Paris, 1990; *Cézanne in Provence*, exh. cat., National Gallery of Art, Washington, Philip Conisbee and Denis Coutagne (eds.), New Haven, 2006. In a letter to his son of 8.9.1906, Cézanne himself confirmed that the idea of painting in series was inherent to his own work: "Here on the bank of the river the motifs multiply, the same subject seen from a different angle offers subject for study of the most powerful interest and so varied that I think I could occupy myself for months without changing place, by turning now more to the right, now more to the left", in: *Cézanne in Provence*, exh. cat., National Gallery of Art, Washington DC et al., New Haven, 2006, p. 283. ► 61 Tanaka Hidemichi, "Cézanne and 'Japonisme'", in: *Artibus et Historiae*, vol. 22, no. 44, 2001, pp. 204–210. A woman known by name to the author of this essay purchased a number of Japanese woodblock prints that came from Jas de Bouffan, Cézanne's estate in Aix. It is not certain, however, whether they belonged to Cézanne (verbal message from the woman to Oliver Wick, Zurich, in March 2014). The woman sold them a few years ago to an antiquarian in Geneva. We received the information that Cézanne is thought to have owned woodblock prints from Geneviève Lacambre, Paris, in December 2013, for which we hereby extend our sincere thanks. ► 62 Cf. esp. Tanaka, "Cézanne and 'Japonisme'" (see note 61); Mabuchi, "Japonisme et naturalisme", in: *Le Japonisme*, exh. cat., Galeries nationales du Grand Palais, Paris, et al., Paris, 1988, p. 40. ► 63 The Japanese series as inspiration for the European artists was already established by Louis Aubert in *Les maîtres de l'estampe japonaise*, Paris, 1914, pp. 249–251. ► 64 John Coplans, *Serial Imagery*, exh. cat., Pasadena Museum of Art et al., Pasadena, 1968; *The Repeating Image* (see note 42).

Belinda Thomson, Japonisme *in the works of Van Gogh, Gauguin, Bernard and Anquetin*

► 1 "Il est incontestable que l'imagerie japonaise a fait s'ouvrir bien des yeux. Vous n'avez pas tant à vous émouvoir de notre impressionnisme, c'est vous qui l'avez inventé", Félix Régamey, cited in: Omoto Keiko and Francis Macouin, *Quand le Japon s'ouvrit au monde, Émile Guimet et les arts d'Asie*, Paris, 1990 (new edition: 2005), p. 100. Unless otherwise specified, all quotations in English have been translated by the author of this essay. ► 2 "[…] le vieux Japon s'écroule […] J'assiste à la fin de ce monde merveilleux, artistique, poétique, plein de douceur qui s'en va sombrer dans le sombre fatras de la civilisation occidentale", letter from Régamey to his mother, 1876, cited in: Omoto and Macouin, *Quand le Japon* (see note 1), pp. 66, 68. ► 3 In attempting to bring some new thinking to this important topic, I have not attempted to deal with every aspect. For further reading on Van Gogh and Japan, see the general bibliography – in particular, Kōdera Tsukasa, "Van Gogh's utopian Japonisme", in: *Catalogue of the Van Gogh Museum's Collection of Japanese Prints*, Amsterdam, 1991, pp. 11–45. On Gauguin and Japanese prints, see the pioneering article by Yvonne Thirion, "L'influence de l'estampe japonaise dans l'œuvre de Gauguin", in: *Gazette des Beaux-Arts*, no. 47, Jan.–Apr. 1958, pp. 95–114. ► 4 Louis van Tilborgh, *Van Gogh and Japan*, Amsterdam, 2006, p. 7. ► 5 For a suggestive reading of Van Gogh's *Japonisme*, see Elizabeth C. Childs's essay, "Seeking the studio of the south: Van Gogh, Gauguin and Avant-Garde Identity", in: *Van Gogh and the Painters of the Petit Boulevard*, Saint Louis Art Museum, Saint Louis, 2001, pp. 119–135. ► 6 For further considerations of Gauguin and Van Gogh's contrasting relationship with Japanese art, see Douglas Druick and Peter Kort Zegers, *Van Gogh and Gauguin: The Studio of the South*, Art Institute of Chicago and Van Gogh Museum, Amsterdam, New York and London, 2001; Debora Silverman, *Van Gogh and Gauguin: The Search for Sacred Art*, New York, 2000. For Bernard, see *Émile Bernard 1868–1941. A Pioneer of Modern Art*, Städtische Kunsthalle, Mannheim, and Van Gogh Museum, Amsterdam, Zwolle, 1990; Fred Leeman, *Émile Bernard*, Paris, 2013. For Anquetin, see Frédéric Destrémau, *Louis Anquetin ou la Passion d'être peintre*, Galerie Brame & Lorenceau, Paris, 1991. ► 7 All references to and quotations from Van Gogh's letters cite the online edition of Leo Jansen, Hans Luijten and Nienke Bakker: www.vangoghletters.org, letter no. 640 to Theo Van Gogh, 15.7.1888. ► 8 Van Gogh, *Letters* (see note 7), letter no. 325 to Anthon van Rappard, on or about 5.3.1883. ► 9 Ibid., letter no. 360 to Theo Van Gogh, 7.6.1883. ► 10 Régamey's Japanese-inspired chromolithographs illustrated Philippe Burty's article on the Japanese poetess, Komati in *L'Art*, vol. 2, 1875. ► 11 The going rate charged by Bing was 5 sous, but Vincent and Theo Van Gogh seem to have been offered a discount. Van Gogh, *Letters* (see note 7), letter no. 642 to Theo Van Gogh, 15.7.1888. ► 12 Van Tilborgh, *Van Gogh* (see note 4), pp. 18–19. ► 13 Van Gogh, *Letters* (see note 7), letter nos 640 and 642 to Theo Van Gogh, 15.7.1888. ► 14 Ibid., letter no. 640 to Theo Van Gogh, 15.7.1888. ► 15 "Il y a chez Bing un grenier, là il y a un tas de 10 mille crepons, paysages, figures, crepons anciens aussi. Il te laissera un dimanche choisir toi-même, alors prends pas mal d'anciennes feuilles aussi", ibid. ► 16 Ibid., letter no. 626 to his sister Willemien, 16–20.7.1888. The suggestion he may wish for more prints to be sent down appears in letter no. 640 to Theo of 15.7.1888. ► 17 This intriguing point is made by Childs, "Seeking the studio" (see note 5), p. 120, at note 27. ► 18 This special issue of *Paris illustré* from 4.5.1886 included an article by the Japanese art dealer Hayashi Tadamasa. ► 19 Émile Bernard in the introduction to *Lettres de Vincent van Gogh à Émile Bernard*, Paris, 1911, p. 12. ► 20 In letter 640 to Theo from 15.7.1888, he alludes to this informal decoration of their Paris apartment: "Ton apartement ne serait pas ce qu'il est sans les japonaiseries continuellement." ("Your apartment wouldn't be what it is without the constant presence of Japanese prints."). ► 21 On this topic, see Griselda Pollock, "On Not Seeing Provence: Van Gogh and the Landscape of Consolation", in: *Framing France: The Representation of Landscape in France, 1870–1914*, Richard Thomson (ed.), Manchester and New York, 1998, pp. 81–118. ► 22 Van Gogh, *Letters* (see note 7), letter no. 590 to his sister Willemien, on or about 30.3.1888. ► 23 "saisir […] ce qui est essentiel", ibid., letter no. 596 to Bernard, on or about 12.4.1888. ► 24 Ibid.; in letter no. 652 to Theo of 31.7.1888, Vincent Van Gogh describes a plunging view of a coal barge on the Rhone and the figures working on it in terms of Hokusai. *Quay with Men Unloading Sand Barges*, which he painted three weeks later and described in letter no. 669 to Bernard, was effectively a variant of this view. ► 25 From September 1888 onwards, Van Gogh frequently used the word "figurines" as shorthand for such diminutive Japanese-inspired figures. ► 26 Van Gogh had read about Buddhist bonzes in Pierre Loti's novel *Madame Chrysanthème* in the summer of 1888. However, in *Promenades japonaises* (1880), Guimet had described these contrasting traits and Régamey had illustrated the shaven-headed bonzes. ► 27 "Voyons, on aime la peinture Japonaise, on en a subi l'influence – tous les impressionistes ont ca en commun – et on n'irait pas au Japon c. à d. ce qui est l'equivalent du Japon, le midi. – Je crois donc qu'encore après tout l'avenir de l'art nouveau est dans le midi", Van Gogh, *Letters* (see note 7), letter no. 620 to Theo Van Gogh, 5.6.1888. ► 28 "il a paru, il parait, un article sur Anquetin dans Revue indépend. où on le nommerait le chef d'une nouvelle tendance où le japonisme etait plus accusé encore etc. Je ne l'ai pas lu mais enfin – le chef du petit Boulevard est sans aucun doute Seurat et dans la japonaiserie le petit Bernard a été plus loin peut etre qu'Anquetin", ibid. ► 29 Édouard Dujardin, "Aux XX et aux Indépendants. Le cloisonisme (1)", in: *La Revue indépendante*, March 1888, pp. 487–492. ► 30 The exhibition was held at the Grand-Bouillon/Restaurant du Chalet in Avenue de Clichy. See *Van Gogh and the Birth of Cloisonism*, exh. cat., Art Gallery of Ontario, Toronto, and Van Gogh Museum, Amsterdam, Bogomila Welsh-Ovcharov (ed.), Toronto, 1981, and Cornelia Homburg, *Vincent Van Gogh and the Painters of the Petit Boulevard*, Saint Louis Art Museum, New York, 2001. ► 31 "[…] il est évident qu'une sensation différente serait obtenue par une coloration différente […] à travers une vitre jaune – c'est le cas du *Faucheur*, – sensation de plein soleil", Dujardin, "Aux XX" (see note 29), p. 491. ► 32 Held in another cafe run by Mr Volpini, it was entitled *L'Exposition de peintures du groupe impressionniste et synthétiste*. ► 33 See *Paul Gauguin: Paris, 1889*, exh. cat., Cleveland Museum of Art and Van Gogh Museum, Amsterdam, Ostfildern, 2009. ► 34 "[…] ce serait une fête pour moi que de passer une matinee avec toi dans la galerie des Hollandais. Tout cela ne se décrit guère. Mais devant les tableaux je pourrais te montrer des merveilles et des miracles qui pour moi font que les primitifs n'ont pas du tout en premier lieu et le plus directement mon admiration. […] les primitifs comme les japonais me paraissent […] de L'ÉCRITURE À LA PLUME, cela m'intéresse infiniment […] mais une chose complete, une perfection nous rend l'infini tangible." ("It would be a treat for me to spend a morning with you in the Dutch gallery. All that is barely describable. But in front of the paintings I could show you marvels and miracles that are the reason that, for me, the primitives really don't have my admiration first and foremost and most directly. […] the primitives as well as the Japanese, seem to me [...] like WRITING WITH A PEN; they interest me infinitely [...] but something complete, a perfection, makes the infinite tangible to us."), Van Gogh, *Letters* (see note 7), letter no. 649 to Bernard, 29.7.1888. ► 35 "Car le japonais fait abstraction du reflet posant ses teintes plates l'une à côté de l'autre – des traits caractéristiques arrêtant naivement des mouvements ou des formes." ("Because the Japanese disregards reflection, placing his solid tints one beside the other – characteristic lines naively marking off movements or shapes."), ibid., letter no. 622 to Bernard, 7.6.1888. ► 36 A letter from Gauguin to Bernard written around 4.11.1888 hints at this ongoing discussion about the role of shadows and how their absence in Japanese prints was not detrimental to the impression of *plein air* and warmth; see *Correspondance de Paul Gauguin*, Victor Merlhès (ed.), Paris, 1984, p. 270. ► 37 "[...] pourquoi avons-nous tant aimé les japonais? Parce qu'ils nous rapportaient nos synthèses perdues dans des amusements et des minuties de 5 siècles", in: *Émile Bernard, Les lettres d'un artiste (1884–1941)*, Neil McWilliam (ed.), Dijon, 2012, letter from Bernard (in Florence) to Andries Bonger, 14.5.1893, p. 138 (trans. Belinda Thomson). p. 138. ► 38 Gauguin's *Still Life with Horse's Head* of 1886 (Bridgestone Museum of Art, Tokyo) includes Japanese fans and a puppet. ► 39 This fan was not located and feared lost at the time of Zingg's publication on Gauguin's fans; see Jean-Paul Zingg, *Les Éventails de Paul Gauguin*, Paris, 2001, cat. XVII, p. 50 and p. 91. ► 40 "tout à fait japonais par un [word crossed out] sauvage du Pérou", letter from Gauguin to Schuffenecker, 8.7.1888: "Pelouse vert-Véronèze pur dégradant jusqu'au jaune de chrome *sans exécution* comme les crépons japonais", in: *Correspondance de Paul Gauguin* (see note 36), letter from Gauguin to Vincent Van Gogh, 24 or 25.7.1888, p. 198 and p. 201. ► 41 In a letter to Bernard of late October/early November 1888, Gauguin mentions seeing in Arles subjects: "je vois du Puvis coloré à faire, mélangé de Japon" ("I see coloured Puvis to do, mixed with Japan"), ibid., p. 270. ► 42 See the discussion in Belinda Thomson, *Gauguin's Vision*, National Galleries of Scotland, Edinburgh, 2005, pp. 43–44. ► 43 Gauguin exhibited the painting with this title at Les XX in early 1889. See *Gauguin, Les XX et la Libre Esthétique*, Musée d'Art moderne et d'Art contemporain de la Ville de Liège, Liège, 1995, p. 62. ► 44 See Belinda Thomson, "Making the Familiar Strange", in: *Gauguin: Maker of Myth*, exh. cat., Tate Modern, London, and National Gallery of Art, Washington, London, 2010, pp. 93–95. ► 45 This print, which resembles certain designs by Kunisada, has not as yet been identified. ► 46 I would like to thank Sandra Gianfreda for alerting me to the possible identification of this print, in: Jens Peter Munk and Kirsten Olesen, *Post-Impressionism*, Copenhagen, 1993, p. 100. ► 47 "J'ai installé notre immense atelier avec des étoffes lithographies P.G.O. et Bernard, japonais, etc. C'est superbe [...]" ("I decorated our huge atelier with textiles, lithographs from P.G.O. and Bernard, Japanese prints, etc. It looks wonderful [...]"), *Lettres de Gauguin à sa femme et à ses amis*, Maurice Malingue (ed.), Paris, 1946, letter from Gauguin to Bernard, LXXXIX, around Oct. 1889, p. 169. ► 48 "Les murs de l'atelier resplendissaient cependant de ses études claires et gaies, au-dessus desquelles, à deux ou trois mètres de hauteur, courait une sorte de frise faite d'estampes juxtaposées d'Hokousai et d'Outamaro. Ces estampes, ainsi que de curieux dessins japonais originaux, appartenaient à Gauguin, qui avait en outre piqué ça et là quelques photographies d'après des œuvres connues de Manet et de Puvis de Chavannes. Une estampe d'Outamaro, d'une valeur de 300 francs, avait été cédée par Joyant à l'artiste en échange de tableaux", in: Jean de Rotonchamp, *Paul Gauguin, 1848–1903*, Paris, 1906 (new edition: 1925), p. 77. ► 49 Gauguin, *Avant et après*, trans. Van Wyck Brooks as *The Intimate Journals of Paul Gauguin*, London, 1923, p. 54. ► 50 "Nous-mêmes, d'ailleurs, à part Gauguin qui reste avec Sérusier et ses élèves dans l'imitation du crépon et des sculptures cambodgiennes, nous avons évolué vers l'art classique, sentant là la grande force de l'avenir, l'art classique de Manet, de Puvis, de Corot, l'art classique si mal compris jusqu'alors." ("Besides, we ourselves, apart from Gauguin who is still, along with Sérusier and his pupils, imitating Japanese prints and Cambodian sculpture, have evolved in the direction of classical art, feeling that it constitutes the great force for the future, the classical art of Manet, Puvis, Corot, the classical art that has been so poorly understood hitherto."), in: *Émile Bernard* (see note 37), letter from Bernard to A. Bonger, 20.12.1900, p. 673.

Claire Guitton, *"Discovering new horizons and liberties" –*
Japonisme *and the decorative arts in France*

► 1 "[...] un petit livre bizarrement broché, à couverture rouge (qui servait) à caler des porcelaines expédiées par des Français établis au Japon", "Léonce Bénédite, Félix Bracquemond, l'animalier", in: *Art et Décoration*, vol. 17, Jan.–June 1905, pp. 39–40. Unless otherwise specified, all quotations in English have been translated by the translator of this essay. ► 2 Jean-Paul Bouillon stresses the difficulty of precisely dating this "discovery", which probably occurred some years later; see Jean-Paul Bouillon, "Remarques sur le Japonisme de Bracquemond", in: *Japonisme in Art. An International Symposium*, Society for the Study of Japonisme (ed.), Tokyo, 1980, p. 84. ► 3 While *Japonisme* can be seen clearly in this ensemble, it should also be said that the form of the individual pieces of this service and the blue decorative edge must be seen in the context of the French tradition of the eighteenth century. Not all of the motifs come from Japanese woodblock prints – Bracquemond also partly returned to motifs from earlier works. Finally, not all of the motifs were placed "randomly"; instead a trinomial arrangement can often be discerned very clearly; cf. *La France regarde le Japon: l'influence des peintres japonais sur les arts décoratifs*, exh. cat., Tokyo National Museum, Tokyo and Paris, 2008; *Félix Bracquemond et les arts décoratifs: du japonisme à l'Art nouveau*, exh. cat., Musée National Adrien-Dubouché, Limoges et al., Jean-Paul Bouillon (ed.), Paris, 2005; *Le Service Rousseau: art, industrie et japonisme*, exh. cat., Musée d'Orsay, Paris, Jean-Paul Bouillon et al. (ed.), Paris, 1988. ► 4 Geneviève Lacambre, "Hokusai and the French diplomats. Some remarks on the collection of Baron de Chassiron", in: *The Documented Image. Visions in Art History*, Gabriel P. Weisberg and Laurinda S. Dixon (eds.), Syracuse, 1987, pp. 72–73; *Vous avez dit japonisme?*, exh. cat., Musée Gallé-Juillet, Creil, Sabine Pasdelou (ed.), Chéroy, 2010, pp. 23–27 and pp. 61–62. ► 5 In this *Recueil*, Japan appeared as one source of inspiration among many, which also included Persia, China and Italy, in particular. Some motifs from the *Manga* appeared some months later, in December, also in Baron Chassiron's account of his journey (*Notes sur le Japon, la Chine et l'Inde, 1858, 1859, 1860*, Paris, 1861). See *Le Japonisme*, exh. cat., Galeries nationales du Grand Palais, Paris et al., Paris, 1988, p. 26. The *Recueil* could also be accessed in a number of libraries and municipal schools outside Paris; cf. *Vous avez dit japonisme?* (see note 4), p. 67, at note 36. ► 6 *L'art pour tous*, Émile Reiber and Claude Sauvageot (eds.), Paris, 1861–1906 (Japanese objects made public from 1868); Auguste Racinet, *L'ornement polychrome*, Paris, 1869; Émile Reiber, *Premier volume des albums-Reiber, bibliothèque portative des arts du dessin*, Paris, 1877. The most notable and known publications in France at the time include: Christopher Dresser, *The Art of Decorative Design*, London, 1862; Thomas William Cutler, *A Grammar of Japanese Ornament and Design*, London, 1879/1880; George Ashdown Audsley, *The Ornamental Arts of Japan*, London, 1880; cf. "Chronologie", in: *Le Japonisme* (see note 5), pp. 60–123. ► 7 Siegfried Bing, "Programme", in: *Le Japon artistique. Documents d'Art et d'Industrie*, issue 1, May 1888, p. 5. The magazine was also published in German and English. ► 8 Manuela Moscatiello, *Le japonisme de Giuseppe de Nittis: un peintre italien en France à la fin du XIXe siècle*, Berne et al., 2011, pp. 60–66. ► 9 Michel Beurdeley and Michèle Maubeuge, *Edmond de Goncourt chez lui*, Nancy, 1991. ► 10 Florence Rionnet, *Le rôle de la Maison Barbedienne (1834–1954) dans la diffusion de la sculpture aux XIXe et XXe siècles: considérations sur les bronzes d'édition et l'histoire du goût*, doctoral dissertation 2006 (unpublished), p. 52. ► 11 *Meubles d'art, styles Renaissance, Louis 16 et dans le goût Japonais. Œuvres décoratives d'Ed. Lièvre. Meubles anciens, bronzes, faïences, tableaux*, auc. cat., Paris, 1887, pp. 70–94. ► 12 Tsuchida Ruriko, "Gallé et l'esthétique japonaise", in: *Nature et symbolisme "Influences du Japon"*, exh. cat., Musée départemental Georges de La Tour, Vic-sur-Seille, François Le Tacon (ed.), Metz, 2009, p. 29. ► 13 Tsuchida Ruriko, "Gallé et l'esthétique japonaise", in: *Nature et symbolisme* (see note 12), pp. 29–30. ► 14 See the essay by Gregory Irvine in this publication. ► 15 Philippe Burty, "Le musée oriental à l'Union central", in: *Le Rappel*, 25.10.1869, p. 2, cited in: Michel Maucuer, "La copie des objets asiatiques au XIXe siècle: Émile Reiber, Théodore Deck, et la collection Cernuschi", in: *La revue des musées de France*, no. 3, June 2011, p. 81. ► 16 "[...] pendant plus de quinze jours, il (Reiber) passa toutes ses matinées à dessiner au Palais de l'Industrie et rapportait de ses séances les plus savoureux croquis qui devaient lui rendre tant de services dans les adaptations qu'il allait en faire dans la maison Christofle", Henri Bouilhet cited in: *L'émail français au XIXe siècle: le renouveau dans l'orfèvrerie et la bijouterie française*, 12e Biennale internationale des arts du feu de Limoges, Limoges, 1994, p. 70; Marc Bascou, "Émile Reiber. Le Japon pour tous", in *L'Objet d'art*, no. 13, Dec. 1988–Jan. 1989, p. 56. ► 17 He used his sketches to illustrate most of the plates comprising his *Premier Volume des Albums-Reiber. Bibliothèque portative des arts du dessin*. With this collection, directed "at all members of the artistic family of France", Reiber wanted to provide the artists' imagination with "new nutrition"; cf. Geneviève Lacambre, "La diffusion de l'art d'Extrême-Orient comme modèle pour les artistes: l'exemple de la collection Cernuschi", in: *Ebisu*, no. 19, 1998, p. 129 (contributions to the colloquium *Henri Cernuschi [1821–1896] – homme politique, financier et collectionneur d'art asiatique*, Maison franco-japonaise, Tokyo, 1998). ► 18 Cf. Maucuer, "La copie" (see note 15), pp. 81–82. ► 19 Odile Nouvel-Kammerer, in: *La Revue des musées de France*, Dec. 2005, no. 5, p. 89. I wish to express my deep gratitude at this point to Ms Audrey Gay-Mazuel, curator at Musée des Arts décoratifs, who provided me with access to the dossier of this object. ► 20 Jules Champfleury, "La mode des japoniaiseries", in: *La vie parisienne*, 21.11.1868, pp. 862–863, reprinted in Geneviève and Jean Lacambre, *Champfleury. Son regard et celui de Baudelaire*, Paris 1990, pp. 143–145. "Japoniaiseries" is a neologism by Champfleury, composed of the terms "Japon" and "niaiserie" (nonsense) alluding sarcastically to the term "Japonaiserie", which was common at the time, and which not only referred to Japanese objects, but also to French artists' dealing with Japan. Cf. Ikegami Chūji, "James Tissot, 'Drawing Instructor' of Tokugawa Akitake", in: *Japonisme in Art* (see note 2), p. 152. ► 21 See Ernest Chesneau, *L'Art japonais: conférence faite à l'Union centrale des Beaux-Arts appliqués à l'industrie*, 19.2.1869, Paris, 1869, p. 28. ► 22 "le pastiche japonais", Louis Gonse, *L'Art japonais*, Paris 1883, vol. 1, p. II. ► 23 "une aveugle singerie", Bing, "Programme" (see note 7), p. 6. ► 24 "Japon de surface", Louis Gonse, "L'art japonais et son influence sur le goût européen", in: *Revue des arts décoratifs*, April 1898, p. 111. ► 25 Gonse, *L'Art japonais* (see note 22), p. II. ► 26 "poursuivre une pensée originale", Philippe Burty, "La Poterie et la porcelaine au Japon par M. Ph. Burty" (first talk, 18.10.1884), in: *Revue des arts décoratifs*, 1884–1885, p. 392. ► 27 "les lois rigoureuses que nous nommons nos styles", in: Bing, "Programme" (see note 7), p. 6. ► 28 Chesneau, *L'Art japonais* (see note 21), p. 28. ► 29 "saines doctrines", Gonse, *L'Art japonais* (see note 22), p. II. ► 30 "d'une supériorité écrasante pour nos praticiens"; "Les Japonais n'ont ni secrets ni trucs que nous n'ayons déjà utilisés. Ce qui les met hors pair, c'est la conscience dans le travail, c'est le respect et l'amour de leur œuvre, c'est l'adresse même de leur mains", ibid, vol. 2, chapter 5 "La sculpture", p. 74. ► 31 "notre civilisation à la vapeur", ibid, p. 95. ► 32 "[…] l'union des arts, petits et grands, est parfaite là-bas", Ary Renan, "La Mangua de Hokusaï", in: *Le Japon artistique. Documents d'Art et d'Industrie*, issue 8, Dec. 1888, p. 94. ► 33 Gonse was amazed at the fact that "[…] à tous les degrés de l'échelle, depuis le plus humble ouvrier jusqu'au *tshiajin* le plus accompli, ce pays semble vivre pour le culte de l'art" ([…] "this land seems to live for the glorification of art at all levels of society, from the simplest worker to the complete *tshiajin*"), Louis Gonse, "Le génie des Japonais dans le décor", in: *Le Japon artistique. Documents d'Art et d'Industrie*, issue 2, June 1888, p. 14. ► 34 "seul maître", Bing, "Programme" (see note 7), p. 7. ► 35 Japanese art is only one of many sources within this "back-to-nature" movement, which was also fostered by a growing interest in Gothic art and in the art of the eighteenth century, to name just a few examples. ► 36 Yamane Ikunobu, "L'influence du japonisme dans l'œuvre d'Émile Gallé", in: *Annales de l'Est*, 55th year, special edition, 2005, pp. 54–55 (contributions to the colloquium *Hommage à Émile Gallé*, Nancy 2004), ► 37 Gonse, *L'Art japonais* (see note 22), vol. 1, chapter 2, "Le pays, la race", pp. 96–100. ► 38 "[…] c'est le retour à la nature que nous indique l'art japonais, c'est le chemin de ce monde infini qui nous enveloppe et que nous ne voyons pas. Il aura fallu lire les albums japonais et voir leur céramique, leurs laques et leurs bronzes, pour nous rappeler que nous avons comme eux un ciel, des champs, des bois, des eaux, peuplés d'oiseaux, de fleurs, d'herbes, d'insectes et de poissons aux couleurs innombrables", Josse (Lucien Falize), "L'art japonais à propos de l'exposition organisée par M. Gonse. Lettres de M. Josse à Monsieur Louis Gonse, directeur de la *Gazette des Beaux-Arts*," in: *Revue des arts décoratifs*, 1882–1883, vol. 3, p. 363. ► 39 "[…] une fleur vaut un homme", Ary Renan, "La Mangua de Hokusaï (suite et fin)", in: *Le Japon artistique. Documents d'Art et d'Industrie*, issue 9, January 1889, p. 113. ► 40 "[…] la forme ne dérive pas, comme en notre vieux monde, d'un principe architectural […]. Plus souple est la forme japonaise: inspirée de la fleur, du fruit, des choses de la nature, elle n'est pas corrigée par la règle, ni mesurée par le compas, elle reste libre, pittoresque, osée", Lucien Falize, "Travaux d'orfèvre", in: *Le Japon artistique. Documents d'Art et d'Industrie*, issue 5, Sept. 1888, p. 52. ► 41 "[…] la nature elle-même est le point de départ de tout", Émile Gallé, 1884, cited in: Tsuchida, "Gallé" (see note 12), p. 33. ► 42 The example is cited in Valérie Thomas, "L'art japonais, une source d'influence dans les dessins de l'atelier de Gallé?", in: *Nature et symbolisme* (see note 12), p. 48. ► 43 "L'Exposition universelle de 1878 nous révéla sur la céramique du Japon un fait que nous ignorions complètement", in: Burty, "La Poterie" (see note 26), vol. 5, p. 386. ► 44 "vitrine étroite et sans mise en scène […] des pots, de petits vases, de petites coupes", ibid. ► 45 "[…] il s'en fallut d'assez peu que l'on ne les classât parmi les objets sauvages", ibid. ► 46 "[…] lors de l'Exposition universelle de 1878, la section d'art japonais le (Carriès) saisit tout particulièrement, et la poterie entre les autres objets. Il y revint fréquemment, avec enthousiasme, avec une inquiète curiosité, en parla, y repensa souvent", Arsène Alexandre, *Jean Carriès, imagier et potier, étude d'une œuvre et d'une vie*, Paris, 1895, p. 121. More detailed information on Carriès can be found in: *Jean Carriès, 1855–1894, La matière de l'étrange*, exh. cat., Musée du Petit Palais, Paris, Amélie Simier (ed.), Paris, 2007. ► 47 Siegfried Bing, "La céramique", in: Gonse, *L'Art japonais* (see note 22), vol. 2, pp. 239–334. ► 48 Philippe Burty, "La poterie au Japon I", in: *Le Japon artistique. Documents d'art et d'industrie*, issue 17, Sept. 1889, pp. 53–63, and Philippe Burty, "La poterie au Japon II", in: *Le Japon artistique. Documents d'art et d'industrie*, issue 18, Oct. 1889, pp. 69–79. ► 49 *L'Art Nouveau: La Maison Bing*, exh. cat., Van Gogh Museum, Amsterdam et al., Gabriel P. Weisberg, Edwin Becker and Évelyne Possémé (eds.), Stuttgart, 2004, p. 25. ► 50 See Christine Shimizu, in: *Satsuma: de l'exotisme au japonisme*, exh. cat., Musée national de céramique, Sèvres, Paris/Sèvres, 2007, pp. 149–150 and p. 152. ► 51 See Christine Shimizu, "Rodin et l'art du grès japonais", in: *Rodin, le rêve japonais*, exh. cat., Musée Rodin, Paris, Paris, 2007, pp. 221–226. ► 52 "Cette bouteille n'a d'autre décor que l'éclat de ces émaux, coulant les uns par-dessus les autres avec un abandon plein de franchise", *Le Japon artistique. Documents d'Art et d'Industrie*, issue 8, Dec. 1888, p. 105. ► 53 "ce maître charmeur dont l'artiste japonais a de tout temps aimé à provoquer les caprices heureux", Bing, "La céramique" (see note 47), p. 255. ► 54 "Là où nous croirions à des accidents de fabrication, il faudrait se garer de ce faux jugement. Ce sont souvent des négligences pleines de coquetterie", Philippe Burty, "La Poterie et la porcelaine au Japon par M. Ph. Burty" (third talk, 25.10.1884), in: *Revue des arts décoratifs*, 1884–1885, vol. 5, p. 417. ► 55 "Je recommence mon ancienne vie, fruste, sauvage, mal élevé. Je ne veux pas être à tout prix un Français moderne, c'est-à-dire superficiel", letter from Jean Carriès to Aline Ménard-Dorian, cited by: Alexandre, in: *Jean Carriès* (see note 46), p. 147. ► 56 "tout à fait japonais par un sauvage du Pérou", letter from Gauguin to Schuffenecker 8.7.1888, cited by: Françoise Cachin, in: *Gauguin*, exh. cat., Galeries nationales du Grand Palais, Paris et al., Paris, 1989, p. 145. ► 57 Bing, "Programme" (see note 7), p. 7.

Ursula Perucchi-Petri, *The Nabi and East Asian art – Pierre Bonnard, Maurice Denis, Félix Vallotton and Édouard Vuillard*

► 1 For more on the Nabi, see Ursula Perucchi-Petri, *Die Nabis und Japan. Das Frühwerk von Bonnard, Vuillard und Denis*, Munich, 1976. The Nabi included, for a while, artists as diverse as Henri-Gabriel Ibels, Georges Lacombe, Aristide Maillol, Paul-Elie Ranson, Jòzsef Rippl-Rònai, Kerr-Xavier Roussel, Paul Sérusier and Jan Verkade. See *Die Nabis. Propheten der Moderne*, exh. cat., Kunsthaus Zürich, Zurich, Galeries nationales du Grand Palais, Paris, Claire Frèches-Thory and Ursula Perucchi-Petri (eds.), Munich, 2000. Within the scope of this essay, my focus is on the artists in this group for whom Japanese art was an important inspiration. ► 2 "Se rappeler qu'un tableau – avant d'être un cheval de bataille, une femme nue, ou une quelconque anecdote – est essentiellement une surface plane recouverte de couleurs en un certain ordre assemblées", Maurice Denis, "Définition du Néo-Traditionnisme", in: *Art et Critique*, 1890, reprinted in Maurice Denis, *Théories 1890–1910: Du Symbolisme et de Gauguin vers un nouvel ordre classique*, Paris, 1912. This translation by Peter Collier: Maurice Denis, "Definition of Neo-Traditionism", in: *Art in Theory 1815–1900*, Charles Harrison, Paul Wood, Jason Gaiger (eds.), Oxford, 1998, p. 863. ► 3 Ibid., p. 866. ► 4 Bonnard, dubbed by Fénéon as "le Nabi très japonard" (the very Japanese Nabi), also regarded Japanese woodblock prints as folk art. In a letter to Hedy Hahnloser-Bühler from 4.1.1946, he wrote: "In my youth I was enchanted by the magnificent colority of Japanese *crepons* – a kind of work on paper entirely in the style of folk art", cited in: Annette Vaillant, *Bonnard ou le bonheur de voir*, Neuchâtel, 1965, p. 182. Maurice Denis mentioned Japanese kakemonos in 1890 in the same breath as other examples of early art admired by the Nabi such as medieval glass windows, Egyptian paintings and Byzantine mosaics; see Denis, "Définition" (see note 2, p. 866). ► 5 "C'est là que je trouvais pour un ou deux sous des crépons ou des papiers de riz froissés aux couleurs étonnantes", cited in: Antoine Terrasse, *Pierre Bonnard*, Paris, 1967, p. 24. Unless otherwise specified, all quotations in English have been translated by the translator of this essay. ► 6 "Gauguin, Sérusier se réfèrent en fait au passé. Mais là ce que j'avais devant moi, c'était quelque chose de bien vivant, d'extrêmement savant", ibid. ► 7 It should be noted that many caricaturists, popular printmakers and Chat Noir artists were also influenced by Japanese art; cf. Karen Woodbridge Smith, *Japonisme and the Circle of Le Chat Noir*, doctoral dissertation 1976, Ann Arbor 1980 (microfiche). ► 8 Dietrich Seckel, *Einführung in die Kunst Ostasiens*, Munich, 1960, p. 384. ► 9 Dietrich Seckel, *Buddhistische Kunst Ostasiens*, Stuttgart, 1957, p. 150. ► 10 According to Maurice Denis: "Il n'y a pas lieu de copier, de reproduire la nature telle que nous la voyons, mais de la 'représenter', la transposer en un jeu de couleurs vives, inscrites dans une arabesque simple, expressive, originale […]" ("Instead of copying nature as one perceived it, one should 'represent' it, transmute it into a play of vivid colours, emphasising simple, expressive, original arabesques […]"), cited in: Maurice Denis, "Paul Sérusier, sa vie, son œuvre", in: *Paul Sérusier, ABC de la peinture*, Paris, 1942, p. 43. ► 11 The first version shown here has a somewhat more sketchy and graphic character than the final version in oils now hanging in the Musée d'Orsay in Paris. ► 12 Just how much Denis was interested in Japanese art is evident from his own personal collection of 94 Japanese woodblock prints, most of them from the nineteenth century, by Kunisada, Kuniyoshi and Eisen, among others. He also kept several front-page covers from the magazine *Le Japon artistique*.

This collection is still in the hands of his family. Vuillard also collected more than 70 Japanese woodblock prints as well as ink drawings and sketchbooks by Hokusai and Kitao Masayoshi. His library included W. de Seidlitz, *Les Estampes Japonaises*, trans. P. André Lemoisne, Paris, 1911, and two books by Noguchi Yone, *L'Art du Japon, Kōrin* and *L'Art du Japon, Hiroshige*, Paris and Brussels, 1926. ► 13 In his article about "Néo-Traditionnisme" from 1890, Denis posited: "Mais l'illustration, c'est la décoration d'un livre!" – "Trouver cette décoration sans servitude du texte, sans exacte correspondance de sujet avec l'écriture; mais plutôt une broderie d'arabesque sur les pages [...]" ("Illustration is the decoration of a book [...] without subservience to the text, without exact correspondence of the subject with writing; but rather like an embroidery of arabesques on the pages, an accompaniment of expressive lines", cited in: Dario Gamboni, *The Brush and the Pen*, trans. Mary Whittall, Chicago, 2011, p. 243. ► 14 "J'avais compris au contact de ces frustes images populaires que la couleur pouvait comme ici exprimer toutes choses sans besoin de relief ou de modelé. Il m'apparut qu'il était possible de traduire lumière, formes et caractère rien qu'avec la couleur, sans faire appel aux valeurs", cited in: Terrasse, *Pierre Bonnard* (see note 5), p. 10. ► 15 Hans R. Hahnloser mentions a conversation with Bonnard: "When asked what he actually owed to the Japanese, Bonnard responded humbly and almost paradoxically, 'the chequered pattern'". *Hauptwerke des Kunstmuseums Winterthur*, Kunstverein Winterthur (ed.), Winterthur, 1949, p. 135. This response is not quite as banal as it sounds; such patterns, especially chequered fabrics, do indeed play a prominent role in Bonnard's work, and he found inspiration for them in the richly patterned kimonos featured in Japanese woodblock prints. ► 16 Seckel, *Einführung* (see note 8), p. 310. ► 17 *The Mustard Seed Garden Manual of Painting*, trans. from the Chinese by Mai-Mai Sze, Princeton, 1978. ► 18 Seckel, *Einführung* (see note 8), p. 375. ► 19 "Représenter sur une surface plane, des masses et des objets situés dans l'espace, tel est le problème du dessin [...] L'œil du peintre donne aux objets une valeur humaine, et reproduit les choses telles que les voit un œil humain. Et cette vision est mobile. Et cette vision est variable", cited in: Terrasse, *Pierre Bonnard* (see note 5), pp. 162–163. ► 20 The version presented here is one of an edition of 110 lithographs printed by Bonnard between 1894 and 1895 after his original distemper painting. For details, see Colta Ives, "City life", in: *Pierre Bonnard – The Graphic Art*, exh. cat., The Metropolitan Museum of Art et. al, Colta Ives, Helen Giambruni and Sasha M. Newman (eds.), New York, 1989, pp. 111–116. Colta Ives uses the earlier title *Promenade*. ► 21 Seckel, *Einführung* (see note 8), p. 380. ► 22 Ibid., p. 71. ► 23 Maxime Vallotton and Charles Goerg, *Felix Vallotton, Catalogue raisonné de l'œuvre grave*, Geneva, 1972, no. 51. Vallotton had a small collection of Japanese woodblock prints by artists such as Utamaro and Kunisada as well as a Chinese ink painting depicting a wedding ceremony. Today, works from the former Vallotton Collection are housed in the Fondation Félix Vallotton, Lausanne. ► 24 Seckel, *Einführung* (see note 8), p. 218. Because the three-part or multi-part woodblock print cycles by Japanese artists were often torn apart over the years, Europeans tended to overinterpret the cropped aspect of the individual prints. ► 25 "La découpure stricte dans la vision donne presque toujours quelque chose de faux. La composition au second degré consiste à faire rentrer certains éléments de vision qui sont en dehors de ce rectangle", cited in: Michel Terrasse, *Bonnard, du dessin au tableau*, Paris, 1996, p. 204. ► 26 See Ursula Perucchi-Petri, "Japonisme in Bonnard's Early and Late Work", in: *Pierre Bonnard early and late*, exh. cat., The Phillips Collection, Washington DC, London, 2002, pp. 190–203; Ursula Perucchi-Petri, "Pierre Bonnard und die ostasiatische Kunst", in: *Pierre Bonnard. Magier der Farbe*, exh. cat., Von der Heydt-Museum, Wuppertal, Gerhard Finckh and Peter Kropmanns (eds.), Wuppertal, 2010, pp. 48–59.

Peter Kropmanns, *More confirmation than inspiration –*
Japonisme *in French painting of the early twentieth century*

► 1 Shigemi Inaga, "The Making of Hokusai's Reputation in the Context of Japonisme", in: *Japan Review*, 2003, 15, pp. 77–100. ► 2 Cf. Geneviève Lacambre and Suzanne Esmein, "Chronologie", in: *Le Japonisme*, exh. cat., Galeries nationales du Grand Palais, Paris and Tokyo, Paris, 1988, pp. 60–123. ► 3 A helpful introduction to this subject matter is Takashina Shūji, "Problèmes du Japonisme", in: *Le Japonisme* (see note 2), pp. 16–21. A research work structured in large part by motif, such as Siegfried Wichmann, *Japonisme: Ostasien – Europa, Begegnungen in der Kunst des 19. und 20. Jahrhundert*, Herrsching, 1980, naturally has its merits as well. ► 4 Klaus Berger, *Japonisme in Western Painting from Whistler to Matisse*, trans. David Britt, Cambridge, 1992, p. 313. ► 5 The word "japonard", used as an adjective only with regard to Bonnard, is a neologism constructed from the combination of "japonais" (Japanese) and the artist's last name. On Bonnard's early *Japonisme*, see Ursula Perucchi-Petri's essay in this volume. ► 6 Ursula Perucchi-Petri, "Pierre Bonnard und die ostasiatische Kunst", in: *Bonnard: Magier der Farbe*, exh. cat., Von der Heydt-Museum, Wuppertal, Gerhard Finckh and Peter Kropmanns (eds.), Wuppertal, 2010, pp. 49–59. ► 7 In this regard, Michel Terrasse distinguishes between the influence ("influence") of Japanese artists on Bonnard *that did not occur* and the education ("enseignement") which he received from these artists *that did occur* (Michel Terrasse, *Bonnard: Du dessin au tableau*, Paris, 1996, p. 17). We have selected an anonymous photograph taken of Bonnard's atelier in rue de Douai, Paris, between 1905 and 1910 as evidence for Bonnard's passion for collecting Japanese woodblock prints; a more commonly used example is the 1946 photograph taken by Brassaï (Gyula Halász) in Bonnard's studio in Le Cannet, *Mur chez Bonnard (estampe japonaise)*. ► 8 "C'est là (dans les Grands-Magasins) que j'ai trouvé pour un ou deux sous des crêpons ou des papiers de riz froissés aux couleurs étonnantes [...] Je remplis les murs de ma chambre de cette imagerie naïve et criarde [...] Ce que j'avais devant moi c'était quelque chose de bien vivant, extrêmement savant", Antoine Terrasse, *Pierre Bonnard*, Paris 1967, p. 24, taken from Gaston Diehl's notes of a conversation, *Comœdia*, 10.7.1943. Cf. Antoine Terrasse, *Bonnard, étude biographique et critique*, Geneva 1964, pp. 20–24. Unless otherwise specified, all quotations in English have been translated by the translator of this essay. ► 9 Henri Matisse in conversation with Jacques Guenne (*L'art vivant*, no. 18, 15.9.1925), cited in: Henri Matisse, *Écrits et propos sur l'art*, Dominique Fourcade (ed.), Paris, 1992, p. 83. ► 10 In connection with relativising Matisse's interest in Japan, it should be noted that Matisse made a variety of costume paintings; for example, he painted his wife as a Spanish guitar player in 1903. ► 11 Cf. the drawing by André Derain, *Matisse and His Wife at Collioure*, 1905, inv./acc. no. 2004.60, Metropolitan Museum of Art, New York. ► 12 Cf. *Matisse, His Art and His Textiles: The Fabric of Dreams*, exh. cat., Royal Academy of Arts, London, Metropolitan Museum of Art, New York and Musée Matisse, Le Cateau-Cambrésis, London, 2004. ► 13 Geneviève Lacambre, "Gustave Moreau et le Japon", in: *Revue de l'Art*, no. 85, 1989, pp. 64–75. A homage to the Japanese colour woodblock print is also extant from Georges Rouault (1871–1958), the student of Moreau, Fauve and first curator of Musée Gustave Moreau (*Study from a Japanese Colour Woodblock Print*, 1925). This drawing may be another reference by Rouault to the early period of *Japonisme* in the 1860s, when Moreau, who remained an authority for him throughout his life, was among the pioneering discoverers of Japanese colour woodblock prints. ► 14 "Je t'écris avec un pinceau japonais épatant", in: Albert Marquet to Henri Matisse, March 1899, in: *Matisse–Marquet: Correspondance 1898–1947*, Claudine Grammont (ed.), Lausanne, 2008, p. 24 (see the front cover illustration and document 1 next to p. 72). ► 15 Henri Matisse to Albert Marquet, 15.4.1909, in: *Matisse–Marquet* 2008 (see note 14), p. 64. Here, the identification of the museum (formerly Königgrätzer Strasse, destroyed in 1945) differs from that in *Matisse–Marquet*, p. 64 (at note 85). ► 16 "Arriver à ne pas tracer un point qui ne fût vivant. Combien de fois l'ai-je entendu citer ce mot d'Hokusaï", Marcelle Marquet in: *Albert Marquet: 1875–1947*, exh. cat., Fondation de l'Hermitage, Lausanne, Lausanne, 1988, p. 16. ► 17 "Lorsque je vois Hokusaï je pense à notre Marquet – et vice versa – je n'entends pas imitation d'Hokusaï mais similitude", Henri Matisse in: *Le Point*, no. 27, Dec. 1943, cited in: Matisse, *Écrits et propos* (see note 9), p. 159. ► 18 The sitter's headdress suggests that the painting within the painting had as its model one of the portraits of Naniwaya Okita by Utamaro. ► 19 Cf. fig. in: *Bonnard* (see note 6), pp. 312–313. ► 20 Michel Terrasse, *Bonnard. Du dessin au tableau*, Paris, 1996, p. 274. ► 21 Pierre Bonnard, letter to Hedy Hahnloser 4.1.1946, cited in: Annette Vaillant, *Bonnard ou le bonheur de voir*, Neuchâtel, 1965, p. 182. ► 22 "À vrai dire, ces estampes étaient des médiocres reproductions, et cependant je ne devais pas connaître la même émotion quand il me fut donné de voir les originaux. Ceux-ci n'apportaient plus la fraîcheur d'une révélation", Henri Matisse in conversation with Jacques Guenne (*L'art vivant*, no. 18, 15.9.1925), cited in: Matisse 1992 (see note 9), p. 83. ► 23 "Bonnard m'a dit la même chose et il a ajouté que lorsqu'il avait vu les originaux il s'est trouvé un peu déçu. Cela s'explique par la patine et un peu de décoloration des vieux tirages. Peut-être si nous n'avions eu que ces originaux à regarder, n'aurions-nous pas été impressionnés, comme par les retirages", Henri Matisse, letter to André Rouveyre, 22.2.1948, cited in: *Matisse/Rouveyre, Correspondance*, Hanne Finsen (ed.), Paris, 2001, p. 45. ► 24 Berger, *Japonisme* (see note 4), p. 314. ► 25 Ibid., p. 306, as well as bibliographic information assembled by the author. ► 26 "Quelle leçon de pureté, d'harmonie", Henri Matisse in conversation with Jacques Guenne (*L'art vivant*, no. 18, 15.9.1925), cited in: Matisse, *Écrits et propos* (see note 9), p. 83. ► 27 Robert Reiff, "Matisse and Torii Kiyonaga", in: *Arts Magazine*, 1981, 55, no. 6, p. 164 (at note 4). ► 28 Albert C. Barnes, "Matisse and the Japanese tradition", in: Albert C. Barnes and Violette de Maza, *The Art of Henri Matisse*, New York, 1933, excerpts of which are reprinted in Berger, *Japonisme* (see note 4), pp. 374–378; Reiff, "Matisse" (see note 27); details on this discussion among Schneider,

Barr and Flam with additional references to the literature may be found in Peter Kropmanns, "'Quelle leçon de pureté, d'harmonie …' – À propos de Matisse, Bonnard et le Japonisme", in: *Matisse et Bonnard. Lumière de la Méditerranée*, exh. cat., Kawamura Memorial Museum of Art and The Museum of Modern Art, Hayama, Tokyo, 2008, supplement in French, pp. 13–16. ► 29 Here, we follow Barnes's (see note 28) concluding discussion on the problem of not always being able to unambiguously identify Japanese elements in the art of Matisse or to separate them from other elements. ► 30 Alfred H. Barr, Jr., *Matisse: His art and his public*, New York, 1951, p. 90. ► 31 "La couleur existe en elle-même, possède une beauté propre. Ce sont les crépons japonais que nous achetions pour quelques sous rue de Seine qui nous l'ont révélée. J'ai compris alors que l'on pouvait travailler avec des couleurs expressives qui ne sont pas obligatoirement des couleurs descriptives. Une fois l'œil désencrassé, nettoyé par les crépons japonais, j'étais apte à recevoir vraiment les couleurs en raison de leur pouvoir émotif", Henri Matisse, "Le chemin de la couleur", from a conversation with Gaston Diehl (*Art Présent*, no. 2, 1947), cited in: Matisse, *Écrits et propos* (see note 9), p. 203. ► 32 "Les Orientaux se sont servis du noir comme couleur, notamment les Japonais dans les estampes", Henri Matisse, "Le Noir est une couleur" (*Derrière le miroir*, no. 1, Dec. 1946), cited in: Matisse, *Écrits et propos* (see note 9), p. 203. Somewhat later, in 1947, Matisse again acknowledged Japanese colour woodblock print artists, apparently with reference to Edmond de Goncourt's foreword to *Hokousaï : l'art japonais au XVIIIe siècle*, Paris, 1896, p. XII (*Jazz*, cf. Matisse, *Écrits et propos* [see note 9], p. 239). Fourcade noted that Louis Aragon remembered from his meetings with Matisse that the artist liked to quote Hokusai: "If I were to live longer, I would be able to paint." Matisse is said to have added: "Put another way: In the end I do not know how to draw anymore", by which he meant, as Fourcade documented with reference to another remark of Matisse's, that he had set aside his school training and found his own language as a draftsman (Matisse, *Écrits et propos* [see note 9], p. 237). Matisse's interest in Japanese art is also apparently attested by a letter from 1926, in which his son-in-law Georges Duthuit mentioned a dreadful ("lamentable") publication by Henri Focillon on the graphic art of Hokusai (Georges Duthuit, undated letter to Henri Matisse [late Oct. 1926], in: Georges Duthuit, *Écrits sur Matisse*, Rémi Labrusse (ed.), Paris, 1992, p. 244). ► 33 Takashina, "Problèmes" (see note 3), p. 19. ► 34 "Et tous y trouvèrent une confirmation plutôt qu'une inspiration à leurs façons personnelles de voir, de sentir, de comprendre et d'interpréter la nature." Ernest Chesneau, "L'Exposition universelle: Le Japon à Paris", in: *Gazette des Beaux-Arts*, vol. 18, Paris, 1.9.1878, p. 396.

Sabine Bradel, *Of brocades and heroes – variations in Japanese colour woodblock prints*

► 1 Peter Kornicki, *The Book in Japan*, Honolulu, 2001, p. 57. ► 2 *Hokusai and Hiroshige: Great Japanese Prints from the James A. Michener Collection*, Yoko Woodson (ed.), Seattle, 1998, p. 32. ► 3 *The Floating World Revisited*, Donald Jenkins (ed.), Portland, 1993, p. 6. ► 4 Julie Nelson Davis, *Utamaro and the Spectacle of Beauty*, Honolulu, 2007, p. 69. ► 5 Ellis Tinios, "Kunisada and the Last Flowering of Ukiyo-e Prints", in: *Print Quarterly*, vol. 8, no. 4, Dec. 1991, p. 348. ► 6 *Competition and Collaboration. Japanese Prints of the Utagawa School*, Laura J. Mueller (ed.), Leiden, 2007, p. 18. ► 7 Robert Schaap, *Hiroshige's journey in the 60-odd provinces*, Leiden, 2004, p. 12. ► 8 *Hokusai and Hiroshige* (see note 2), pp. 37–38. ► 9 *Competition and Collaboration* (see note 6), p. 17.

Ricard Bru, *"Art is never chaste" – Picasso and erotic* Japonisme

► 1 For an introduction to and interpretation of this work, see Theodore Reff, "Manet's Portrait of Zola", in: *The Burlington Magazine*, vol. 117, no. 862, Jan. 1975, pp. 35–44. ► 2 James Laver, *Whistler*, London, 1930, p. 111. ► 3 For a general discussion of the spread and influence of Japanese prints in the West, see Ricard Bru, *Erotic Japonisme: The Influence of Japanese Sexual Imagery on Western Art*, Leiden, 2013. For a discussion of the same subject in the context of erotic art production in Japan, see the catalogue of a recent exhibition held at the British Museum, *Shunga: sex and pleasure in Japanese art*, London, 2013. ► 4 "J'ai acheté l'autre jour des albums d'obscénités japonaises. Cela me réjouit, m'amuse, m'enchante l'œil. Je regarde cela en dehors de l'obscénité, qui y est et qui semble ne pas y être et que je ne vois pas, tant elle disparaît sous la fantaisie. La violence des lignes, l'imprévu de la conjonction, l'arrangement des accessoires, le caprice des poses et des choses, le pittoresque et pour ainsi dire le paysage des parties génitales", Edmond and Jules de Goncourt, *Journal: Mémoires de la vie littérarie*, revised edition by Robert Ricatte, Paris, 1989, vol. 1, p. 1013; English cited in: Bru, *Erotic Japonisme* (see note 3), p. 479. ► 5 Guillaume Apollinaire, *Propos sur Picasso*, Paris, Bibliothèque Littéraire Jacques Doucet, pp. 875–877, cited in: *Picasso Apollinaire: Correspondance*, Pierre Caizergues and Hélène Seckel (eds.), Paris, 1992, p. 203. ► 6 For a discussion of Picasso and the *shunga* prints, see *Secret Images: Picasso and the Japanese Erotic Print*, Ricard Bru and Malén Gual (eds.), London, 2010 (originally published as *Imatges secretes: Picasso i l'estampa eròtica japonesa*, exh. cat., Museu Picasso, Barcelona, [Barcelona, 2009]). ► 7 Okamoto Tarō, *Seishun Pikaso*, Tokyo, 1953, pp. 109–110 (in Japanese). ► 8 Brassaï, *Conversations with Picasso*, trans. Jane Marie Todd, Chicago, 1999, p. 223.

Shops selling Far Eastern art

1 À la Porte chinoise, Place de la Bourse 29 (1826/1831–1850), Rue Vivienne 36 (from 1850–1886), run by Monsieur Bouillette
2 À l'Empire chinois (or céleste), run by Monsieur Decelle, Rue Vivienne 45 (1856/57–1862), Rue Vivienne 55 (1862–1874), Rue Vivienne 53 (1874–1885)
3 Au Céleste Empire, run by J.-G. Houssaye, Rue Saint-Marc 20 (extant until 1870)
4 La Jonque chinoise, run by Monsieur et Madame Desoye, Rue de Rivoli 220 (1862–1878), Rue de Rivoli 221 (1877–1888)
5 Shop of Auguste Sichel, Rue Pigalle 11 (1876–1884), Rue de Clichy 37 (1884–1887)
6 Shops of Siegfried Bing, Rue Chauchat 19 (1878–1896), Rue de Provence 23 (1880–1894), Rue Bleue 13 (1881–1889), Rue de la Paix 19 (1882–1884)
7 Kiryū Kōshō Kaisha, Boulevard des Capucines 10/ Rue Taitbout 54 (1880–1884)
8 Shop of Philippe und Octave Sichel, Rue Pigalle 11 / Rue Blanche 23 (1885–1893)
9 Wakai, Hayashi et Cie, 7 cité d'Hauteville (1884–1886); run by Hayashi alone, Rue de la Victoire 65 (1886–1900)
10 Shop of Florine Langweil, Boulevard des Italiens 4 (1889–1904), Place Saint Georges 26 (1904–1914)

Exhibitions

11 World fairs (1867, 1878, 1889 and 1900)
12 Musée Oriental in the Palais de l'Industrie, 10 April–10 November 1869, organised by the Union centrale des Beaux-Arts appliquée à l'Industrie
13 Galerie Georges Petit, Rue de Sèze 8, exhibition *Exposition rétrospective de l'Art japonais*, organised by Louis Gonse, April–May 1883
14 Café du Tambourin, Boulevard de Clichy 62, exhibition of Japanese woodblock prints organised by Vincent Van Gogh, February/March 1887
15 École des Beaux-Arts, Quai Malaquais, exhibition *Exposition de la gravure japonaise* organised by Siegfried Bing, 25 April–22 May 1890
16 Galeries Durand-Ruel, Rue Le Peletier 11, exhibition of woodblock prints by Hiroshige and Utamaro organised by Siegfried Bing, 22 January–20 February 1893

Museums

17 Musée Guimet, opened in 1889 (Émile Guimet Collection)
18 Musée Cernuschi, opened in1898 (Henri Cernuschi Collection)
19 Musée d'Ennery, Avenue du Bois de Boulogne, today Avenue Foch 59, opened in 1908, (Clémence and Adolphe Philippe d'Ennery Collection)

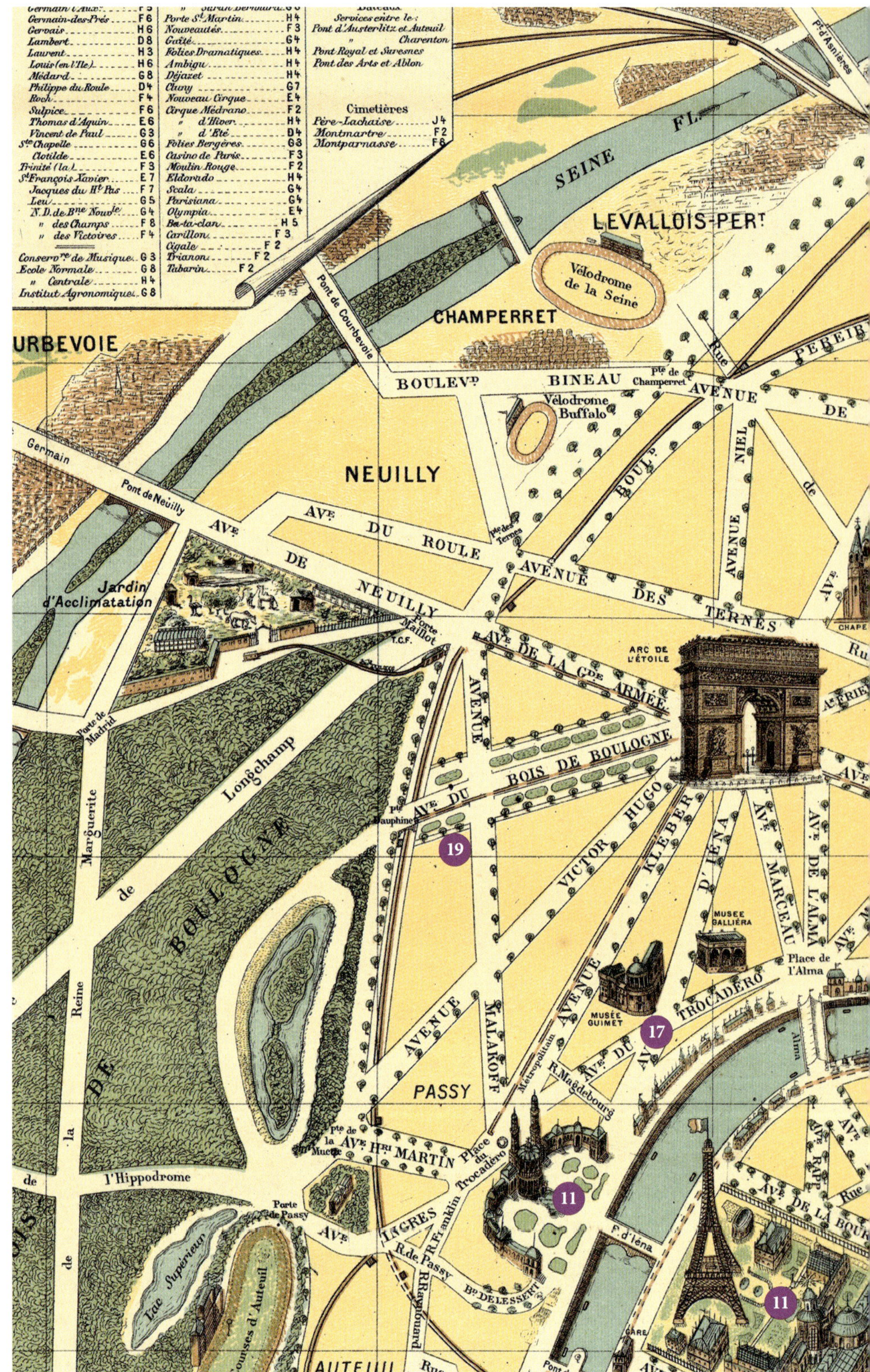

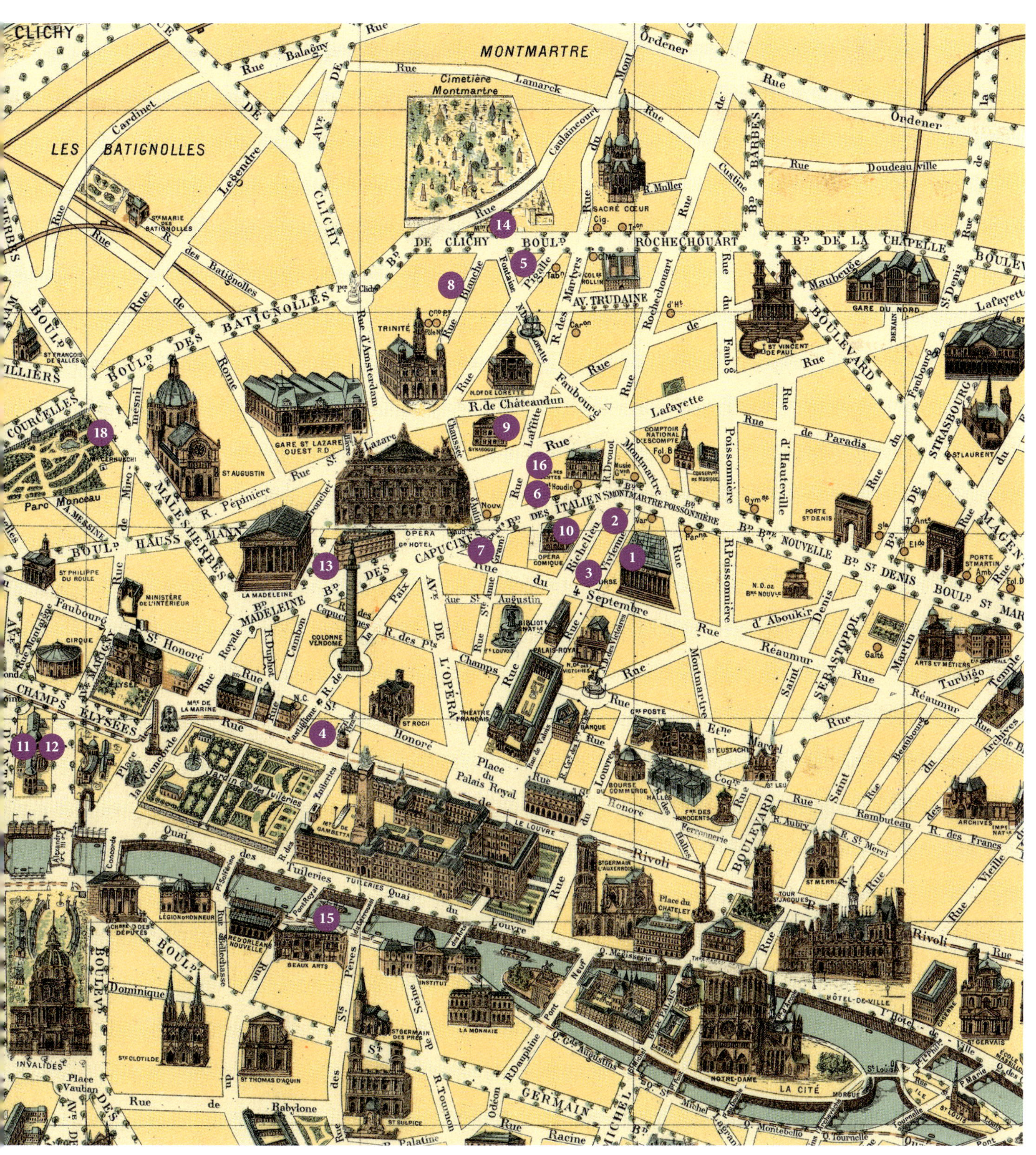

L. Guilmin, *New Map of Paris,* 1899, Bibliothèque nationale de France (detail).
The most important sites where Japanese art could be seen and/or purchased are shown.
The map does not contain all streets.

Chronology

On *Japonisme*
(compiled by Juliana Gocke)

1853/54

- In response to American pressure, Japan reopens its ports to the rest of the world after 215 years of almost complete isolation. The arrival of Admiral Matthew C. Perry at Edo Bay in 1853 is followed by the signing of the Treaty of Kanagawa with the USA on 31 March 1854.
- Enjoying a stable domestic economy and facing the threat of Catholicisation by Portuguese and Spanish missionaries, Japan had progressively cut itself off from the outside world starting in 1616 to the point where, from 1639 onwards, only trade with China and the Netherlands was permitted. During the period of isolation, it was only under strict conditions that Japanese were allowed to travel abroad.

1855

- First world fair in Paris. Japanese objects are exhibited in the Dutch pavilion.

1855–1858

- Signing of trade agreements between Japan and the Netherlands, Russia, England and France.

1861

- In *Recueil de dessins pour l'art et l'industrie*, a collection of images by Adalbert de Beaumont and Eugène V. Collinot, published in several volumes between 1859 and 1873, Japanese motifs begin to serve as source imagery for artists for the first time from 1861 onwards.
- The book *Notes sur le Japon, la Chine et l'Inde 1858, 1859, 1860* by Baron Charles de Chassiron – who travelled to China and Japan in his role as a French diplomat – contains the first facsimiles of Japanese woodblock prints, including some from Katsushika Hokusai's *Manga*.
- Charles Baudelaire is among the first collectors of Japanese woodblock prints; in a letter to Arsène Houssaye, he writes: "It is quite some time since I received a parcel of Japanese items. I have divided them among my friends, and have put three of them aside for you […]."
- In his *Journal* on 8 June, Jules de Goncourt notes his purchase of Japanese prints in the shop À la Porte chinoise in rue Vivienne in Paris: "Recently in *La Porte Chinoise* I bought some Japanese drawings printed on paper that is like a fabric, with the woolliness and elasticity of wool. I have never seen anything in art so wonderful, so imaginative, so admirable and poetic. These are subtle tones like the tones of pen-and-ink drawings, as luminous as enamels; poses, costumes, faces, women that are like something out of a dream; the simplicity of the primitive school, captivating and with an individual quality surpassing that of Dürer; a magic that intoxicates the eyes, like a perfume of the Orient. Wonderful art, natural, as multilayered as blossom, as fascinating as a magic mirror."

1862

- World fair in London. In the so-called "Japanese Court", Sir Rutherford Alcock exhibits 614 Japanese artefacts, mostly from his own collection, acquired on his travels in Japan and for the first time including woodblock prints.
- In addition to the existing shops selling Asian wares – À la Porte chinoise (opened in 1826) and À l'Empire chinois (1856), both in rue Vivienne – La Jonque chinoise, run by a couple named Desoye, opens in rue de Rivoli. This shop trading in Far Eastern objects and artworks is frequented by writers, such as Edmond de Goncourt and Charles Baudelaire, and artists – among them, Édouard Manet, Edgar Degas, James McNeill Whistler and Claude Monet.

1863

- Felice Beato travels to Japan and remains there until 1884. One of the most important photographers of his day, he sets up a studio in Yokohama which he runs until 1877. He supplies the West with hand-coloured photographs of Japanese genre scenes and landscapes.

1867

- World fair in Paris. Japan takes part officially for the first time. The 1,308 items selected for exhibition show aspects of Japanese life and include models of Japanese houses, a variety of objects and the art of *ukiyo-e*. The Japanese presence inspires many French artists – James Tissot, for example – to collect Japanese art. Félix Bracquemond exhibits his *Service Rousseau*, featuring motifs of which some are taken from woodblock prints by Katsushika Hokusai and Utagawa Hiroshige (p. 252).
- Prince Tokugawa Akitake attends the exhibition as a representative of the Tokugawa government and stays in Paris until 1868 to study. James Tissot becomes his drawing tutor.
- *The Société Japonaise du Jing-lar* is founded: Henri Fantin-Latour, Félix Bracquemond, Jules Jacquemart, Philippe Burty, Zacharie Astruc and Alphonse Hirsch attend monthly meetings at the house of Marc L. E. Solon, director of the Sèvres porcelain manufactory.
- After the example of "Chinoiserie", the Goncourt brothers coin the expression "Japonaiserie", referring primarily to Japanese products.

1868

- Start of the Meiji Restoration, a period marked by the restoration of the imperial power and the modernisation of Japan after the Western model in the areas of law, administration, economics, the military and commerce. Edo, the capital of Japan, is given its modern name, Tokyo.
- Zacharie Astruc publishes his article "Le Japon chez nous" in the periodical *L'Étendard*, listing in it the names of writers and artists who collect Japanese art, among them Alfred Stevens, James Tissot, Ernest Chesneau, Jules Champfleury, Marc L. E. Solon, Félix Bracquemond, Henri Fantin-Latour, Philippe Burty, the Goncourt brothers, Édouard Manet, Claude Monet and himself.

1869

- On 19 February, Ernest Chesneau gives a lecture on Japanese art at the Union centrale des Beaux-Arts appliqués à l'industrie.
- 10 April–10 November: In the annual exhibition of French decorative arts held in the Palais de l'Industrie, the Union centrale des Beaux-Arts appliqués à l'industrie organises a "Musée Oriental", in which various Chinese, Indian, Persian and Japanese objects from private Paris collections, including Japanese items from the holdings of Philippe Burty, are displayed.

1870

- Franco-Prussian War 1870–1871.
- Aimé Humbert publishes *Le Japon illustré (2 vols)*.

1871

- On their travels in the Far East, Henri Cernuschi, a Milanese banker, and the art critic Théodore Duret acquire numerous Japanese objects. Two years later, Cernuschi organises the *Exposition des Beaux-Arts de l'Extrême-Orient*, featuring these items, in the Palais de l'Industrie.

1872

- The term "Japonisme" is first used by the art critic Philippe Burty in his series of articles published under that title in *La Renaissance littéraire et artistique*. The articles describe various aspects of Japanese manners and customs. It is not until 1875 that Burty defines the term in the English periodical *The Academy*: "What is called here 'le Japonisme' is the study of the art and genius of Japan."

1873

- The art critics Jules Claretie and Ernest Chesneau use the term "Japonisme" in its modern sense – namely, of creative engagement with Japanese art on the part of artists in France: Claretie in his book *Peintres et sculpteurs contemporains* and Chesneau in his article "Le japonisme dans les arts" printed in the periodical *Musée universel*. In this article, Chesneau claims to have coined the term himself.
- World fair in Vienna. Japan's first official participation under the Meiji government, with 6,000 works representing the whole of Japanese culture (tools, foodstuff, but also art, including a great diversity of objects made of silk, lacquerware, porcelain, bronze and leather, as well as sculptures, paintings and drawings). Outside the exhibition are a Japanese garden and the recreation of a Japanese village.

1874

- Kiryū Kōshō Kaisha is the first manufactory and trading company in Japan to be founded under the Meiji government.
- 15 April–15 May: First exhibition by the impressionists in the studio of the photographer Nadar in Paris.

1875

- At his ceramics manufacturing business, which he and Jean-Baptiste Ernest Leullier founded in rue du Faubourg Saint-Denis in Paris in 1863, Siegfried Bing begins displaying and selling Japanese and Chinese artefacts.

1876

- Émile Guimet and Félix Régamey undertake a six-month journey to China, Japan and South East Asia.

1878

- World Fair in Paris. Organised by the imperial commissioner Wakai Kenzaburō and Hayashi Tadamasa, the Japanese display features a Japanese pavilion in the form of a wooden palace. Among the 430 Japanese items on display are bronzes and lacquerware from the collections of Philippe Burty, Émile Guimet, Henri Cernuschi and Siegfried Bing. After the exhibition, Hayashi quickly becomes an important collector and mediator of Japanese art.
- After mounting a successful display at the world fair, Siegfried Bing opens his own gallery of Chinese and Japanese art in rue Chauchat in Paris.
- Ernest Chesneau publishes "Le Japon à Paris" in the periodical *Gazette des Beaux-Arts*. In it, he lists artists and collectors who are inspired by Japanese art or who take pleasure in it: Édouard Manet, James Tissot, Henri Fantin-Latour, Alphonse Hirsch, Edgar Degas, Claude Monet, Félix Bracquemond, Marc L. E. Solon, Edmond und Jules de Goncourt, Jules Champfleury, Philippe Burty, Émile Zola, Ferdinand Barbedienne,

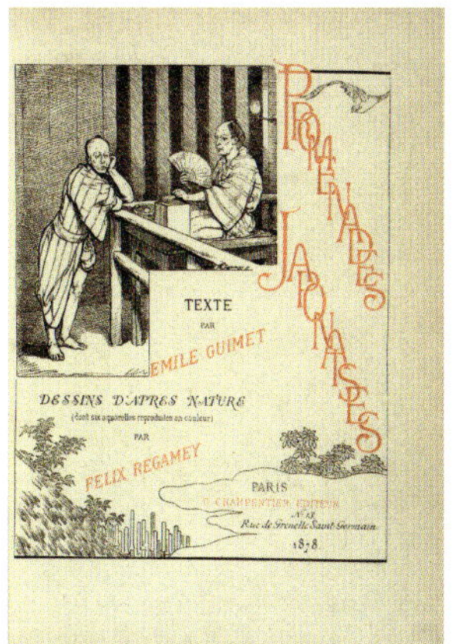

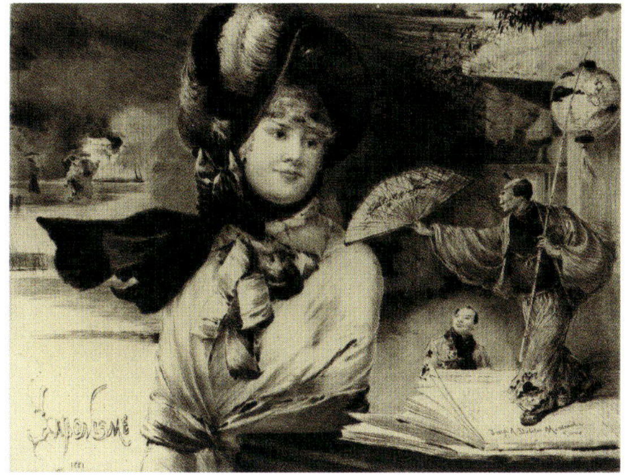

1 Émile Guimet, *Promenades japonaises*, illustrations by Félix Régamey, Paris, 1878

2 Henry Somm, *Japonisme*, 1881, Bibliothèque nationale de France

Charles Christofle, Henri Bouilhet, Lucien Falize, Henri Cernuschi, Théodore Duret, Émile Guimet and Félix Régamey.

- Paris department stores such as Au Bon Marché and Au Printemps put Japanese woodblock prints on sale at modest prices. Here, artists such as Camille Moreau-Nélaton, Pierre Bonnard and Édouard Vuillard stock up on prints of various kinds.
- In Émile Guimet's book *Promenades japonaises*, Félix Régamey illustrates the account of their joint journey to Asia in 1876. The illustrations include reproductions of works by the Japanese artists Katsushika Hokusai and Kawanabe Kyōsai (fig. 1). A sequel, *Promenades japonaises: Tokio–Nikko*, appears two years later.
- 28 November: During a meeting at the house of Philippe Burty, the Japanese artist Watanabe Seitei paints some watercolours. Edmond de Goncourt, Edgar Degas, Édouard Manet and Giuseppe De Nittis are present.

1879

- Émile Guimet opens the Musée des Religions in Lyon with a library and school.

1880

- Siegfried Bing's first visit to Japan.

1881

- After his return from Japan, Siegfried Bing opens three new shops selling Far Eastern objects – in rue de Provence, rue Bleue and rue de la Paix. His import shop in rue de Provence is a meeting place for Vincent Van Gogh, Émile Bernard and Louis Anquetin.
- Théodore Duret publishes his article "L'Art japonais" in the periodical *Gazette des Beaux-Arts*, with illustrations by Hokusai, Hokkei and Hiroshige.
- Félix Régamey illustrates the Japanese novel *Okoma* by Takizawa Bakin.

1883

- April–May: In collaboration with Hayashi Tadamasa and Wakai Kenzaburō, Louis Gonse organises a major exhibition of Japanese art, encompassing 3,000 exhibits, at Galerie Georges Petit. Louis Gonse, Philippe Burty, Siegfried Bing, Théodore Duret and Alphonse Hirsch contribute by lending items from their collections. Henri de Toulouse-Lautrec and Camille Pissarro are among the fascinated visitors. On 24 April 1883, Pissarro writes to his son: "Duret, Gonse – of the Gazette des Beaux-Arts – Burty, Hirsch, the painter, and others have put on an Exposition Japonaise at Petit's – wonderful. What I have found in all the art of that astonishing people is that there is nothing that leaps to the eye, but a serenity, a grandeur, an extraordinary unity, a rather muted radiance, and yet everything *is* radiant; an amazing austerity, and what taste!" Following the success of the exhibition, Gonse publishes *L'Art japonais*, initially in two volumes – the first systematic history of Japanese art to appear in France. Three years later, he publishes a new, abridged edition in a single volume.

1884

- Hayashi Tadamasa and Wakai Kenzaburō open a shop selling Japanese artworks in the Cité d'Hauteville in Paris, which Hayashi moves to rue de la Victoire two years later.

1885

- Van Gogh adorns the walls of his Antwerp studio with Japanese prints. On 28 November, he writes to his brother Theo: "My studio's quite tolerable, mainly because I've pinned a set of Japanese prints on the walls that I find very diverting. You know, those little female figures in gardens or on the shore, horsemen, flowers, gnarled thorn branches."

1887

- February/March: Vincent Van Gogh organises an exhibition of Japanese woodblock prints – probably mostly from Siegfried Bing's collection – in Café Le Tambourin. On 15 July 1888, Van Gogh writes to his brother: "The exhibition of Japanese prints that I had at the Tambourin hat quite an influence on Anquetin and Bernard, but it was such a disaster."

1888

- The painter Louis Dumoulin travels around Japan.
- On 20 February, Vincent Van Gogh arrives in Arles, where he spends several months and feels as if he were in Japan: "I'm always saying to myself *that I'm in Japan here*," he writes to his sister Willemien on 9 September.
- Pierre Loti publishes the novel *Madame Chrysanthème*, which is an international success and which Vincent Van Gogh also reads. Inspired to paint *La Mousmé* (National Gallery of Art, Washington DC), Van Gogh writes on 29 July: "Now, if you know what a '*mousmé*' is (you'll know when you've read Loti's Madame Chrysanthème) – I've just painted one. [...] A mousmé is a Japanese girl – Provençale in this case – aged between 12 and 14."
- In May, Siegfried Bing publishes the first monthly issue of *Le Japon artistique*. The magazine appears 36 times, in three languages, in France, Germany, England and the United States, before ceasing publication in 1891 (fig. 3).
- 28 May: Opening of *Exposition historique de l'art de la gravure au Japon* in Siegfried Bing's shop in rue de Provence.
- December: Galerie Bernheim-Jeune presents a large exhibition of Japanese art including prints from the collections of Siegfried Bing, Philippe Burty, Henri Cernuschi and Louis Gonse.
- At the Académie Julian, Paul Sérusier founds the group "Les Nabis", meaning the prophets or enlightened ones. Pierre Bonnard, Paul Ranson, René Piot, Ker-Xavier Roussel and Édouard Vuillard are early members of the group, joined later by Aristide Maillol und Félix Vallotton.

1889

- Japan becomes a constitutional monarchy.
- World fair in Paris marking the hundredth anniversary of the French Revolution. Inauguration of the Eiffel Tower and the Galerie des Machines. A total of 675 Japanese objects from the collections of Siegfried Bing and Louis Gonse are displayed, as well as a number of illustrated Japanese books and woodblock prints. Édouard Manet, Fantin-Latour, Claude Monet, Camille Pissarro, Paul Cézanne und Théodore Rousseau are represented with a number of works.
- 1 December: Opening of the Musée Guimet in Paris with the collection of Émile Guimet from Lyon.

1890

- 25 April–22 May: In the École des Beaux-Arts, Siegfried Bing organises an exhibition giving a historical overview of the art of the Japanese woodblock print from the eighteenth century to 1860 with 760 prints and 430 illustrated books. Among the visitors are Pierre Bonnard, Félix Vallotton, Henri de Toulouse-Lautrec and Mary Cassatt. Cassatt writes in a letter to her friend Berthe Morisot: "Seriously, *you must not* miss that. You who want to make color prints you couldn't dream of anything more beautiful. I dream of it and don't think of anything but color on copper. [...] You *must* see the Japanese – *come as soon as you can*." An exhibition catalogue is published: *Exposition de la gravure japonaise*.

1891

- In collaboration with Hayashi Tadamasa, and after years of preparation, Edmond de Goncourt publishes *Outamaro: Le peintre des maisons vertes*, the first biography of Kitagawa Utamaro.

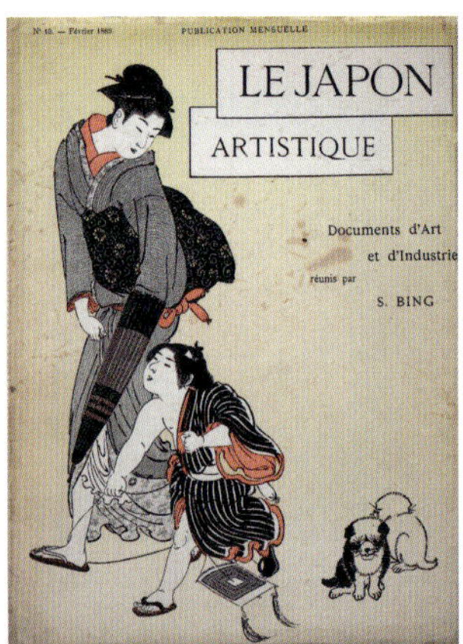

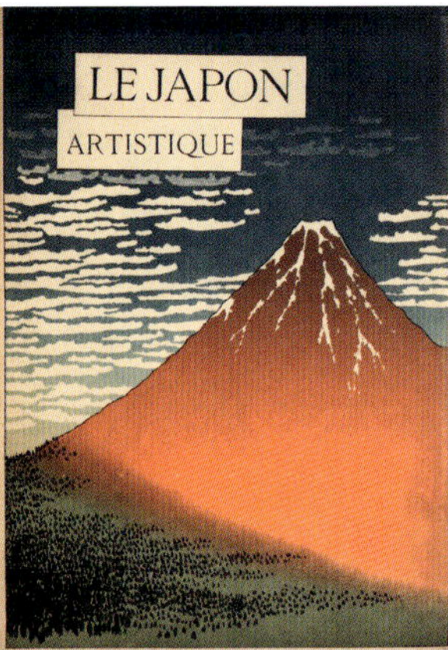

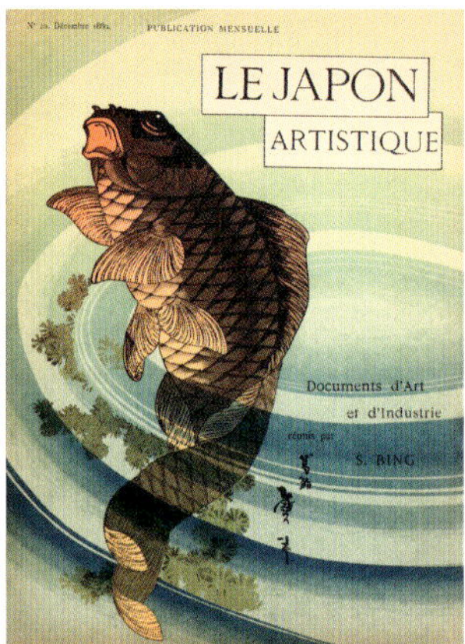

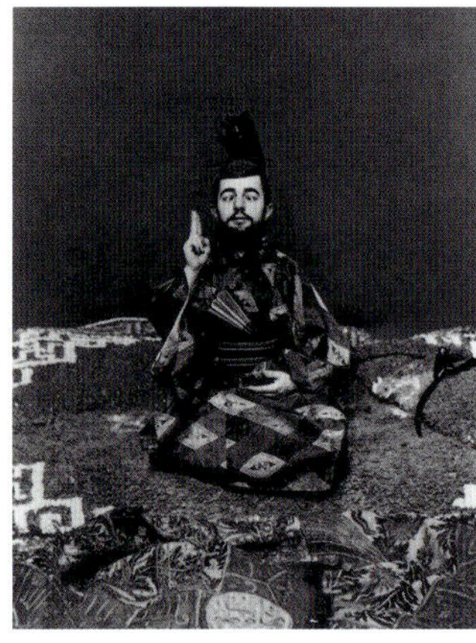

- March: Philippe Burty's collection is sold at Siegfried Bing's shop and at Galerie Durand-Ruel.
- Félix Régamey publishes *Le Japon pratique* with a hundred of his own drawings.

1893

- 22 January–20 February: Exhibition organised by Siegfried Bing at Galerie Durand-Ruel in Paris showing over 300 woodblock prints by Utagawa Hiroshige and Kitagawa Utamaro. Visitors include Camille Pissarro, Claude Monet and Auguste Rodin. Filled with enthusiasm, Pissarro writes to his son Lucien: "It's absolutely overwhelming and wonderfully arranged. Only small rooms, painted in muted pink and pistachio green, really exquisite, and the prints are simply marvellous. An artistic event! […] Dash it all, this show certainly proves us right! There are grey sunsets which are amazingly impressionist." In another letter, he adds: "The Japanese exhibition is magnificent. Hiroshigué [sic] is a splendid impressionist. Monet, Rodin and I are thrilled. How glad I am that I painted my snow pictures and floods: these Japanese artists confirm my faith in our position." A catalogue compiled by Siegfried Bing, *Estampes d'Outamaro et Hiroshighé*, is published in conjunction with the show.
- On his estate at Giverny, Claude Monet has a garden laid out with a water-lily pond and a Japanese-style bridge, which inspires him with many subjects for paintings.

1894

- The Sino-Japanese War, from which Japan emerges as the victor.
- Clémence d'Ennery bequeaths her collection of Far Eastern art, assembled from the 1840s onwards, to the French state. In 1908, Musée d'Ennery, which houses the collection, is opened in her former *hôtel particulier*.

1895

- 26 December: Siegfried Bing ceases to deal only in Asian art: after major alterations to his shops in rue de Chauchat and rue Provence, he opens his new gallery, L'Art Nouveau, which gives its name to a new modern art movement.

1896

- The periodical *La Revue blanche* publishes three articles by Siegfried Bing on Katsushika Hokusai: "La vie et l'œuvre de Hok'saï", "L'art japonais avant Hok'saï" and "La jeunesse de Hok'saï – Shunro". At the same time, Edmond de Goncourt publishes his work *Hokousaï: L'Art japonais au XVIIIième siècle*.

1897

- March: Auction of the collection of the brothers Edmond and Jules de Goncourt at the Hôtel Drouot. It includes Japanese and Chinese art objects and various paintings and prints. The catalogue *Arts de l'Extrême-Orient, objets d'art japonais et chinois* appears, with a preface by Siegfried Bing.

1898

- Opening of Musée Cernuschi in Paris.

1900

- World fair in Paris. The Japanese section is under the direction of Hayashi Tadamasa and comprises 2,128 exhibits. There are also a Japanese garden and teahouse on the grounds of the Palais du Trocadéro.

1902

- June: Hayashi Tadamasa sells his collection at the Hôtel Drouot before returning to Japan. It contains prints, drawings and illustrated books from Japan.

1903

- April: The collection of Edmond Taigny is sold by auction at the Hôtel Drouot; Taigny had already sold parts of his collection here in 1893.
- June: The collection of Paul Brenot, with various Chinese and Japanese objects in porcelain, bronze, lacquerware and enamel as well as fabrics, is auctioned off at the Hôtel Drouot, Paris.

1904

- Auction of the collection of Charles Gillot at Galerie Durand-Ruel in Paris.

1905

- Japan wins the war against Russia.

1906

- After Siegfried Bing's death, his collection is sold by auction at Galerie Durand-Ruel.

Around 1905 onwards

- In France, the craze for all things Japanese gradually subsides. For artists like Pierre Bonnard, Henri Matisse, André Derain and Pablo Picasso, however, Japanese art continues to be an important source of inspiration.

On Museum Folkwang's Japanese Collection
(compiled by Christoph Dorsz)

1898

- In August, Karl Ernst Osthaus (1874–1921) engages in preliminary discussions with Justus Brinckmann about establishing a museum of applied art in Hagen. Brinckmann, the director of the Museum für Kunst und Gewerbe Hamburg, sells the young collector his first Japanese art objects.

1899

- During the summer, Brinckmann introduces Osthaus to the Berlin art dealer Hermann Paechter. In the years that follow, Paechter's gallery, "R. Wagner", procures hundreds of Japanese art objects for Osthaus's museum.

1900

- On Brinckmann's recommendation, Osthaus has a meeting with Siegfried Bing on the occasion of the Paris World Fair. The young collector acquires two small lacquer boxes previously owned by Georg Oeder.

1901

- In the spring, Osthaus buys some netsukes from Paechter originating from the collection of Marcus B. Huish. Brinckmann arranges for some selected tea ceramics to be brought to Hagen.

1902

- Museum Folkwang opens its doors on 9 July. Japanese art is the focus of the second special exhibition that the museum holds; Osthaus gives a lecture on *Japanese Utensils* at this exhibition's opening on 7 December.

1903

- On 4 January, Osthaus gives a lecture on *Japanese Decorative Art* in the museum. In April, he purchases from Bing more than thirty objects from the collection of Edmond Taigny, including some kakemonos. In addition, he chooses several writing boxes from Bing's stock. At the same time, he obtains works in lacquer, tea ceramics and sword hand guards from R. Wagner. In early June, he spends considerable sums on purchases at the auction of the collection of Paul Brenot (fig. 5). Never again does Osthaus spend as much money on the Japanese Collection as in this year.

1904

- In early February, Osthaus makes major purchases at the *Vente Gillot* (auction of the collection of Charles Gillot), among them a Noh theatre costume. At the

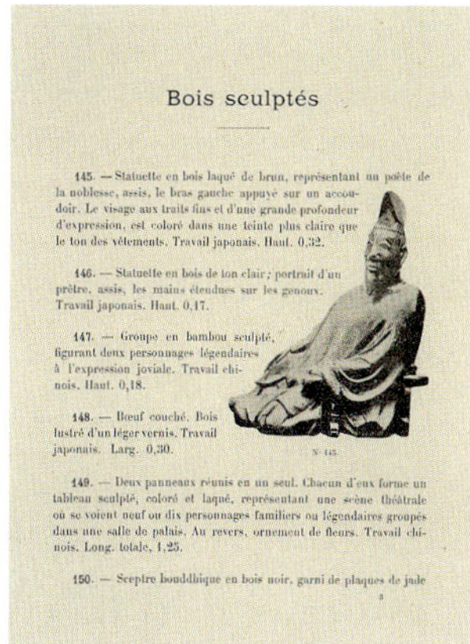

Bois sculptés

145. — Statuette en bois laqué de brun, représentant un poète de la noblesse, assis, le bras gauche appuyé sur un accoudoir. Le visage aux traits fins et d'une grande profondeur d'expression, est coloré dans une teinte plus claire que le ton des vêtements. Travail japonais. Haut. 0,32.

146. — Statuette en bois de ton clair; portrait d'un prêtre, assis, les mains étendues sur les genoux. Travail japonais. Haut. 0,17.

147. — Groupe en bambou sculpté, figurant deux personnages légendaires à l'expression joviale. Travail chinois. Haut. 0,18.

148. — Bœuf couché. Bois lustré d'un léger vernis. Travail japonais. Larg. 0,30.

N° 145.

149. — Deux panneaux réunis en un seul. Chacun d'eux forme un tableau sculpté, coloré et laqué, représentant une scène théâtrale où se voient neuf ou dix personnages familiers ou légendaires groupés dans une salle de palais. Au revers, ornement de fleurs. Travail chinois. Long. totale, 1,25.

150. — Sceptre bouddhique en bois noir, garni de plaques de jade

3

3 *Le Japon artistique*, ed. Siegfried Bing, issue 10, February 1889; issue 12, April 1889; issue 20, December 1889

4 Anonymous, *Toulouse-Lautrec in a Kimono*, circa 1892, Musée Toulouse-Lautrec, Albi, France

5 *Objets d'art de la Chine et du Japon [...] formant la collection de M. Paul Brenot*, Hôtel Drouot auction catalogue, Paris, 5–10.6.1903, p. 3 (showing a wooden sculpture of the Japanese poet *Kakinomoto no Hitomaro*, which Karl Ernst Osthaus acquired for Museum Folkwang, p. 233)

same time, he acquires an old wooden statue of Shō Kannon on the Paris art market. In June, after his second journey to Tunis, Osthaus holds a large exhibition of textiles in his own possession, which includes Japanese fabrics and dyeing stencils. In the summer, he buys a considerable collection of colour woodblock prints, produced by the most important masters of *ukiyo-e*, from the Leipzig antique dealer Karl W. Hiersemann.

1905

- The East Asian collection in the upper vestibule of the museum is enlarged by the addition of further display cabinets. In the March issue of *Die Rheinlande*, Max Creutz publishes a report containing what is still the most important account of Museum Folkwang's collection of Japanese art.

1906

- In January, Osthaus buys lacquerware items and woodblock prints from the Berlin art dealers Rex & Co. At the third German Exhibition of Decorative Arts in Dresden, his wife Gertrud is able to exhibit a portfolio of photographs of the East Asian collection in the room devoted to Hagen. On behalf of Galerie Miethke in Vienna, the painter Carl Moll arranges for a Japanese statue of a priest – no longer in existence – to be brought to Hagen.

1907

- At the beginning of the year, Osthaus purchases an unidentified Japanese colour woodblock print triptych and a scroll painting on the Berlin art market.

1909

- The art historian Wilhelm Niemeyer introduces Osthaus to Paul Vautier, who has assembled an exquisite collection of Japanese art in Tokyo.

1910

- In January, the museum exhibits Japanese colour woodblock prints and the new acquisitions from Vautier's collection: tea ceramics and theatre masks. Osthaus now occasionally buys Japanese art objects from the Amsterdam art dealers Van Veen & Co. Japanese colour woodblock prints and dyeing stencils are shown in the October exhibition.

1911

- Japanese theatre masks and colour woodblock prints form part of the theatre exhibition held in March. The young art history student Karl With visits Hagen, and Osthaus invites him to spend some time in the museum as an assistant. Deutsches Museum für Kunst in Handel und Gewerbe organises the travelling exhibition *Flechtarbeiten* (Basketwork), which includes ikebana baskets and tatami mats.

1912

- In the May exhibition, Japanese silk fabrics from Deutsches Museum für Kunst in Handel und Gewerbe are displayed.

1913

- The East Asian collection is once again expanded with the addition of further display cases. With, the former assistant, travels to Japan, where he makes numerous purchases on the museum's behalf.

1914

- Osthaus uses Japanese objects of high value, among them a *gigaku* mask bought in 1904 at the *Vente Gillot*, to pay for a number of lacquerware items chosen by With at the art dealer's H. Saenger in Hamburg. In July, in its last exhibition before the outbreak of the First World War, the museum displays the new acquisitions from Japan.

1916

- On 11 November, With gives a lecture at the museum on *Early Buddhist Sculpture in East Asia*, the subject of his dissertation.

1917

- Paula Deetjen, a sister-in-law of Osthaus's, produces a new set of photographs of the museum's Japanese art objects.

1919

- In April, the Berlin auction house Rudolph Lepke auctions off a relatively large mixed lot of paintings and decorative artefacts from the museum's collection, including about twenty Japanese art objects. With's two-volume dissertation *Buddhist Sculpture in Japan up to the Beginning of the Eighth Century* appears with a dedication to Osthaus. During the summer, the dedicatee writes two enthusiastic reviews of it.

1920

- In March, With acquires Japanese art objects for the museum by auction at Rudolph Lepke's. The three items – a gold lacquer box and two paintings – are no longer in the collection.

1921

- On 24 February, shortly before the death of Osthaus, who is staying in Merano, With gives a lecture on *Asian Sculpture*.

1922

- The Folkwang collections are sold. On 29 October, Museum Folkwang in Essen is opened. A number of selected Japanese art objects form part of the first presentation of the collection in the Hans-Goldschmidt-Haus.

Glossary

In the following – as in the entire catalogue – all Japanese terms prevalent in the English language are written as they appear in the *New Oxford Spelling Dictionary* (3rd edition, 2005); all other Japanese terms not found in this reference work are written in italics and begin with a lower-case letter.

Japanese woodblock prints
(compiled by Sabine Bradel)

abuna-e
"Daring picture"; erotic image but, unlike the *shunga*, with no sexual content

aiban
Paper format (approx. 34.2 × 22.5 cm)

banzuke
Theatre programme

benizuri-e
A kind of colour print made from 1740 onwards, which uses two or three colour blocks in addition to the line block and in which a red plant-derived pigment (*beni*) predominates

bijin-ga
Portrait of a beautiful person, especially a woman

bokashi
Gradation of colour; a printing technique developed in the nineteenth century

chirimen-e
"Crepe printing"; a technique popular from the 1830s onwards in which, following the normal printing process, the picture was mechanically crinkled to give the impression that it had been printed on creped silk; the subsequent reduction in the size of the paper made the colours appear brighter

chūban
Medium-sized paper format for ceremonial use (*daihōsho*) (approx. 28 × 20 cm)

chūban (daikō hōsho)
Slightly wider medium-sized paper format for ceremonial use *(daikō hōsho)* (approx. 29 × 22 cm)

chūtanzaku
Medium-sized vertical-format print with a poem (approx. 38 × 13 cm)

ehon
"Picture book", a woodblock-printed book in which illustrations take up more space than text

e-goyomi
Calendar with indications of the month and year hidden in the picture

fūkei-ga
Picture of a landscape

fūzoku-ga
Picture of manners and customs

giga
Humorous picture, caricature

harimaze-e
Prints made from the second half of the nineteenth century onwards by one or several artists, with at least two illustrations not necessarily related to one another; the illustrations were set in cartouches intended to be cut out and tacked to walls, sliding doors, fans, etc.

hashira-e
"Pillar picture"; tall, narrow paper format (between 66 × 10 cm and 68.5 × 15 cm); pictures in this format could be mounted on the wooden pillars supporting the house

hosoban
Narrow paper format (approx. 31.5 × 14 cm)

hyōbanki
Book of critiques of actors and courtesans

ichimai-e
Composition on a single sheet

kamuro
A courtesan's girl apprentice

kanban
Sign or announcement poster at a theatre, tea house or shop

kentō
Registration mark to ensure that the paper is correctly aligned with the printing blocks

kiwame
Circular seal of the censoring authority, incorporated into the prints from 1791 to 1842

meisho-e
Depiction of a famous location

mon
Crest or insignia of a dynasty of actors or of a house of pleasure

musha-e
Portrait of warriors and heroes

nigao-e
Portrait that does not idealise facial features

nikuhitsu-ga
Painting in the style of the *ukiyo-e* woodblock prints – usually, though not always, executed by woodblock artists

nishiki-e
"Brocade print"; polychrome print developed in 1764/1765 with more than five colour blocks in addition to the line block

ōban
Large paper format (approx. 38 × 26 cm)

ōkubi-e
"Large head picture"; a bust portrait in three-quarter profile

onnagata
Kabuki actor specialising in female roles

ōtanzakuban
Paper format, approx. 38 × 17 cm

shunga
"Spring picture"; picture with erotic content

sumizuri-e
Black-and-white line print

surimono
Small-format, high-quality private commission produced in limited editions to commemorate special occasions; often a combination of a picture and poems

tan-e
Early hand-coloured line print in which a red mineral pigment (*tan*) predominates

ukiyo-e
Popular art genre of the Edo period (1603–1868), practised in the form of the woodblock print (*moku hanga*) and painting (*nikuhitsu-ga* or *nikuhitsu ukiyo-e*)

urushi-e
"Lacquer picture"; early hand-coloured line print in which certain areas were given a lacquer-like lustre through the addition of glue to the ink

yakusha-e
Portrait of an actor

Yoshiwara
Licensed pleasure district in Edo

yūjo
Courtesan

Japanese objects
(compiled by Antje Papist-Matsuo)

bundai
Low writing desk, often covered with lacquer decoration

byōbu
Folding screen, usually with six panels; originally made for protection against the weather, the paper-covered panels developed into surfaces for painting and calligraphy

chaire
Small earthenware tea jar used to contain the powdered green tea for the tea ceremony; *chaire* exist in various forms

chanoyu
"Hot water for tea"; term for the ritual art of preparing and drinking powdered green tea

chawan
Tea bowl; unlike the Western teacup, the Japanese tea bowl has no handle; the shape and size of tea bowls make them suitable for holding with both hands

fukusa
A square silk cloth used for the cleansing of utensils before the tea is prepared

fusuma
Sliding door with a wooden frame, usually fitted with paper on each side, often painted or covered with decorative paper

ikakeji
A lacquer ground sprinkled with a layer of fine powdered metal (gold or silver) covering it entirely

ikebana
Traditional Japanese art of flower arranging, distinguished by various styles; the basic style consists of three flowering twigs arranged in an asymmetrical triangle

inro
Medicine container comprising several parts, originally used to hold stamping ink; inros are usually made of richly lacquered wood but also of ivory or metal; the individual compartments are joined by a cord laced through cord runners on both sides, with an *ojime* ("cord fastener") drawing the cords together; a netsuke acts as a toggle to hold the cord securely in place

kakemono
Vertical-format hanging scroll, with a painting or calligraphy mounted on it

karaori
Opulent costume worn for female roles in Noh theatre; originally a traditional type of weaving in Japan, in which the decoration looks like embroidery

katagami
Japanese paper stencils made of impregnated paper, used for dyeing fabrics for kimonos, curtains and banners

katatsuki
"Protruding shoulder", type of container, a form of *chaire*; the wide "shoulder" is the principal characteristic of this form

kyōgen
Type of traditional Japanese theatre which developed alongside Noh theatre; it is performed in Noh theatre, without masks, as a light interlude

makie
Decorative technique in which fine particles of gold, silver or coloured lacquer are sprinkled onto a drawing previously made on a wet lacquer ground, creating an image ("sprinkled picture"); fundamental techniques are the "polished sprinkled picture" (*togidashi*), the "flat sprinkled picture" (*hiramakie*) and the "raised sprinkled picture" (*takamakie*)

*makimono (*also *emakimono)*
Horizontal-format pictorial scroll, which is unrolled from right to left to view the painting mounted on it, or a written text

nashiji
"Pear skin ground"; the sprinkling of irregularly shaped flakes of metal onto a wet lacquer ground, which is then overlaid with a transparent lacquer

netsuke
Carved security toggle for inros or tobacco containers

Noh
Traditional Japanese dance theatre that developed in the fourteenth century under Buddhist and popular influence; the actors wear masks to play the roles of women, gods and demons

sadō
"Way of tea"; a term describing the Japanese tea ceremony as a spiritual and artistic discipline in life

seto and *mino*
Japanese ceramics were produced in the kilns of Seto and Mino; famous for *shino* ware; their origins go back to the late sixteenth century

suzuribako
Writing box with lacquer decoration, which contained the implements needed for writing such as a grinding stone, ink stone, brushes, water dropper and paper knife

takatori
Japanese ceramics produced in Shikoku; they were first made around the late sixteenth or early seventeenth centuries by Korean potters

tebako
"Hand box"; a rectangular cosmetic box with lacquer decoration, forming part of a luxurious trousseau

temmoku type
Tea bowl with a small foot and conical sides; named after Chinese Jian ware from Tianmu Mountain in Fujian Province

tsuba
Decorated sword hand guard situated between the blade and the grip of a sword and intended to protect the hand

urushi
Japanese name for the natural raw material from East Asia that is gathered as a resinous sap from the lacquer tree and processed to make lacquer

Exhibited works

NOTES

General:
Dimensions are specified in terms of height × width × depth in centimetres.

Works on paper:
Due to their extreme sensitivity to light, the majority of works on paper cannot be shown at both exhibition venues. For this reason, two sets of works have been assembled for Essen and Zurich respectively. Works that are exhibited in Essen only are indicated as such ("Only in Essen"); works only shown in Zurich likewise bear the designation "Only in Zurich".

Japanese artefacts:
Works that stem from important former French collections of the nineteenth century are designated with "Formerly Collection", with the name of the respective artist given, if known. Unless otherwise indicated, the artefacts belong to Museum Folkwang, Essen.

Japanese woodblock prints:
Artists are listed according to their artist's name, not their surname. A Japanese title is only given if the respective woodblock print bears an inscription, or if it is the title commonly used. Unless otherwise specified, the technique refers to the colour woodblock print (*nishiki-e*); the format is *ōban* (approx. 38 × 26 cm). Works from former artists' collections are designated with "Sheet formerly in Collection", with the name of the respective artist given; this also applies to sheets from other important nineteenth-century French collections. If a different sheet with the same motif belonged to an artist's collection, then this is specified with "Motif also in Collection", with the name of the respective artist given. For conservational reasons, a small number of sheets must be replaced after two months for the three-and-a-half-month duration of the exhibition in Essen.

France

PAINTINGS AND PASTELS

► 1 Émile Bernard (1868–1941)
The Wave / La vague, 1892
Oil on fibreboard on canvas, 57.8 × 85.2 cm
Collection of the Ackland Art Museum,
The University of North Carolina at Chapel Hill,
Ackland Fund
p. 215

► 2 Pierre Bonnard (1867–1947)
Decorative Panneaux – Women in the Garden / Panneaux décoratifs – Femmes au jardin, 1890/1891
Distemper over charcoal, pencil and white chalk on paper, mounted on canvas, each 154 × 47 cm
Kunsthaus Zürich, Vereinigung Zürcher Kunstfreunde, Geschenk Ernst Gamper, 1984
p. 279

► 3 Pierre Bonnard
Women with a Dog / Femmes au chien, 1891
Oil on canvas, 40 × 32 cm
Sterling and Francine Clark Art Institute, Williamstown, Massachusetts, USA, 1979.23
Only in Essen, p. 289

► 4 Pierre Bonnard
The Passerby / La passante, 1894
Oil on wood, 36 × 25 cm
Private Swiss Collection
Only in Essen, p. 288

► 5 Pierre Bonnard
Female Nude in the Mirror / Nu au miroir, 1910
Oil on canvas, 124 × 48 cm
Wallraf-Richartz-Museum & Fondation Corboud, Cologne
Only in Essen, p. 329

► 6 Gustave Caillebotte (1848–1894)
Four Vases with Chrysanthemums / Quatre vases de chrysanthèmes, circa 1893
Oil on canvas, 54 × 65 cm
Private Collection
p. 165

► 7 Paul Cézanne (1839–1906)
Mont Sainte-Victoire / Montagne Sainte-Victoire, circa 1890
Oil on canvas, 65 × 92 cm
Musée d'Orsay, Paris, donation de la petite-fille d'Auguste Pellerin, 1969
Only in Essen, p. 179

► 8 Paul Cézanne
View of Mont Sainte-Victoire Seen from Les Lauves / Le mont Sainte-Victoire vu des Lauves, 1904/1906
Oil on canvas, 59.9 × 72.2 cm
Kunstmuseum Basel
p. 181

► 9 Paul Cézanne
View of Mont Sainte-Victoire Seen from Les Lauves / Le mont Sainte-Victoire vu des Lauves, 1904/1906
Oil on canvas, 54 × 73 cm
Viktor and Marianne Langen Collection
p. 180

► 10 Gustave Courbet (1819–1877)
The Wave / La vague, 1869
Oil on canvas, 63 × 92 cm
Städel Museum, Frankfurt am Main, Eigentum des Städelschen Museums-Vereins e.V.
Only in Essen, p. 169

► 11 Gustave Courbet
The Wave / La vague, circa 1869
Oil on canvas, 46 × 55 cm
Scottish National Gallery, Edinburgh
Only in Zurich, p. 166

► 12 Gustave Courbet
The Wave / La vague, 1870
Oil on canvas, 45 × 59 cm
Museum Folkwang, Essen
p. 168

► 13 Giuseppe De Nittis (1846–1884)
Portrait of a Lady / Figure de dame, 1880
Oil on canvas, 71 × 38 cm
Pinacoteca Giuseppe De Nittis, Barletta
p. 111

► 14 Edgar Degas (1834–1917)
Orchestra Musicians / Musiciens à l'orchestre, 1872 (reworked 1874–1876)
Oil on canvas, 69 × 49 cm
Städel Museum, Frankfurt am Main
Only in Essen, p. 205

► 15 Edgar Degas
Dancers Mounting the Stairs / Danseuses montant un escalier, 1886/1890
Oil on canvas, 39 × 90 cm
Musée d'Orsay, Paris, legs du comte Isaac de Camondo, 1911
p. 206

► 16 Edgar Degas
Before the Ballet / Le foyer de la danse, 1890/1892
Oil on canvas, 40 × 88.9 cm
National Gallery of Art, Washington, Widener Collection, 1942.9.19
p. 207

► 17 Edgar Degas
Ballet Dancer / Danseuse, scène de ballet, 1891
Oil on mahogany, 22 × 15.8 cm
Hamburger Kunsthalle
Only in Essen, p. 204

► 18 Edgar Degas
Morning Toilette / La coiffure, 1892/1895
Oil on canvas, 82 × 87 cm
The National Museum of Art, Architecture and Design, Oslo
Only in Essen, p. 161

► 19 Edgar Degas
Breakfast after the Bath / Le petit déjeuner après le bain, circa 1894
Charcoal and pastel on vellum paper, 104 × 68.5 cm
Collection Triton Foundation
p. 158

► 20 Edgar Degas
Breakfast after the Bath (The Bath) / Le petit déjeuner après le bain (Le bain), circa 1895/1898
Pastel on paper on cardboard, 82.5 × 79 cm
Fondation Beyeler, Riehen/Basel, Sammlung Beyeler
p. 159

► 21 Edgar Degas
Breakfast after the Bath / Le petit déjeuner à la sortie du bain, circa 1895–1898
Pastel on paper, 121 × 92 cm
Private Collection
Only in Zurich, p. 157

► 22 Maurice Denis (1870–1943)
Self-Portrait beneath Trees / Portrait de l'artiste sous les arbres, circa 1891
Oil on canvas, 21.5 × 80 cm
Private Collection
p. 294

► 23 Maurice Denis
July / Juillet, 1892
Oil on canvas, 38.4 × 61.5 cm
Arp Museum Bahnhof Rolandseck / Sammlung Rau für UNICEF
Only in Essen, p. 295

► 24 Maurice Denis
Portrait of Madame Ranson, in Green / Portrait de Madame Ranson, en vert, 1893
Oil on canvas, 124 × 42 cm
Private Collection
p. 277

► 25 Maurice Denis
Virginal Spring / Virginal printemps, 1894
Oil on canvas, 57 × 32.5 cm
Kunsthaus Zürich, Geschenk der Hulda und Gustav Zumsteg-Stiftung
p. 298

► 26 Louis Dumoulin (1860–1924)
Theatre District in Yokohama / Quartier des théâtres à Yokohama, circa 1888
Oil on canvas, 100 × 73 cm
Musée National des Arts Asiatiques Guimet, Paris
p. 130

► 27 Louis Dumoulin
Festival in Nikkō (Festival of Shōgun Ieyasu) / Fête à Nikkō (Fête du shogun Yeyasu), 1888/1889
Oil on canvas, 55 × 46 cm
Musée National des Arts Asiatiques Guimet, Paris
p. 130

► 28 Louis Dumoulin
The Sacred Bridge over the Daiya River in Nikkō / Pont sacré sur la rivière Daiya à Nikkō, 1888/1889
Oil on canvas, 74 × 100 cm
Musée National des Arts Asiatiques Guimet, Paris
p. 131

► 29 James Ensor (1860–1949)
Fans and Fabrics / Éventails et étoffes, circa 1906
Oil on canvas, 47.5 × 55.5 cm
Kunsthaus Zürich, Fonds Gustav Henneberg
p. 328

► 30 Henri Fantin-Latour (1836–1904)
Blossoming Rhododendron Branch / Rhododendron, 1874
Oil on canvas, 54 × 57 cm
Wallraf-Richartz-Museum & Fondation Corboud, Cologne
p. 163

► 31 Paul Gauguin (1848–1903)
Arlésiennes (Mistral), 1888
Oil on jute, 73 × 92 cm
The Art Institute of Chicago, Mr. and Mrs. Lewis Larned Coburn Memorial Collection
p. 217

► 32 Paul Gauguin
Blue Trees: "Your Turn Will Come, My Beauty!" / Les arbres bleus – "Vous y passerez, la belle!", 1888
Oil on jute sackcloth, 93 × 73 cm
Ordrupgaard
Only in Essen, p. 68

► 33 Paul Gauguin
The Kelp Gatherers (II) / Ramasseuses de varech (II), 1889
Oil on canvas, 87 × 123.1 cm
Museum Folkwang, Essen
p. 211

► 34 Paul Gauguin
Still Life with Onions and Japanese Woodcut / Nature morte aux oignons, circa 1889
Oil on canvas, mounted on cardboard, 40.3 × 51.5 cm
Ny Carlsberg Glyptotek, Copenhagen
Only in Essen, p. 125

► 35 Paul Gauguin
Reclining Tahitian Women / Arearea no varua ino (Sous l'empire du revenant), 1894
Oil on canvas, 60 × 98 cm
Ny Carlsberg Glyptotek, Copenhagen
Only in Zurich, p. 225

► 36 Paul Gauguin
Riders on the Beach (I) / Cavaliers sur la plage (I), 1902
Oil on canvas, 65.6 × 75.9 cm
Museum Folkwang, Essen
Only in Essen, p. 224

► 37 Vincent Van Gogh (1853–1890)
The Courtesan (after Eisen) / Japonaiserie (d'après Kesaï Yeisen), 1887
Oil on cotton, 110.3 × 60 cm
Van Gogh Museum, Amsterdam (Vincent van Gogh Foundation)
p. 123

► 38 Vincent Van Gogh
Portrait of Père Tanguy / Le père Tanguy, 1887
Oil on canvas, 65 × 51 cm
Private Collection
Only in Zurich, p. 20

► 39 Vincent Van Gogh
Quay with Men Unloading Sand Barges / Les bateaux amarrés, 1888
Oil on canvas, 55.1 × 66.2 cm
Museum Folkwang, Essen
p. 10

► 40 Vincent Van Gogh
Sower with Setting Sun / Le semeur, 1888
Oil on canvas, 73 × 92 cm
Stiftung Sammlung E. G. Bührle, Zürich
p. 223

► 41 Vincent Van Gogh
A Corner of the Asylum and the Garden with a Heavy, Sawed-Off Tree / Le parc de l'hôpital, à Saint-Rémy, 1889
Oil on canvas, 75 × 93.5 cm
Museum Folkwang, Essen
p. 219

► 42 Georges Lacombe (1868–1916)
The Violet Wave / Lame violette, 1896–1897
Oil on canvas, 47.5 × 62.5 cm
The George Economou Collection, Athens
p. 171

► 43 Édouard Manet (1832–1883)
Basket of Flowers / Panier fleuri, 1880
Oil on canvas, 65 × 81 cm
Private Collection, courtesy of Galerie Beck & Eggeling, Düsseldorf
p. 121

► 44 Henri Matisse (1869–1954)
La Japonaise: Woman beside the Water / La Japonaise au bord de l'eau, 1905
Oil and pencil on canvas, 35.2 × 28.2 cm
The Museum of Modern Art, New York, purchase and partial anonymous gift, 1983
p. 94

► 45 Henri Matisse
Interior with Black Notebook / Nice, cahier noir, 1918
Oil on canvas, 33 × 40.7 cm
Hahnloser/Jaeggli Stiftung, Winterthur
Only in Essen, p. 327

► 46 Claude Monet (1840–1926)
Vase of Poppies / Vase de pavots, 1883
Oil on canvas, 100 × 60 cm
Museum Boijmans Van Beuningen, Rotterdam, on loan from the Foundation Willem van der Vorm
p. 120

► 47 Claude Monet
Rocks at Belle-Île / Rochers à Belle-Île, 1886
Oil on canvas, 59.5 × 73 cm
Ny Carlsberg Glyptotek, Copenhagen
Only in Essen, p. 176

► 48 Claude Monet
The Rock Pyramids at Port-Coton in the Sun / Les pyramides de Port-Coton, effet de soleil, 1886
Oil on canvas, 64 × 64 cm
Private Collection, courtesy of Thomas Ammann Fine Art AG, Zurich
Only in Zurich, p. 177

► 49 Claude Monet
Bed of Chrysanthemums / Massif de chrysanthèmes, 1897
Oil on canvas, 130.8 × 88.9 cm
Private Collection
p. 307

► 50 Claude Monet
Water-Lily Pond / Le bassin aux nymphéas, 1899
Oil on canvas, 89 × 93 cm
State Pushkin Museum of Fine Arts, Moscow
Only in Zurich, p. 304

► 51 Claude Monet
Bridge over a Pond of Water Lilies / Le bassin des nymphéas, 1899
Oil on canvas, 92.7 × 73.7 cm
The Metropolitan Museum of Art, H. O. Havemeyer Collection, Bequest of Mrs. H. O. Havemeyer, 1929 (29.100.113)
Only in Essen, p. 305

► 52 Claude Monet
The Artist's Garden in Giverny / Le jardin aux iris, Giverny, 1900
Oil on canvas, 89.5 × 92 cm
Yale University Art Gallery, Collection of Mr. and Mrs. Paul Mellon, B.A. 1929, L.H.D.H 1967
p. 302

► 53 Claude Monet
Water-Lily Pond with Irises / Le bassin aux nymphéas avec iris, 1914/1922
Oil on canvas, 200 × 600 cm
Kunsthaus Zürich, Geschenk Emil G. Bührle
Only in Zurich, pp. 310–311

► 54 Claude Monet
Water-Lilies / Nymphéas, circa 1915
Oil on canvas, 151.4 × 201 cm
Bayerische Staatsgemäldesammlungen – Neue Pinakothek, Munich
Only in Essen, p. 308

► 55 Claude Monet
The Water-Lily Pond / Le bassin aux nymphéas, circa 1916
Oil on canvas, 130.5 × 200.5 cm
Museum Folkwang, Essen
p. 313

► 56 Claude Monet
Water-Lilies / Nymphéas, 1916/1919
Oil on canvas, 200 × 180 cm
Fondation Beyeler, Riehen/Basel, Sammlung Beyeler
p. 309

► 57 Claude Monet
The Water-Lily Pond at Giverny / Coin de l'étang à Giverny, 1917
Oil on canvas, 117 × 83 cm
Musée de Grenoble
p. 315

► 58 Claude Monet
The Water-Lily Pond /
Coin du bassin aux nymphéas, 1918
Oil on canvas, 120 × 89 cm
Collection des Musées d'art et d'histoire de la Ville de Genève, dépôt Fondation Garengo
p. 314

► 59 Paul Ranson (1864–1909)
Coastline / Rivage, 1889
Oil on canvas, 59.9 × 73 cm
Kunsthaus Zürich,
Schenkung Ottilie Roederstein, 1920
p. 296

► 60 Paul Ranson
Female Nude Arranging Her Hair at the Edge of a Pond / Nu se coiffant au bord de l'étang, circa 1897
Oil on canvas, 91 × 70 cm
Private Collection
p. 299

► 61 Odilon Redon (1840–1916)
The Japanese Warrior Vase /
Vase au guerrier japonais, circa 1905
Pastel and chalk on paper, mounted on cardboard, 90.5 × 71.5 cm
Courtesy of Galleri K, Oslo
p. 127

► 62 Pierre Auguste Renoir (1841–1919)
Still Life with Bouquet /
Nature morte au bouquet, 1871
Oil on canvas, 74 × 60 cm
The Museum of Fine Arts, Houston, The Robert Lee Blaffer Memorial Collection, gift of Sarah Campbell Blaffer
p. 58

► 63 Paul Sérusier (1864–1927)
Small Landscape with Seaweed Gatherers /
Petit paysage avec pêcheurs de varech, circa 1889
Oil on cardboard, 21.9 × 33.2 cm
Städel Museum, Frankfurt am Main
Only in Essen, p. 210

► 64 Paul Sérusier
Washerwomen at the Laïta River /
Les laveuses à la Laïta, 1892
Oil on canvas, 73.2 × 92.2 cm
Musée d'Orsay, Paris, donation de Mlle Boutaric, 1980
p. 297

► 65 Alfred Stevens (1823–1906)
The Letter of Separation /
La lettre de rupture, circa 1867
Oil on canvas, 74.5 × 54.5 cm
Musée d'Orsay, Paris
p. 110

► 66 Alfred Stevens
The Japanese Mask /
Le masque japonais, circa 1874/1875
Oil on canvas, 97 × 70 cm
Collection of Diane B. Wilsey
p. 115

► 67 James Jacques Joseph Tissot (1836–1902)
Young Women Looking at Japanese Articles /
Jeunes femmes regardant des objets japonais, 1869
Oil on canvas, 70.5 × 50.2 cm
Cincinnati Art Museum, gift of Henry M. Goodyear, M.D., 1984.217
p. 107

► 68 James Jacques Joseph Tissot
The Japanese Scroll /
Le rouleau horizontal japonais, circa 1872
Oil on canvas, 38.7 × 57.2 cm
Private Collection
p. 113

► 69 Édouard Vuillard (1868–1940)
A Seamstress / Couseuse à la grande étoffe, 1892
Oil on canvas, 64.5 × 53.7 cm
Saint Louis Art Museum, gift of Sidney M. Shoenberg Sr.
p. 275

► 70 Édouard Vuillard
Large Interior with Six Persons /
Le grand intérieur aux six personnages, 1897
Oil on canvas, 88 × 193 cm
Kunsthaus Zürich
Only in Zurich, p. 293

► 71 Édouard Vuillard
Family in the Garden / Dans le jardin, chez Vallotton, 1898
Oil on cardboard, 26.8 × 111 cm
Staatsgalerie Stuttgart
Only in Essen, p. 274

► 72 Édouard Vuillard
Madame Vuillard Arranging Her Hair /
La coiffure, 1900
Oil on cardboard, mounted on wood, 49.5 × 35.5 cm
The Henry Barber Trust, the Barber Institute of Fine Arts, University of Birmingham
p. 292

► 73 James Abbott McNeill Whistler (1834–1903)
Variations in Violet and Green, 1871
Oil on canvas, 61.5 × 36 cm
Musée d'Orsay, Paris
Only in Zurich, p. 203

► 74 James Abbott McNeill Whistler
Nocturne: Blue and Silver – Cremorne Lights, 1872
Oil on canvas, 50.2 × 74.3 cm
Tate, bequeathed by Arthur Studd, 1919
p. 202

DRAWINGS

► 75 Félix Régamey (1844–1907)
Squatting Priest / Prêtre accroupi, 1876
Pencil, ink and watercolour on paper, heightened in white, 75 × 54 cm (total frame dimensions, framed with five other drawings)
Musée National des Arts Asiatiques Guimet, Paris
Only in Essen

► 76 Félix Régamey
Sanctuary in Kyoto / Sanctuaire à Kyoto, 1876
Pencil, ink and watercolour on paper, heightened in white, 75 × 54 cm (total frame dimensions; framed with three other drawings, among them *View of Arashiyama in Kyoto*)
Musée National des Arts Asiatiques Guimet, Paris
Only in Essen, p. 133

► 77 Félix Régamey
Dance / Danse, 1876
Pencil, ink and watercolour on paper, heightened in white, 75 × 54 cm (total frame dimensions; framed with one other drawing)
Musée National des Arts Asiatiques Guimet, Paris
Only in Essen, p. 132

► 78 Félix Régamey
Standing Figure / Personnage debout, 1876
Pencil, ink and watercolour on paper, heightened in white, 75 × 54 cm (total frame dimensions; framed with seven other drawings)
Musée National des Arts Asiatiques Guimet, Paris
Only in Zurich, p. 132

► 79 Félix Régamey
Altar and Ceremony / Autel et cérémonie, 1876
Pencil, ink and watercolour on paper, heightened in white, 75 × 54 cm (total frame dimensions; framed with one other drawing)
Musée National des Arts Asiatiques Guimet, Paris
Only in Zurich

► 80 Henry Somm (1844–1907)
Japanese Grammar / Grammaire japonaise, circa 1868–1870
Paperback album with cloth in floral decor, covered, 79 pages
Pen and brown ink on paper
14.4 × 9.8 cm
Musée d'Orsay, Paris
Formerly in the possession of Philippe Burty

FANS AND FAN PAINTINGS

► 81 Pierre Bonnard (1867–1947)
Women and Flowers /
Femmes dans un bois, circa 1891
Pencil, watercolour, pen and brown ink on vellum paper, 29 × 59 cm
Triton Foundation Collection
p. 298

► 82 Pierre Bonnard
Promenaders and Riders in the Avenue du Bois /
Promeneurs et cavaliers, avenue du Bois, 1894
Gouache and Chinese ink on fan, 37 × 73 cm
Adrien Maeght Collection, Saint Paul
Only in Zurich, p. 280

► 83 Giuseppe De Nittis (1846–1884)
Nature (Fan) / Nature (éventail), 1883
Watercolour on silk, 28 × 55 cm
Pinacoteca Giuseppe De Nittis, Barletta

► 84 Edgar Degas (1834–1917)
Dancers Behind the Scenes / Danseuses au repos dans les coulisses, circa 1878/1879
Gouache and gilt painting on silk, 29 × 59 cm
E. W. K. Bern
Only in Zurich, p. 204

► 85 Paul Gauguin (1848–1903)
Little Cat Eating out of Bowl /
Petit chat mangeant dans une écuelle, 1888
Gouache on paper, 20 × 42.5 cm
Private Collection
p. 216

► 86 Henri de Toulouse-Lautrec (1864–1901)
At Circus Fernando / Au cirque Fernando, 1888
Black and red ink on white paper, 21 × 66 cm
Musée Toulouse-Lautrec, Albi, France
Only in Essen, p. 280

► 87 Félix Vallotton (1865–1925)
Fan / Éventail, circa 1896–1898
Pen, brush and Chinese ink on Japanese paper, mounted on bamboo, 39 × 70 × 4.5 cm
Musée départemental Maurice Denis, Saint-Germain-en-Laye
Only in Essen, p. 280

► 88a–g Émile Bernard (1868–1941)
Bretonneries, 1889
Series of zincographs with watercolour and gouache
Kunsthalle Mannheim
Only in Essen

a *Bretonneries (Title Page) / Bretonneries (Page de titre)*
31.3 × 24.5 cm (image and sheet)
p. 212

b *Bretons in a Boat / Le retour du pardon* or *Bretons en barque*
31 × 24 cm (image), 31.5 × 24.5 cm (sheet)

c *Breton Women Hanging Washing / Bretonnes étendant le linge*
25 × 31.7 cm (image and sheet)
p. 213

d *Breton Women Making Haystacks / Bretonnes faisant les foins*
25.2 × 32.8 cm (image and sheet)
p. 213

e *Breton Women Feeding the Pigs / Bretonnes nourrisant les cochons*
24.5 × 31.8 cm (image and sheet)
p. 213

f *Breton Wedding / La noce en Bretagne*
23.3 × 29.3 cm (image and sheet)
p. 213

g *Breton Women Harvesting Crops / Bretonnes faisant la moisson*
24.4 × 30.5 cm (image and sheet, trimmed at the edges)

► 89 Pierre Bonnard (1867–1947)
France-Champagne, 1891
Colour lithograph on paper,
approx. 80 × 61 cm (sheet)
Bibliothèque de Genève, affiches, SGA 120.46
Only in Zurich, p. 197

► 90a–b Pierre Bonnard
La Revue blanche, 1894
Colour lithograph on paper
80 × 61 cm (sheet)
a Staatsgalerie Stuttgart / Graphische Sammlung
Only in Essen, p. 196
b Coninx-Stiftung, Zürich
Only in Zurich

► 91a–o Félix Buhot (1847–1898)
Japonisme, 1883
Series of ten etchings
Edition of 150, of which 100 printed on Dutch laid paper

▸ *Cover and Bookplate / Couverture et ex-libris*
Etching and aquatint on brown laid paper,
25.7 × 17.7 cm (image, cover), 10.7 × 13.7 cm (image, bookplate), each 31.8 × 47.6 cm (sheet)
a Institut national d'histoire de l'art, Bibliothèque, collections Jacques Doucet
Only in Essen

▸ *Cover / Page de titre*
Etching on Dutch laid paper, 25.7 × 17.7 cm (image), 31.9 × 22.8 cm (sheet)
b Institut national d'histoire de l'art, Bibliothèque, collections Jacques Doucet
Only in Essen, p. 118
Etching on paper, 25.7 × 17.7 cm (image), 44.5 × 30.8 cm (sheet)
c Musée Thomas Henry, Cherbourg-Octeville
Only in Zurich

▸ *Carved Wooden Mask / Masque en bois sculpté*
Sheet 1, etching on Dutch laid paper,
18.2 × 14.4 cm (image), 31.3 × 22.5 cm (sheet)
d Institut national d'histoire de l'art, Bibliothèque, collections Jacques Doucet
Only in Essen, p. 119
Etching on paper, 18.2 × 14.4 cm (image), 45 × 30.5 cm (sheet)
e Musée Thomas Henry, Cherbourg-Octeville
Only in Zurich

▸ *Ivory Medicine Container / Pharmacie ivoire*
Sheet 2, etching on Dutch laid paper,
18.8 × 14.7 cm (image), 31.7 × 22.5 cm (sheet)
f Institut national d'histoire de l'art, Bibliothèque, collections Jacques Doucet
Only in Essen, p. 119

▸ *Bronze Genius / Génie bronze*
Sheet 3, etching on Dutch laid paper,
18.8 × 14.8 cm (image), 31.5 × 22.5 cm (sheet)
g Institut national d'histoire de l'art, Bibliothèque, collections Jacques Doucet
Only in Essen
Etching on paper, 18.8 × 14.8 cm (image), 45 × 30.5 cm (sheet)
h Musée Thomas Henry, Cherbourg-Octeville
Only in Zurich

▸ *Porcelain Tea Jar / Boîte à thé porcelaine*
Sheet 4, etching and drypoint on Dutch laid paper,
20.9 × 15 cm (image), 31.4 × 22.6 cm (sheet)
i Institut national d'histoire de l'art, Bibliothèque, collections Jacques Doucet
Only in Essen

▸ *Lacquered Pewter Vase / Vase étain laqué*
Sheet 5, etching on Dutch laid paper,
21 × 15 cm (image), 31.3 × 22.8 cm (sheet)
j Institut national d'histoire de l'art, Bibliothèque, collections Jacques Doucet
Only in Essen

▸ *Bronze Horseman / Cavalier bronze*
Sheet 6, etching on Dutch laid paper,
23.8 × 16 cm (image), 31.3 × 22.5 cm (sheet)
k Institut national d'histoire de l'art, Bibliothèque, collections Jacques Doucet
Only in Essen

▸ *Bronze Inkwell* or *Bronze Toad / Bronze encrier* ou *Crapaud bronze*
Sheet 7, etching, aquatint and drypoint on Dutch laid paper, 21.4 × 15.3 cm (image),
31.4 × 22.3 cm (sheet)
l Institut national d'histoire de l'art, Bibliothèque, collections Jacques Doucet
Only in Essen, p. 118
Etching on paper, 21.4 × 15.3 cm (image),
42.3 × 30.2 cm (sheet)
m Musée Thomas Henry, Cherbourg-Octeville
Only in Zurich

▸ *The Barque of Dai-Ko-Ku, Wood / Barque de Dai-Ko-Ku, bois*
Sheet 8, etching on Dutch laid paper,
26.2 × 34.7 cm (image), 31.5 × 44.8 cm (sheet)
n Institut national d'histoire de l'art, Bibliothèque, collections Jacques Doucet
Only in Essen

▸ *Bookplate: Butterfly and Dragonfly / Ex-libris papillon et libellule*
Sheet 9, etching, aquatint and drypoint on Dutch laid paper, 10.8 × 13.6 cm (image),
31.3 × 22.6 cm (sheet)
o Institut national d'histoire de l'art, Bibliothèque, collections Jacques Doucet
Only in Essen

► 92a–j Mary Cassatt (1844–1926)
Series of ten sheets (*The Ten*), 1890–1891
Colour drypoint and aquatint
Bibliothèque nationale de France

▸ *The Bath* (also *The Tub*)
17th state (of 17), 31.2 × 25 cm (image),
36.6 × 26.6 cm (sheet)
a Inv. no. D 14151
Only in Essen, p. 189
14th state (of 17), 31.2 × 25 cm (image),
42.5 × 30 cm (sheet)
b Inv. no. A 09272
Only in Zurich

▸ *The Lamp*
4th state (of 4), 32 × 25.3 cm (image),
44.5 × 28.3 cm (sheet)
c Inv. no. D 14151
Only in Essen

▸ *The Letter*
4th state (of 4), 34.4 × 22.6 cm (image),
43.5 × 30.5 cm (sheet)
d Inv. no. A 09272
Only in Zurich, p. 191

▸ *Mother's Kiss*
5th state (of 5), 34.5 × 22.7 cm (image),
37.1 × 27.8 cm (sheet)
e Inv. no. D 14151
Only in Essen
5th state (of 5), 34.5 × 22.7 cm (image),
43.5 × 30.5 cm (sheet)
f Inv. no. A 09272
Only in Zurich

▸ *Maternal Caress*
6th state (of 6), 36.7 × 26.8 cm (image),
44.6 × 28 cm (sheet)
g Inv. no. D 14151
Only in Essen, p. 190
6th state (of 6), 36.7 × 26.8 cm (image),
43.5 × 30 cm (sheet)
h Inv. no. A 09272
Only in Zurich

▸ *Afternoon Tea Party*
5th state (of 5), 34.2 × 26.3 cm (image),
43.6 × 30.5 cm (sheet)
i Inv. no. D 14151
Only in Essen

▸ *The Coiffure*
5th state (of 5), 36.7 × 26.7 cm (image),
43.5 × 30 cm (sheet)
j Inv. no. A 09272
Only in Zurich, p. 190

► 93 Jules Chéret (1836–1932)
Poster for the Exposition de la gravure japonaise, *École des Beaux-Arts, Paris / Exposition de la gravure japonaise,* 1890
Colour lithograph on paper,
82.5 × 117.5 cm (sheet)
Museum für Kunst und Gewerbe Hamburg
Only in Essen, p. 96

► 94a–b Edgar Degas (1834–1917)
Mary Cassatt at the Louvre: The Paintings Gallery / Au Louvre: La peinture (Mary Cassatt), 1879–1880
Soft ground etching, drypoint, etching, aquatint and *crayon électrique*, 20th state (of 20),
30.5 × 12.6 cm (image), 36.5 × 27.5 cm (sheet)
a Kunsthalle Bremen – Kupferstichkabinett – Der Kunstverein in Bremen
Only in Essen, p. 185
Soft ground etching, drypoint, etching, aquatint, 7th state (of 20), 30 × 12.5 cm (image),
42.4 × 28.8 cm (sheet)
b Kupferstich-Kabinett,
Staatliche Kunstsammlungen Dresden
Only in Zurich

► 95a–t Pablo Picasso (1881–1973)
Raphael and the Fornarina / Raphaël et la Fornarina, 1968
26 of 347 etchings from the *Suite 347*

▸ *Raphael and the Fornarina II / Raphaël et la Fornarina II,* 29.8.1968
28 × 39 cm (image), 45 × 54 cm (sheet)
a Private Collection
Only in Essen, p. 319
b Fondation Jean et Suzanne Planque, Lausanne
Only in Zurich

▸ *Raphael and the Fornarina III / Raphaël et la Fornarina III,* 31.8.1968
17 × 20.5 cm (image), 28 × 33 cm (sheet)
c Private Collection
Only in Essen
d Fondation Jean et Suzanne Planque, Lausanne
Only in Zurich

▸ *Raphael and the Fornarina XI / Raphaël et la Fornarina XI,* 2.9.1968
14.8 × 20.9 cm (image), 25 × 32.5 cm (sheet)
e Private Collection
Only in Essen
f Fondation Jean et Suzanne Planque, Lausanne
Only in Zurich

▸ *Raphael and the Fornarina XIII / Raphaël et la Fornarina XIII,* 3.9.1968
14.8 × 20.9 cm (image), 25 × 32.5 cm (sheet)
g Private Collection
Only in Essen
h Fondation Jean et Suzanne Planque, Lausanne
Only in Zurich

▸ *Raphael and the Fornarina XIV / Raphaël et la Fornarina XIV,* 3.9.1968
14.8 × 20.9 cm (image), 25 × 32.5 cm (sheet)
i Private Collection
Only in Essen
j Fondation Jean et Suzanne Planque, Lausanne
Only in Zurich, p. 321

▸ *Raphael and the Fornarina XVI / Raphaël et la Fornarina XVI,* 4.9.1968
14.8 × 20.9 cm (image), 25 × 32.5 cm (sheet)
k Private Collection
Only in Essen
l Fondation Jean et Suzanne Planque, Lausanne
Only in Zurich, p. 325

▸ *Raphael and the Fornarina XVII / Raphaël et la Fornarina XVII,* 4.9.1968
14.8 × 20.9 cm (image), 25 × 32.5 cm (sheet)
m Private Collection
Only in Essen, p. 322
n Fondation Jean et Suzanne Planque, Lausanne
Only in Zurich

▸ *Raphael and the Fornarina XIX / Raphaël et la Fornarina XIX,* 5.9.1968
15 × 20.5 cm (image), 28 × 34.5 cm (sheet)
o Private Collection
Only in Essen, p. 322
p Fondation Jean et Suzanne Planque, Lausanne
Only in Zurich

▸ *Raphael and the Fornarina XX / Raphaël et la Fornarina XX,* 7.9.1968
14.8 × 20.9 cm (image), 25 × 32.5 cm (sheet)
q Private Collection
Only in Essen, p. 323
r Fondation Jean et Suzanne Planque, Lausanne
Only in Zurich

▸ *Raphael and the Fornarina XXII / Raphaël et la Fornarina XXII,* 8.9.1968
15 × 20.5 cm (image), 28 × 34.5 cm (sheet)
s Private Collection
Only in Essen, p. 323
t Fondation Jean et Suzanne Planque, Lausanne
Only in Zurich

► 96 Félix Régamey (1844–1907)
Poster for *Okoma. Roman japonais illustré,* 1883
Colour lithograph on paper, 23.5 × 34 cm (sheet)
Museum für Kunst und Gewerbe Hamburg
Only in Zurich

► 97 Henri Rivière (1864–1951)
Study, The Wave / Étude de vagues, La vague, 1893
Colour lithograph, 29.3 × 46 cm (image),
42 × 58.6 cm (sheet)
Kupferstich-Kabinett,
Staatliche Kunstsammlungen Dresden
Only in Essen

► 98a–e Henri Rivière
Series *The Magic Hours / La féerie des heures*
Colour lithographs on paper
Staatsgalerie Stuttgart / Graphische Sammlung

a *Dawn / L'aube,* 1901
Sheet 1, 24 × 60 cm (image), 30.1 × 67.7 cm (sheet)
p. 194

b *Mist / La brume,* 1901
Sheet 4, 59.6 × 24 cm (image), 67 × 31 cm (sheet)

c *Crescent / Le premier quartier,* 1901
Sheet 5, 59.6 × 24 cm (image), 67 × 31 cm (sheet)
p. 195

d *The Shower / L'averse,* 1901
Sheet 7, 24 × 59.9 cm (image), 30 × 67.6 cm (sheet)
p. 194

e *Quiet Sea / Le calme plat,* 1902
Sheet 11, 24 × 59.8 cm (image),
30.1 × 67.9 cm (sheet)
p. 194

► 99a Henri Rivière
36 Views of the Eiffel Tower / Les trente-six vues de la tour Eiffel, 1902
Foreword by Arsène Alexandre
36 colour lithographs,
23.3 × 29.3 × 1.6 cm (inner book)
Kupferstich-Kabinett,
Staatliche Kunstsammlungen Dresden

b–k As individual sheets:
Musée Carnavalet – Histoire de Paris

b *Frontispiece / Frontispice*
Sheet 1, 17 × 21.2 cm (image),
22.7 × 26.8 cm (sheet)
Only in Essen, p. 193

c *The Tower under Construction, View from the Trocadéro / La tour en construction, vue du Trocadéro*
Sheet 3, 17 × 21.2 cm (image),
22.7 × 26.8 cm (sheet)
Only in Essen, p. 193

d *View from the Rue Beethoven / Rue Beethoven*
Sheet 5, 21.2 × 17 cm (image),
26.8 × 22.7 cm (sheet)
Only in Zurich

e *View from Notre-Dame / De Notre-Dame*
Sheet 9, 21.2 × 17 cm (image),
26.8 × 22.7 cm (sheet)
Only in Essen

f *View from the Point-du-Jour / Du Point-du-Jour*
Sheet 11, 17 × 21.2 cm (image),
22.7 × 26.8 cm (sheet)
Only in Zurich, p. 193

g *View from the Rue Lamarck / De la rue Lamarck*
Sheet 14, 17 × 21.2 cm (image),
22.7 × 26.8 cm (sheet)
Only in Zurich

h *View from the Quai de Passy through the Rain / Du quai de Passy, par la pluie*
Sheet 16, 17 × 21.2 cm (image),
22.7 × 26.8 cm (sheet)
Only in Zurich

i *View from the Rue des Abbesses / De la rue des Abbesses*
Sheet 19, 17 × 21.2 cm (image),
22.7 × 26.8 cm (sheet)
Only in Essen

j *View from the Pier / De l'Estacade,* 1902
Sheet 33, 17 × 21.2 cm (image),
22.7 × 26.8 cm (sheet)
Only in Zurich

k *View from the Jardins du Trocadéro, in the Autumn / Des jardins du Trocadéro, l'automne*
Sheet 34, 17 × 21.2 cm (image),
22.7 × 26.8 cm (sheet)
Only in Essen

► 100a–b Henry Somm (1844–1907)
Japonisme, 1881
Drypoint, 24.3 × 32 cm (image),
31 × 40.3 cm (sheet)
a Bibliothèque nationale de France
Only in Essen, p. 347
Etching, drypoint, steel brush, 24.3 × 32 cm (image), 26.6 × 35.5 cm (sheet)
b Cabinet d'arts graphiques des Musées d'art et d'histoire, Genève
Only in Zurich

► 101 Henri de Toulouse-Lautrec (1864–1901)
Ambassadeurs, Aristide Bruant in His Cabaret / Ambassadeurs, Aristide Bruant dans son cabaret, 1892
Colour lithograph on paper,
152.4 × 99.3 cm (sheet)
Museum Folkwang /
Deutsches Plakat Museum, Essen
p. 199

- ▸ 102a–b Henri de Toulouse-Lautrec
  Divan Japonais, 1893
  Colour lithograph on paper
  80.7 × 61 cm (sheet)
  a Museum Folkwang, Essen
  Only in Essen, p. 198
  80.8 × 62.5 cm (sheet)
  b Kunsthaus Zürich, Grafische Sammlung
  Only in Zurich

- ▸ 103 Henri de Toulouse-Lautrec
  Jane Avril, 1893
  Colour lithograph on paper, 129.4 × 95 cm (sheet)
  Kunsthaus Zürich, Grafische Sammlung
  Only in Zurich

- ▸ 104 Henri de Toulouse-Lautrec
  Le Matin, 1893
  Colour lithograph on paper, 82.8 × 59.5 cm (sheet)
  Museum Folkwang /
  Deutsches Plakat Museum, Essen
  p. 198

- ▸ 105 Henri de Toulouse-Lautrec
  Reine de Joie by Victor Joze /
  Reine de Joie par Victor Joze, 1893
  Colour lithograph on paper,
  151.2 × 100 cm (sheet)
  Museum Folkwang /
  Deutsches Plakat Museum, Essen

- ▸ 106 Félix Vallotton (1865–1925)
  The Jungfrau / La Jungfrau, 1892
  Woodcut, 14.5 × 25.5 cm (image),
  25.2 × 36.9 cm (sheet)
  Kunsthaus Zürich, Grafische Sammlung

- ▸ 107 Félix Vallotton
  The "Bon Marché" Department Store /
  Le Bon Marché, 1893
  Woodcut, 20 × 25.9 cm (image),
  23.6 × 33 cm (sheet)
  Kunsthaus Zürich, Grafische Sammlung
  p. 285

- ▸ 108 Félix Vallotton
  The Gust of Wind / Le coup de vent, 1894
  Woodcut, 18 × 22.4 cm (image),
  25.3 × 31 cm (sheet)
  Kunsthaus Zürich, Grafische Sammlung
  p. 284

- ▸ 109 Félix Vallotton
  The Bath / Le bain, 1894
  Woodcut, 18.1 × 22.5 cm (image),
  21.5 × 25.5 cm (sheet)
  Kunsthaus Zürich, Grafische Sammlung

- ▸ 110 Félix Vallotton
  The Shower / L'averse, 1894
  Woodcut, 18 × 22.5 cm (image),
  25.3 × 32.2 cm (sheet)
  Kunsthaus Zürich, Grafische Sammlung
  p. 285

- ▸ 111 Félix Vallotton
  The 1st of January / Le 1er janvier, 1896
  Woodcut, 17.6 × 22.3 cm (image),
  42.6 × 56.5 cm (sheet)
  Kunsthaus Zürich, Grafische Sammlung
  p. 285

- ▸ 112 Félix Vallotton
  Laziness / La paresse, 1896
  Woodcut, 17.7 × 22.2 cm (image)
  E. W. K. Bern
  p. 283

PHOTOGRAPHS

- ▸ 113 Felice Beato (1832–1909)
  The Bronze Statue of Dai-Bouts, Kamakura, 1863
  Albumen print, 24 × 29 cm
  Sammlung P. + R. Herzog, Basel
  Only in Zurich, p. 134

- ▸ 114 Felice Beato, attributed to
  "1585. Betto, or Horse Boy", 1863–1868
  Albumen print, hand-coloured,
  26.3 × 20.5 cm
  Museum Folkwang, Essen

- ▸ 115 Felice Beato
  Litter Bearers, circa 1865
  Albumen print, coloured, 22.1 × 28.3 cm (image)
  Sammlung P. + R. Herzog, Basel
  Only in Zurich

- ▸ 116 Felice Beato
  Woman Playing the Shamisen, circa 1865
  Albumen print, hand-coloured,
  27.4 × 22.2 cm (image)
  Sammlung P. + R. Herzog, Basel
  Only in Zurich, p. 137

- ▸ 117 Felice Beato
  View of Mount Fuji / "Fusiyama", 1867
  Albumen print, hand-coloured, 19.6 × 24.4 cm
  Museum Ludwig Köln / Fotografische Sammlung /
  Sammlung Lebeck
  Only in Essen, p. 135

- ▸ 118 Felice Beato
  Litter Bearers, circa 1868
  Albumen print, hand-coloured,
  21.2 × 26.5 cm (image)
  Museum Ludwig Köln / Fotografische Sammlung /
  Sammlung Lebeck
  Only in Essen, p. 136

- ▸ 119 Felice Beato
  Japanese Woman with Two Mirrors, before 1881
  Albumen print, hand-coloured, 24.4 × 19.6 cm
  Museum Ludwig Köln / Fotografische Sammlung /
  Sammlung Lebeck
  Only in Essen

- ▸ 120 Ogawa Kazumasa (1860–1929)
  Sattatoge Pass and Mt. Fuji / "P. 91 Fujijama (Tokaido)", circa 1885/1890
  Albumen print, hand-coloured, 22 × 27.6 cm
  Sammlung P. + R. Herzog, Basel
  Only in Zurich

- ▸ 121 Kusakabe Kimbei (1841–1932)
  "641. Wisteria at Kameido, Tokio",
  2nd half of 19th c.
  Albumen print, hand-coloured, 19.9 × 26 cm
  Museum Ludwig Köln / Fotografische Sammlung /
  Sammlung Lebeck
  Only in Essen

- ▸ 122 Kusakabe Kimbei
  Umbrella Maker, circa 1880
  Albumen print, hand-coloured, 20.6 × 26.5 cm
  Museum Ludwig Köln / Fotografische Sammlung /
  Sammlung Lebeck
  Only in Essen, p. 136

- ▸ 123 Kusakabe Kimbei
  "103. Selling Flowers", 1885–1895
  Albumen print, hand-coloured, 20.8 × 26.5 cm
  Museum Folkwang, Essen

- ▸ 124 Tamamura Kōzaburō (b. 1856)
  A Wisteria Trellis at Kameido Shrine in Tokyo /
  "A499. Wysteria vine", 2nd half of 19th c.
  Albumen print, hand-coloured, 18.5 × 24.3 cm
  Sammlung P. + R. Herzog, Basel
  Only in Zurich, p. 134

- ▸ 125 Baron Raimund von Stillfried-Ratenicz (1839–1911)
  Hairdressing, 2nd half of 19th c.
  Albumen print, hand-coloured, 24 × 19 cm
  Sammlung P. + R. Herzog, Basel
  Only in Zurich

- ▸ 126 Unknown artist
  "D 96, Dancers", 2nd half of 19th c.
  Albumen print, hand-coloured, 19.8 × 25.3 cm
  Museum Ludwig Köln / Fotografische Sammlung /
  Sammlung Lebeck
  Only in Essen, p. 136

- ▸ 127 Unknown artist
  Nagoya, circa 1885/1890
  Albumen print, hand-coloured, 21.7 × 27.8 cm
  Sammlung P. + R. Herzog, Basel
  Only in Zurich

- ▸ 128 Unknown artist
  Basket Seller, circa 1885/1890
  Albumen print, hand-coloured, 19.2 × 24.8 cm
  Sammlung P. + R. Herzog, Basel
  Only in Zurich

ARTEFACTS

Bronze

- ▸ 129 Édouard Lièvre (1828–1886; designer) / Maison Ferdinand Barbedienne (founded in 1838) / Masayoshi (active circa 1790–1834; bronze artist) / unknown Japanese bronze artist (2nd half of 19th c.)
  Jardiniere, 19th c. (Japan), 1870/1880
  (Lièvre and Barbedienne)
  Motif: dragons, tortoises, cranes,
  chimaeras and bamboo
  Bronze, chased, pierced and patinated,
  159 × 64 × 60 cm
  Les Arts Décoratifs, musée des
  Arts décoratifs, Paris
  p. 78

Faience and earthenware

- ▸ 130 Barluet et Cie (1876–1884; Creil et Montereau faience manufactory)
  Plate, circa 1879
  Part of the *Service Japon*
  Motif: blossoming branches in blue
  Faience, H 2.1 cm, Ø 25.4 cm
  Les Arts Décoratifs, musée des
  Arts décoratifs, Paris
  Service Japon formerly also in Monet's possession
  p. 126

► 131 Félix Bracquemond (1833–1914; designer) and François-Eugène Rousseau (1827 –1891; designer and entrepreneur) / Lebeuf Milliet & Cie (1840–1876; Creil et Montereau faience manufactory)
Platter, 1866
Part of the *Service Rousseau* (designed in 1866)
Motif: crayfish and eggplants after Utagawa Hiroshige (*Large Fish* series)
Earthenware, white, motifs in transfer decor painted underglaze in various colours, 6.3 × 44.8 × 38.8 cm
Les Arts Décoratifs, musée des Arts décoratifs, Paris
Probably exhibited at the Paris World Fair of 1867
p. 252

► 132 Félix Bracquemond and François-Eugène Rousseau / Lebeuf Milliet & Cie
Deep Plate, 1866
Part of the *Service Rousseau* (designed in 1866)
Motif: cock after Katsushika Hokusai (*Manga*, vol. 1)
Earthenware, white, motifs in transfer decor painted underglaze in various colours, H 3.4 cm, Ø 24.4 cm
Les Arts Décoratifs, musée des Arts décoratifs, Paris
Probably exhibited at the Paris World Fair of 1867
p. 252

► 133 Félix Bracquemond and François-Eugène Rousseau / Lebeuf Milliet & Cie
Vegetable Bowl (triangular), 1866/1876
Part of the *Service Rousseau* (designed in 1866)
Motif: chrysanthemums, birds and insects, in part after Katsushika Hokusai's *Manga*
Earthenware, white, motifs in transfer decor painted underglaze in various colours, H 13 cm, Ø 27.7 cm
Les Arts Décoratifs, musée des Arts décoratifs, Paris
p. 252

► 134 Joseph Théodore Deck (1823–1891) / Edmond Lachenal (1855–1930) (painted decoration)
Wall Plate with Branch of Peonies, circa 1870–1880
Faience, white body, thrown or cast, painted, glazed, H 5 cm, Ø 40.2 cm
Museum für Angewandte Kunst Köln (MAKK)
p. 112

► 135 Genlis et Rudhard (1864?–1890?) (faience manufactory)
Vase, 1865/1874
Motif: Japanese women setting cranes free, after a woodblock print by Utagawa Kunisada II
Faience, glazed, painted, H 34.5 cm, Ø 16.4 cm
Les Arts Décoratifs, musée des Arts décoratifs, Paris
p. 122

► 136 Camille Moreau-Nélaton (1840–1897)
Vase with Handles, with Basketwork Decor, 1883
Earthenware, reddish-brown body, thrown, painted in barbotine technique, glazed, H 32.7 cm, Ø 20.5 cm
Museum für Angewandte Kunst Köln (MAKK)
p. 116

Glass

► 137 Daum Frères (glassworks founded in 1878)
Vase with Poppies, circa 1897
Glass, etched und decorated in relief, H 15 cm, Ø 17 cm
Musée départemental Maurice Denis, Saint-Germain-en-Laye

► 138 Escalier de Cristal (manufacturer, company founded in 1809)
Bowl with Mounted Dragon, circa 1875
Motif: two carps with flowers and waves
Crystal, cut, enamel-painted, bronze (mounting), H 28 cm, Ø 46 cm
Collection D. Travert, France
Only in Zurich, p. 257

► 139 Escalier de Cristal
Vase with Mounted Elephant Heads, 1883–1885
Motif: the god Hotei as a singing musician with a moon lute, after an illustration in *L'Art japonais* by Louis Gonse (1883, vol. 1)
Colourless glass, freely formed, decor in shallow rock crystal cut and shallow relief etching painted with matt glaze paint and burnish gold, martelé structures on lower section of sides, two gilded bronze handles, H 22.4 cm, Ø 14 cm
Stiftung Museum Kunstpalast, Düsseldorf – Glasmuseum Hentrich – Sammlung Gerda Koepff
Only in Essen

► 140 Émile Gallé (1846–1904)
Vase with Carp Motif, 1878
Motif: carp after Katsushika Hokusai (*Manga*, vol. 13)
Clair de lune glass, mould-blown, enamel-painted, H 28 cm, Ø 22 cm
Les Arts Décoratifs, musée des Arts décoratifs, Paris
Exhibited at the Paris World Fair of 1878
p. 256

► 141 Émile Gallé
Vase, 1898
Motif: water lilies
Glass, partially flashed (violet, yellow), marquetry decor, etched, inclusions (white, yellow and green), bronze base, H 48.3 cm, Ø 23.8 cm
Collection Musée Ariana, Ville de Genève
Only in Zurich

► 142 Émile Gallé
Vase, 1898/1900
Motif: irises
Glass, blown, flashed, marquetry technique, deep-cut, H 22 cm, Ø 6 cm
Les Arts Décoratifs, musée des Arts décoratifs, Paris
p. 306

► 143 Émile Gallé
Vase, circa 1898–1900
Motif: water lilies
Glass, mould-blown, pinched into quatrefoil shape, fine-bubbled greyish-brown patinage on colourless ground, multilayered and marbled in grey-green-violet partially relief-decorated with martelé cut, H 13.5 cm, Ø 16.7 cm
Stiftung Museum Kunstpalast, Düsseldorf – Glasmuseum Hentrich
p. 312

► 144 Émile Gallé
Vase with Flower and Vine Decor, 1900
Motif: flowers, vines, and three quatrefoil reserves in the manner of Japanese hand guards for swords (tsubas)
Glass, mould-blown, colourless ground with applied torn silvery metal foil, flashed (greyish brown), etched decor, H 16.7 cm, Ø 9.1 cm
Stiftung Museum Kunstpalast, Düsseldorf – Glasmuseum Hentrich
p. 261

► 145 Émile Gallé
Vase, circa 1901–1903
Motif: chrysanthemums
Glass, mould-blown, on colourless ground, flashed (cream-coloured beneath opaque brownish red), flower motif as applied relief, accented with torn silvery metal foil (leaves), semi-matt polished, H 40.8 cm, Ø 15.4 cm
Stiftung Museum Kunstpalast, Düsseldorf – Glasmuseum Hentrich
p. 306

► 146 Émile Gallé
Vase, circa 1903
Motif: irises
Glass, mould-blown, on colourless ground, flashed (violet and yellowish brown), interior surface frosted, exterior acid-polished, etched decor, H 39.6 cm, Ø 17.8 cm
Stiftung Museum Kunstpalast, Düsseldorf – Glasmuseum Hentrich

► 147 François-Eugène Rousseau (1827–1891; designer and entrepreneur) / Ernest Léveillé (1841–1913; designer) / Escalier de Cristal? (manufacturer, company founded in 1808)
Bowl with Mounted Bronze Motif, before 1880
Motif: two bamboo branches and a carp, branch with crouching rat (mounted)
Glass, colourless, freely formed, decor glaze-painted, interior drawing and contours in mixed gold, mounted motif in gilded bronze, 4.6 × 24.6 × 22.8 cm
Stiftung Museum Kunstpalast, Düsseldorf – Glasmuseum Hentrich – Sammlung Gerda Koepff
Only in Essen

► 148 François-Eugène Rousseau
Jardiniere, circa 1884
Motif: blossoming branch
Glass, blown, flashed, deep-cut, 14 × 23 × 17 cm
Les Arts Décoratifs, musée des Arts décoratifs, Paris
p. 117

► 149 François-Eugène Rousseau and/or Ernest Léveillé / Appert Frères (1865–1931; manufacturer)
Covered Vase with Base, circa 1888–1890
Motif: carp, waves and stylised aquatic plants (lotus)
Glass, colourless with spotty powder meldings, mould-blown with compressed air, rim of mouth ground flat, decor in simple relief etching, body finished with fine sanding and engraving, gilded bronze fittings, 48.5 × 22.8 × 18.2 cm
Stiftung Museum Kunstpalast, Düsseldorf – Glasmuseum Hentrich – Sammlung Gerda Koepff
Only in Essen, p. 255

Stoneware

► 150 Alexandre Bigot (1862–1927)
Vase, 1905
Stoneware, sand-coloured body, thrown, engobe-coated, glazed,
H 26.5 cm, Ø 24 cm
Museum für Angewandte Kunst Köln (MAKK)

► 151 Jean Carriès (1855–1894)
Bottle, 1888–1894
Stoneware, glazed, with drip glaze,
31.6 × 18.3 cm
Petit Palais, Musée des Beaux-Arts de la Ville de Paris

► 152 Jean Carriès
Dented Vase, 1888–1894
Stoneware, glazed, with drip glaze, 15.9 × 15.5 cm
Petit Palais, Musée des Beaux-Arts de la Ville de Paris
p. 265

► 153 Jean Carriès
Gourd Vase, circa 1890
Stoneware with drip glaze, H 14 cm, Ø 9 cm
Hetjens-Museum, Deutsches Keramikmuseum

► 154 Jean Carriès
Elongated Spherical Vase, circa 1890
Stoneware, grey body, olive-green feldspar underlying glaze, white drip glaze, gilded neck,
H 17.8 cm, Ø 14.4 cm
Museum für Kunst und Gewerbe Hamburg
p. 263

► 155 Jean Carriès
Vase, 1892
Stoneware, glazed, with drip glaze,
H 19.6 cm, Ø 15.3 cm
Petit Palais, Musée des Beaux-Arts de la Ville de Paris
p. 269

► 156 Ernest Chaplet (1835–1909)
Vase with Wave Decor, 1886/1887
Motif: fish jumping in the waves
Stoneware, light-grey body, partially unglazed, green in lower section, glazed greenish blue, crests of waves in white slip, applied in relief-like manner (barbotine technique),
H 21.2 cm, Ø 13.4 cm
Designmuseum Danmark
p. 170

► 157 Pierre Adrien Dalpayrat (1844–1910)
Vase, late 19th c.
Stoneware with drip glaze, H 16.5 cm, Ø 21.5 cm
Hetjens-Museum, Deutsches Keramikmuseum

► 158 Pierre Adrien Dalpayrat
Gourd Vase, circa 1895
Stoneware with drip glaze, H 16.5 cm, Ø 21 cm
Hetjens-Museum, Deutsches Keramikmuseum
p. 266

► 159 Albert Louis Dammouse (1848–1926)
Vase, circa 1890
Motif: chrysanthemums and butterfly
Stoneware, underlying glaze, enamel, edged in gold, H 23 cm, Ø 13.5 cm
Hetjens-Museum, Deutsches Keramikmuseum

► 160 Albert Louis Dammouse
Wall Plate, circa 1899
Motif: poppy
Stoneware, olive-coloured underlying glaze, motifs in brownish red and greenish grey-blue, painted with clay slip and coated with lead glaze,
H 4.6 cm, Ø 33.8 cm
Museum für Kunst und Gewerbe Hamburg
Exhibited at the Paris World Fair of 1900

► 161 Auguste Delaherche (1857–1940)
Bowl, 1908
Stoneware with drip glaze, H 7.6 cm, Ø 20.7 cm
Museum für Angewandte Kunst Köln (MAKK)

► 162 Paul Jeanneney (1861–1920)
Jar with Grooved Sides, circa 1898
Stoneware, grey body, light olive-grey and brown feldspar glazes, bluish-green drip glaze, ivory lid,
H 11.2 cm, Ø 10.7 cm
Museum für Kunst und Gewerbe Hamburg
p. 264

► 163 Paul Jeanneney
Vase, late 19th c. / early 20th c.
Stoneware, glazed, yellowish with green drip glaze,
H 23.7 cm, Ø 21.5 cm
Musée Rodin, Paris
Formerly Rodin Collection

► 164 Paul Jeanneney
Bowl, circa 1900
Stoneware, glazed, H 7.5 cm, Ø 19.5 cm
Les Arts Décoratifs, musée des Arts décoratifs, Paris
p. 270

► 165 Paul Jeanneney
Bowl, circa 1900
Stoneware, glazed, H 7 cm, Ø 10 cm
Les Arts Décoratifs, musée des Arts décoratifs, Paris
p. 270

► 166 Paul Jeanneney
Vase, circa 1900
Stoneware, glazed, H 17.5 cm, Ø 11.5 cm
Les Arts Décoratifs, musée des Arts décoratifs, Paris
Exhibited at the Paris World Fair of 1900
p. 266

Sculpture

► 167 Auguste Rodin (1840–1917) (sculptor) / Paul Jeanneney (1861–1920) (manufacturer)
Balzac, Monumental Head / Tête monumentale de Balzac, probably 1899
Stoneware, brown and beige-yellow glaze, formed in a mould after a plaster model,
47.5 × 44.6 × 38.2 cm
Musée Rodin, Paris
p. 271

Other materials

► 168a–b Pierre Bonnard (1867–1947)
Nannies' Promenade, Frieze of Carriages / Promenade des nourrices, frise des fiacres,
1894/1897
Four-panel screen, lithographs in five colours, each 143 × 46 cm
a Private Collection, courtesy of Städel Museum, Frankfurt am Main
Only in Essen, p. 86
b Jules Maeght Collection, San Francisco
Only in Zurich

► 169 René Lalique (1860–1945)
Comb with Chrysanthemum Decor, 1899–1900
Greyish-brown horn, gold, enamel and opals,
16.2 × 9 cm
Museum für Kunst und Gewerbe Hamburg
p. 164

► 170 Félix Vallotton (1865–1925)
The Girl with the Little Cat (Bonbonniere) / La fillette au chaton (bonbonnière), circa 1896
Wood, lacquered, with intarsia, 5.2 × 15.2 × 15.2 cm
Musée départemental Maurice Denis, Saint-Germain-en-Laye
p. 281

► 171 Gabriel-Frédéric Viardot (1830–1906)
The Small Letter Box / La petite boîte aux lettres, 2nd half of 19th c.
Wood, mother-of-pearl inlays, 46 × 26 × 18.5 cm
Collection Musée Clemenceau, Paris
Formerly Collection Georges Clemenceau
Only in Zurich

Japan

PAINTINGS

Kakemonos

► 172 Japan, in the style of Katsushika Hokusai (1760–1849)
Plum Blossoms in the Moonlight, 19th c.
Ink on paper, 135.4 × 21.5 cm (picture)
Two seals right: Katsushika and Taitō

► 173 Kano Yōsen-in Korenobu (1753–1808)
Herons on a Meadow in the Snow, after 1794
Ink on silk, 144.5 × 55.5 cm (picture)
Inscr. lower right: Yōsen-in hōin hitsu (brush of Yōsen-in with title hōin = Dharma seal), seal: Fujiwara Korenonbu no in
Formerly in the Edmond Taigny Collection
p. 231

► 174 After Isoda Koryūsai (1735–1790)
Lady and Two Boys Playing Blind Man's Buff, after 1781/1782
Ink and paint on silk, 64.8 × 28.8 cm (picture)
Inscr. lower right: Hokkyō Koryūsai ga (picture by Koryūsai, with title *hokkyō* = Dharma bridge), seal: hitherto unidentified
Formerly in the Edmond Taigny Collection

► 175 Soga Shōhaku (1730–1781)
Landscape with Scholar in a Boat, Fishing, 18th c.
Ink on paper, 27.8 × 55.4 cm (image)
Inscr. left.: Shōhaku hitsu, seal: Shiryū
Formerly in the Edmond Taigny Collection

Fan leaves

► 176 Katsushika Hokusai (1760–1849)
Seated Woman, circa 1808/1809
Ink and light paint on paper with *mica*, signed: Hokusai X, 17 × 44.1 cm
Museen der Stadt Regensburg, Historisches Museum
Only in Zurich

► 177 Katsushika Hokusai
Mushrooms and Maple Leaves, 1820–1834
Ink and paint on silk, signed:
Saki no Hokusai Itsu hitsu, 17.3 × 46 cm
Museen der Stadt Regensburg, Historisches Museum
Only in Essen

► 178 Unknown artist
Bird on Plum Blossom Branch, probably 17th c.
Ink, paint, silver? and gold on paper, 18.3 × 45.4 cm
Museen der Stadt Regensburg, Historisches Museum
Only in Essen, p. 117

► 179 Unknown artist
Blossoming Cherry Tree on Brown Ground,
probably 19th c.
Ink, paint, gold? and silver? on paper,
17.7 × 54.7 cm
Museen der Stadt Regensburg, Historisches Museum
Only in Zurich

► 180 Unknown artist
Blue Flower with Dragonfly, probably 19th c.
Paint on silk, signed: wa X, 15.2 × 50.2 cm
Museen der Stadt Regensburg, Historisches Museum
Only in Zurich

► 181 Kitagawa Utamaro (1753–1806)
Woman Reading, 2nd half of 18th / early 19th c.
Ink and paint on paper with mica, signed:
Utamaro hitsu, 17.7 × 48.2 cm
Museen der Stadt Regensburg, Historisches Museum
Only in Essen

Folding screens *(byōbu)*

► 182 Tsukioka Sessai (d. 1839)
Carps, late Edo period, 1839 or before
Pair of six-panel screens, ink on gold,
on cloth-covered paper, each 166.7 x 365 x 1.5 cm
Museum DKM, Duisburg
Only in Zurich, pp. 258–259

► 183 Hara Zaimei (1778–1844)
Blossoming Cherry Tree on Gold Ground,
late Edo period, early 19th c.
Six-panel screen, drawing ink on gold and paper,
174 × 374.4 cm
Musée National des Arts Asiatiques Guimet, Paris
Only in Essen, pp. 108–109

WOODBLOCK PRINTS

Single sheets

► 184 Keisai (Ikeda) Eisen (1790–1848)
Chrysanthemums (Kiku), 1830s
Publisher: Echigoya Chōōhachi
Baur Foundation, Geneva
Only in Zurich, p. 164

► 185 Hosoda Eishi (Chōbunsai) (1756–1829)
The Courtesan Ōgino of the Ōgiya House and her Kamuros Isami and Susami (Ōgiya uchi Ōgino, Isami, Susami), 1792–1793
Publisher: Nishimuraya Yohachi
hashira-e
Kunsthalle Bremen – Kupferstichkabinett –
Der Kunstverein in Bremen
Only in Zurich

► 186 Hosoda Eishi (Chōbunsai)
Women Catching Fireflies (Hotarugari), 1796–1797
Publisher: Izumiya Ichibei (Kansendō)
ōban triptych
Kupferstich-Kabinett,
Staatliche Kunstsammlungen Dresden
Only in Zurich
Motif also in the Monet Collection

► 187 Hosoda Eishō (Chōkōsai)
(active circa 1780–1800)
Beauties Shaving their Eyebrows (Mayu-wo-soru-bijin), circa 1793–1799
Publisher: Yamaguchiya Chūemon Chūsuke
hashira-e
Bibliothèque nationale de France
Sheet formerly in the Rivière Collection
Only in Essen

► 188 Kikugawa Eizan (1787–1867)
Woman Dressed for Travelling and Holding an Inscribed Fan (Ōgi o motsu tabisugata no bijin),
1804–1817
Publisher: unknown
hashira-e
Bibliothèque nationale de France
Sheet formerly in the Rivière Collection
Only in Essen, p. 184

► 189 Kikugawa Eizan
The Hour of the Snake: Toshie from the Daimonjiya House (Hiru minokoku Daimonjiya uchi),
1812–1820
From the series *The Twelve Hours in the Pleasure Quarters (Seirō jūniji)*, publisher: Eirakiya Kichibei (Tenjudo)
Staatsgalerie Stuttgart / Graphische Sammlung /
Sammlung Schloß Fachsenfeld
p. 144

► 190a–b Kikugawa Eizan
The Courtesan Hinaaya of the Chōjiya House (Chōjiya uchi Hinaaya), 1814–1817
From the series *Parody of the Seven Divinities of Good Luck by Courtesans (Keisei mitate shichi fuku-jin)*, publisher: Iwatoya Kisaburō
a Van Gogh Museum, Amsterdam (Vincent van Gogh Foundation)
Sheet formerly in the Van Gogh Collection
Only in Essen, p. 145
b Kunsthalle Bremen – Kupferstichkabinett –
Der Kunstverein in Bremen
Only in Zurich

► 191 Suzuki Harunobu (1725–1770)
Parody of the Chapter "Evening Winds" of the Tale of Prince Genji (Mitate Yūgao), circa 1765
Publisher: no mark
chūban, left sheet of a diptych
Baur Foundation, Geneva
Only in Zurich

► 192 Suzuki Harunobu
Girls after the Bath (Summer), 1766–1767
Publisher: no mark
chūban
Staatliche Museen zu Berlin,
Museum für Asiatische Kunst
Only in Zurich

► 193 Suzuki Harunobu
The Sleeping Tea-boy (Chabōzu), circa 1767
Publisher: no mark
chūban
Staatliche Museen zu Berlin, Museum für
Asiatische Kunst
Only in Essen

► 194 Suzuki Harunobu
Viewing the Moon, 1767–1768
Publisher: no mark
chūban
Staatliche Museen zu Berlin, Museum für
Asiatische Kunst
Only in Essen, p. 188

► 195 Suzuki Harunobu
Woman Holding Insect Cage, and Small Boy (Mushikago mochi bijin), circa 1767/1768
Publisher: no mark
chūban
Museen der Stadt Regensburg, Historisches Museum
Only in Essen, p. 188

► 196 Suzuki Harunobu
Picking Irises in the Rain (Uchū no ayame tsumami), circa 1767/1768
Publisher: no mark
chūban
Museen der Stadt Regensburg, Historisches Museum
Only in Essen, p. 141

► 197 Utagawa Hiroshige (1797–1858)
Lobster and Shrimp (Ise ebi, Shiba ebi),
circa 1832–1833
From the series *Large Fish*, publisher: Nishimura Yohachi (Eijudō)
Kunsthalle Bremen – Kupferstichkabinett –
Der Kunstverein in Bremen
Only in Essen, p. 253
Motif also in the Rivière Collection

► 198a–h Utagawa Hiroshige
Series *53 Stations of the Tōkaidō Road (Tōkaidō gojūsan tsugi no uchi)*, publisher:
Takenouchi Magohachi (Hōeidō)

▸ *Hakone, View of the Lake (Hakone kosui zu)*,
1833–1834
Sheet 11 (10th station)
a Kunsthalle Bremen – Kupferstichkabinett –
Der Kunstverein in Bremen
Only in Essen
b Kupferstich-Kabinett,
Staatliche Kunstsammlungen Dresden
Only in Zurich, p. 149
Motif also in the Rivière Collection

▸ *Mishima, Morning Mist (Mishima asagiri)*,
1833–1834
Sheet 12 (11th station)
c Kunsthalle Bremen – Kupferstichkabinett –
Der Kunstverein in Bremen
Only in Essen
d Staatliche Museen zu Berlin, Museum für
Asiatische Kunst
Only in Zurich, p. 148
Motif also in the Rivière Collection

▸ *Yūi: Satta Peak (Yūi Satta mine)*, 1833–1834
Sheet 17 (16th station)
e Bibliothèque nationale de France
Sheet formerly in the Rivière Collection
Only in Zurich, p. 148
f Kunsthalle Bremen – Kupferstichkabinett – Der Kunstverein in Bremen
Only in Essen
Motif also in the Monet Collection

▸ *Sudden Rain at Shōno (Shōno hakuu)*, 1833–1834
Sheet 46 (45th station)
g Museen der Stadt Regensburg, Historisches Museum
Only in Essen
h Museum für Kunst und Gewerbe Hamburg
Only in Zurich, p. 149
Motif also in the Rivière Collection

► 199a–b Utagawa Hiroshige
Series *Famous Views of Edo in the Four Seasons (Shiki Kōto meisho)*
chūtanzaku
Staatliche Museen zu Berlin, Museum für Asiatische Kunst
Only in Essen

a *Moon Over Ryogoku, Summer (Natsu, Ryōgoku no tsuki)*, 1834–1835
Publisher: no mark

b *Winter: Snow on the Sumida River (Fuyu Sumidagawa no Yuki)*, 1834–1835
Publisher: Kawaguchiya Shōzō (Shōeidō, Eisendō)

► 200 Utagawa Hiroshige
Carp (Koi), circa 1840–1842
From the series *Large Fish (Uo zukushi)*, publisher: Yamadaya Shōjirō
Baur Foundation, Geneva
Only in Zurich
Motif also in the Monet Collection

► 201 Utagawa Hiroshige
View of Futamigaura (Futamigaura no zu), 1847–1852
Triptych from the series *Famous Places in Ise (Ise meisho)*, publisher: Sanoya Kihei (Sanoki, Kikakudō)
ōban triptych
Fondation Claude Monet, Giverny, Académie des Beaux-Arts
Sheet formerly in the Monet Collection
pp. 172–173

► 202a–g Utagawa Hiroshige
Series *Famous Places in the Sixty-Odd Provinces (Rokujū yoshū meisho zue)*, publisher: Koshimuraya Heisuke

▸ *Tango Province: Ama no hashidate (Tango Ama no Hashidate)*, 1853
a Museen der Stadt Regensburg, Historisches Museum
Only in Essen, p. 209

▸ *Mimasaka Province: Yamabushi Valley (Mimasaka Yamabushidani)*, 1853
b Museen der Stadt Regensburg, Historisches Museum
Only in Essen
Motif also in the Rivière Collection

▸ *Awa Province: Naruto Whirlpools (Awa, Naruto no fūha)*, 1855
c Museum für Kunst und Gewerbe Hamburg
Sheet formerly in the Edmond and Jules de Goncourt Collection
Only in Essen
d Staatliche Museen zu Berlin, Museum für Asiatische Kunst
Only in Essen, p. 175
Motif also in the Monet Collection

▸ *Chikuzen Province: Hakozaki, the Road through the Sea (Chikuzen Hakozaki, kaichū no michi)*, 1855
e Staatliche Museen zu Berlin, Museum für Asiatische Kunst
Only in Zurich

▸ *Satsuma Province: Bō Bay, The Two-Sword Rocks (Satsuma Bō no ura Sokenseki)*, 1856
f Museen der Stadt Regensburg, Historisches Museum
Only in Essen, p. 174
g Kupferstich-Kabinett, Staatliche Kunstsammlungen Dresden
Only in Zurich
Motif also in the Monet, Rivière and Rodin collections

► 203a–r Utagawa Hiroshige
Series *One Hundred Famous Views of Edo (Meisho Edo hyakkei)*, publisher: Uoya Eikichi

▸ *The Kawaguchi Ferry and Zenkōji Temple (Kawaguchi no watashi Zenkōji)*, 1857
Sheet 20
a Museen der Stadt Regensburg, Historisches Museum
Only in Essen, p. 208
b Staatliche Museen zu Berlin, Museum für Asiatische Kunst
Only in Zurich
Motif also in the Van Gogh Collection

▸ *Plum Estate, Kameido (Kameido ume yashiki)*, 1857
Sheet 30
c Museum für Kunst und Gewerbe Hamburg
Sheet formerly in the Edmond and Jules de Goncourt Collection
Only in Zurich
d Private Collection
Only in Essen, p. 221
Motif also in the Van Gogh and Rivière collections

▸ *Yoroi Ferry, Koami-chō (Yoroi no watashi Koami-chō)*, 1857
Sheet 46
e Bibliothèque nationale de France
Formerly in the Rivière Collection
Only in Zurich, p. 209
f Kupferstich-Kabinett, Staatliche Kunstsammlungen Dresden
Only in Essen

▸ *Rain Shower above the Great Bridge at Atake (Ōhashi Atake no yūdachi)*, 1857
Sheet 58
g Bibliothèque nationale de France
Sheet formerly in the Rivière Collection
Only in Essen, p. 46
h Museum für Kunst und Gewerbe Hamburg
Only in Zurich
Motif also in the Van Gogh and Monet collections

▸ *Horikiri Iris Garden (Horikiri no hana ayame)*, 1857
Sheet 64
i Museum für Kunst und Gewerbe Hamburg
Sheet formerly in the Edmond and Jules de Goncourt Collection
Only in Zurich
j Museen der Stadt Regensburg, Historisches Museum
Only in Essen, p. 303
Motif also in the Rivière Collection

▸ *Inside Kameido Tenjin Shrine (Kameido Tenjin keidai)*, 1856
Sheet 65
k Bibliothèque nationale de France
Sheet formerly in the Rivière Collection
Only in Zurich, p. 303
l Designmuseum Danmark
Only in Essen

▸ *Dyers' Quarter, Kanda (Kanda Konyachou)*, 1857
Sheet 75
m Musée National des Arts Asiatiques Guimet, Paris
Only in Essen
Motif also in the Rivière Collection

▸ *Naitō Shinjuku at Yotsuya (Yotsuya Naitō Shinjuku)*, 1857
Sheet 86
n Designmuseum Danmark
Only in Essen, p. 214
o Musée National des Arts Asiatiques Guimet, Paris
Only in Zurich

▸ *Maples, Tekona Shrine and Bridge at Mama (Mama no momiji Tekona no yashiro Tsugihashi)*, 1857
Sheet 94
p Baur Foundation, Geneva
Only in Zurich, p. 220
Motif also in the Van Gogh and Rivière collections

▸ *Kinryūzan Temple, Asakusa (Asakusa Kinryūzan)*, 1856
Sheet 99
q Museen der Stadt Regensburg, Historisches Museum
Only in Essen

▸ *Asakusa Ricefields and Torinomachi Festival (Asakusa tanbo Torinomachi mōde)*, 1857
Sheet 101
r Musée National des Arts Asiatiques Guimet, Paris
Only in Zurich
Motif also in the Monet and Rivière collections

► 204a–e Utagawa Hiroshige
Series *36 Views of Mount Fuji (Fuji sanjūrokkei)*, publisher: Tsutaya Kichizō (Kōeidō)

▸ *Fuji at Left from the Tōkaidō (Tōkaidō hidari Fuji)*, 1858
a Van Gogh Museum, Amsterdam (Vincent van Gogh Foundation)
Sheet formerly in the Van Gogh Collection
Only in Zurich, p. 218
b Kunsthalle Bremen – Kupferstichkabinett – Der Kunstverein in Bremen
Only in Essen

▸ *Futamigaura in Ise Province (Ise Futamigaura)*, 1858
c Fondation Claude Monet, Giverny, Académie des Beaux-Arts
Sheet formerly in the Monet Collection
p. 174

▸ *The Sea off Satta in Suruga Province (Suruga Satta kaijō)*, 1858
d Staatliche Museen zu Berlin, Museum für Asiatische Kunst
Only in Zurich

▸ *Koganei in Musashi Province (Musashi Koganei)*, 1858
e Museum für Kunst und Gewerbe Hamburg
Only in Essen, p. 208
Motif also in the Rivière Collection

► 205a–u Katsushika Hokusai (1760–1849)
Series *36 Views of Mount Fuji (Fugaku sanjūrokkei)*, publisher: Nishimuraya Yohachi (Eijudō)

▸ *Fuji from the Tea Plantation of Katakura in Suruga Province (Suruga Katakura chaen no Fuji)*, 1830–1831
a Kunsthalle Bremen – Kupferstichkabinett – Der Kunstverein in Bremen
Only in Essen
b Baur Foundation, Geneva
Only in Zurich, p. 178
Motif also in the Rivière Collection

▸ *Mishima Pass in Kai Province (Kōshū Mishima goe)*, 1830–1831
c Baur Foundation, Geneva
Only in Zurich, p. 146
Motif also in the Rivière Collection

▸ *Under the Wave off Kanagawa (Kanagawa oki nami ura)*, 1830–1831
d Private Collection
Sheet formerly in the Henri Vever Collection
Only in Essen, p. 167
e Museum für Kunst und Gewerbe Hamburg
Only in Zurich, p. 26
Motif also in the Monet and Rivière collections

▸ *Ejiri in Suruga Province (Sunshū Ejiri)*, 1830–1831
f Museen der Stadt Regensburg, Historisches Museum
Only in Essen, p. 192
g Museum für Kunst und Gewerbe Hamburg
Only in Zurich
Motif also in the Monet and Rivière collections

▸ *Hodogaya on the Tōkaidō (Tōkaidō Hodogaya)*, 1830–1831
h Bibliothèque nationale de France
Sheet formerly in the Rivière Collection
Only in Essen, p. 192

▸ *Kajikazawa in Kai Province (Kōshū Kajikazawa)*, 1830–1831
i Bibliothèque nationale de France
Sheet formerly in the Rivière Collection
Only in Zurich
j Museum für Kunst und Gewerbe Hamburg (inv. no. IE 1897.54)
Sheet formerly in the Edmond and Jules de Goncourt Collection
Only in Essen
k Museum für Kunst und Gewerbe Hamburg (inv. no. IE 1896.394)
Only in Essen
Motif also in the Monet Collection

▸ *Shower beneath the Summit (Sanka hakuu)*, 1830–1831
l Kupferstich-Kabinett, Staatliche Kunstsammlungen Dresden
Only in Essen
m Baur Foundation, Geneva
Only in Zurich
Motif also in the Rivière Collection

▸ *Snowy Morning at Koishikawa (Koishikawa yuki no ashita)*, 1830–1831
n Kupferstich-Kabinett, Staatliche Kunstsammlungen Dresden
Only in Essen, p. 178
Motif also in the Rivière Collection

▸ *South Wind, Clear Sky (Gaifū kaisei)*, 1830–1831
o Bibliothèque nationale de France
Sheet formerly in the Rivière Collection
Only in Zurich, p. 147
p Museum für Kunst und Gewerbe Hamburg
Only in Essen
q Baur Foundation, Geneva (blue version)
Only in Zurich
Motif also in the Monet Collection

Under Mannen Bridge at Fukagawa (Fukagawa Mannenbashi no shita), 1830–1831
r Museum für Kunst und Gewerbe Hamburg
Only in Zurich, p. 146
Motif also in the Rivière Collection

▸ *Ushibori in Jōshū Province (Jōshū Ushibori)*, 1830–1831
s Bibliothèque nationale de France
Sheet formerly in the Rivière Collection
Only in Zurich, p. 192
t Museum für Kunst und Gewerbe Hamburg
Only in Essen
u Kupferstich-Kabinett, Staatliche Kunstsammlungen Dresden
Only in Essen

► 206a–b Katsushika Hokusai
Series *Large Flowers*, publisher: Nishimuraya Yohachi (Eijudō)
Fondation Claude Monet, Giverny, Académie des Beaux-Arts

a *Chrysanthemums and Horsefly (Kiku ni abu)*, 1833–1834
Sheet formerly in the Monet Collection
p. 162

b *Peonies and Butterfly (Botani ni chō)*, 1833–1834
Sheet formerly in the Monet Collection
p. 162

► 207 Katsushika Hokusai
Bullfinch and Weeping Cherry (Uso, shidarezakura), circa 1834
From the series *Small Flowers*, publisher: Nishimuraya Yohachi (Eijudō)?
chūban
Museen der Stadt Regensburg, Historisches Museum
Only in Essen

► 208 After Torii Kiyonaga (1752–1815)
Interior of a Bathhouse (Onna yu), circa 1850–1875 (after a woodblock print of circa 1787)
Publisher: no mark
chūban diptych
Stadtmuseum Oldenburg, Grafiksammlung
Only in Essen
Motif also in the Degas Collection (first version, p. 63)

► 209 Utagawa Kunisada (Toyokuni III) (1786–1864)
Yoyotose of the Sanomatsuya (Sanomatsuya uchi Yoyotose), 1825
Publisher: Nishimuraya Yohachi (Eijudō)
Private Collection
Sheet formerly in the Denis Collection

► 210 Utagawa Kunisada (Toyokuni III)
The Splendour of Butterflies and Peonies in the Garden (Sono kochō botan no hanabusa), 1849
Publisher: Tsutaya Kichizō (Kōeidō)
ōban triptych
Van Gogh Museum, Amsterdam (Vincent van Gogh Foundation)
Sheet formerly in the Van Gogh Collection
Only in Essen, pp. 290–291

► 211 Utagawa Kunisada (Toyokuni III)
Munesada, Kuronushi and Komachi at the Pass of Ōsaka, 1850
From the kabuki drama *The Young poet Onono Komachi in Twelve Layers of Festive Silk*, play *Snow and Love Piled Up at the Seki-no-to Barrier Gate (Tsumoru koi yuki seki no to)*, actors: Sawamura Chōjūrō V in the role of Munesada, Ichikawa Ebizō V in the role of Kuronushi and Onoe Baikō IV in the role of Komachi, publisher: Ebiya Rinnosuke
ōban triptych
Stiftung Museum Kunstpalast, Düsseldorf
Only in Essen

► 212 Utagawa Kunisada (Toyokuni III)
Ichikawa Ebizō V (formerly Danjūrō VII) in the Role of the Bandit Ishikawa Goemon (Ishikawa Goemon, Godaime Ichikawa Ebizō), 1851
From the kabuki drama *Eternal Help – The Beach of Masago*, publisher: Ōtaya Takichi (Hori Takichi)
Top sheet of a vertical *ōban* diptych
Stiftung Museum Kunstpalast, Düsseldorf
Only in Essen

► 213 Utagawa Kunisada (Toyokuni III)
Yume no Ichirobei in the Manner of Zhang Shun (Chōjun) (Chōjun ni hisu Yume no Ichirobei), 1859
From the series *Stories of the Most Outstanding Men of our Day (Tōsei kōdanshiden)*, publisher: Hayashiya Shōgorō
Stiftung Museum Kunstpalast, Düsseldorf
Only in Zurich, p. 124

► 214 Utagawa Kunisada (Toyokuni III)
The Actor Nakamura Shikan in the Role of the Nun Shōgetsu (Shōgetsuni), 1860
Publisher: Kiya Sōjirō
Crepe print (*chirimen-e*)
Musée Rodin, Paris
Sheet formerly in the Rodin Collection
Only in Zurich

► 215 Utagawa Kunisada (Toyokuni III)
Ōtomo Kuronushi and the Cherry Blossom Spirit Sumizome (Ōtomo no Kuronushi, Sumizome Sakura no Sei), 1860
Actors: Nakamura Shikan IV in the role of Ōtomo Kuronushi and Sawamura Tanosuke III in the role of the cherry blossom spirit Sumizome, play: *Snow and Love Piled Up at the Seki-no-to Barrier Gate (Tsumoru koi yuki seki no to)*, publisher: Ebiya Rinnosuke
Crepe print (*chirimen-e*), *ōban* diptych
Musée Rodin, Paris
Sheet formerly in the Rodin Collection
Only in Essen, p. 150

- ► 216 Utagawa Kunisada (Toyokuni III)
Nakamura Shikan VI in the Role of Washi no Chōkichi (Washi no Chōkichi), 1861
From the kabuki drama *Five Saviours of the Oppressed in their Best Years (Hanazoroi gonin otoko)*, publisher: Seiseidō Kagaya Kichiemon (Kichibei)
Stiftung Museum Kunstpalast, Düsseldorf
Only in Essen, p. 151

- ► 217 Utagawa Kunisada (Toyokuni III)
The Helmet: Duchess Kaoyo Recognises the Helmet of Yoshisada by his Scent, 1862
First act of the kabuki drama *Template for Calligraphy: A Treasury of Faithful Samurai (Kanadehon Chūshingura)*, publisher: Hirookaya Kōsuke (Eisendō)
ōban triptych
Stiftung Museum Kunstpalast, Düsseldorf
Only in Zurich, pp. 152–153

- ► 218 Utagawa Kunisada (Toyokuni III)
Ichimura Kakitsu in the Role of Motada Jirō (Motada Jirō), 1863
From the series *Toyokuni's Contest of the Magic Arts*, publisher: Hiranoya Shinzō (Aikindō)
Stiftung Museum Kunstpalast, Düsseldorf
Only in Zurich

- ► 219 Utagawa Kuniyoshi (1797–1861)
Okon's Lover Fukuoka Mitsugu, 1843–1847
From the series *Mirror of Virtuous Women (Teijo misao kagami)*, publisher: Kojimaya Jūbei
ōban, sheet from a polyptych
Private Collection
Sheet formerly in the Denis Collection
p. 286

- ► 220 Utagawa Kuniyoshi
The Actor Ichimura Uzaemon XII in the Role of the Princess Yaegaki (Yaegaki), 1848
Publisher: Minatoya Kohei
Private Collection
Sheet formerly in the Denis Collection
p. 278

- ► 221 Utagawa Kuniyoshi
The Actor Seki Sanjūro III in the Role of Giheiji Obaba and the Actor Bandō Shūka in the Role of Danshichi Okaji, 1852
Play: *Shinzō tsurifune kidan (Giheiji Obaba Danshichi Okaji)*, publisher: Iseya Kanekichi
Private Collection
Sheet formerly in the Denis Collection
p. 287

- ► 222a–b Utagawa Kuniyoshi
The Ide Crystal River in Yamashiro Province (Yamashiro kuni Ide no Tamagawa), circa 1847
Triptych from an untitled series of the *Six Crystal Rivers (Mu Tamagawa)*, publisher: Sanoya Kihei (Sanoki, Kikakudō)
ōban triptych
a Museen der Stadt Regensburg, Historisches Museum
Only in Essen
b Baur Foundation, Geneva
Only in Zurich
Motif also in the Monet Collection

- ► 223 Utagawa Sadakage (active circa 1818–1844)
Elegant Play of Flowers (Fūryū hana asobi zu), 1818–1830
Publisher: Iseya Rihei
Private Collection
Sheet formerly in the Denis Collection
p. 286

- ► 224a–b Katsushika Taito II (active circa 1830–1844)
Carp (Koi), circa 1830–1844
Publisher: Echigoya Chōhachi
ōban harimaze-e (trimmed)
a Museen der Stadt Regensburg, Historisches Museum
Only in Essen
b Staatliche Museen zu Berlin, Museum für Asiatische Kunst
Only in Zurich, p. 254

- ► 225 Unknown artist
Heroic Stories of Japan (Nihon buyōden), Meiji period (1868–1912)
Publisher: no mark
Crepe print (*chirimen-e*)
Private Collection
Sheet formerly in the Denis Collection

- ► 226 Unknown artist
Ono-no-Otsu, Meiji period (1868–1912)
From the series *Mirror of Renowned Women from Ancient and Modern Times (Kokon meifu kagami)*, publisher: no mark
Crepe print (*chirimen-e*)
Private Collection
Sheet formerly in the Denis Collection

- ► 227 Kitagawa Utamaro (1753–1806)
The Hour of the Snake (Mi no koku), 1794–1795
From the series *Twelve Hours of the Green Houses (Seirō jūni toki tsuzuki)*, publisher: Tsutaya Jūzaburō
Musée National des Arts Asiatiques Guimet, Paris
Only in Essen, p. 156

- ► 228 Kitagawa Utamaro
Needlework (Harishigoto), 1794–1795
Publisher: Uemura Yohei
Left sheet of an *ōban* triptych
Bibliothèque nationale de France
Sheet formerly in the Rivière Collection
Only in Essen

- ► 229 Kitagawa Utamaro
The Hour of the Horse (Uma no koku), circa 1794–1795
From the series *The Sundial of Young Women (Musume hidokei)*, publisher: Murataya Jirobei (Eiyūdō)
Musée National des Arts Asiatiques Guimet, Paris
Only in Essen

- ► 230a–b Kitagawa Utamaro
Kisegawa of the Matsubaya (Matsubaya Kisegawa), 1795–1796
From the series *Charm Contest of Five Belles (Gonin bijin aikyō kurabe)*, publisher: Ōmiya Gonkurō
a Staatliche Museen zu Berlin, Museum für Asiatische Kunst
Only in Essen, p. 143
b Kupferstich-Kabinett, Staatliche Kunstsammlungen Dresden
Only in Essen
Motif also in the Monet Collection

- ► 231 Kitagawa Utamaro
Episode in Musashino of the "Tales of Ise" (Ise monogatari Musashino), 1796
Publisher: Tsutaya Jūsaburō
Middle sheet of an *ōban* triptych
Baur Foundation, Geneva
Only in Zurich, p. 278

- ► 232 Kitagawa Utamaro
Lady with a Fan, circa 1796
Publisher: Izumiya Ichibei (Kansendō)
Baur Foundation, Geneva
Only in Zurich, p. 142

- ► 233a–b Kitagawa Utamaro
Series *Manners and Customs of Eight Views of the Floating World (Fūzoku ukiyo hakkei)*, publisher: Ise-Yo
Baur Foundation, Geneva
Only in Zurich

  a *Evening Snow in the Mood of Awakening (Neoki no bosetsu)*, 1797
  p. 186

  b *Clearing Weather during the Toilette (Mijimai seiran)*, 1797
  p. 142

- ► 234 Kitagawa Utamaro
Hairdresser (kamiyui), 1798–1799
From the series *Twelve Types of Women's Handicraft (Fujin tewasa jūniko)*, publisher: Wakasaya Yoichi (Jakurindō)
Staatliche Museen zu Berlin, Museum für Asiatische Kunst
Only in Essen, p. 160

- ► 235 Kitagawa Utamaro
Before the Mirror (Kyōdai mae), 1799–1800
Publisher: Ōmiya Gonkurō
Museen der Stadt Regensburg, Historisches Museum
Only in Essen
Motif also in the Monet Collection

- ► 236 Kitagawa Utamaro
Peeping (Nozoki), circa 1799–1800
Publisher: Ōmiya Gonkurō
Bibliothèque nationale de France
Sheet formerly in the Rivière Collection
Only in Essen

- ► 237 Kitagawa Utamaro
Wisteria and Peony (Fuji ni botan), circa 1801
From the series *Comparison of the Flower Arrangements of Beautiful Women (Tenshō bijin ikebana awase)*, publisher: Izumiya Ichibei (Kansendō)
Kunsthalle Bremen – Kupferstichkabinett – Der Kunstverein in Bremen
Only in Zurich
Motif also in the Monet Collection

- ► 238 Kitagawa Utamaro
The Sound of the Teahouse Bell (Chamise no kane no oto), 1802
From the series *Eight Views of the Floating World (Ukiyo hakkei)*, publisher: Izumiya Ichibei (Kansendō)
hashira-e
Kunsthalle Bremen – Kupferstichkabinett – Der Kunstverein in Bremen
Only in Zurich, p. 276

► 239 Kitagawa Utamaro
The Hour of the Snake (Mi no koku zu), 1802
From the series *Customs of Beauties Around the Clock (Fūzoku bijin tokei)*, publisher: Izumiya Ichibei (Kansendō)
Staatliche Museen zu Berlin, Museum für Asiatische Kunst
Only in Zurich

► 240 Kitagawa Utamaro
Mother Bouncing Baby (Haha to ko, takai takai), circa 1803
Publisher: Izumiya Ichibei (Kansendō)
Museum für Kunst und Gewerbe Hamburg
Only in Zurich

► 241 Kitagawa Utamaro
Mother and Child, circa 1804
From the series *Twelve Views of Beautiful Girls, Compared with Famous Regions (Meisho fūkei bijin jūni sō)*, publisher: no mark
Staatliche Museen zu Berlin, Museum für Asiatische Kunst
Only in Essen, p. 187
Motif also in the Monet Collection

► 242 Utagawa Yoshimaru II (1844–1907)
New Prints of Worms and Insects (Shinpan chūrui), 1883
Publisher: Okui Chūbei
Van Gogh Museum, Amsterdam (Vincent van Gogh Foundation)
Sheet formerly in the Van Gogh Collection
Only in Essen, p. 72

► 243 Utagawa Yoshitora (active circa 1845–1880)
Cherry Blossom Time, 1847–1852
Publisher: Kinkyōdō
ōban triptych
Van Gogh Museum, Amsterdam (Vincent van Gogh Foundation)
Copy formerly in the Van Gogh Collection
Only in Zurich

Books and albums

► 244 Utagawa Hiroshige (1797–1858)
A Picture Album of the Floating World (Ukiyo Ryūsai gafu), circa 1830
Vol. 3, publisher: Eirakuya Tōshirō
Colour woodblock print, *ehon*
Private Collection
Sheet formerly in the Denis Collection

► 245 Utagawa Hiroshige
Large Fish (Uo zukushi), circa 1832–1833 / circa 1840–1842
34 sheets from two series, publishers: Nishimura Yohachi (Eijudō) / Yamada Shōjirō
24.6 × 18.4 × 1.5 cm (*ōban* fan-fold bound)
Lehmbruck Museum, Duisburg
Motifs also in the Monet, Moreau-Nélaton, Rivière and Rodin collections

► 246 Utagawa Hiroshige II (1826–1869)
Kannon Hall Built on a Cliff at Kasamori-ji Temple in Kazusa Province (Kazusa Kasamori-ji iwazukuri Kannon), 1859
From the series *One Hundred Famous Views in the Various Provinces (Shokoku meisho hyakkei)*, publisher: Uoya Eikichi
Crepe print (*chirimen-e*), 21.8 × 16 × 1.8 cm (*ōban*, bound with other woodblock prints in an album)
Lehmbruck Museum, Duisburg
Motif also in the Bonnard Collection

► 247 Katsushika Hokusai (1760–1849)
One Hundred Views of Mount Fuji (Fugaku hyakkei), 1835
Vol. 2 (of 3), publisher: Nishimura Yūzō
Woodblock print, printed in monochrome shades of black and grey, *ehon*
Private Collection
Copy formerly in the Lacombe Collection
p. 170
Copies of this volume also in the Monet and presumably also Van Gogh collections

► 248a–n Katsushika Hokusai
Transmitting the Spirit, Revealing the Form of Things: Random Sketches by Hokusai (Denshin Kaishu Hokusai Manga), 1814–1878
Publisher: Eirakuya Tōshirō, Kadomaruya Jinsuke, Hanabusaya Heikichi or Takekawa Tōbei
Colour woodblock prints, *ehon*
Copies of these volumes also in the Bracquemond and Gallé collections (exactly which volumes has not been determined with certainty in every case)

▸ Vol. 1, 19th c. (1st ed. 1814)
a Private Collection
Only in Essen
b Sammlung P. + R. Herzog, Basel
Only in Zurich

▸ Vol. 2, 19th c. (1st ed. 1815)
c Museen der Stadt Regensburg, Historisches Museum
Only in Essen
d Sammlung P. + R. Herzog, Basel
Only in Zurich
Copies of this volume in the Moreau-Nélaton and presumably also Manet collections

▸ Vol. 3, 19th c. (1st ed. 1815)
e Sammlung P. + R. Herzog, Basel
Only in Zurich

▸ Vol. 4, 19th c. (1st ed. 1816)
f Museen der Stadt Regensburg, Historisches Museum
Only in Essen
g Sammlung P. + R. Herzog, Basel
Only in Zurich
Copy of this volume in the Monet Collection

▸ Vol. 6, 19th c. (1st ed. 1817)
h Museen der Stadt Regensburg, Historisches Museum
Only in Essen
Copies of this volume in the Monet and Vuillard collections

▸ Vol. 7, 19th c. (1st ed. 1817)
i Museen der Stadt Regensburg, Historisches Museum
Only in Essen
j Sammlung P. + R. Herzog, Basel
Only in Zurich
Copies of this volume in the Gallé and Monet collections

▸ Vol. 9, 19th c. (1st ed. 1819)
k Museen der Stadt Regensburg, Historisches Museum
Only in Essen
l Sammlung P. + R. Herzog, Basel
Only in Zurich
Copy of this volume in the Monet Collection

▸ Vol. 13, 19th c. (1st ed. 1849)
m Museen der Stadt Regensburg, Historisches Museum
Only in Essen
n Sammlung P. + R. Herzog, Basel
Only in Zurich, p. 256
Copies of this volume in the Monet and presumably also Gallé collections

► 249 Torii Kiyonaga (1752–1815)
First Bath of the New Year (Yudono hajime), 1787
Sheet 6 from the album *Colors of the Triple Dawn (Saishiki mitsu no asa)*, publisher: Nishimuraya Yohachi
Sheet from an *ehon*
Staatliche Museen zu Berlin, Museum für Asiatische Kunst
Only in Zurich

► 250 Utagawa Kunisada (Toyokuni III) (1786–1864)
Divers at Ise Making Abalone Strips (Ise no ama nagaawabi tsukuru no zu), 1860
Publisher: Kagaya Kichiemon (Kichibei)
ōban triptych, fan-fold bound with other woodblock prints
Museum Angewandte Kunst, Frankfurt am Main
Only in Essen
Motif also in the Monet Collection

► 251 Kitao Masayoshi (1764–1824)
The Method of Simplified Drawing (Ryakuga shiki), 1795
Publisher: Surahaya Ichibei
Colour woodblock print, *ehon*
Musée Rodin, Paris
Volume formerly in the Rodin Collection
Copy of the volume also in the Vuillard Collection

► 252a–f Kitao Masayoshi
Double-page from the volume *The Method of Simplified Drawing for Plants and Flowers (Sōka ryakuga shiki)*, 1813
Publisher: Suharaya Ichibei
Black and polychrome printing without contours
Sheets from an *ehon*
Staatliche Museen zu Berlin, Museum für Asiatische Kunst
Copy of the volume in the Monet Collection

a *Iris (Ayame)* (right), *Aster and Lycoris (Sanhichi, manyūsage)* (left)
Only in Essen

b *Star Lily and Small Chrysanthemums (Himeyuri, kogiku)* (right), *Poppy (Keshi)* (left)
Only in Essen

c *Brassica japonica (Mizunagi)* (right), *nenuphar japonicum (Kōhone)* (left)
Only in Essen

d *Iris (Kakitsubata)* (right), *yellow archangel (Yamabuki)* (left)
Only in Essen

e *Chrysanthemums (Kiku)*
Only in Zurich

f *Tragacanth (Gegebana, sakite)* (right), *poppy (Bijinsō keshi)* (left)
Only in Zurich

► 253 Various Japanese artists
Souvenirs of Van Gogh / Souvenirs de Van Gogh (Gōgu no omoide), 19th c.
14 Japanese woodblock prints bound in an album, 41 × 29 cm
Musée National des Arts Asiatiques Guimet, Paris
Sheets formerly in the Van Gogh Collection; then, as an album, formerly in the Paul Gachet Collection

Shunga

► 254 Keisai (Ikeda) Eisen (1790–1848)
Couple in the Summer, circa 1820–1825, from the series *The Secret Language of the Courtesans (Keisai Higo)*
Museen der Stadt Regensburg, Historisches Museum
Only in Essen

► 255a–b Hosoda Eishi (Chōbunsai) (1756–1829)
Series *Blithe Laughter of the Flowers (Hana no ikkyōshō)*, circa 1788
aiban
Museen der Stadt Regensburg, Historisches Museum
Only in Essen

a *Amorous Couple*, circa 1788
Sheet 10

b *Amorous Couple with Lamp*, circa 1788
Sheet 12

► 256 Kikugawa Eizan (1787–1867)
A Man Forcing Sake on a Woman, circa 1804–1811
Sheet (*abuna-e*) from an untitled series of twelve woodblock prints
Museen der Stadt Regensburg, Historisches Museum
Only in Zurich

► 257 Katsushika Hokusai (1760–1849), attributed to
Couple with Mirror, circa 1810
Museen der Stadt Regensburg, Historisches Museum
Only in Essen

► 258 Katsushika Hokusai
Models of Couples (Ehon tsui no hinagata), 1812
Album of twelve woodblock prints
ehon (bound as leporello)
Musée Rodin, Paris
Sheet formerly Rodin Collection
p. 324

► 259 Katsushika Hokusū, attributed to / Katsushika Hokusai (1760–1849)
Album *A Dyer's Saffron (Suetsumuhana)* of twelve woodblock prints, among them a woodblock print by Hokusai from the album *Models of Couples (Ehon tsui no hinagata)*, 1812 (Hokusai) / circa 1830 (Hokusū)
ehon (bound as leporello)
Musée Rodin, Paris
Sheet formerly Rodin Collection
p. 324

► 260a–b Torii Kiyonaga (1752–1815)
Album *Twelve Modern Reflections (Imayō jūni-kagami)*
chūban
Museen der Stadt Regensburg, Historisches Museum

a *Amorous Couple*, circa 1785
Only in Essen

b *Couple with Peony*, circa 1785
Only in Zurich

► 261a–b Torii Kiyonaga
Series *Scrolls of the Sleeve (Sode no maki)*
hashira-e
Private Collection

a *Secret Encounter*, circa 1785
Formerly in the Picasso Collection
p. 320

b *A Middle-Aged Couple*, circa 1785
Formerly in the Picasso Collection
p. 320

► 262 Isoda Koryusai (1735–1790), attributed to
Amorous Couple with Courtesan, circa 1770–1775
chūban
Museen der Stadt Regensburg, Historisches Museum
Only in Essen

► 263 Isoda Koryusai
Amorous Couple between a Screen and a Door, circa 1777
From the series *Twelve Encounters on the Road to Sensuality (Shikidō torikumi jūni-ban)*
Museen der Stadt Regensburg, Historisches Museum
Only in Zurich

► 264 Utagawa Kunisada (Toyokuni III)? (1786–1864)
Makimono with erotic woodblock prints, circa 1840
Comprising eight double pages of a volume, 20 × 250 cm
Musée Rodin, Paris
Formerly in the Rodin Collection

► 265 Katsukawa Shunchō (active circa 1783–1795)
A Pair of Lovers, circa 1783–1795
Sheet from an untitled album of twelve (?) woodblock prints
Private Collection
Formerly in the Picasso Collection
p. 319

► 266 Katsukawa Shunchō
A Pair of Lovers, circa 1790
Sheet 6 from an untitled album of twelve (?) woodblock prints
Private Collection
Formerly in the Picasso Collection

► 267 Katsukawa Shunchō, attributed to
Amorous Couple, Naked, circa 1783–1795
aiban
Museen der Stadt Regensburg, Historisches Museum
Only in Essen

► 268 Katsukawa Shunchō
Amorous Couple, Dressed, circa 1785–1790
aiban
Museen der Stadt Regensburg, Historisches Museum
Only in Zurich

► 269 Katsukawa Shunchō
Amorous Couple, Dotted Coat, circa 1785–1790
aiban
Museen der Stadt Regensburg, Historisches Museum
Only in Zurich

► 270 Katsukawa Shunchō
Amorous Couple, Man with Olive-Green Coat, circa 1785–1790
aiban
Museen der Stadt Regensburg, Historisches Museum
Only in Zurich

► 271 Katsukawa Shunchō, attributed to
Couple Seen through a Screen (tsuitate), circa 1795
Museen der Stadt Regensburg, Historisches Museum
Only in Zurich

► 272 Kitagawa Utamaro (1753–1806)
A Geisha with Her Lover, 1799
Sheet 8 of the series *Unravelling the Threads of Desire (Negai no itoguchi)*
Museen der Stadt Regensburg, Historisches Museum
Only in Zurich

► 273 Kitagawa Utamaro, attributed to
Amorous Couple, circa 1789–1801
chūban (daikō hōsho)
Museen der Stadt Regensburg, Historisches Museum
Only in Zurich

► 274 Kitagawa Utamaro, attributed to
Naked Couple, circa 1789–1801
chūban (daikō hōsho)
Museen der Stadt Regensburg, Historisches Museum
Only in Zurich

► 275 Kitagawa Utamaro
Dressed Couple Lying on Their Fronts, circa 1803
Sheet from an untitled *shunga* album
ōtanzakuban
Museen der Stadt Regensburg, Historisches Museum
Only in Essen

► 276 Kitagawa Utamaro
Couple, circa 1803
Sheet from an untitled *shunga* album
ōtanzakuban
Museen der Stadt Regensburg, Historisches Museum (JS 40)
Only in Essen

► 277 Kitagawa Utamaro
Couple, circa 1803
Sheet from an untitled *shunga* album
ōtanzakuban
Museen der Stadt Regensburg, Historisches Museum (JS 42)
Only in Essen

DYEING STENCILS *(katagami)*

Paper, cut

► 278 *Katagami*, 2nd half of 19th c.
Motif: banana leaves
31.2 × 41.7 cm

► 279 *Katagami*, 2nd half of 19th c.
Motif: waves
41.1 × 62.8 cm
p. 236

► 280 *Katagami*, 2nd half of 19th c.
Motif: two cranes on stylised pine bark in rhombus form
55.8 × 41.7 cm
p. 237

► 281 *Katagami*, circa 1900
Motif: peonies on net-like pattern
30.5 × 41 cm
Musée Rodin, Paris
Formerly in the Rodin Collection
Only in Essen

► 282 *Katagami*, circa 1900
Motif: waves
24.2 × 40.7 cm
Musée Rodin, Paris
Formerly in the Rodin Collection
Only in Essen

► 283 *Katagami*, circa 1900
Motif: fishnets, pebbles and pine bark in fan-shaped pattern
32.1 × 41.1 cm
Musée Rodin, Paris
Formerly in the Rodin Collection
Only in Essen

► 284 *Katagami*, circa 1900
Motif: bows and arrows
24.7 × 41.3 cm
Musée Rodin, Paris
Formerly in the Rodin Collection
Only in Essen, p. 282

► 285 *Katagami*, circa 1900
Motif: stylised chrysanthemums between ivy vines
24.1 × 41.2 cm
Musée Rodin, Paris
Formerly in the Rodin Collection
Only in Essen

► 286 *Katagami*, circa 1900
Motif: plum blossoms alternating with a geometric pattern
25.3 × 41.3 cm
Musée Rodin, Paris
Formerly in the Rodin Collection
Only in Zurich

► 287 *Katagami*, circa 1900
Motif: geometric pattern
24.5 × 41.1 cm
Musée Rodin, Paris
Formerly in the Rodin Collection
Only in Zurich, p. 282

► 288 *Katagami*, circa 1900
Motif: flowers, gourds and bamboo in rhombus-shaped pattern
30.5 × 41.3 cm
Musée Rodin, Paris
Formerly in the Rodin Collection
Only in Zurich, p. 282

► 289 *Katagami*, circa 1900
Motif: circular wisteria blossoms on striped pattern
26.5 × 41.7 cm
Musée Rodin, Paris
Formerly in the Rodin Collection
Only in Zurich

► 290 *Katagami*, circa 1900
Motif: intertwined plum blossoms
25.5 × 41 cm
Musée Rodin, Paris
Formerly in the Rodin Collection
Only in Zurich

ARTEFACTS

Noh robe

► 291 *Noh Robe (atsuita-karaori)*, 18th or early 19th c.
Noh theatre costume / dancing robe
Complex fabric with supplementary weft brocade patterns on coloured silk and strips of gilded paper, lined with linen-weave silk, 170.5 x 140.5 cm
Formerly in the Charles Gillot Collection
p. 235

Theatre masks

Wood, carved and painted with pigments on lime-glue mixture

► 292 Ji'unin
Fudō-myōō-Beshimi, 15th/16th c.
Noh theatre face mask
Demon, combination of Fudō-myōō and Beshimi ("imperturbable king of light")
22.5 × 16 × 9.5 cm
p. 114

► 293 Deme Mitsuteru
Suji-otoko, 16th c.
Noh theatre face mask
Demon, man with bulging veins
19.7 × 14.9 × 8 cm
Formerly in the Charles Gillot Collection
p. 114

► 294 *Ō-beshimi*, early Edo period, 17th c.
Noh theatre face mask
Large Beshimi, used for the mountain demon Tengu
24 × 15.5 × 10.5 cm

► 295 Kodama Ōmi Mitsumasa (died in 1704)
Ko-omote, 17th c.
Noh theatre face mask
Beautiful young woman
21.1 × 13.3 × 6.9 cm
Formerly in the Charles Gillot Collection
p. 234

► 296 *Kitsune*, probably 18th c.
Kyōgen theatre face mask
Fox
24 × 16.4 × 16.7 cm

► 297 *Oto-goze / Okame*, probably 18th c.
Kyōgen theatre face mask
Plump, simple, rather homely woman
19 × 15 × 7.5 cm

Small-scale sculptures

► 298 Bizen?
Daruma (or Bodai Daruma?), 19th c.
Clay, fired, 15.7 × 14.6 × 16.4 cm
Formerly in the Edmond Taigny Collection
p. 232

► 299 *Hitomaro*, probably 19th c.
Sculpture of the Japanese poet Kakinomoto no Hitomaro
Coniferous wood, lacquer, glass, gold bronze, 32.1 × 26.4 × 14.2 cm
Formerly in the Paul Brenot Collection
p. 233

Lacquerware

► 300 *Bowl Stand (temmoku-dai)*, Muromachi period, 15th/16th c.
Stand for a tea bowl; edges adopt the contour of a waternut blossom
Wood, black lacquer, covered with red lacquer, partially rubbed off to create an uneven, decorative pattern (Negoro ware), edge and rims gone over with black lacquer, 9.3 × 15 × 16.3 cm
p. 246

► 301 *Box for Tooth-Blackening Powder (hagurobako)*, late Muromachi period, 16th c.
Motif: a large pine tree with a blossoming wisteria winding around its trunk, in front of it a brocade curtain, in the interior and on the sides scattered wisteria branches
Wood, black lacquer, gold *maki-e* ground, decor in gold *maki-e* techniques and pewter foil inlays, on the bottom black lacquer strewn with isolated flakes of gold, lead rim, 4 × 8.6 × 6.5 cm

► 302 *Incense Box (kōgō)*, Momoyama period, circa 1600
Motif: exterior: lotus vines and crests distributed over the surface, at the centre, within a circular border, a lotus blossom from above; interior: scattered kiri-blossom and star-shaped crests.
Wood, black lacquer, gold *maki-e* ground, decor in *maki-e* techniques in gold and silver as well as larger-scale inlays of gold, silver and pewter foil, lead rim, 5.1 × 9.4 × 7.8 cm

► 303 *Incense Box (kōgō)*, early Edo period, early 17th c.
Motif: exterior: doe; interior: decor of honeysuckle branches with blossoms
Wood, black and brown lacquer, decor in *maki-e* technique and accents in red lacquer, lead rim, 3.4 × 7.9 × 7.9 cm
p. 242

► 304 *Incense Burner (hitorimo)*, mid Edo period, 18th c.
Akoda type with curved sides in the shape of a pumpkin (*akoda-uri*), motif: tops of young pines (*wakamatsu*)
Wood, wood grain imitated with *maki-e* lacquer, decor in gold *maki-e* technique, interior lined with metal, rim and pierced cover of copper-gold alloy, 5.3 × 6.4 × 6.3 cm

► 305 *Stacking Box (jūbako)*, mid Edo period, 18th c.
Three-tiered box for incense of different scents, motif on lid: pair of pheasants on rocks, on the sides plovers (*chidori*) over waves
Wood, black lacquer, gold *maki-e* ground, decor in *maki-e* technique with *harigaki* and regular gold *kirigane* as well as accents in red lacquer, 7.5 × 9.7 × 7.6 cm

► 306 *Writing Box (suzuribako)*, Ritsuō style, late Edo period, late 18th c. / early 19th c.
Motif: "monkey reaching for the moon" (*enkō sokugetsu*)
Bamboo, woven and coated with dark brown lacquer, edges trimmed with black lacquer, decor in black lacquer, red lacquer and gold *maki-e* technique, inlays in metal, lead, ceramic and mother-of-pearl, "Kan" porcelain mark, 5.7 × 27.2 × 19.9 cm (oval)
p. 243

► 307 *Writing Box (suzuribako)*, Ritsuō style, 19th c.
Motif: exterior: the poet Saigyō Hōshi contemplating Mount Fuji; interior: a rocky island landscape surrounded by waves
Wood, black lacquer, decor in *maki-e* techniques in gold and silver, inlays in ivory, glazed ceramic, mother-of-pearl and lead, "Kan" porcelain mark, 4 × 22.5 × 23.3 cm
p. 245

► 308 *Writing Box (suzuribako)*, Meiji period, late 19th c.
Motif: exterior: helmet, musket, powder sack and cannon; interior: a rocky island landscape surrounded by waves
Wood, brown lacquer, decor in *maki-e* techniques in gold and silver and accents in red lacquer, inlays in mother-of-pearl, 5 × 22 × 23.7 cm
Formerly in the Edmond Taigny Collection
p. 244

► 309 *Low Writing Table (bundai)*, Meiji period, late 19th c.
Motif: scattered feathers, on the legs a Chinese coin pattern with rhombus-shaped blossom stars
Wood, black lacquer, decor in polychrome *togidashi maki-e* sprinkled with mother-of-pearl dust, fittings in silver-plated copper, 13.6 × 63 × 32.8 cm
Formerly in the Siegfried Bing Collection
p. 38

► 310 *Writing Box (suzuribako)*, Meiji period, circa 1900
Motif: two carp jumping in waves
Cut entirely from marbled lacquer, decor in cut red lacquer application, inlaid glass and *maki-e* technique, interior carved lacquer, 4.5 × 21.2 × 9.8 cm

Inros

► 311 *Inro*, Edo period, late 18th c.
Motif: blossoming peonies
Five-part, wood, black and brown lacquer, decor in *maki-e* techniques in gold and silver and accents in red lacquer, glass *ojime*, 7.8 × 6.3 × 2 cm
p. 239

► 312 *Inro*, late Edo period, circa 1800
Motif: chrysanthemums on a fence, above them lanterns mounted on a roof, on the back a koto, next to it a kitten and a small lacquerware jar
Five-part, wood, black lacquer with polychrome *togidashi maki-e* sprinkled with mother-of-pearl dust, *hirameji* along the cord guide, gold lacquer signature "Made by Min(koku?)" and red lacquer mark, amber *ojime*, 7.9 × 6.2 × 2.4 cm

► 313 *Inro*, Rimpa style, late Edo period, early 19th c.
Motif: blossoming irises
Five-part, wood, gold *maki-e* ground (with extremely fine sprinkled flakes of gold), high *maki-e* depiction, mother-of-pearl inlays and lead, 6.5 × 5.2 × 2.4 cm
p. 238

► 314 *Inro*, Rimpa style, late Edo period, early 19th c.
Motif: sailing ship on waves after a design by Yamada Jōkasai (18th c.)
Six-part, wood, glossy black lacquer ground *(roiro)*, decor in *maki-e* techniques in silver, gold and red lacquer, inlays in pewter, *ojime*, 9.4 × 5.3 × 2.6 cm
p. 238

► 315 *Inro*, late Edo period, 19th c.
Motif: two hares sitting among *tokusa* grasses
Four-part, wood, black lacquer, decor in *maki-e* techniques in gold and silver and accents in red lacquer, mother-of-pearl inlays, gold lacquer signature "Kajikawa" and red lacquer mark in tsubo form, 7.1 × 5 × 2.2 cm
Formerly in the Paul Brenot Collection
p. 239

► 316 *Inro*, late Meiji period, late 19th c.
Motif: two ducks among rushes
Four-part, wood, black lacquer, small amount of coloured lacquer, silver ground *(ginji)* and depiction in the ink-painting style *(sumi-e togidashi)*, gold lacquer signature "Ippō (Yanagisawa)" and red lacquer mark, rock crystal?, *ojime*, 7.4 × 7.9 × 1.8 cm

► 317 *Inro*, Meiji period, late 19th c.
Motif: pine tree and flying cranes
Five-part, wood, gold *maki-e* ground, decor in *maki-e* techniques in gold, 7.9 × 5.8 × 2.2 cm

Netsukes

► 318 *Toad Sitting in a Tree Trunk*, late 18th c.
Light boxwood / fruit wood?, 2.6 × 4.4 × 2.6 cm
Formerly in the Marcus B. Huish Collection

► 319 *Laughing? Dancer*, late 18th c.
Ivory, 7.7 × 2.1 × 1.2 cm

► 320 *Skull with Snake*, 18th/19th c.
Boxwood, ivory, lacquer or horn?, 2.9 × 2.9 × 3.4 cm
Formerly in the Marcus B. Huish Collection

► 321 *Laughing Man (Dancer?)*, early 19th c.
Ivory, 5.7 × 2.8 × 1.9 cm
Formerly in the Marcus B. Huish Collection

► 322 *Ōni (Demon) as Thunder God Raiden*, early 19th c.
Boxwood, with (former) inlays in ivory, mother-of-pearl, horn, lacquer or silver, 2.8 × 4.1 × 2.3 cm
p. 241

► 323 *Two Dancers with a Shishimai Mask*, 1st half of / mid 19th c.
Ivory, 3.3 × 3.4 × 2.2 cm

► 324 *The Thunder God Raiden with his Drum, Sitting in the Clouds*, mid 19th c.
Boxwood, and ivory with inlays in horn, 2.6 × 3.9 × 3.8 cm

► 325 *Hare between Waves*, mid 19th c.
Boxwood, with inlays in horn, 3.2 × 3.8 × 2.1 cm

► 326 *Rat*, mid 19th c.
Boxwood, with inlays in horn, 3 × 4.2 × 3.2 cm
Formerly in the Marcus B. Huish Collection
p. 240

► 327 *Three Puppies on a Straw Mat*, 2nd half of 19th c.
Ivory with inlays in wood/metal/horn? and gold lacquer applications, rubbed in (carbon black) pigments, 2.1 × 5 × 3.8 cm
p. 240

► 328 *Octopus in a Food Storage Jar*, 19th c.
Boxwood, with inlays in horn and ivory, 5.1 × 3.2 × 3 cm
p. 241

► 329 *Old Man, Laughing, with Tengu Mask on his Back*, 19th c.
Boxwood, remnants of mother-of-pearl inlays?, 3.4 × 3.2 × 4.3 cm

Ceramics

► 330 *Tea Bowl (chawan), temmoku* type, Seto, Edo period, 17th c.
Stoneware, ochre-coloured glaze, H 7 cm, Ø 12.2 cm
p. 246

► 331 *Tea Bowl (chawan)*, Edo period, 17th/18th c.
Raku, lead glaze, H 8.4 cm, Ø 11.5 cm
p. 268

► 332 *Tea Bowl (chawan)*, Edo period, 17th/18th c.
Raku, lead glaze, H 9.2 cm, Ø 11.9 cm

► 333 *Tea Bowl (chawan)*, Edo period, 17th/18th c.
Raku, engobe and lead glaze, H 6.8 cm, Ø 11.5 cm

► 334 *Tea Bowl (chawan)*, Shigaraki style, Edo period, 17th/18th c.
Raku, vertical grooves, H 9.8 cm, Ø 11.9 cm
p. 268

► 335 *Tea Bowl (chawan)*, Hagi, Edo period, 17th/18th c.
Stoneware, white rice straw ash glaze, H 8.8 cm, Ø 14.5 cm

► 336 *Tea Jar (chaire) with Straight Shoulder*, Seto, katatsuki type, Edo period, late 17th/18th c.
Stoneware, iron glaze, ivory lid, H 9.7 cm, Ø 7.6 cm
p. 247

► 337 *Pair of Covered Vases*, Arita, Imari style, Edo period, 18th c.
Motif: figures in a landscape
Porcelain, painted, gilded, each H 54.7 cm, Ø 29.4 cm
Musée Rodin, Paris
Formerly in the Rodin Collection
p. 106

► 338 *Tea Bowl (chawan) in the Shape of a Shoe (kutsugata)*, Mino, Oribe type, Edo period, 18th c.
Stoneware, green and white glaze painted with iron, 7 × 14.8 × 13.3 cm
p. 265

► 339 *Food or Tea Bowl (chawan)*, Mino, Oribe type, Edo period, 18th c.
Stoneware, cream-coloured glaze with brown spiral decor in interior, small copper green and red dots, gold and red lacquer repairs, H 8.9 cm, Ø 13.9 cm
p. 262

► 340 *Tea Jar (chaire)*, Seto, Edo period, 18th c.
Stoneware, engobe and wood ash glaze, ivory lid, 9.7 × 5.9 × 5.9 cm
p. 264

► 341 *Tea Bowl (chawan)*, Mino, Shino type, Edo period, 18th c.
Stoneware, white glaze, pronounced turning grooves, gold lacquer repairs, 8.9 × 13.9 × 13.9 cm
p. 248

- ► 342 *Covered Vase*, Fukagawa Manufactory, 1878 or before
Motif: lion, rocks, wave, vine ornaments
Porcelain, painted, gilded, H 138 cm, Ø 63 cm
Collection Musée Ariana, Ville de Genève
Exhibited at the 1878 World Fair in Paris (prize of honour)
Only in Zurich

- ► 343 Akahada
Tea Bowl (chawan), 19th c.
Motif: Mount Fuji
Stoneware with iron glaze, 9.5 × 9.8 × 9 cm
Formerly in the Edmond Taigny Collection
p. 249

- ► 344 *Vase*, 19th c.
Stoneware, various-coloured glazes, H 17 cm, Ø 12.5 cm
Hetjens-Museum, Deutsches Keramikmuseum
p. 267

- ► 345 *Double Gourd Vase*, 19th c.
Stoneware, variously coloured glossy drip glazes, H 10 cm, Ø 8.5 cm
Hetjens-Museum, Deutsches Keramikmuseum
p. 267

Baskets

- ► 346 *Flower Basket with Handle*, last third of 19th c.
Bamboo, 20.3 × 25 × 24.7 cm
p. 116

- ► 347 *Bowl Basket*, last third of 19th c.
Bamboo and rattan, H 10.3 cm, Ø 29 cm
p. 116

- ► 348 *Flower Basket for Hanging*, last third of 19th c.
Bamboo and rattan in scale pattern, platelets in the form of plovers (*chidori*) and metal ring, H 25.2 cm, Ø 15.2 cm
p. 116

Tsubas

- ► 349 *Tsuba*, circa 1650–1700
Motif: lotus leaves
Pierced iron, 7.6 × 7.1 × 0.5 cm
Inscr. verso (trans.): Made by Kinai, resident of Echizen Province
Formerly in the Philippe Burty Collection, then Paul Brenot Collection
p. 28

- ► 350 *Tsuba*, circa 1700–1750
Motif: stylised waves
Pierced iron, 8.2 × 8.1 × 0.5 cm
Formerly in the Paul Brenot Collection

- ► 351 *Tsuba*, circa 1750–1800
Motif: chrysanthemums and geometric pattern
Pierced iron, H 0.5 cm, Ø 7.9 cm
Formerly in the Paul Brenot Collection
p. 260

- ► 352 *Tsuba*, circa 1750–1800
Motif: crane
Pierced iron, applied copper alloy, possibly *shibuichi* (copper/silver) with *shakudō* (copper/gold), 8.1 × 7.7 × 0.6 cm
p. 260

- ► 353 *Tsuba*, circa 1750–1800
Motif: cherry blossoms over stylised stream
Pierced iron, applied *shakudō* (copper/gold) and copper, 7.5 × 7.3 × 0.5 cm
Inscr. recto (trans.): Made by Suruga, resident of Echizen Province
Presumably formerly in the Paul Brenot Collection

- ► 354 *Tsuba*, circa 1750–1800
Motif: monkey
Pierced iron, applied copper alloy and possibly *shakudō* (copper/gold), 6.1 × 5.6 × 0.8 cm

- ► 355 *Tsuba*, circa 1750–1800
Motif: parallel diagonal ridges (depicting rain?)
Pierced iron, applied copper, H 0.5 cm, Ø 8.15 cm
Inscr. verso: (trans.): Made by Kinai, resident of Echizen Province
Formerly in the Philippe Burty Collection, then Paul Brenot Collection

- ► 356 *Tsuba*, circa 1800–1850
Motif: long-tailed birds
Pierced iron, 7.5 × 7.2 × 0.5 cm
Formerly in the Paul Brenot Collection

- ► 357 *Tsuba*, circa 1800–1850
Motif: cherry blossoms
Pierced iron, applied copper and gold, 7 × 6.7 × 0.4 cm
Inscr. recto (trans.): Suruga Takuoki, resident of Inshu Province
Presumably formerly in the Paul Brenot Collection
p. 260

Documentation

- ► 358 Takizawa Bakin
Okoma, 1883
Illustrations by Félix Régamey, drawings by Shigamei
Paris: E. Plon & Cie., 31 × 24.5 cm
Private Collection

- ► 359a–e Siegfried Bing (ed.)
Le Japon artistique: Documents d'Art et d'Industrie, 1888–1891 (nos 1–36)
Paris: Marpon et Flammarion, 33.4 × 24.7 cm
Private Collection

  a No. 10 (Feb. 1889)
  b No. 12 (Apr. 1889)
  c No. 16 (Aug. 1889)
  d No. 19 (Nov. 1889)
  e No. 20 (Dec. 1889)
  p. 348

- ► 360 Siegfried Bing (ed.)
Exposition de la gravure japonaise ouverte à l'École des Beaux-Arts, 1890
Paris: L'École des Beaux-Arts, 26.5 × 19 cm
Private Collection

- ► 361 Edmond de Goncourt
Hokousaï (L'art japonais au XVIIIe siècle), 1896
Paris: G. Charpentier et E. Fasquelle, 18 × 14 cm
Museum für Kunst und Gewerbe Hamburg

- ► 362 Louis Gonse
L'Art japonais, 1883
Paris: A. Quantin, 2 vols, each 35.5 × 27 cm
Bibliothek Museum Folkwang, Essen

- ► 363 Émile Guimet
Promenades japonaises, 1878
Illustrations by Félix Régamey
Paris: G. Charpentier, 29 × 21 cm
Museum für Kunst und Gewerbe Hamburg
Copy formerly in the possession of Edmond de Goncourt
p. 347

- ► 364 Aimé Humbert
Le Japon illustré, 1870
Drawings by E. Bayard, H. Catenasi, Aug. Ciceri et al.
Paris: L. Hachette, 2 vols, each 35 × 27 cm
Museum für Kunst und Gewerbe Hamburg

- ► 365 Pierre Loti
Madame Chrysanthème, 1888
Engravings by Guillaume Frères after drawings and watercolours by Rossi and Myrbach
Paris: Calmann Lévy, 23.4 × 16 cm
Private Collection

- ► 366 *Objets d'art de la Chine et du Japon. Porcelaines, bronzes, laques, émaux cloisonnés, gardes de sabre, étoffes etc. formant la collection de M. Paul Brenot*, 1903
Catalogue of the auction at the Hôtel Drouot, 5–10 June 1903 (s.l., s.n.), 31 × 23 cm
Museum für Kunst und Gewerbe Hamburg
p. 349

- ► 367 *Paris illustré: Le Japon*, nos 45 and 46, May 1886
46 × 33 cm
Van Gogh Museum, Amsterdam (Vincent van Gogh Foundation)
Formerly in the possession of Van Gogh
Only in Essen, p. 71

- ► 368 Félix Régamey
Le Japon pratique, 1891
Paris: J. Hetzel & Cie., 18 × 12 cm
Museum für Kunst und Gewerbe Hamburg

Select bibliography

General literature on *Japonisme*

Akiyama Terukazu, *L'âge du japonisme. La France et le Japon dans la deuxième moitié du XIXe siècle*, Société Franco-Japonaise d'Art et d'Archéologie, Tokyo and Kinokuniya, 1983.

Klaus Berger, *Japonismus in der westlichen Malerei 1860–1920*, Munich, 1980; English: *Japonisme in Western Painting from Whistler to Matisse*, Cambridge, 1992.

Chantal Bouchon et al. (ed.), *Katagami. Les pochoirs japonais et le japonisme*, exh. cat., Maison de la culture du Japon, Paris, Paris, 2007.

Karin Breuer (ed.), *Japanesque: The Japanese Print in the Era of Impressionism*, exh. cat., Fine Arts Museums of San Francisco, Munich, London and New York, 2010.

Ricard Bru, *Japonismo: La Fascinación por el arte japonés*, exh. cat., Obra Social "La Caixa", Barcelona, 2013; Catalan: *Japonism: La fascinació per l'art japonès*, Caixa Forum Madrid, 2013.

Ricard Bru, *Erotic Japonisme. The Influence of Japanese Sexual Imagery on Western Art*, Leiden, 2013.

Jacques de Caso, "1861: Hokusai rue Jacob", in: *The Burlington Magazine*, vol. 111, no. 798, Sept. 1969, pp. 562–565.

Françoise Chappuis et al. (ed.), *D'Outremer et d'Orient mystique: les itinéraires d'Émile Guimet*, Sully-la-Tour, 2001.

Timothy Clark et al. (ed.), *Shunga. Sex and pleasure in Japanese Art*, exh. cat., The British Museum, London, London, 2013.

Doris Croissant et al. (ed.), *Japan und Europa 1543–1929*, exh. cat., 43. Berliner Festwochen, Martin-Gropius-Bau Berlin, Berlin, 1993 (with separate essay collection).

Claudia Däubler-Hauschke et al. (ed.), *Impressionismus und Japanmode: Edgar Degas, James McNeill Whistler*, exh. cat., Städtische Galerie, Überlingen, Petersberg, 2009.

Claudia Delank, *Das imaginäre Japan in der Kunst: "Japanbilder" vom Jugendstil bis zum Bauhaus*, Munich, 1996.

Jacques Dufwa, *Winds from the East. A study in the Art of Manet, Degas, Monet and Whistler 1856–1886*, Stockholm, 1981.

Elisa Evett, *The Critical Reception of Japanese Art in Late Nineteenth-Century Europe*, doctoral dissertation 1980, Ann Arbor, 1982.

Phylis Anne Floyd, *Japonism in context: documentation, criticism, aesthetic reactions*, doctoral dissertation 1983, Ann Arbor, 1983.

Phylis Anne Floyd, "Documentary Evidence for the Availability of Japanese Imagery in Europe in Nineteenth-Century Public Collections", in: *Art Bulletin*, vol. 68, no. 1, 1986, pp. 105–141.

Daniel Hedinger, *Im Wettstreit mit dem Westen: Japans Zeitalter der Ausstellungen 1854–1941* (Reihe d. Globalgeschichte), Frankfurt am Main and New York, 2011.

Jan Walsh Hokenson, *Japan, France and East-West Aesthetics: French literature, 1867–2000*, Madison, N.J., 2004.

Horst-Janssen-Museum (ed.), *Paris im Japanfieber. Meisterwerke des japanischen Farbholzschnitts begeistern französische Künstler von Degas bis Vallotton*, exh. cat., Horst-Janssen-Museum, Oldenburg, Oldenburg, 2007.

Inaga Shigemi, "Une esthétique de rencontre, ou l'affinité de l'impressionnisme avec le japonisme comme un malentendu et sa conséquence paradoxale au cours de l'implantation de l'impressionnisme au Japon", in: *Word & Image* (First International Conference on Word & Image / Premier Congrès international de texte et image), vol. 4, no. 1, Jan.–Mar. 1988, pp. 139–147.

Inaga Shigemi, "Impressionnisme et japonisme: histoire d'un malentendu créateur", in: *Nouvelles de l'estampe*, no. 159, 1998, pp. 6–21.

Gregory Irvine (ed.), *Japonisme and the rise of the modern art movement: The Arts of the Meiji Period*, London, 2013.

Deborah Johnson, "Japanese Prints in Europe before 1840", in: *The Burlington Magazine*, vol. 124, no. 95, June 1982, pp. 343–348.

Geneviève Lacambre, "Hokusai and the French diplomats. Some remarks on the collection of Baron de Chassiron", in: *The Documented Image. Visions in Art History*, Gabriel P. Weisberg et al. (ed.), Syracuse, 1987, pp. 71–85.

Geneviève Lacambre (ed.), *Le Japonisme*, exh. cat., Galeries nationales du Grand Palais, Paris / Musée national d'Art Occidental, Tokyo, Paris, 1988.

Geneviève Lacambre, "Les collectionneurs japonisants au temps des Goncourt", in: *Cahiers Edmond et Jules de Goncourt*, no. 4, 1995–1996, pp. 164–170.

Geneviève Lacambre, "La diffusion de l'art d'Extrême-Orient comme modèle pour les artistes: l'exemple de la collection Cernuschi", in: *Ebisu*, vol. 19, 1998, pp. 123–134.

Geneviève Lacambre, "Le japonisme du XIXe siècle: nouvelles orientations de la recherche", in: *Regards et discours européens sur le Japon et l'Inde au XIXe siècle*, Université de Limoges, conference proceedings, 3–4 June 1998, Limoges, 2000.

Geneviève Lacambre, "Le Japonisme: exotisme et assimilation", in: *L'Oriente: storia di una figura nelle arti occidentali (1700–2000)* (Studi inter artes 1), Dal Settecento al Novecento, Paolo Amalfitano et al. (ed.), Rome, 2007, pp. 625–634.

Lionel Lambourne, *Japonisme. Cultural Crossings between Japan and the West*, London, 2005.

Deborah Levitt-Pasturel, "Critical Response to Japan at the Paris 1878 Exposition Universelle", in: *Gazette des Beaux-Arts*, no. 119, Feb. 1992, pp. 68–80.

Mae Michiko, "Nipponspiration als transkulturelle Grenzüberschreitung in der Kunst. Japonismus und japanische Populärkultur", in: *Nipponspiration. Japonismus und japanische Populärkultur im deutschsprachigen Raum*, Mae Michiko et al. (ed.), Cologne, 2013, pp. 21–48.

Francesco Morena et al. (ed.), *Giapponismo. Suggestioni dall'Estremo Oriente dai Macchiaioli agli anni Trenta*, exh. cat., Palazzo Pitti, Florence, Livorno, 2012.

Manuela Moscatiello, "A craze for auctions. Japanese art on sale in 19th century Paris", in: *La revue Andon*, no. 90, 2011, pp. 22–45.

Nakamura Hiroko, *La connaissance et l'interprétation de Hokusai en France dans la seconde moitié du XIXe siècle*, doctoral dissertation 2006, 3 vols (microfiche).

Susan J. Napier, *From Impressionism to Anime: Japan as Fantasy and Fan Cult in the Mind of the West*, New York, 2007.

Niiro Keiko, *L'image du Japon en France entre 1860 et 1915*, doctoral dissertation 1997, Villeneuve-d'Ascq (book on demand).

Omoto Keiko and Francis Macouin, *Quand le Japon s'ouvrit au monde*, Paris, 1990.

Max Put, *Plunder and pleasure: Japanese Art in the West 1860–1930*, Leiden, 2000.

Charlotte von Rappard-Boon, "Japonism, the first years 1856–1876", in: *Liber amicorum Karl G. Boon*, Jaap de Hoop Scheffe (ed.), Amsterdam, 1974, pp. 110–121.

Leopold Reidemeister (ed.), *Der Japonismus in der Malerei und Graphik des 19. Jahrhunderts*, exh. cat., Staatliche Museen der Stiftung Preußischer Kulturbesitz im Haus am Waldsee, Berlin, 1965.

Patricia Rochard (ed.), *Japan, Quelle der Inspiration: Japanische Kunst und europäische Moderne um 1900* (Internationale Tage Ingelheim), exh. cat., Internationale Tage im Alten Rathaus der Stadt Ingelheim, Ingelheim, 2001.

John Sandberg, "The discovery of Japanese prints in the 19th century before 1867", in: *Gazette des Beaux-Arts*, no. 71, May–June 1968, pp. 295–302.

Hans-Günther Schwarz et al. (ed.), *Kirschblütenträume: Japans Einfluss auf die Kunst der Moderne*, exh. cat., Kurpfälzisches Museum der Stadt Heidelberg, Heidelberg, 2012.

William Leonard Schwartz, "The Priority of the Goncourts' Discovery of Japanese Art", in: *PMLA*, vol. 42, no. 3, Sept. 1927, pp. 798–806.

René Sieffert (ed.), *Le Japon et la France: images d'une découverte*, Paris, 1974.

Yvonne Thirion, "Le japonisme en France dans la seconde moitié du XIXe siècle, à la faveur de la diffusion de l'estampe japonaise", in: *Cahiers de l'Association Internationale des Études Françaises*, no. 13, 1961, pp. 117–130.

Tokyo National Museum (ed.), *Arts of East and West from World Expositions 1855–1900; Paris, Vienna and Chicago. Commemorating the 2005 World Exposition, Aichi, Japan*, exh. cat., Tokyo National Museum / Osaka Municipal Museum of Art / Nagoy City Museum, Aichi, 2004.

Diane N. Towle, *Spaces of Japonisme and the Art of Whistler, Van Gogh, and Monet: Collecting, Decoration and the Japanese Other*, doctoral dissertation 2013, Saint Louis, 2013.

Chantal Valluy and Lucie Prost, *Adolphe Philippe d'Ennery, collectionneur, 1811–1899*, doctoral dissertation 1975 (unpublished).

Gabriel P. Weisberg, "Samuel Bing: Patron of Art Nouveau. Part 1: The Appreciation of Japanese Art", in: *The Connoisseur*, vol. 172, Oct. 1969, pp. 119–125.

Gabriel P. Weisberg (ed.), *Japonisme: Japanese Influence on French Art 1854–1910*, exh. cat., The Cleveland Museum of Art, Cleveland, et al., Cleveland, 1975.

Gabriel P. Weisberg, "The Creation of Japonisme", in: *The Origins of L'Art Nouveau: The Bing Empire*, exh. cat., The Van Gogh Museum, Amsterdam / Musée des Arts decoratifs, Paris, Paris, Amsterdam et al., 2004, pp. 51–71; German: "Die Entstehung des Japonismus", in: *L'Art Nouveau: La Maison Bing*, Stuttgart, 2004, pp. 51–71.

Gabriel P. Weisberg (ed.), *The Orient Expressed. Japan's Influence on Western Art, 1854–1918*, exh. cat., Museum of Art, Mississippi / McNay Art Museum, San Antonio, Texas, Seattle, 2011.

Gabriel P. and Yvonne M. L. Weisberg, *Japonisme: an annotated bibliography*, New York, 1990.

Western Sources of Japanese Art and Japonism V: Œuvres choisies de critiques d'art, marchands d'art et collectionneurs sur le japonisme, Tokyo, 2010.

Siegfried Wichmann (ed.), *Weltkulturen und Moderne Kunst, die Begegnung der europäischen Kunst und Musik im 19. und 20. Jahrhundert mit Asien, Afrika, Ozeanien, Afro- und Indo-Amerika*, held by the organising committee for the 20th Olympic Games, Munich, 1972, exh. cat., Haus der Kunst, Munich, Munich, 1972.

Siegfried Wichmann, *Japonismus: Ostasien – Europa, Begegnungen in der Kunst des 19. und 20. Jahrhunderts,*

Herrsching, 1980; English: *Japonisme: The Japanese Influence on Western Art in the Nineteenth and Twentieth Centuries*, New York, 1981.
Yamada Chisaburō F. (ed.), *Japonisme in Art. An international Symposium*, The Society for the Study of Japonisme, Tokyo, 1980.

On artist's collections

Geneviève Aitken and Marianne Delafond, *La collection d'estampes japonaises de Claude Monet à Giverny*, Paris, 1983.
Marianne Delafond (ed.), *Les estampes japonaises de Claude Monet*, exh. cat., Musée Marmottan Monet, Paris, Paris, 2006.
Colta Ives, "Degas, Japanese Prints and Japonisme", in: *The Private Collection of Edgar Degas*, exh. cat., The Metropolitan Museum of Art, New York, Anne Dumas et al. (ed.), New York, 1997, pp. 247–260.
Daniel Marchesseau (ed.), *Monet au Musée Marmottan et dans les collections suisses, estampes japonaises*, exh. cat., Fondation Pierre Gianadda, Martigny, Martigny, 2011.
Manuela Moscatiello, "La collection d'art japonais de Giuseppe De Nittis", in: *Arts asiatiques*, vol. 59, 2004, pp. 126–133.
Charlotte van Rappard-Boon et al. (ed.), *Catalogue of the Japanese Prints. Van Gogh Museum's Collection*, Van Gogh Museum Amsterdam, Zwolle, 1991 (revised edition: 2006).
Shizuoka Prefectural Museum of Art (ed.), *Rodin et le Japon*, exh. cat., Shizuoka Prefectural Museum of Art / Aichi Prefectural Museum of Art, Tokyo, 2001.
Dominique Viéville (ed.), *Rodin: Le rêve japonais*, exh. cat., Musée Rodin, Paris, Paris, 2007.
Watanabe Toshio, "Eishi prints in Whistler's Studio", in: *The Burlington Magazine*, vol. 128, no. 1005, Dec. 1986, pp. 873–880.
Gabriel P. Weisberg, "Les albums ukiyo-e de la collection de Camille Moreau: source nouvelle pour le Japonisme", in: *Nouvelles de l'estampe 23*, Sept.–Oct. 1975, pp. 18–21.

On painting

Natalie Adamson, "Japonisme and Odilon Redon's decorative painting: the search for a lost paradise", in: *Apollo*, vol. 146, no. 428, 1997, pp. 12–21.
Matthias Arnold, *Van Gogh und seine Vorbilder. Eine künstlerische Selbstfindung*, Munich, 1997.
Nienke Bakker, "Colour and Japonisme", in: *The real Van Gogh. The artist and his letters*, exh. cat., Royal Academy of Arts, London, London, 2010, pp. 92–123.
Christoph Becker (ed.), *Monets Garten*, exh. cat., Kunsthaus Zürich, Ostfildern-Ruit, 2004.
Monika Bincsik, "A simple worshipper of the eternal Buddha: the japonisme of Vincent van Gogh", in: *Van Gogh in Budapest*, exh. cat., Museum of Fine Arts, Budapest, Budapest, 2006, pp. 399–413.
Jocelyn Bouquillard, "Vagues japonaises: L'influence des 'images du monde flottant'", in: *Vagues: autour des paysages de mer de Gustave Courbet*, exh. cat., Musée Malraux, Le Havre, Paris, 2004, pp. 38–43.
David Bromfield, "Japanese Art, Monet and the Formation of Impressionism: Cultural Exchange and Appropriation in Later Nineteenth Century European Art", in: *Recovering the Orient: Artists, Scholars, Appropriations*, Andrew Gerstle and Anthony Milner (eds.), London and Canberra, 1995, pp. 7–43.
Gilles Chazal et al. (ed.), *Giuseppe de Nittis. La modernité élégante*, exh. cat., Petit Palais, Musée des Beaux-Arts de la Ville de Paris, Paris, 2010.
Bernard Dorival, "Le corsage à carreaux et les japonismes de Bonnard", in: *La Revue du Louvre et des Musées de France*, 1969, no. 1, pp. 21–24.
Vincenzo Farinella, "Le bionde allegrie della natura. Qualche verifica sul giapponismo di Monet", in: *Monet*, Radolphe Rapetti (ed.), conference proceedings, Treviso, 16–17 Jan. 2002, Conegliano 2003, pp. 218–229.
Nathalie Gallissot, "Le Japon rêvé de James Tissot", in: *James Tissot et ses maîtres*, exh. cat., Musée des Beaux-Arts de Nantes, Cyrille Sciama (ed.), Paris and Nantes, 2005, pp. 47–67.
David E. Gliem, "Revisiting Bonnard's Japonisme", in: *Open Inquiry Archive*, vol. 1, no. 7, 2012 (www.openinquiryarchive.net, last accessed 9.7.2014).
Marijke de Groot, "'Japonaiserie forever': Vincent van Gogh and Japan", in: *The Low Countries*, 1999, no. 7, pp. 143–151.
Joop M. Joosten, "Claude Monet's Discovery: Japanese Prints Given Away", in: *Holland as Wrapping Paper, Monet in Holland*, exh. cat., Rijksmuseum Vincent Van Gogh Museum, Amsterdam, Zwolle, 1986, pp. 72–82.
Jay Martin Kloner, *The Influence of Japanese Prints on Édouard Manet and Paul Gauguin*, doctoral dissertation 1968, Ann Arbor, 1971 (microfiche).
Kobayashi Taichirō, "Hokusai et Degas sur la peinture Franco-Japonaise en France et au Japon", in: *International Symposium on History of Eastern and Western Cultural Contacts*, Japanese National Commission for Unesco (ed.), Tokyo, 1959, pp. 69–75.
Kōdera Tsukasa, "Japan as Primitivistic Utopia: Van Gogh's Japonisme Portraits", in: *Simiolus: Netherlands Quarterly for the History of Art*, vol. 14, no. 3/4, 1984, pp. 189–208.
Kôdera Tsukasa, "Van Gogh's Utopian Japonisme", in: *Catalogue of the Japanese Prints. Van Gogh Museum's Collection*, Van Gogh Museum Amsterdam, Zwolle, 1991 (revised edition: 2006), pp. 11–46.
Peter Kropmanns, "'Quelle leçon de pureté, d'harmonie …' À propos de Matisse, Bonnard et le Japonisme", in: *Matisse et Bonnard. Lumière de la Méditerranée*, exh. cat., Kawamura Memorial Museum of Art / The Museum of Modern Art, Hayama, Tokyo, 2008, pp. 25–29; supplement in French, pp. 13–16.
Mabuchi Akiko, "Van Gogh and Japan", in: *Vincent van Gogh*, exh. cat., National Museum Western Art, Tokyo / Nagoya City Museum, Nagoya, Tokyo, 1985, pp. 154–179.
Mabuchi Akiko, "Claude Monet's Japonisme: Nature and Decoration", in: *Monet. A Retrospective*, exh. cat., Bridgestone Museum of Art / Nagoya City Art Museum / Hiroshima Museum of Art, Nagoya, 1994, pp. 232–238.
Matsumoto Kaoru, *Cézanne and Hokusai: The Image of the Mountain*, doctoral dissertation 1993, Montreal, 1993.
Linda Merrill, "Whistler and the 'Lange Lijzen'", in: *The Burlington Magazine*, vol. 136, no. 1099, Oct. 1994, pp. 683–690.
Manuela Moscatiello, *Le japonisme de Giuseppe De Nittis: Un peintre italien en France à la fin du XIXe siècle*, doctoral dissertation 2007, Berne and New York, 2011.
The National Museum of Modern Art (ed.), *Vincent van Gogh and Japan*, exh. cat., The National Museum of Modern Art, Kyoto / Setagaya Art Museum Tokyo, Kyoto, 1992.
Omoto Keiko, *Van Gogh, pèlerinages japonais à Auvers*, Paris, 2009.
Fred Orton, "Vincent van Gogh in Paris, 1886–1887: Vincent's Interest in Japanese Prints", in: *Vincent: Bulletin of the Rijikmuseum Vincent van Gogh*, vol. 1, no. 3, 1971, pp. 2–12.
Ursula Perucchi-Petri, *Die Nabis und Japan. Das Frühwerk von Bonnard, Vuillard und Denis*, doctoral dissertation 1972, Munich, 1976.
Ursula Perucchi-Petri, "Maurice Denis et le Japon", in: *La Revue du Louvre et des Musées de France*, no. 4, Oct. 1982, pp. 260–265.
Ursula Perucchi-Petri, "Vuillard et le Japon", in: *Vuillard*, exh. cat., Musée des Beaux-Arts, Lyon / Fondation Caixa de Pensions, Barcelona / Musée des Beaux-Arts, Nantes, Paris, 1990, pp. 137–158.
Ursula Peruchi-Petri, "Die Nabis und der Japonismus", in: *Die Nabis: Propheten der Moderne*, exh. cat., Kunsthaus Zürich / Galeries nationales du Grand Palais, Paris, Munich, 1993, pp. 33–59.
Ursula Perucchi-Petri, "Japonisme in Bonnard's Early and Late Work", in: *Pierre Bonnard early and late*, exh. cat., The Phillips Collection, Washington DC, Washington DC, 2002, pp. 190–203.
Ursula Perucchi-Petri, "Pierre Bonnard und die ostasiatische Kunst", in: *Pierre Bonnard. Magier der Farbe*, exh. cat., Von der Heydt-Museum, Wuppertal, Wuppertal, 2010, pp. 48–59.
Brigitte Ranson Bitker, "Paul-Elie Ranson, 1861–1909: le Nabi plus japonard que le japonard", in: *Nouvelles de l'estampe*, no. 129, 1993, pp. 11–24.
Eliza E. Rathbone, "Monet, Japonisme, and Effets de Neige", in: *Impressionists in Winter: Effets de Neige*, exh. cat., The Phillips Collection, Washington DC / The Fine Arts Museum San Francisco, Charles S. Moffett et al. (ed.), London, 1998, pp. 25–37.
Theodore Reff, "Manet's Portrait of Zola", in: *The Burlington Magazine*, vol. 117, no. 862, Jan. 1975, pp. 34–44.
Robert Reiff, "Matisse and Torii Kiyonaga", in: *Arts magazine*, vol. 55, no. 6, pp. 164–167.
Marc Restellini (ed.), *Van Gogh. Rêves de Japon*, exh. cat., Pinacothèque de Paris, Paris, 2012.
Mark Roskill, *Van Gogh, Gauguin and the Impressionist Circle*, London, 1970.
John Sandberg, "Japonisme and Whistler", in: *The Burlington Magazine*, vol. 106, no. 740, Nov. 1964, pp. 500–507.
Shinoda Yūjirō, *Degas. Der Einzug des Japanischen in die französische Malerei*, inaugural dissertation 1957, Tokyo, 1957.
Shinoda Yūjirō, "Der Einzug des Japanischen in die französische Malerei. Hokusai und Degas", in: *Wege zu Edgar Degas*, Wilhelm Schmid (ed.), Munich, 1988, pp. 288–297.
Virgina Spate et al. (ed.), *Monet & Japan*, exh. cat., National Gallery of Australia, Canberra / Art Gallery of Western Australia, Perth, Canberra, 2001.
Sugiyama Naoko, "Vallotton, un japonisme incontestable?", in: *Félix Vallotton. Le feu sous la glace*, exh. cat., Galeries nationales du Grand Palais, Paris, Paris, 2013, pp. 240–249.
Takumi Hideo, "Claude Monet and Japan", in: *Monet et ses amis*, exh. cat., Museum of Modern Art, Ibaraki, Ibaraki, 1988, pp. 33–41.
Tanaka Hidemichi, "Cézanne and 'japonisme'", in: *Artibus et historiae*, vol. 22, no. 44, 2001, pp. 201–220.
Yvonne Thirion, "L'Influence de l'estampe japonaise sur la peinture française dans la seconde moitié du XIXe siècle", in: *Musées de France*, no. 8, 1948, pp. 229–234.
Yvonne Thirion, "L'influence de l'estampe japonaise dans l'œuvre de Gauguin", in: *Gazette des Beaux-Arts*, no. 47, Jan.–Apr. 1956, pp. 95–114.

Louis van Tilborgh, *Van Gogh and Japan*, Amsterdam, 2006.

Patrick Vauday, "Résonnance de l'impressionnisme et du japonisme: Monet", in: *La Décolonisation du tableau: art et politique au XIX*[e] *siècle: Delacroix, Gauguin, Monet*, Paris, 2006, pp. 125–169.

Jill De Vonyar and Richard Kendall, *Degas and the Art of Japan*, exh. cat., Reading Public Museum, Reading, Pennsylvania, New Haven and London, 2007.

Frank Whitford, *Japanese Prints and Western Painters*, London, 1977.

Siegfried Wichmann, "Bewegung als Eigenexistenz im Werk Hokusais und in den Pastellen und Zeichnungen von Edgar Degas", in: *Wege zu Edgar Degas*, Wilhelm Schmid (ed.), Munich, 1988, pp. 281–287.

On prints

Jennifer T. Criss, *Japonisme and beyond in the art of Marie Bracquemond, Mary Cassatt, and Berthe Morisot, 1867–1895*, doctoral dissertation 2007, Philadelphia, 2007.

Danièle Devynck (ed.), *Toulouse-Lautrec & le japonisme*, exh. cat., Musée Toulouse-Lautrec, Albi, Albi, 1991.

Joseph Faulkner, *Japonisme: the influence of Japanese art in French printmaking 1860–1910*, Chicago, 1979.

David E. Gliem, "Japonisme and Bonnard's Invention of the Modern Poster", in: *Japan Studies Association Journal*, no. 1, 2008, pp. 17–38.

Elizabeth Harvey-Lee, "Japonisme in printmaking", in: *Antique collecting*, vol. 29, no. 10, Apr. 1995, pp. 20–25.

Colta Feller Ives (ed.), *The Great Wave: The Influence of Japanese Woodcuts on French Prints*, exh. cat., Metropolitan Museum of Art, New York, New York, 1974.

Kanagawa prefectural museum of modern art (ed.), *Henri Rivière – Maître français de l'Ukiyo-e*, exh. cat., Kanagawa prefectural museum of modern art, Kamakura / Yamaguchi prefectural museum of art, Yamagata and Tokyo, 2009.

Elizabeth K. Menon, "Henry Somm's Japonisme, 1881 in context", in: *Gazette des Beaux-Arts*, vol. 119, no. 1477, Feb. 1992, pp. 89–98.

Siegmar Nahser et al. (ed.), *Faszination Japan. Japanischer Holzschnitt und europäische Graphik 1870–1914*, exh. cat., Altes Museum, Staatliche Museen zu Berlin, Berlin, 1984.

Museo Picasso de Barcelona (ed.), *Secret Images: Picasso and the Japanese Erotic Print*, exh. cat., Museo Picasso de Barcelona, London, 2012; Museo Picasso de Barcelona (ed.); Catalan: *Imágenes Secretas: Picasso y la Estampa erotica japonesa*, Barcelona, 2009.

Valérie Sueur-Hermel (ed.), *Henri Rivière: entre impressionnisme et japonisme*, exh. cat., Bibliothèque nationale de France, Paris, Paris, 2009.

Gabriel P. Weisberg, "Buhot's Japonisme Portfolio Revisited", in: *Cantor Arts Center Journal*, vol. 6, 2010, pp. 34–35.

On photography

Terry Bennett, *Old Japanese Photographs: Collector's Data Guide*, London, 2006.

Terry Bennett, *Photography in Japan 1853–1912*, Tokyo, 2006.

Anne Lacoste (ed.), *Felice Beato: A Photographer on the Eastern Road*, exh. cat., J. Paul Getty Museum, Los Angeles, Los Angeles, 2010.

Bettina Lockemann, *Das Fremde sehen: Der europäische Blick auf Japan in der künstlerischen Dokumentarfotografie*, Bielefeld, 2008.

Claudia Gabriele Philipp et al. (ed.), *Felice Beato in Japan: Photographien zum Ende der Feudalzeit, 1863–1873*, exh. cat., Fotomuseum im Münchner Stadtmuseum / Museum für Kunst und Gewerbe Hamburg / Japanisch-Deutsches Zentrum Berlin, Heidelberg, 1991.

On the decorative arts

Marie-Amélie Anquetil, *Éventails de Maurice Denis*, exh. cat., Musée du Prieuré, Saint-Germain-en-Laye, Saint-Germain-en-Laye, 1983.

Geneviève Aubry et al. (ed.), *Rêves de Japon: japonisme et arts appliqués*, exh. cat., Musée de la faïence, Sarreguemines, Sarreguemines, 2008.

Anne Bouquillon et al. (ed.), *Satsuma: de l'exotisme au japonisme*, exh. cat., Musée national de céramique, Sèvres, Paris and Sèvres, 2007.

Jean-Paul Bouillon (ed.), *Art, industrie et japonisme: "Le service Rousseau"*, exh. cat., Musée d'Orsay, Paris, Paris, 1988.

Jean-Paul Bouillon (ed.), *Félix Bracquemond et les arts décoratifs: du japonisme à l'Art nouveau*, exh. cat., Musée national Adrien-Dubouché, Limoges / Deutsches Porzellanmuseum, Selb-Plößberg / Musée Départemental de l'Oise, Beauvais, Paris, 2005.

Martin Eidelberg, "Bracquemond, Delâtre and the discovery of Japanese prints", in: *The Burlington Magazine*, vol. 123, no. 937, Apr. 1981, pp. 220–227.

Marc Gerstein, "Degas's Fans", in: *The Art Bulletin*, vol. 64, no. 1, Mar. 1982, pp. 105–118.

Katharina Henkel and Carolin Bohlmann, *Garten des Lebens. Ein Wandschirm von Pierre Bonnard*, publication accompanying the exhibition, Alte Nationalgalerie, Staatliche Museen zu Berlin, Cologne, 2002.

Monika Kopplin, *Das Fächerblatt von Manet bis Kokoschka. Europäische Traditionen und japanische Einflüsse*, Saulgau, 1981.

François Le Tacon (ed.), *Émile Gallé: Nature & symbolisme, influences du Japon*, exh. cat., Musée Départemental Georges de La Tour, Vic-sur-Seille, Metz, 2009.

Michel Maucuer, "La copie des objets asiatiques au XIXe siècle: Émile Reiber, Théodore Deck, et la collection Cernuschi", in: *La Revue du Louvre et des Musées de France*, no. 3, Paris, 2011, pp. 80–90.

Miura Atsushi et al. (ed.), *La France regarde le Japon: l'influence des peintres japonais sur les arts décoratifs français dans la seconde moitié du XIX*[ème] *siècle*, exh. cat., Tokyo National Museum, Tokyo and Paris, 2008.

Musée d'art et d'histoire et al. (ed.) *Jean Carriès, 1855–1894, ou La terre viscérale*, exh. cat., Musée Leblanc-Duvernoy, Auxerre, Auxerre and Saint-Amand-en-Puisaye, 2007.

Édouard Papet (ed.), "Une autre polychromie: plâtres platinés, bronzes et sculptures céramiques de Jean-Joseph Carriès", in: *Quarante-huit / Quatorze: La revue du Musée d'Orsay*, 2004, pp. 72–83.

Sabine Pasdelou, *Vous avez dit Japonisme?*, exh. cat., Musée Gallé-Juillet, Creil, Chéroy, 2010.

Anne Sefrioui, *Éventails impressionistes*, Paris, 2012.

Philippe Thiébaut, "Contribution à une histoire du mobilier japonisant: les créations de l'Escalier de Cristal", in: *Revue de l'art*, vol. 85, 1989, pp. 76–83.

Tsuchida Ruriko et al. (ed.), *Gallé and japonisme*, exh. cat., Suntory Museum of Art, Tokyo / Suntory Museum, Osaka, Tokyo, 2008.

Gabriel P. Weisberg, "Félix Bracquemond & Japanese Influence in Ceramic Decoration", in: *The Art Bulletin*, vol. 51, Sept. 1969, pp. 277–280.

Yamane Ikunobu, "L'influence du japonisme dans l'œuvre d'Émile Gallé", in: *Annales de l'Est*, vol. 55, no. 2, 2005, pp. 51–65.

Jean-Pierre Zingg, *Les éventails de Paul Gauguin*, Paris 1996; English: *The Fans of Paul Gauguin*, Paris, 2001.

Short biographies of the authors

Geneviève Aitken, received her diploma from the École du Louvre and a bachelor's degree in history and history of art from Université Paris IV. From 1990 to 2009, deputy director of the department for new technologies and delegate for documentary studies at Centre de Recherche et de Restauration des Musées de France. Currently responsible for the documentation of the Musée Rodin collections. A specialist on the Nabi artists and organiser of the exhibition *Artistes et théâtre d'avant-garde, programmes illustrés 1890–1900* (1990). Editor of the catalogue on Monet's collection of Japanese woodblock prints (1983) and catalogues on Huguette Berès's collections of Japanese woodblock prints (2002 and 2003).

Sabine Bradel, studied art history, Japanese studies and English at the University of Trier; completed her studies in October 2011 after a year abroad in Tokyo undertaking research for her master's thesis on Suzuki Harunobu. Since February 2012, research assistant at the Department of East Asian Art History at the University of Zurich; currently preparing a doctoral dissertation on the Japanese colour woodblock print of the sixteenth to the eighteenth centuries. Contributions on this subject in the exhibition catalogues *Bonnard, Vallotton, Vuillard im Bann des japanischen Holzschnitts* (Winterthur, 2013) and *Szenen aus der fließenden Welt* (Paderborn, Neuss 2007/2008), among others. Papers on the Japanese colour woodblock print held at Museum Rietberg (Zurich, 2013) and Villa Flora (Winterthur, 2013/2014).

Ricard Bru, former professor of nineteenth-century art history at the University of Barcelona – today, at the city's Instituto de Cultura. Curator of the recent exhibitions *Japonisme. La fascinació per l'art japonès* (Barcelona, 2013) and *Secret Images. Picasso and the Japanese Erotic Print* (Barcelona, 2009). Academic publications on *Japonisme* and Japanese art in Europe: *Erotic Japonisme. The Influence of Japanese Sexual Imagery on Western Art* (2013) and *Els orígens del Japonisme a Barcelona* (2010). Regular lectures in Europe and Japan, publications on the subject of *Japonisme* in international academic journals and contributions to various book publications and exhibitions – most recently, *Shunga: sex and pleasure in Japanese art* (London, 2013).

Christoph Dorsz, studied history of art, classical archaeology and medieval German in Bochum. Since 2011, research associate at the Institut für Kunst- und Designwissenschaft at Folkwang University of the Arts. Curator of the exhibition *Der Folkwang Impuls. Das Museum von 1902 bis heute* held at Osthaus Museum Hagen in 2012.

Sandra Gianfreda, born in Biel/Bienne, Switzerland. Studied history of art and architecture as well as psychology in Berne and Rome; completed her doctoral dissertation on the half-figure history painting of the seicento in 2001. Co-editor of the German translation of Leon Battista Alberti's treatise *On Painting*. From 1998 to 2002, research assistant at the Department of Modern Art History in Berne; subsequently, research fellowship at Kunstmuseum Basel in the nineteenth-century art and classic modernism department. From 2005 to 2009, curator at Kunstmuseum Winterthur. Since late 2009, project manager and curator for special exhibitions – most recently, the exhibition *The Ecstasy of Colour – Munch, Matisse and the Expressionists* (2012/2013). Exhibitions and publications on classic modernism and contemporary art.

Claire Guitton, studied history at Université Paris X Nanterre and history of art as well as museum studies at the École du Louvre in Paris and the Ruprecht-Karls-Universität in Heidelberg; second master's thesis on the late works of Paul Cézanne and Claude Monet. Internship in the context of exhibition preparations for *Emil Nolde* (Grand Palais, Paris, et al., 2008/2009). After an internship at Musée Rodin, temporary delegate for documentary studies while preparing the catalogue raisonné on the marble sculptures of Auguste Rodin (forthcoming autumn 2015). In 2011/2012, tutorial at the École du Louvre. Since 2013, research assistant in the project office for special exhibitions at Museum Folkwang, Essen.

Ulrike Hofer, studied history of art and philosophy in Vienna and Lausanne; master's thesis on primitivism in the work and life of Max Pechstein (2009). From 2008 to 2010, freelance work at the Ludwig Boltzmann-Institut für Kriegsfolgen-Forschung in Vienna. Took the further education course *Kunstkritik und Kuratorisches Wissen* (art criticism and curatorial expertise) in Bochum in 2010/2011. Since 2011, research assistant in the project office for special exhibitions at Museum Folkwang, Essen. Collaboration in the exhibition *The Ecstasy of Colour – Munch, Matisse and the Expressionists* (2012/2013).

Gregory Irvine, senior curator from 1992 to 2014 in the Asian Department of the Victoria and Albert Museum, London, with responsibility for the collections of Japanese metalwork, focusing on arms, armour and cloisonné enamels. Former curator in the Department of Japanese Antiquities of the British Museum. Regular study trips to Japan over the years; research on the use of masks in Japan's religious ceremonies and rituals, in folk performance and in traditional theatre. In 2012/2013, exchange fellow at Staatliche Kunstsammlungen Dresden; in November 2008, visiting professor at Ritsumeikan University, Kyoto; founding member and co-chair of JACUK (Japanese Art Collections in the UK) as well as member of numerous academic and/or cultural associations and committees, etc. Extensive publications – recently, *Japonisme and the Rise of the Modern Art Movement: the Arts of the Meiji Period* (London, 2013) and *Japanese Cloisonné Enamels* (London, 2011), among others.

Peter Kropmanns, studied history of art and Romance studies in Würzburg and Bonn; wrote his doctoral thesis in Berlin on Henri Matisse. Art critic and journalist, specialist translator, exhibition curator and author; since many years, a resident of Paris. Numerous publications on classic modernism, particularly on French and German art, the artistic exchange between France and Germany, and individual artists of the Parisian artistic circle in the late nineteenth and early twentieth centuries.

Mario-Andreas von Lüttichau, born in Munich in 1952. Studied history of art in Munich and received his doctorate in 1983. Various internships at the State Museums in Munich; from 1986 to 1988, research assistant at Berlinische Galerie for twentieth-century art; from 1988 to 1991, research assistant at Kunstmuseum Bonn. Since 1991, curator for paintings and sculptures of the nineteenth and twentieth centuries at Museum Folkwang, Essen. Teaching assignments in art history in Bonn and Düsseldorf. Exhibitions and publications on nineteenth- and twentieth-century art.

Mae Michiko, professor of literature and cultural studies and Chair in Modern Japan (cultural studies) at the Heinrich Heine University of Düsseldorf. Wrote her doctoral dissertation on Robert Musil at Saarland University. Teaching and research at the University of Marburg (1984–1993) and the University of Vienna (1992/1993). Appointed to the University of Düsseldorf in 1993; between 1995 and 2001, vice-rector of this institution. Visiting professor at various Japanese universities and co-editor of the series *Geschlecht und Gesellschaft*. Author of numerous publications in the fields of transcultural and gender studies, multicultural civil society in Japan and modern Japanese literature. Recent publications on the subject *Japonismus und japanische Populärkultur im deutschsprachigen Raum* (co-edited with E. Scherer, Böhlau, 2013).

Antje Papist-Matsuo, studied history of art, East Asian art history, sinology and classical archaeology in Cologne. From 2000 to 2005, research associate at the department for East Asian art history at the Art History Institute, Freie Universität Berlin. In 2005/2006, visiting scholar at Kokugakuin University in Tokyo. Academic collaboration in research projects of the FU Berlin, such as master–student relationships in East Asian art, as well as teaching assignments. Since 2013, intern at Museum für Asiatische Kunst, East Asian Art Collection, Berlin; curator of the exhibition held there entitled *Ikeda Iwao: Bambus und Lack* (2013). Research focus on Japanese decorative arts, especially lacquerware (dissertation on Japanese Negoro lacquerware). Numerous publications – as co-editor, for instance, of *Long Life. Festschrift in Honour of Roger Goepper* (Frankfurt am Main, 2006) and author of the exhibition catalogue *A Japanese Taste for Lacquers. The Klaus F. Naumann Collection* (Berlin, 2006). Since 2014, co-editor (with Jeong-Hee Lee Kalisch) of the series *Studies of East Asian Art History*, Freie Universität Berlin/Studien für Ostasiatische Kunstgeschichte, Freie Universität Berlin.

Ursula Perucchi-Petri, studied European and East Asian art history at the universities of Heidelberg, Paris and Zurich. Doctoral dissertation on *Die Nabis und Japan – Das Frühwerk von Bonnard, Vuillard und Denis* (published in 1976). From 1975 to 1995, head of the Collection of Prints and Drawings and, from 1980, vicedirector of Kunsthaus Zürich. From 1995 to 2005, curator at Museum Villa Flora, Winterthur. Numerous exhibitions and publications – in particular, on the Nabi artists (Bonnard, Vuillard, Vallotton, Denis, etc.), the ZERO group (1979), American minimal and conceptual artists (Sol LeWitt, Judd, Ryman, Sandback, Tuttle, Nauman, etc., 1994/1995) as well as video art (since 1981).

Belinda Thomson, independent scholar specialising in French art and, since 2011, Honorary Professor in Art History at the University of Edinburgh. Received a bachelor's degree in French and art history at the University of East Anglia in 1975, spending a year at the Sorbonne from 1973 to 1974; completed her master's degree in art history in 1976 at the Courtauld Institute of Art, London, specialising in Symbolism and submitting a dissertation on Maurice Denis. From 1977 to 1983, research assistant at the Open University, subsequently lecturing part-time at Manchester Metropolitan University and at the University of Edinburgh.

Photo credits

- Lent courtesy of the Ackland Art Museum, The University of North Carolina at Chapel Hill, Ackland Fund: p. 215
- M. Aeschimann, Geneva: pp. 319 b., 320
- akg-images: p. 74 l.
- Akita Museum of Modern Art: p. 24 l.
- Thomas Ammann Fine Art AG, Zurich: p. 177
- Archiv Ursula Perucchi-Petri: pp. 91 l., 92 l.
- The Art Institute of Chicago: p. 217
- © Städel Museum – ARTOTHEK: pp. 169, 210; © U. Edelmann – Städel Museum – ARTOTHEK: p. 205; © Stiftung Museum Kunstpalast – ARTOTHEK: pp. 124, 151–153, 255, 261, 306 b., 312
- Photo Les Arts Décoratifs, Paris / Jean Tholance. Tous droits réservés: pp. 56 l., 78, 80 m., 117 b., 122, 126, 252, 256 b., 266 r., 270, 306 t
- The Barber Institute of Fine Arts, University of Birmingham: p. 292
- Baur Foundation, Geneva: pp. 142, 146 b., 164 b., 178 b., 186, 220, 278 b.
- Robert Bayer, Basel: pp. 159, 309
- Beck & Eggeling, Düsseldorf: p. 121
- Anders Sune Berg: p. 68
- Bibliothèque de Genève: p. 197
- Bibliothèque des Arts décoratifs, Paris: p. 56 r.
- Bibliothèque nationale de France: pp. 30 m., 30 r., 34 r., 36, 46, 48 l., 147, 148 b., 184, 189–191, 192 m., 192 b., 209 b., 303 b., 344–345, 347 r.
- Bildarchiv Foto Marburg, Paula Deetjen: pp. 40 m., 40 r., 42 l., 42 m., 42 r.; Dr. Franz Stoedtner, Berlin: p. 41
- bpk / Bayerische Staatsgemäldesammlungen: p. 308; bpk / Staatsbibliothek zu Berlin: pp. 26 l., p. 66 l.; bpk / CNAC-MNAM / Philippe Migeat: pp. 100 l., 100 r.; bpk / Hamburger Kunsthalle / Elke Walford: p. 204 t.; bpk / The Metropolitan Museum of Art: pp. 24 r., 305; bpk / RMN / Christian Jean: p. 99 l.; bpk / RMN / Estate Brassaï: p. 330; bpk / RMN – Grand Palais: pp. 62 l., 118–119; bpk / RMN – Grand Palais (musée Guimet, Paris): pp. 130–132; bpk / RMN – Grand Palais (musée Guimet, Paris) / Harry Bréjat: p. 156; bpk / RMN – Grand Palais (musée Guimet, Paris) / Thierry Ollivier: pp. 70 l., 108–109; bpk / RMN – Grand Palais (musée Guimet, Paris) / Ravaux: p. 133; bpk / RMN – Grand Palais / Hervé Lewandowski: pp. 61 r., 89, 179, 206; bpk / RMN – Grand Palais / Paris, Musée d'Orsay / Patrice Schmidt: p. 203; bpk / RMN – Grand Palais / René-Gabriel Ojéda: pp. 81 l., 88 r.; bpk / RMN / Hervé Lewandowski: pp. 110, 297
- Brame & Lorenceau (ed.), *Anquetin. La Passion d'être Peintre*, exh. cat., Galerie Brame & Lorenceau, Paris, Paris, 1991, p. 92: p. 73
- The Bridgeman Art Library: Detroit Institute of Arts, USA / Gift of Dexter M. Ferry Jr. / The Bridgeman Art Library: p. 67; Christie's Images / The Bridgeman Art Library: pp. 100 m., 307; Musée de l'Annonciade, Saint-Tropez / Giraudon / Bridgeman Images: p. 91 r.; Museum of Fine Arts, Houston, Texas, USA / Gift of Audrey Jones Beck, © 2014 Succession H. Matisse / DACS, London / The Bridgeman Art Library: p. 101
- Cincinnati Art Museum: p. 107
- The Cleveland Museum of Art: p. 84 (fig. 6)
- The Cummer Museum of Art & Gardens, Jacksonville: p. 61 l.
- Designmuseum Danmark, Pernille Klemp: pp. 84 (fig. 9), 170 b., 214
- © Droits réservés: pp. 280 t., 281
- Hughes Dubois, Paris: p. 257
- The George Economou Collection, Athens: p. 171
- Fondation Beyeler, Riehen/Basel: p. 180
- Fondation Claude Monet, Giverny, Académie des Beaux-Arts: pp. 48 r., 162, 172–173, 174 b.
- Freer Gallery of Art, Smithsonian Institution, Washington, DC: p. 60 (fig. 1)
- Hans Hansen, Hamburg 2009: pp. 38, 114, 233–234, 240 b., 241 l., 245, 248, 265 r.
- Harvard Art Museums / Fogg Museum, Imaging Department, © President and Fellows of Harvard College: pp. 22 r., 72 r.
- Sammlung P. + R. Herzog, Basel: pp. 134, 137, 256 t.
- Hetjens-Museum, Deutsches Keramikmuseum: pp. 266 l., 267
- Børre Høstland: p. 161
- Japan Print Gallery: p. 76
- Collection Claire Joyes: p. 54 r.
- E. W. K. Bern: pp. 204 b., 283
- Kōbe City Museum: p. 25
- Kunsthalle Bremen – Kupferstichkabinett – Der Kunstverein in Bremen: p. 185; Karen Blindow: pp. 253, 276
- Kunsthalle Mannheim: pp. 212–213
- Kunsthaus Zürich: pp. 279, 284–285, 293, 296, 298 t., 310–311, 321, 325, 328
- Kunstmuseum Basel, Martin P. Bühler: p. 181
- Kunstmuseum Bern: p. 331
- Kupferstich-Kabinett, Staatliche Kunstsammlungen Dresden, Herbert Boswank: pp. 149 b., 178 t.
- Rémi Labrusse und Jacqueline Munck (ed.), *Matisse – Derain. La vérité du fauvisme*, Paris, 2005, p. 68: p. 96 r.
- Lenders: pp. 20, 84 (fig. 8), 91 m., 113, 115, 157, 165, 170 t., 216, 277, 278 t., 286–287, 294, 299, 319 t., 322–323, 348 l.
- Collection Adrien Maeght, Saint Paul: p. 280 m.
- Markus Mühlheim, Prolith SA, Switzerland: p. 288
- © MuMa Le Havre / Florian Kleinefenn: p. 99 r.
- Musée d'art et d'histoire, Ville de Genève: Jean Marc Yersin: p. 314
- Musée des Beaux-Arts de Dijon, François Jay: p. 60 (fig. 3)
- Musée Carnavalet / Roger-Viollet: p. 193
- Musée Cernuschi / Roger-Viollet: p. 81 r.
- © Musée de Grenoble: p. 315
- Musée Rodin: p. 53; Christian Baraja: p. 271; Jean de Calan: pp. 22 l., 150, 282, 324; Luc and Lala Joubert: p. 106
- Musée Toulouse-Lautrec, Albi, Tarn, France: p. 348 r.; cliché François Pons: p. 280 t.
- Museen der Stadt Regensburg, Historisches Museum: pp. 117 t., 141, 174 t., 188 r., 192 t., 208 t., 209 t., 303 t.
- Museum Folkwang, Essen, Jens Nober: pp. 10, 28, 42 r., 43 l., 72 m., 88 l., 116 l., 167–168, 198–199, 211, 219, 221, 224, 231–232, 235–239, 240 t., 241 r., 242–244, 246–247, 249, 260, 262, 264 l., 268, 313
- Museum für Kunst und Gewerbe Hamburg: pp. 26 r., 27 r., 40 l., 44, 96 l., 146 t., 149 t., 164 t., 208 b., 263, 264 r., 347 l., 349
- 2014. Museum of Fine Arts, Boston: pp. 27 l., 60 (fig. 4), 62 r., 63, 77, 80 r.
- The Museum of Fine Arts, Houston: p. 58
- 2014. Digital image, The Museum of Modern Art, New York/Scala, Florence: pp. 74 m., 94
- Nancy, musée de l'Ecole de Nancy, cliché Claude Philippot: p. 84 (fig. 7)
- Image courtesy of the National Gallery of Art, Washington: pp. 93, 207
- Nevill Keating Pictures, London: p. 97
- Ny Carlsberg Glyptotek, Copenhagen, Ole Haupt: pp. 125, 176, 225
- Ōtani Memorial Art Museum, Nishinomiya City: p. 22 m.
- David Park Curry, *James McNeill Whistler. Uneasy Pieces*, Virginia Museum of Fine Arts, Richmond, New York, 2004, p. 121: p. 60 (fig. 2)
- Reto Pedrini, Zurich: p. 327
- Petit Palais / Roger-Viollet: pp. 265 l., 269
- Ronald Pickvance, *Gauguin and the School of Pont-Aven*, exh. cat., Indianapolis Museum of Art, Indianapolis, Indiana et al., London, 1994, p. 36: p. 74 r.
- Collection Philippe Piguet, Paris: p. 54 l.
- Pinacoteca Giuseppe De Nittis, Barletta: p. 111
- Private Collection / Archive of the owners: pp. 52 l., 88 m., 96 m.
- Rheinisches Bildarchiv Köln, rba_d036870: p. 116 r.; rba_d036871: p. 112; rba_c002985: p. 329; rba_c001086: p. 163; rba_d037108-rba_d037111: pp. 135–136
- Saint Louis Art Museum: p. 275
- Antoine Salomon and Guy Cogeval, *Vuillard. Le Regard innombrable. Catalogue critique des peintures et pastels*, vol. 1, Paris, 2003, p. 377, cat. V-18.2: p. 92 r.
- The Samuel Courtauld Trust, The Courtauld Gallery, London: p. 52 r.
- Peter Schälchli, Zurich: p. 295
- Scottish National Gallery: p. 166
- SIK Zurich (J. P. Kuhn): p. 223
- Courtesy of Sotheby's London: p. 127
- Staatliche Museen zu Berlin, Museum für Asiatische Kunst, Jürgen Liepe: p. 143; photo courtesy of Art Research Center, Ritsumeikan University, Kyoto: pp. 148 t., 160, 175, 187, 188 l., 254
- Staatsgalerie Stuttgart: pp. 144, 194–196, 274
- State Pushkin Museum of Fine Arts, Moscow: p. 304
- Sterling and Francine Clark Art Institute, Williamstown, Massachusetts, USA, Michael Agee: p. 289
- Stiftung DKM, Werner J. Hannappel: pp. 258–259
- Studio Tromp, Rotterdam: p. 120
- Tate, London 2014: p. 202
- Tehran Museum of Contemporary Art, Tehran: p. 85
- TNM Image Archives: p. 31
- Collection Triton Foundation: pp. 158, 298 b.
- Universitätsbibliothek Heidelberg, *Recueil de dessins pour l'art et l'industrie*, 1859 (96 G 44 RES); plate 31: p. 80 l.
- Van Gogh Museum, Amsterdam (Vincent van Gogh Foundation): pp. 34 l., 49, 70 m., 70 r., 71, 72 l., 123, 145, 218, 290–291
- © Victoria and Albert Museum, London: pp. 30 l., 30 r., 32 l., 32 r., 33, 34 m., 66 r.
- Yale University Art Gallery, New Haven, Connecticut: p. 302
- Horst Ziegenfusz: p. 86

Copyrights

Monet, Gauguin, Van Gogh …
Japanese Inspirations

The exhibition and the catalogue were conceived by Museum Folkwang and realised in collaboration with Kunsthaus Zürich.

Museum Folkwang, Essen
27 September 2014 to 18 January 2015

Kunsthaus Zürich
20 February to 10 May 2015

Exhibition

Director: Tobia Bezzola
Curator and project management: Sandra Gianfreda
Research assistants: Claire Guitton and Ulrike Hofer
Administration head: Holger Peters
Registrars: Susanne Brüning and Alexandra Seese
Restoration support: Silke Zeich, Frederike Breder and Christiane Schneider
Press and marketing: Anka Grosser and Anna Sophie Littmann
Education and information: Peter Daners and Annika Schank
Visitor services: Stefanie Dixon
Facility management: Kay Zetzsche
Exhibition design: Dieter Thiel, Basle
Coordination / exhibition technology: Alexandra Klein and Daniel Wimmer / Reiner Baldau, Sefa Bespinar, Tim Czastrau, Anatoli Marcin, Olaf Masuch, Michael Peters, Klaus Schlüter, Frank Sternberg, Gerd Ufer, Henrik Weiß, Till Wellner, Alina Wenzel and Stephan Zmudzinski

Museum Folkwang
Museumsplatz 1
45128 Essen
Tel. 0201 88 45 000
Fax 0201 88 9145 000

Publication

Editor: Museum Folkwang, Essen
Conception: Sandra Gianfreda, in cooperation with Claire Guitton and Ulrike Hofer
Editorial assistants: Claire Guitton and Ulrike Hofer
Translations from the German:
Helen Atkins (chronologies; glossary), Brian Currid (greeting; texts by Christoph Dorsz, p. 39; Mario-Andreas von Lüttichau, pp. 154, 326; Ulrike Hofer, pp. 182, 200, 272; Ricard Bru, p. 316), Ishbel Flett (text by Ursula Perucchi-Petri, p. 87), Carolyn Kelly (texts by Geneviève Aitken, p. 47; Claire Guitton, pp. 79, 128, 250, 300), Ariane Kossack (foreword; texts by Mario-Andreas von Lüttichau, p. 104; Antje Papist-Matsuo, p. 226), Benjamin Letzler (text by Peter Kropmanns, p. 95) and Judith Rosenthal (introduction; index of exhibited works; texts by Mae Michiko, p. 21; Sandra Gianfreda, p. 59; Sabine Bradel, p. 138)
Copy-editing: Edition Folkwang/Steidl, Ariane Kossack
Book design: Steidl Design / Sarah Winter, Julia Melzner
Scans: Steidl's digital darkroom
Image editing: Steidl's digital darkroom / Judith Lange
Total production and printing: Steidl, Göttingen

First edition 2014

Edition Folkwang/Steidl
Düstere Str. 4
37073 Göttingen
Tel. 0551 49 60 60
Fax 0551 49 60 649
mail@steidl.de
www.steidl.de/www.steidlville.com

ISBN 978-3-86930-899-9
Printed in Germany